I0818475

Smith Street Books and Never Too Small respectfully acknowledge the Wurundjeri People of the Kulin Nation, who are the Traditional Owners of the land on which we work, and we pay our respects to their Elders past and present.

Never Too Small

Vol. 2

Reinventing Small Space Living

Never Too Small

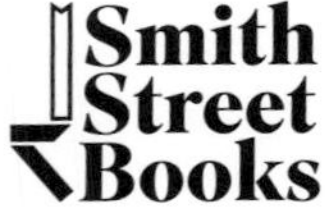

Created by Colin Chee

Vol. 2

Reinventing Small Space Living

Written by Joel Beath & Camilla Janse van Vuuren

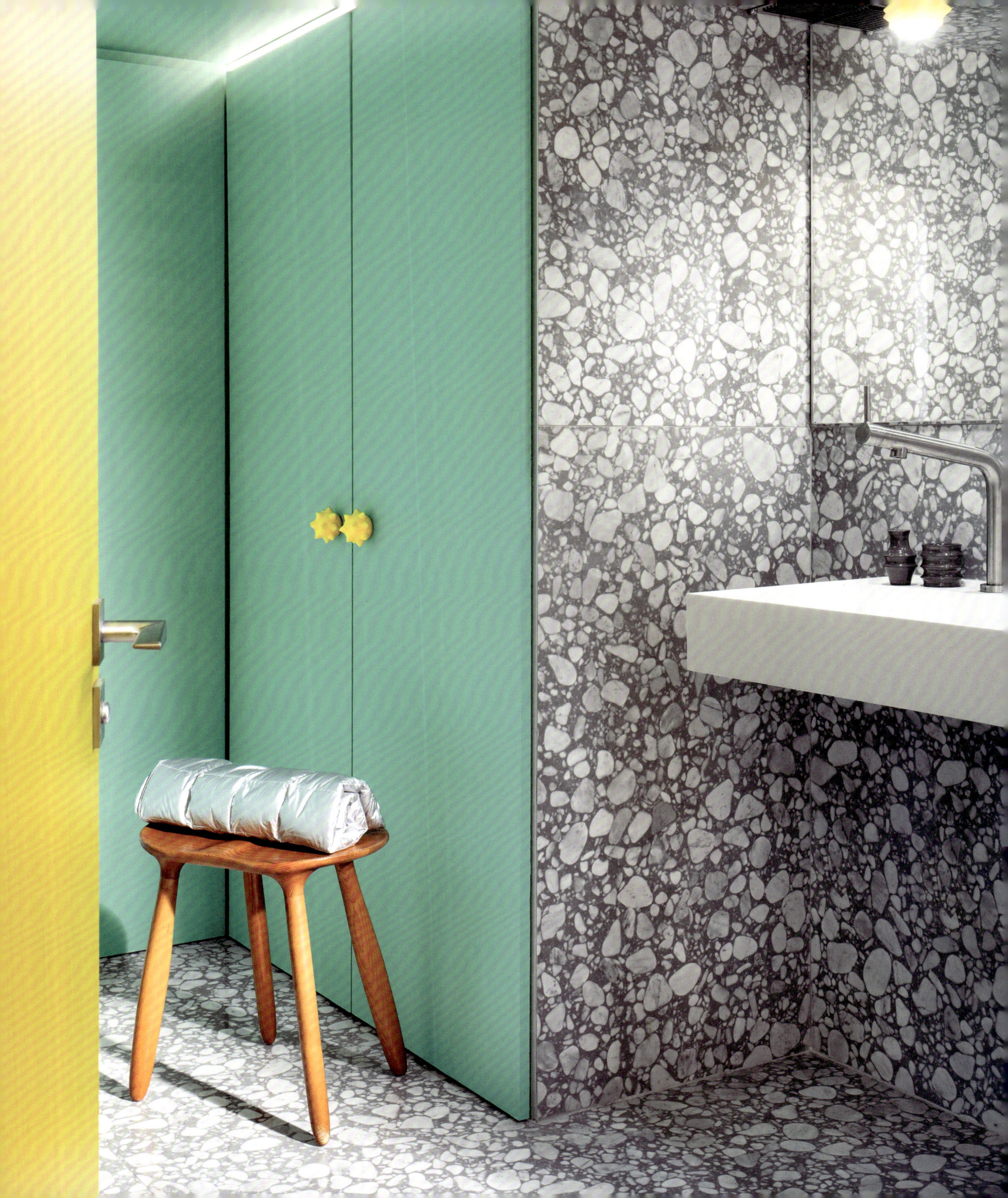

Introduction

Given the increasing pressures on expanding urban areas, we at Never Too Small are more convinced than ever that embracing small-footprint living is the answer. As the world becomes more populated and natural resources face mounting strain, we believe a small-footprint mindset is the solution to urban densification.

But what does adopting a small-footprint mindset entail? It's not merely about constructing tiny apartments, but rather about designing and building them thoughtfully. It involves adapting or refurbishing existing buildings – or underutilised spaces, such as the airspace around a train station carpark – to enhance their energy performance rather than demolishing and rebuilding them. Essentially, it's about maximising the potential of what already exists.

When new construction is necessary, we need to carefully consider how materials and methods will minimise our impact on the natural environment. We currently pull up approximately 100 billion tonnes of raw material from the planet each year and the building industry accounts for nearly half of these material needs. Each of us bears responsibility to do what we can within our means.

We believe the most environmentally friendly buildings are the ones that already exist. In this second volume of *Never Too Small*, we explore how small-scale design can adapt to existing buildings – employing a people-centric approach to small-footprint living which respects individual styles, narratives, cultural backgrounds, age groups and various household types.

Consequently, we have dedicated a section to family homes, recognising the need for city living to accommodate the raising of future generations. An integral part of achieving this lies in the layout: that's why we have included before and after floor plans of every home featured in the book. By studying them closely, we can observe the positive impact these changes have on the residents. Delving into the images and the floor plans also lets us get a deeper understanding of the residents themselves, as if we were personally acquainted with their way of life.

Within these pages, we are thrilled to share examples of architects and designers who experiment with sustainable and salvaged materials, as well as explore the possibilities of repurposing heritage buildings. Our six sections – Adaptive Reuse, Addition and Subtraction, Experimental Approaches, Family-Friendly Homes, Multifunctional Spaces and Sustainable Solutions – were carefully curated to provide you with uplifting and inspiring examples from around the world of outstanding small-footprint design.

A small-footprint mindset extends beyond the realm of the home itself. For this way of living to thrive, our cities must be adapted to support it. The concept of 20-minute neighbourhoods has guided urban-planning decisions in our hometown of Melbourne since 2018 and we are enthusiastically waiting for more cities worldwide to adopt a similar framework for sustainable, high-density growth.

If we successfully embrace all these principles, our cities will become the solution to our population and climate challenges. By reducing greenfield development and instead accommodating more people in proximity to amenities and opportunities within connected and flourishing communities, these hurdles can be overcome.

This book, a follow up to *Never Too Small: Reimagining Small Space Living*, was designed to inspire. We create to inspire and, in turn, are inspired by your creativity. And even if you don't live in a small home, you can still be an ally.

We're making progress and we hope you love the book. Thanks for being with us on the journey!

Architect and designer Anthony Authié's Parisian home features bursts of colour and one-of-a-kind 3D-printed details that align with his goal of a 'fully-fledged and unique aesthetic'.

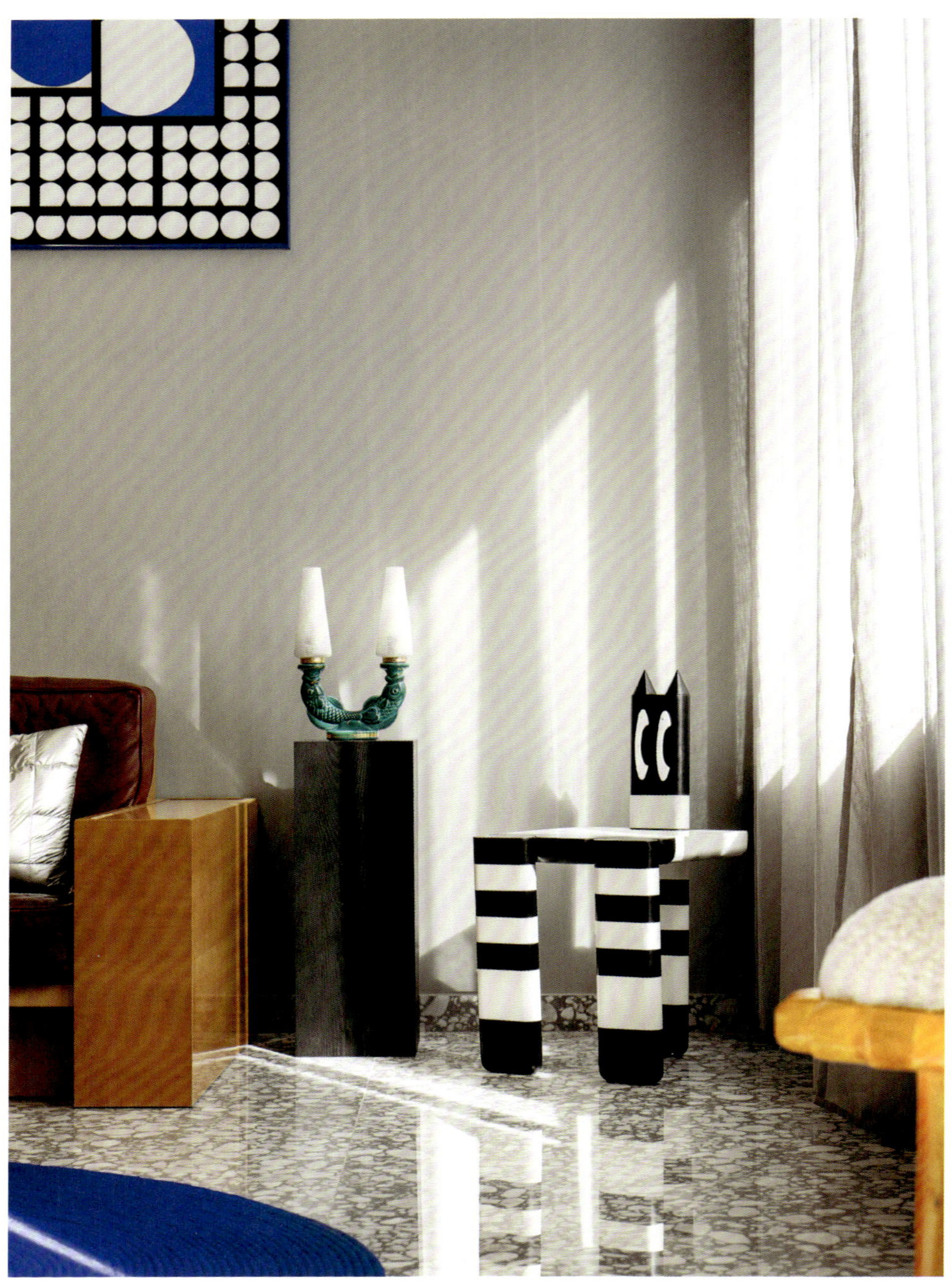

Authié's 'Bandit Chair' sits in good company alongside various pieces made by his friends.

Addition and subtraction

This section explores how renovating a small home poses challenges and opportunities that can be solved by subtracting or adding elements through the design process. Subtracting elements declutters and maximises space, while adding elements optimises storage and introduces functionalities. beâCHâlet in Sydney (page 12) and Casa Cubo in Buenos Aires (page 22) showcase resourcefulness and space optimisation in small-home designs.

Multifunctional spaces

Multifunctional spaces maximise space efficiency in small homes, saving valuable square footage and creating a more spacious feel. They provide flexibility and adaptability, easily transforming to suit changing needs. Sydney's Mark II (page 96) is a great example of this with simple built-in cabinets, a Murphy bed and a hidden desk, allowing the living room to turn into a sleeping space, a home office and a living room depending on the time of day.

Adaptive reuse

In an era of urbanisation and environmental consciousness, adaptive reuse repurposes existing structures into functional, eco-friendly homes. Adaptive reuse conserves resources, reduces costs and honours the unique character and history of buildings. The architects of Monolocale EFFE (page 162) in Mantova, Italy, exemplify adaptive reuse. Uncovering a centuries-old wall during excavation, the designers incorporated it as a central element, preserving its historical significance in this remarkable transformation.

Experimental approaches

Experimental approaches in small-home design challenge traditional constraints and unleash creativity. They encourage us to question norms and reimagine spaces. The Maximalist Mini Loft (page 198) in Paris is a highly personalised space that uses bold colours and textures, while Barcelona's EG112 simple dwelling (page 208) integrates an open bathroom with a nautical theme. These examples show how experimentation enhances functionality and creates unique atmospheres, proving that even accessible solutions can be transformed into extraordinary designs.

Sustainability solutions

This section explores how sustainability is integral to small-footprint design. These projects blend creativity, efficiency and conscious decision-making. They consider environmental impact, utilising innovative strategies like passive heating and cooling, encourage finite resource use and energy conservation. Jourdain (page 228) in Paris showcases affordability and sustainability with French pine plywood furniture and salvaged items.

Family-friendly homes

Small homes near urban centres are increasingly chosen by families for their amenities and community. This section showcases creative designs that have adapted to changing family needs. F-house (page 266) in Osaka, is a remarkable example, maximising every inch of space by expanding horizontally. Its loft serves as storage and a playful haven for children, demonstrating how compact spaces can be transformed into functional and enjoyable family homes.

1

Renovating or redesigning a small space presents a unique set of challenges and opportunities. With limited space available, every element added or removed can have a profound impact on the storage, privacy, layout and overall functionality of a home. The ability to strategically subtract and add elements is crucial to creating a harmonious and efficient living space.

Subtracting elements allows for decluttering and maximising the use of available space. By carefully assessing the existing layout, one can identify unnecessary or underutilised components that can be removed to free up valuable room. This process involves critically evaluating each element, considering its purpose, functionality and contribution to the overall design. Removing certain features can create new possibilities, heighten a sense of openness and improve the flow between different zones.

On the other hand, adding elements can introduce new functionalities. In a small space, every inch matters and well-thought-out additions can make a significant difference. By considering the specific needs and preferences of the occupants, new elements can be strategically incorporated to improve storage, increase privacy or enable multifunctional spaces. Whether it's clever built-in storage solutions, innovative room dividers or creative furniture choices, the possibilities for adding elements are vast.

Designed by architect/owner Matt Reynolds as his Sydney homebase, beâCHâlet showcases an extreme DIY approach with a focus on storage for books and treasured items. The design emphasises resourcefulness and flexibility in a small-footprint design.

Addition and Subtraction

Similarly, architects/owners Torunn Vaksvik Skarstad and Matías Michatek designed their home in Buenos Aires, Casa Cubo, with an emphasis on functionality and multipurpose design elements. One such example is a staircase that cleverly conceals a hidden bathroom and storage.

In Marvila, Portugal, KEMA studio faced a challenging floor plan with varying heights. To overcome this, the entrance was relocated to the middle of the apartment, allowing for a flexible reconfiguration of the space. The attic apartment was expanded to maximise the existing floor space and the design embraces the low end of the tapered ceiling with two clever niches.

IT's House in Taipei City boasts a standout feature in its staircase, which serves as storage and adds a touch of organic beauty to the space. The sleeping area benefits from a large floor-to-ceiling glass window, providing an opportunity to enjoy natural light and the surrounds. This design blends functionality and aesthetics harmoniously.

Balancing the process of subtracting and adding elements is key to achieving an optimal small-footprint design, and each decision should be purposeful and mindful of the overall space constraints. The goal is to create homes where every element serves a specific purpose and contributes to the overall aesthetic and usability of the space.

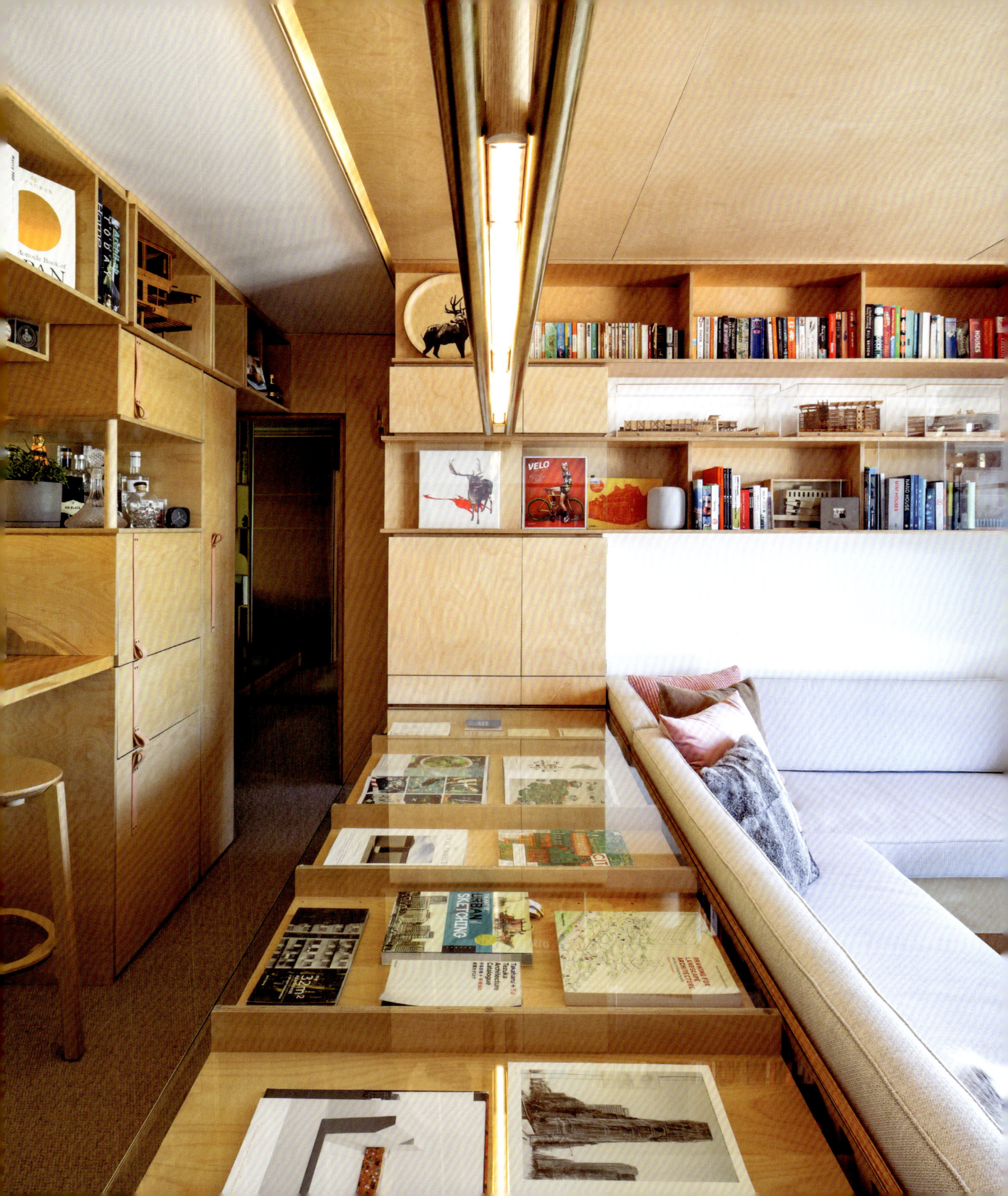
VELO
URBAN SKETCHING
HOUSES

beâCHâlet

51m² / 549ft²
mattr.studio
Bronte, Sydney

One of the prettiest city beaches in the world, certainly in Australia, is a small patch of sand just 10 kilometres south of the Sydney CBD. With its ocean pool, popular cafes and pre-dawn fitness groups, Bronte Beach is a hub of activity for locals and visitors alike who flock to the beach at the slightest sign of sunshine.

Such a destination comes with a serious price tag, and even the smallest, most dilapidated of homes demands a significant investment. With a keen eye for the potential of a small unit in an upscale area, Matt Reynolds, of mattr.studio, saw an opportunity to transform this run-down apartment into a luxurious retreat, now known as beâCHâlet.

Reynolds was attracted by the 'views to the ocean, car parking near the beach and the opportunity to improve possibly the worst-kept unit in the complex'. Inspired by the sleek efficiency of Japanese and Scandinavian architecture, as well as the ingenious use of space found in yachts and caravans, Reynolds's custom joinery allowed for an adaptable space with a surprising amount of storage.

The 'Japandi' style is evident immediately upon entry with a Japanese genkan-inspired space inside the front door. There is a place to sit and remove your shoes, and here the bench is enhanced with a seat that folds forward to reveal a hidden storage compartment.

One of the major changes to the floor plan was the removal of the wall that separated the entry from the kitchen. In its place, Reynolds introduced multifunctional joinery.

These custom-made elements blend style and functionality, most evidently in the open-plan living-dining area. This space features a floating bookcase that wraps around the walls, acting as a device that ties the whole space together. A sliding panel made of pegboard opens to reveal the television and more display shelves, and the panel can slide the entire length of the wall back into the entryway. A home gymnasium is concealed behind a curtain and a two-piece couch can be reconfigured to turn the living room into a stand-alone guest bedroom.

The kitchen is generous for the space, with full-size appliances and a large prep area. The overhead cupboards are finished in gloss black Perspex to match the drawers and doors below the bench, while the cupboards on the window side are enclosed with clear Perspex sliding screens to allow daylight into the kitchen through the window and the glassware. The cork floor tiles are finished with Black Japan stain and add yet another unique touch to the home.

The two bedrooms in beâCHâlet are a study in functionality and design. The main bedroom features a bed on a raised platform with hidden long-term storage and easily accessible drawers underneath. A wall of joinery includes a wardrobe, drawers and cupboard space for clothing. The mirrored wardrobe and mirrors at each end of the room bounce light off each other and create a sense of more space. The second bedroom is multifunctional: it's a guest room, an additional workspace with a fold-out desk and a storage area for Reynolds's collection of sporting equipment with a unique bike-storage wall.

Reynolds's home is a hit in the neighbourhood, and he notes visitors remark 'on the attention to detail, the sense of cosiness, as well as the practicality of the apartment – how everything has a purpose'. It's also a fine example of how reinventing existing properties rather than rebuilding is the way of the future.

PAGE 12 The floating bookcase wraps around the interior of the living-dining room and proudly displays Reynolds's books and other curiosities.

AFTER

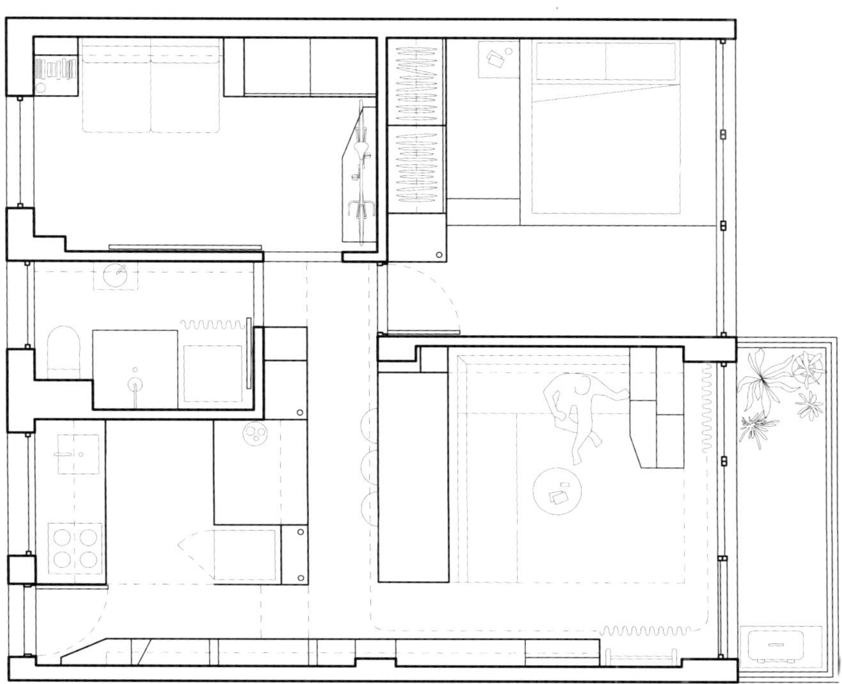

BEFORE

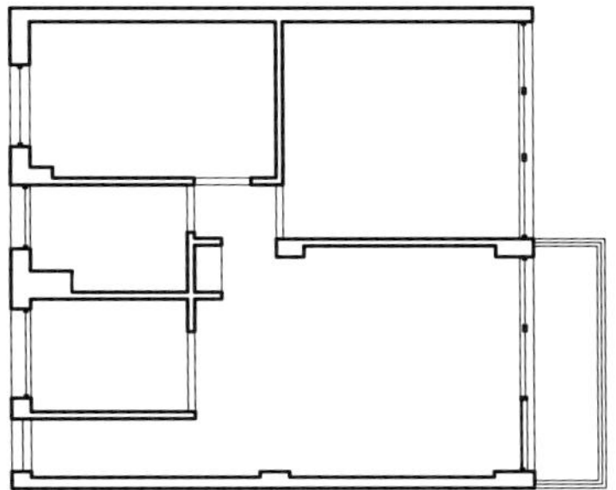

Scale 1:100

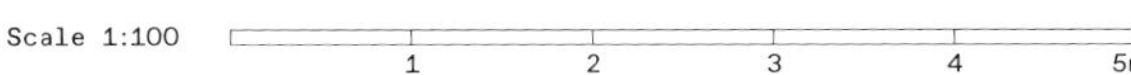

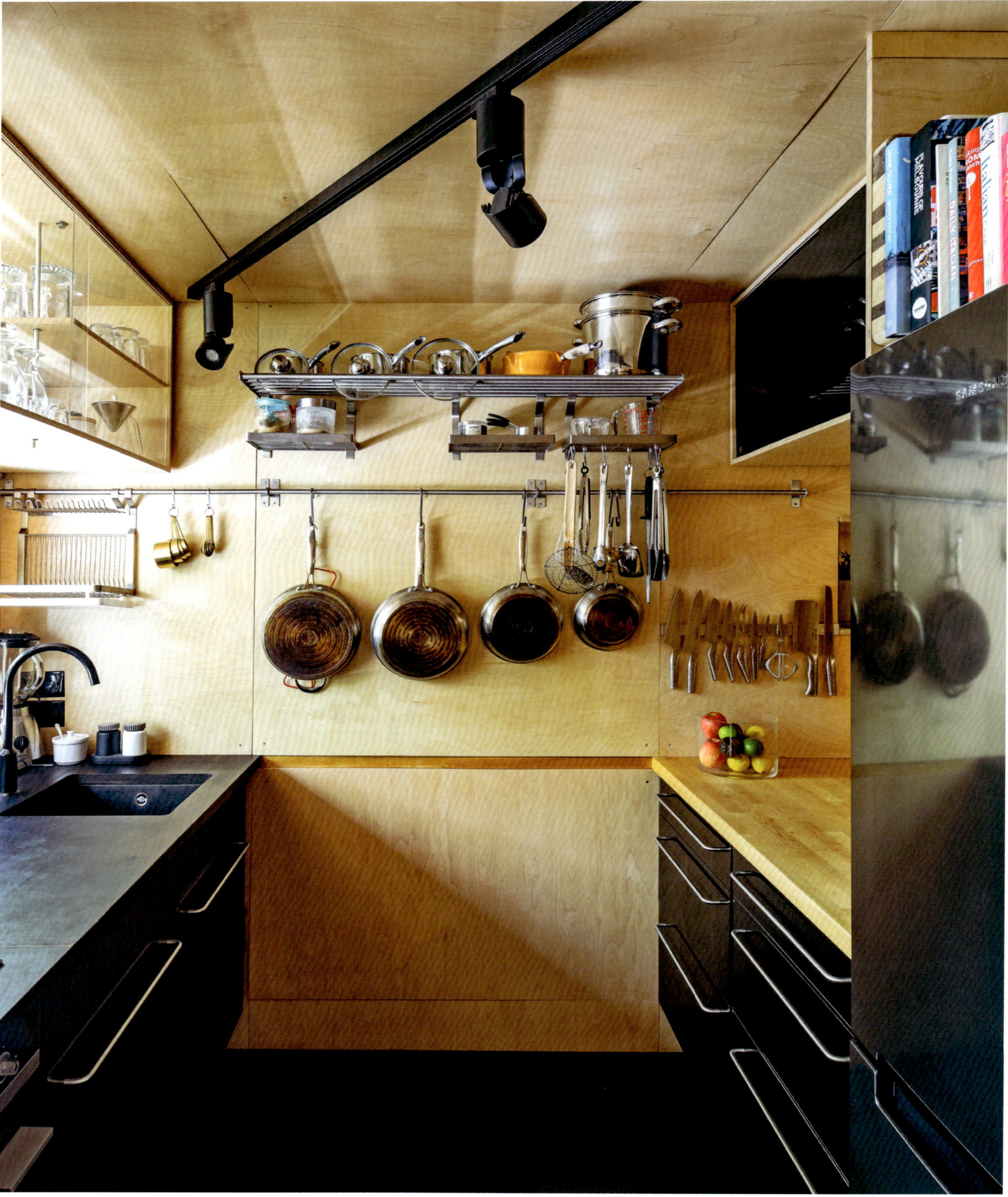
FLAVOURS OF MELBOURNE
DAILY ITALIAN
Italian

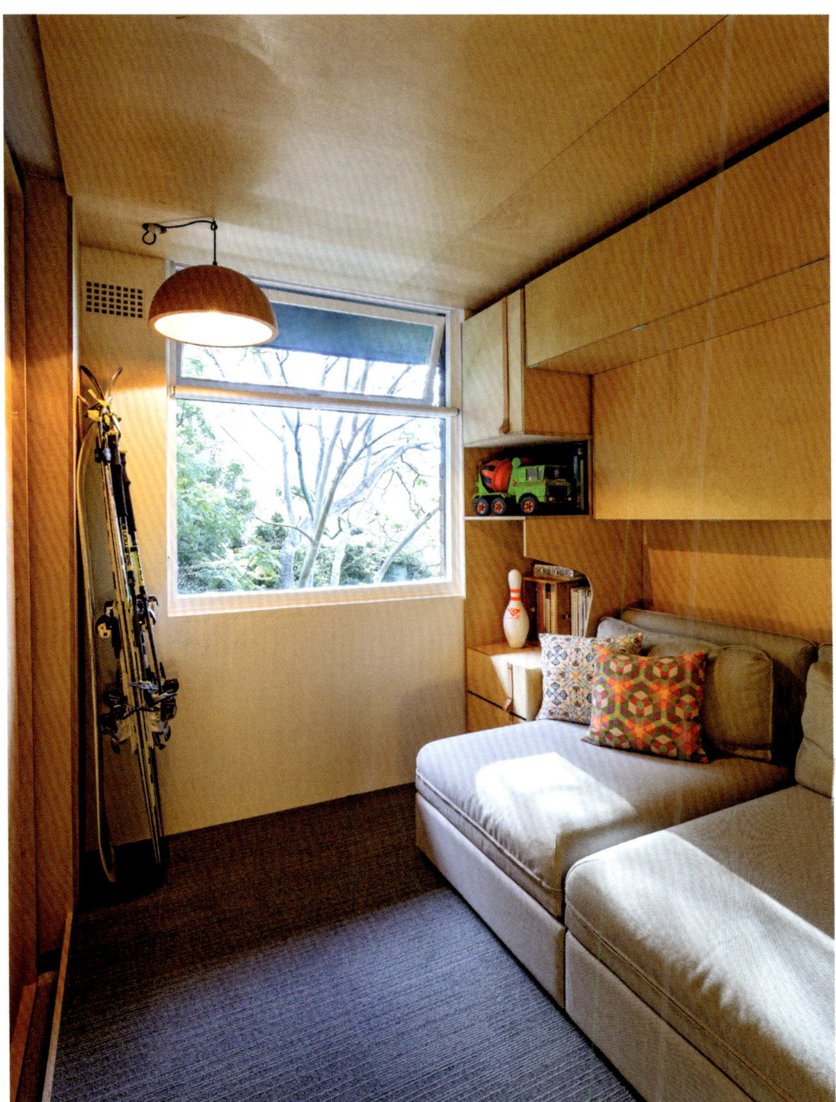

OPPOSITE Additional storage can be created in otherwise blank spaces by integrating rails and hooks.

LEFT Bright, uncluttered spaces with wooden features are often found in Japandi-style homes.

... visitors remark 'on the attention to detail, the sense of cosiness, as well as the practicality of the apartment – how everything has a purpose'.

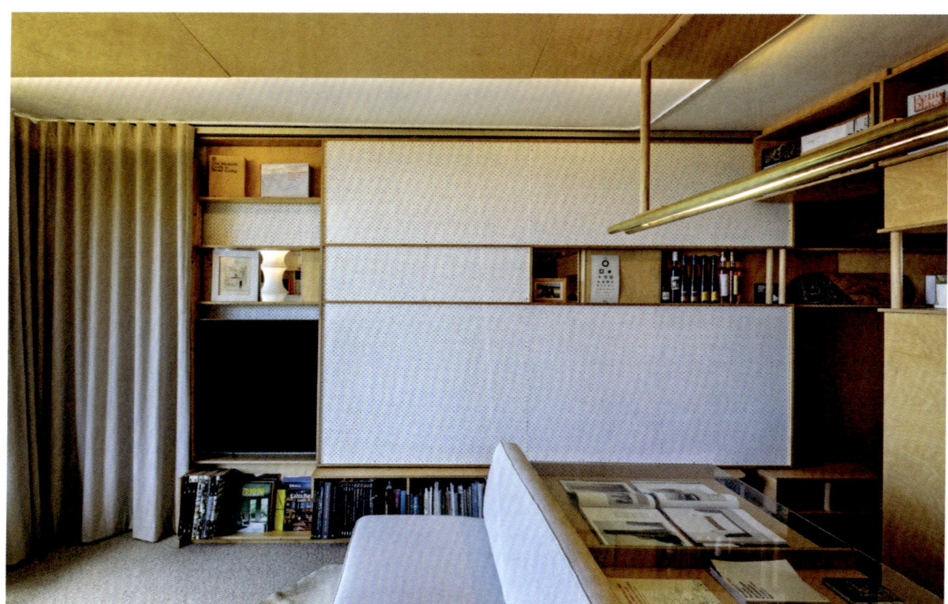

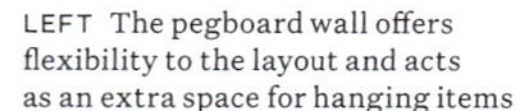

LEFT The pegboard wall offers flexibility to the layout and acts as an extra space for hanging items.

BELOW The sliding panel is an ingenious way to reveal various functions of the design when required.

OPPOSITE No space was left unutilised in Reynolds's genkan-inspired entry.

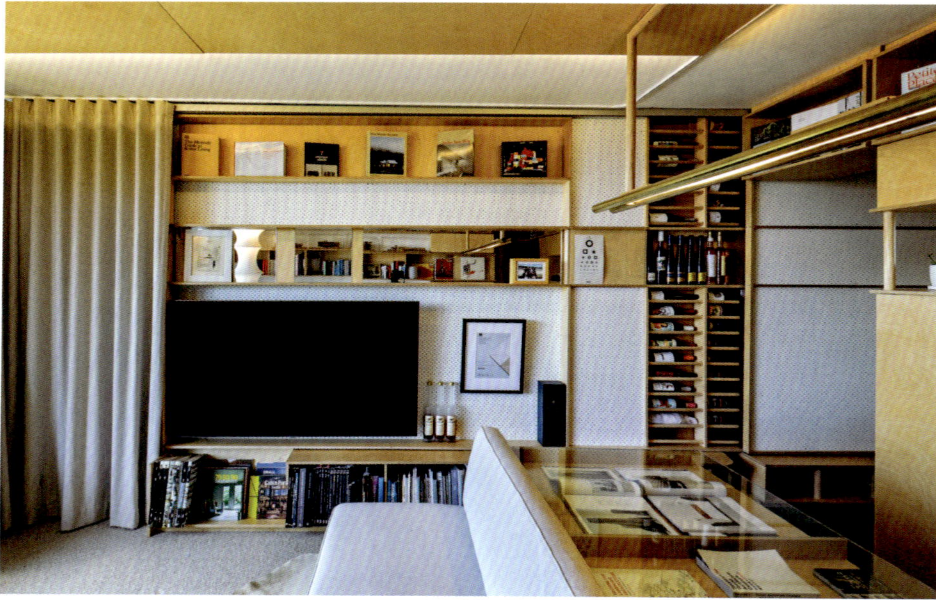

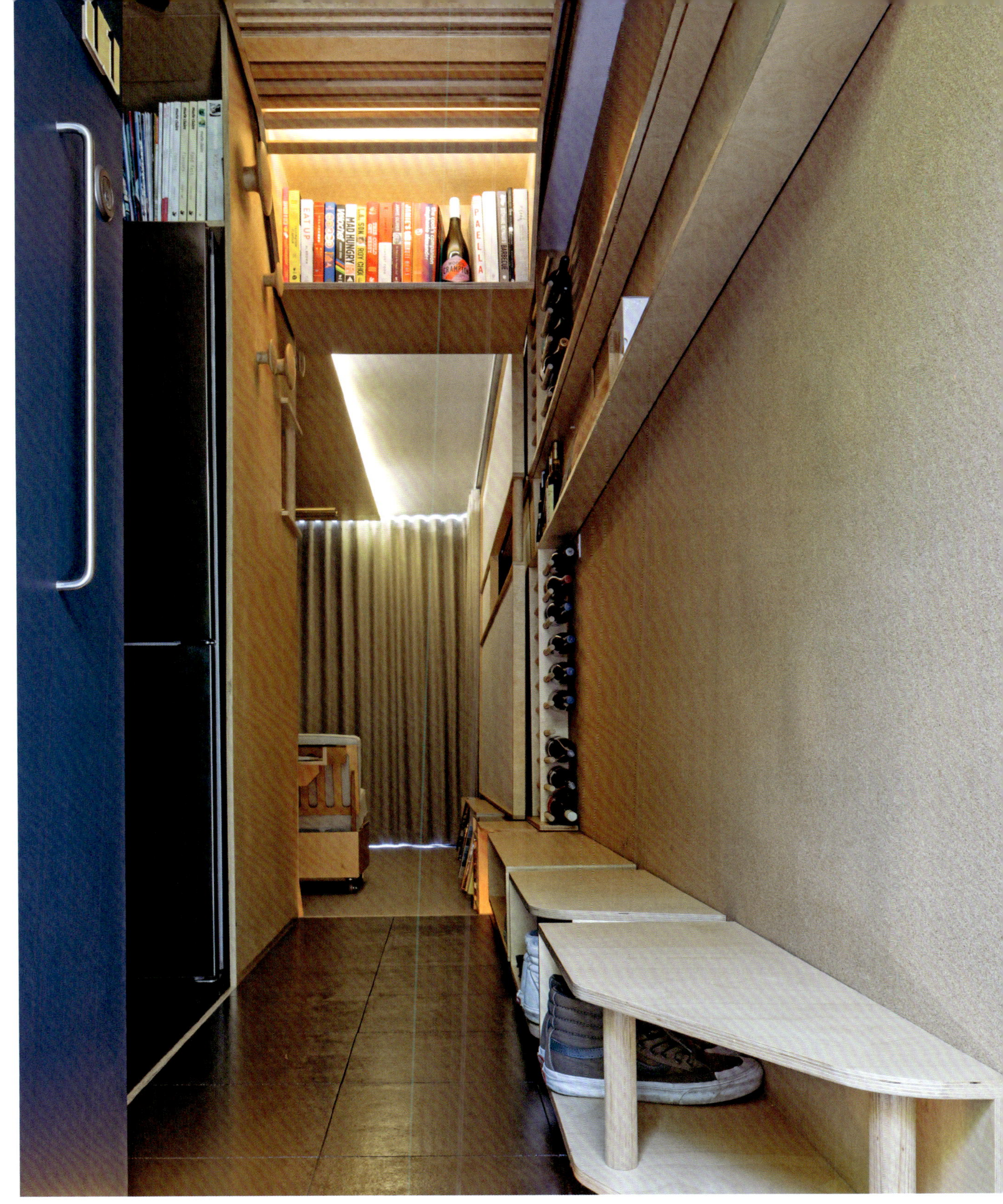

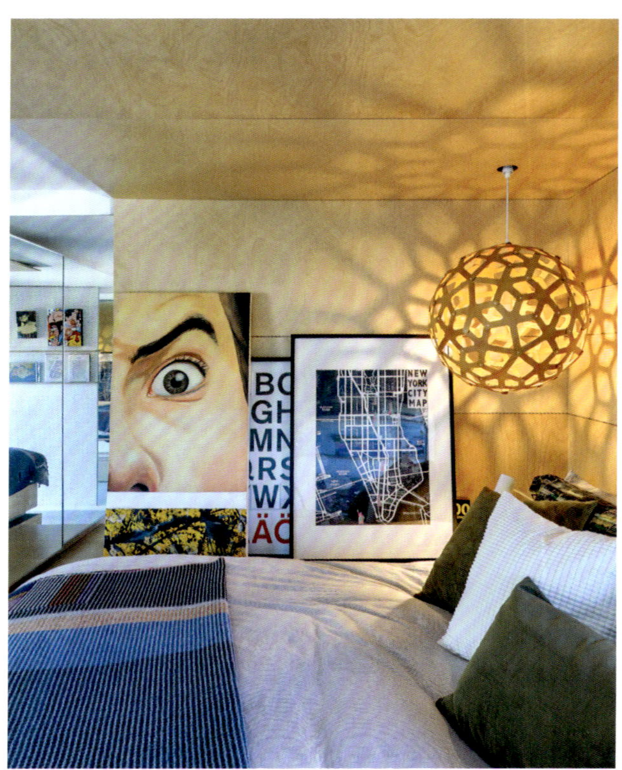
NEW
YORK
CITY
MAP

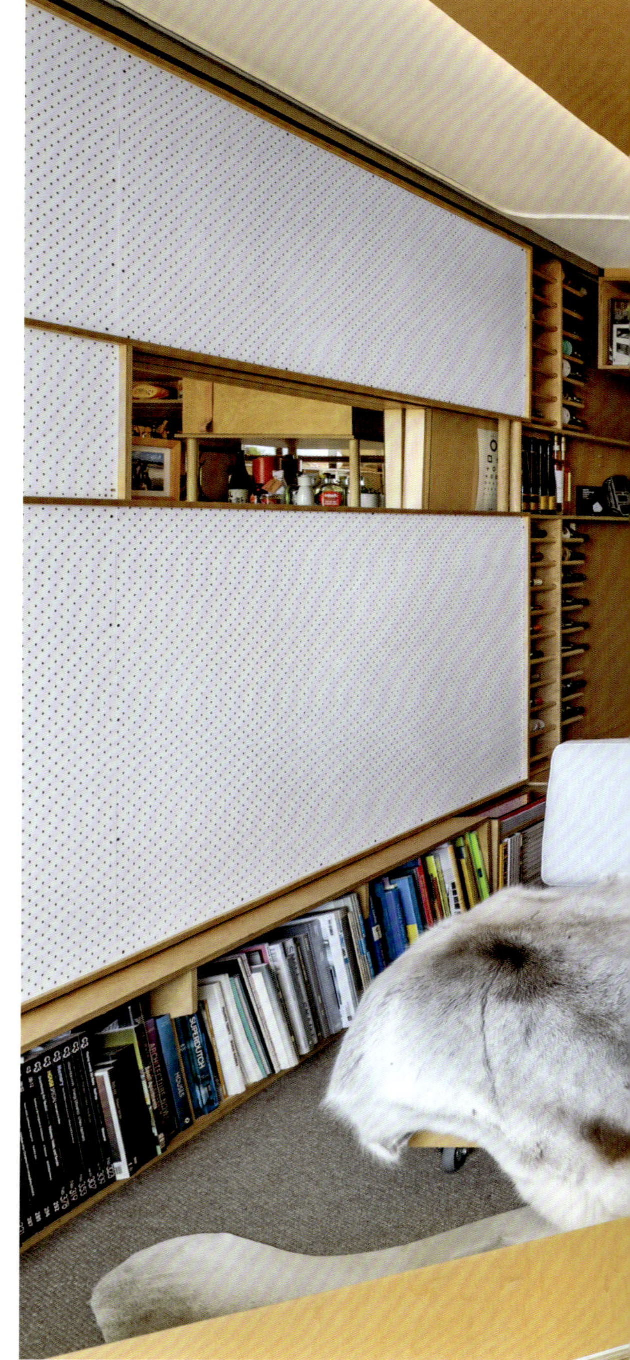

OPPOSITE Mirrors are one of the very best ways to make a space feel lighter and larger.

BELOW Despite its size, beâCHâlet has ample seating area and room to relax.

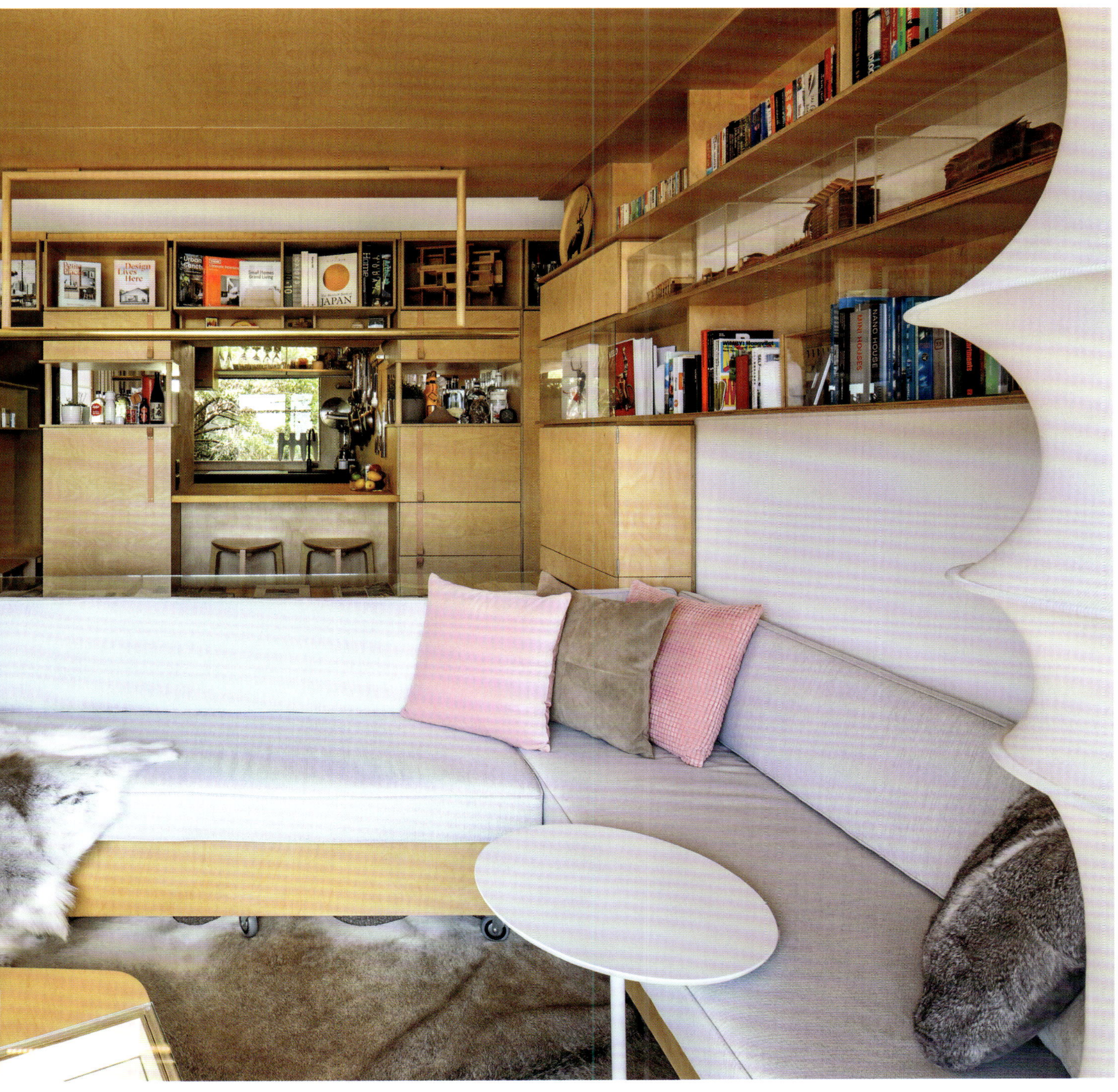

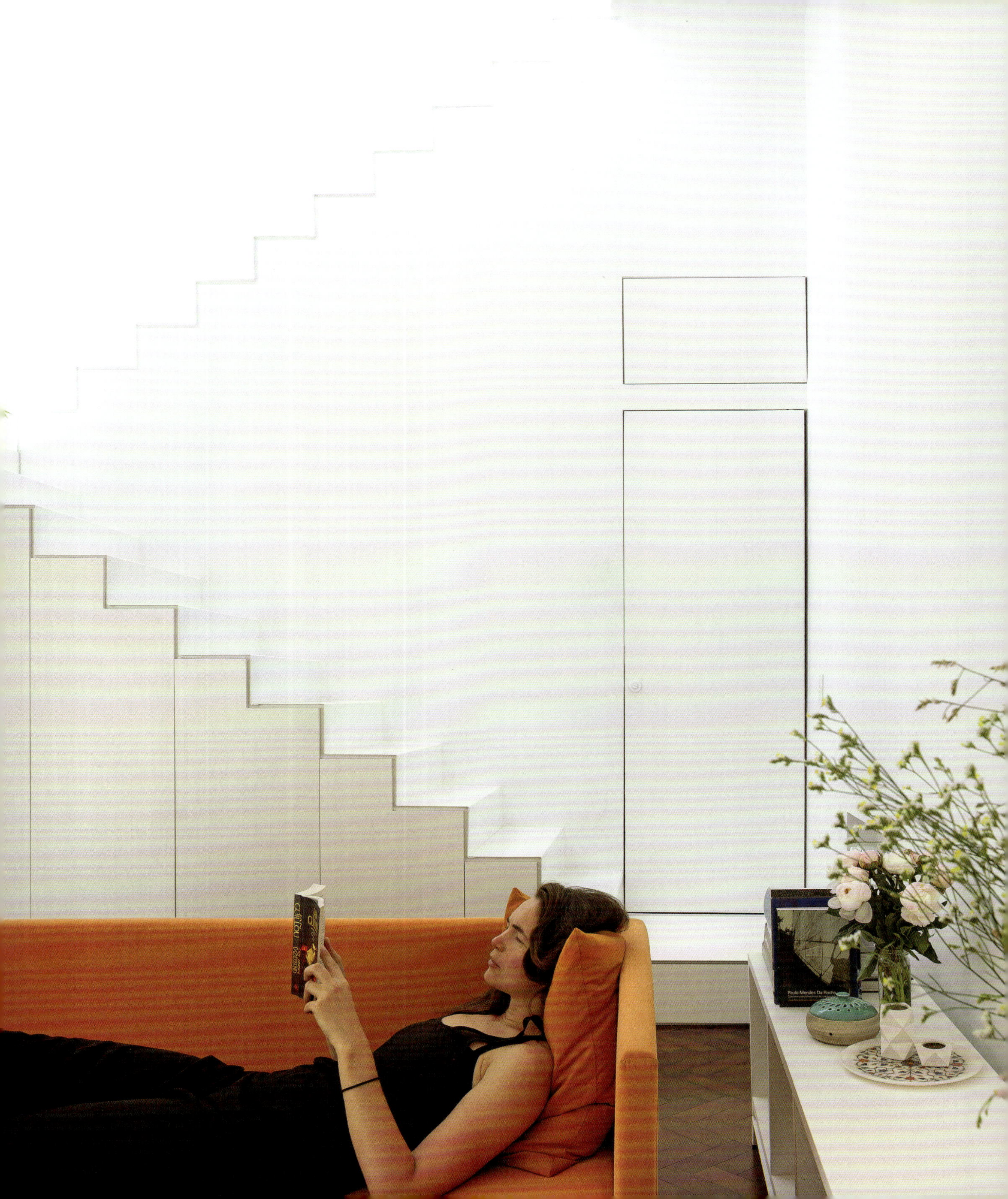

Paulo Mendes Da Rocha

Casa Cubo

59m² / 635ft²
Arqs. MichatekSkarstad
Parque Chacabuco, Buenos Aires

Architects and owners Torunn Vaksvik Skarstad and Matías Michatek are originally from cold climates so their home, Casa Cubo, in Buenos Aires celebrates the city's indoor/outdoor culture.

'We very much liked the fact that the lot the property sits on is 7 sq m (75 sq ft) and therefore decided on a total height of 7 m (23 ft),' Skarstad explains. 'Hence, the name Casa Cubo.'

PAGE 22 The outline of the stairs is a subtle-yet-graphic backdrop to the living room.

RIGHT Light streams in from above in the plant-filled patio – one of the original elements of the home.

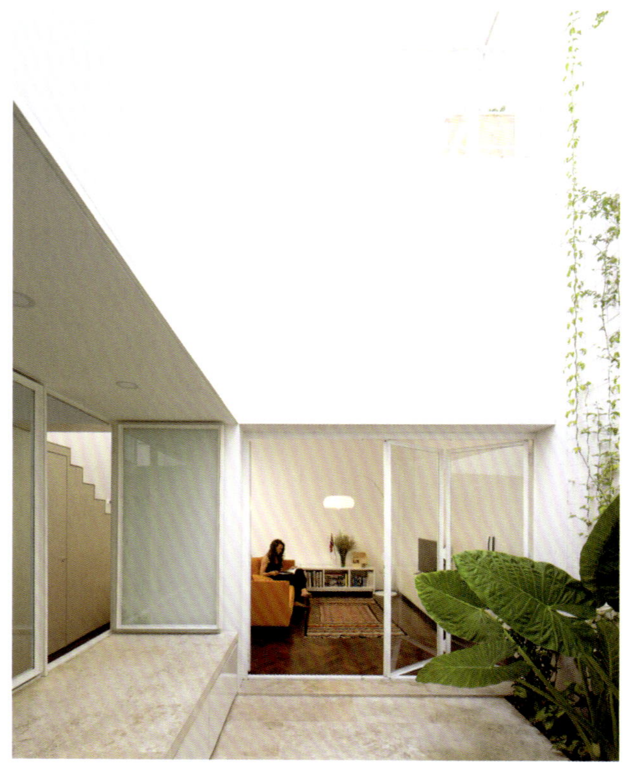

The apartment was originally completely oriented towards a central patio. In fact, all the rooms could only be accessed through the patio and had no connecting doors between them. Skarstad and Michatek changed the floor plan dramatically, and also added one-and-a-half storeys to accommodate a new office, kitchen and dining room. The additional storey is a simple metal framework with a light galvanised steel roof.

'We were always more focused on the potential of the structure and how we could make the best of the space rather than our specific wishes,' recalls Michatek.

Despite the drastic changes to the floor plan, the patio remains an important element as it's how you enter the home. It's a simple yet lush, plant-filled welcome and the apartment's first indoor/outdoor connection. Lining one of the patio's walls is a bench nook with drawers underneath for storing tools and gardening equipment.

The patio leads directly into the living room. All the furnishings and decor are lower to the ground, showcasing the bright, white walls, voluminous space overhead and the outline of the unembellished and striking feature stairs. The two storage units, housing books and the television, were custom made.

The primary bedroom sits just off the living room. The small niche that runs along the side of the bed doubles as bedside storage. Rather inventively, the drawers of the patio bench can be accessed from inside the bedroom too and provide additional storage for clothes.

The central focus of the home is the staircase: it looks like a pencil line drawing on a white sheet of paper. Made of metal, this multifunctional structure takes up minimal space and is the understated showpiece of the atrium.

Tucked away in the long and narrow section under the stairs is a bathroom. It's compact but has just enough room for a vanity, toilet and full-sized shower. On the other side of the stairs is a powder room for guests.

A small office sits just off the landing of the first set of stairs. One of the office walls is also made of metal sheeting and acts as a giant magnetic board for work notes. A large casement window fills the entire end wall and opens fully so the space is well-ventilated and flooded with natural light.

AFTER

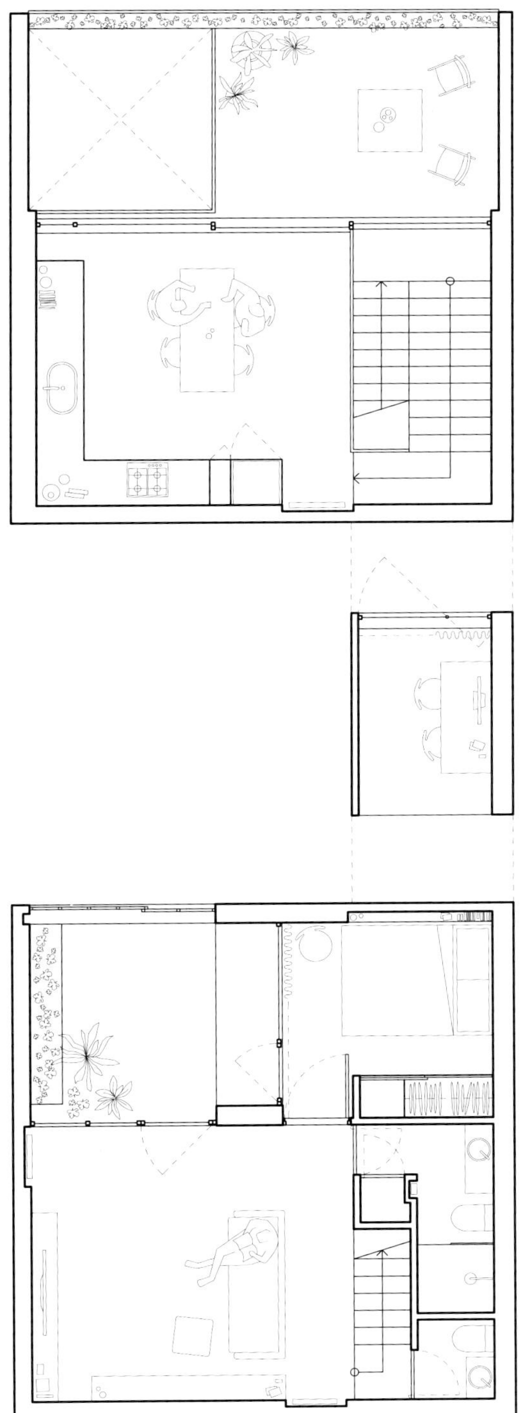

Scale 1:100

BEFORE

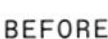

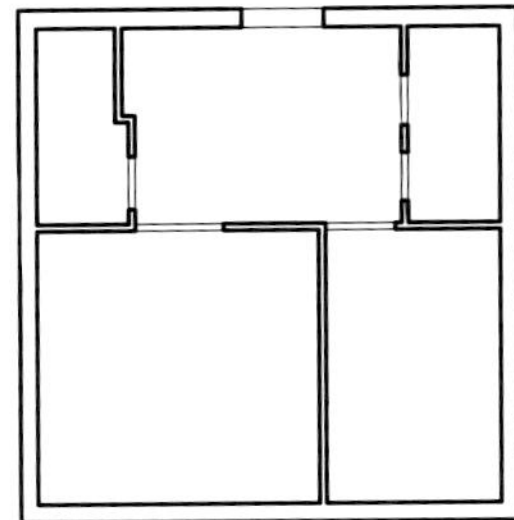

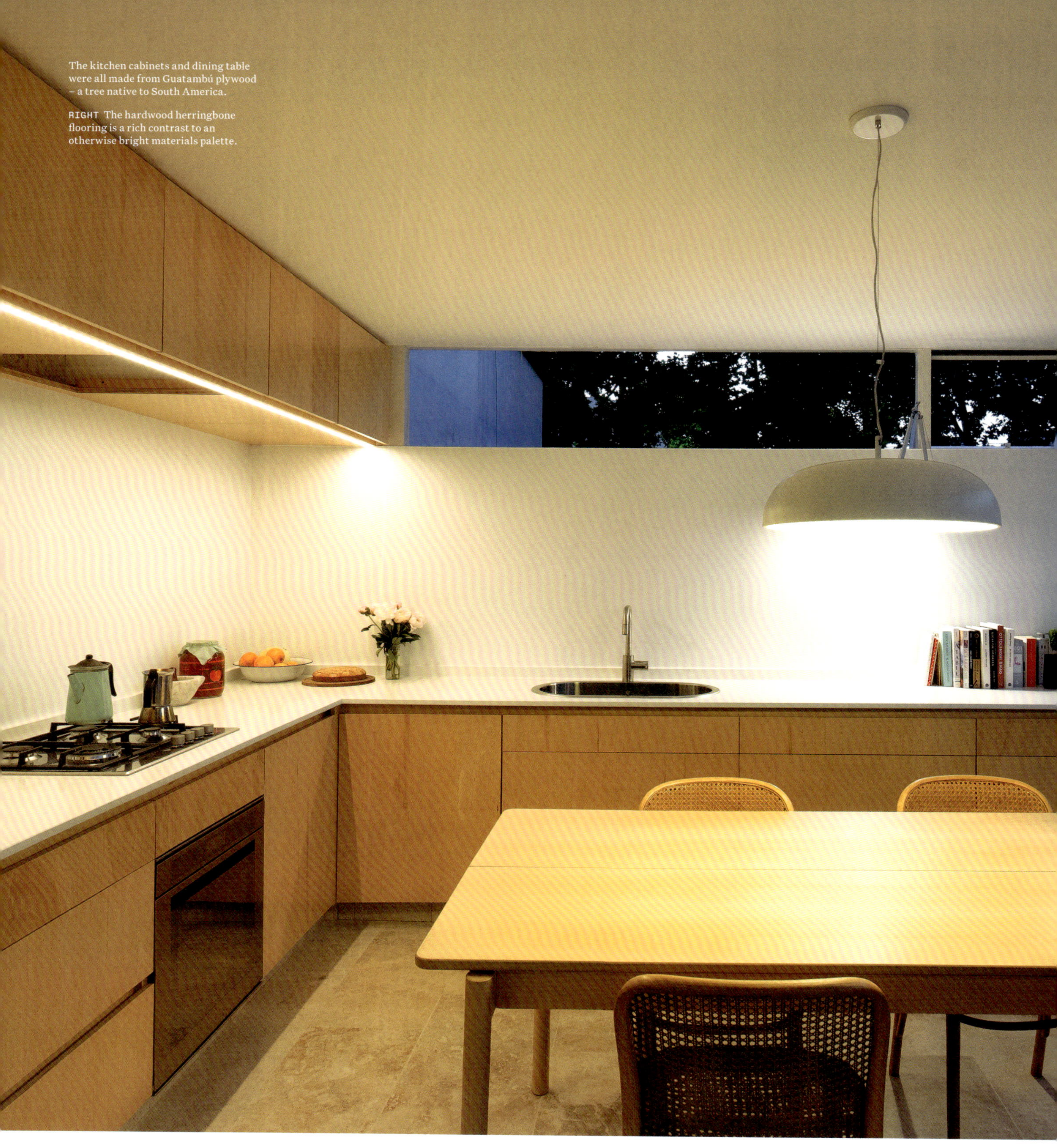

The kitchen cabinets and dining table were all made from Guatambú plywood – a tree native to South America.

RIGHT The hardwood herringbone flooring is a rich contrast to an otherwise bright materials palette.

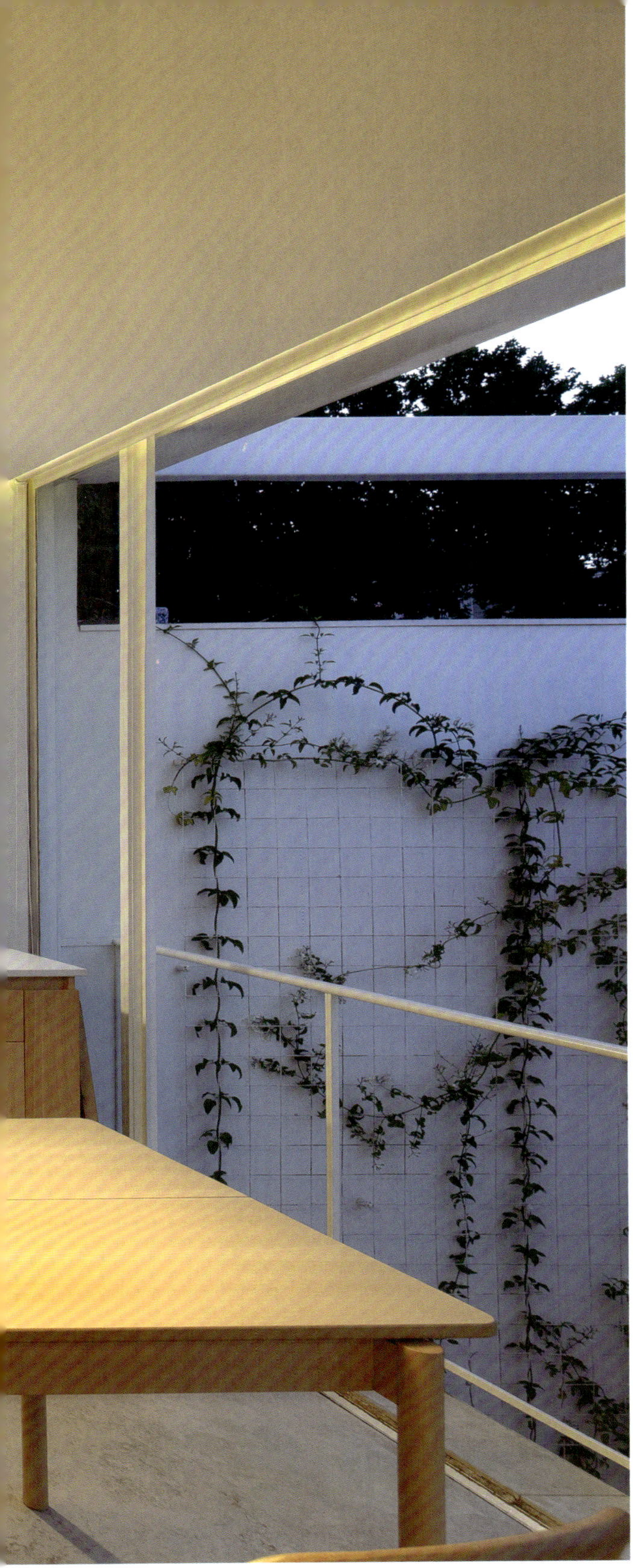

This mostly white and minimal home feels anything but cold or restrained.

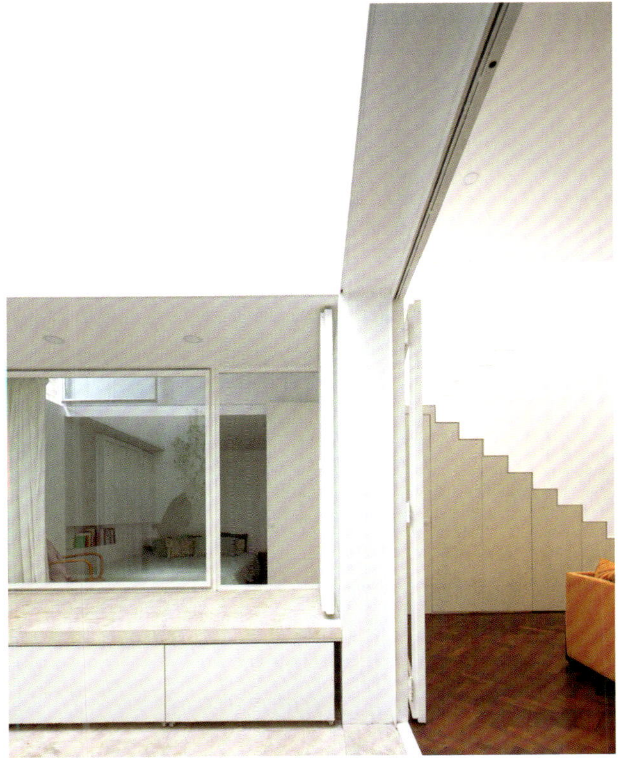

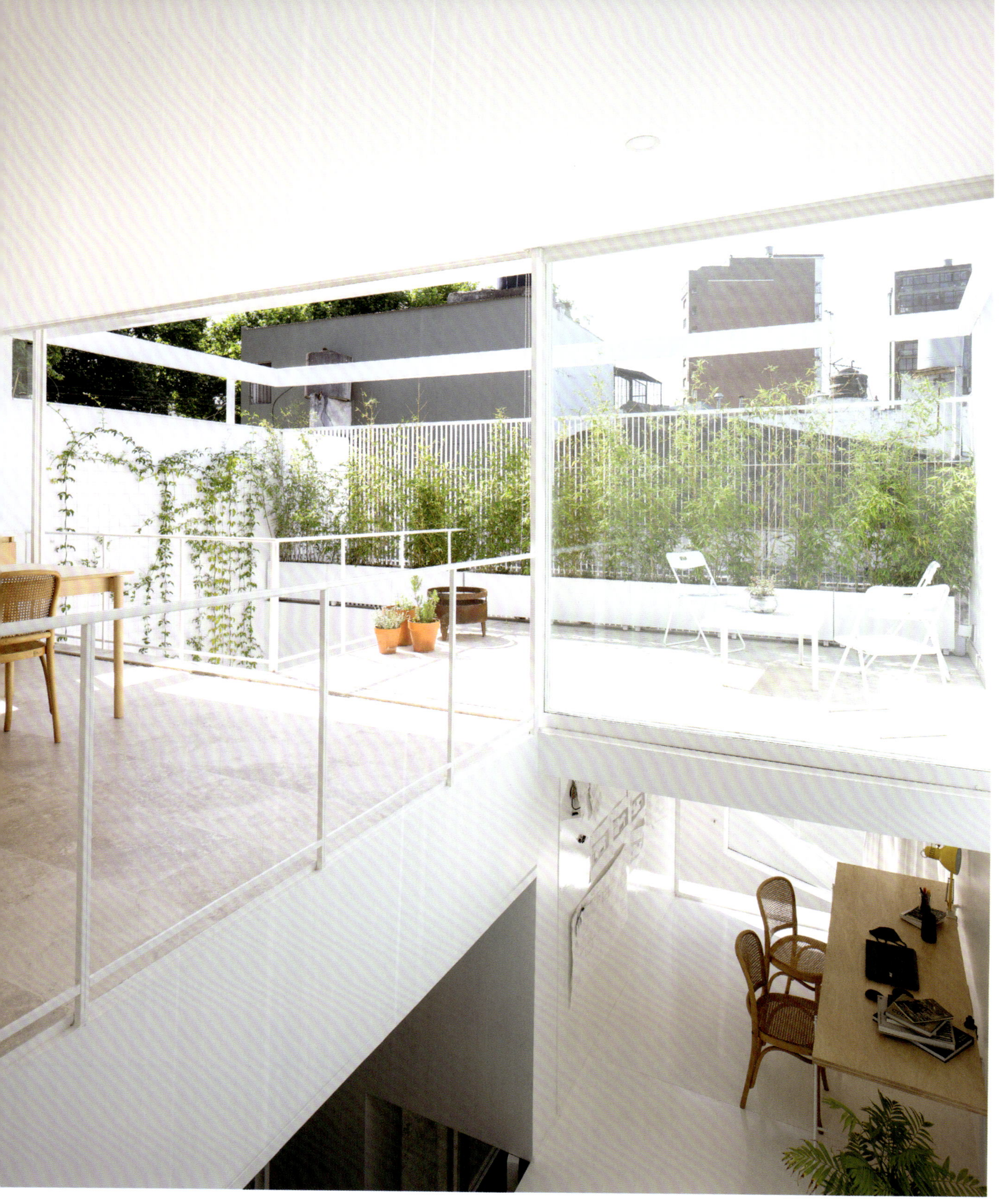

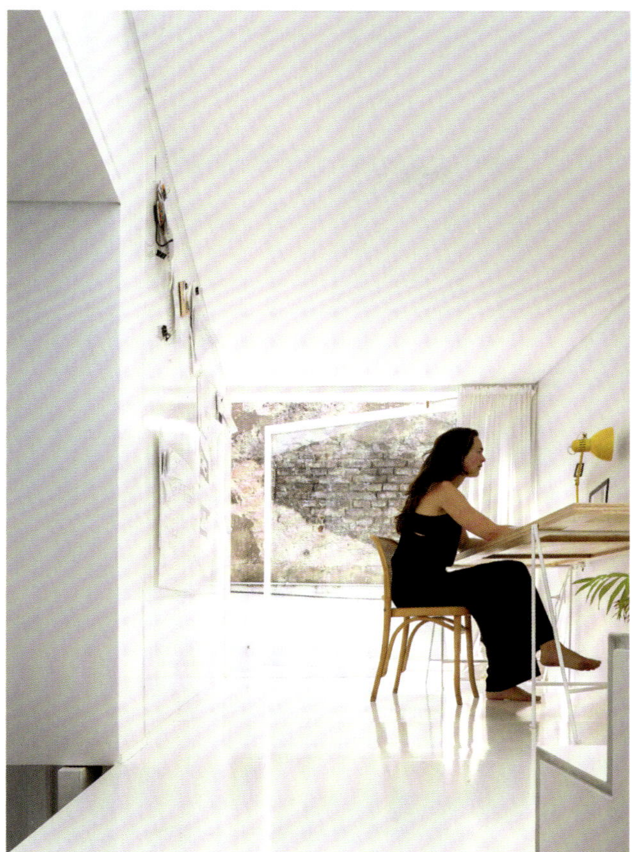

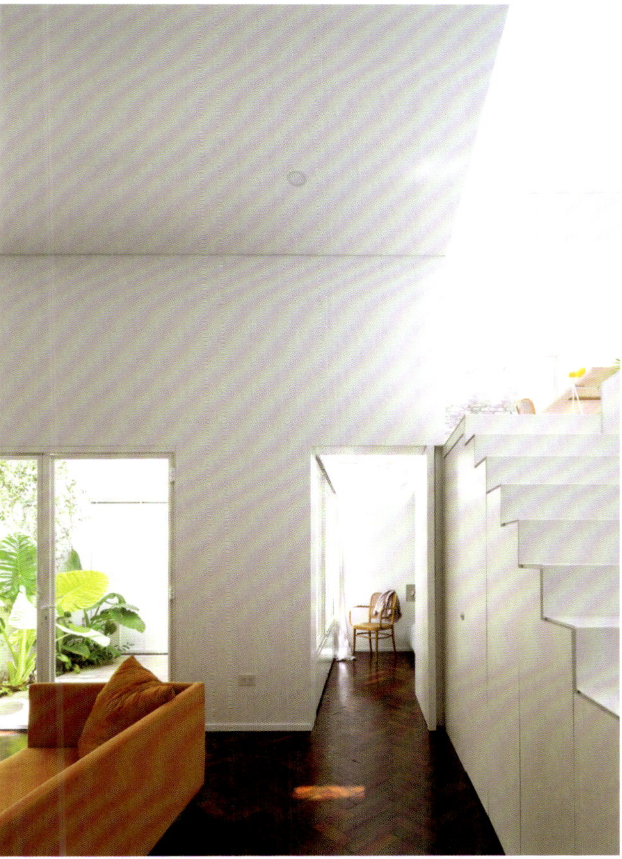

OPPOSITE The kitchen and dining areas meld seamlessly with the terrace, making the space ideal for al fresco dining.

TOP LEFT The simple light-filled office features notes hung on a magnetic wall.

TOP RIGHT A view to the patio and bedroom from the living room.

From the office, another small set of stairs leads up to the kitchen, the dining area and the terrace. Windows line two of the walls and this level seems to consist as much of sky as it does glass and wood.

The sleek and minimal kitchen cabinets and the beautiful dining room table are made from Guatambú plywood (a native tree to South America) and were custom designed by Skarstad and Michatek.

Glass-panelled sliding doors open out onto the generous terrace where white metal planters, filled with thriving bamboo, line the railing. The planters were custom designed by the duo and welded on site (as were the windows and staircase railing).

This mostly white and minimal home feels anything but cold or restrained. Light flows easily throughout, reaching its crescendo on the top storey where indoor/outdoor celebrations are, by the space's very existence, unending.

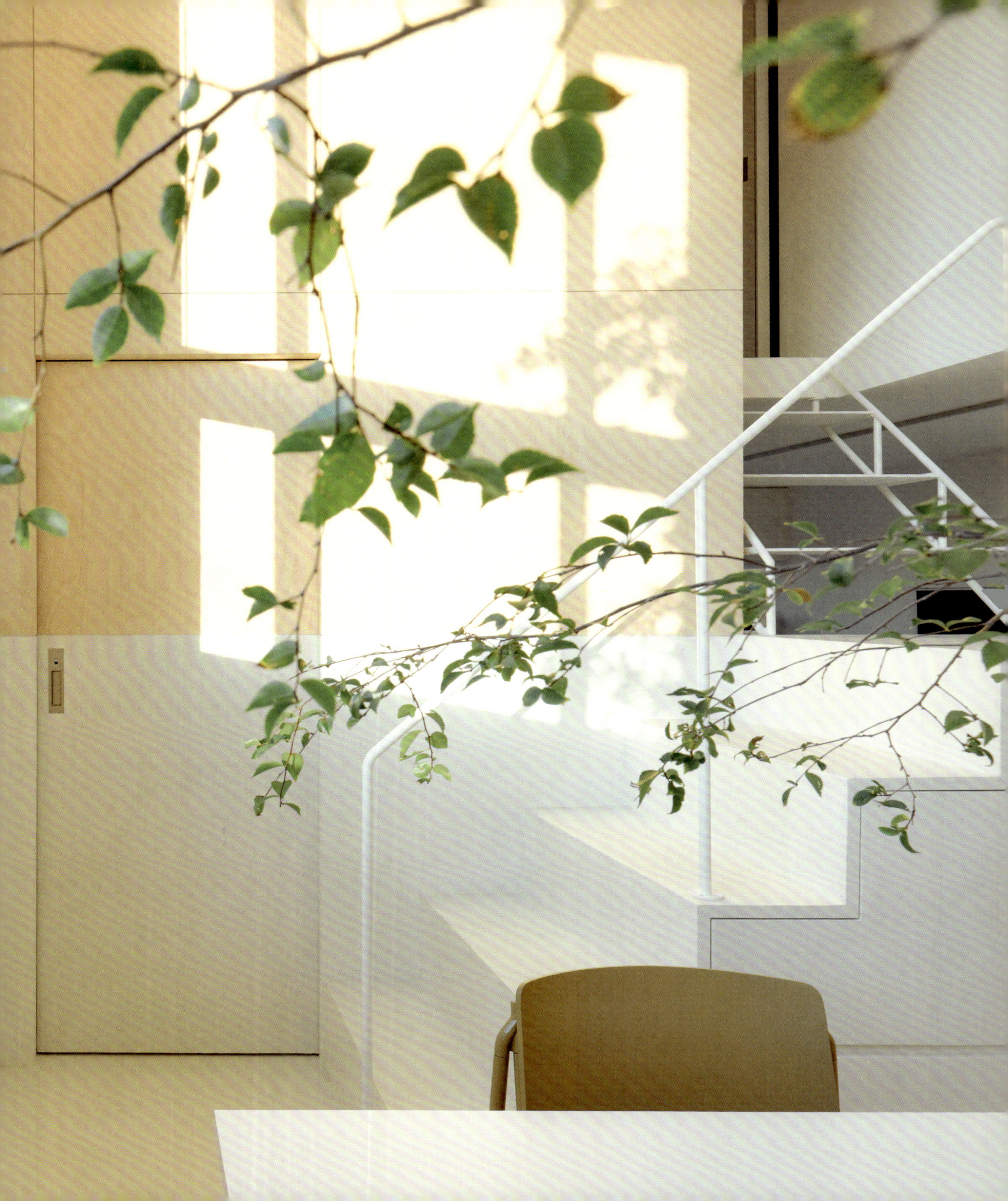

IT's House

$70m^2$ / $753ft^2$
2 Books Design
Wenshan District,
Taipei City

The design of this home was inspired by the owners' two cats, Millie and Hana. 'They like to look out the window, lying around and basking in the sun,' architect Jeff Weng explains.

Making the link between pet cats and architecture is surprisingly easy in IT's House with its sun-filled spaces and clean, bright aesthetic.

Located in an apartment building in the south of Taipei City, Taiwan, adjacent to the Jingmei River, the home's footprint was reduced to 70 sq m (753 sq ft) to let in more light. The footprint of the mezzanine level, added by the previous owner, was reduced to open the vertical volume and ease the crowded feel of this level.

The staircase's direction and material was also changed to 'increase transparency in the space and reduce the sense of oppression caused by bulky stairs'. In their place are metal-truss stairs with a stacked birch plywood and cement base.

The front door opens to a round wall cabinet, deliberately oversized to appear like a window in the entryway. The hallway connects to the living room and the kitchen. A line of lights from the entrance to the kitchen acts as a visual guide, lengthens the entire depth of field and makes the living room appear more open.

The kitchen is located at the end of the entryway. The clients didn't need a dining room table near the kitchen, so an island was installed instead. The kitchen's ceiling tapers and in the tallest area there was room for a plywood storage cabinet containing a washing machine and clothes dryer. The refrigerator stands flush with the cupboards in a niche. A small balcony accessed through sliding doors in the kitchen is a compact-yet-welcome outdoor space.

A Togo sofa placed adjacent to the kitchen island defines the living room area. The wall-mounted television with cords and accompanying tech embedded in a base cabinet ensures the floor space below is clean and clear.

The bedroom is located upstairs, and a solid glass wall allows for little visual interruption between the two storeys. Weng says of the bed's placement next to the glass, 'you can sit on the edge of the bed and enjoy the night sky before going to sleep'.

A bathroom and dressing room adjoin the bedroom. Rather than using tiles, the walls have been painted with a mineral paint and any gaps between surfaces have been sealed to increase the minimal feel of the space. The basin has a concrete-like texture to blend in as much as possible with the concrete look of the hand-troweled walls. Stainless steel accessories were used to 'emphasise the delicacy of stainless steel and the roughness of mineral paint,' explains Weng. 'The contrast strengthens the texture of the two.'

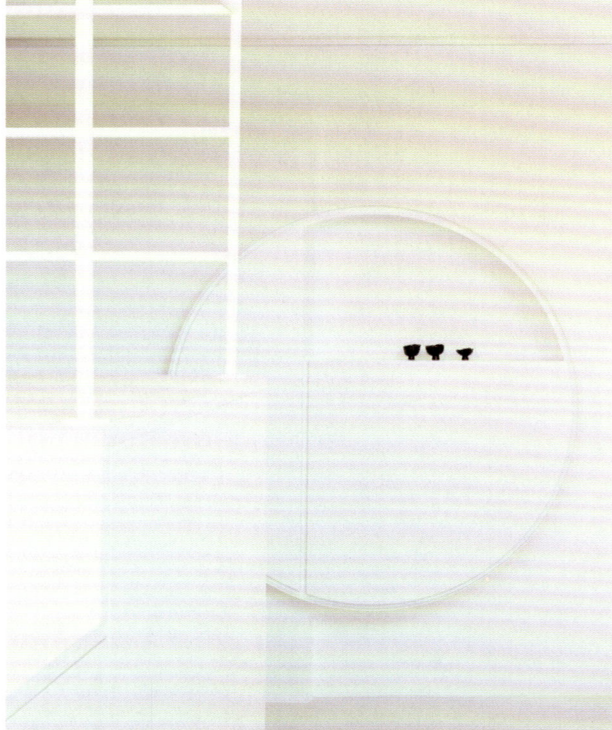

PAGE 30 Architect Jeff Weng believes that 'every corner of a small space should be fully utilised, but making full use of it does not only focus on storage. More often, these corners are used to achieve a certain space atmosphere'.

RIGHT At the entrance, an oversized round wall cabinet mimics the shape of a window.

AFTER

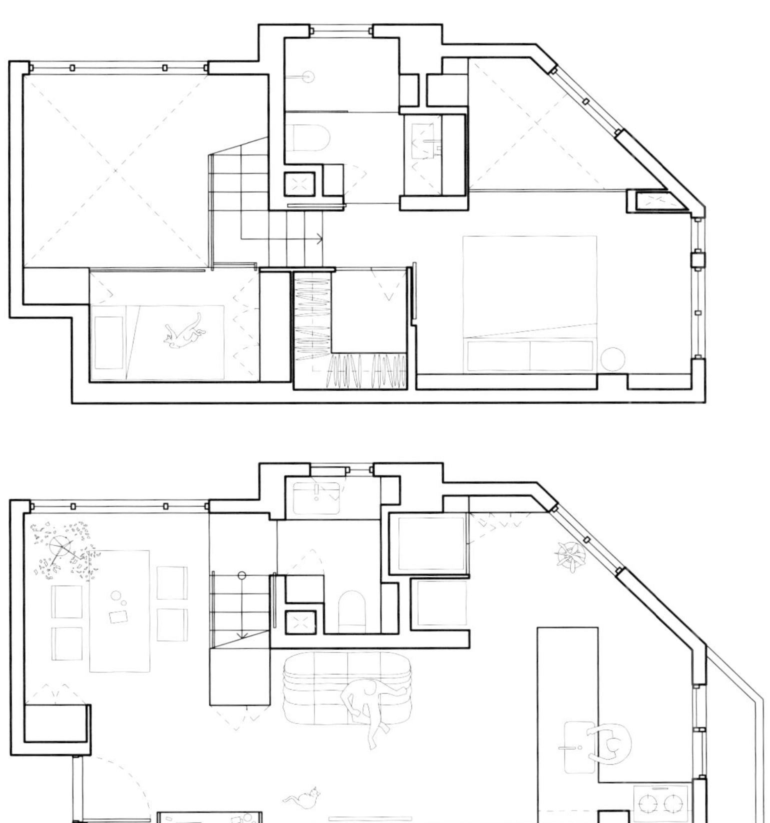

BEFORE

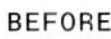

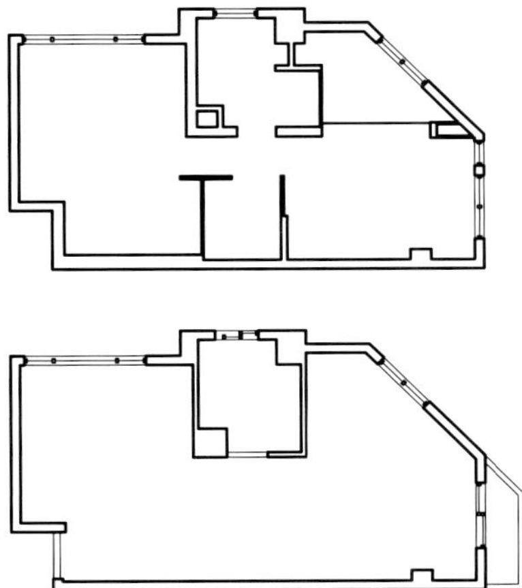

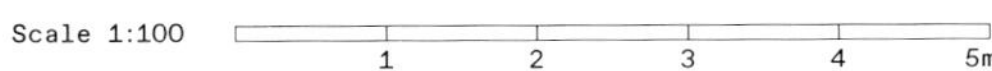

BELOW The staircase was originally orientated in the opposite direction, but now also functions as concealed storage and hides the cats' litter box.

OPPOSITE A Togo sofa adds soft, buttery texture to the living room.

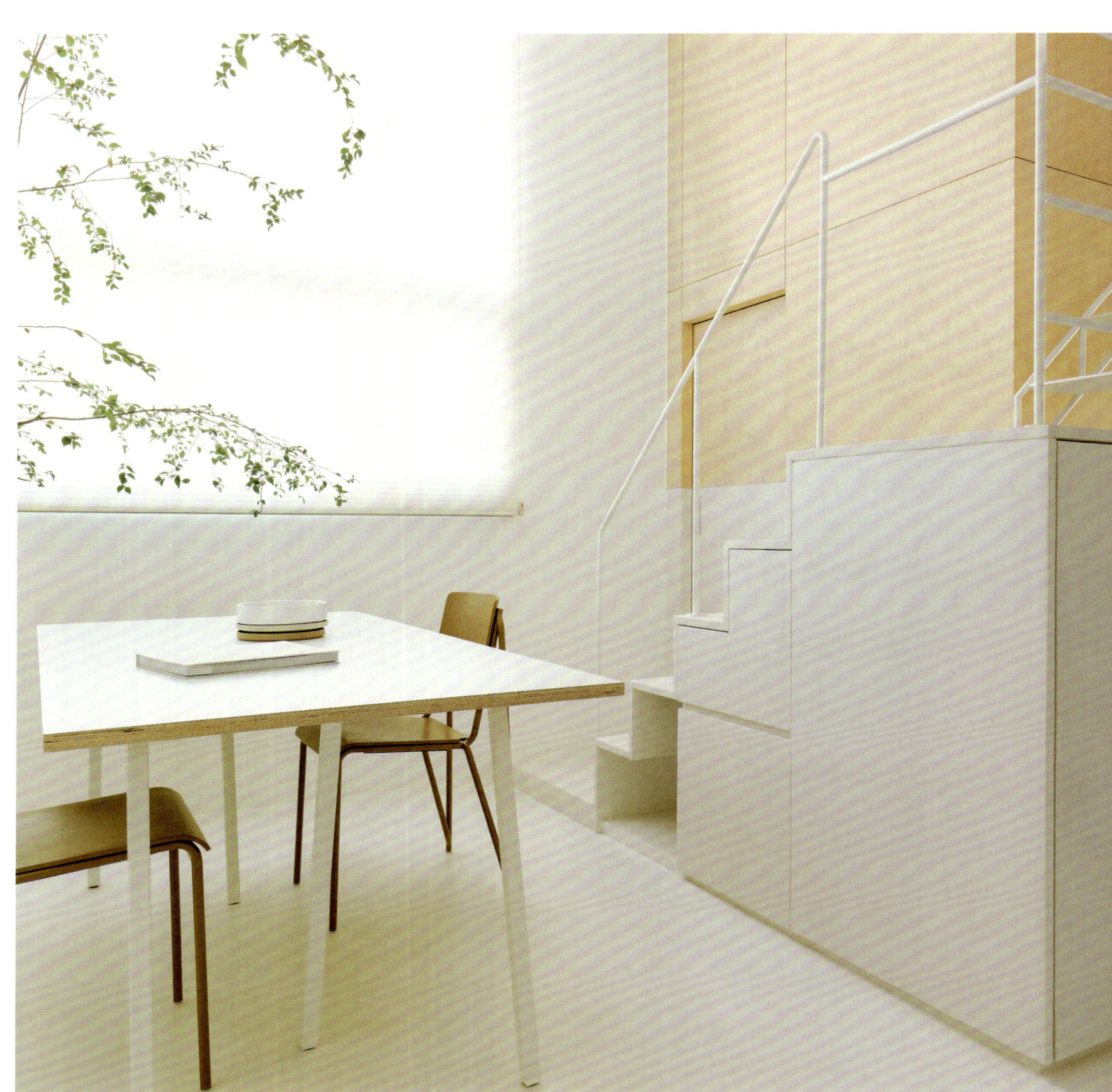

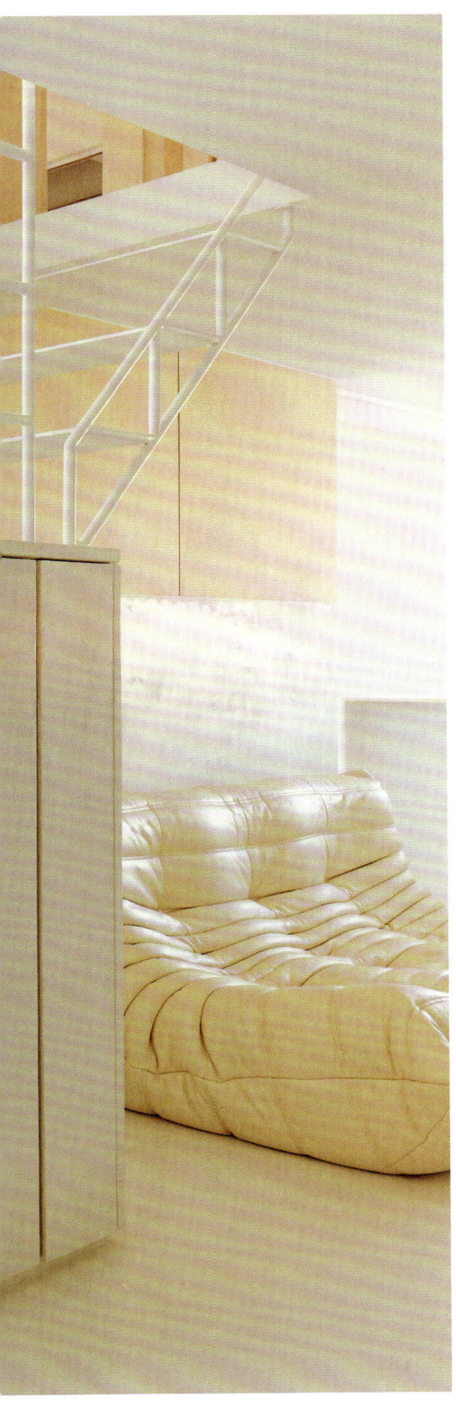

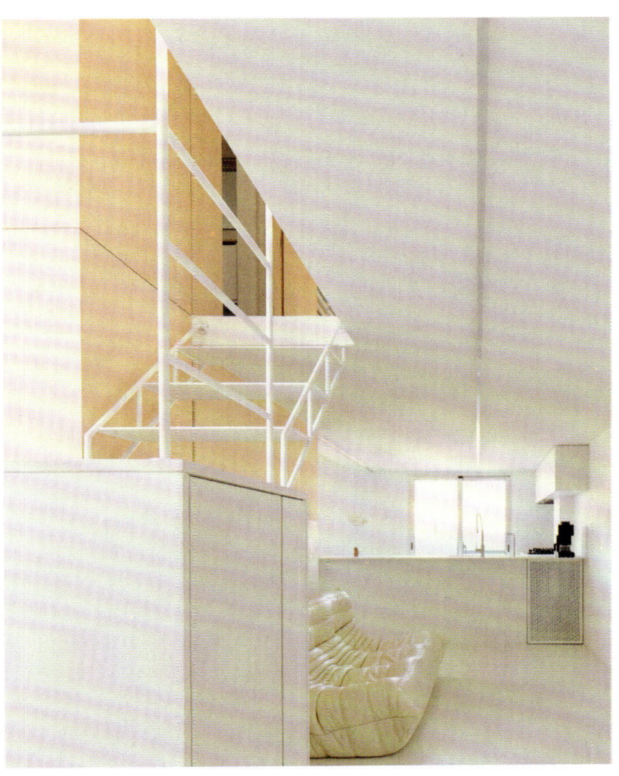

Back downstairs, a light-filled workspace was created just off the kitchen next to a pair of large windows. The generous worktable can be transformed into a dining table on the odd occasion one is needed. The base of the staircase also houses lockers for storage and the cats' litter boxes.

Weng describes the aesthetic of IT's House as 'delicate, relaxed, minimal and chaste' and it is an apt description. The home is calm, free of distractions and clutter, and perfectly suited to the humans and cats who live here.

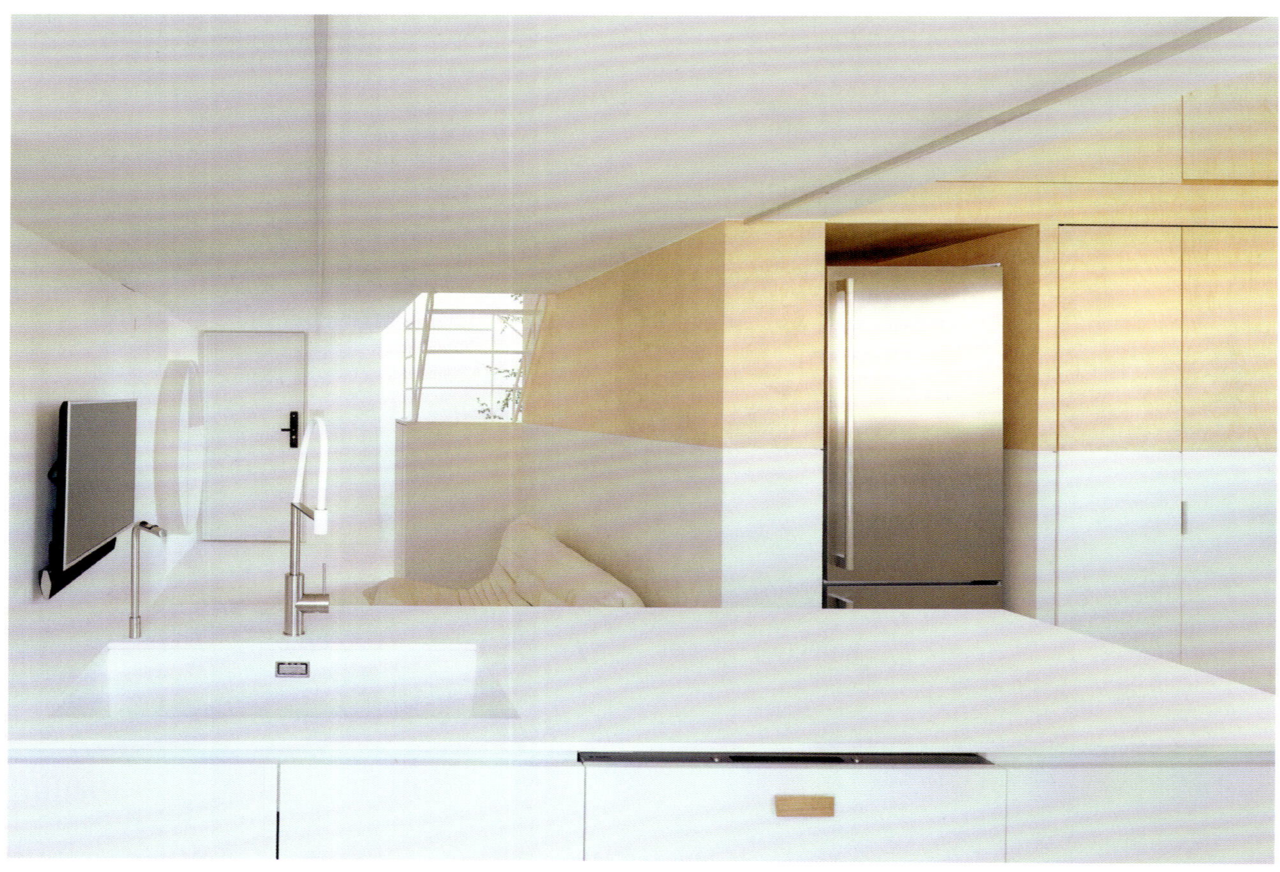

ABOVE The view from the kitchen highlights the impressive staircase made with a cement base and stacked birch plywood. Or as Weng describes it, 'the main vertical visual of the room'.

OPPOSITE A glass wall in the bedroom allows for a sense of serenity and simplicity between the two storeys.

Making the link between pet cats and architecture is surprisingly easy in IT's House with its sun-filled spaces and clean, bright aesthetic.

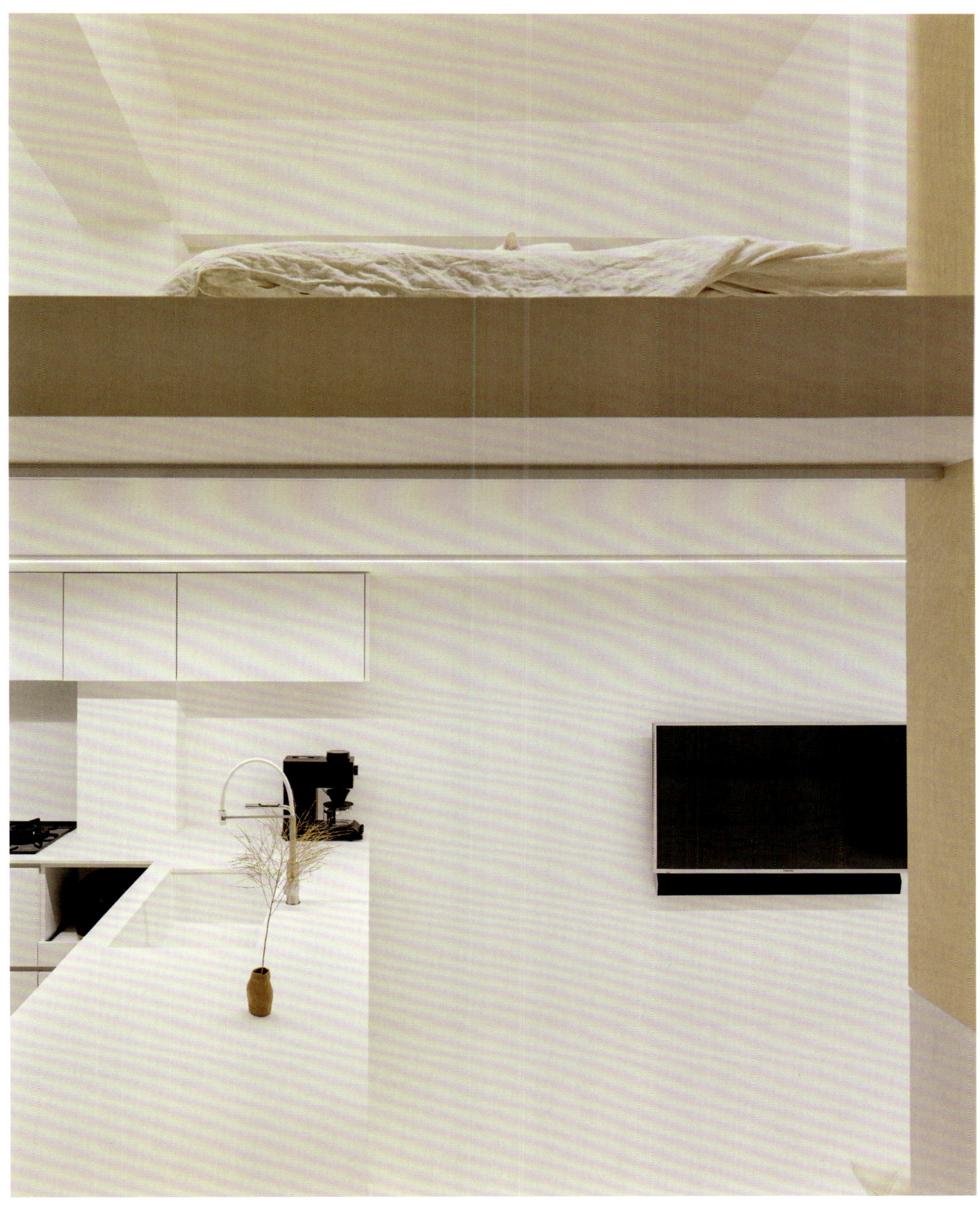

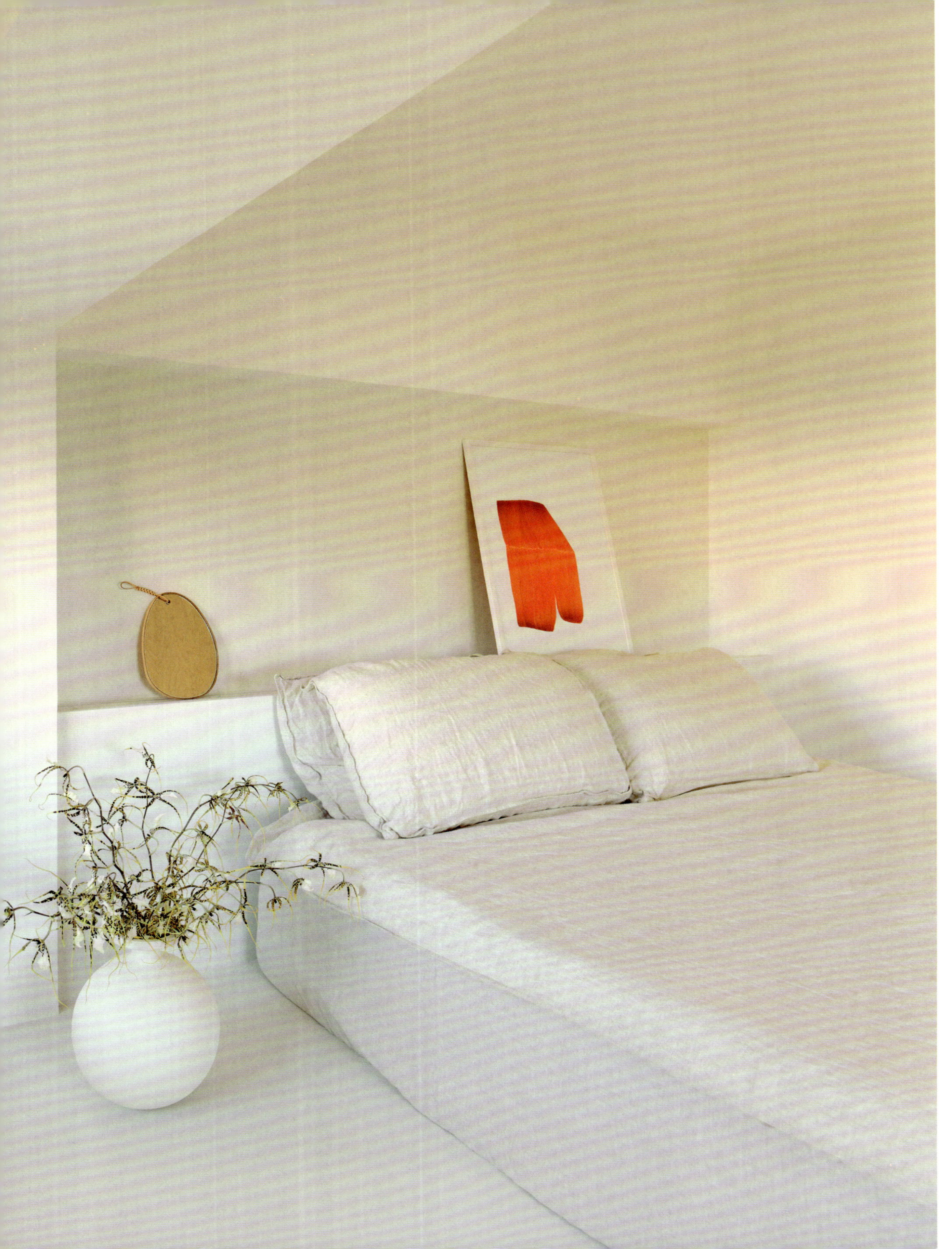

OPPOSITE Weng's philosophy is that even in a small space corners can create a certain 'space atmosphere'.

BOTTOM LEFT The concrete sink in the bathroom is a tactile contrast to the stainless steel hardware.

BOTTOM RIGHT A mineral paint was used in the bathroom and the dressing room to add texture and create a sense of continuity.

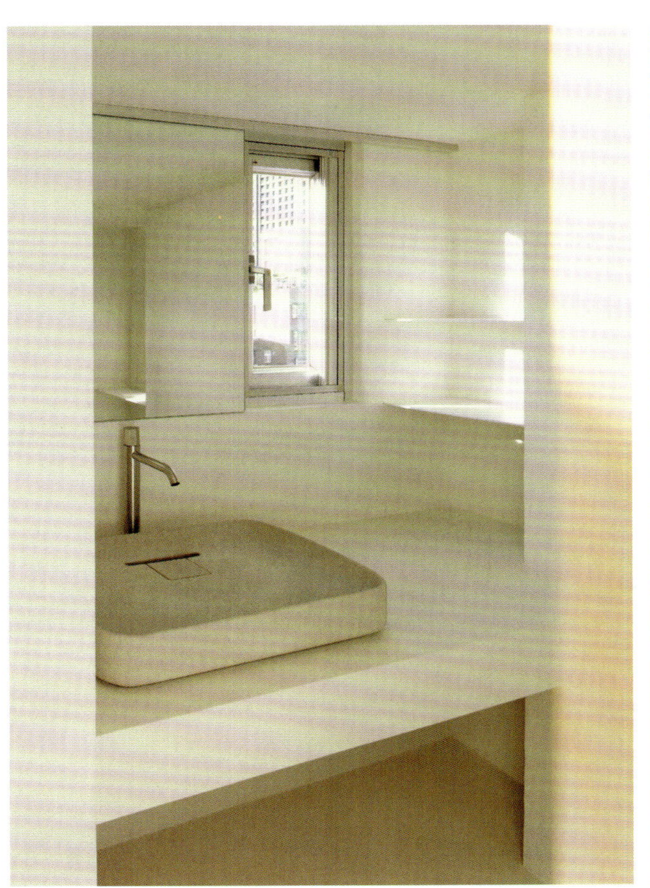

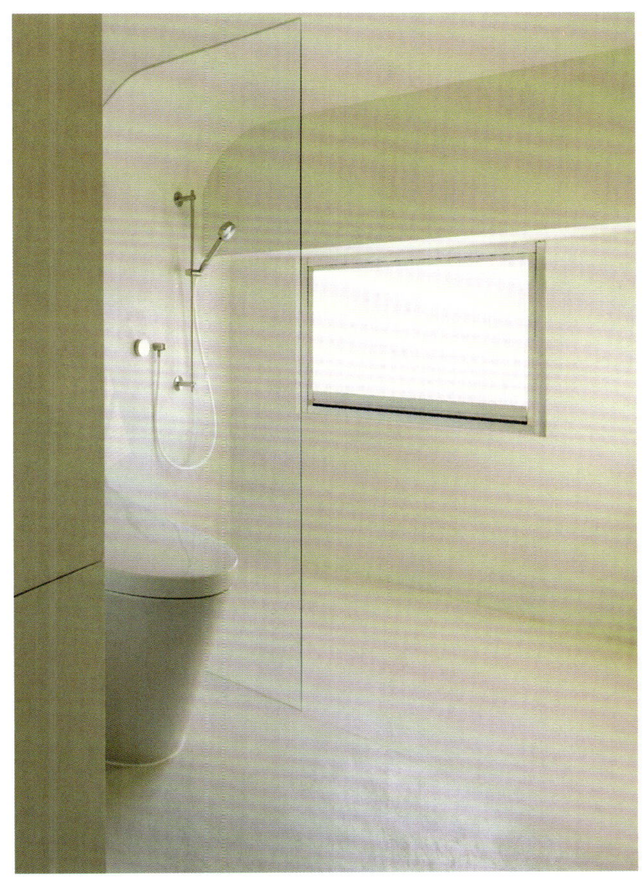

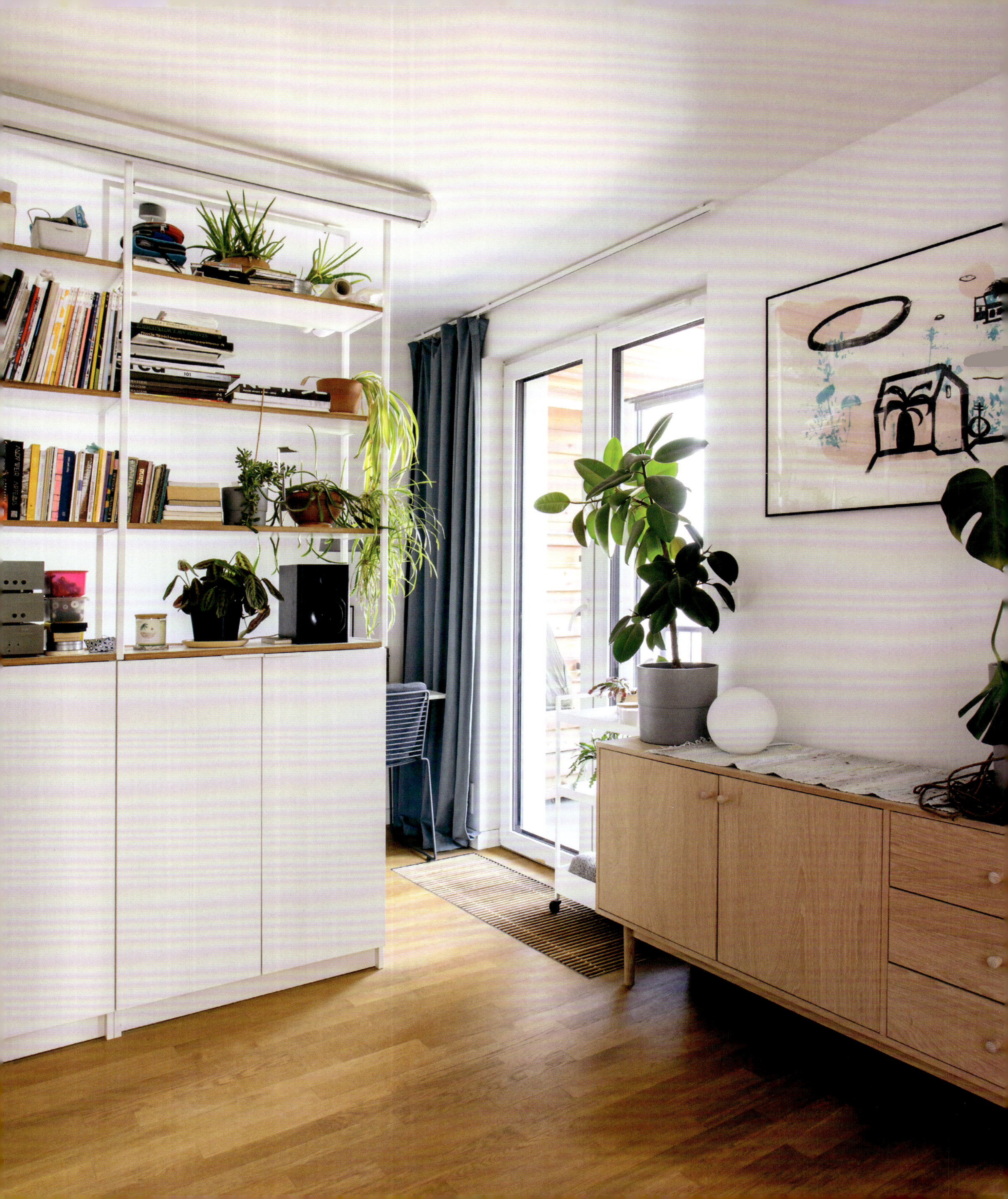

Lwowska

32m² / 344ft²
pigalopus
Podgórze, Kraków

Illustrating the power of skillful interior architecture, Karolina Chodur and Malvina Borowiec of pigalopus made no structural changes to Lwowska. Instead, using multifunctional furniture conducive to future configurations of the space, they were able to create a bright, airy and interesting 32-sq-m (344-sq-ft) home.

Lwowska is in a relatively new building near the city centre of Podgórze in Kraków, Poland. Chodur, who lives in the apartment with her partner and their dog, Wichura, fell in love with the windows and the light in the space. The goal was to make the living area feel as spacious as possible and to divide the space into smaller zones without adding any walls or sacrificing the light and flow of the home.

The entryway has a niche for storing coats and shoes and a pill-shaped mirror, which reflects the living area. A line of grey tiles defines the entrance zone. The rest of the floor is oak parquet, which was chosen to bring warmth underfoot.

Chodur and Borowiec were inspired by modern Belgian architects, such as Dries Otten and B-ILD Architects, who play with geometric forms and colours, and create bright and welcoming interiors with a twist.

One of Lwowska's 'twists' is a floor-to-ceiling shelving unit, used to separate the living and sleeping areas. Made from an IKEA bookshelf and customised with new doors, a steel frame and birch plywood for shelves, it can be moved around if a future resident desires.

The lower cupboards can be accessed from the living room and the bedroom, and act as both a bedside table and a 'fun window' between the two zones. In the sleeping area, the bed frame sits high off the floor to allow for easy access to storage underneath it.

In the eating area, a round kitchen table allows for ease of movement. The kitchen is finished in white ensuring it continues the theme of a neutral backdrop and notable features include a granite sink and an oak benchtop. An additional benchtop was added in front of the window as precious food-prep real estate with a view.

'It was important to design the main lighting in such a way that it did not mark the exact location of the furniture below,' Borowiec says of keeping the lighting design fluid for future configurations of the space.

Lwowska may only be a 32-sq-m (344-sq-ft) apartment, but it is harmoniously teeming with function and personality. It successfully fulfills the current owners' every need, while embracing a 'less is more' philosophy and remaining neutral and flexible enough for future dwellers.

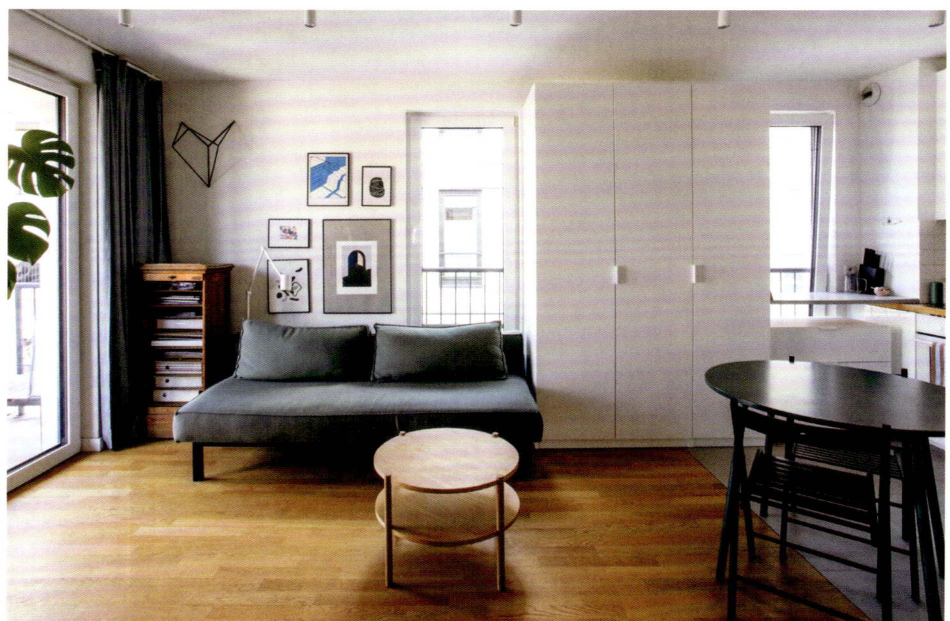

PAGE 40 Plants, an oak dresser and a graphic print hanging above it set the welcoming tone of Lwowska.

RIGHT Furniture selection is crucial in a small space. The open-plan living and kitchen area has a fold-out sleeper for guests and round tables to make moving around the space easy.

AFTER

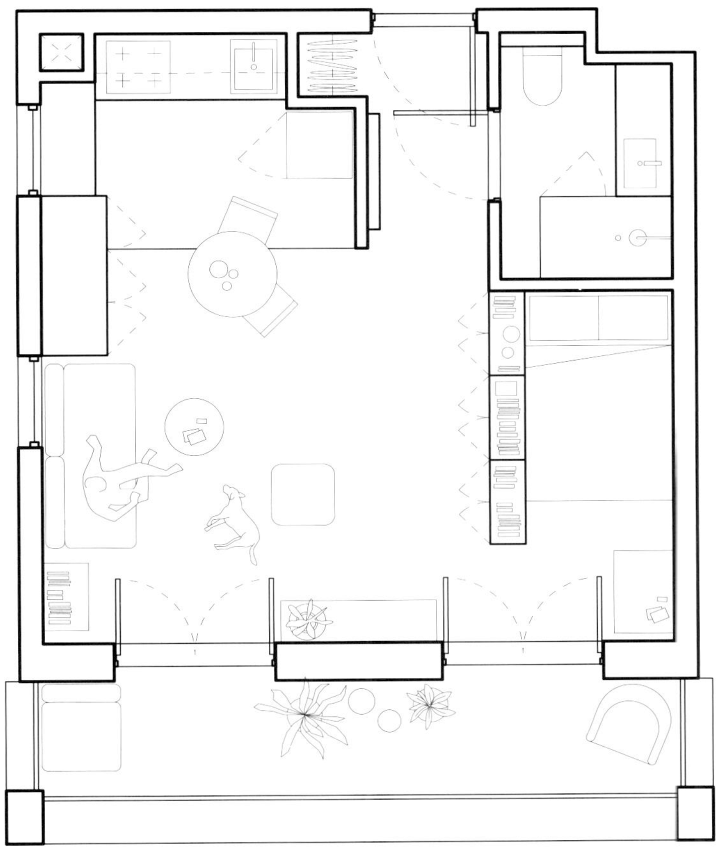

BEFORE

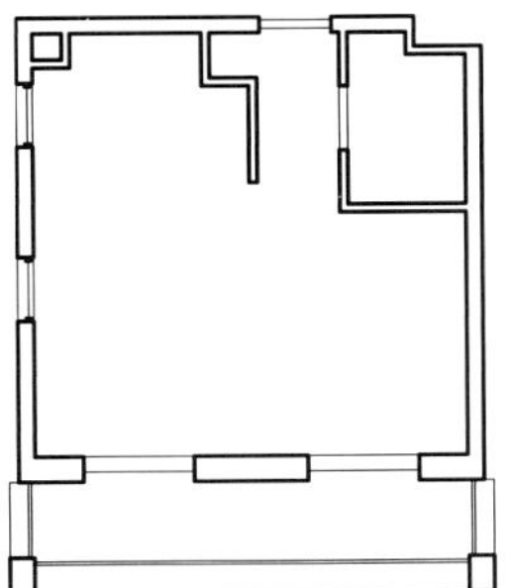

Scale 1:100

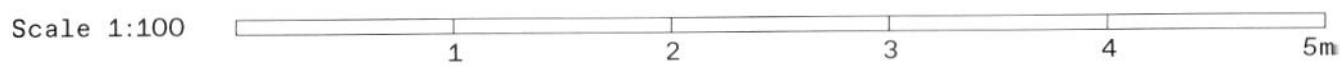

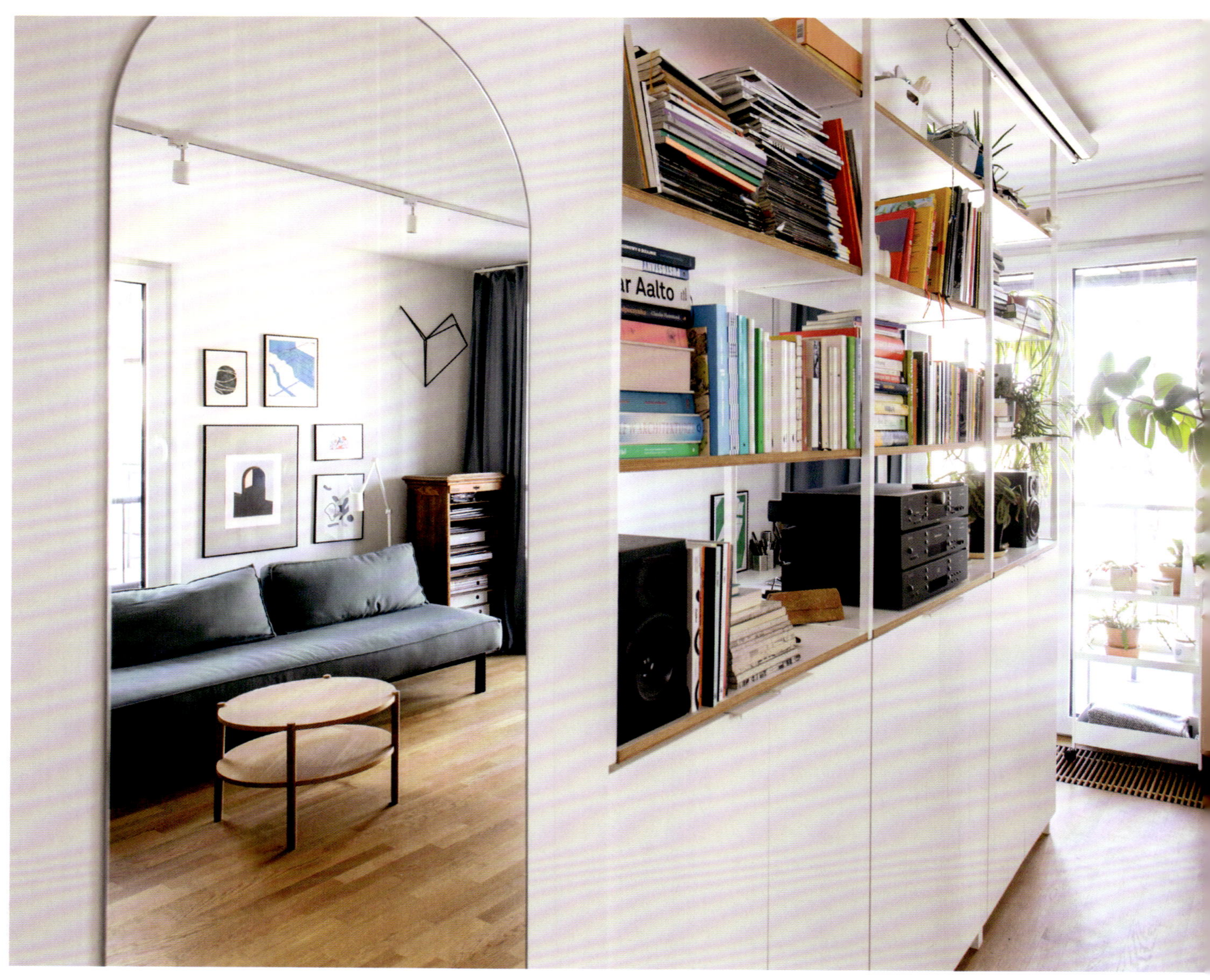

ABOVE An arched mirror in the entry is a clever space-enhancing design choice.

OPPOSITE The lighting was designed so that the configuration of the spaces could be flexible for future occupants.

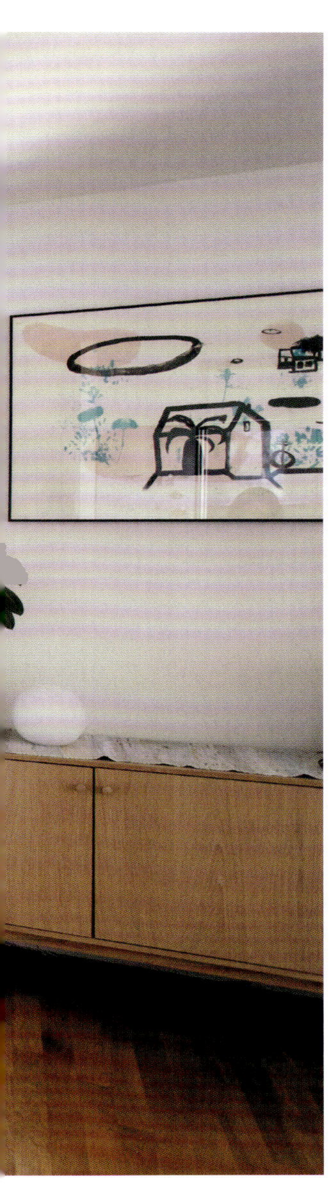

Chodur and Borowiec were inspired by modern Belgian architects, such as Dries Otten and B-ILD Architects, who play with geometric forms and colours, and create bright and welcoming interiors with a twist.

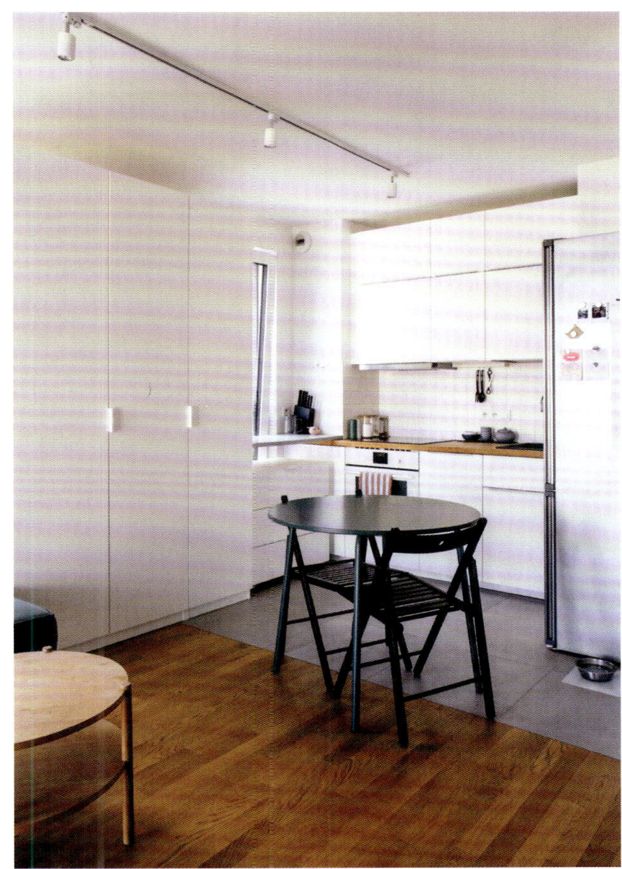

BELOW The bedroom niche is compact but inviting. A lower section of the bookself is used as bedside storage.

RIGHT The bookshelf – a customised IKEA piece – is not only functional but creates a divide between the bedroom and living area.

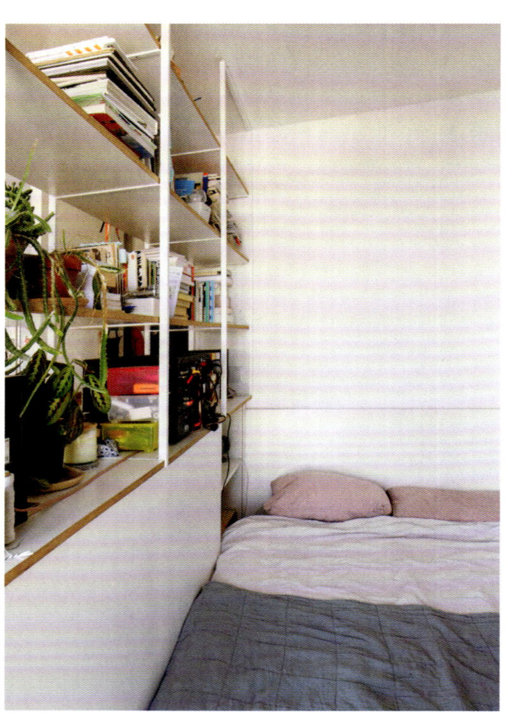

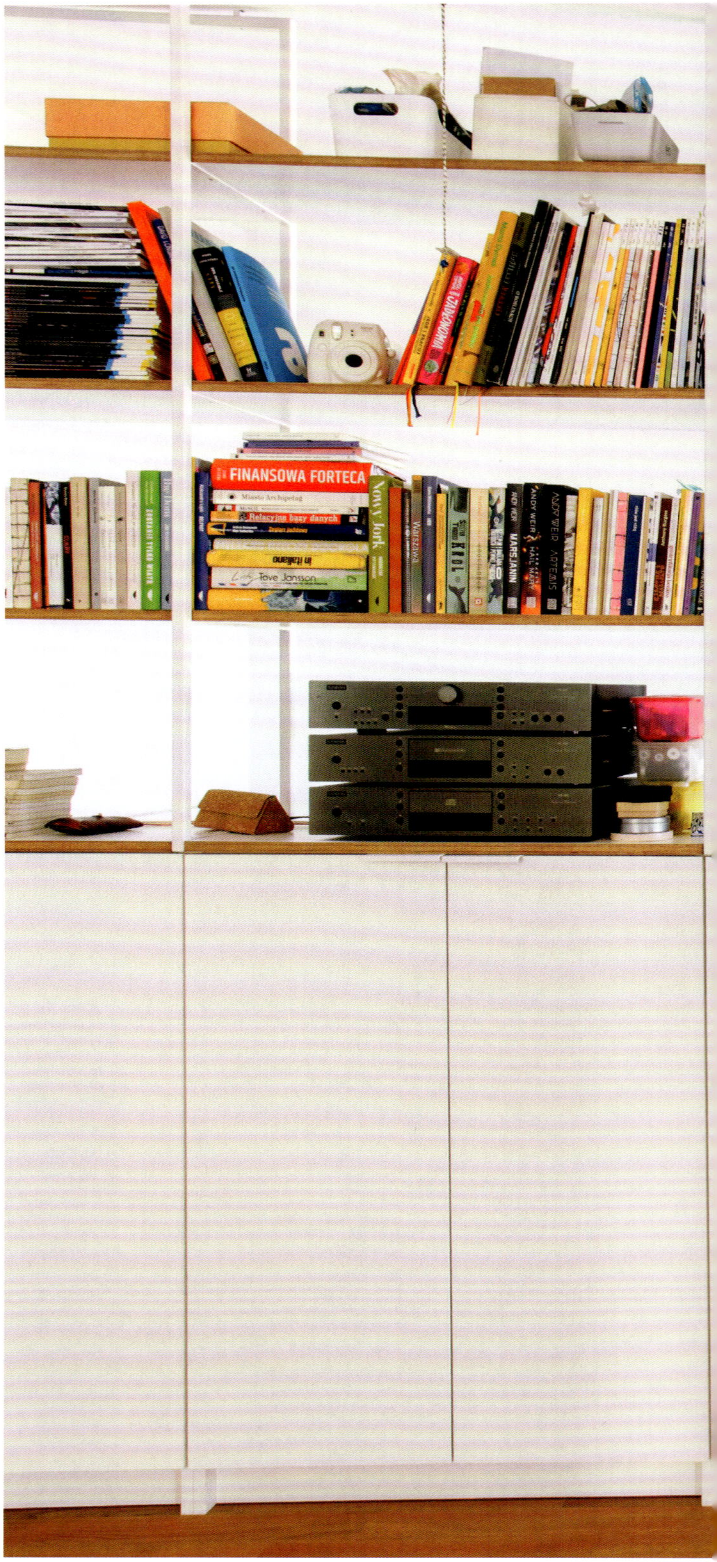

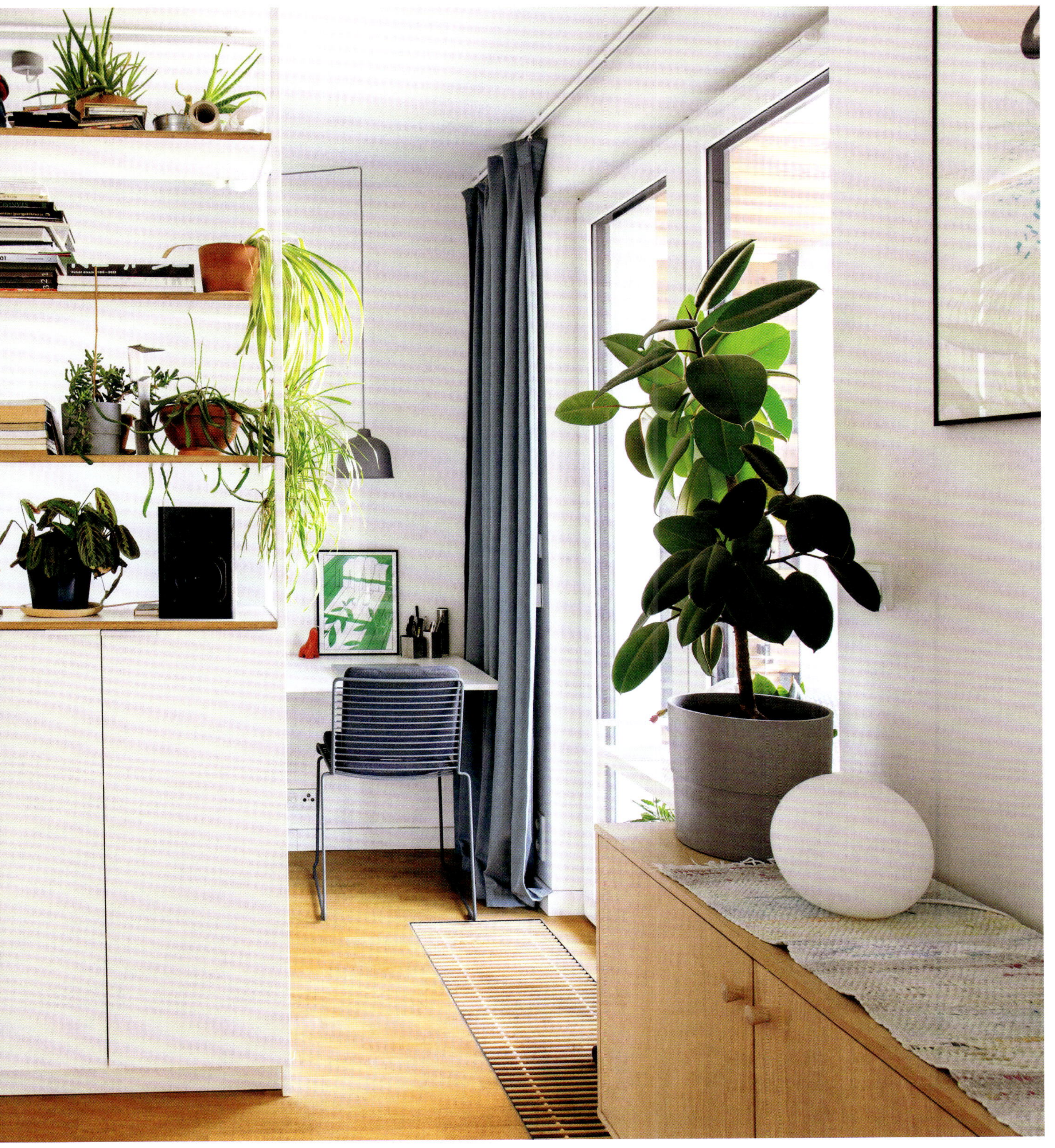

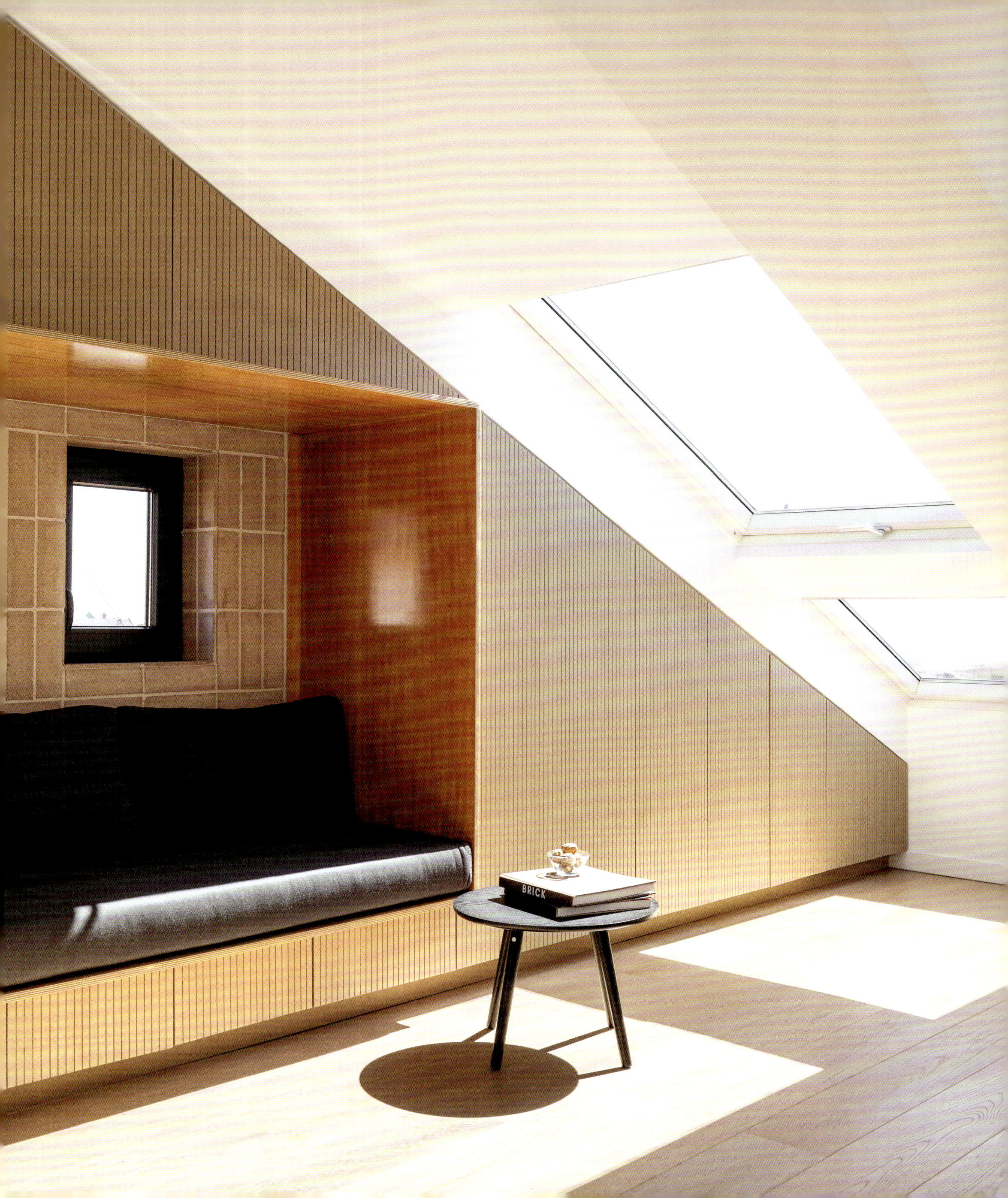
BRICK

Marvila Attic

60m^2 / 645ft^2
KEMA studio
Marvila, Lisbon

Nestled in the vibrant Marvila district of Lisbon, Portugal, sits a remarkable example of urban rejuvenation. This unique space, once an attic, is contained within the roofline of a small apartment located in one of the district's oldest buildings. Tasked with the challenge of breathing new life into this aging space in a heritage-protected treasure from the early 20th century, Eliza Borkowska, Magdalena Czapluk and their team at KEMA studio embarked on a journey to transform the apartment into a modern haven, while preserving its historical charm.

The apartment, perched atop the building, boasts a unique architectural shape that follows the roof's contours, tapering from half a metre at its lowest point to approximately three metres at its peak. The original dwelling was tucked away with limited access and a layout consisting of a kitchen, two small rooms and a toilet, so the renovation team's main objective was to open the apartment up to its surroundings. This view includes breathtaking views of the majestic Tagus River.

To achieve this, they embarked on a comprehensive redesign, demolishing all the internal walls to make an open-plan space encompassing the kitchen, dining area and living room. In addition, they crafted a compact yet comfortable bedroom. Sustainability played a pivotal role throughout the renovation, with materials such as fibre cement panels, coloured wood fibre panels, plywood, metal and brick tiles thoughtfully incorporated. In the entry, the walls and the door are adorned with beige fibres and cement panels, exuding an inviting ambience.

The living room ingeniously utilises the available area beneath the sloped roof. Two niches were crafted along the wall: one serves as a kitchenette and the other as a couch that can comfortably accommodate three people. The couch is also the exact width of a single bed, making it ideal for guests. The backrest of the couch features handcrafted brick tiles, while a small window enhances light and airflow along the entire rear wall.

Storage solutions have been integrated into the gable wall, providing ample space for possessions while also accommodating part of the kitchen. These areas were cleverly constructed using coloured MDF with push-to-open panels. Four new skylights and two additional windows were also strategically placed, flooding the living space with an abundance of natural light. At the heart of the room sits a circular dining table with seating for four.

The bedroom, though compact, is a perfect sanctuary with enough room to accommodate a double bed and a closet near the entrance. The scale of the room is enhanced by a skylight positioned directly above the bed.

PAGE 48 A custom-made niche with built-ins and an integrated couch is a great example of how additions can enhance a small footprint.

BELOW Skylights cut into the angled roof and flood the space with light.

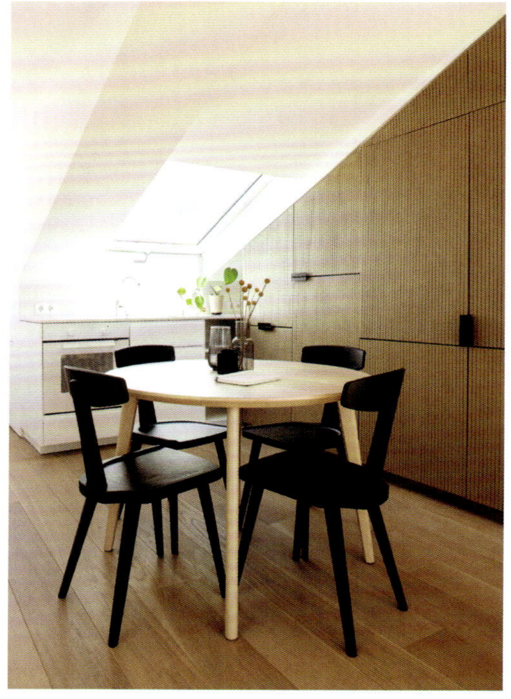

AFTER

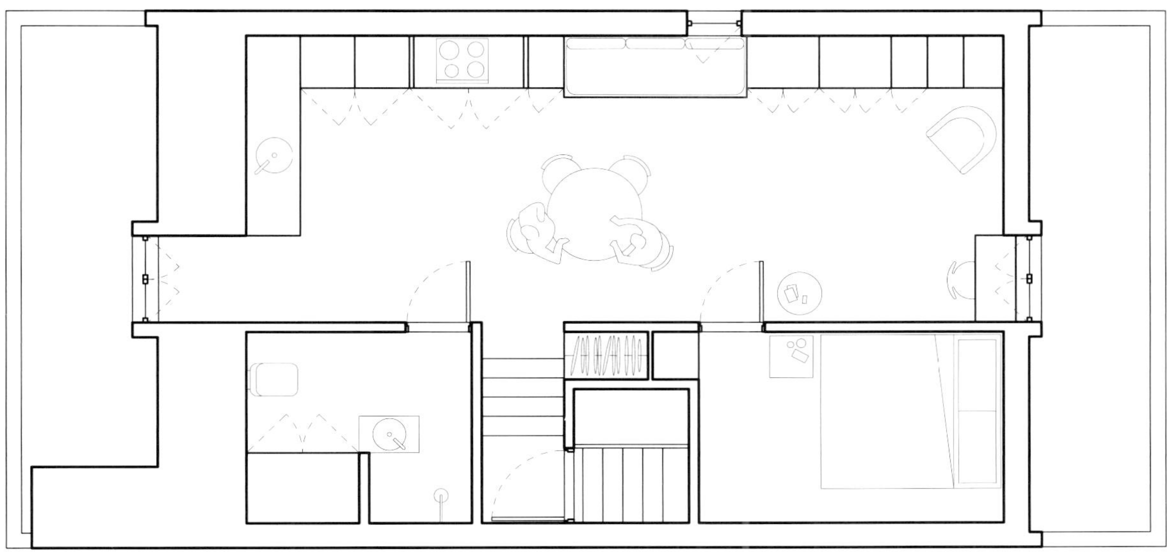

BEFORE

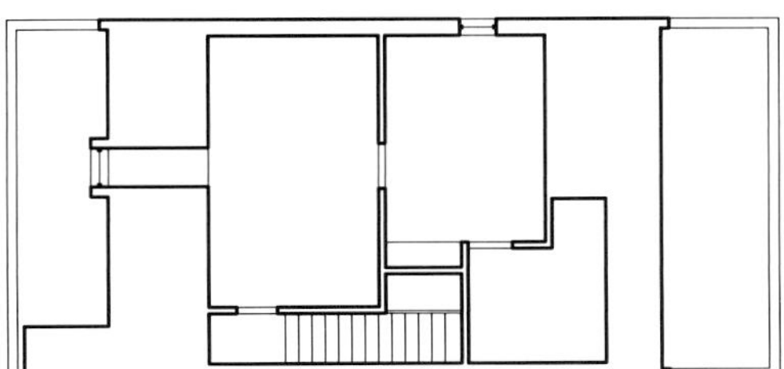

Scale 1:100

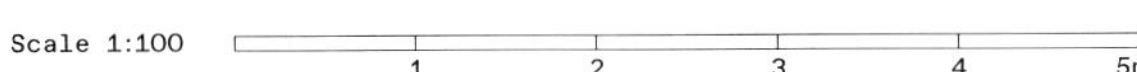

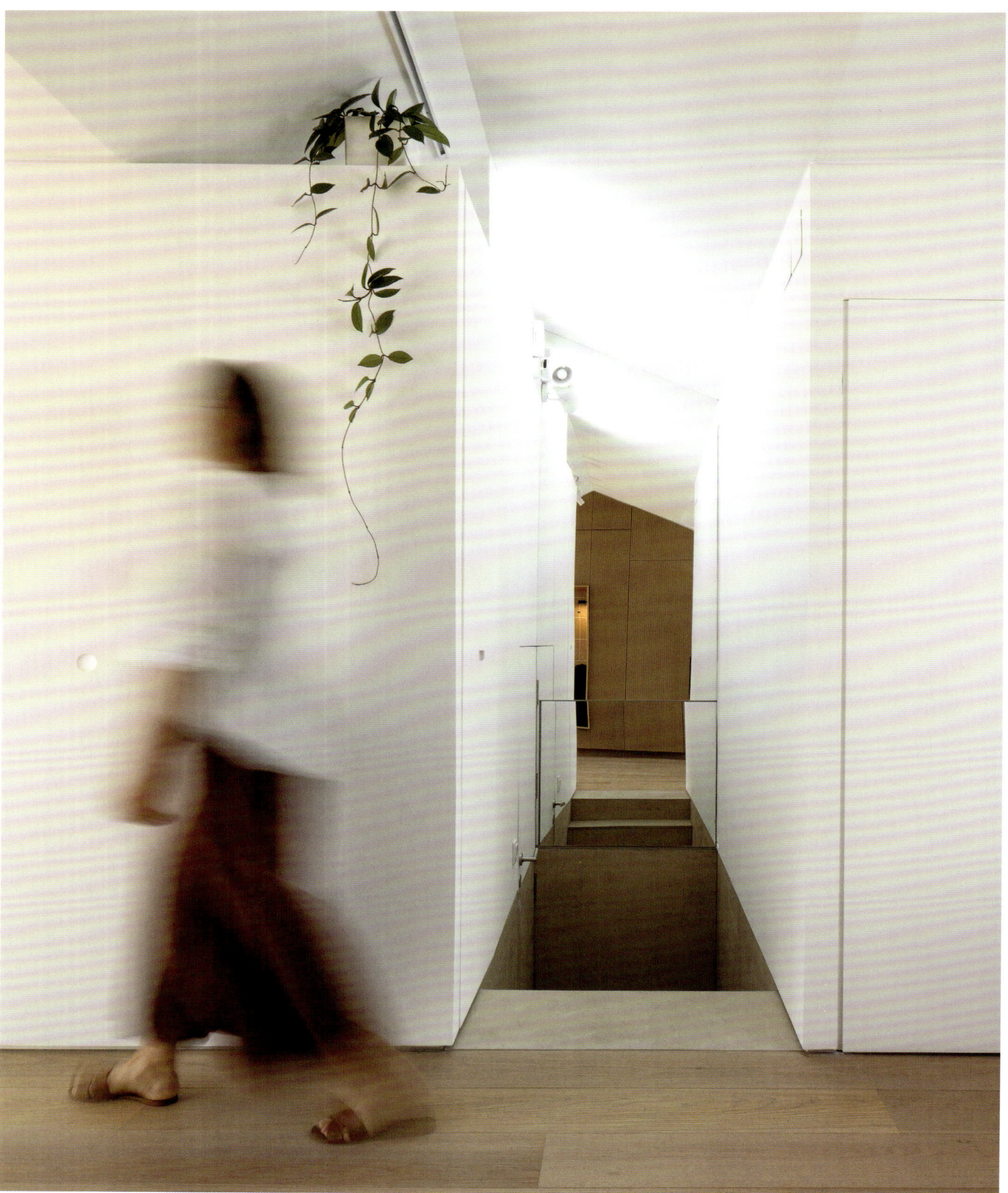

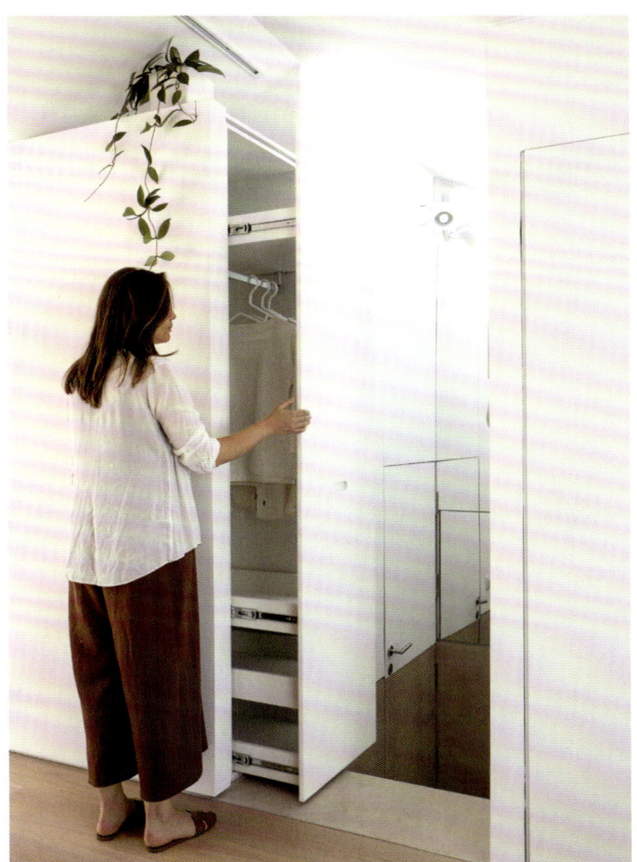

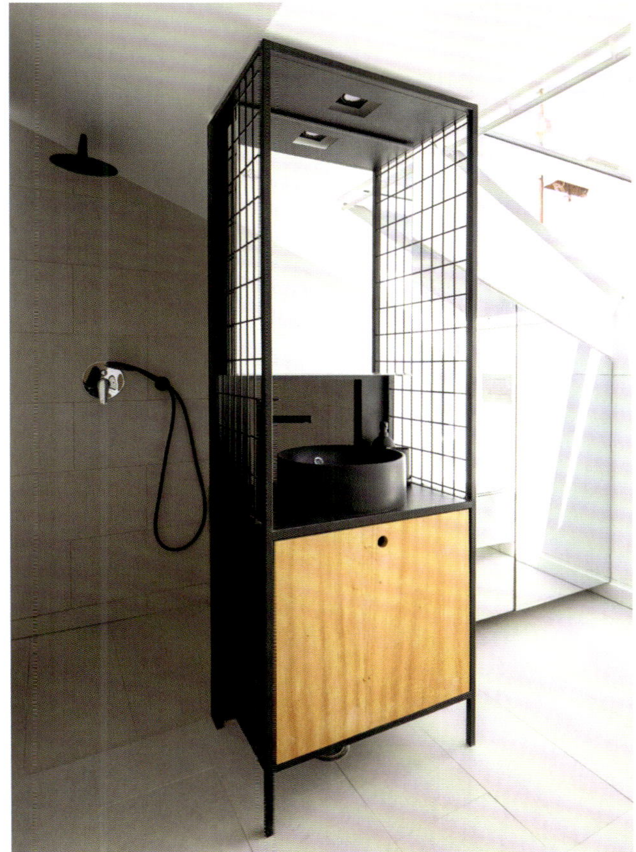

OPPOSITE A simple and light materials palette allows the unique shape of the apartment to be the hero.

TOP LEFT Sliding panels hide additional storage space.

TOP RIGHT The custom bathroom vanity was inspired by Marvila's industrial past.

The bathroom, a new addition to the apartment, has undergone a remarkable transformation, emerging as a bright and pristine area complete with all necessary amenities. Despite its location in a nook, the shower receives lots of light from a floating glass window positioned in the corner of the room and a light integrated into the custom-made vanity. This unique vanity, crafted from a blend of metal and wood, has meaning beyond its fine design and function. 'This element is our tribute to the industrial spirit of Marvila that can be observed throughout the neighbourhood,' say the architects.

Throughout the design process, the team at KEMA studio expertly optimised the available space without compromising on comfort. By skilfully harnessing and amplifying natural light, they created a sense of openness and spaciousness rarely experienced within a compact apartment of this type.

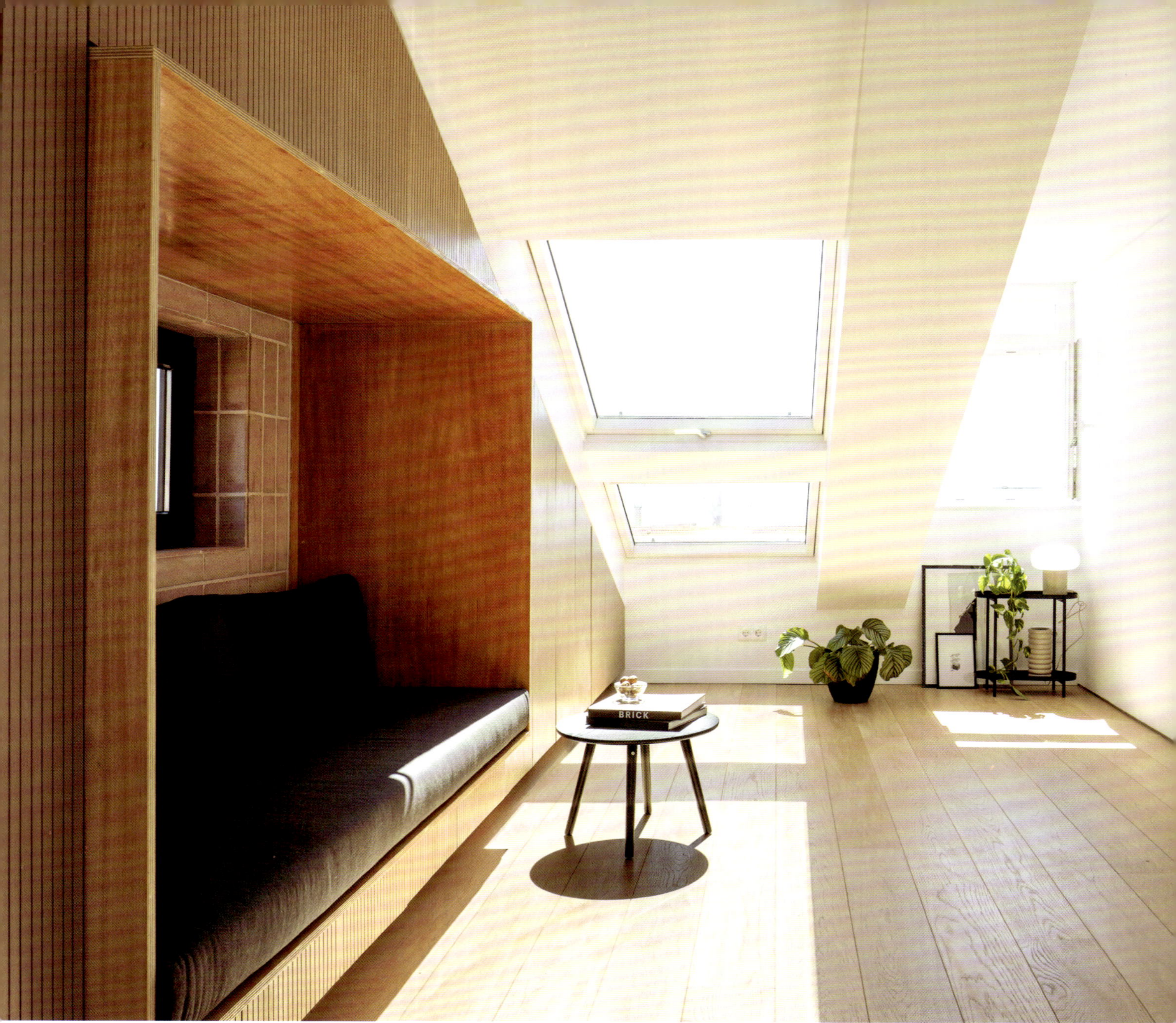
BRICK

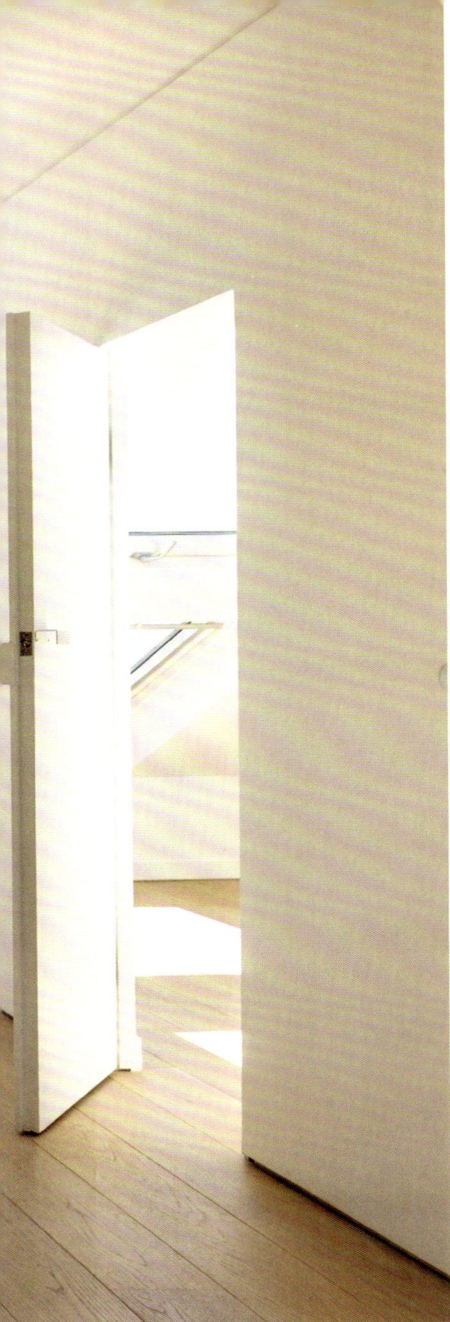

OPPOSITE The extremes in ceiling height provided inspiration rather than being a hindrance to the design.

BELOW The stove and rangehood are hidden to create a seamless look when not in use.

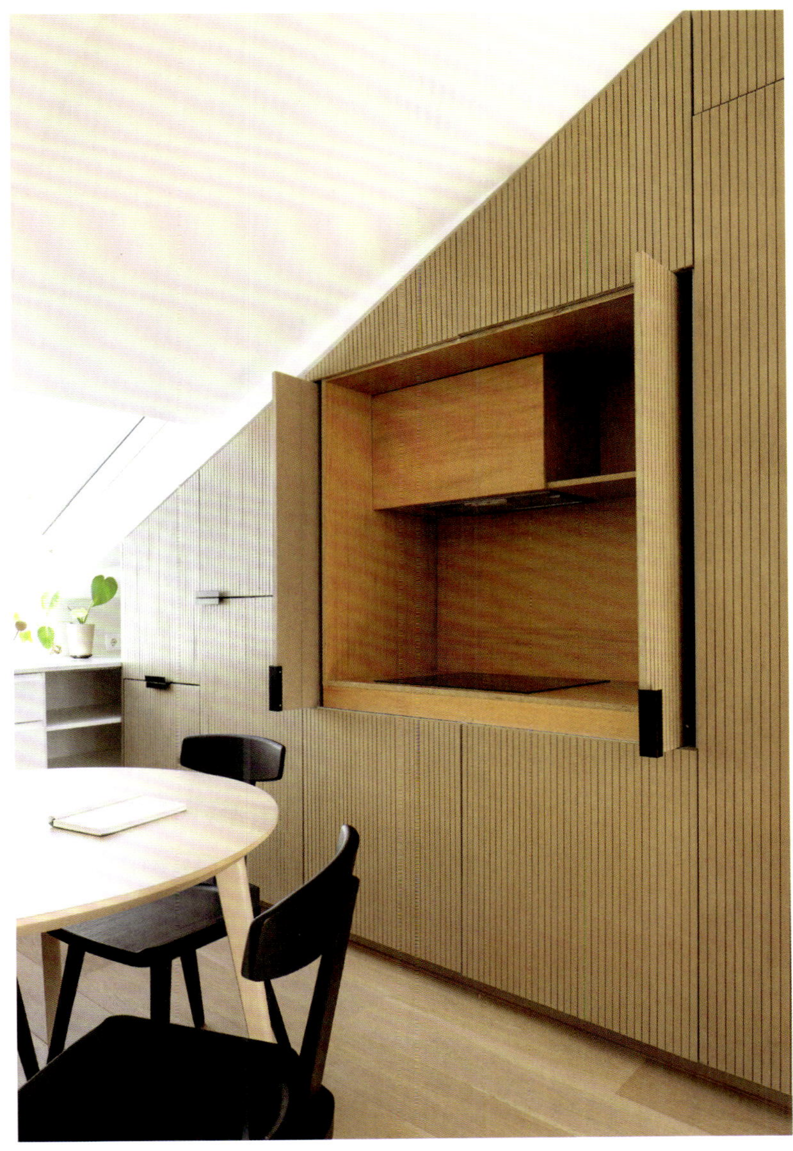

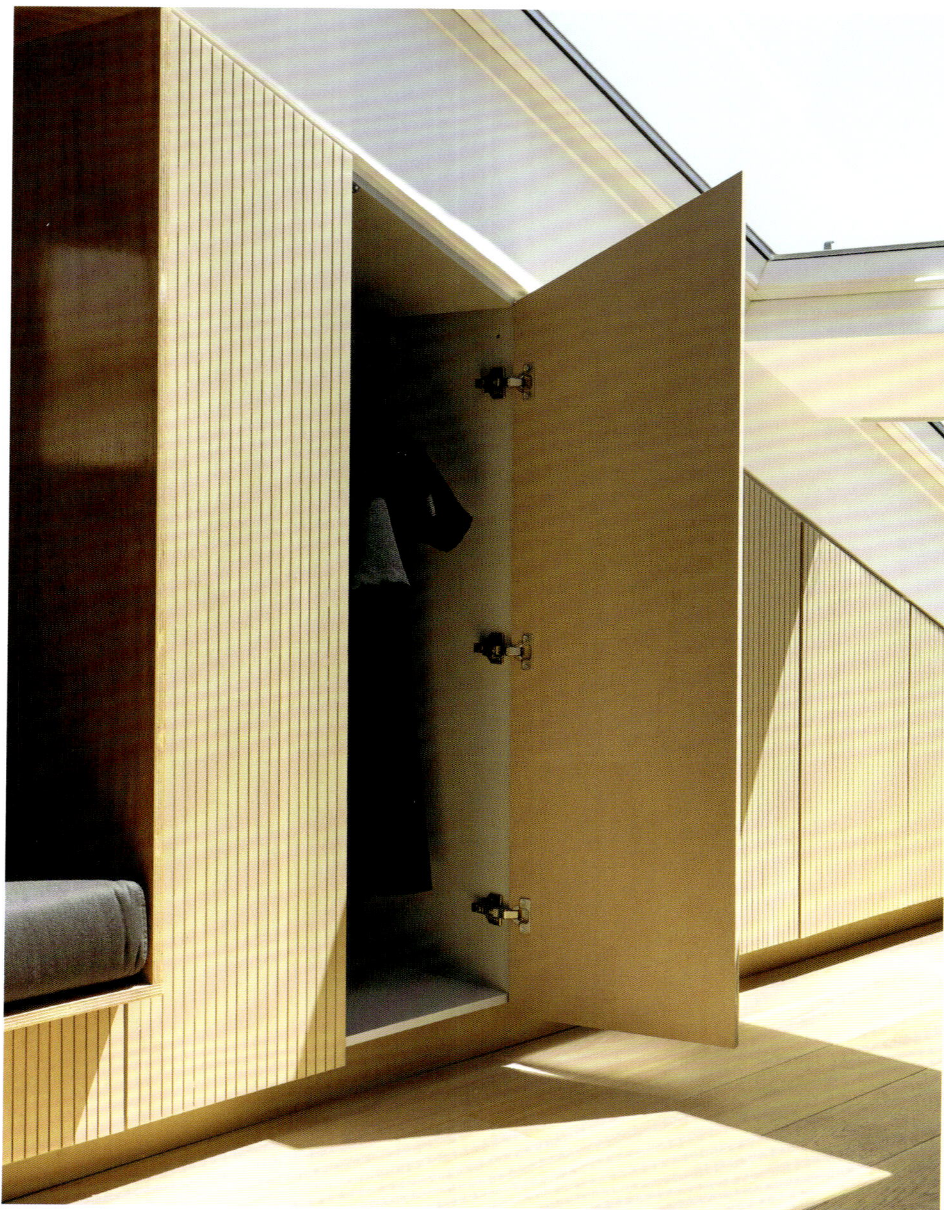

LEFT Despite a minimal design, the apartment has ample storage so that the space remains uncluttered.

OPPOSITE The gable ceiling was embraced and the design configured around it.

‘The apartment, perched atop the building, boasts a unique architectural shape that follows the roof’s contours.’

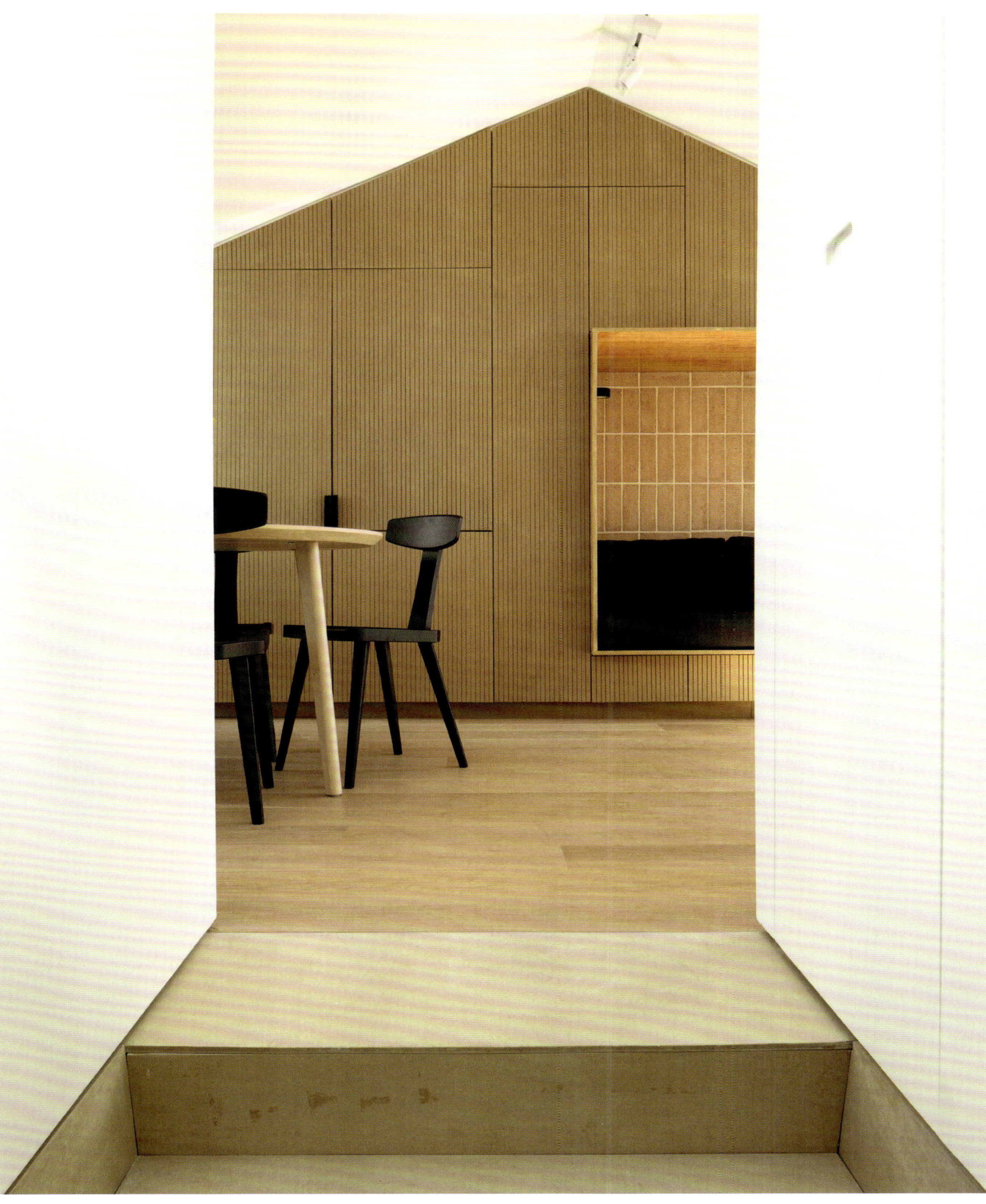

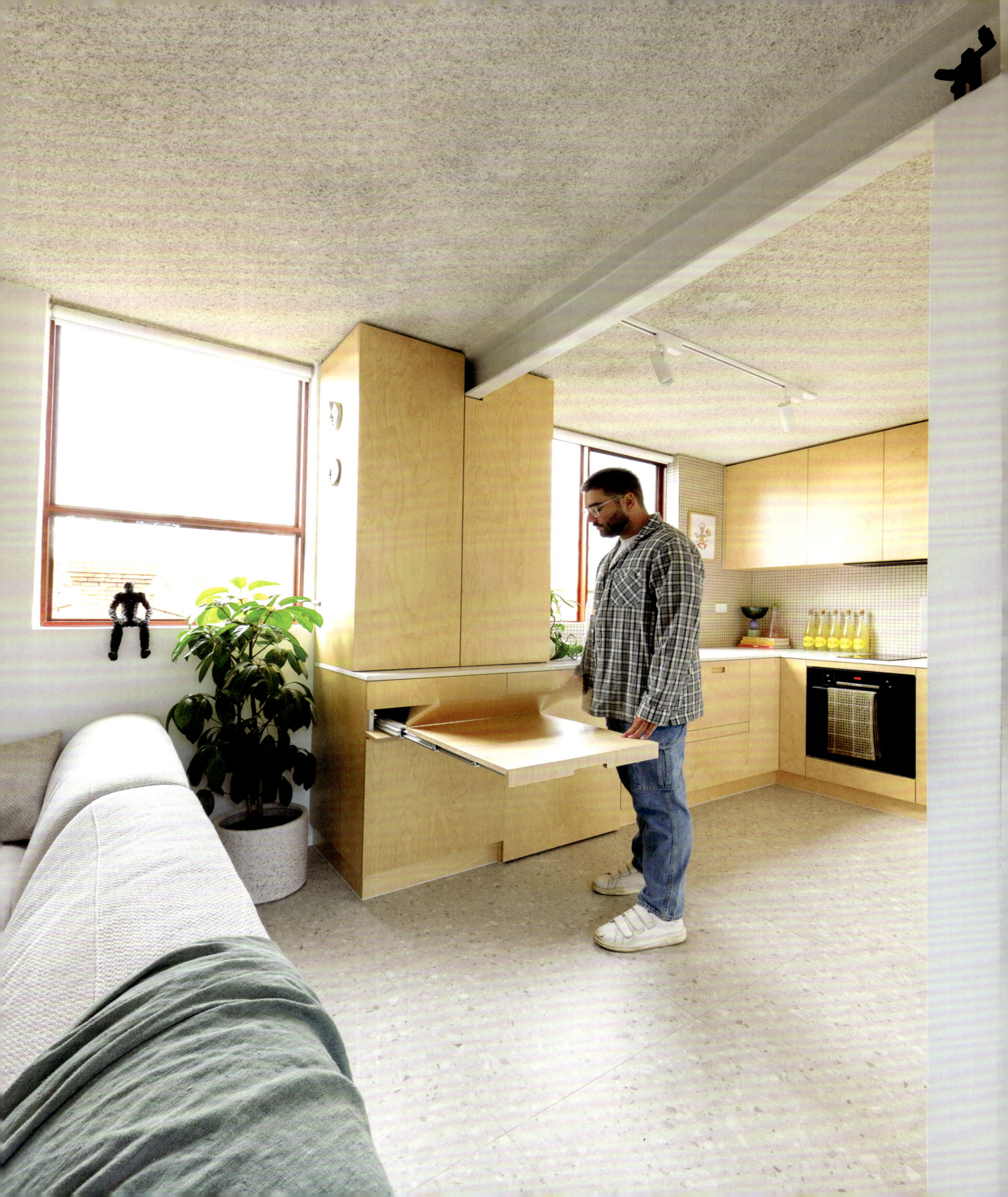

Park Street Apartment

42m² / 452ft²
Alex Antoniadis
Brunswick, Melbourne

In a world where demolishing older buildings is commonplace, adapting them to modern living is a sustainable and cost-effective solution. With their structural integrity and character, older buildings can provide unique living spaces that reflect the architectural elements of a particular era while being modern and comfortable.

The boom of residential complexes in the inner city is a special thread of Melbourne's layered architectural history. This Brunswick complex is nestled in a heritage precinct surrounded by Edwardian and Victorian dwellings, two of Melbourne's iconic 19th-century parks and a vibrant commercial strip on Sydney Road, Brunswick.

The owner, Alex Antoniadis, an urban planner and lover of post-war architecture, purchased what was an ordinary apartment and transformed it into a unique living space that complements an internal courtyard garden.

The goal was to optimise the apartment's functionality by designing an open-plan living area. The wall dividing the kitchen and living area was unnecessary and hindered views and natural light from the east, so it was removed.

The design concept focused on four objectives: the ability to watch television from the kitchen, minimising visual clutter by concealing the kitchen, designing a space for socialising and including ample bench space.

Upon entering the open living space, a window is visible between the pantry and a three-seater couch. Given the apartment's limited size, the function, layout and placement of the couch required careful consideration as it needed to serve a dual purpose. It had to provide easy access to the kitchen while also acting as a barrier to define and separate the space.

The custom kitchen is clad in timber birch plywood that houses an integrated fridge, a dishwasher, a washing machine, a retractable table and ample storage. The kitchen/dining space retracts in and out of the cupboard space to create a flexible area that can be used for other purposes.

The bedroom has a queen-sized bed, a full-sized wall-to-wall wardrobe with sliding doors and a large desk that looks out to the internal courtyard. The bathroom has the same fluted glass door as the bedroom to provide privacy and natural light. Sage-green tiles were chosen to add a pop of colour and the floor-to-ceiling tiling makes the ceilings look higher. The floating vanity contains drawers and storage above it, and there are three panels of glass mirror with integrated storage behind them.

The apartment's flooring is locally sourced grey terrazzo tiles that make the apartment feel larger. A popcorn ceiling pays homage to the original design. The choice of materials, colours and lighting give the design continuity and makes the apartment feel like a seamless space.

Antoniadis believes that 'demolition of a building should be an absolute last resort and, too often, particularly in Australian cities, demolition is viewed as a more cost-effective solution'. In fact, his renovation exemplifies that it is possible to live in a stylish, sustainable and comfortable home that also reflects the history of a place.

PAGE 58 Timber birch plywood provides a strong and low-cost solution for custom joinery.

BELOW Understanding how light affects your home is critical in setting up how you utilise zones. Here the office space takes advantage of a large window.

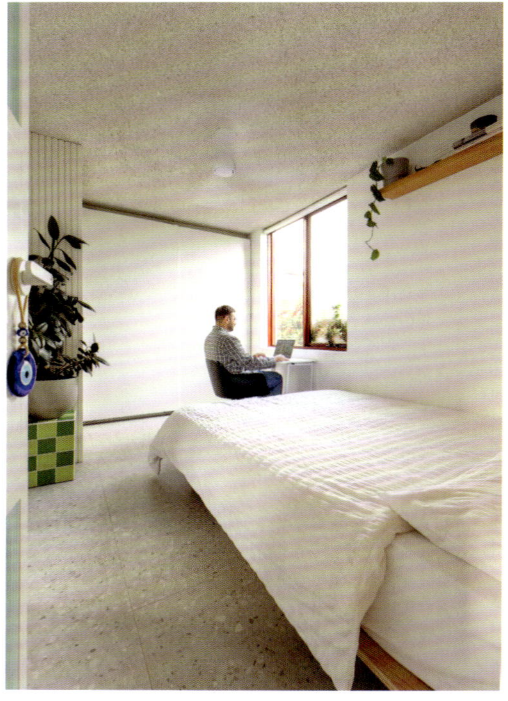

AFTER

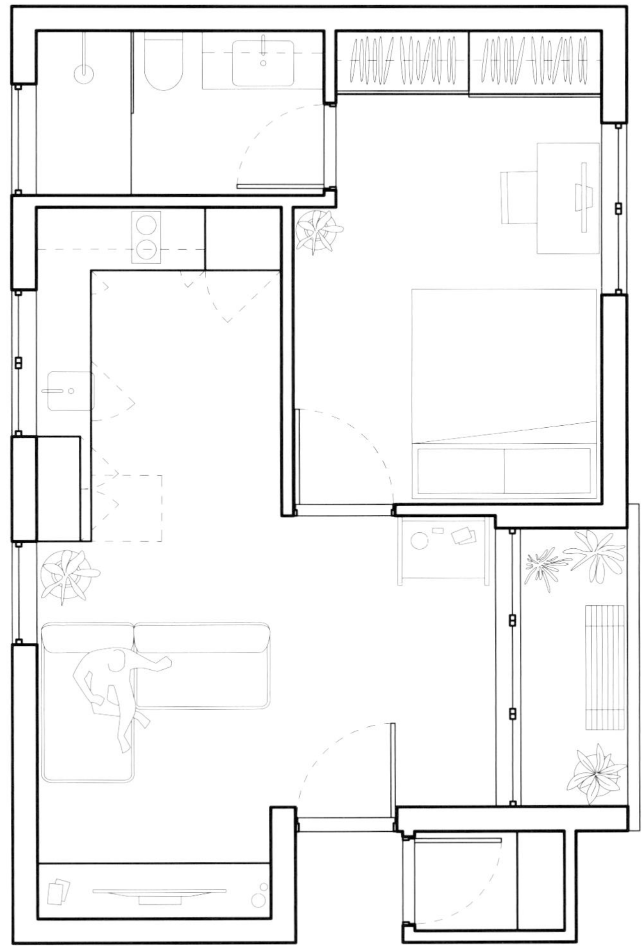

BEFORE

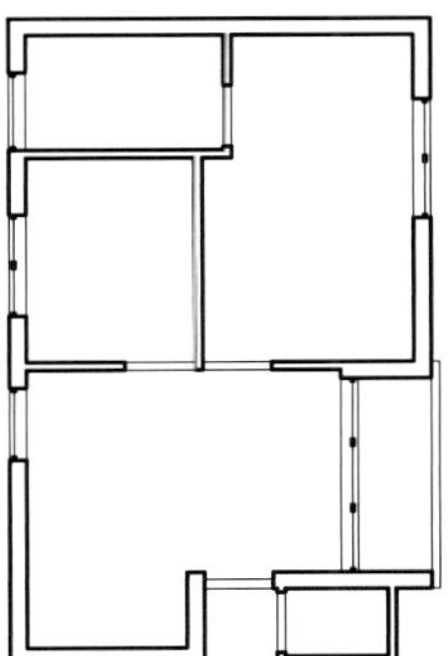

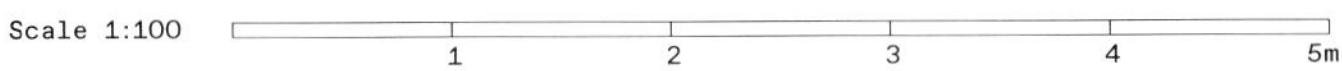

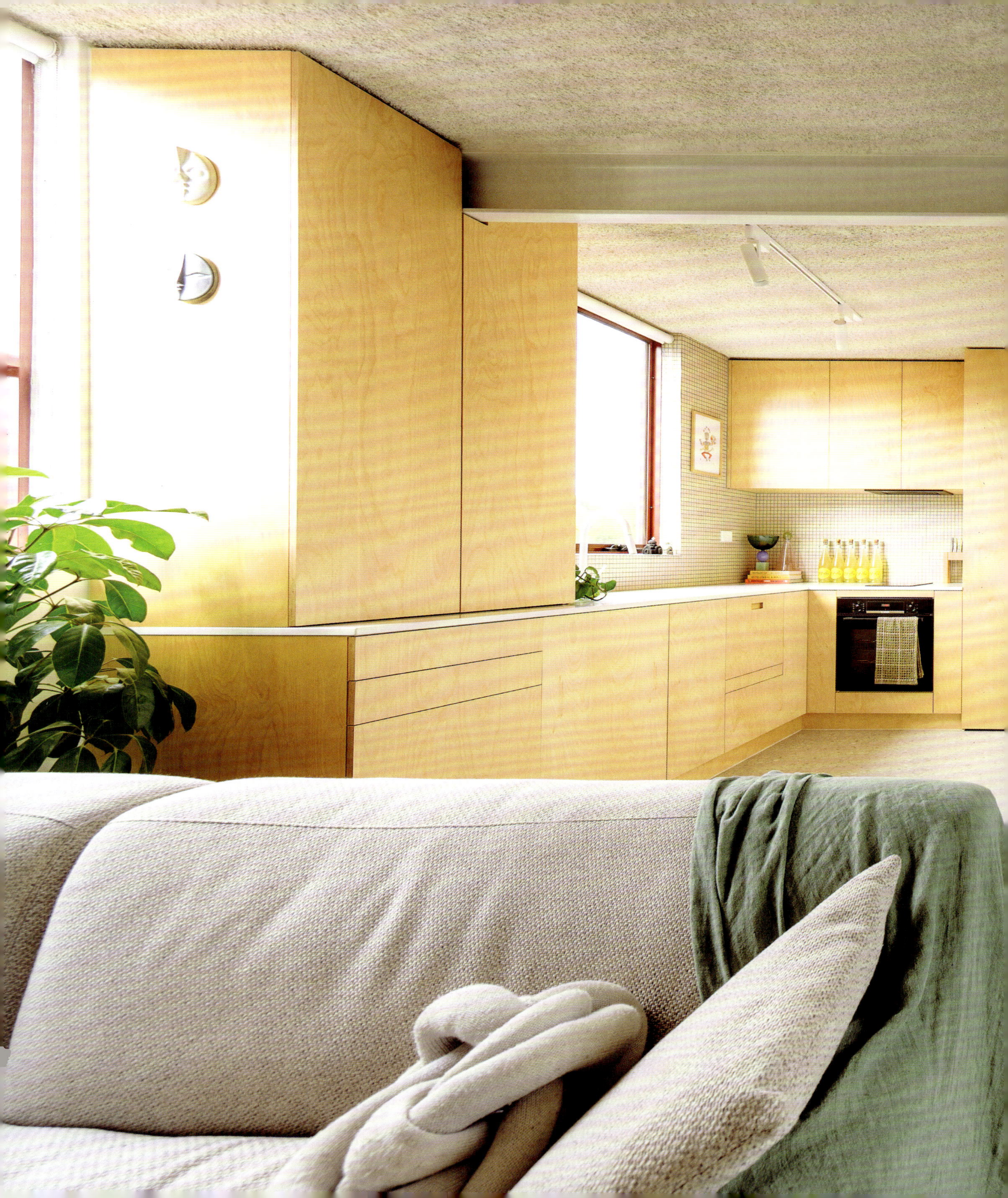

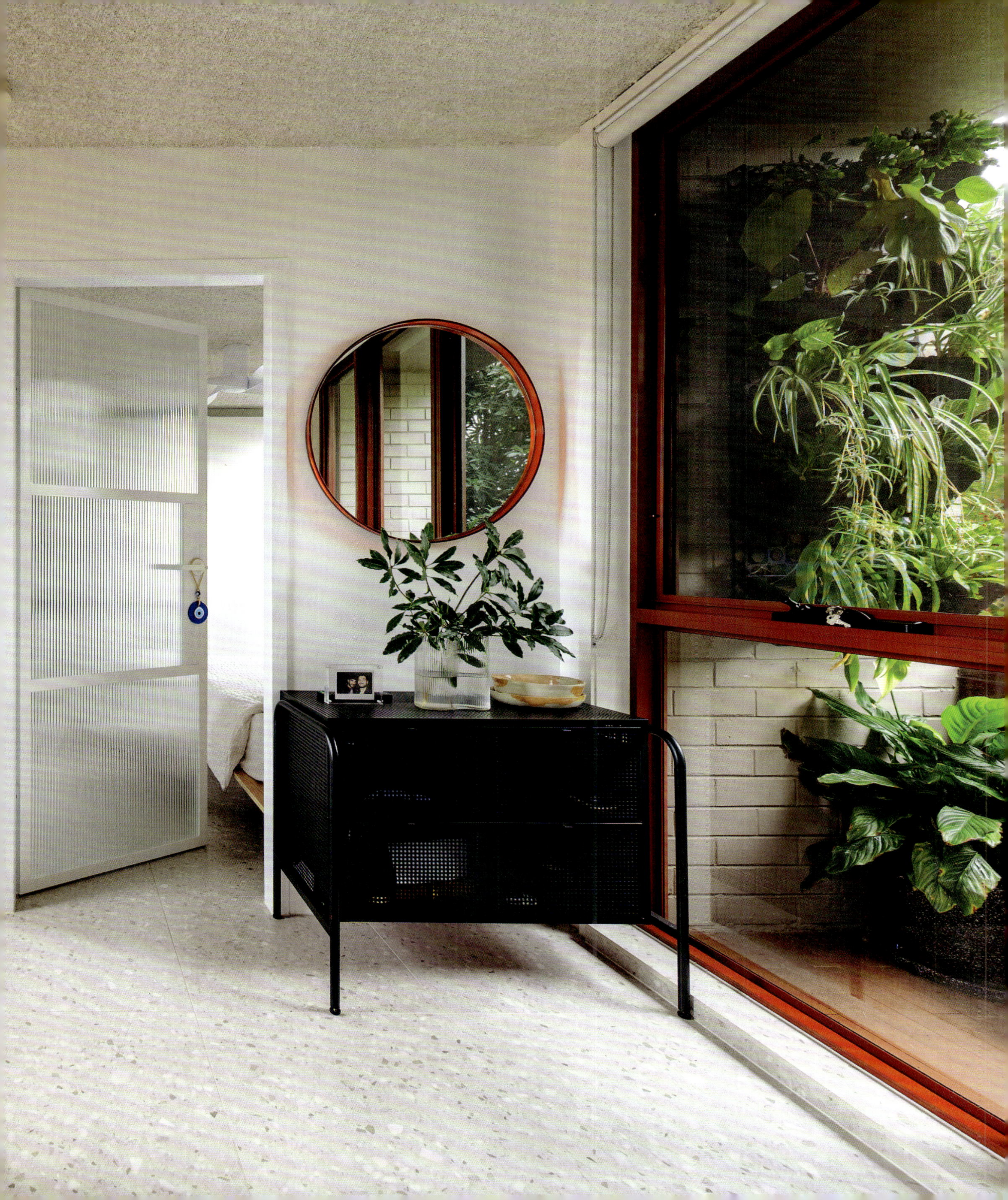

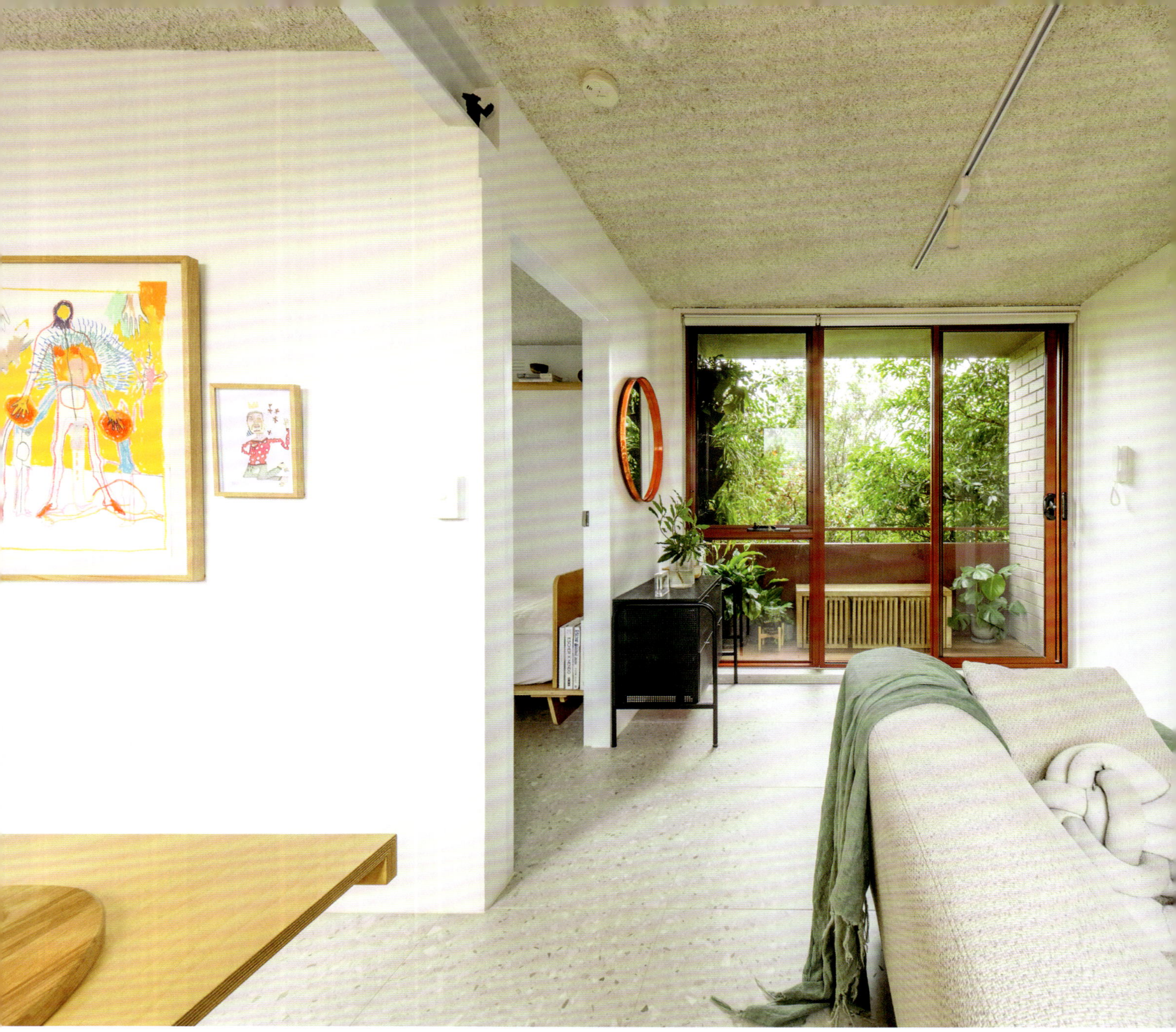

Antoniadis believes that 'demolition of a building should be an absolute last resort . . .'

PREVIOUS PAGE Birch plywood, grey terrazzo floors and white walls make the apartment feel light and airy.

OPPOSITE Full-height glass windows frame the leafy outlook.

BELOW What could have been an awkward nook was transformed into the entertainment area.

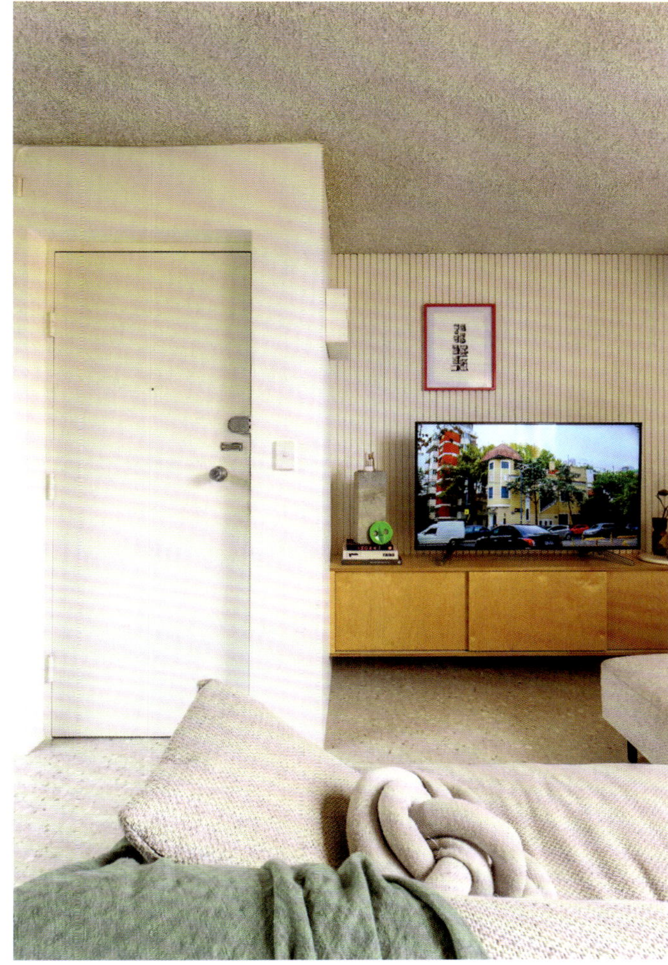

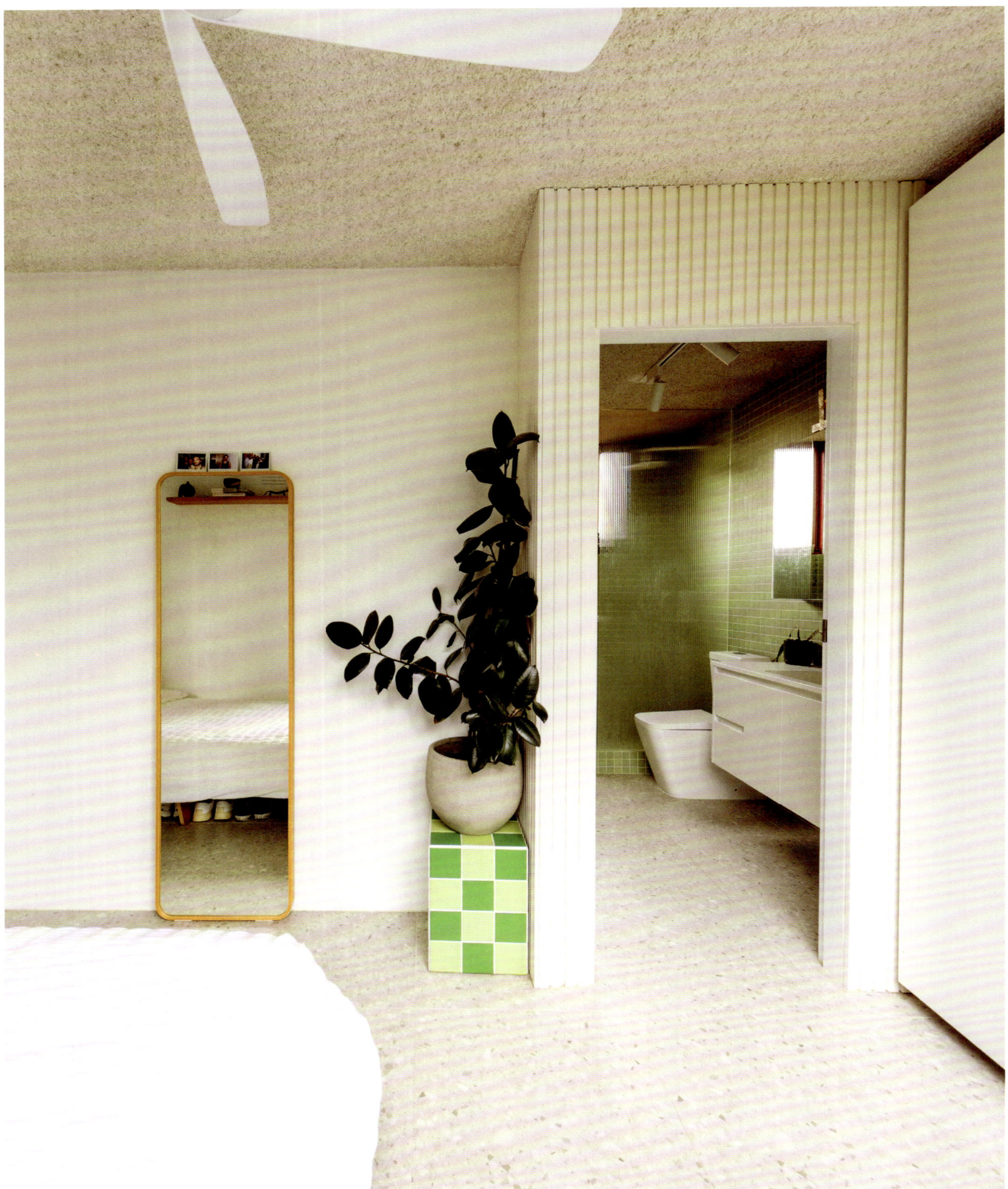

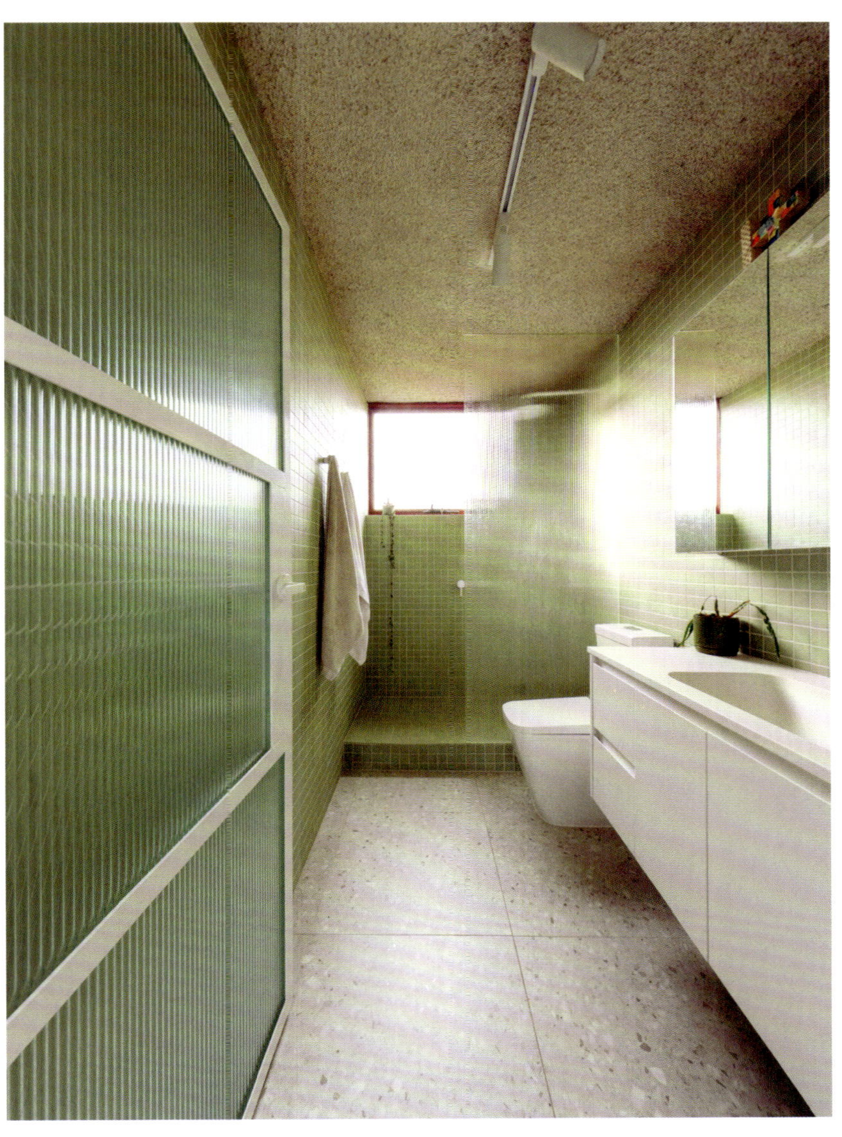

OPPOSITE Reflection is always important. Here, a strategically placed mirror opens up the bedroom.

ABOVE Sage-green tiles add a pop of colour and separate the bathroom design from the rest of the home.

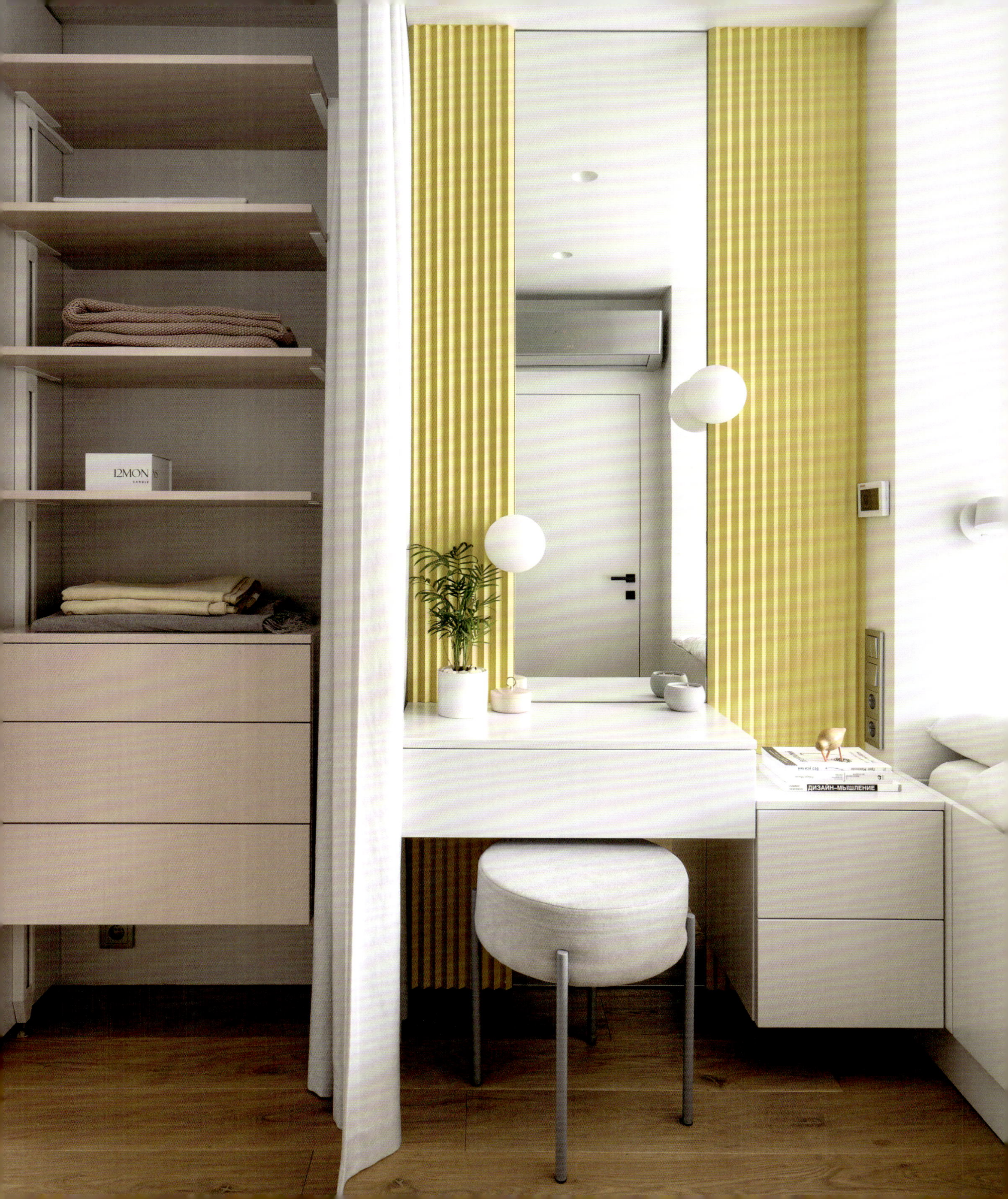
ДИЗАЙН-МЫШЛЕНИЕ

Pinkyellow

32m² / 344ft²
Olha Bondar Design
Fayna Town, Kyiv

Pinkyellow, an apartment in a building in central Kyiv, Ukraine, still exists. Not long ago, it wouldn't be necessary to acknowledge this, but in a city that has been partly destroyed by senseless invasion, Pinkyellow's existence is a reminder of lives forever changed. In showcasing this home, we are reminded that a whole country's worth of stories are on hold. Our hope is that one day soon these stories will recommence.

Completed in 2019, Fayna Town, the modern residential complex that houses Pinkyellow, was originally Kyiv's vegetable factory and greenhouses. On completion, it was transformed into what was a vibrant community area with shops, cafes, bike paths, schools and parks.

Olha Bondar, interior designer and owner of Olha Bondar Design, took what was an empty, largely raw material 32-sq-m (344-sq-ft) space and turned it into a functioning home with a comfortable living room, fully equipped kitchen and a bedroom with a dressing room.

Working with her client's colour palette brief of blue, pink and yellow (with a base of very light grey), Bondar incorporated gentle tones of these colours throughout.

This palette is introduced in the entry hall. To the right is a muted pink wall and a floor-to-ceiling mirror to 'expand the look of the space'. On the left is a built-in wardrobe for outerwear and shoes. There is also a second closet housing the boiler and washing machine.

The entrance leads directly into the living room: a couch with a low back allows the space to hold a full-sized seating area without creating a visual block in any direction.

Directly behind the couch is a high-top dining area that separates the living room and kitchen. This small bar lets two people to comfortably eat or work while looking out towards the living room.

The kitchen is compact but fully equipped. The fridge is hidden in a niche within the walls of the kitchen. The pink door, the same colour as the walls, creates a seamless surface. On the small display area above the sink, there is room for glassware, a vase or personal belongings.

The area around the kitchen window was painted yellow to 'create a portal that would add warm sunlight to the kitchen even on a cloudy day'. This is a simple but incredibly impactful idea.

The bedroom is located through a door in the living room. The custom-made bed has built-in drawers for blankets and linen. The bedside table and dressing table are mounted to the wall to free up floor space. A large floor-to-ceiling mirror sits behind the dressing table and is framed by a yellow feature wall, echoing the yellow in the kitchen.

There is a dressing room, unexpected for an apartment of this size, but high on the client's wish list, behind a curtain on the opposite side of the room. Built-ins blend into the walls here too.

PAGE 68 A dressing room and dressing table are perhaps considered luxuries in a small space, but at the client's request, they were made possible with compact storage solutions.

BELOW The client wanted a space to 'both relax in and inspire her'. Sorbet pink brings warmth, colour and visual interest to the entryway.

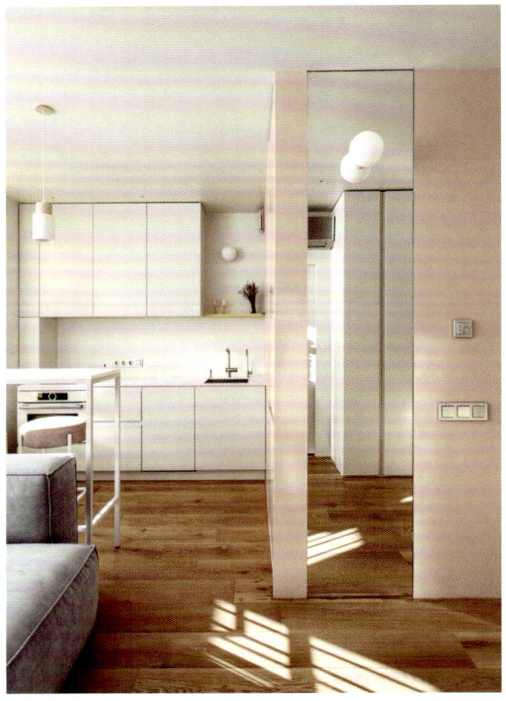

AFTER

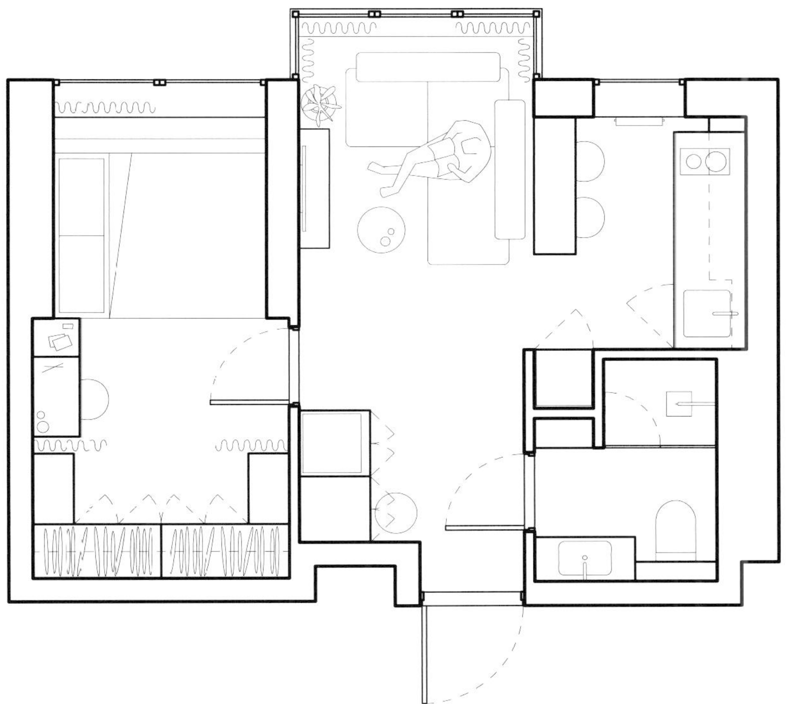

BEFORE

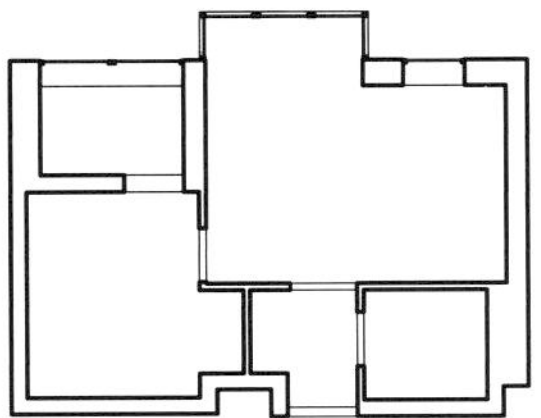

Scale 1:100

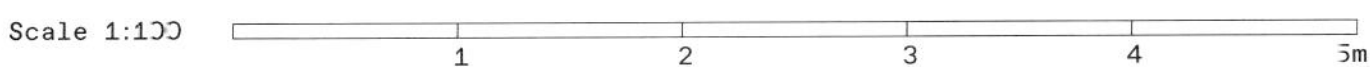

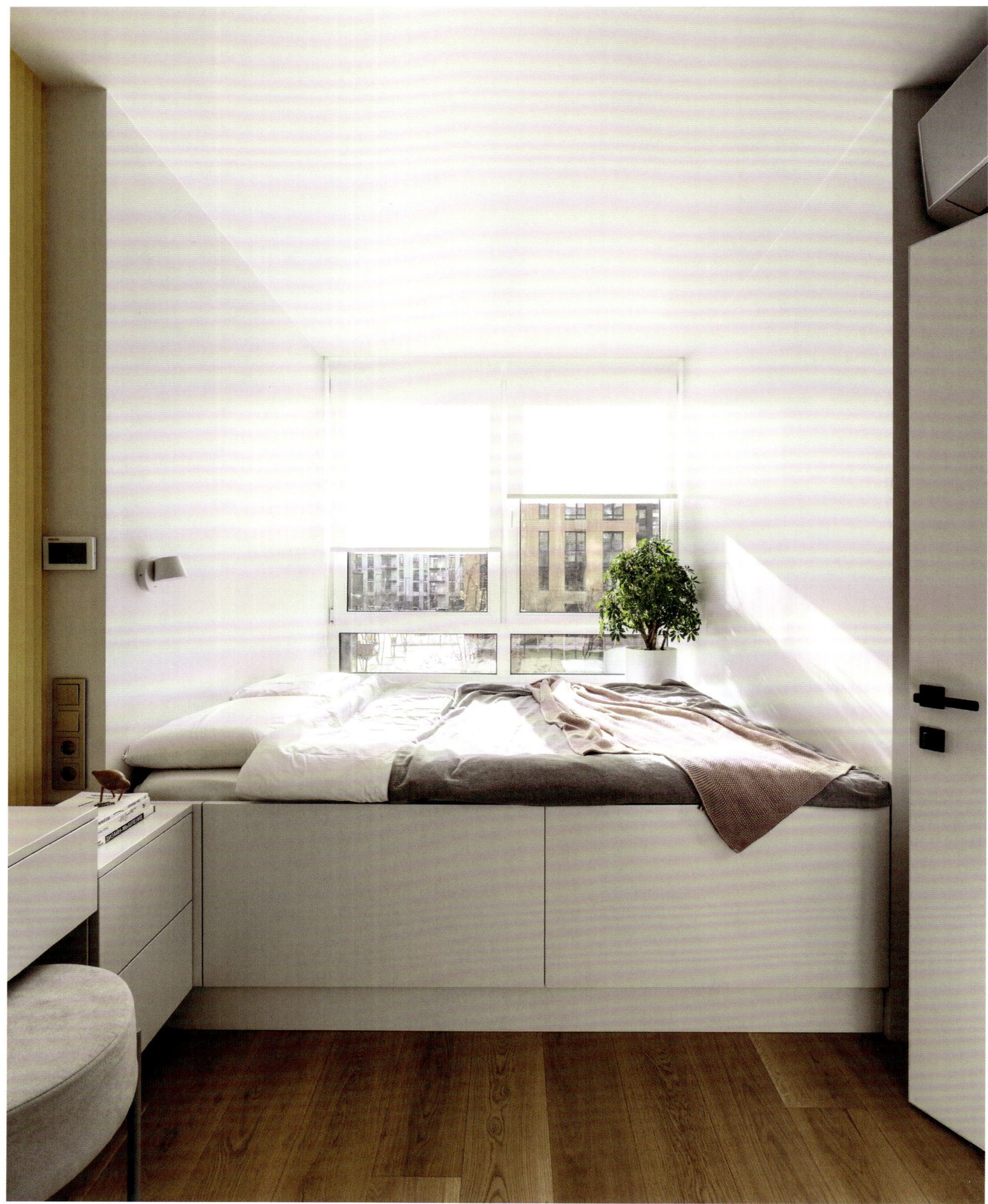

OPPOSITE The custom bed has built-in storage underneath it and, along with the floating bedside table, ensures the compact bedroom is comfortable.

BELOW Integrated tapware and floating elements amplify the sense of space in the bathroom.

RIGHT The kitchen continues the on-theme aesthetic of touches of pink, yellow and blue.

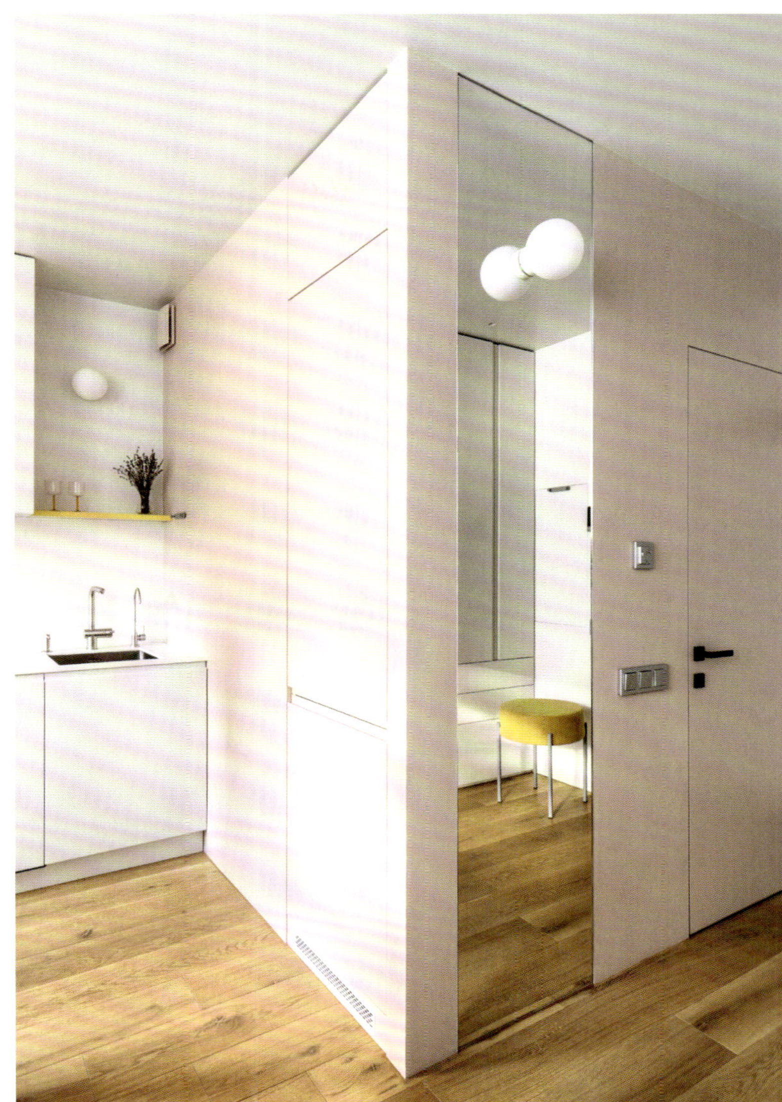

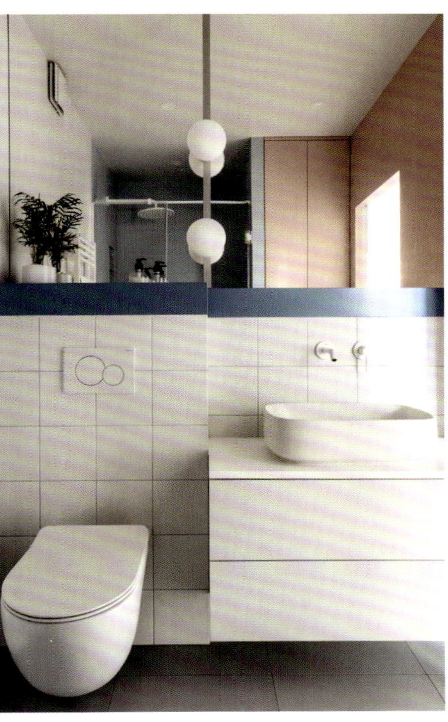

Through a pink door in the entryway is the bathroom. The tapware was built into the wall to free up space for the sink, and the toilet and vanity float above the floor to visually give the room extra space. The built-in closets next to the shower have space for additional storage and a laundry basket.

Pinkyellow is a wonderful example of fulfilling a client's brief through the lens of great design. Like every home in Ukraine, it deserves to be lived in and to have its story continue to unfold.

Like every home in Ukraine, it deserves to be lived in and to have its story continue to unfold.

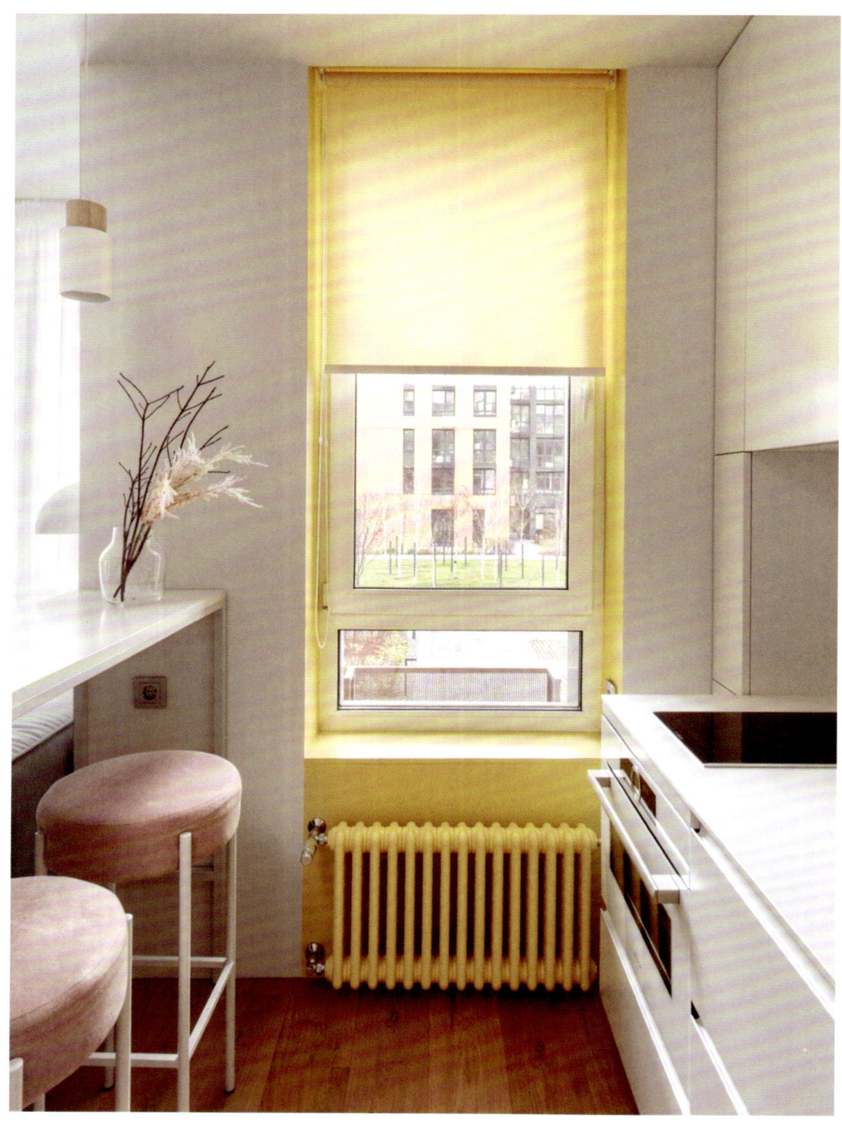

LEFT The kitchen's yellow-framed window is a cheerful focal point.

OPPOSITE A full-sized seating area was made possible by a low-backed couch that doesn't interrupt visual flow.

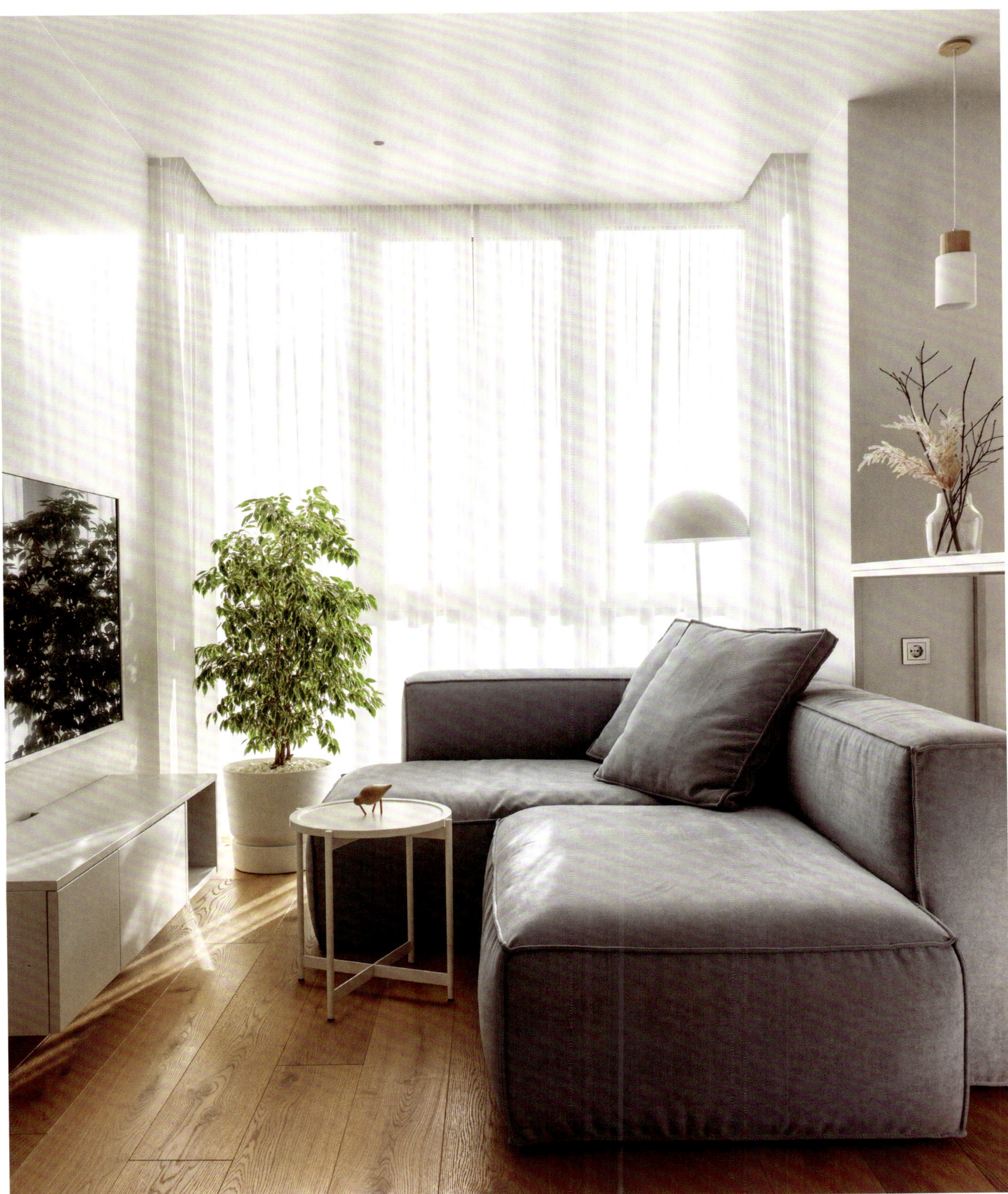

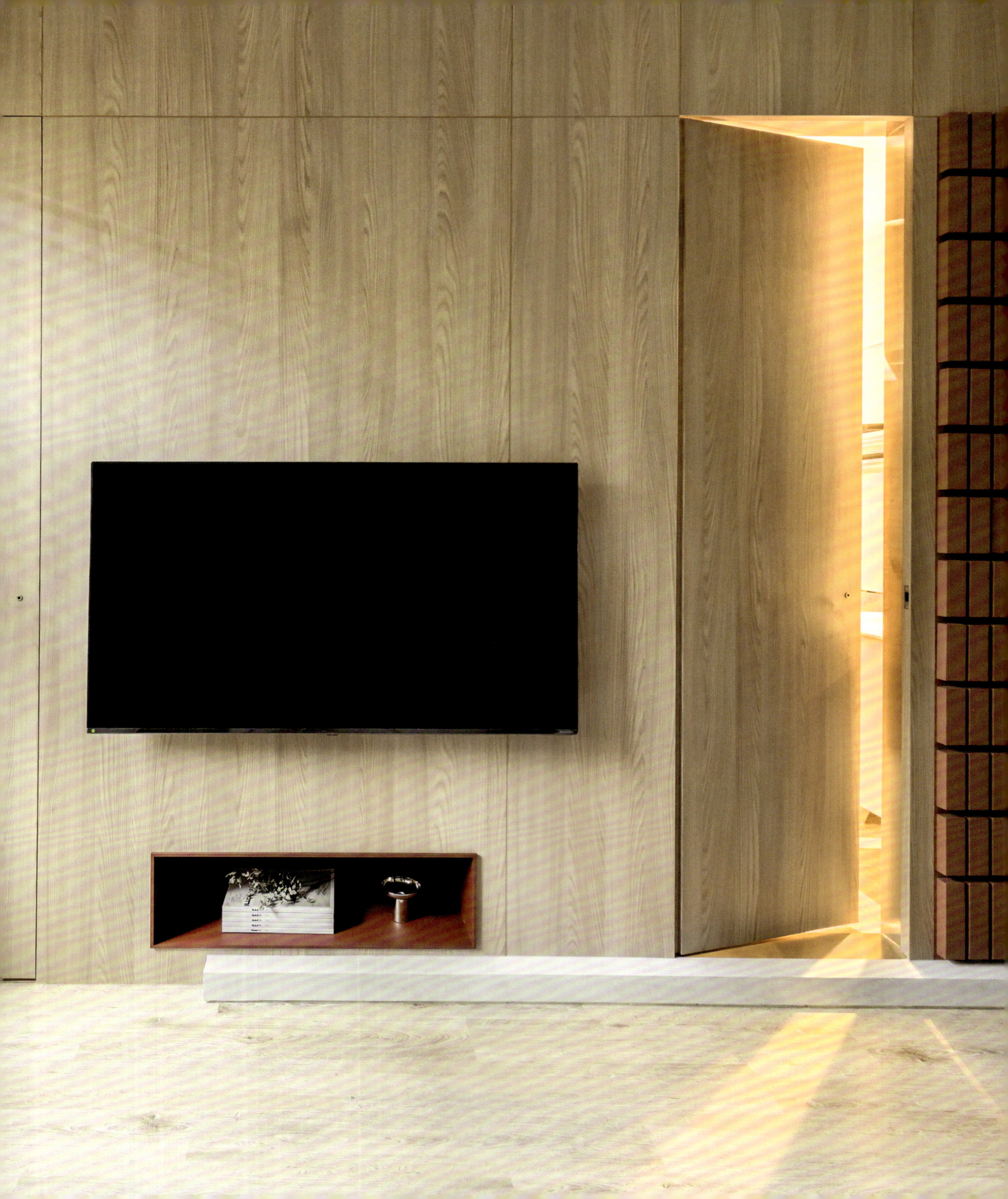

Limit House

28m² / 301ft²
Republic Design
DaTong District, Taipei City

Republic Design's 28-sq-m (310-sq-ft) apartment in Taipei City's DaTong District is a warm and elegant space that pays homage to the traditional colours of the region. Inspired by the earthy reds, greys and light oak wood of the buildings that surround the apartment, the space is both functional and beautiful.

The apartment is in one of the oldest urban areas of Taipei City, close to historic buildings like the Taipei Confucius Temple and one of the largest parks in the city, Yuanshan Park. The client, a businesswoman who frequently travels, only needed a small, maintainable sanctuary, so this compact apartment was ideal for her lifestyle.

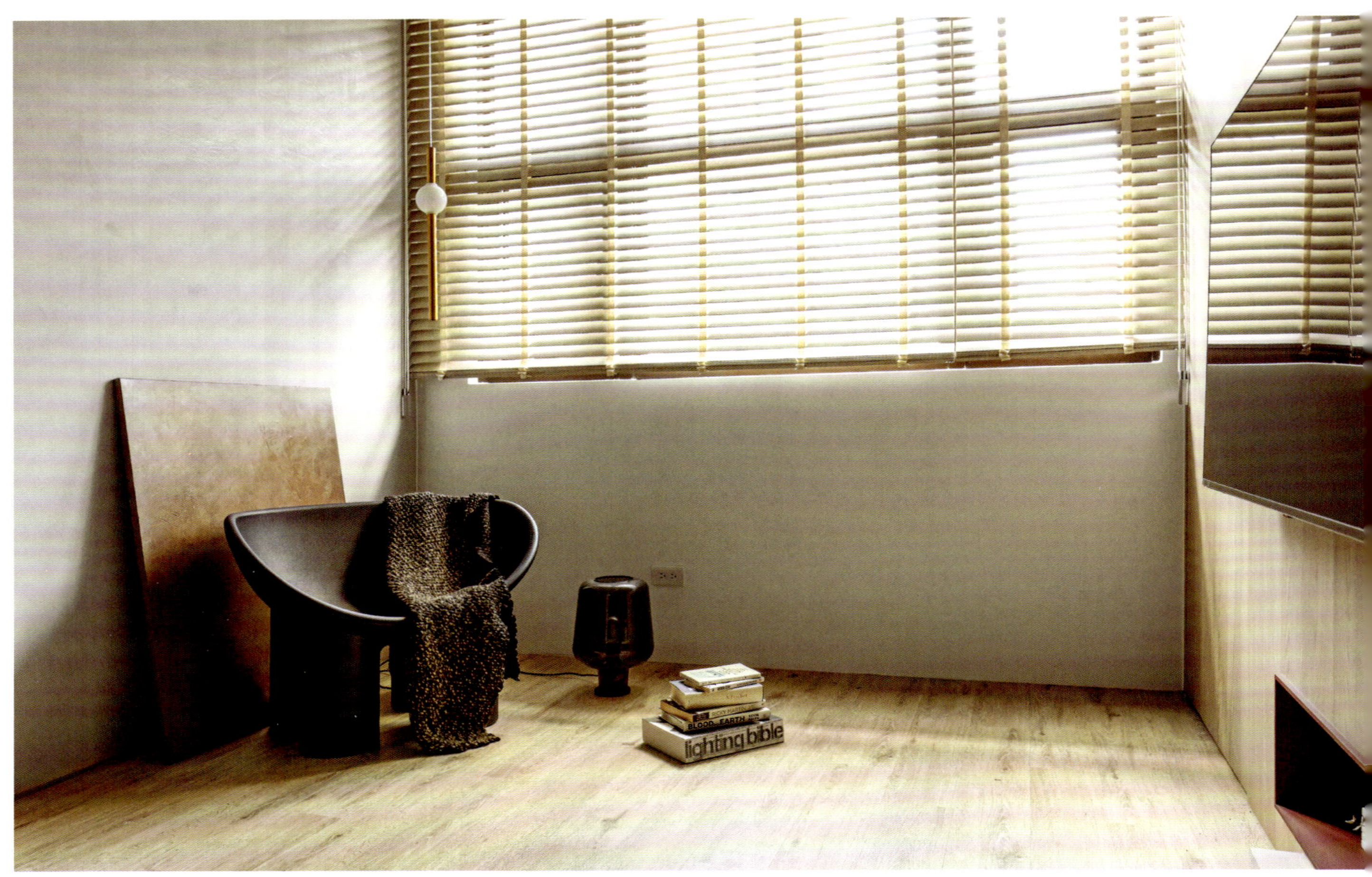

As the client lives alone, there was no need for an entrance hall, so the front door opens directly into the living room. A utility brick wall in the living room, inspired by traditional local colours, has compartments that open and fold to hang coats and store other items in. This wall makes up part of a piece of joinery, featuring a wall-mounted television, that extends all the way to the dining area and kitchen, creating a long pathway in the middle of the apartment.

This leads to a compact dining area that sits between two walls and includes upper and lower storage. The lower storage is finished in matte dark red laminate, which is easy to clean and adds a pop of colour that ties in with the feature brick wall. The kitchen is simple, yet large enough for one person to prepare a meal in. It has a single induction hob, a stainless steel sink, a rangehood, white cabinets and a dishwasher.

As part of the renovation, a mezzanine was added. A compact, foldable staircase, hidden in the ceiling of the mezzanine, leads to extra storage and a guest room.

The bedroom features a single bed and a wardrobe, while a grey full-length mirror reflects natural light and creates the illusion of more space.

Behind a hidden door in the living area, there is a bathroom with terrazzo tiles covering the floor and half of the wall. Glass window blocks in the shower area provide natural light – maximising natural light is one of the hallmarks of Republic Design's approach to small-footprint design.

AFTER

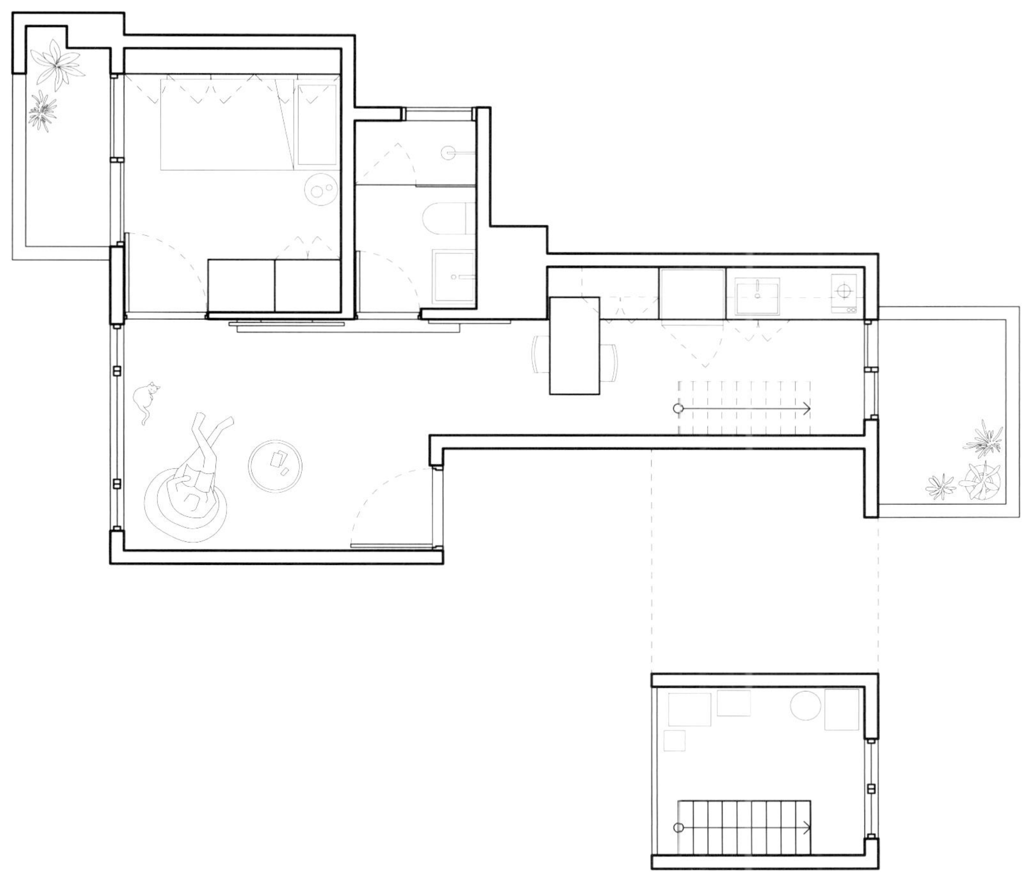

BEFORE

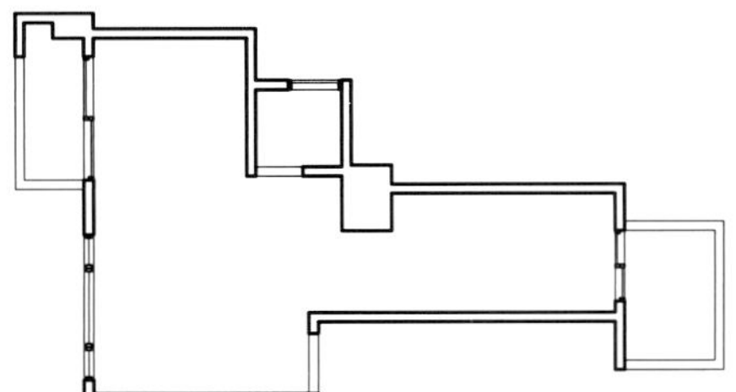

Scale 1:100

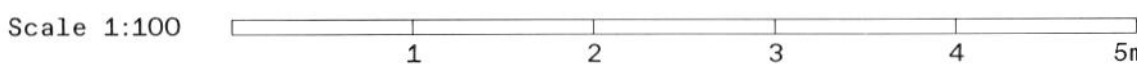

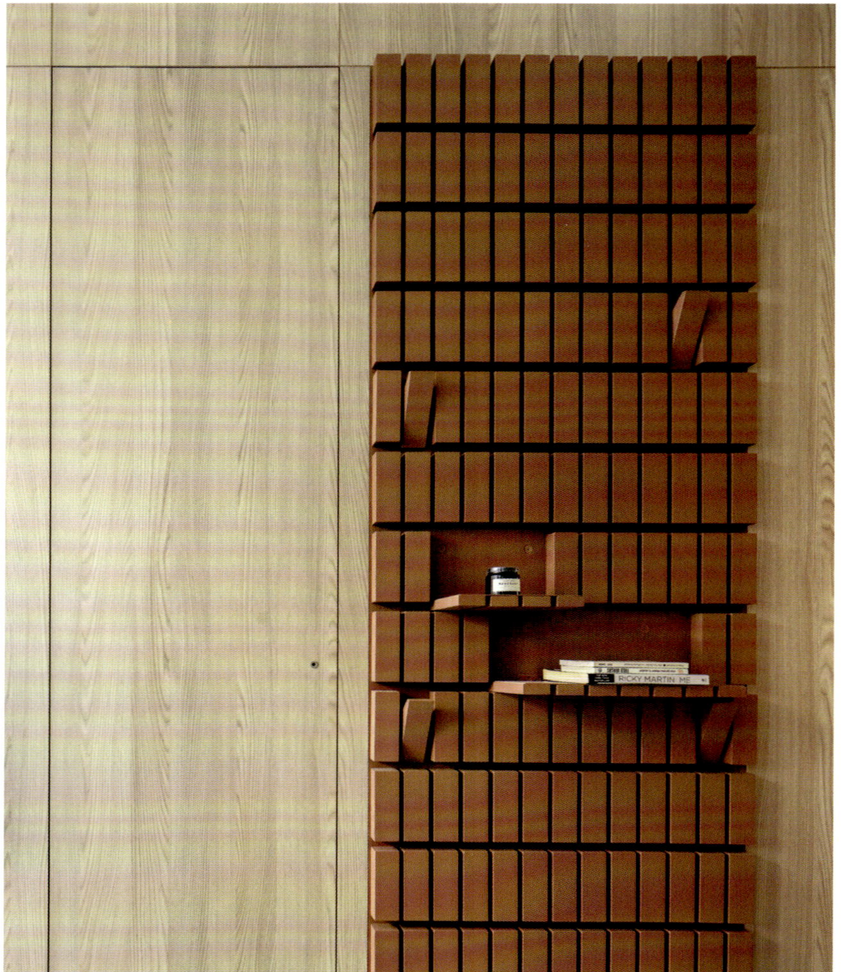

Chris Choo, co-founder and designer at Republic Design, explains: 'Sunlight is the most fundamental element when it comes to small space. The more sunlight gets into the space, the more comfortable you feel, as it reduces the narrow or crowded misconception. We often create a wide-open space, fewer partitions, foldable or modifying furniture as they create an illusion of enlarged space.'

Old apartments can be more affordable for the next generation than newly built homes in urban areas. By renovating and upgrading these spaces, the quality of life can be greatly improved while still preserving the cultural and historical value of these buildings. As Choo explains: 'Despite being a smaller space, [our team] believes that there is more attention than ever on upgrading living conditions and quality of life. A small space does not equal low-cost but is a greater chance to create a neat and elegant space.'

'A small space does not equal low-cost but is a greater chance to create a neat and elegant space.'

PAGE 76 Flush doors and joinery allow feature elements, like the red brick wall, to stand apart.

PAGE 78 Simple-yet-elegant art and furnishings were carefully selected to give the home a gallery-like feel.

OPPOSITE Each brick can be independently moved to create shelving and hooks.

BELOW Glass bricks allow natural light to filter in through the bathroom.

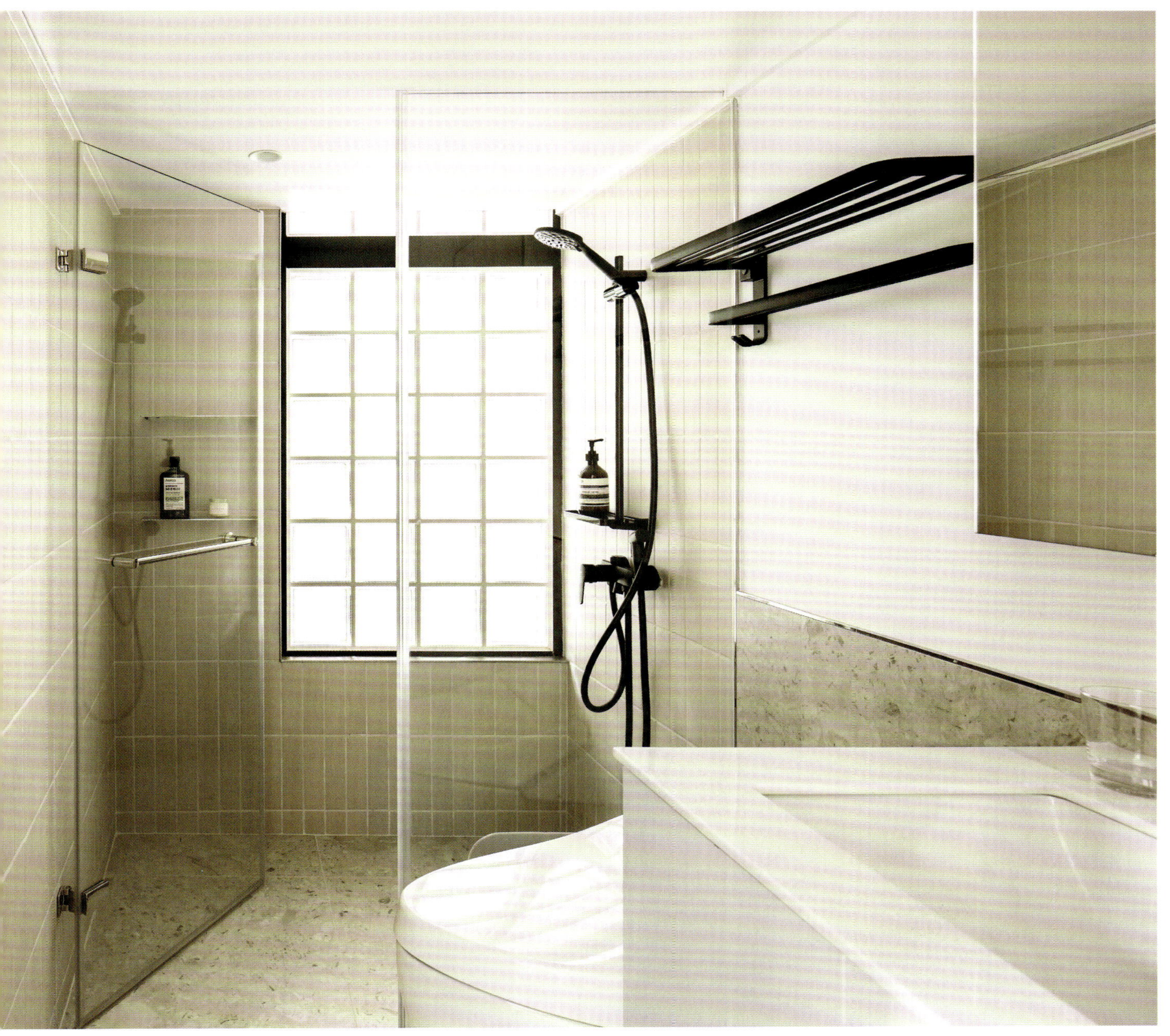

BELOW The earthy colours of Taipei City were the inspiration for the design.

OPPOSITE TOP A loft was added during the renovation to serve as storage and a guest room.

OPPOSITE BOTTOM The darker feature colour on the kitchen benches grounds the design while the lighter colour above creates a sense of height and more space.

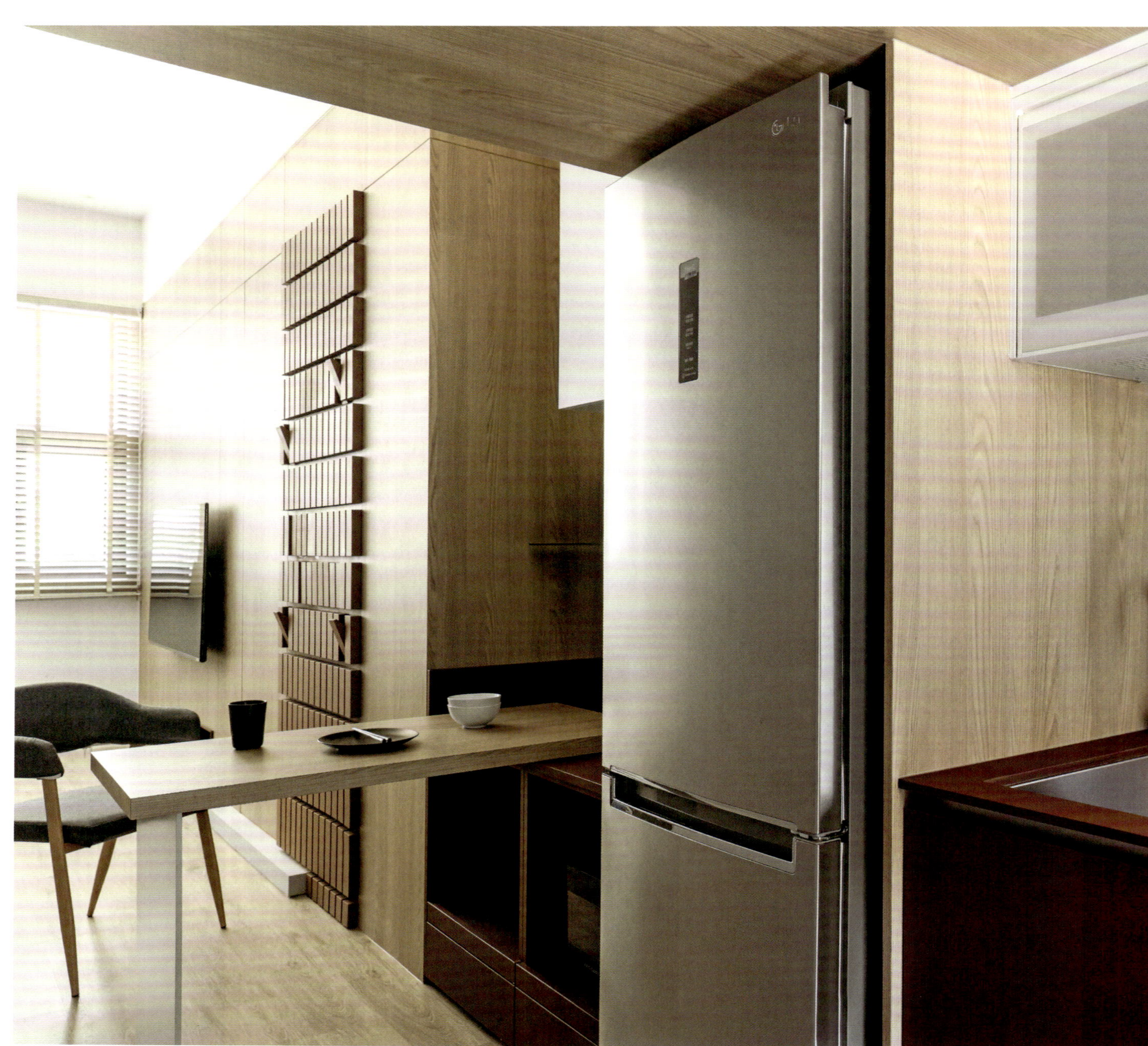

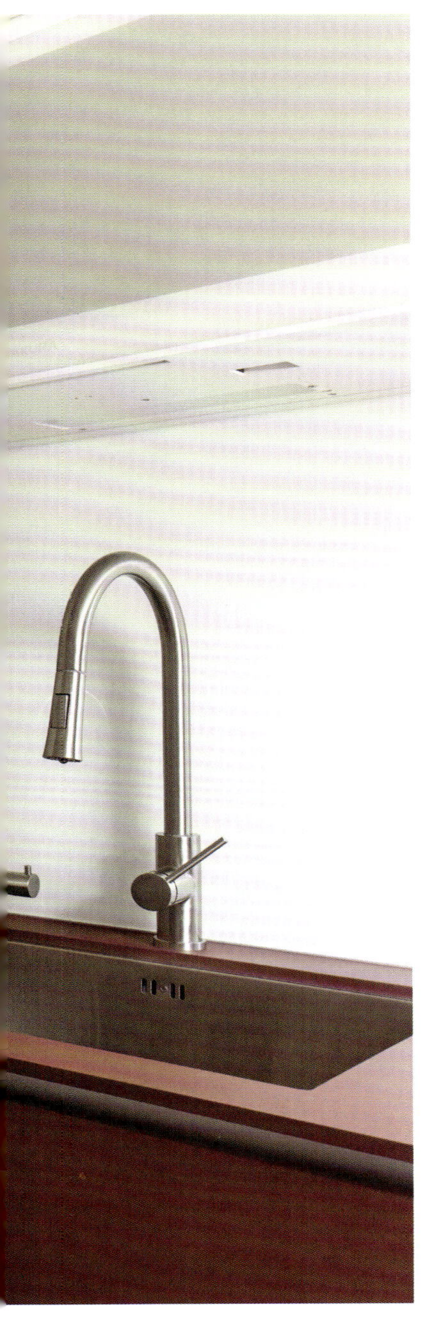

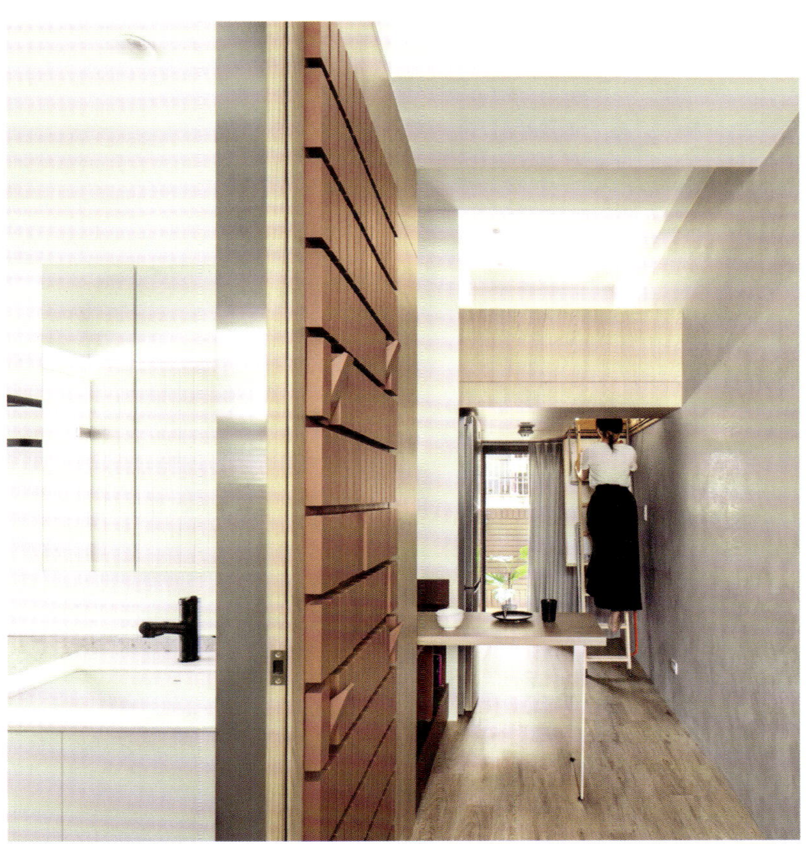

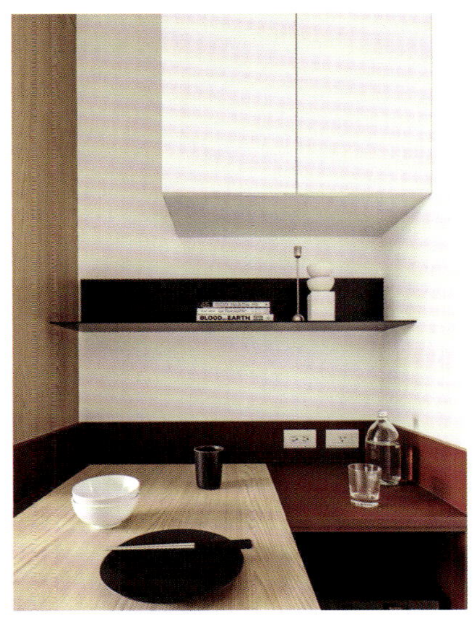

2

One of the reasons multifunctional spaces enhance the overall living experience in small-footprint design is because of their versatility. In a small space, where every square metre matters, spaces designed to serve multiple purposes are often preferred to dedicated rooms. Valuable space is saved and the homes feel spacious and open.

Multifunctional spaces provide flexibility and adaptability. They can be easily transformed to suit changing needs and activities. For example, a living area can be quickly converted into a workspace during the day or transformed into a bedroom at night. This adaptability allows homeowners to make the most of their available space and seamlessly transition between different functions.

There are some stunning multifunctional spaces in this section. Project #13 by Studio Wills + Architects is a remarkable example of this concept. It takes a single unit of a flat and cleverly splits it down the middle, creating an office and a home. By inserting a loft for sleeping and an additional loft for storage in the office, Project #13 optimises its layout without sacrificing functionality. It seamlessly integrates an office within the small home, allowing work and personal life to coexist harmoniously.

Another standout example of a multifunctional home is Mark II by Nicholas Gurney, which was designed to incorporate the client's existing furniture. A joinery unit serves as a television/gaming centre, home office and sleeping area. A sliding door with extendable and retractable cables for the television demonstrates ingenuity and versatility. Additionally, the bathroom doors made of frosted glass play on the concept of borrowing light, which makes the compact inner-Sydney space feel bigger and brighter.

Multifunctional Spaces

Over in Singapore, Waterloo Street takes flexibility to a new level. The client briefed Three-d conceptwerke to design a comfortable and flexible space and the designer's response – furniture on wheels – is an ingenious idea that allows the apartment to be easily reconfigured. For instance, two versatile tables can be joined together to create a larger dining area or workspace. There are also moveable partitions that can be used for privacy or to accommodate guests.

By incorporating multifunctional design principles, small-footprint living becomes more adaptable, efficient and enjoyable.

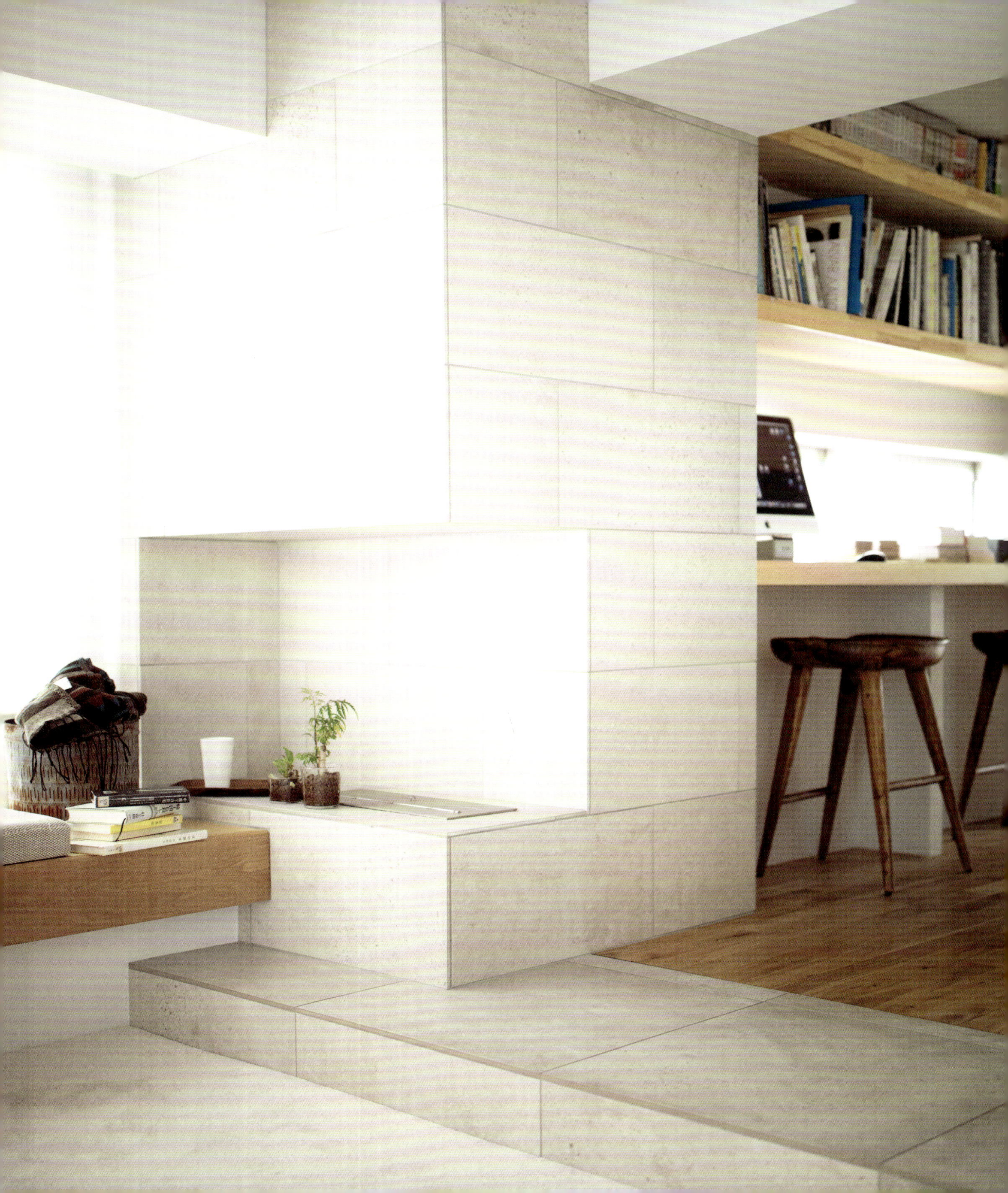

Home in Akatsutsumi

46m² / 495ft²
Small Design Studio
Setagaya, Tokyo

Finding privacy and personal space can be tricky in a densely packed city. However, architect and owner Kumiko Ouchi, of Small Design Studio, was able to create a functional, comfortable and private living space for herself, her partner and their cat, Cochi, five minutes from central Tokyo.

Built in 1979, the building comprises seven apartments, each with a distinctive design. Ouchi modified her apartment to serve as a multipurpose area that seamlessly blends residential and work functions. To achieve this, most of the internal walls in the 46-sq-m (495-sq-ft) space were removed to create an open-concept layout.

Upon entering the apartment, a small entrance hall leads to a walk-in closet, which is the largest storage space in the apartment. The living room is a step lower than the rest of the apartment and features a custom-built 2.2-m (7-ft) bench seat by the window with sliding doors that lead out to a small balcony. A bioethanol fireplace was installed as a replacement for a traditional chimney to make the room feel cosy, as apartment regulations didn't allow for the installation of a wood-burning fireplace.

The kitchen is modest yet efficient, equipped with a gas stove, a fish grill, an oven and a sizeable sink, which satisfies Ouchi's love of cooking.

'We love cooking so the kitchen had to have both functionality and a simple look that would be part of the living room,' she explains. To keep the electric appliances from view, they were placed discreetly on the side of the kitchen that can't be seen from the living room. The wooden base component of the L-shaped kitchen and the small dining table were finished with water-resistant plastering. The refrigerator and compact pantry are neatly tucked away in the corner.

Adjacent to the living room is the office area. The ceiling has a beam at each end of the space which gives the office nook a sturdy-yet-intimate feel. The desk is crafted from laminated wood, with two wall-mounted bookshelves positioned above it and a floor-to-ceiling wardrobe at the end of the office.

The apartment's bathroom and toilet are separated by a mirrored storage cabinet and additional wall-mounted storage beside the sink. The bathroom features a wet room, a popular Japanese bathing concept, that combines a shower and a bathtub in one space. The bathroom also has a washer dryer and a litter box for Cochi.

Ouchi's apartment exemplifies that limited space need not be a hindrance to creating a comfortable and practical living space. As Ouchi says, 'A house is like a container for your life.' This mindset is demonstrated in her home's well-ordered and functional zones.

Tokyo apartments feature heavily on our channel and within our books. It's not favouritism (though we do love Japan). It's because the Japanese approach to simplicity and minimalistic design lends itself so nicely to small-footprint living. After all, the country that invented the bento box was always going to bring that expertise to creating neat, orderly and functional tiny homes.

PAGE 86 A step down is a easy way to create delineation between zones in a small-footprint design.

BELOW Plenty of light reaches the office thanks to the removal of internal walls during the renovation.

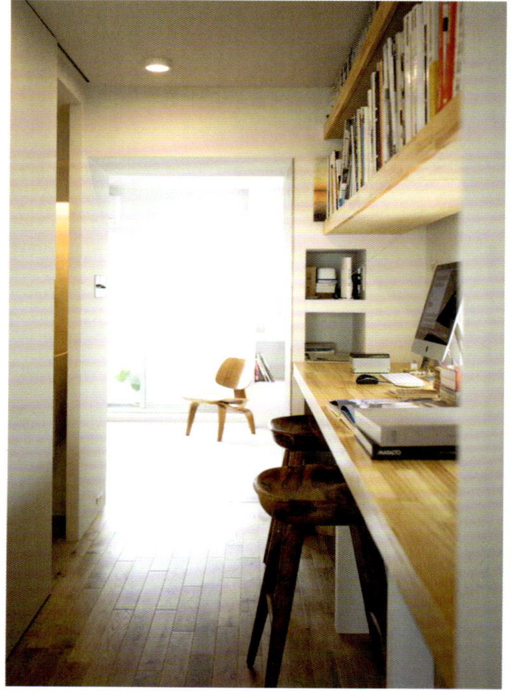

AFTER

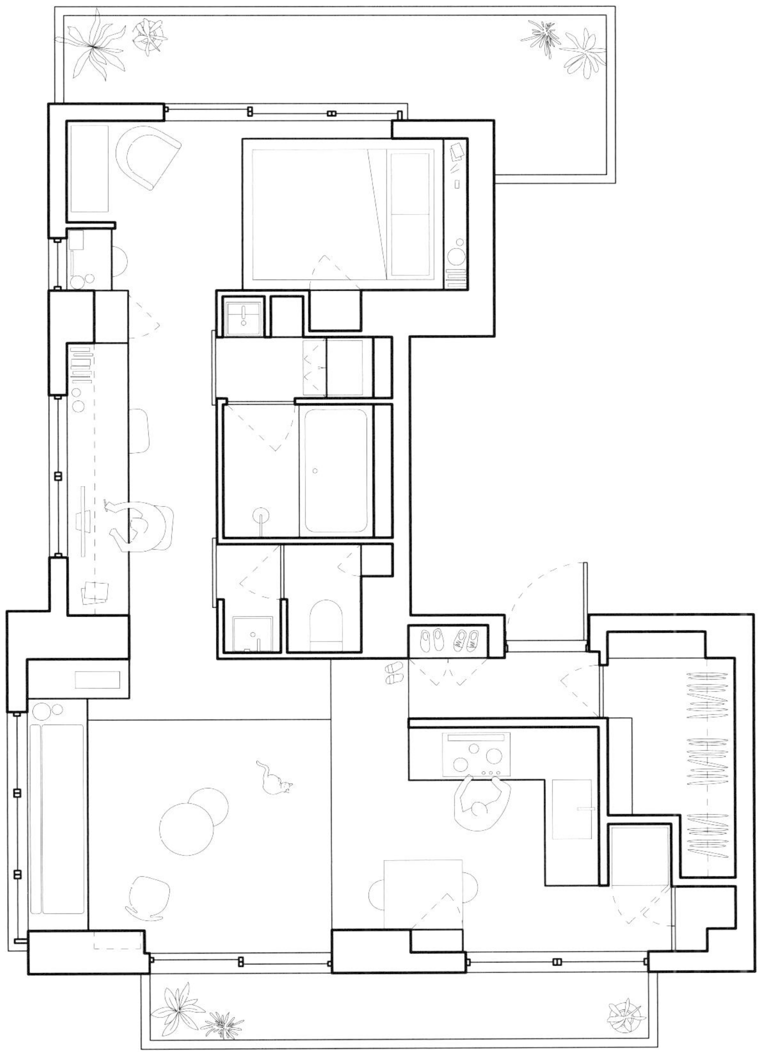

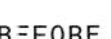

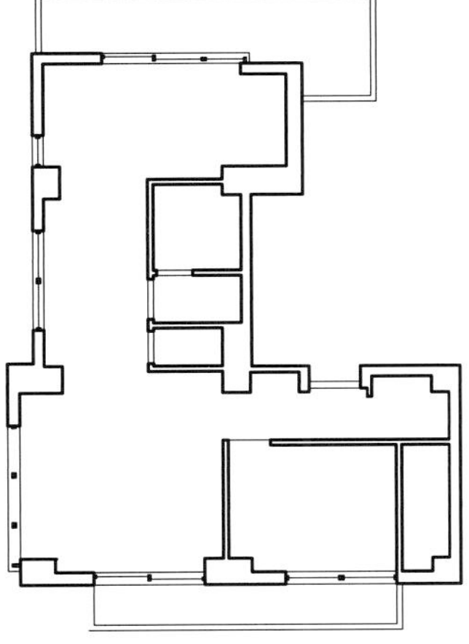

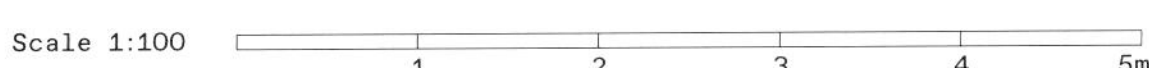

BELOW An L-shaped kitchen is an efficient use of a small space and the additional bench area that comes with it is invaluable.

OPPOSITE Hidden storage is crucial in compact kitchens.

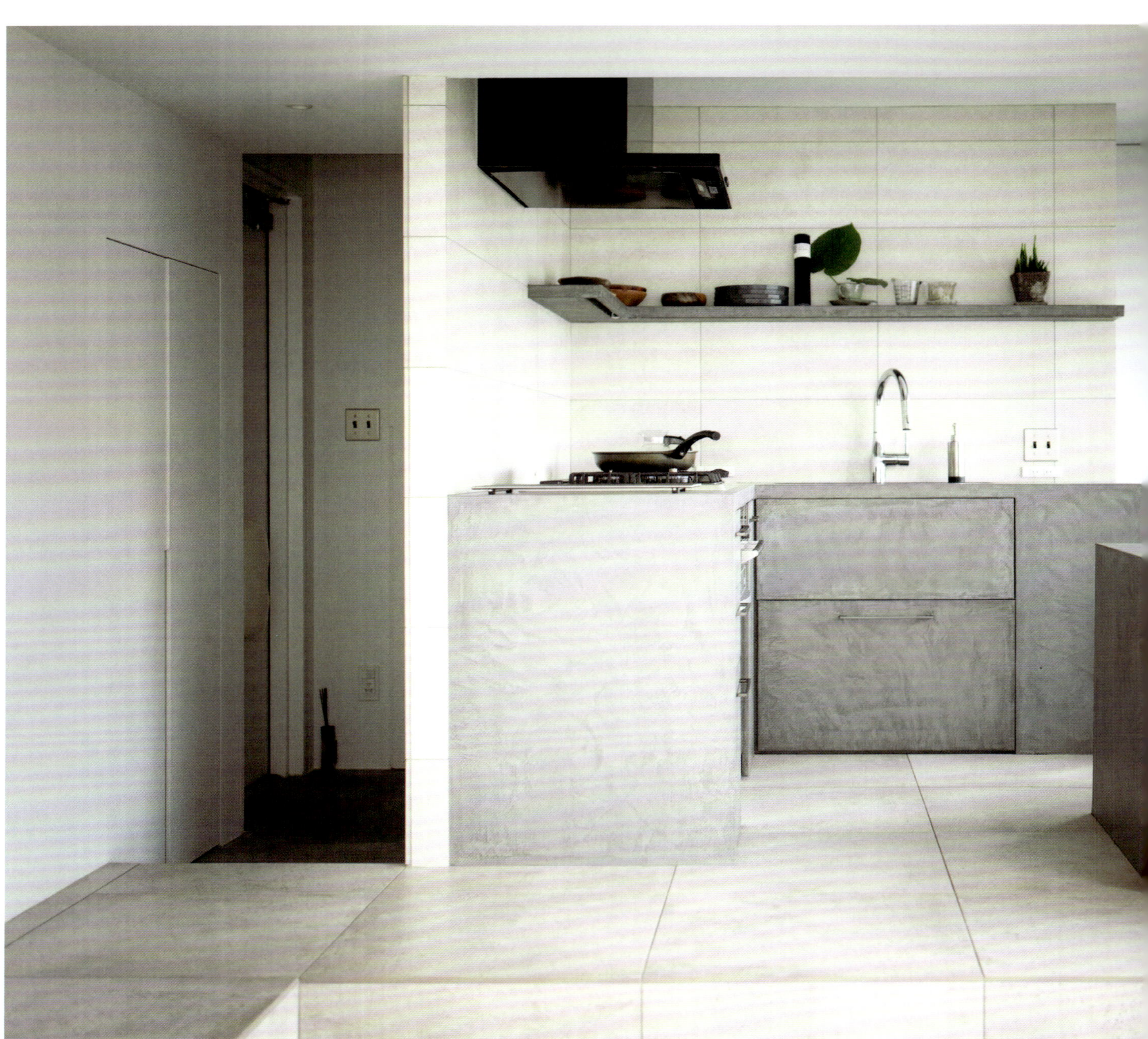

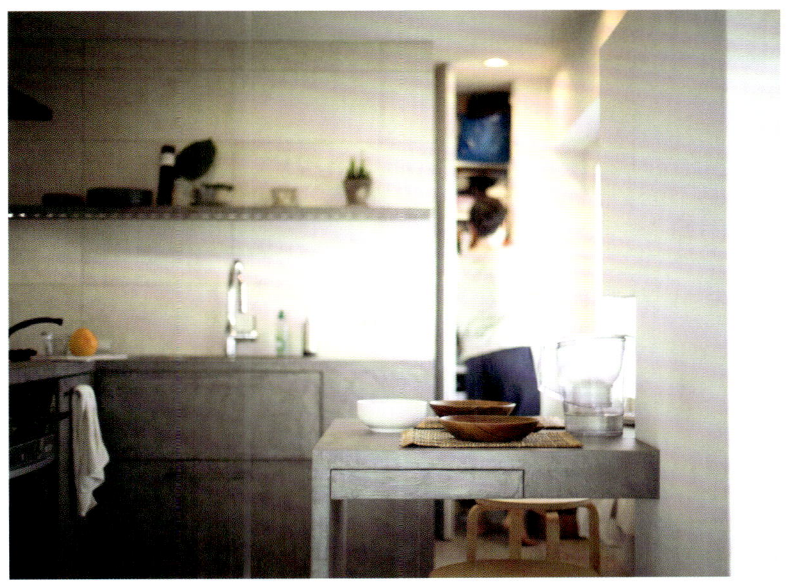

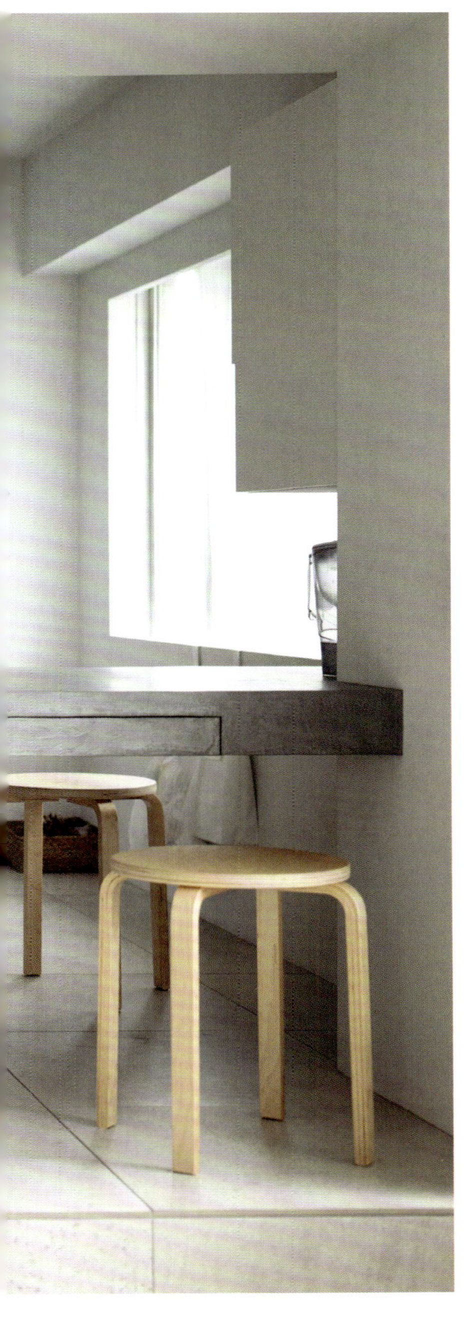

... the Japanese approach to simplicity and minimalistic design lends itself so nicely to small-footprint living.

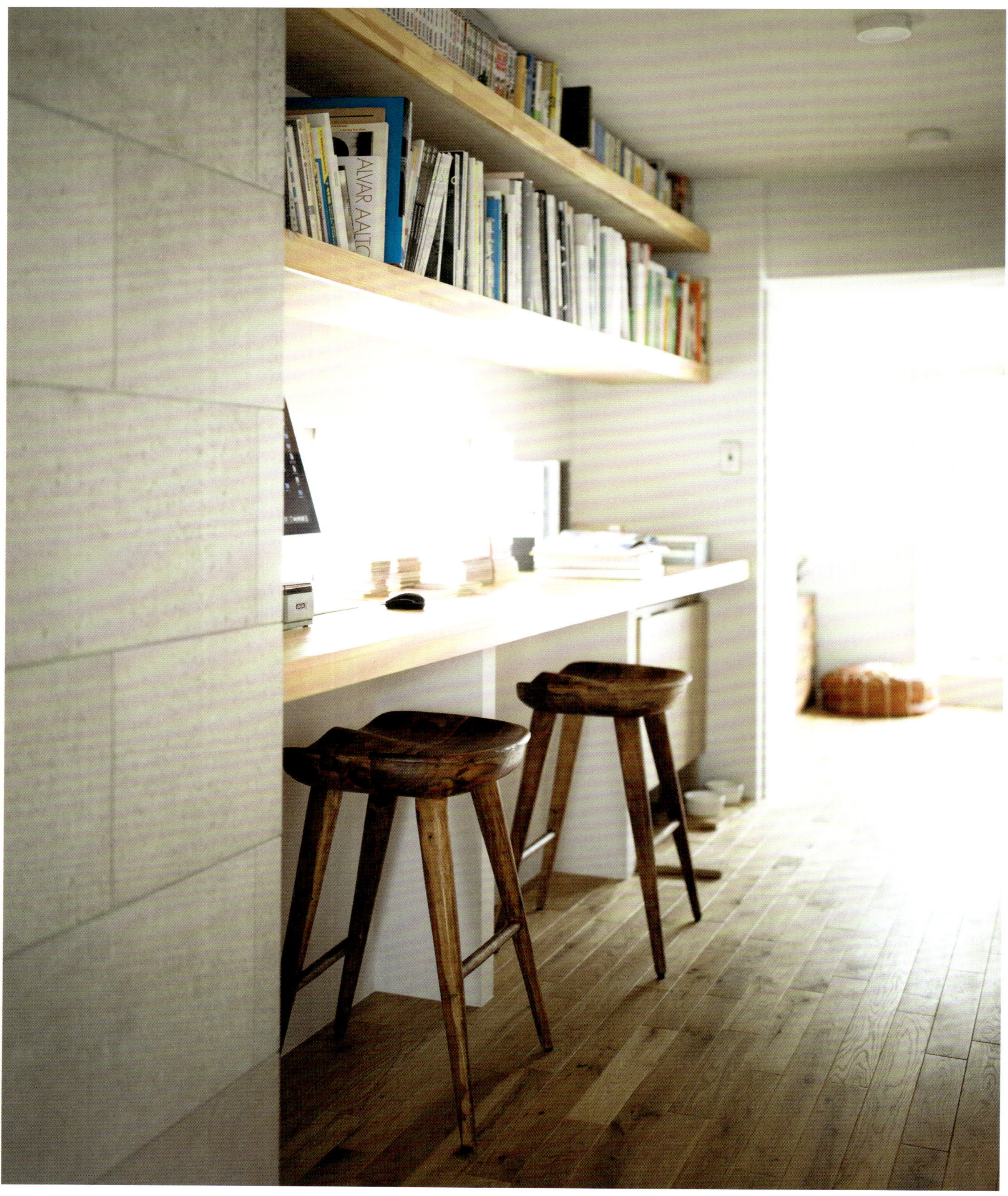
ALVAR AALTO

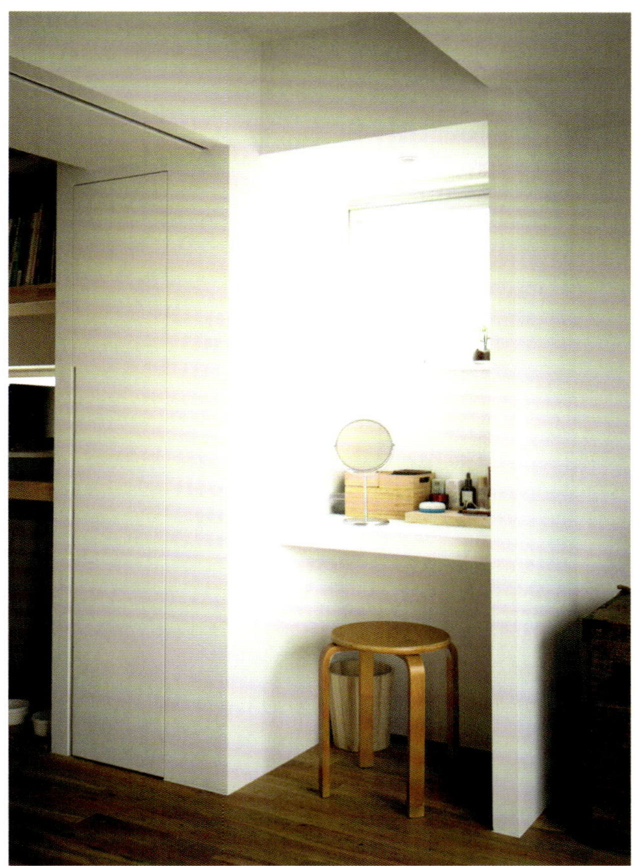

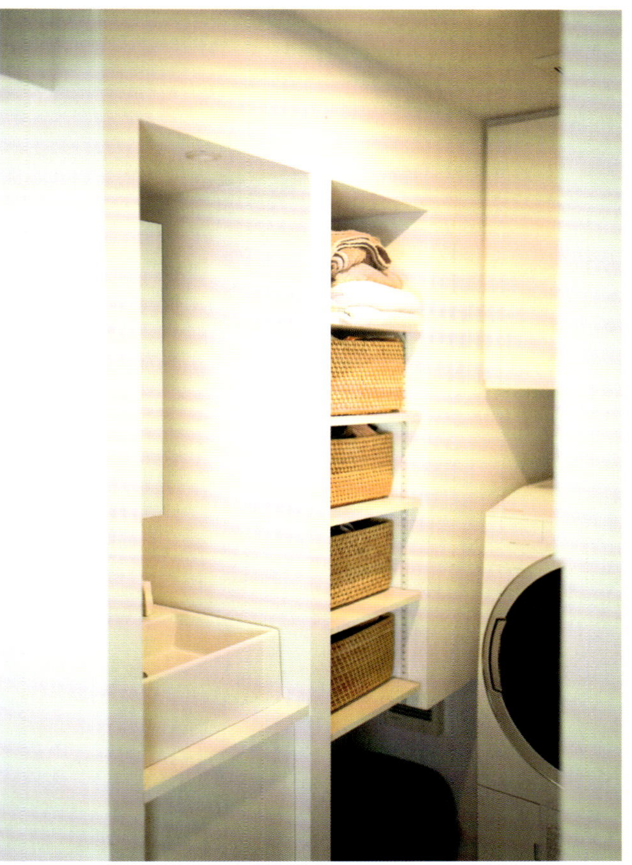

OPPOSITE Timber flooring and wood laminate on the desk and shelves in the office area make the space warm and comfortable despite its compact size.

TOP LEFT A small awkward niche was transformed into a dressing table.

TOP RIGHT Another niche is a hub for the bathroom sink and vanity.

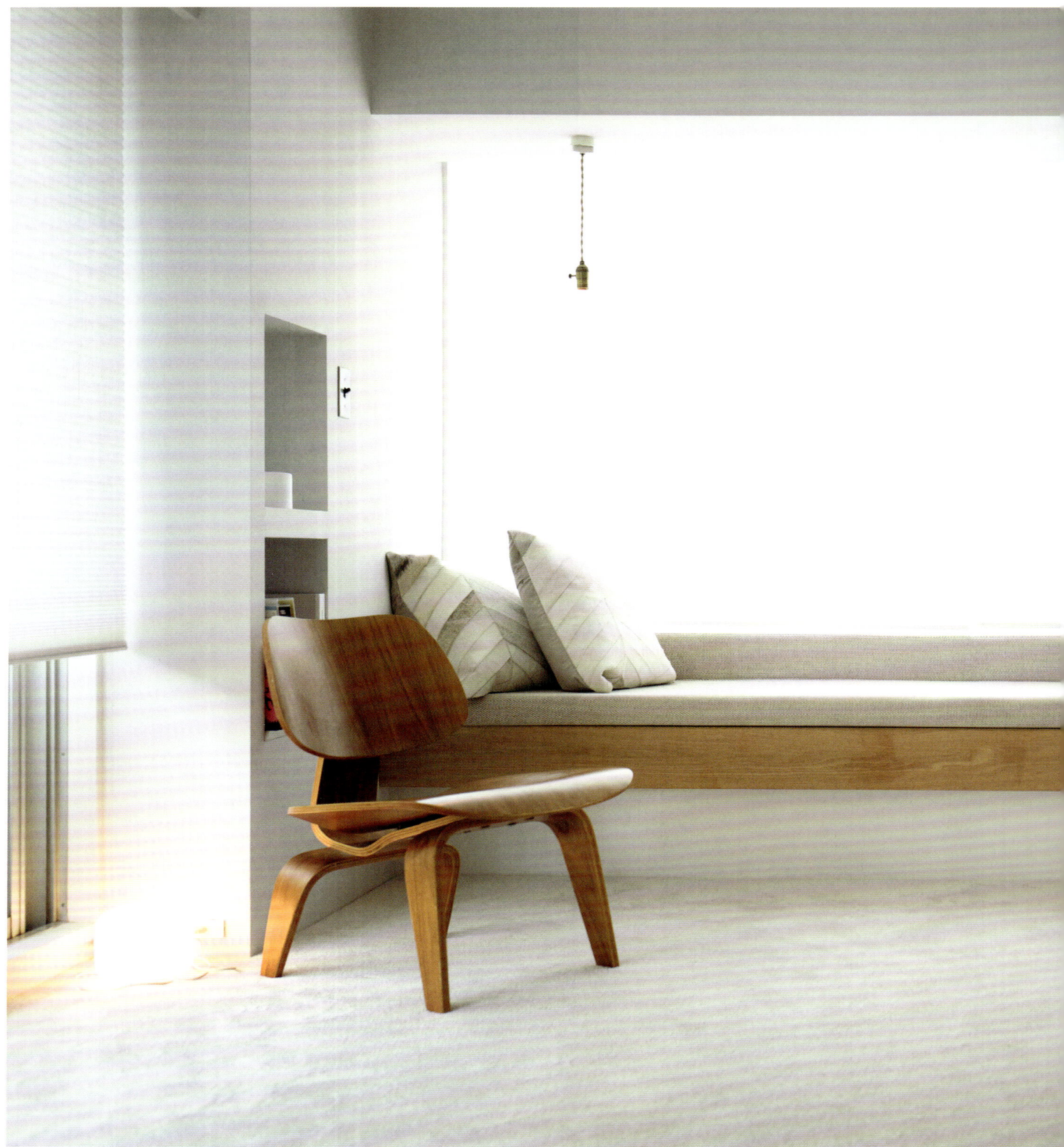

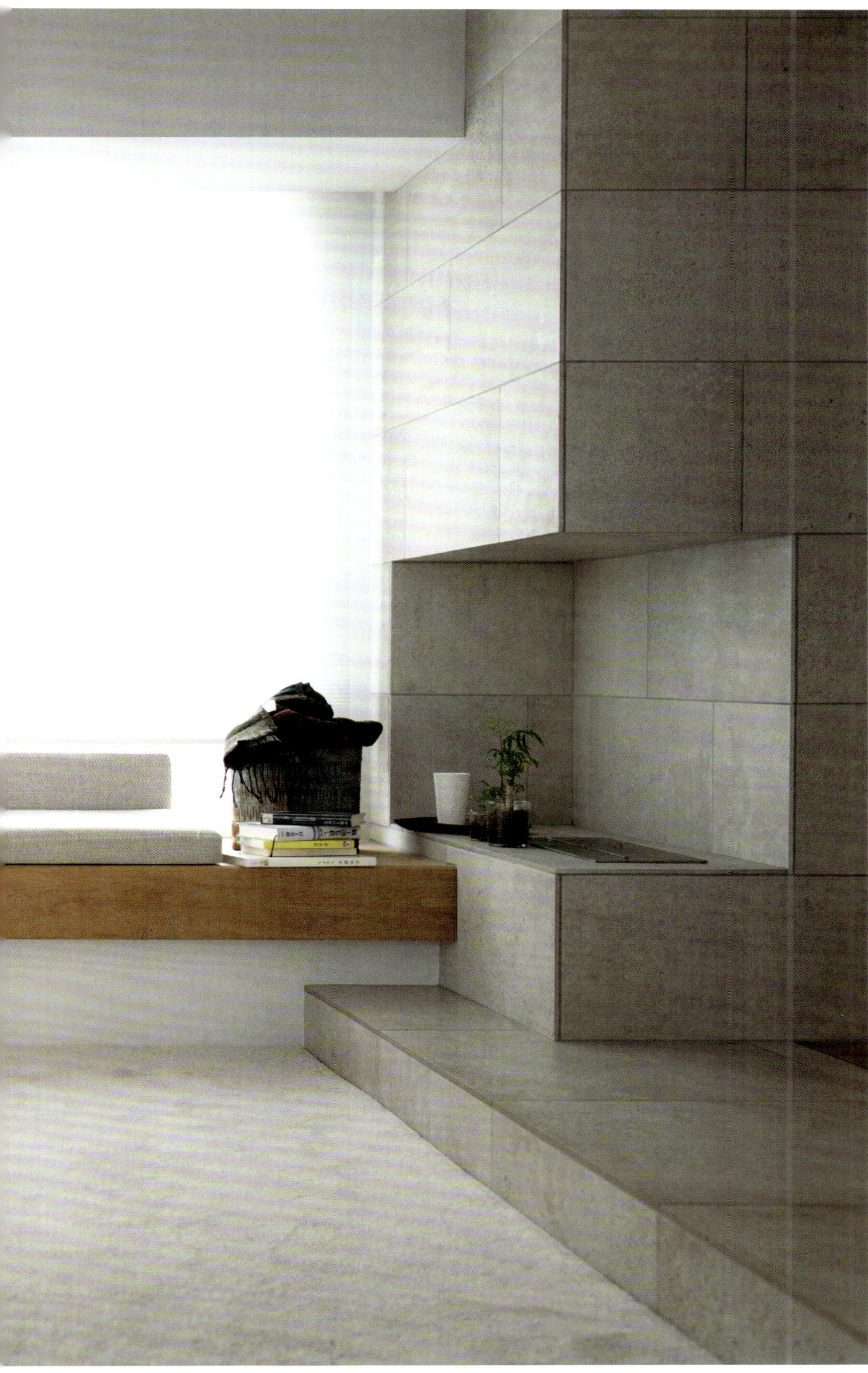

LEFT Simple and light-filled with integrated joinery, this space exemplifies good small-footprint design.

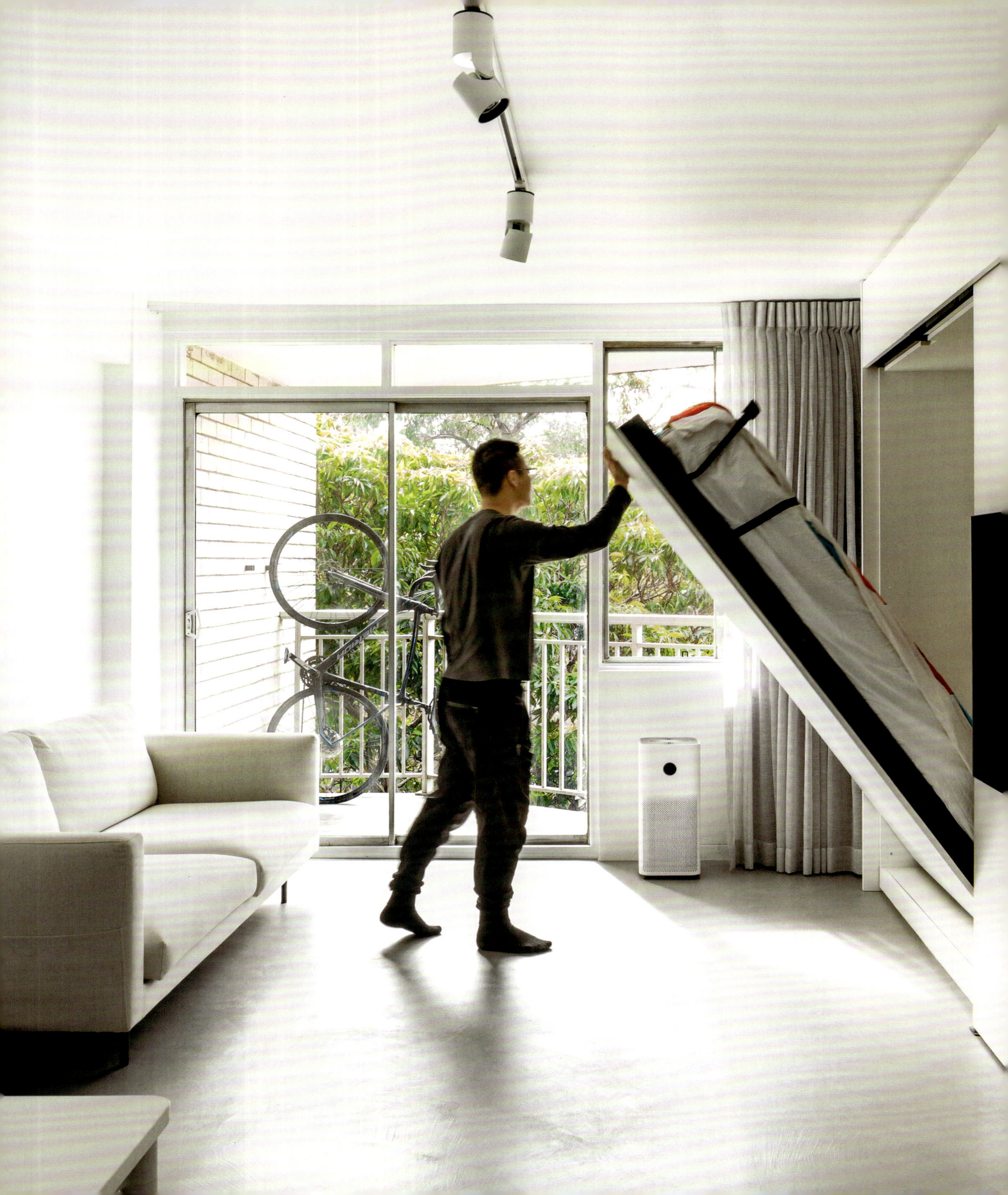

Mark II

27m² / 290ft²
Nicholas Gurney
Rushcutters Bay, Sydney

Located in the heart of Sydney's Rushcutters Bay, this apartment is a masterpiece of minimalism. Built in the mid–1960s, the interior of the 27-sq-m (290-sq-ft) space felt tired. However, the simplicity of the floor plan meant that industrial designer Nicholas Gurney only needed to make small changes. In fact, the only significant structural change was removing the original built-in cupboard that divided the entryway from the kitchen.

The client had a clear vision for how the apartment design could be tailored to their specific requirements and took inspiration from Gurney's previous project, Tara. However, as Gurney explains 'the primary objective for this apartment was to conceal everything in a single unit'.

The concept of streamlining all components into a single joinery unit is a rationalist approach that pushes everything to the perimeter, resulting in an open and flexible layout. To achieve this, Gurney took inspiration from German designer Nils Holger Moorman, who is a favourite of his client. Holger Moorman is known for a minimalistic style that utilises laminated plywood in different hues to achieve a simple-yet-sophisticated look. Gurney used this technique to create the joinery unit that seamlessly flows from the kitchen to general storage, a workspace and a sleeping area.

The L-shaped kitchen was designed to maximise the use of the existing services while also accommodating modern appliances. It features a full-sized dishwasher that flips down, along with an oven and induction cooktop. A hidden cupboard houses the hot water unit and water meter.

The kitchen flows seamlessly into open-plan dining and living areas. The living space is anchored by a simple couch that is oriented towards the television that sits on a sliding panel. The panel conceals the Murphy bed or a recessed workspace, depending on its position. The handle to access the Murphy bed is situated underneath the cabinet fronts above, which falls back into place naturally after use.

As the client works exclusively from home, creating a generous office area that could be hidden when not in use was essential. Adjacent to the workspace, a smaller secondary surface conceals the cable management system. A substantial two-door wardrobe separates the kitchen from the office area.

A combination of sheer and block-out curtains adds ambience to the space. The sheer curtain permits the client to filter natural light in during the day, while the block-out curtains are used at bedtime or when watching a movie.

The integration of all necessary components into a single joinery unit imparts a sense of openness and flow to the apartment. The understated material choices and design result in a minimalistic-yet-inviting aesthetic that feels right at home in the apartment's harbourside locale.

PAGE 96 One piece of custom joinery houses almost all the functions in Mark II.

RIGHT A simple-yet-generous bathroom is the home's only 'room'.

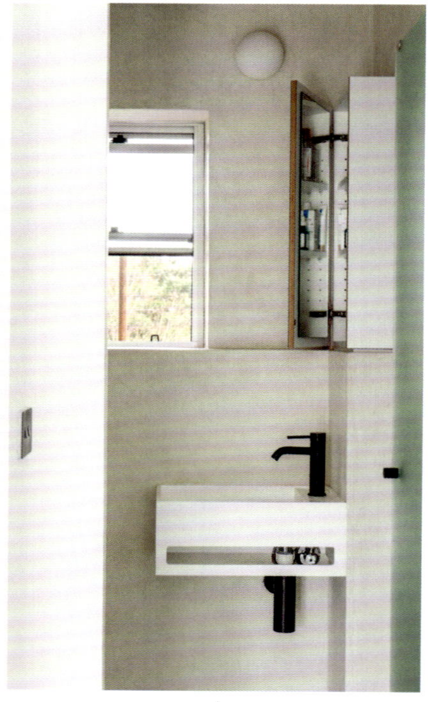

AFTER

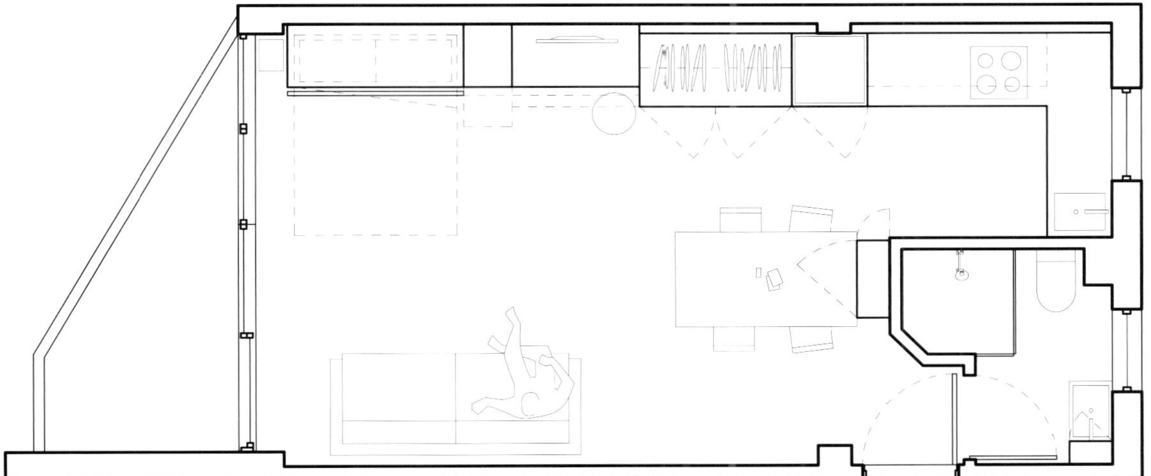

BEFORE

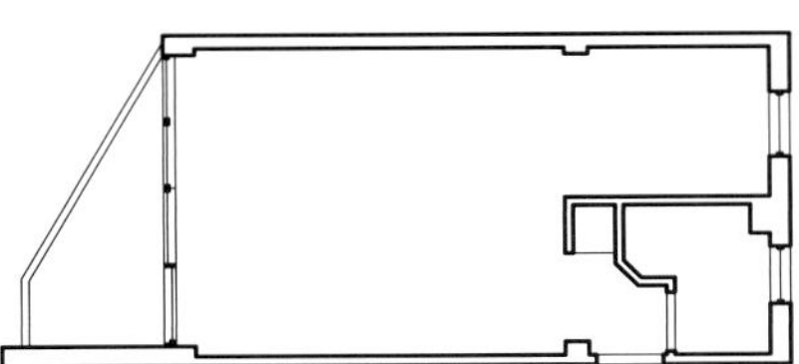

Scale 1:100 — 1 2 3 4 5m

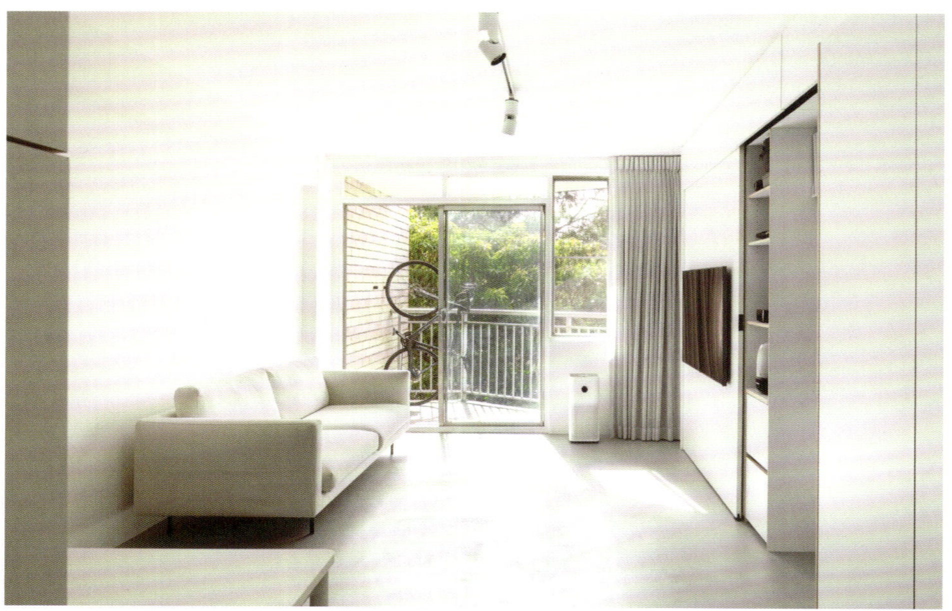

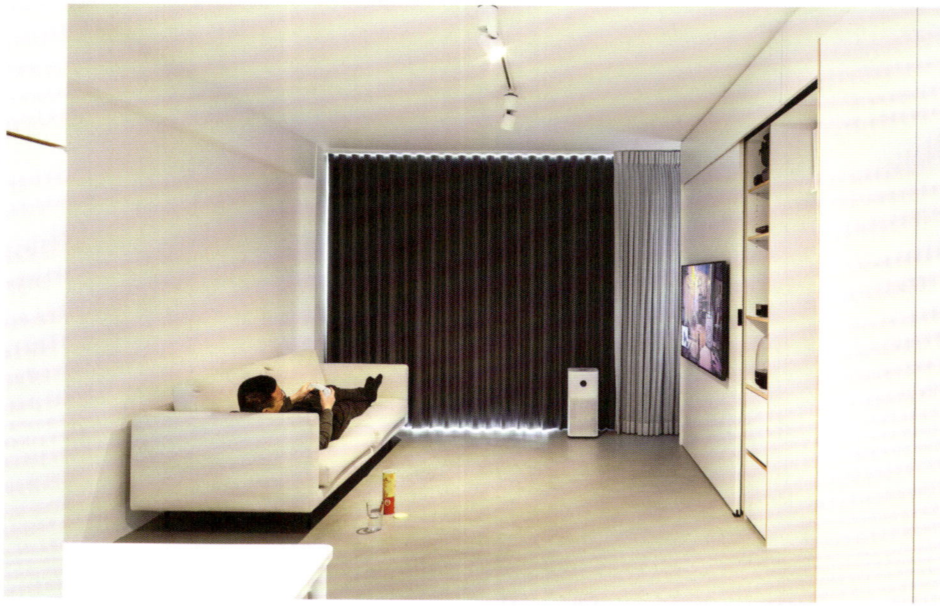

TOP There is plenty of natural light with full-height windows at one end of the apartment.

BOTTOM Block-out curtains also keep out the light when needed.

OPPOSITE A workspace was top of the client's list and it can be hidden when not in use to delineate between business and after hours.

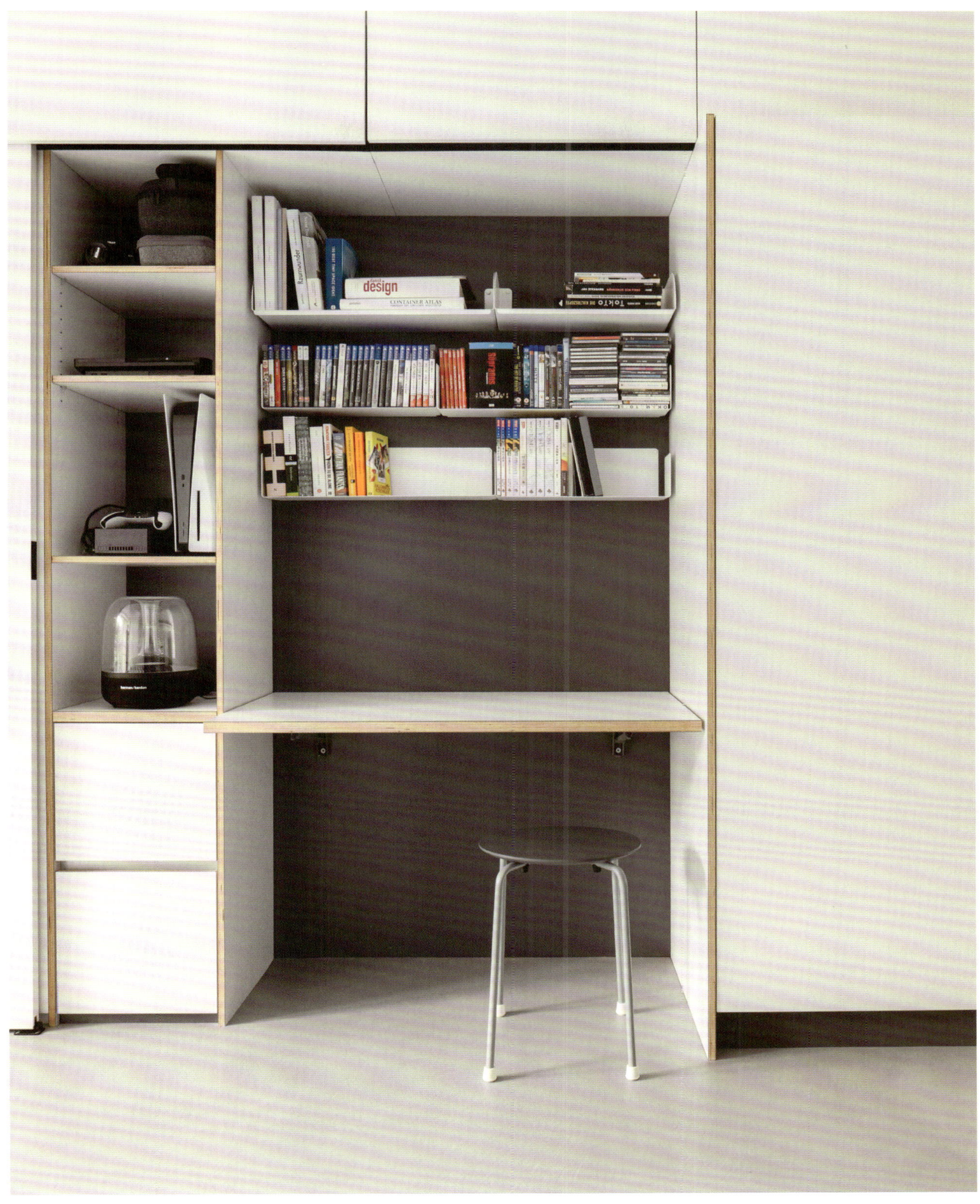
Raumwunder
design
CONTAINER ATLAS

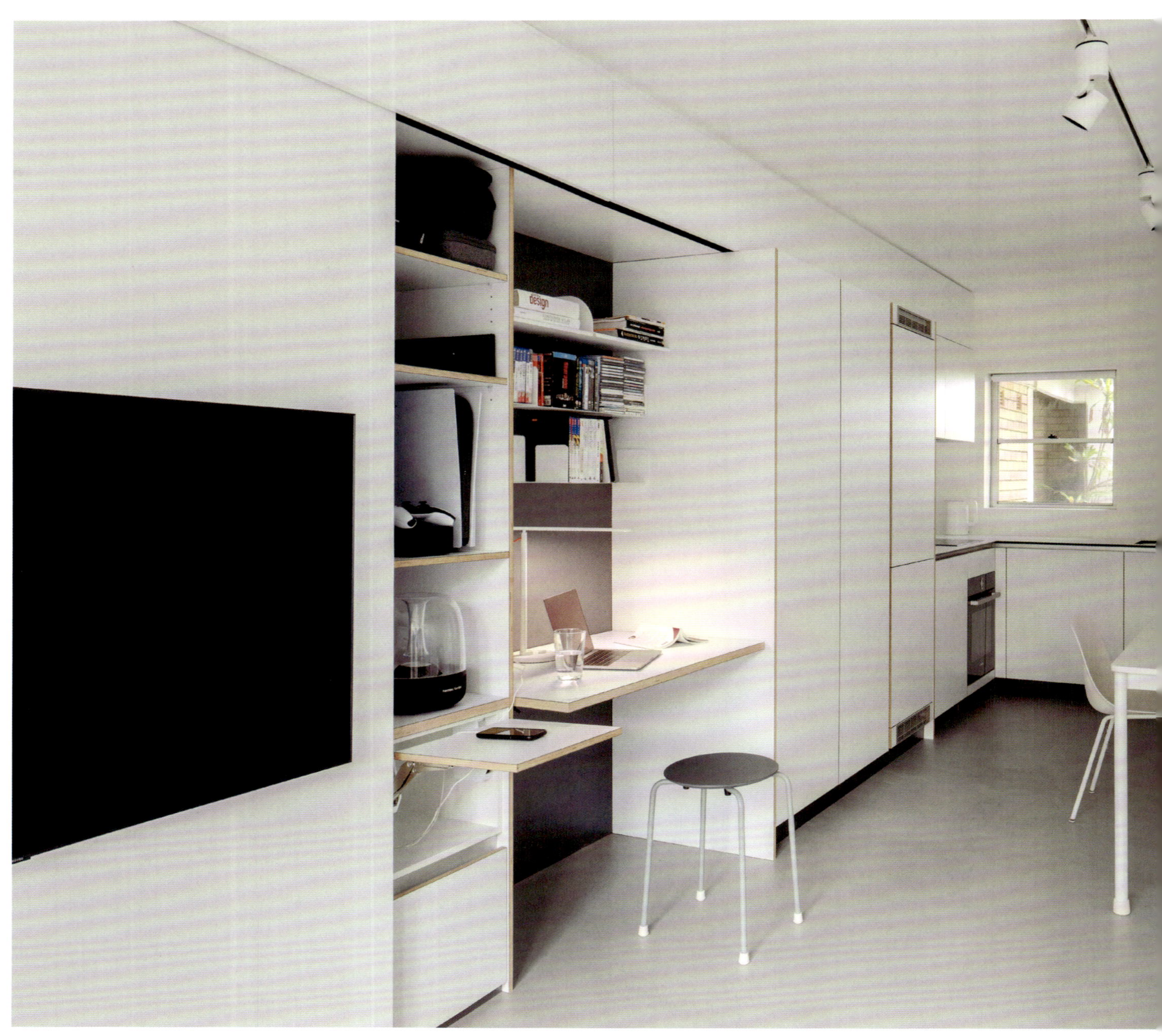

The concept of streamlining all components into a single joinery unit is a rationalist approach.

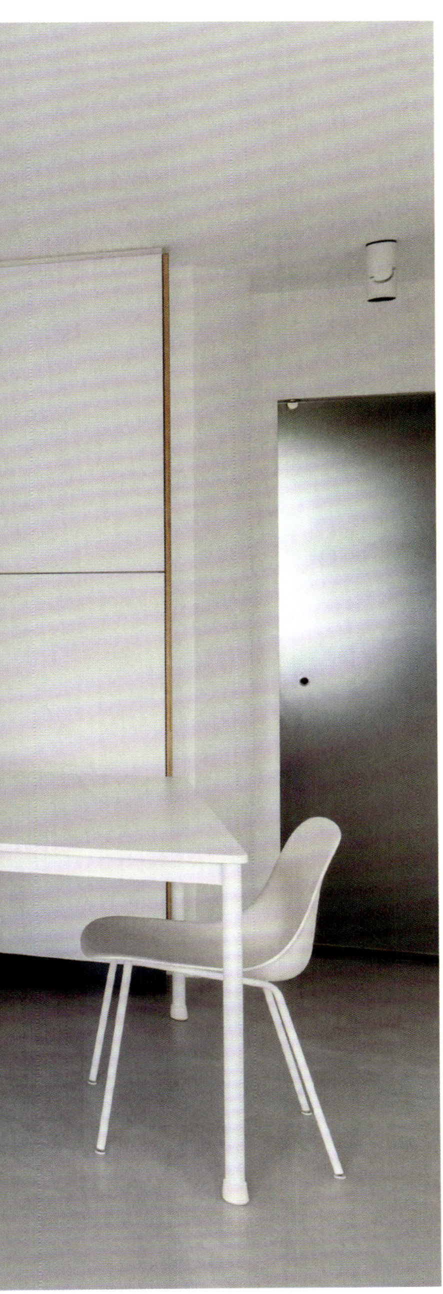

OPPOSITE The custom wall unit stretches from the windows at one end to the kitchen at the other.

BELOW A Murphy bed allows the space to transform from day to night.

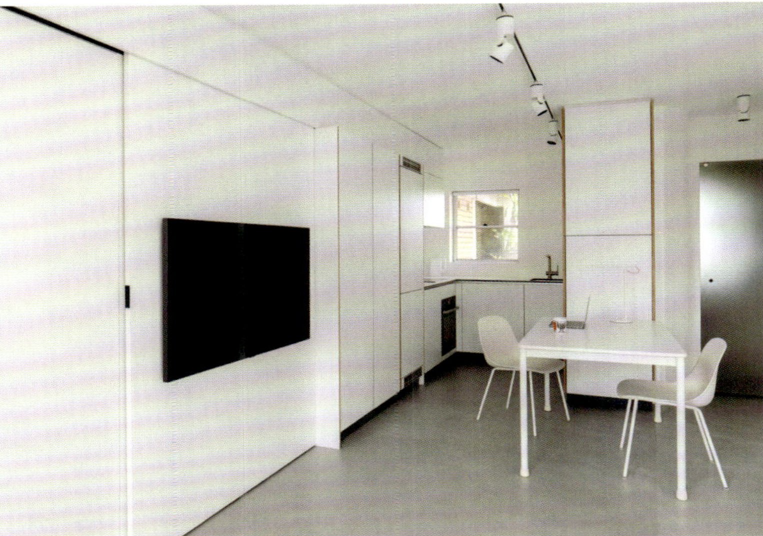

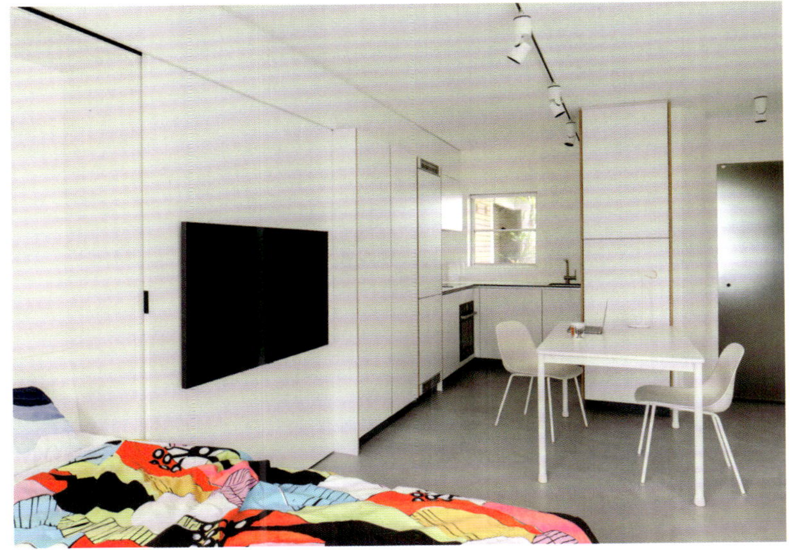

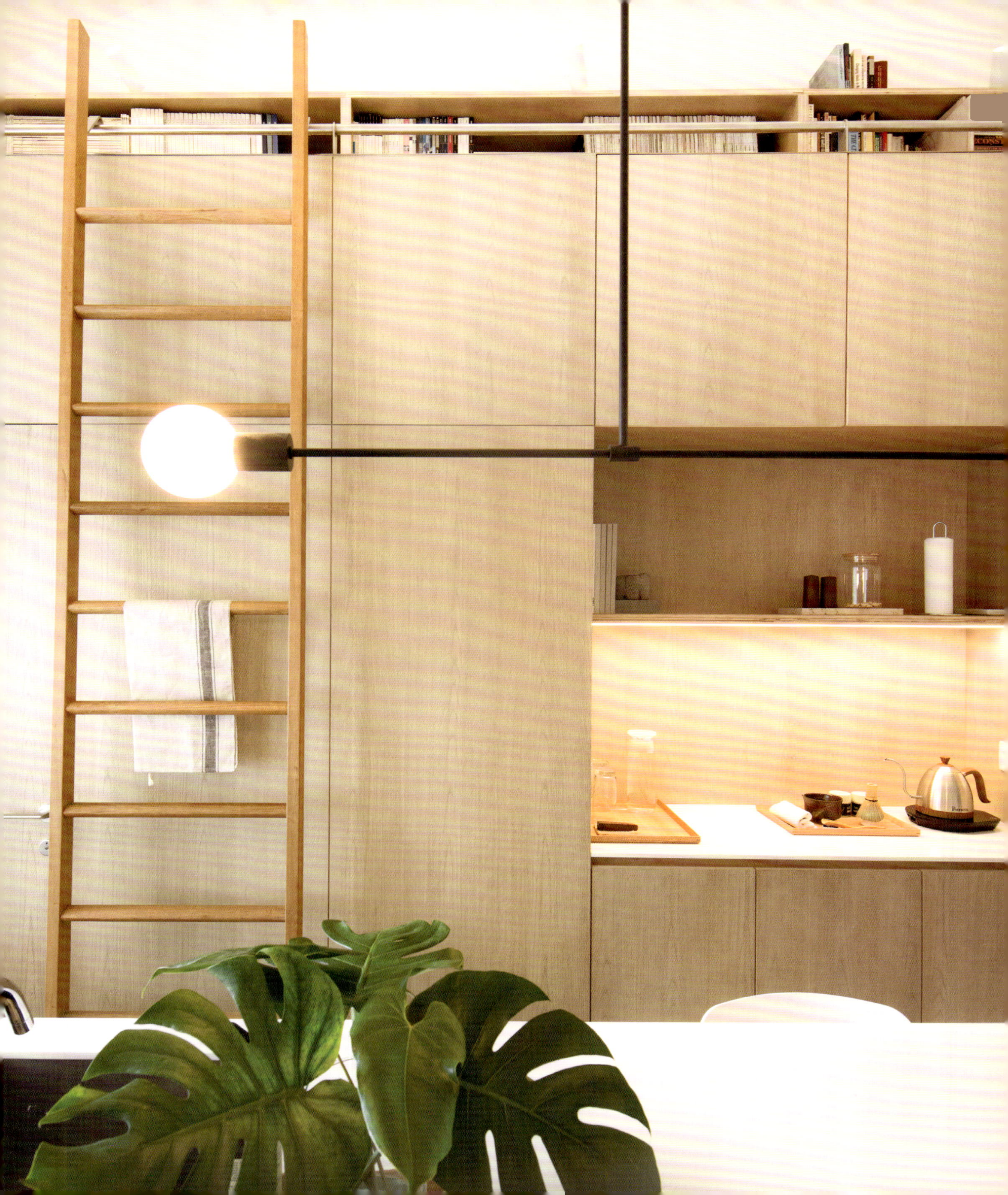

Project #13

64m^2 / 688ft^2
Studio Wills + Architects
Serangoon, Singapore

Over the past few years, there has been a significant shift to working from home. However, the concept of living and working spaces is not new in Singapore, where traditional developments featured shops at street level and living quarters above. When it came time to renovate this home, first built in 1988, it presented Studio Wills + Architects with an opportunity to reinterpret this traditional concept for their client. Rather than an office or shop at street level and a home above, the existing space was divided in half so that the office and house are side by side.

The idea was to design living and working areas that were fully functional and self-sufficient but connected by a shared space. The 64-sq-m (688-sq-ft) apartment originally had two bedrooms and two bathrooms and was meant for single use. However, a wall that divided the space was removed to create a loft between the living and dining areas. This added extra storage above each of the spaces.

PAGE 104 A loft like this one above the kitchen nook is a great use of a high ceiling in a small-footprint space, and is becoming more common.

A shared foyer leads to both the home and office and includes a slimline bench and louvered windows that open to the exterior of the apartment. Glass sliding doors serve as entrances to both spaces. The living room has a sloped high ceiling and a convertible couch for guests. A painting by Kayleigh Goh, a Malaysian artist based in Singapore, adds a touch of elegance to the space.

Adjacent to the living room, there's a white-oak veneer 'space marker' that serves as the largest built-in furniture piece in the home. It also features a walk-in wardrobe and storage. The dining room is situated between the kitchen and the wardrobe and is furnished with a simple white table that can accommodate up to six people. On the other side of the wardrobe, there are built-in shelves that hold a coffee maker, a microwave and a bar fridge. The kitchen area is located under the window on the opposite side and has a separate area for the washing machine.

Across from the washing machine is an apron sink that includes a mirror and under-counter storage. The bathroom includes a WC and an overhead shower, and the sink is located outside of the bathroom. The bathroom is fully tiled with blue homogeneous tiles and features a metal chain, like a rainwater chain, for air-conditioning drainage. The chain allows water to drip onto to a bed of loose pebbles over a floor trap.

The bed, a platform with a futon on top, is positioned above the space marker. It is accessed via timber steps that house integrated drawers and storage. The platform bed features a flip-up storage area and the platform itself has an edge with integrated uplighting for showcasing artwork. A pivot window panel provides a view of the office, which is the most spacious area within the apartment.

The office boasts a long work desk made from three tables joined together in an open configuration. There's a built-in furniture piece, also finished in white oak veneer, that includes bookshelves, a pantry and a hidden door leading to the office bathroom. Across from this built-in is a ledge designated for material samples. In the middle of the space is an island bench with a sink; it's a perfect spot for informal chats over coffee.

By splitting an existing space in half and clearly defining each area's purpose, Studio Wills + Architects has created functional living and working spaces that are fully equipped and independent of each other yet connected by a common space. The design makes use of the existing architecture and adds new features, resulting in a stylish and comfortable home/office space in a great location. The use of louvred windows, a sliding door and a common foyer allows for seamless integration between the two spaces, while still maintaining privacy and individuality.

AFTER

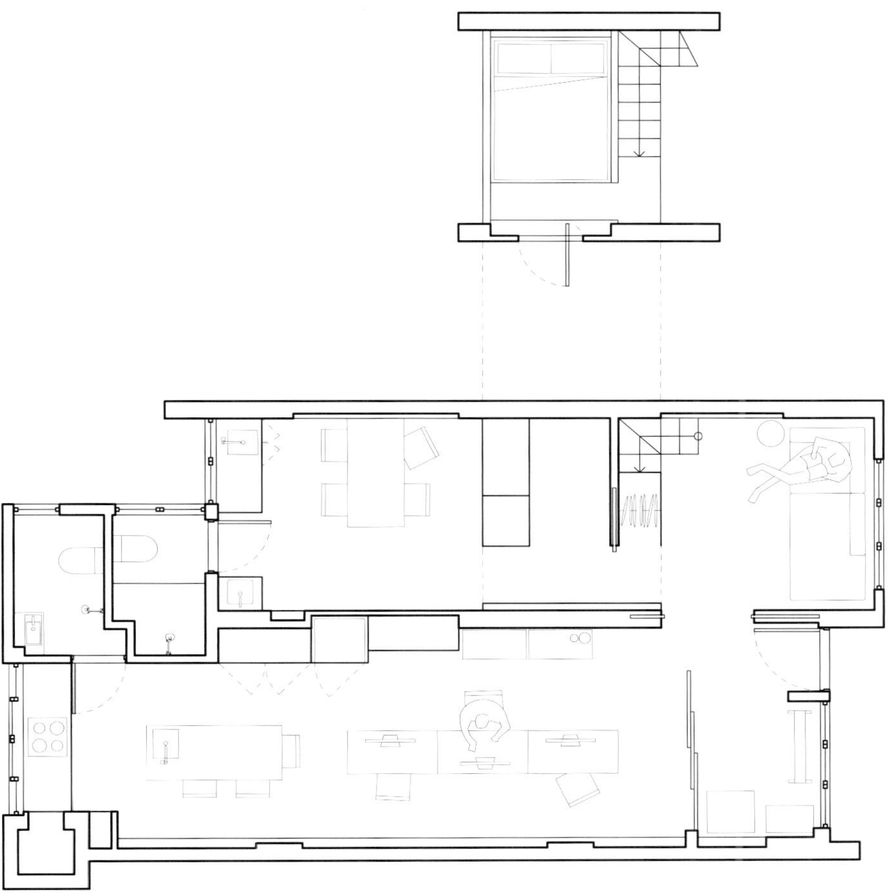

BEFORE

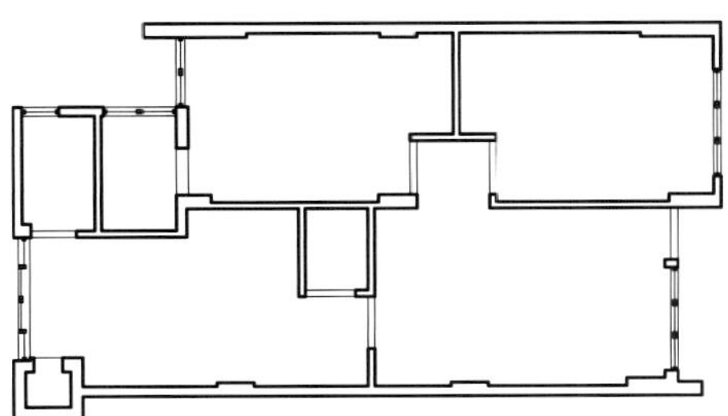

Scale 1:100

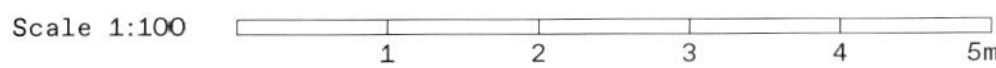

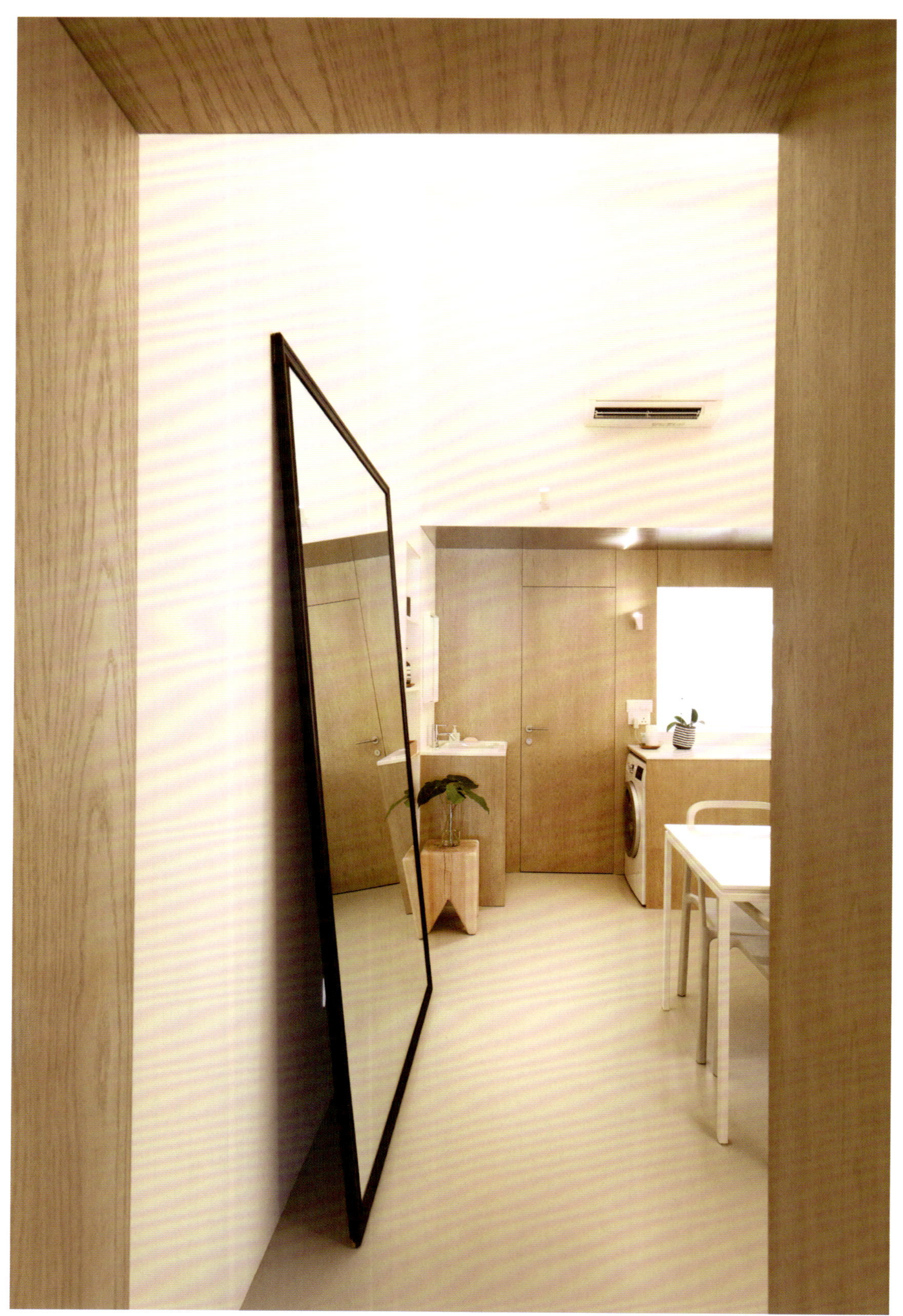

OPPOSITE The combination of timber and a large mirror creates a cosy, light-filled interior.

BELOW Louvres are a wonderful way to transition areas from private to open.

The design makes use of the existing architecture and adds new features.

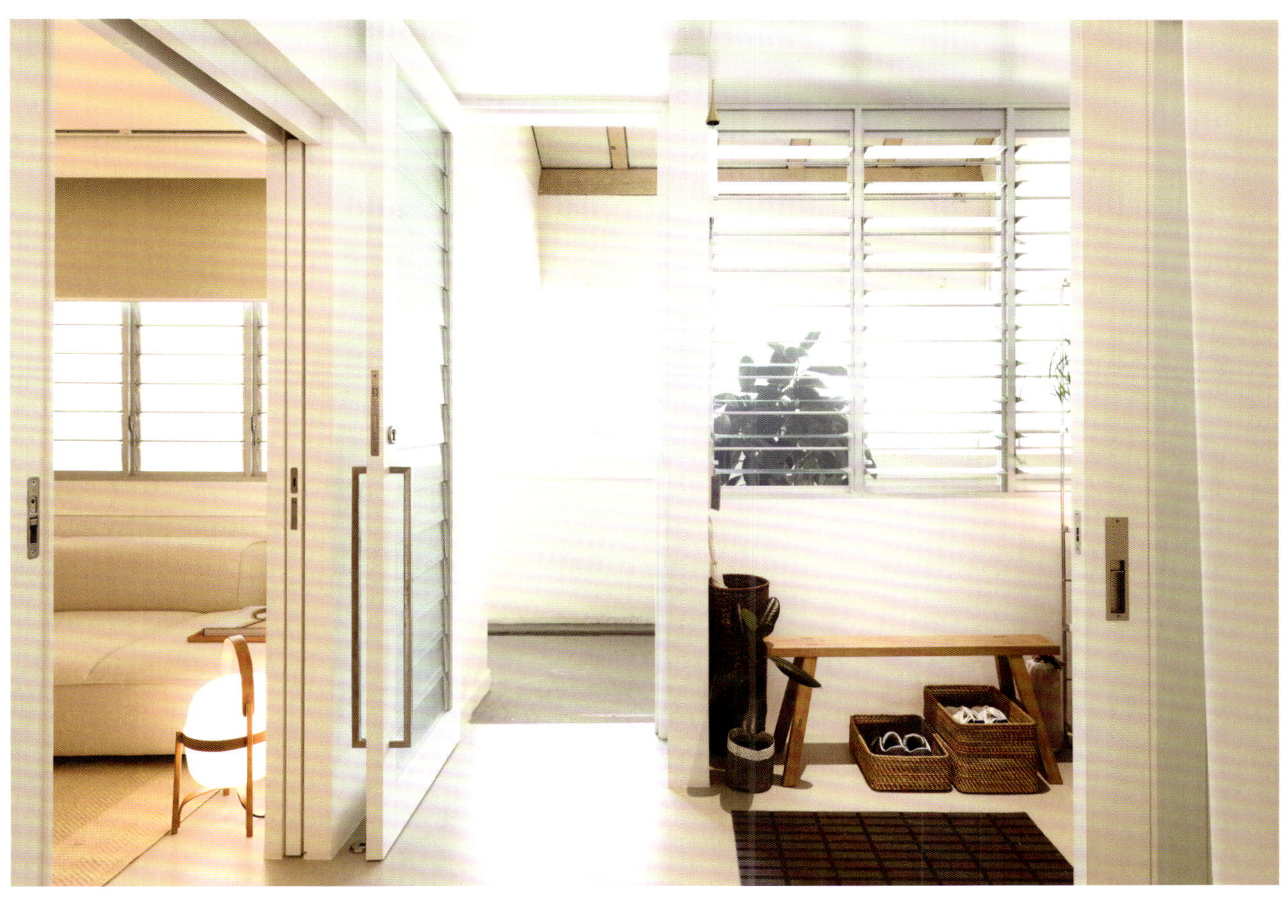

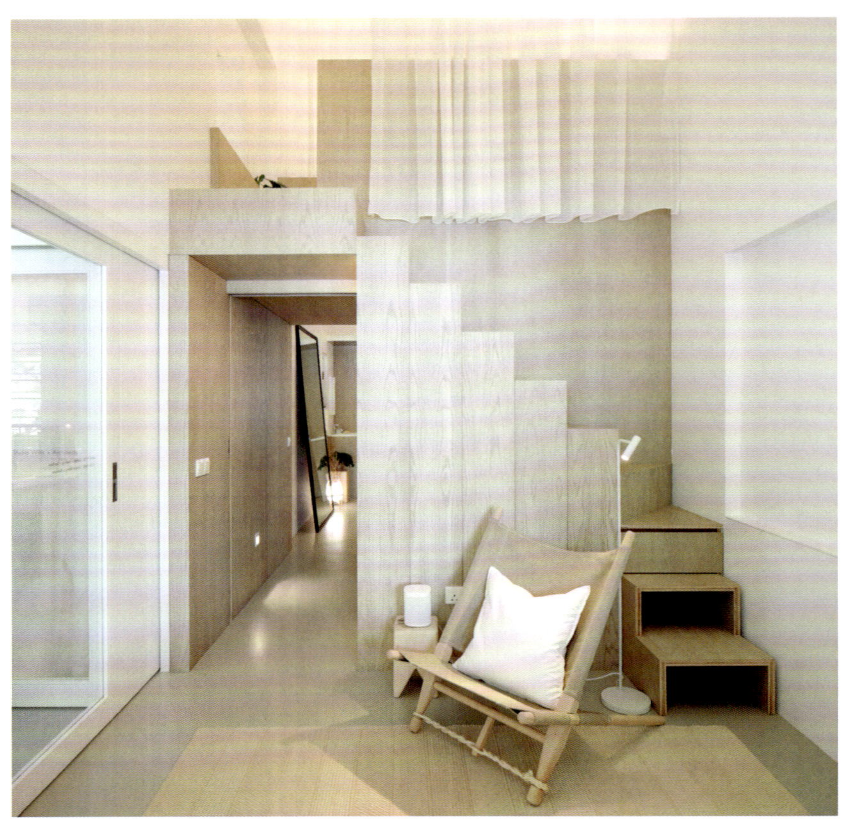

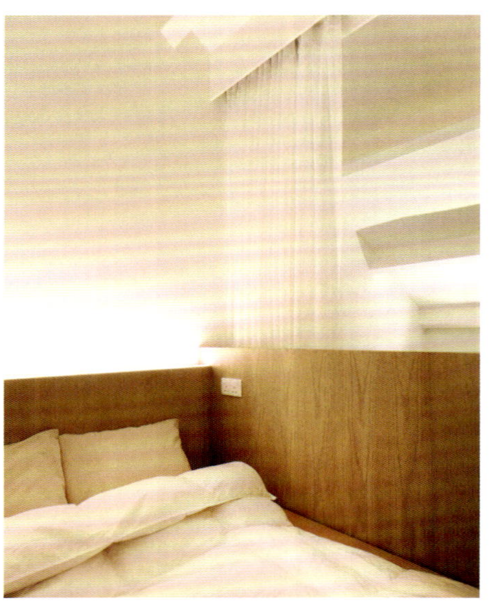

OPPOSITE TOP The stairs are a striking design feature.

OPPOSITE BOTTOM The loft is a wonderful sanctuary for the bedroom.

BELOW A top-down view shows how tightly the stairs have been integrated.

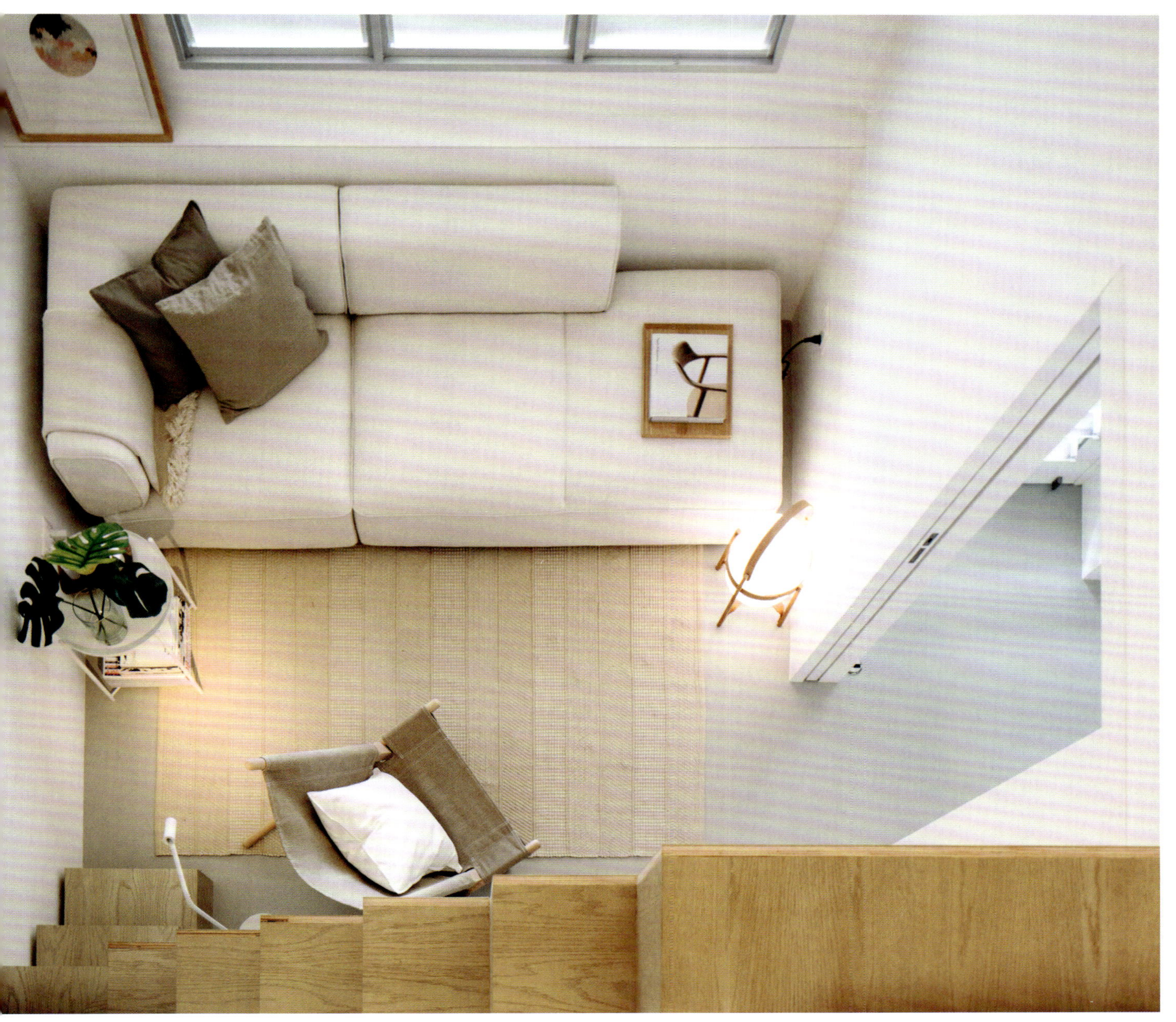

BELOW The loft is private but still open to the floor below so it doesn't feel claustrophobic.

OPPOSITE It was important that the home office was fully separate from the living area so there's space to focus.

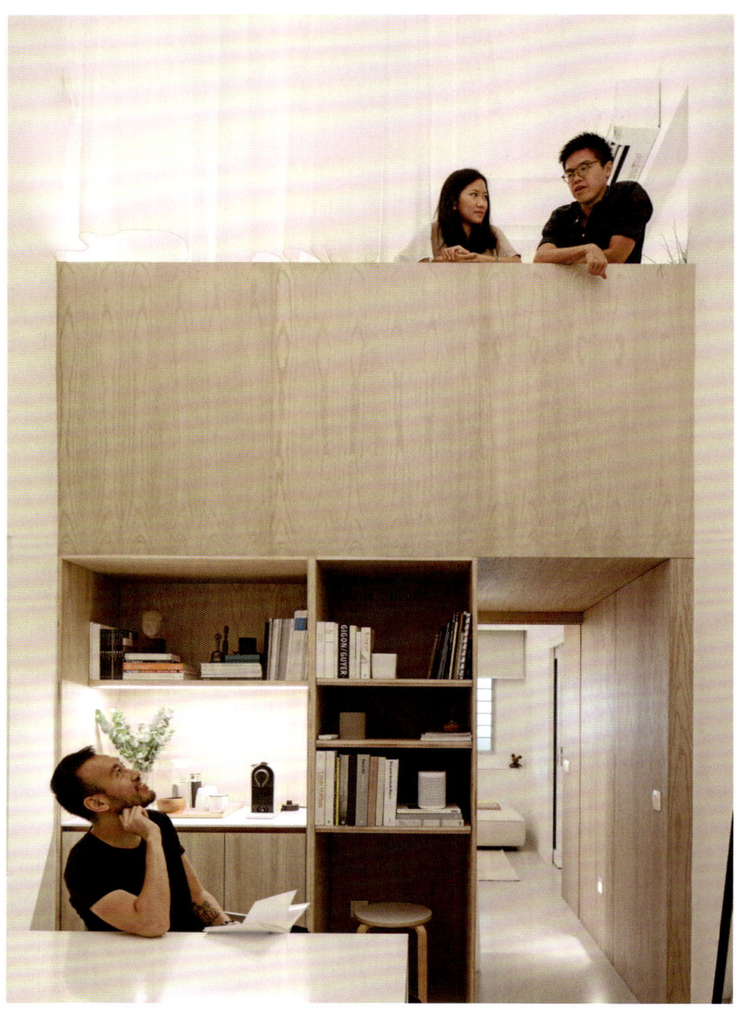

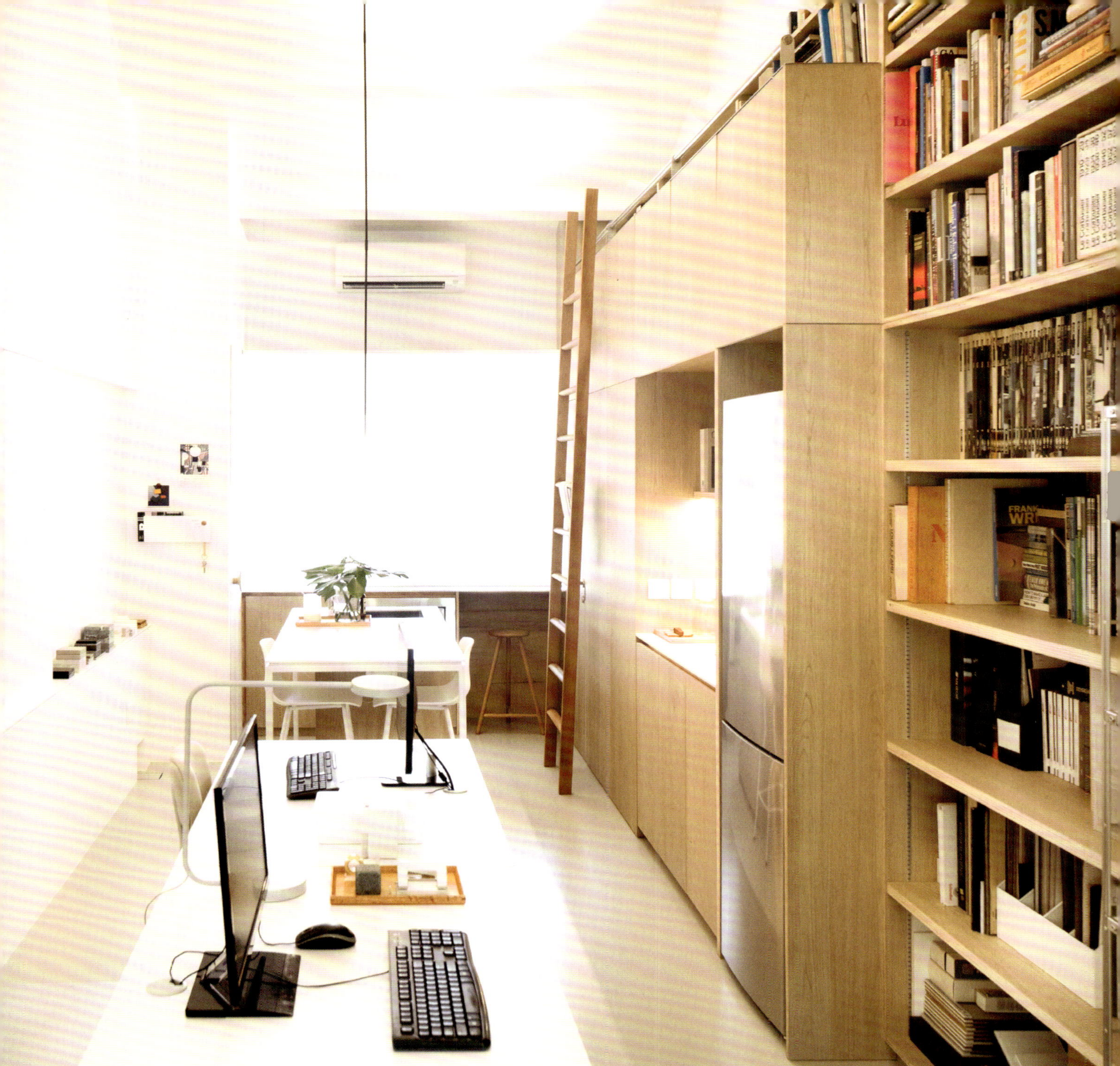

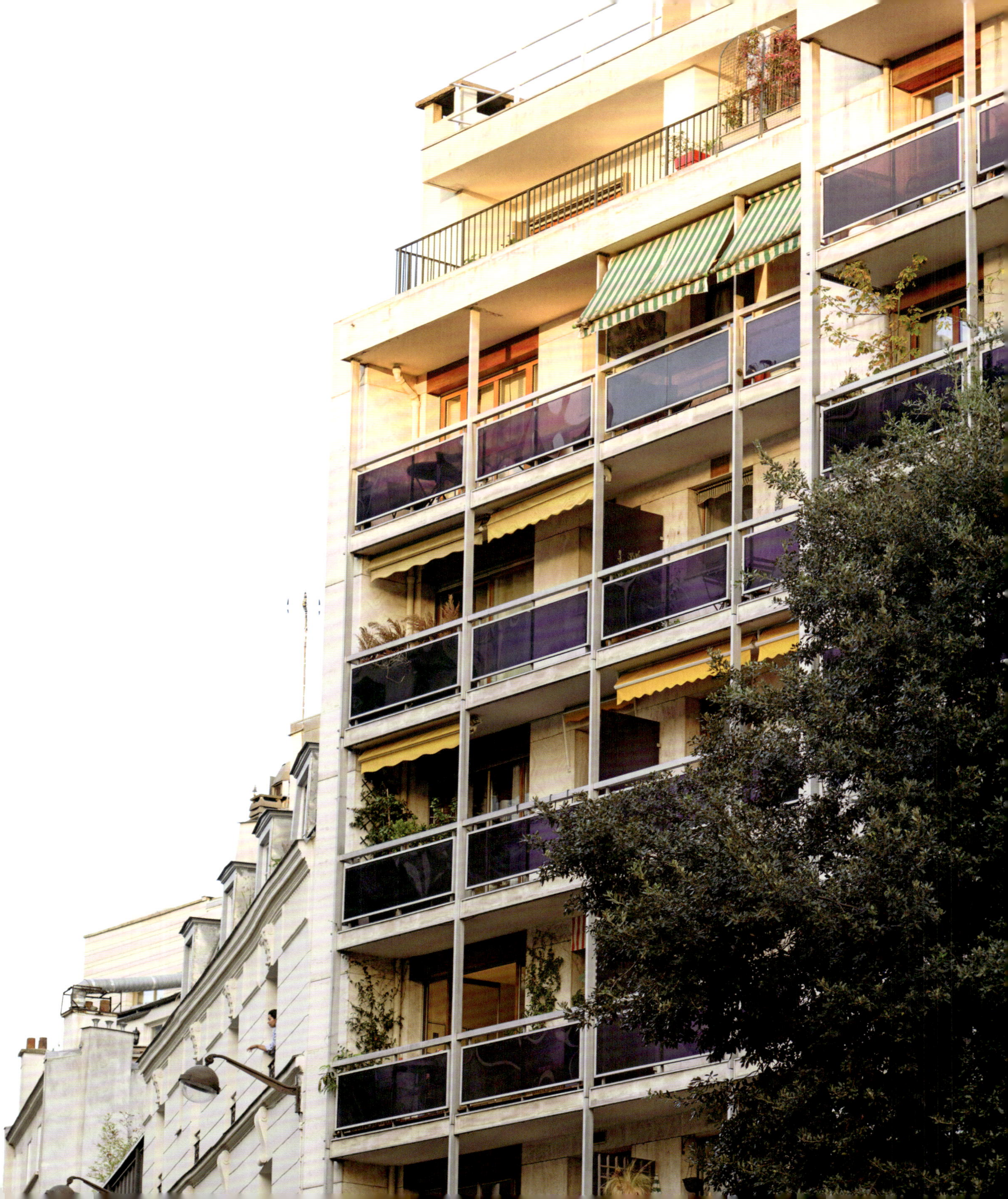

VM36

53m² / 570ft²
JMLC Studio
Pigalle, Paris

Situated on the site of the famous Parisian cabaret Bal Tabarin, this building was completed in the 1970s. While the cabarets that were so popular in this district have gone, the creative spirit of this community remains, along with a respect for the past balanced with a forward-thinking approach to creating resilient and happy communities.

The apartment spans 53 sq m (570 sq ft) and features a charming 8-sq-m (86-sq-ft) terrace. Architect Jean-Malo Le Clerc, designer and founder of JMLC Studio, lives here with his partner. When Le Clerc first discovered the apartment, which had been untouched since the 1990s, it was dilapidated.

Determined to transform it, Le Clerc's design concept revolved around preserving the apartment's 1970s charm while adding modern functionality. He envisioned a tranquil escape from the bustling city. Natural light played a crucial role in the design and there is a great use of mirrors, an open layout and clever placement of windows in the apartment.

The entrance features wood cladding on the ceiling, creating a distinct zone and concealing structural beams. A small yellow room serves as a storage area for bags and clothes, which keeps the living space clutter free.

The kitchen, dining and living areas flow seamlessly, with a mirrored splashback and a ceramic benchtop anchoring the kitchen island. Floor-to-ceiling wooden cabinets hide appliances and maximise storage space.

The living area features a striking green Togo sofa surrounded by pieces from the couple's favourite designers. A retractable desk hidden behind stainless-steel doors allows for a dedicated workspace that can be easily concealed when not in use.

The bedroom exudes a luxurious-hotel-suite ambience. Orange carpet pays homage to the apartment's past and a tapered headboard adds a touch of elegance. Custom-built wardrobes with walnut-finished boat handles provide ample storage. The bathroom is awash in blue with floor-to-ceiling light blue vintage tiles, rounded edges to soften the space even further, and black-and-white marble floor tiles.

The outdoor terrace has a built-in bench with orange-striped cushions and a matching awning, a two-person dining table, built-in furniture and a mix of plants. It's a tranquil space with a Mediterranean-inspired vibe.

Le Clerc's philosophy for designing small spaces centres around maximising functionality, proportion, natural light and circulation. The architect believes in utilising everything efficiently, incorporating smart storage solutions and elements that help make a living environment cohesive.

This transformed apartment exemplifies the importance of repurposing small urban spaces. By breathing new life into existing structures, Jean-Malo showcases the potential for sustainable, personalised living.

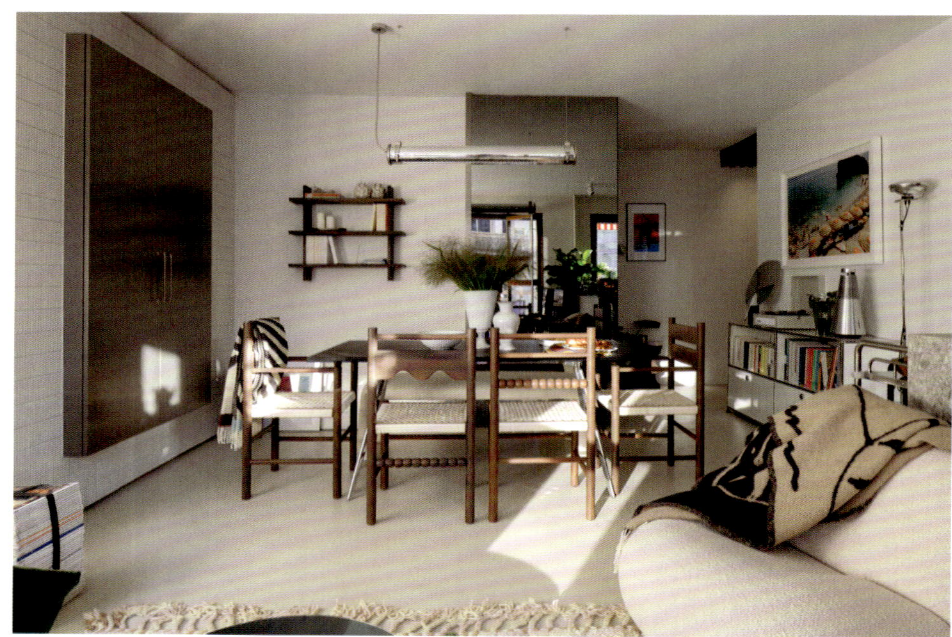

PAGE 114 The distinct exterior of this 1970s apartment complex includes awnings and glass balconies. The generous-sized homes and high ceilings are another bonus of the era.

RIGHT The home is filled with pieces by the couple's favourite designers.

AFTER

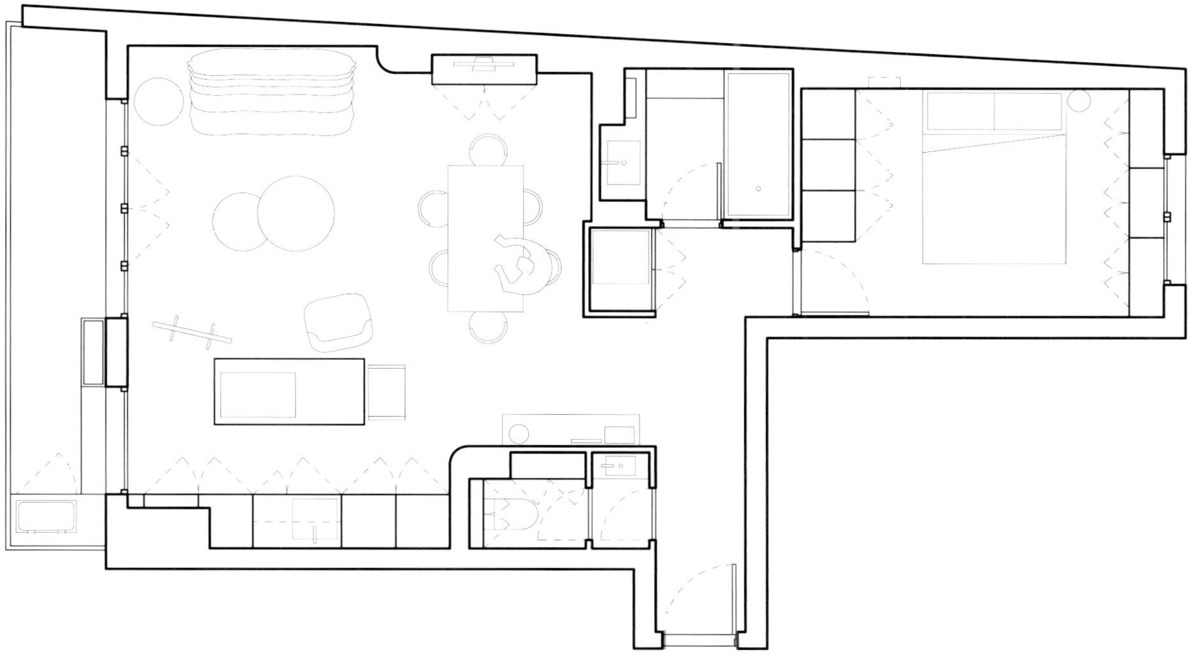

BEFORE

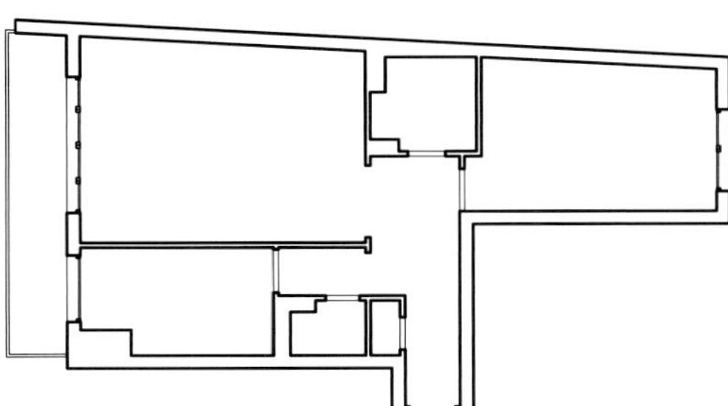

Scale 1:100

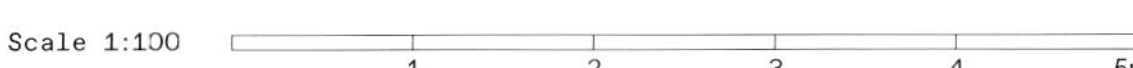

RIGHT With so much natural light, the dark colours in the kitchen help make the home feel cosy.

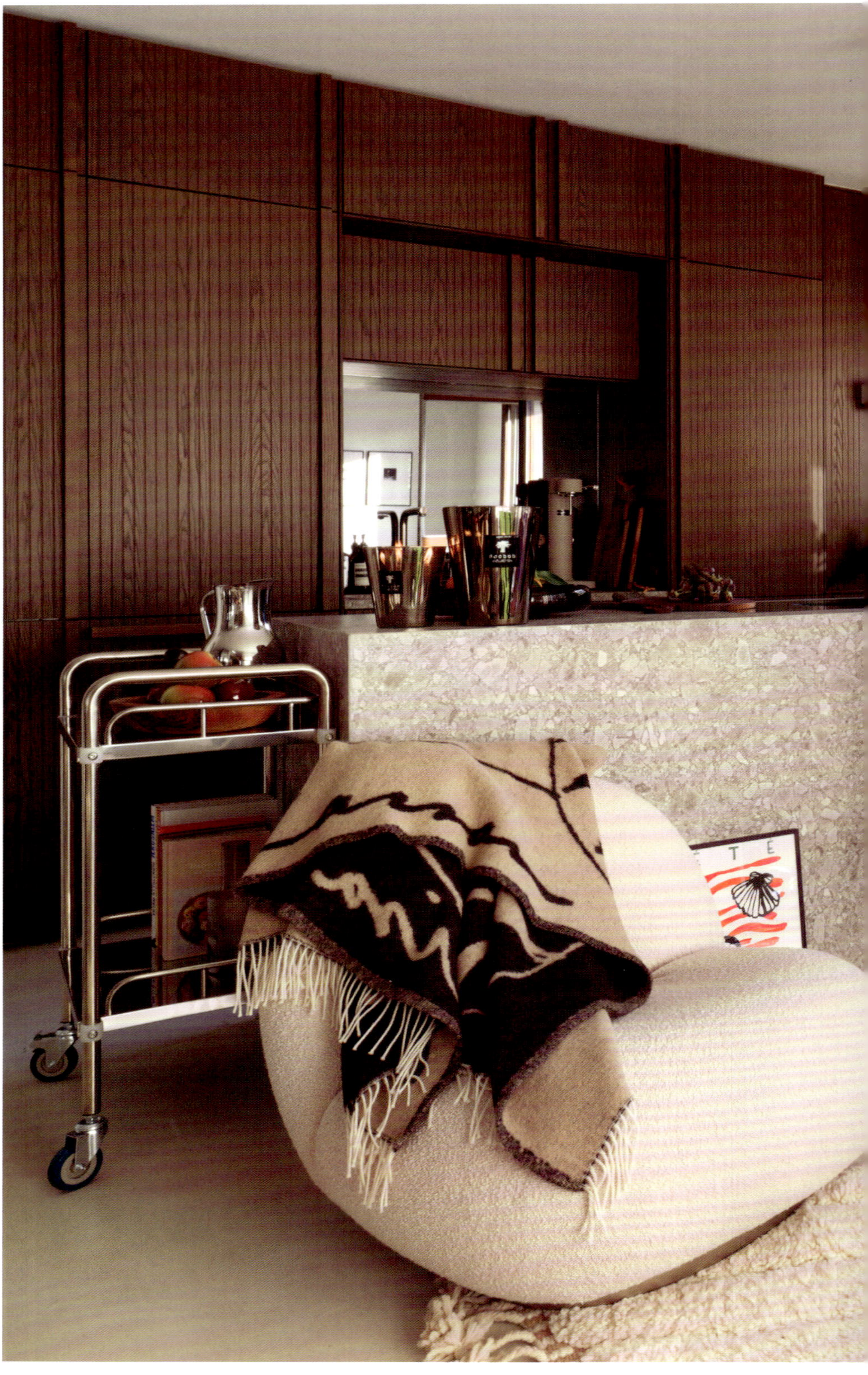

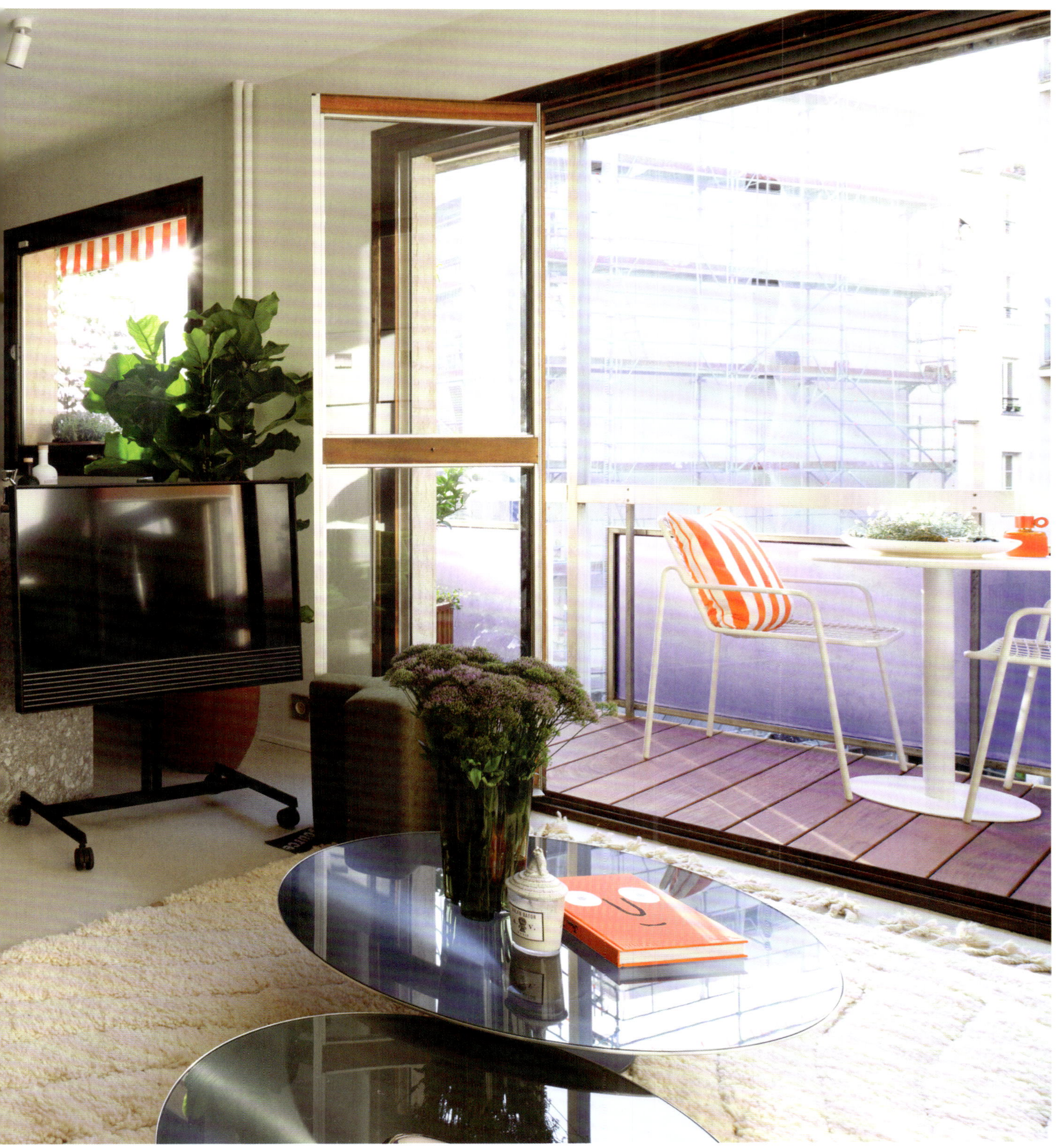

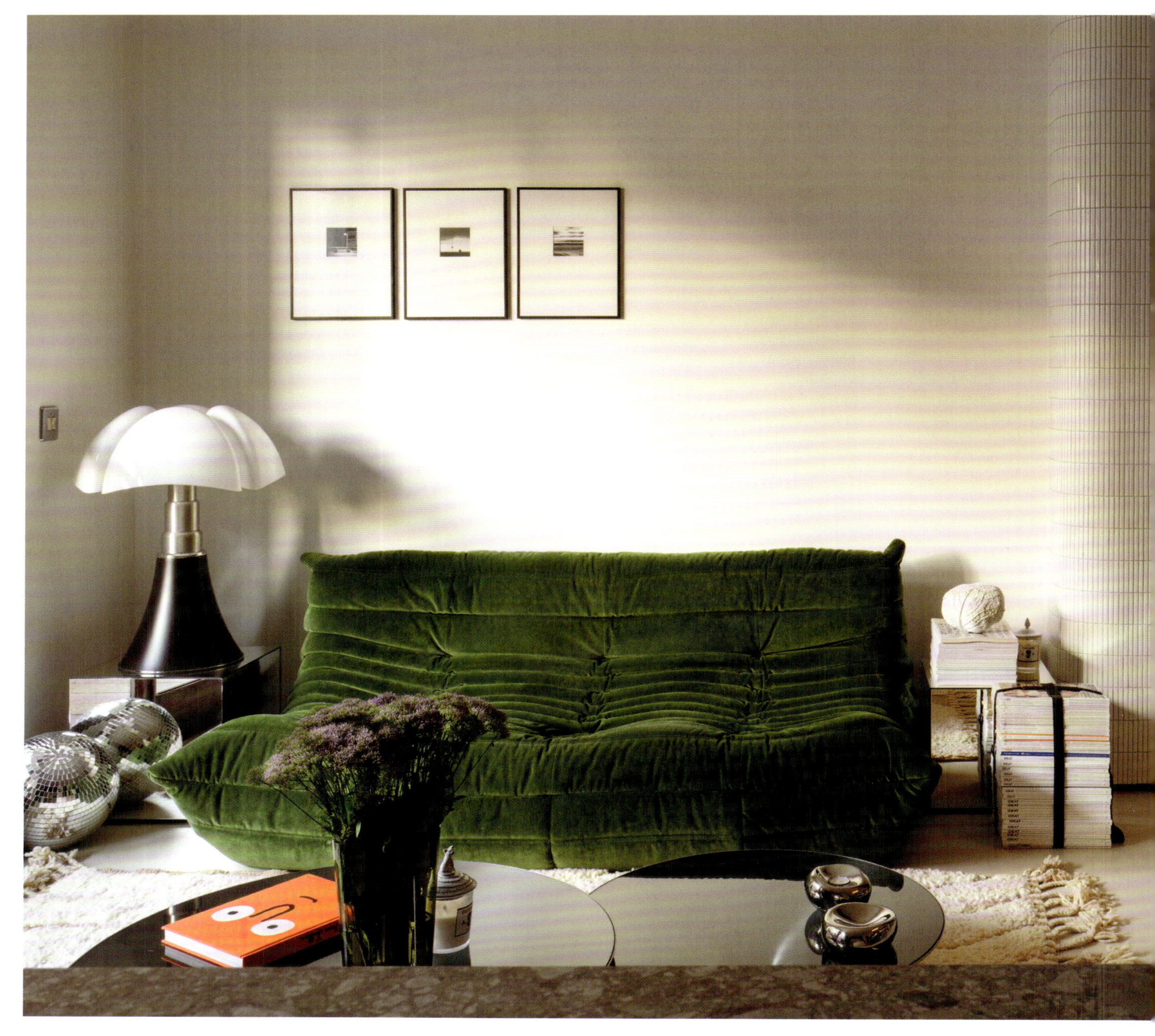

The living area features a striking green Togo sofa surrounded by pieces from the couple's favourite designers.

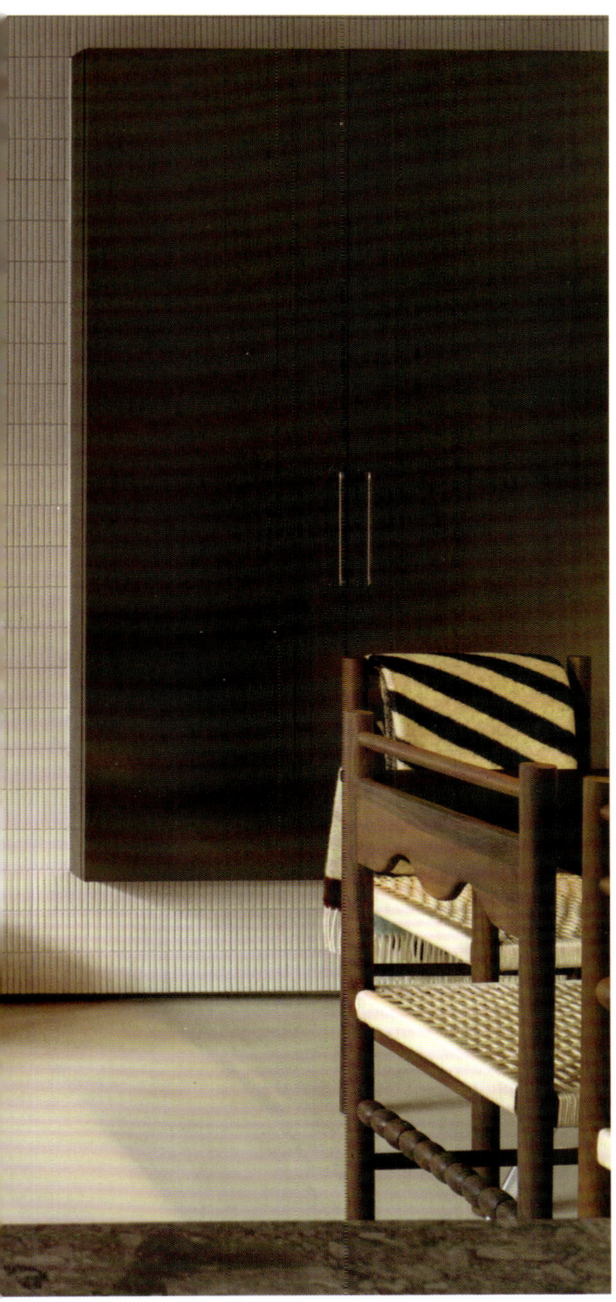

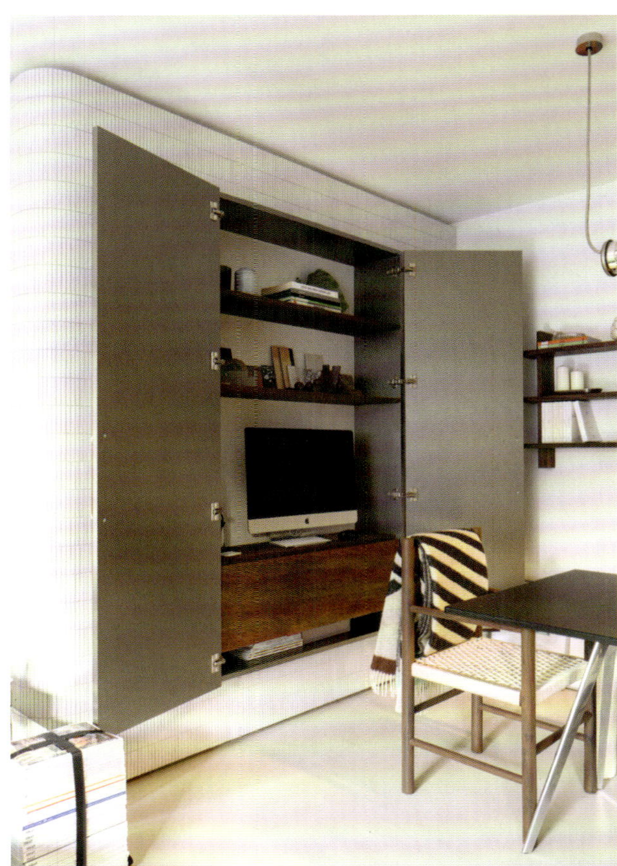

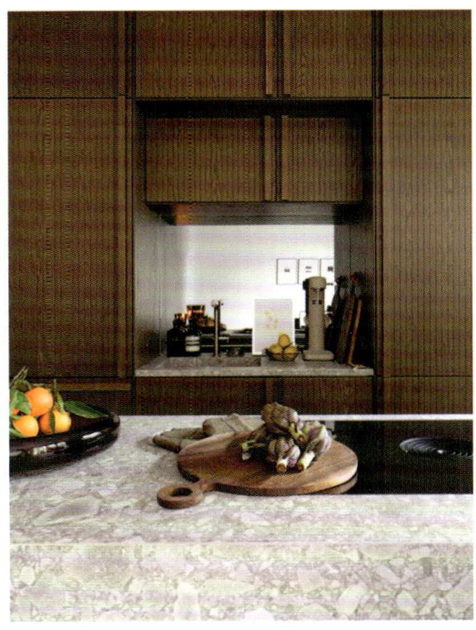

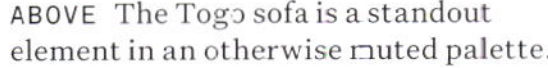

ABOVE The Togo sofa is a standout element in an otherwise muted palette.

TOP RIGHT A stainless steel cabinet hides a neat office space with a fold-down desk.

RIGHT Dark timber offsets the mirrored splashback that feels like a nod to disco days.

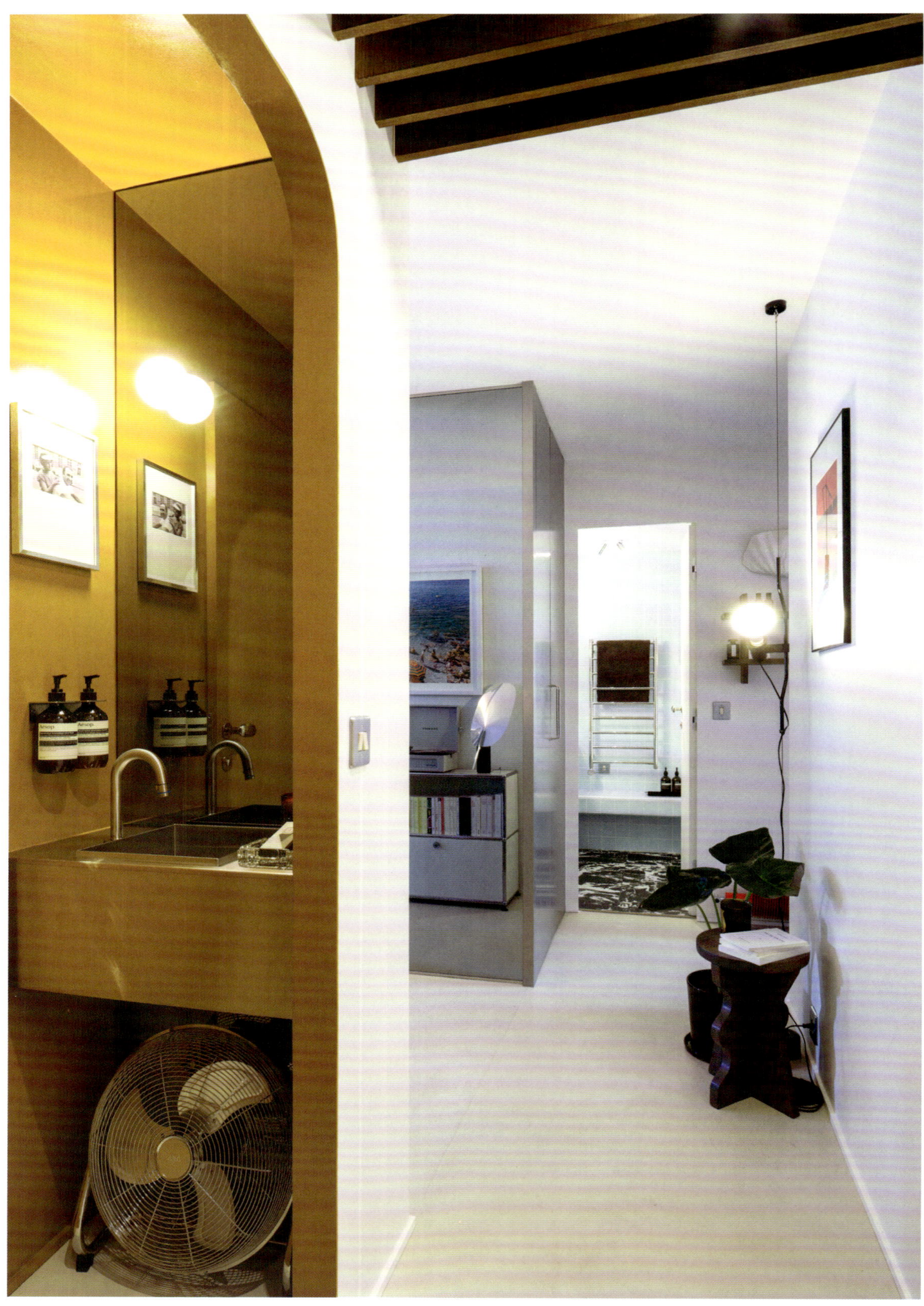
Aesop
Aesop

OPPOSITE The use of bold yellow in the powder room is a creative way of demarcating the zone.

RIGHT Powder blue tiles and frosted glass bounce light around the main bathroom.

BELOW The combination of dark timber and mustard yellow is a modern take on 70s chic.

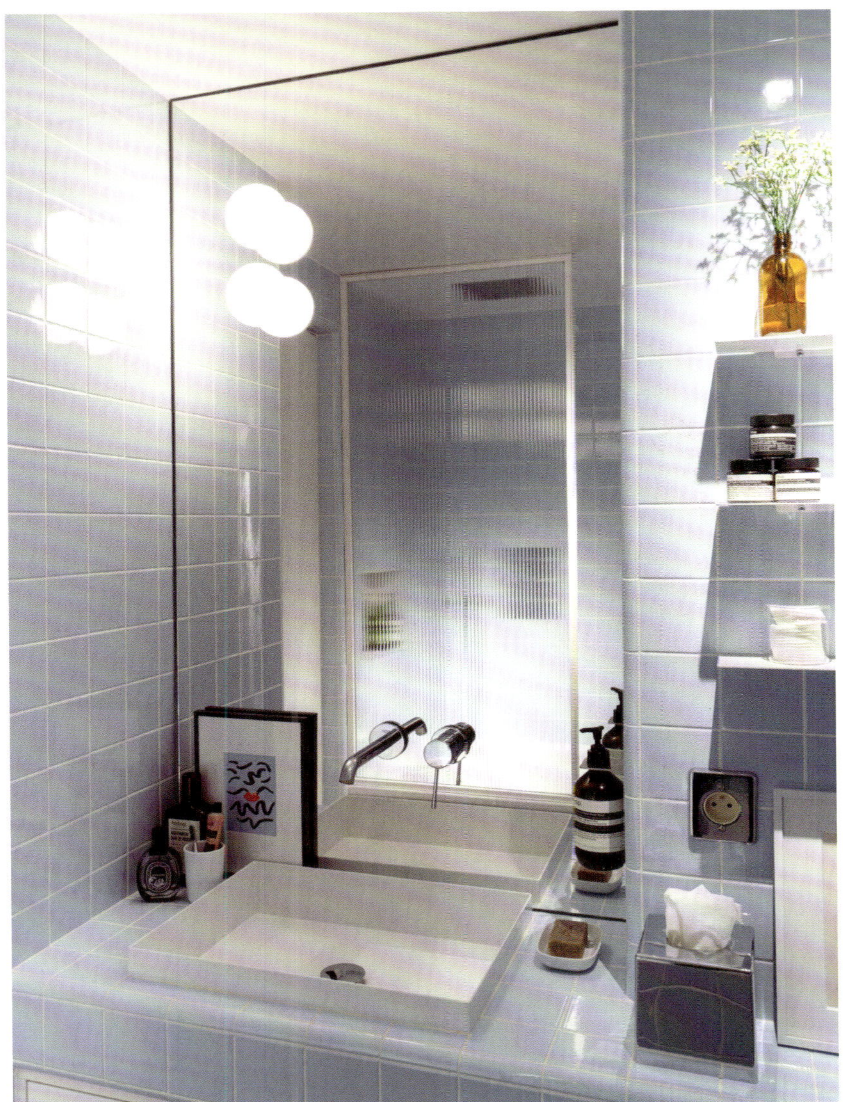

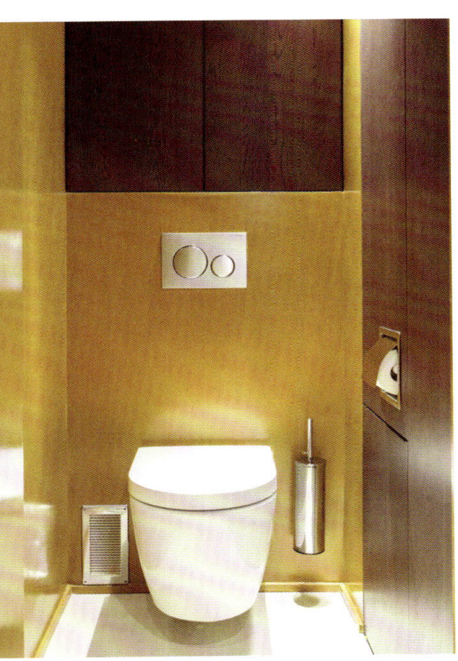

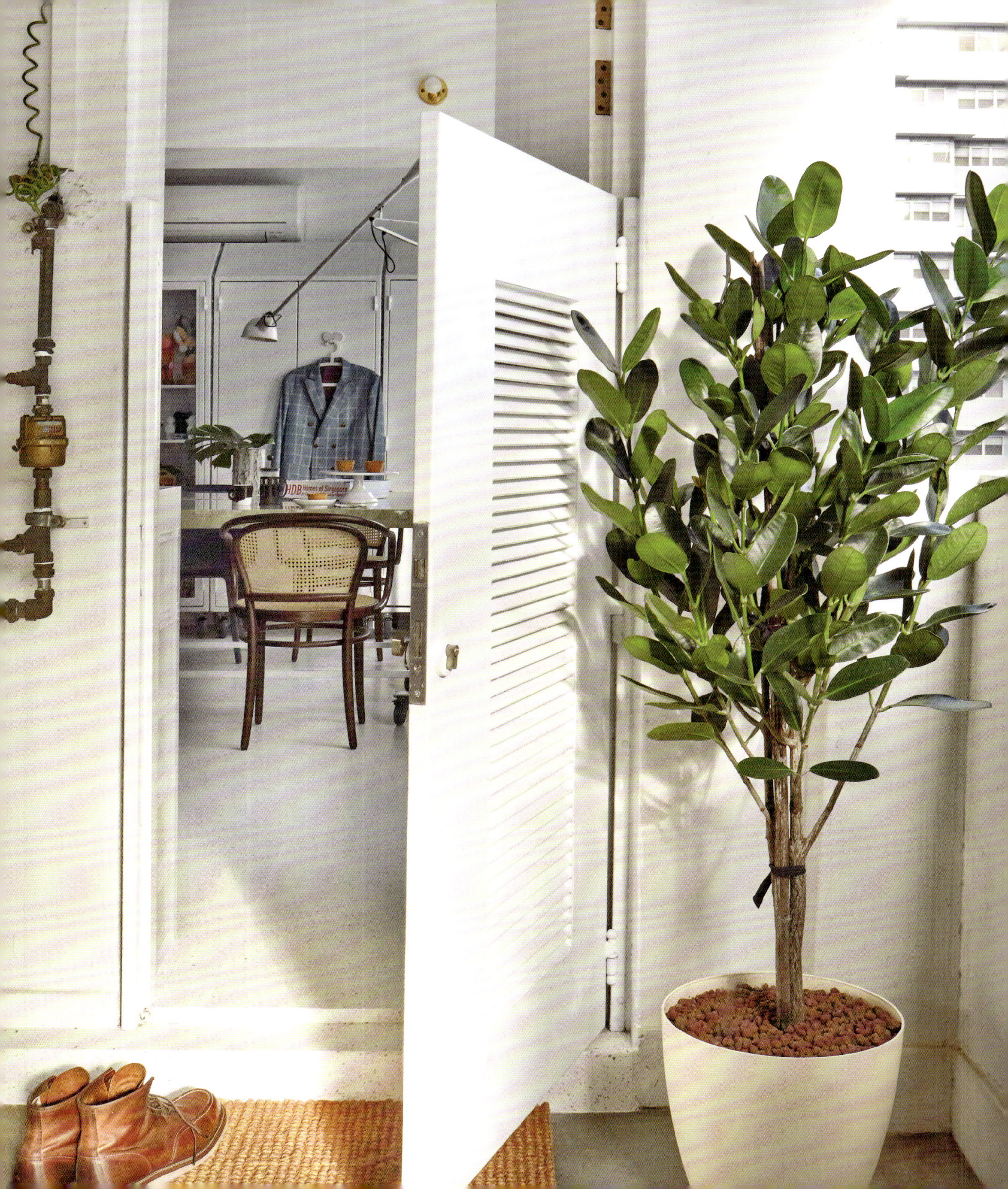
HDB Homes of Singapore

Waterloo Street

59m² / 635ft²
Three-d conceptwerke
Bugis, Singapore

Picture a game of Tetris. Except all the blocks are white. Waterloo Street was created with many moving parts – cabinets, tables and cupboards were all designed to move around the space. Curtains open and close to conceal or reveal a room, and a prized wall lamp swivels to where light is needed.

The apartment sits above five storeys of shops in one of Singapore's Housing Development Board buildings. Built in 1978, it's surrounded by shopping malls, and Hindu and Chinese temples.

The 59-sq-m (635-sq-ft) home went through an impressive make-under to become the light and transitory home it is today. Most of the interior walls were removed to reconfigure the space and the main area of the apartment was kept open plan with zones instead of rooms.

Principal designer Dess Chew and the team at Three-d conceptwerke followed their clients' brief for a 'simple, comfortable, and flexible space where they could enjoy their hobbies', and created a minimal backdrop for the owners' many colourful collectables and collections.

A louvered barn door acts as the entry to the apartment. This unexpected threshold gives a nod to the building's 1970s inception and maintains privacy while helping with ventilation through the stifling Singapore summers.

Inside, the home's minimalist base showcases its maximalist aesthetic. 'To keep the home looking bright, we used white paint, tiles and floors,' explains Chew. 'It allows the client's objects to pop.' And pop they do.

Because the clients didn't want to be locked into specific configurations, two tables on wheels, mostly used for working from home, can be pushed together to form a large dining table when required. An original 265 Paolo Rizzatto wall lamp is adjustable and can be moved to shine light wherever the tables land.

Windows lining the main wall provide ample diffused light. Sitting against the living area wall are modular cabinets on wheels, with pitched roofs for easy cleaning. Designed to be durable and sustainable, they can be recycled when no longer in use.

A large wooden cabinet – a delightful grounding addition – gives the space a warm 1970s feel and provides storage of the couple's collection of kitchenware and knickknacks. Continuing the subtle homage to the 1970s, the fully equipped kitchen is tiled all the way to the ceiling with 10 × 10 cm mosaic tiles.

The glass block walls of the bathroom make the space feel light and airy. The highlight of the bathroom is no doubt the mirror above the vanity, designed to swivel and reveal two small storage shelves.

Curtains are sparingly yet deliberately included and are hung across the entrance to the kitchen and the compact and cosy bedroom. They confine the air conditioning and, if needed, segregate the zones.

Waterloo Street is a great example of the true potential of a flexible, ever-changing space. It is not a blank canvas, but a functioning home full of objects and endless possibilities.

PAGE 124 The louvered barn door – the home's initial nod to the building's 1970s inception – creates privacy while allowing for maximum airflow in the warmer months.

BELOW Square white tiles in the kitchen mirror the glass bricks of the bathroom further in the space.

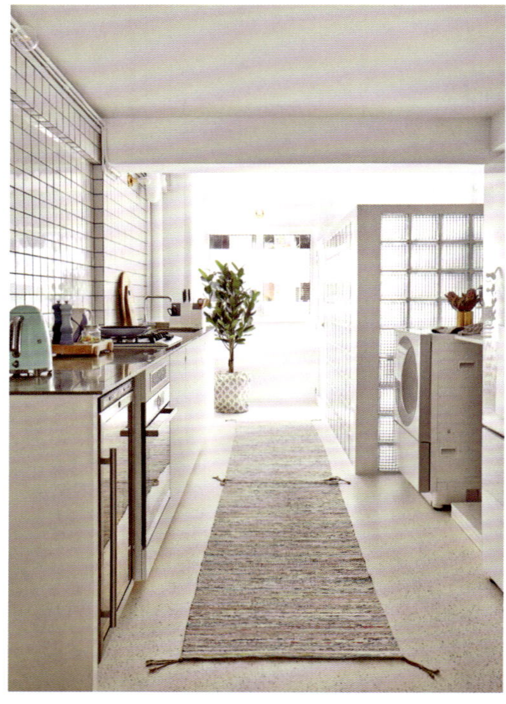

AFTER

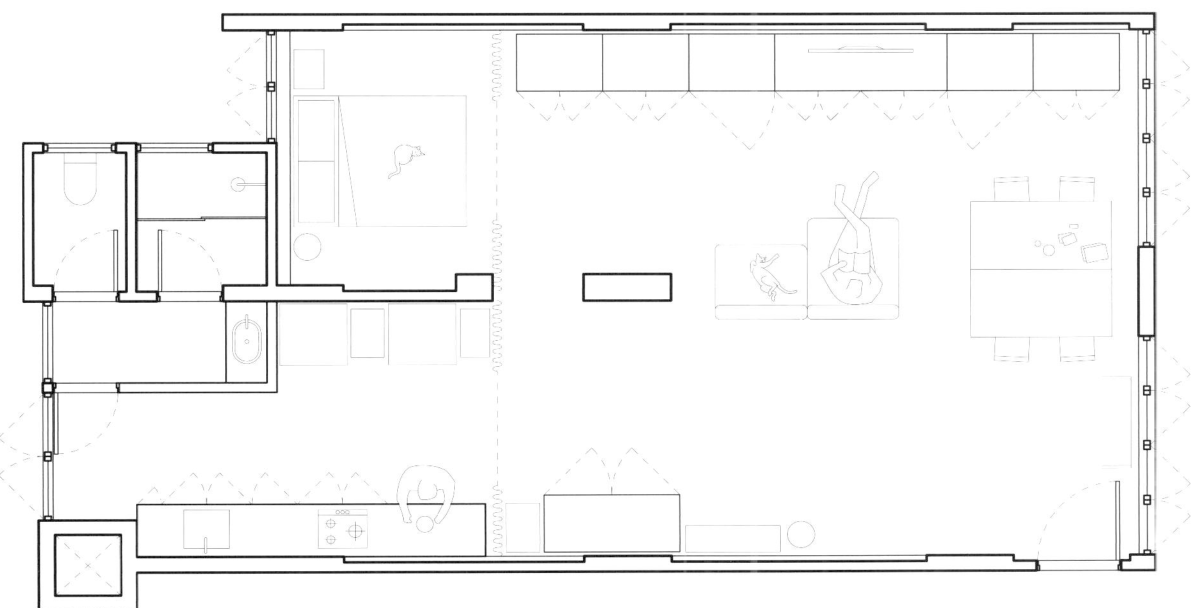

BEFORE

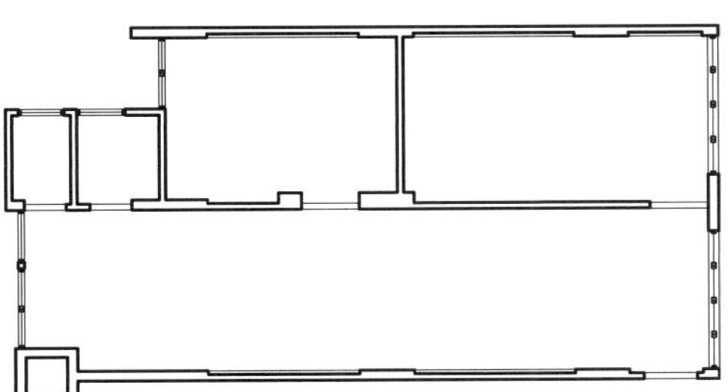

Scale 1:100

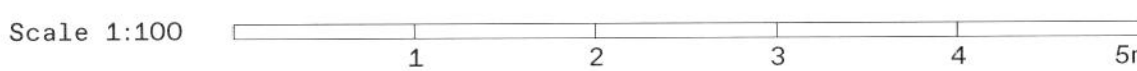

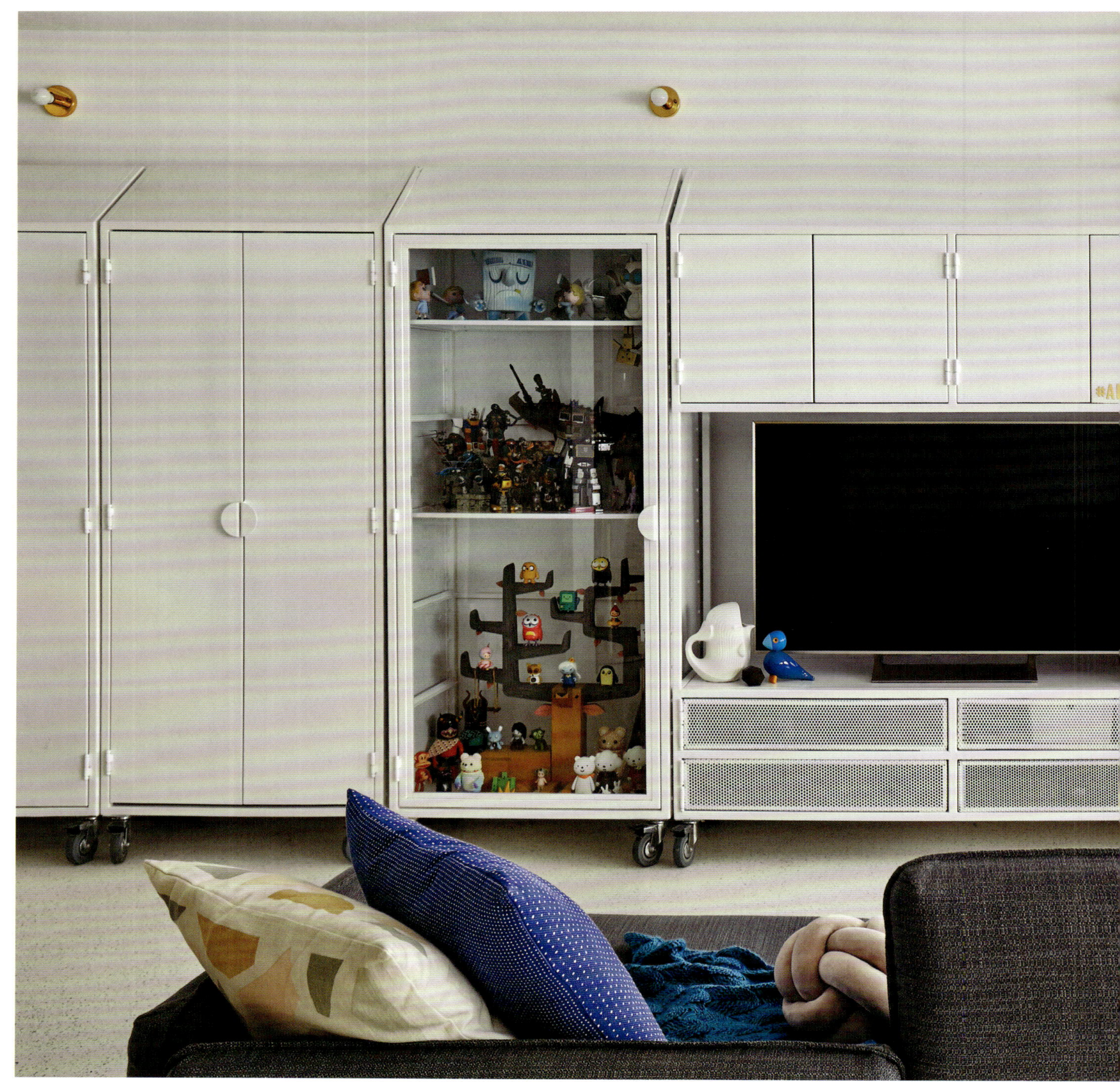

The home's minimalist base showcases its maximalist aesthetic.

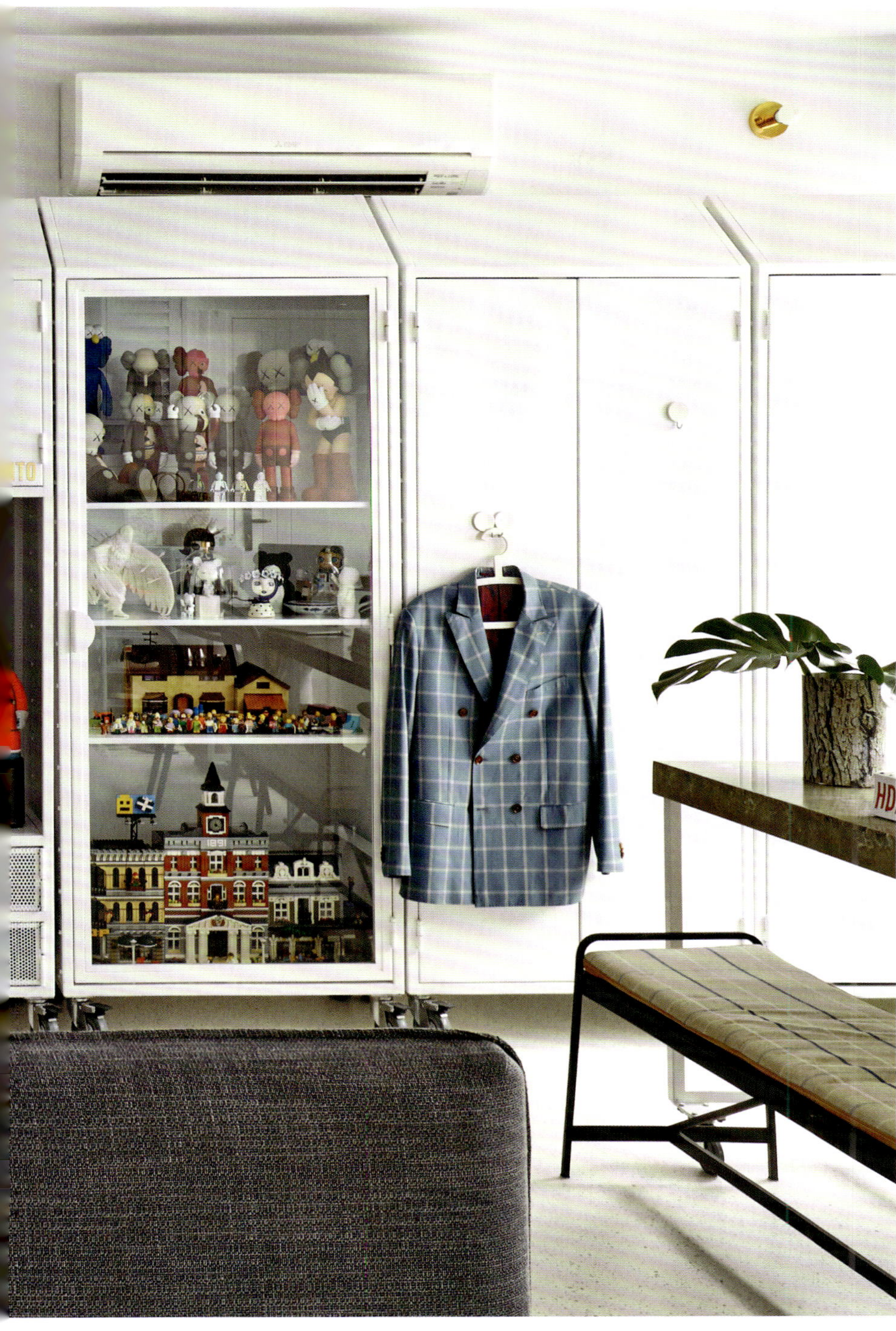

LEFT Custom-built metal cabinets house the couple's collectibles. Their slanted tops make them easy to clean and they were built on wheels so the space can be reconfigured with ease.

BELOW Two large work desks can be pushed together to form a dining table.

RIGHT A neutral backdrop and portable furniture makes for a home that can change and adapt as the owners wish.

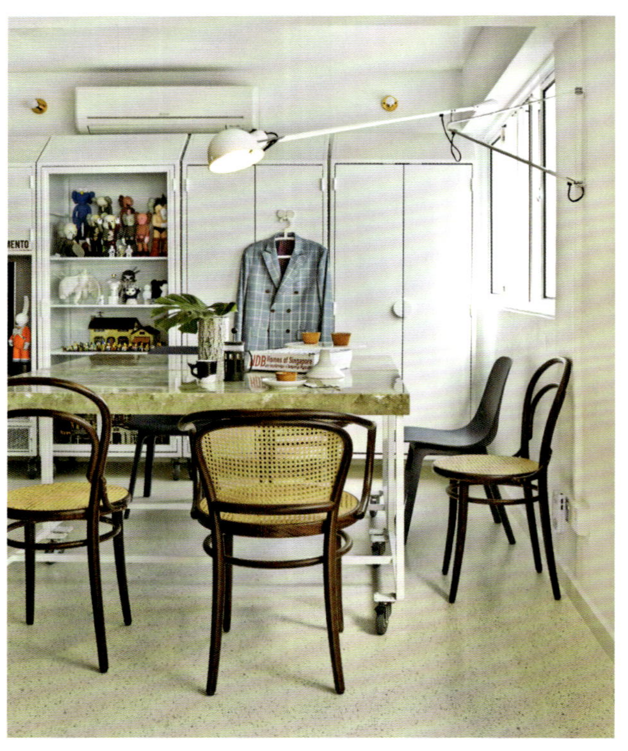

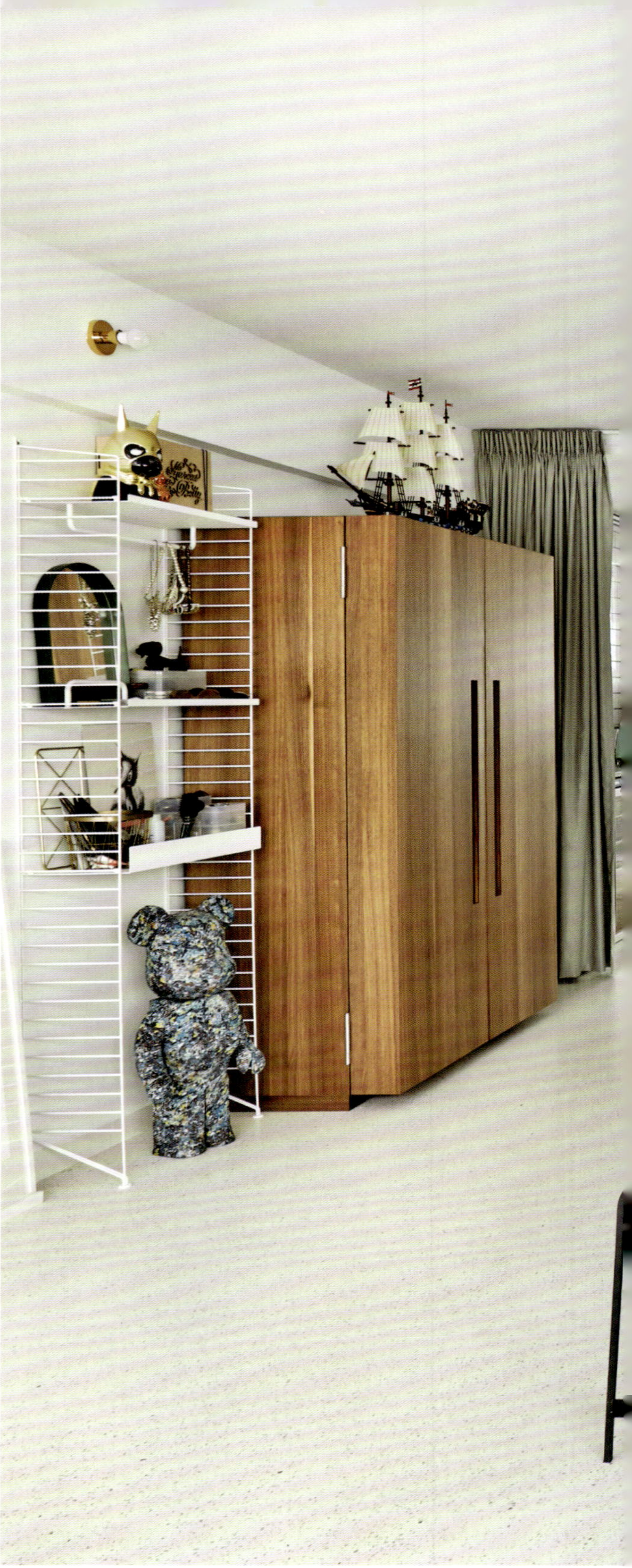

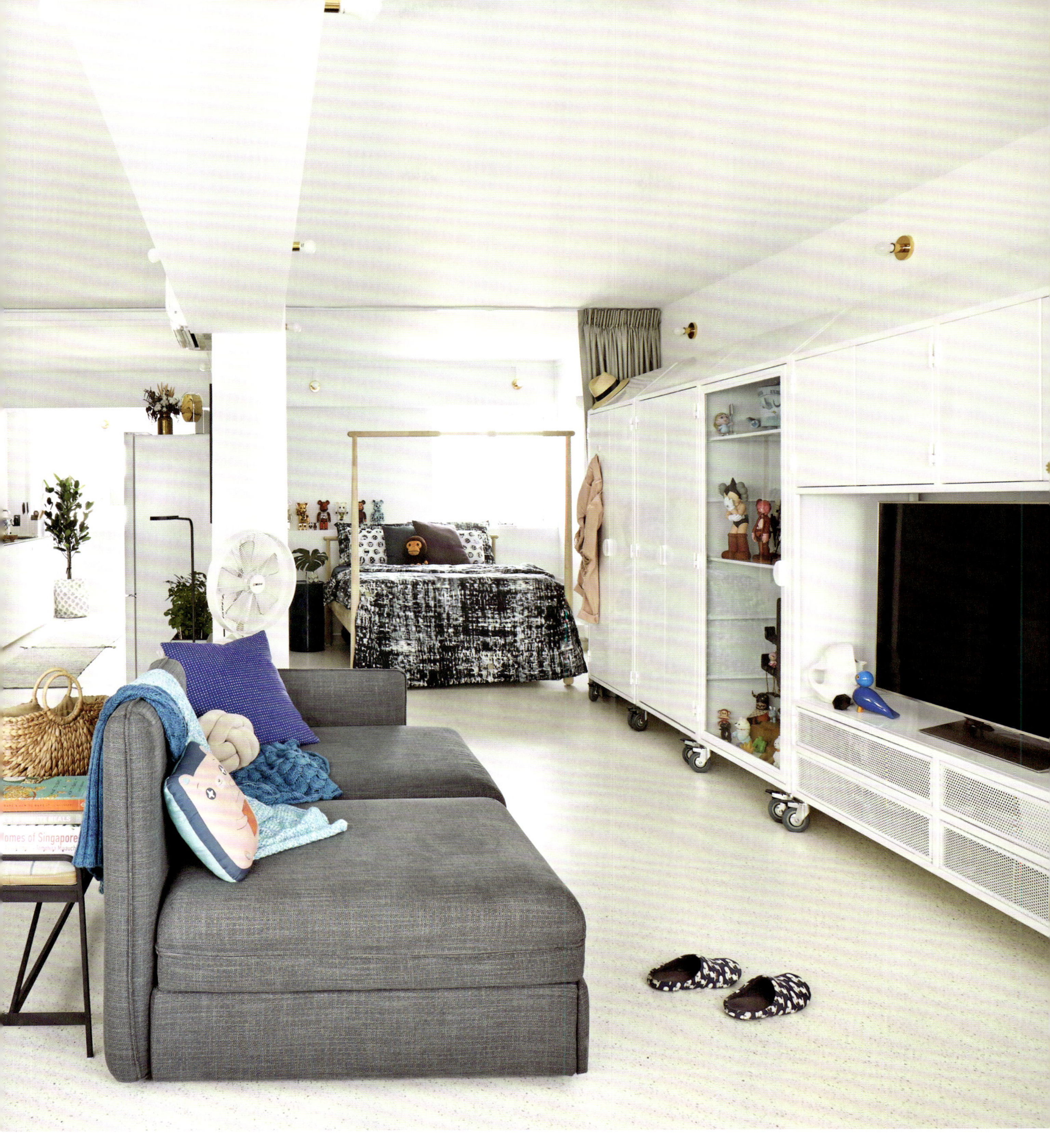

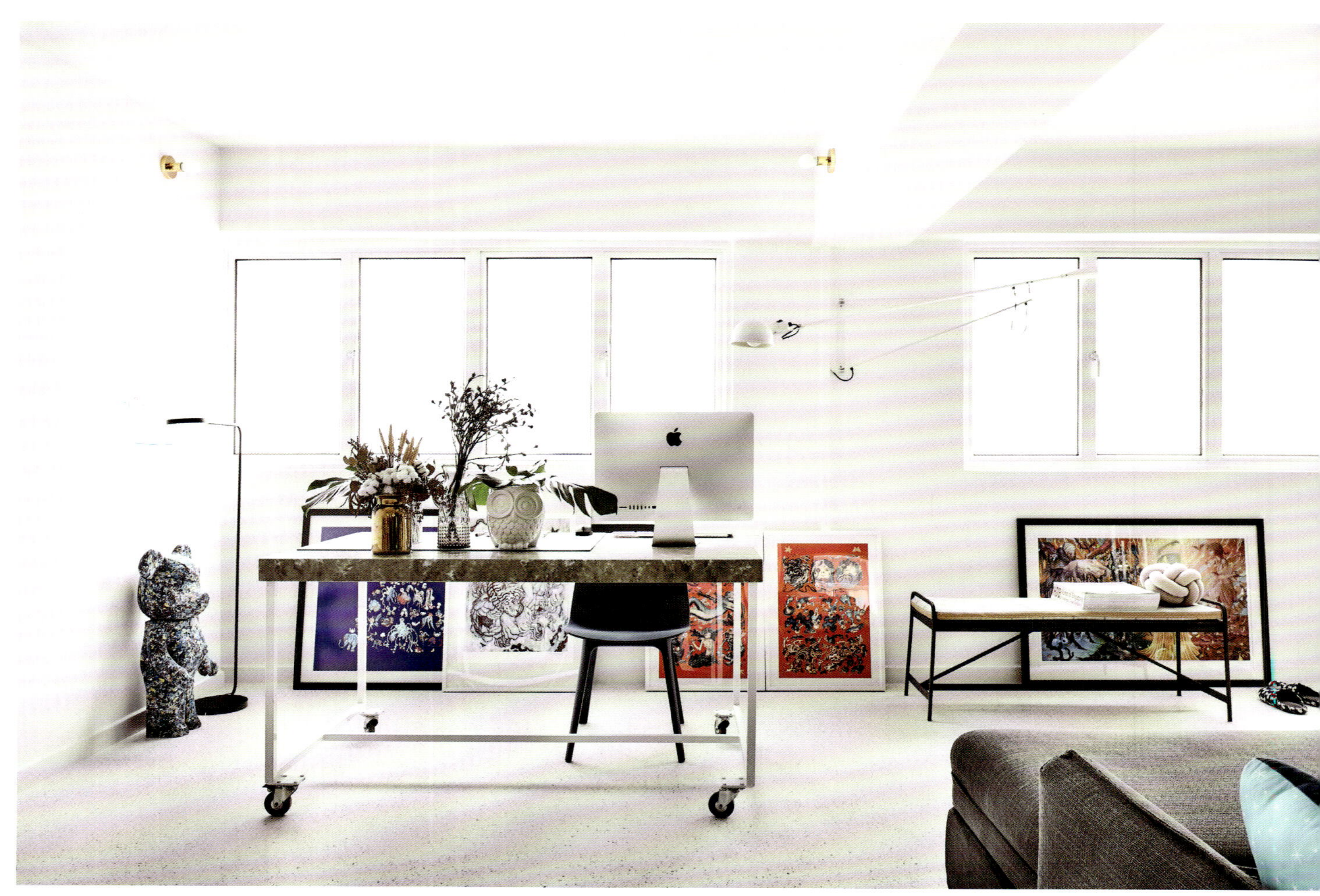

ABOVE An original 265 Paolo Rizzatto wall lamp can be swiveled to illuminate the tables as they move around.

OPPOSITE Materials selection in the bathroom was carefully considered to welcome in the most light.

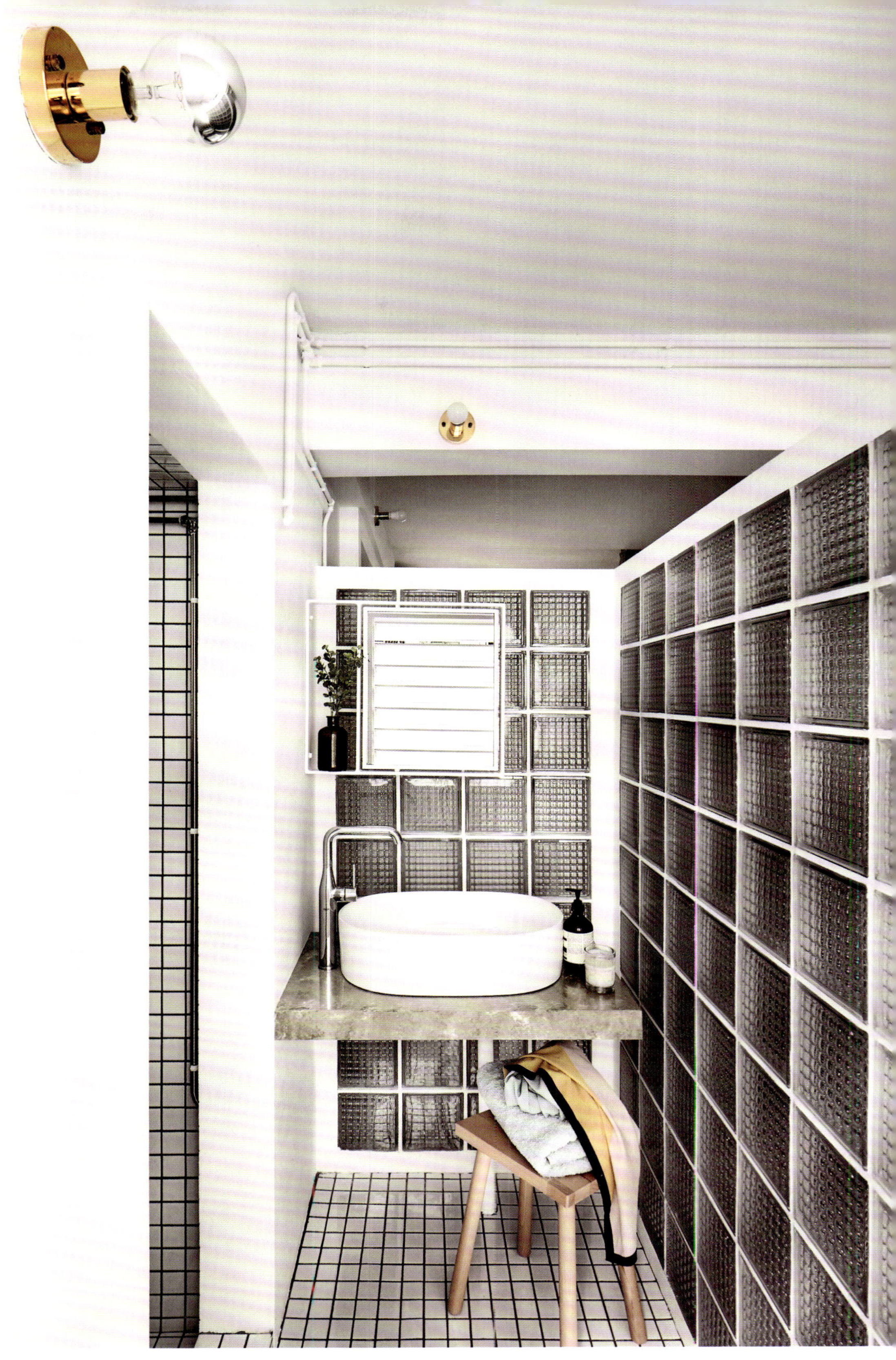

3

In an era defined by rapidly increasing urbanisation and environmental awareness, the need for sustainable living solutions has never been more urgent. As we strive to reduce our carbon footprint and make more efficient use of our resources, the concept of adaptive reuse has emerged as a powerful tool for creating small-footprint homes that embody both functionality and environmental consciousness.

Adaptive reuse is the art of transforming existing structures or spaces into new, purposeful dwellings that meet the evolving needs of modern living. It goes beyond traditional renovation or remodelling, pushing boundaries to reimagine and repurpose buildings in innovative ways. This approach not only offers practical advantages in terms of cost-effectiveness and resource conservation, but also celebrates the unique character and history of the structures being adapted.

In this section, we delve into the realm of adaptive reuse, exploring the possibilities it presents for those seeking to create sustainable and efficient living spaces. These inspiring homes were ingeniously repurposed to fulfil contemporary housing needs while respecting the ecological footprint of the planet.

Nestled within the historic city of Mantova, Monolocale EFFE is a remarkable example of adaptive reuse. The initial stages of excavation revealed a hidden treasure – a centuries-old wall steeped in history and intrigue. Rather than concealing or dismantling this architectural artefact, Archiplanstudio embraced it as a central element of the space.

In the vibrant heart of Athens, the adaptive reuse project Kolonaki invites us to step into the world of a renowned writer's studio. Standing as a testament to the literary

Adaptive Reuse

history of the city, this repurposed space reverently preserves a signature wall that carries the echoes of past luminaries.

The design approach here wholeheartedly celebrates the space's former life. The wall bearing the marks of inspiration remains untouched and serves as a tangible connection to the writer's artistic journey. Through careful restoration and thoughtful arrangement of contemporary elements, Kolonaki seamlessly blends the charm of the old with the convenience of the new and invites its occupants to find inspiration within its storied walls.

Also in Athens, in the suburb of Ilioupoli, what was once a dimly lit and forgotten space has been reborn, offering comfort and functionality to its inhabitants. Through strategic design interventions, natural light now pours into the space and creates a welcoming atmosphere. A splash of blue, which reflects the ocean and reinforces Greece's love affair with this particular shade, is also a standout.

These snapshots exemplify the power of adaptive reuse in small-footprint living.

Beyond the environmental benefits, adaptive reuse offers a host of other advantages. It fosters a sense of community by revitalising neglected areas, preserving the historic fabric of our cities and contributing to urban renewal.

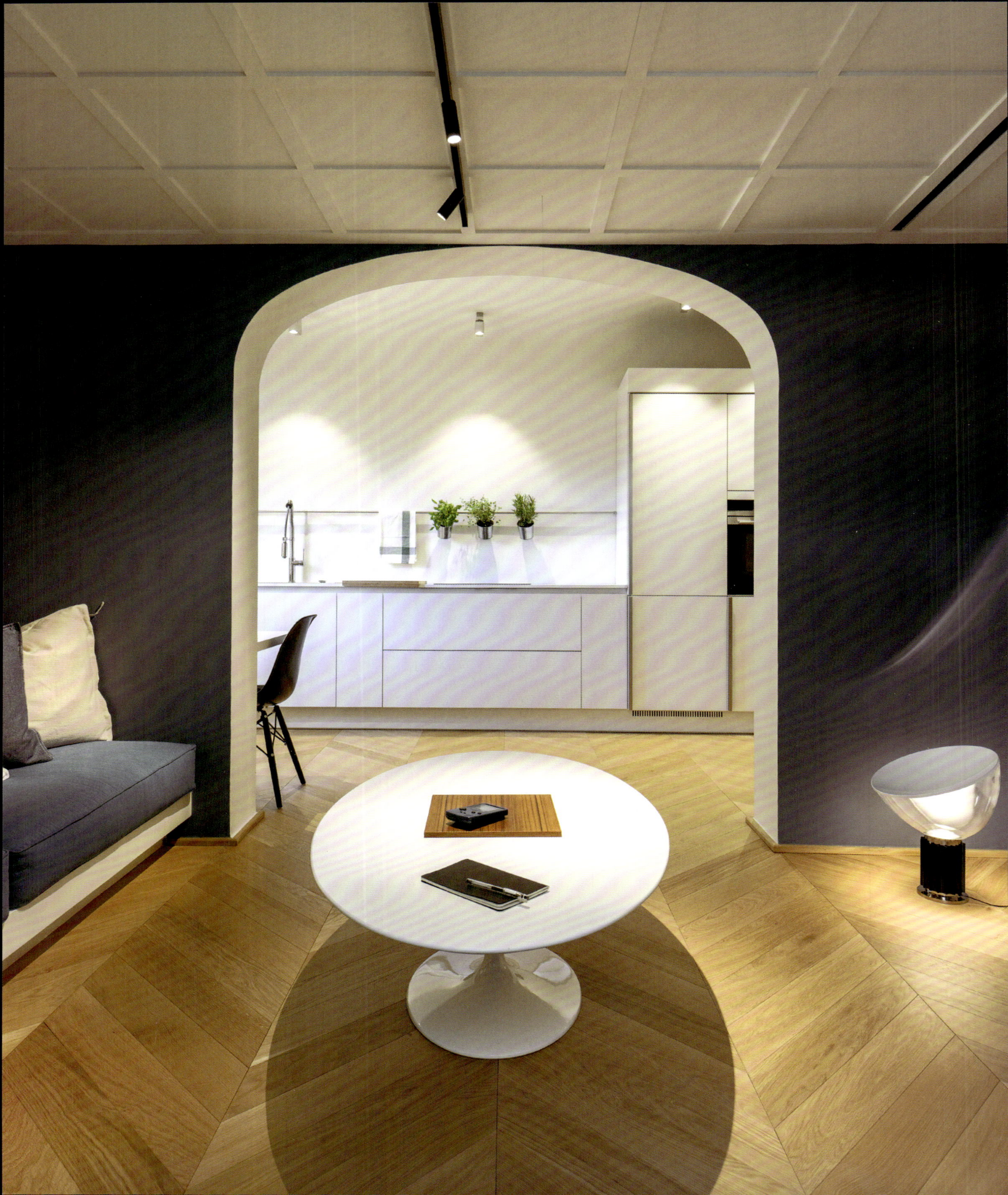

Flat Eleven

50m² / 538ft²
Pierattelli Architetture
Oltrarno, Florence

Architects rarely include small windows. Why design something that doesn't let in a lot of light? But what if that small window perfectly framed a view of the dome of the Renaissance Basilica di Santo Spirito in central Florence?

Flat Eleven is situated in a historic 12th-century building in the Oltarno district of Florence, Italy. This is an area known for its carpenters, restorers, lute makers and blacksmiths, many of whom are still trading today. Palazzo Pitti, a Renaissance palace that houses the largest museum in Florence, sits on the square opposite.

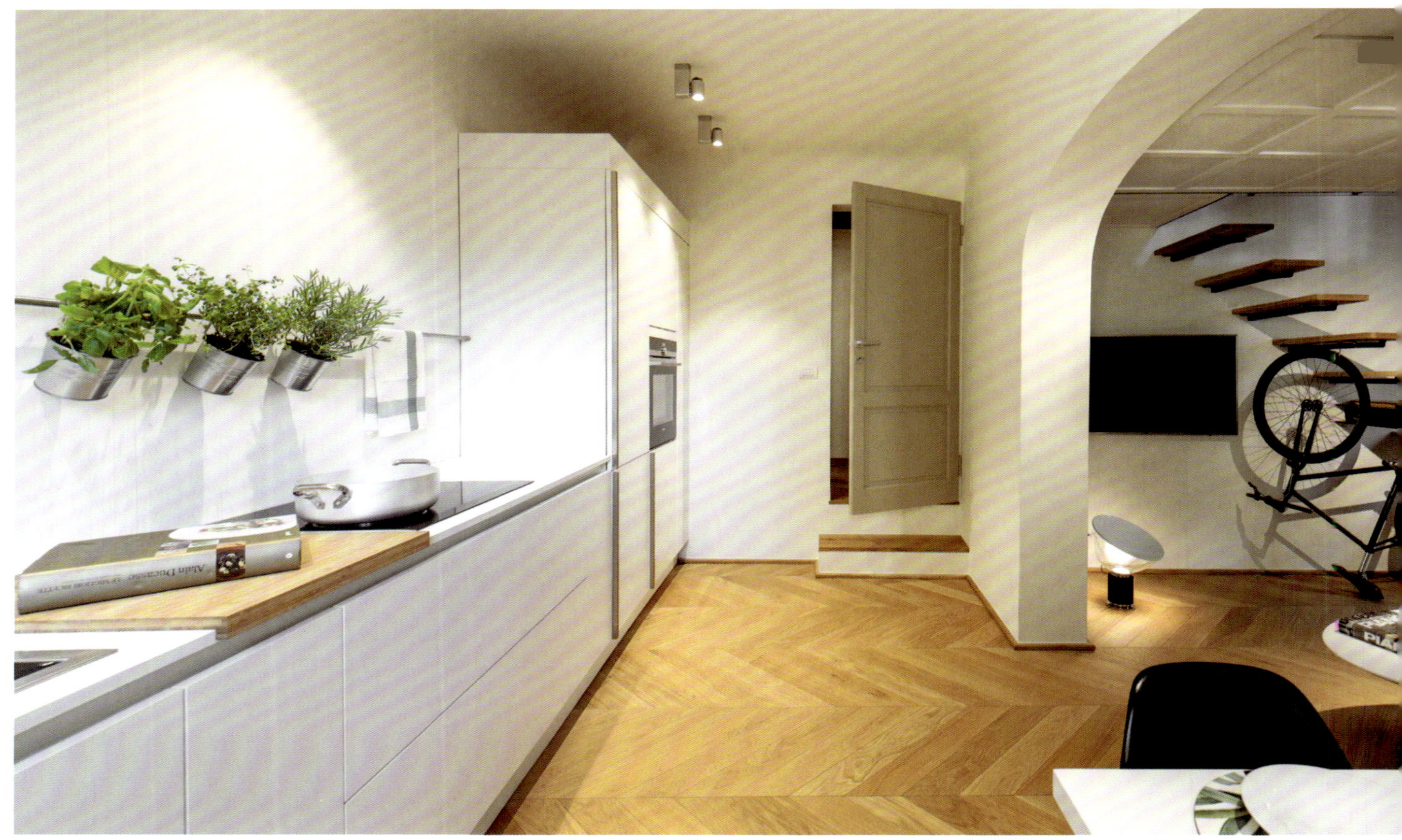

Born from a desire to create a 'bright and open' home for his partner and himself, Claudio Pierattelli and the team at Pierattelli Architetture took a 50-sq-m (538-sq-ft) section of an apartment belonging to his parents and stripped away what wasn't needed, built a separate entrance and a kitchen, and replaced the flooring with French herringbone.

'We wanted to create a precious corner of tranquility in the city,' explains Pierattelli. 'A place where people could find and express themselves.'

The palette of mainly white with accents of deep blue, usually reserved for coastal cottages and beach houses, is unexpected in the centre of this ancient city, but helps create a home that feels at once distinctive and peaceful.

The new entryway perfectly introduces the idea of respite through simplicity. There is a large window that lets in a lot of light and a silver bar to hang coats on – that's it. Once you step down to the main living area, a double-height ceiling is a pleasant surprise that creates a larger sense of space. In fact, every decision was made to allow for a good flow and the maximum amount of light.

A custom-made bench, the base for two-thirds made-to-measure couch cushions and one-third built-in planter, sits along the wall. Since the walls of the apartment aren't parallel, Pierattelli designed one side of the couch shorter than the other to make the room appear symmetrical. Floating shelves line the wall and reach almost all the way to the ceiling. Under the cantilever stairs, the television is mounted on the wall. And, hanging from the stairs, easily accessible but out of the way, a bike is stored, wheels up.

The living room flows easily into the kitchen through a pleasing semicircular arch. All kitchen paraphernalia is concealed by white lacquer wooden cabinets that share the wall with a white and grey marble splashback. Like the cantilever stairs and floating shelves in the living room, the small floating kitchen table was chosen because it frees up space and allows the two chairs to be pushed all the way in when not in use. A small walk-in closet and bathroom are just off the kitchen.

AFTER

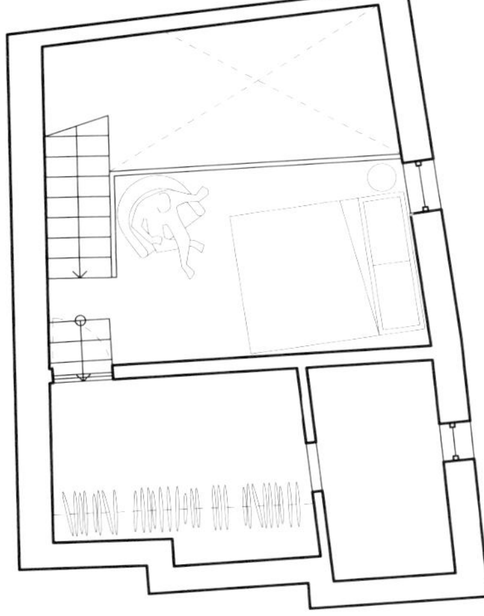

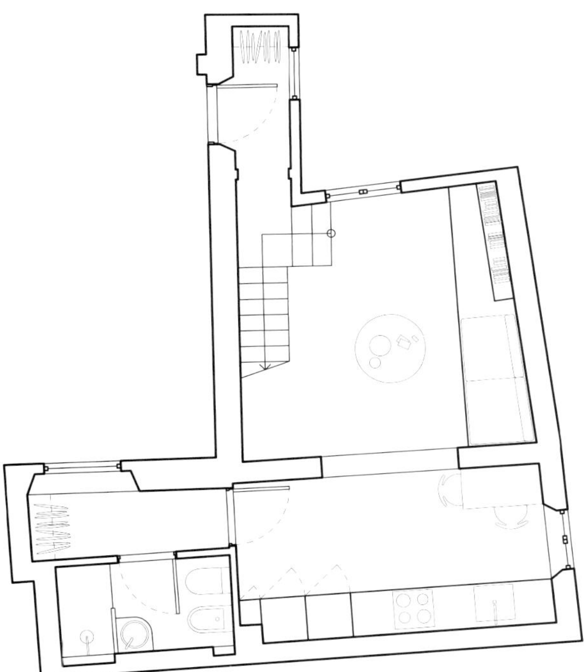

BEFORE

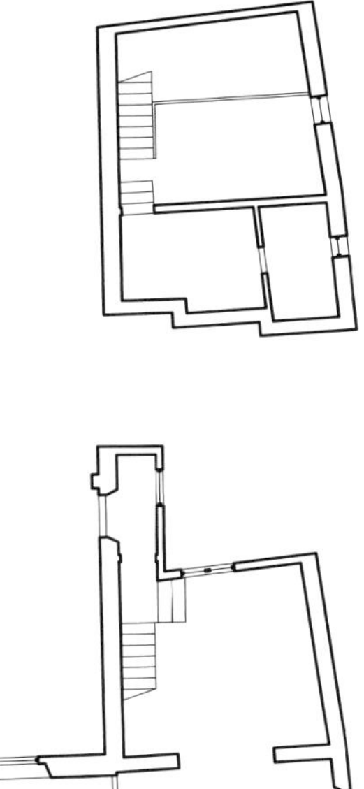

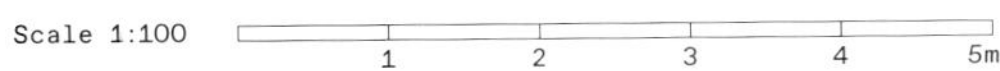

The bedroom sits above the living room in a loft space containing a double bed. A glass balustrade was installed to let as much light in as possible because the only other light source in this space is a small window. However, Pierattelli describes this window as 'the jewel of the flat' because it provides a perfectly framed view of Santo Spirito.

Taking up more than half the loft is a walk-in closet that is used for storage. This allows for the main areas of the home to stay clear and uncluttered. The closet's dark, leafy wallpaper is a delightful contrast to the bright white and blue of the rest of the home.

On living in the city Pierattelli says, '... you have everything you need around the corner ... you can live the life of your neighbourhood'. It's certainly a sage philosophy when the local sites include museums, gardens, monuments, palaces and Renaissance churches.

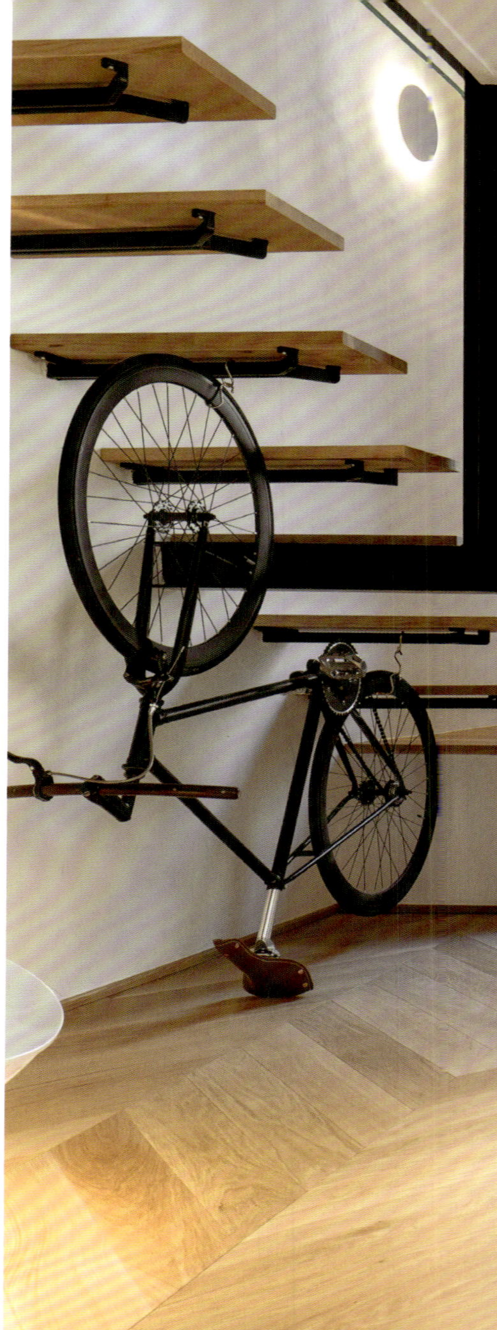

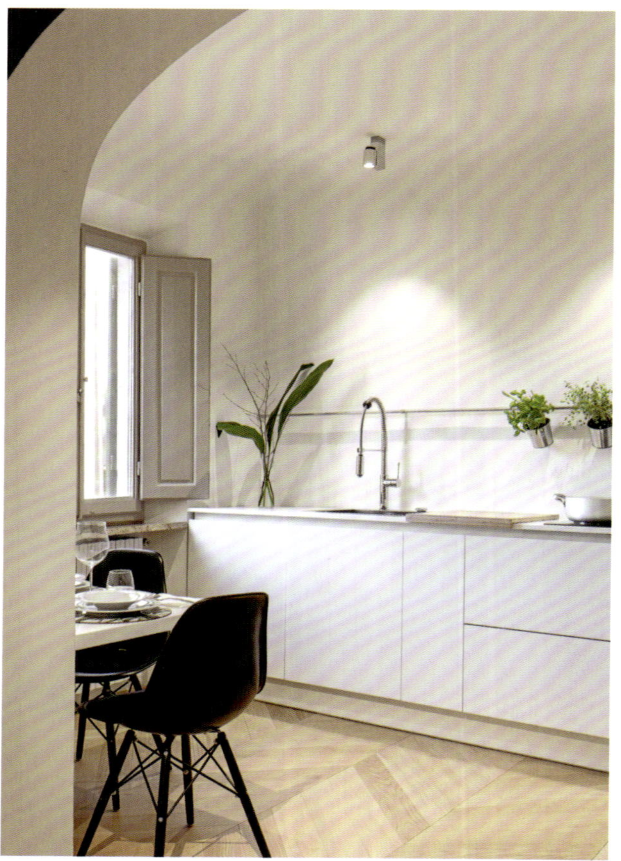

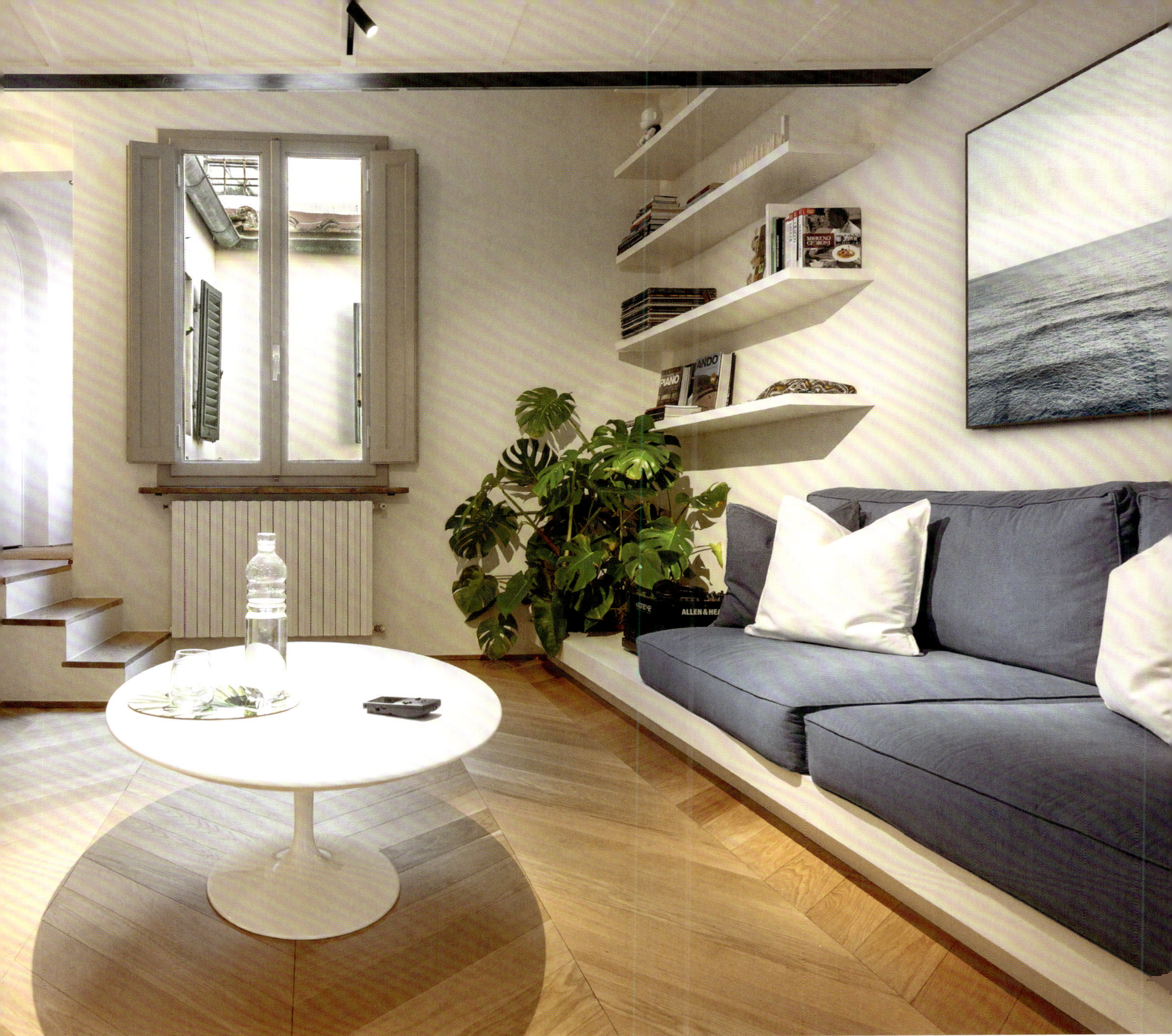

PAGE 136 The team wanted the home to be 'contemporary and youthful but most importantly bright and open'.

PAGE 138 On the home's streamlined aesthetic Pierattelli says 'to help the flat "breathe" I didn't want furniture all over the place'.

OPPOSITE The kitchen is bathed in natural light.

ABOVE The cantilever stairs were left unchanged during the renovation. The lacquered iron beams that support the stairs also double as a great spot for storing Pierattelli's bicycle.

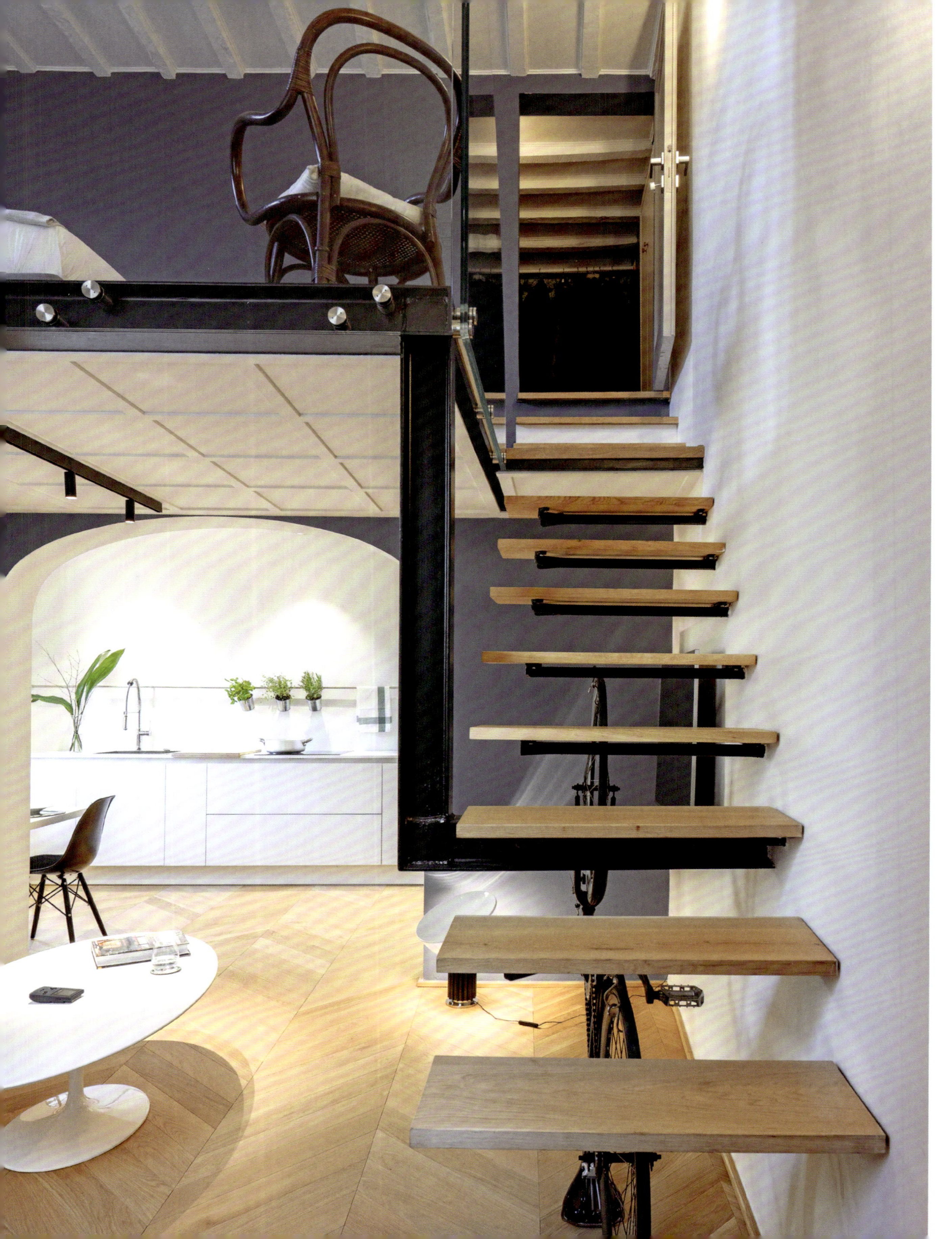

‘We wanted to create a precious corner of tranquility in the city.’

OPPOSITE Up the stairs is a peek into the large walk-in wardrobe just off the bedroom.

BELOW To the right of a wall of floating shelves is the miniature window with a majestic view of the Renaissance Basilica di Santo Spirito.

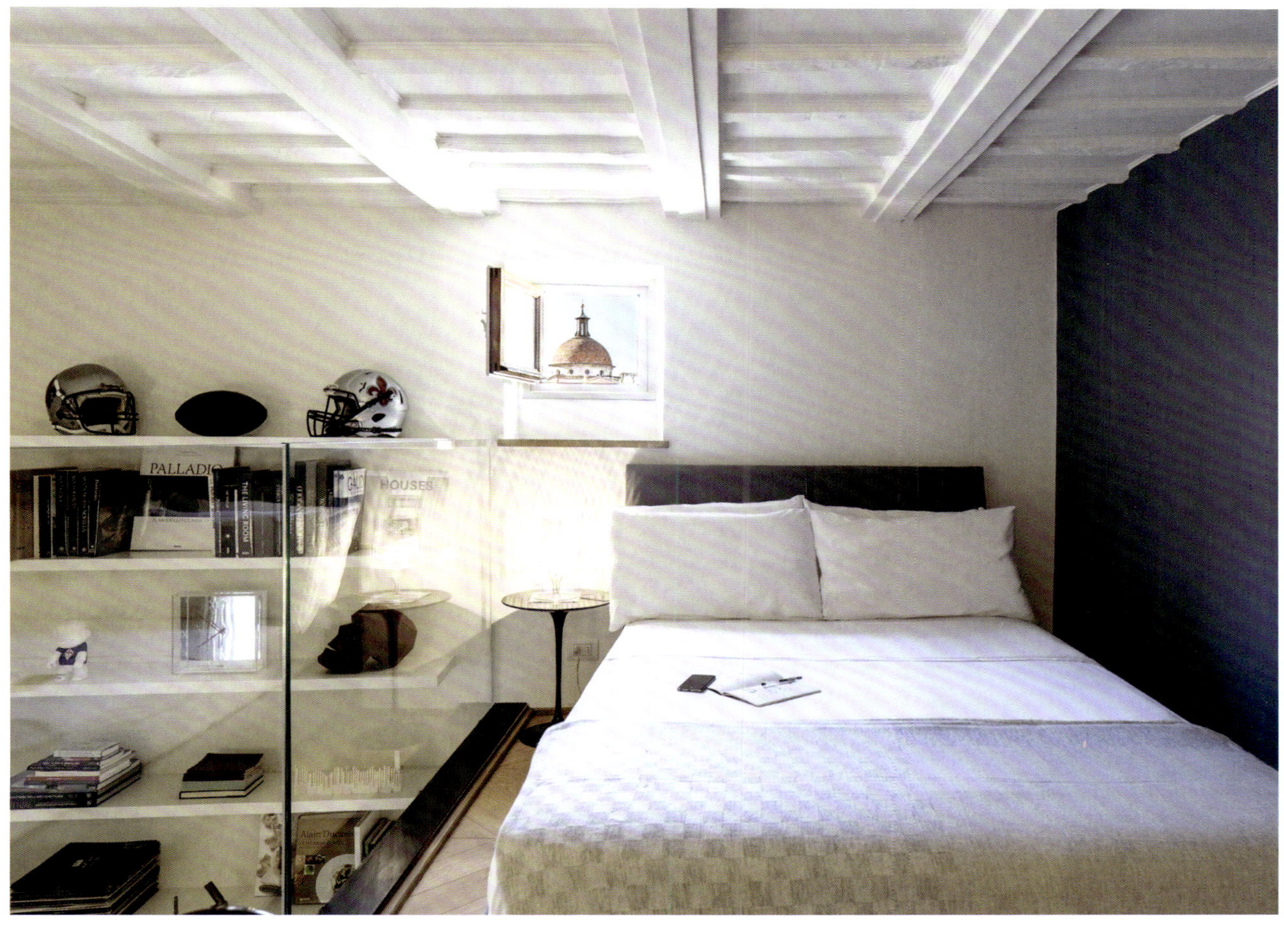

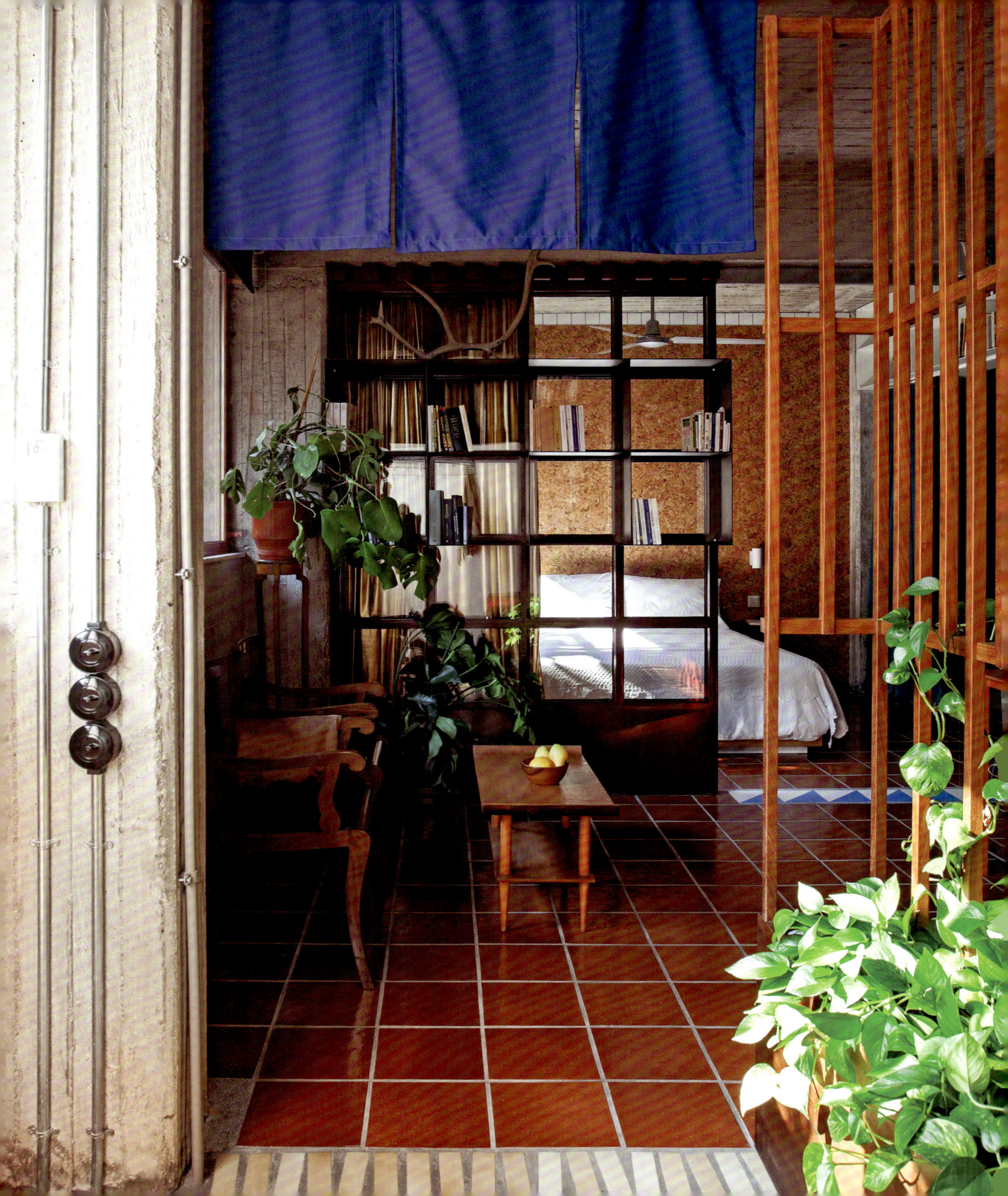

Ilioupoli Apartment

$55m^2$ / $592ft^2$
Point Supreme Architects
Ilioupoli, Athens

Before Ilioupoli became the beautiful 55-sq-m (592-sq-ft) apartment it is today, it was a dark and exposed concrete storage basement in a multigenerational family building in Athens.

Most often, the objective when renovating a space is to open it up, brighten it up, get rid of any cavernous areas. But when architects Konstantinos Pantazis and Marianna Rentzou first saw this basement, they decided to embrace the 'magical cave-like feel of the space'.

‘When we design a small space, we do the opposite of what minimal architecture does,’ explains Rentzou. ‘We try to divide the space into many different areas and introduce many materials.’

This principle is apparent right from the entryway. Custom ceramic floor tiles have been placed seemingly randomly in concrete. A Japanese-inspired wooden partition screen with an integrated planter and a bench with storage space for shoes defines the entry. Next there’s a Noren curtain that conceals the apartment beyond.

Past the curtain, the living area is defined by a coffee table and two simple chairs. A retractable projector screen hangs above so movies can be enjoyed at home. Next to the living area there is a metal bookshelf, chosen for its discreet profile, which creates a natural partition between the living space and bedroom.

The bedroom is further delineated by a line of graphic floor tiles. Behind the bookshelf, a sliding steel partition can be closed in the evenings for privacy and warmth. The two curtains in the bedroom (one a golden orange and one turquoise) hang at different heights to make the space feel bigger and to add visual interest. The cork that covers the wall behind the bed adds another layer of texture and muffles the sound from the street outside.

A custom-made closet sits just outside the bedroom area. It’s accompanied by a generous-sized mirror (again, to create the illusion of more space) and white metal shelves that wrap around a corner. These shelves discreetly conceal a second exit doorway and an air-conditioning unit.

The middle of the apartment centres around a custom steel dining table that comfortably seats six people. The table is placed perpendicular to the windows so that everyone gathered has a front row seat to the dappled sunlight.

To ensure the kitchen doesn’t feel like its own room, there are only two large pieces of cabinetry in the space. The island (which cleverly opens on all four sides) and kitchen cupboards are a warm red laminate. Black Greek marble forms the splashback above the counter.

‘It feels like you are standing in a room that’s bordering a garden,’ Rentzou says of the entranceway partition screen that doubles as a kitchen wall.

A rectangular-shaped window, high up on the other kitchen wall, reveals a blue room beyond. It’s like glimpsing into an aquarium. This is the bathroom. It’s a simple space with a floating bench that ‘creates a sense of the beach’.

Creating a home that is continually visually surprising and delightful in a 55-sq-m (592-sq-ft) space is an impressive achievement. And this is what Ilioupoli has done, all while embracing its basement origins and welcoming in the light.

PAGE 144 Right from the entrance of Ilioupoli Apartment, the architects’ philosophy of dividing the space into different areas and introducing different materials is clear.

AFTER

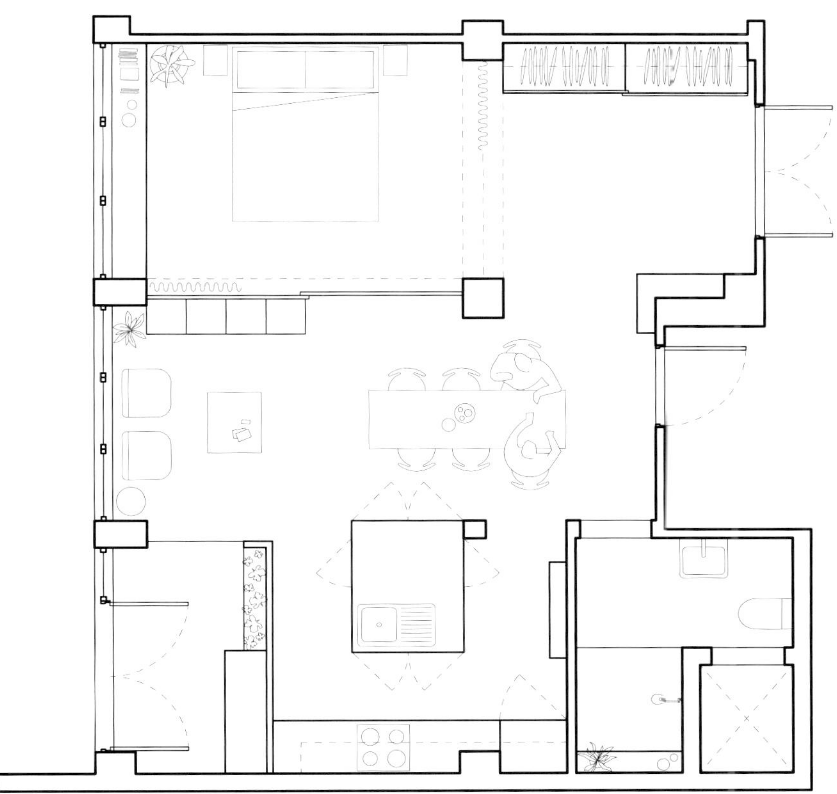

BEFORE

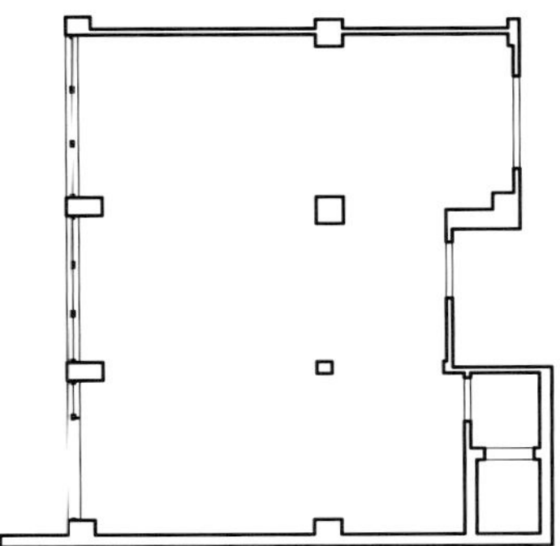

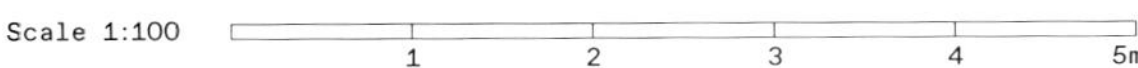

BELOW A partition screen separates the kitchen and entryway but the vertical garden can be enjoyed from both sides.

OPPOSITE The partition casts pleasing shadows on the kitchen's warm red laminate cupboards.

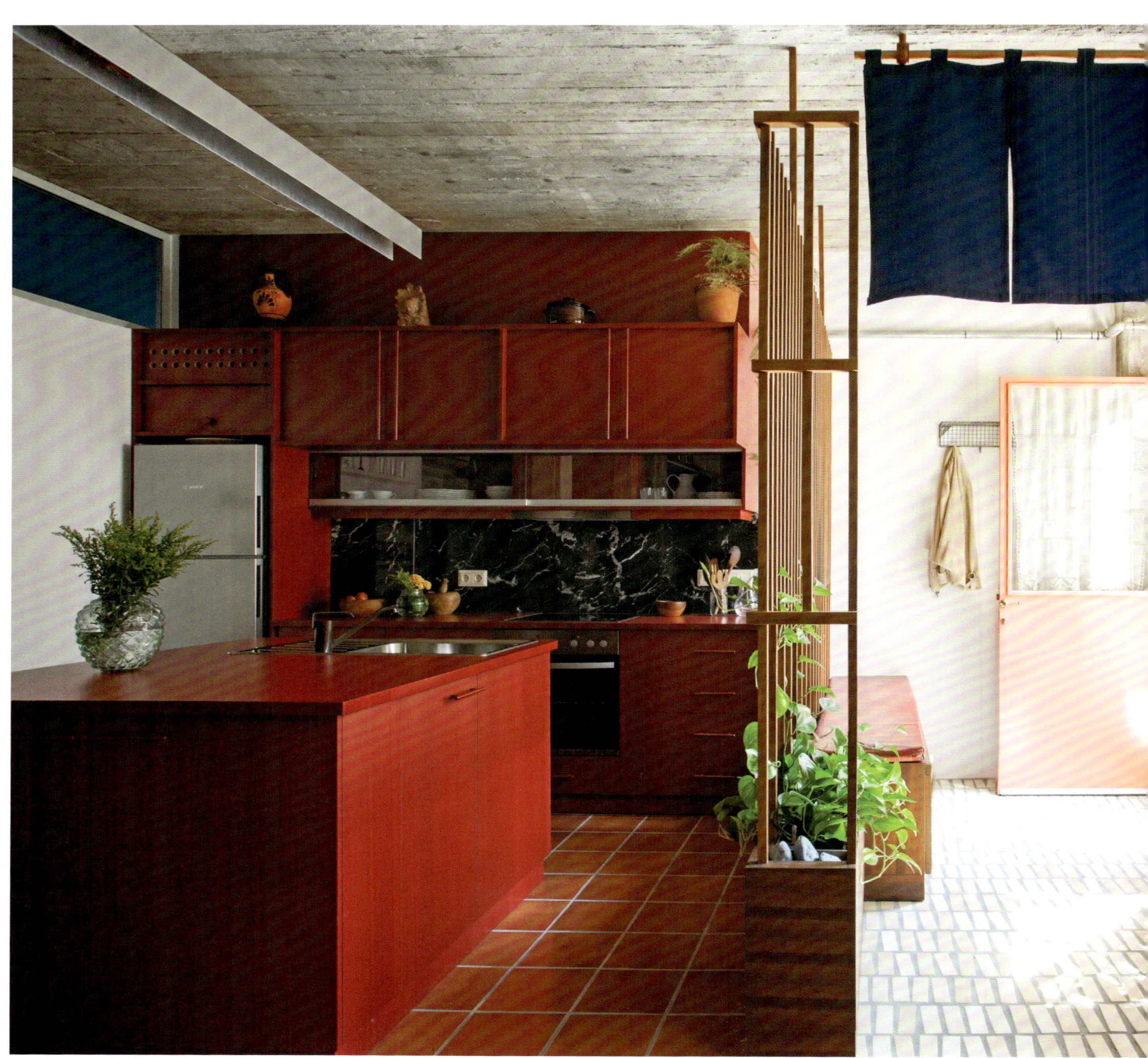

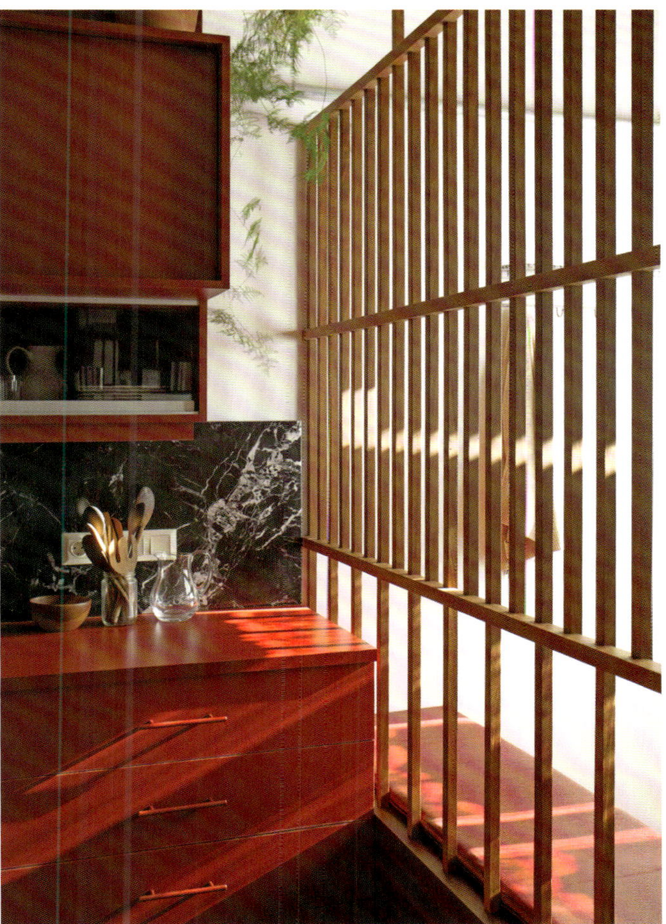

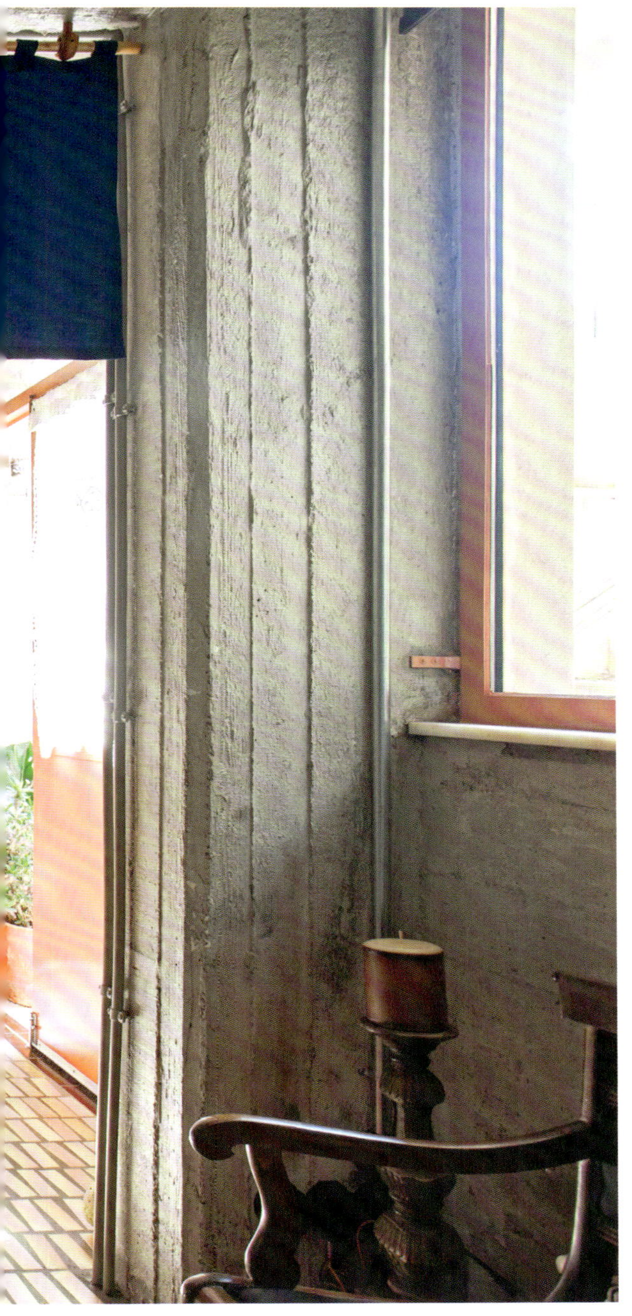

BELOW The large steel table at the centre of the home was custom made and has many uses.

OPPOSITE The bedroom can be made private with a sliding steel partition and an orange curtain. A graphic line of tiles creates a more subtle delineation between the living area and bedroom.

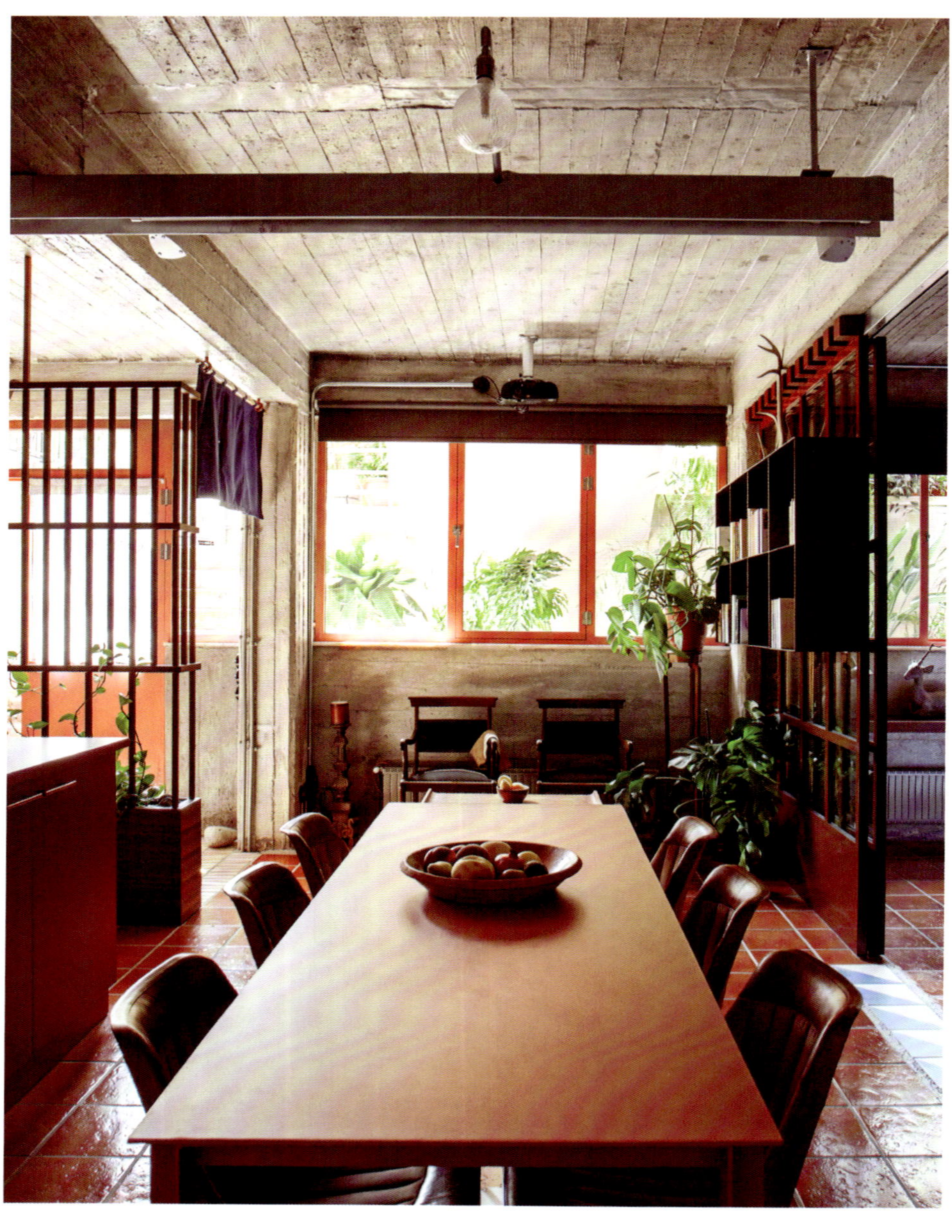

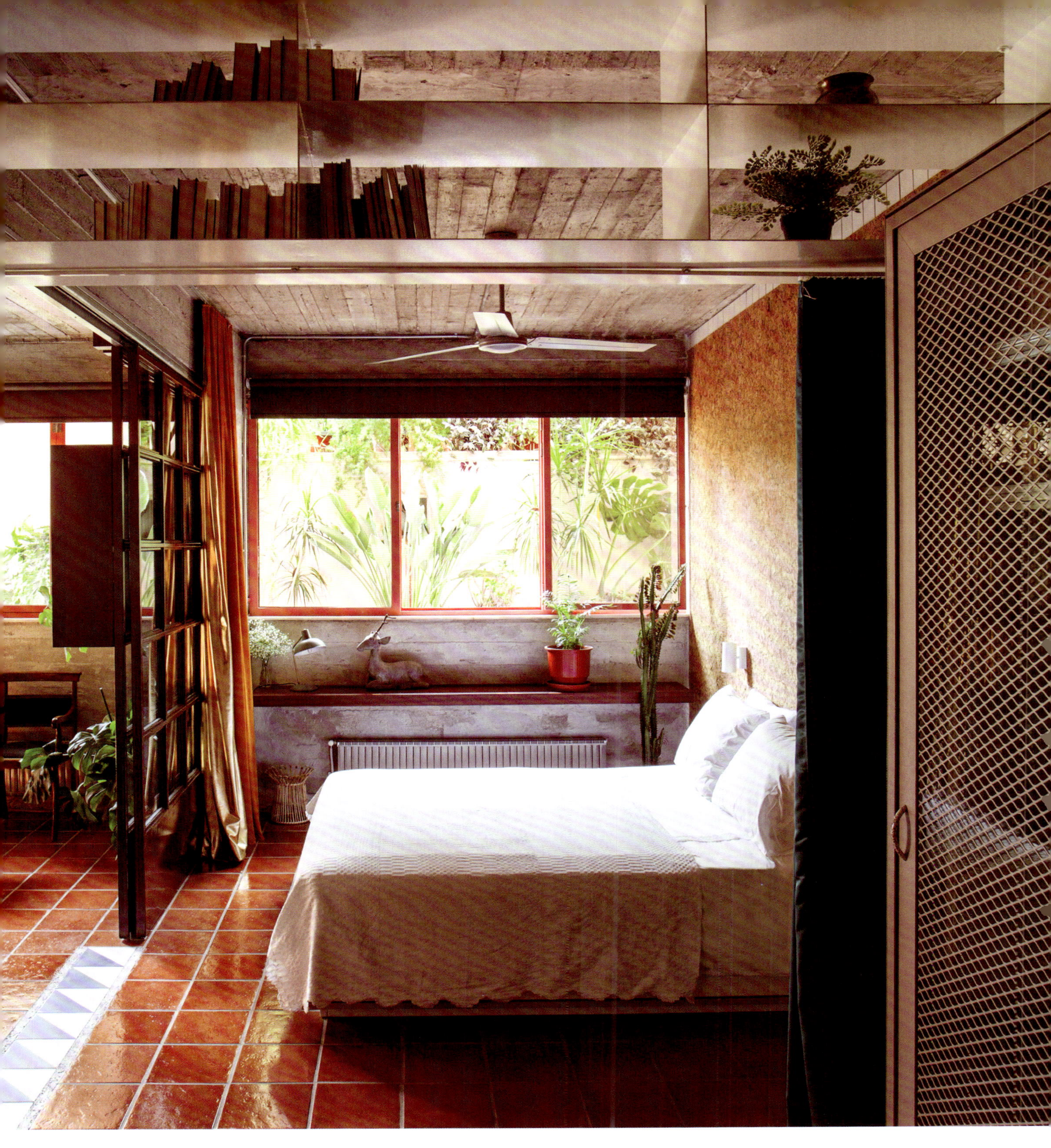

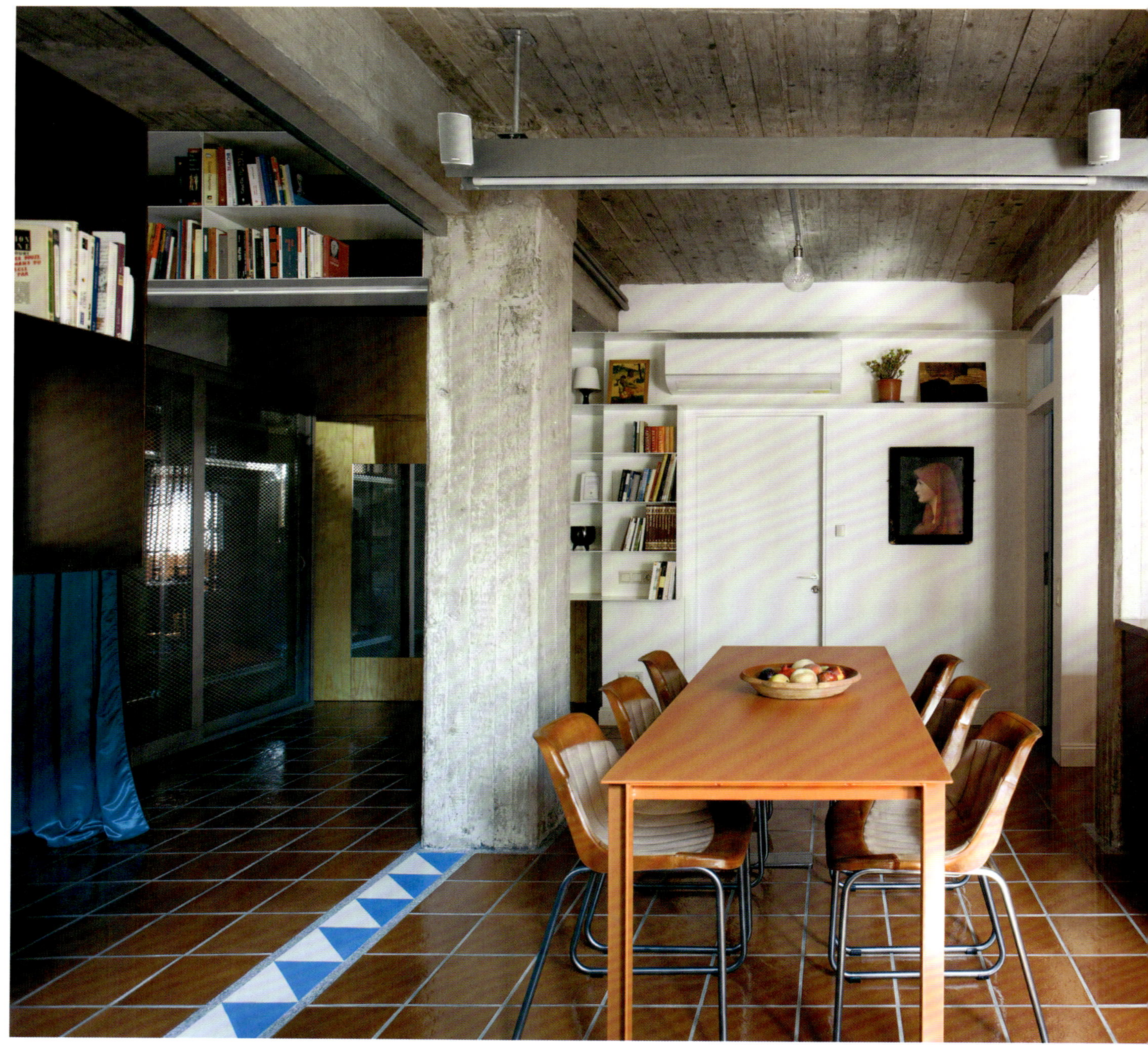

ABOVE The architects chose to treat the space 'as a system (group) of different rooms, but without actually having any walls' so the resulting home is surreal and exciting.

OPPOSITE A glimpse into the bright blue bathroom.

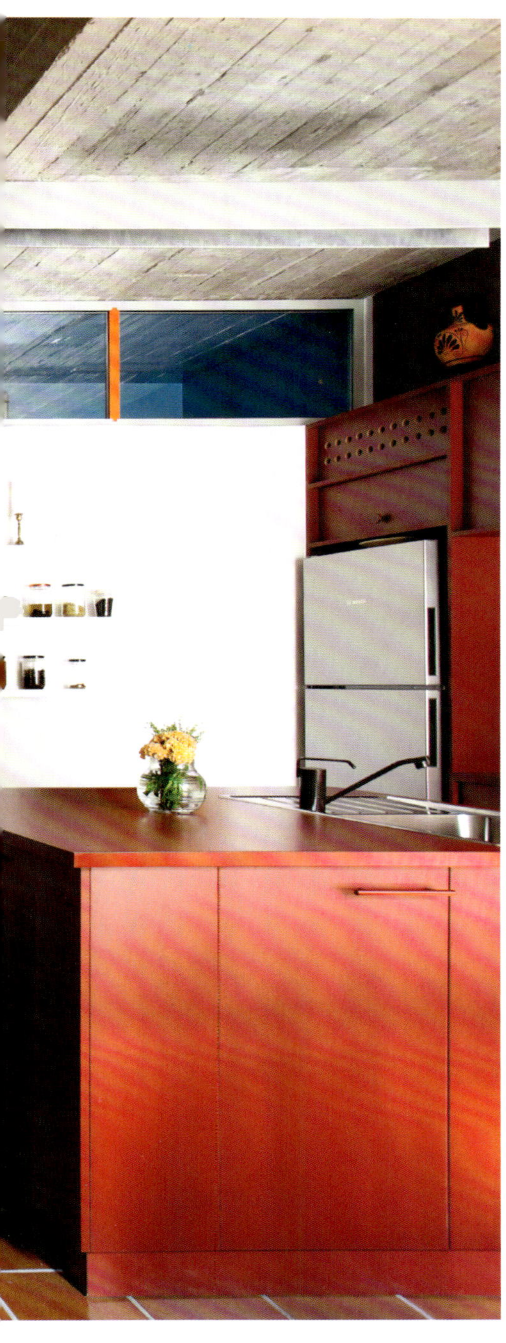

‘We try to divide the space into many different areas and introduce many materials.’

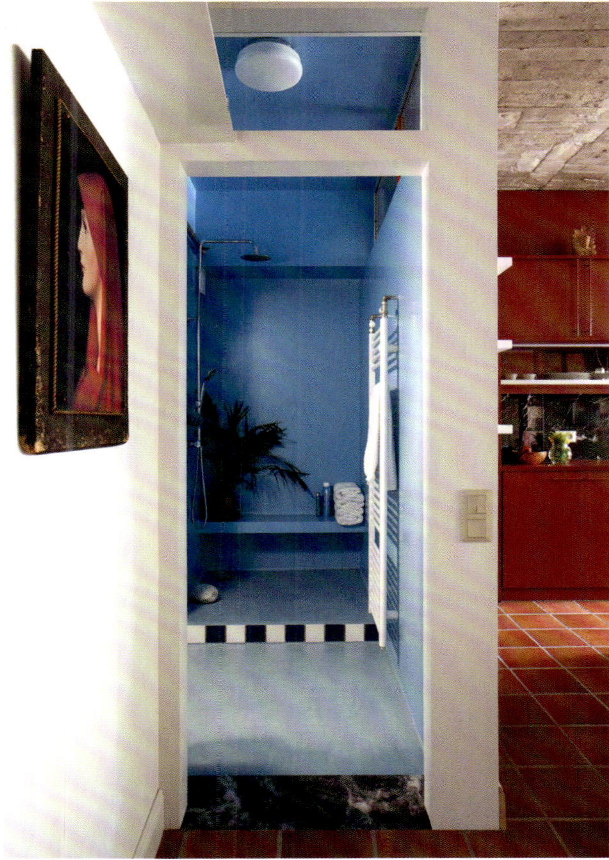

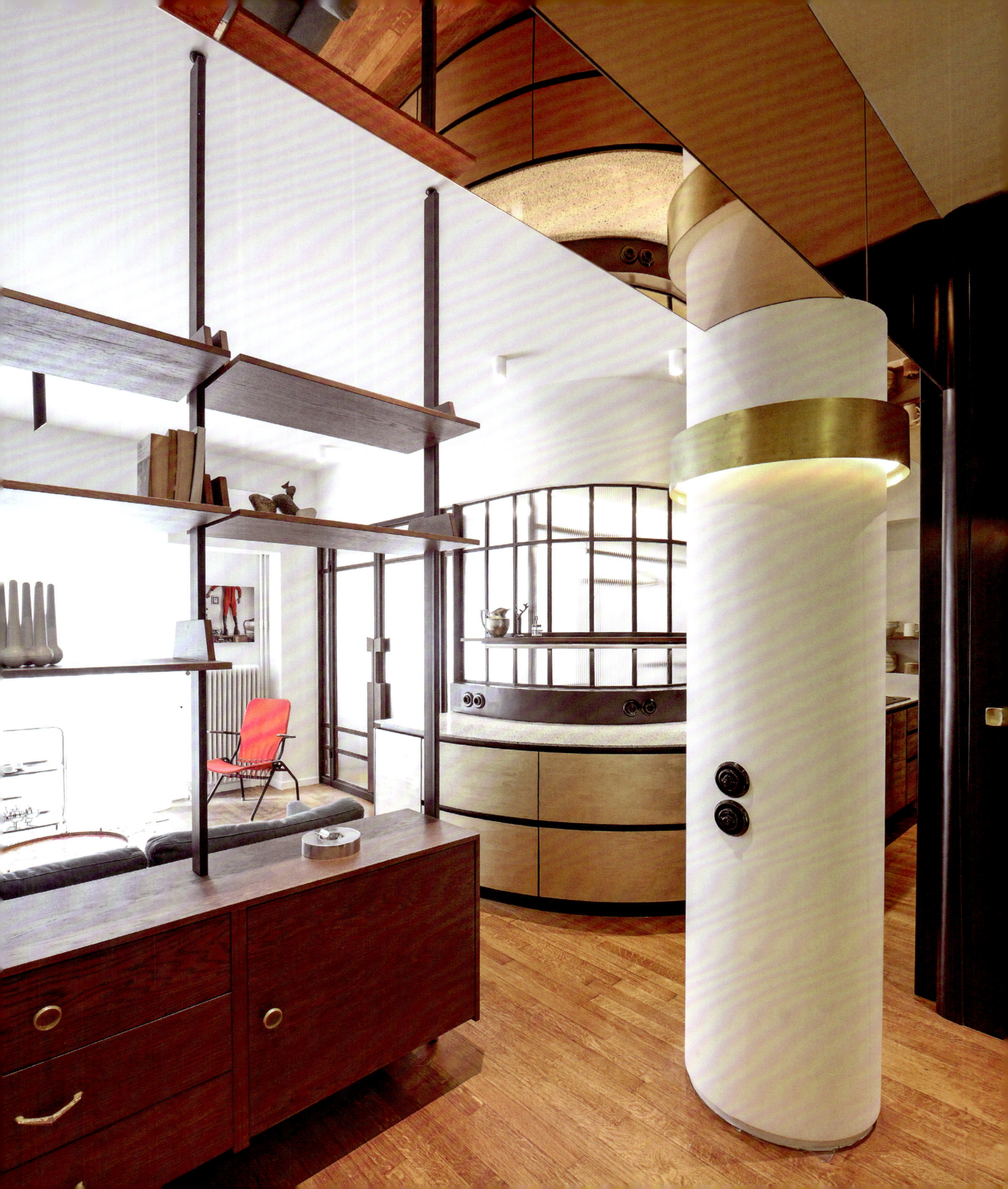

Kolonaki Apartment

$48m^2$ / $516ft^2$
Cluster Architects
Kolonaki, Athens

Situated in the centre of Kolonaki, an upscale suburb of Athens, this apartment, in a complex designed in the 1970s, has undergone an impressive makeover courtesy of Lora Zampara and Michalis Saplaouras of Cluster Architects.

Initially planned as a mixed-use building with commercial space on the ground floor, the building now contains law firms on the upper floors and residential units, while an antique store occupies the ground level.

Zampara and Saplaouras's objective was to design a fully furnished apartment that seamlessly combined practicality, comfort and elegance. In achieving this, the traditional model of a small-footprint refurb was broken as the designers added, rather than removed, walls to maximise the floor plan.

Zampara and Saplaouras encountered a major obstacle during the 48-sq-m (516-sq-ft) apartment's design phase. With just one window and a lone balcony, bringing in ample natural light would be tricky. Due to the neighbours, the hydraulics and plumbing couldn't be moved, so they had to work with that constraint too. The kitchen and bathroom had to remain in the same area as the plumbing, but the rest of the floor plan could be reimagined. Other obstacles discovered during the redevelopment proved to be more of a feature than a hindrance. In a previous life the apartment was an artist's studio and the architects were delighted to find 'a wall full of signatures of famous artists and intellectuals of the 1970s–2000s'. They worked to make sure the wall was 'carefully maintained without any intervention'.

The resulting design is an open, airy space that still maintains privacy. In place of solid walls, Zampara and Saplaouras incorporated translucent walls, Japanese paper and mirrors to optimise natural light and make the atmosphere of the home warm and inviting. A column near the entryway provides a sense of organisation, promoting easy movement throughout the space. The column, which was originally square, was softened by turning it into a circular one and a custom bronze light was added, which transformed it into a striking centerpiece. To brighten the space further, mirrors were strategically placed on the ceiling and the column to reflect and amplify the small amount of available light.

Next to the entrance, a 1960s-inspired perforated wooden partition separates the dining section from the rest of the living area. Custom seating with concealed storage beneath it is complemented by a table and chairs designed in a mid-century-modern style.

The living space is visually separated from the dining area by a tailor-made bookcase with extra storage compartments located at the bottom of the cupboards. A small couch doubles as a guest bed, while a wall-mounted custom-designed floating couch creates the impression of a more spacious environment by freeing up floor space.

The bedroom is enclosed within a metal framework filled with semi-opaque glass, allowing natural light to filter through the apartment. The fitted wardrobe behind the metal construction features light panels made from wood and Japanese paper.

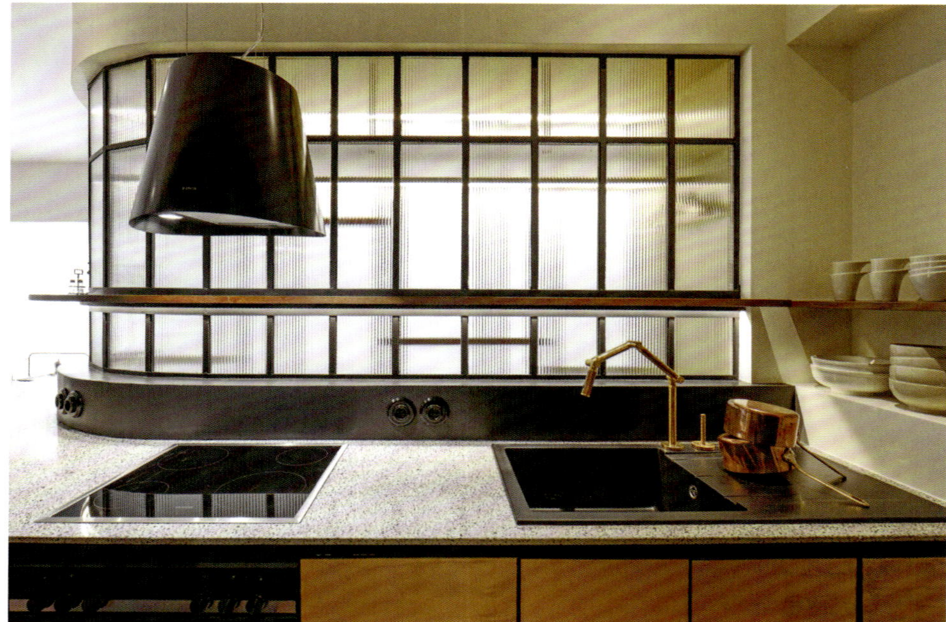

PAGE 154 The column, which was once square, was rounded to create a softer feel to the apartment.

LEFT The kitchen is minimalist but lacks none of the modern amenities.

AFTER

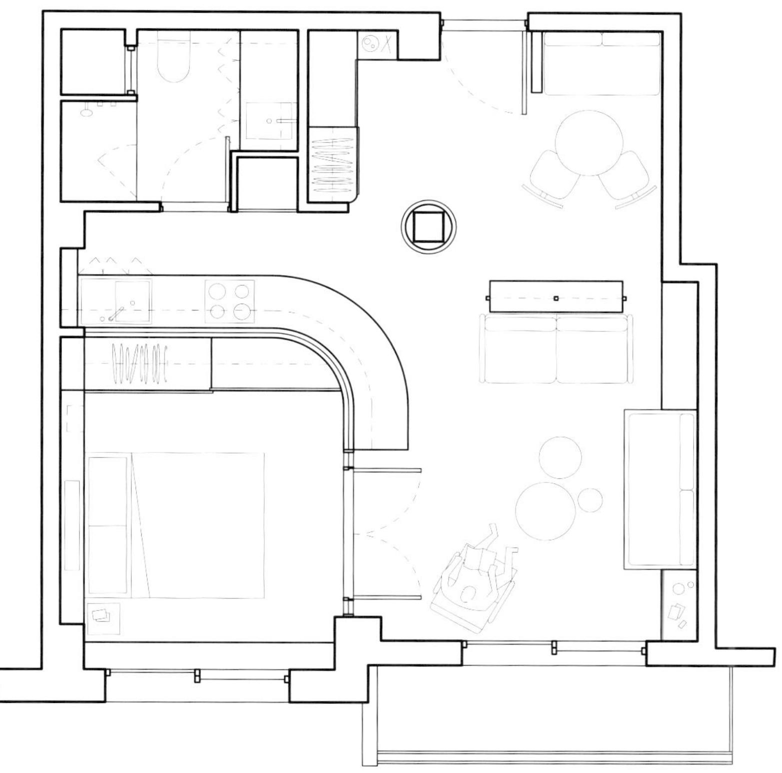

BEFORE

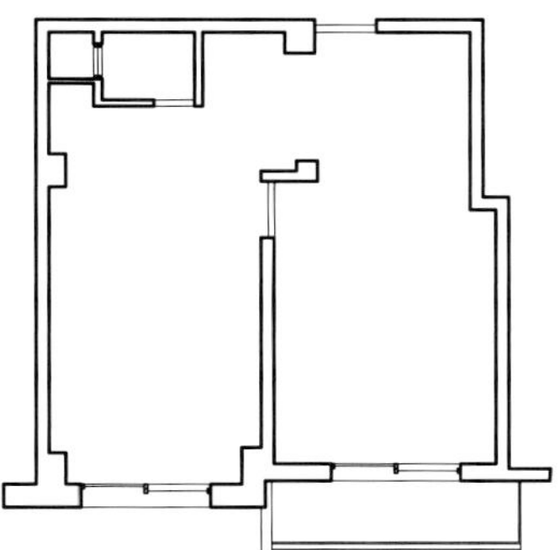

Scale 1:100

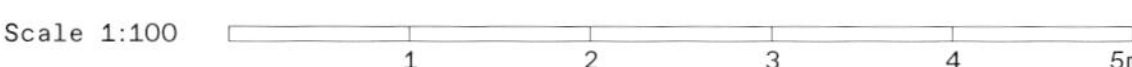

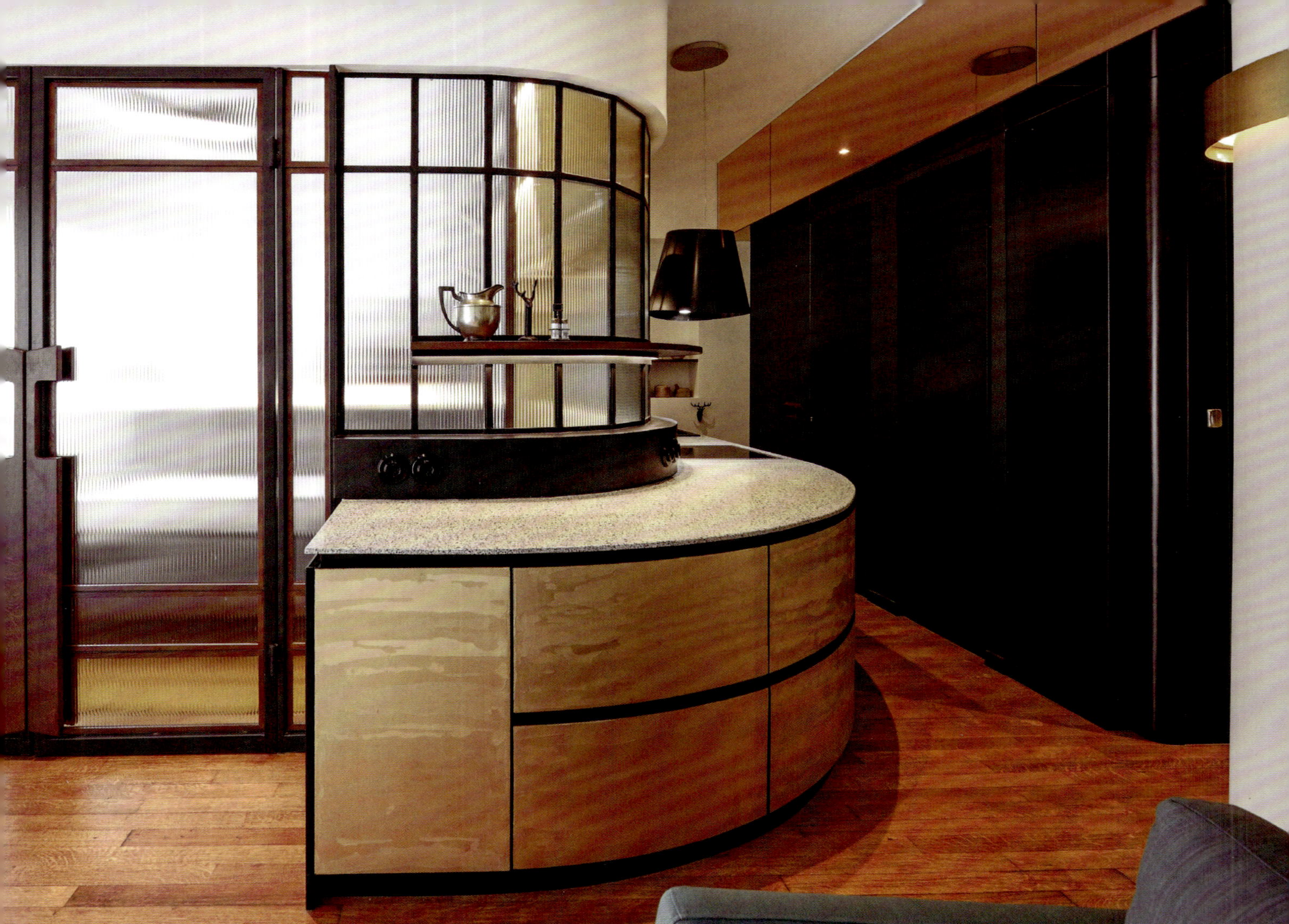

The kitchen wraps around the outside of the bedroom hub and serves as the focal point of the apartment, connecting the living space, bedroom and bathroom. The refrigerator is integrated into a black wall opposite the countertop, and this wall also houses the bathroom at the farthest end. There is no natural light in the bathroom, so to create brightness and enhance the depth of the bathroom, mirrors were added. Large slabs of marble were used for the floor and the shower walls and the scale highlights the natural beauty of the stone.

Kolonaki is a testament to Zampara and Saplaouras's skill for creating functional, comfortable and adaptable design within a limited area. By carefully selecting their materials and coming up with creative solutions to overcome a lack of natural light, they have imbued the space with depth and dimension – and transformed a once-outdated apartment into a stunning, modern home.

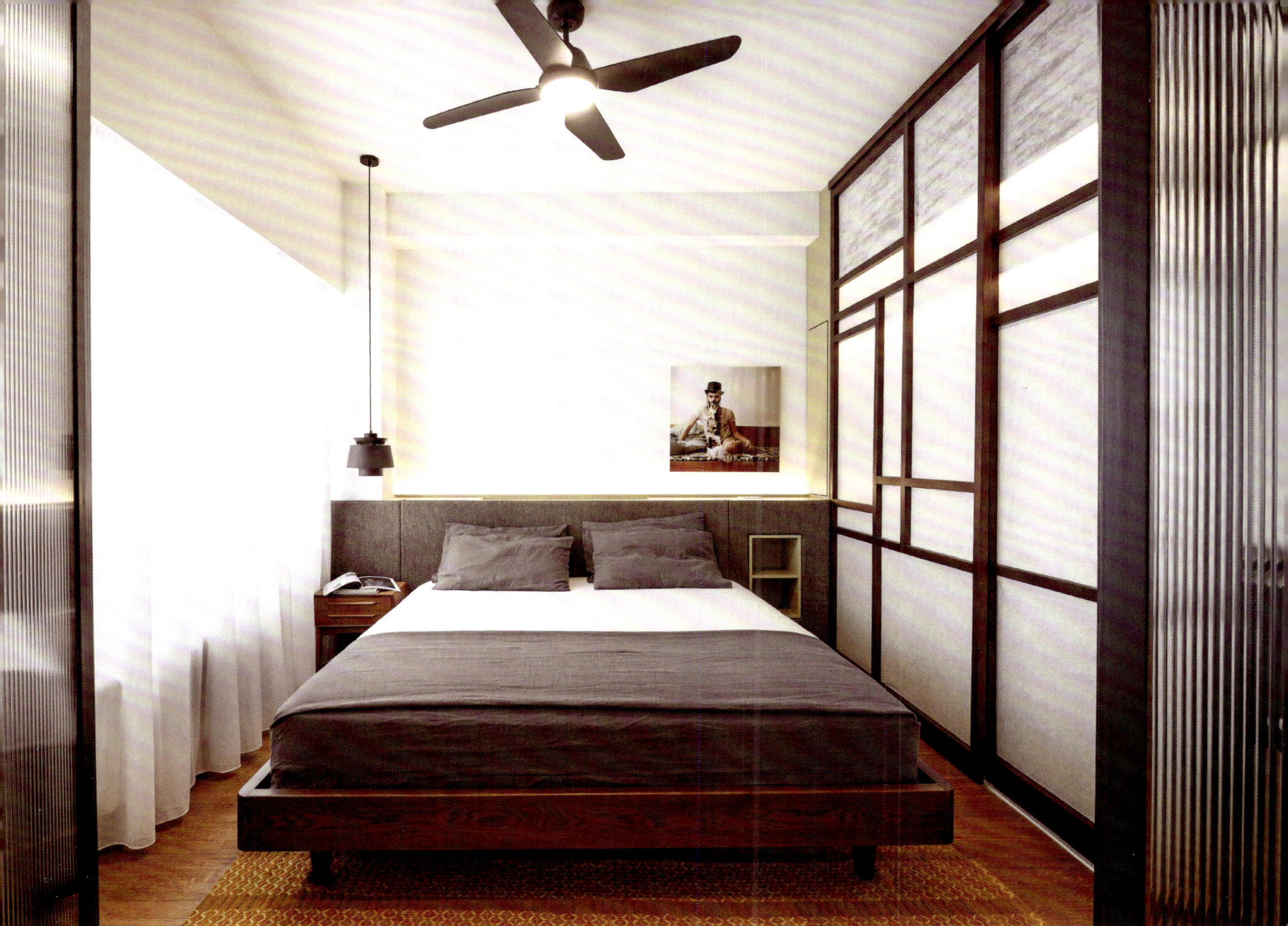

OPPOSITE The shape of the kitchen cleverly curves around the bedroom.

ABOVE A large wraparound window of fluted glass allows the bedroom to enjoy privacy while the kitchen benefits from natural light.

The resulting design is an open, airy space that still maintains privacy.

BELOW The living room makes the most of the natural light with a day bed positioned to soak up the Grecian sun.

OPPOSITE A splash of gold makes the column a feature rather than a eyesore.

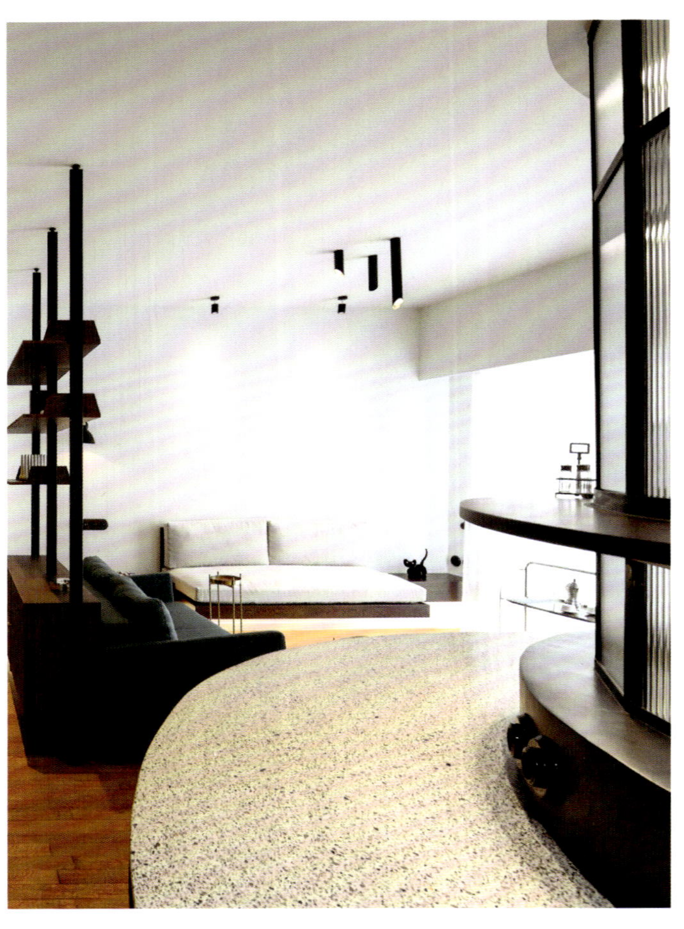

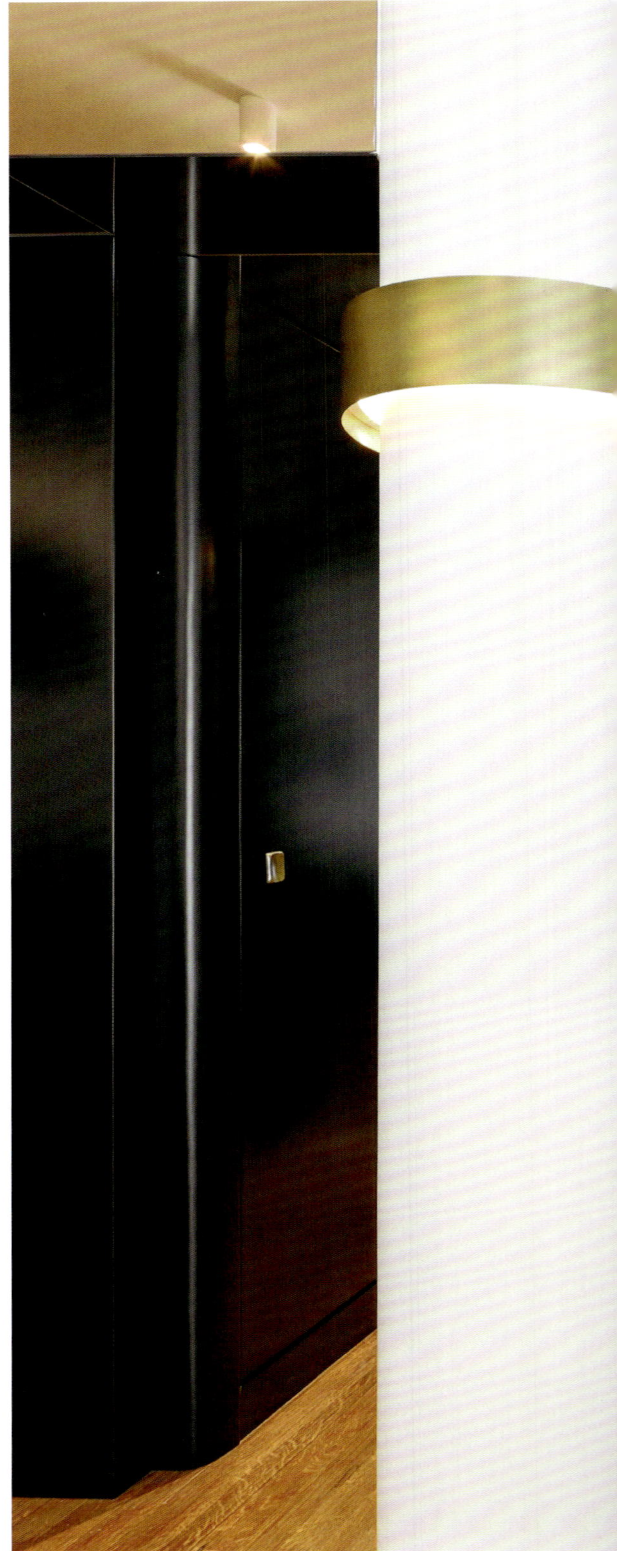

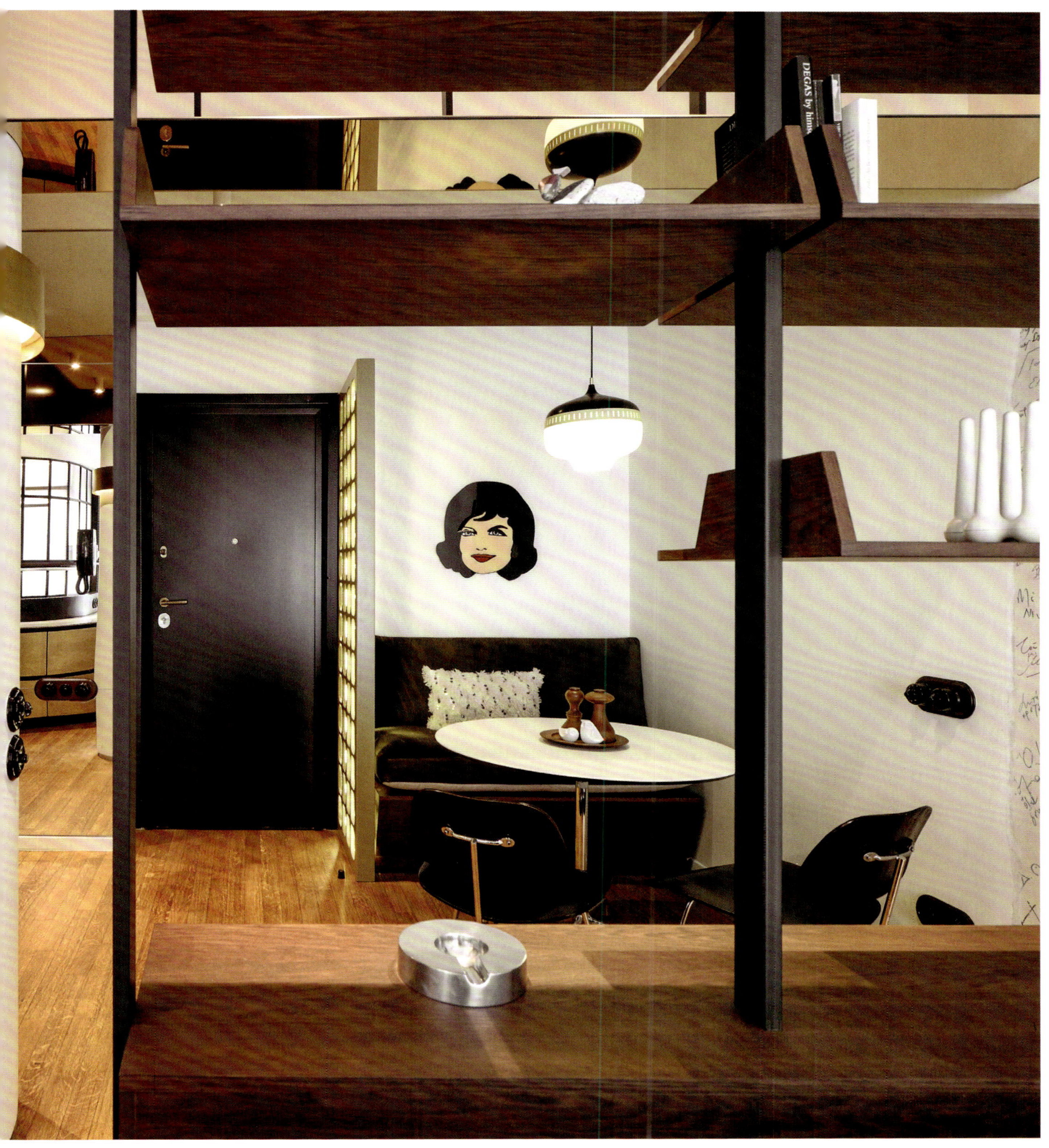

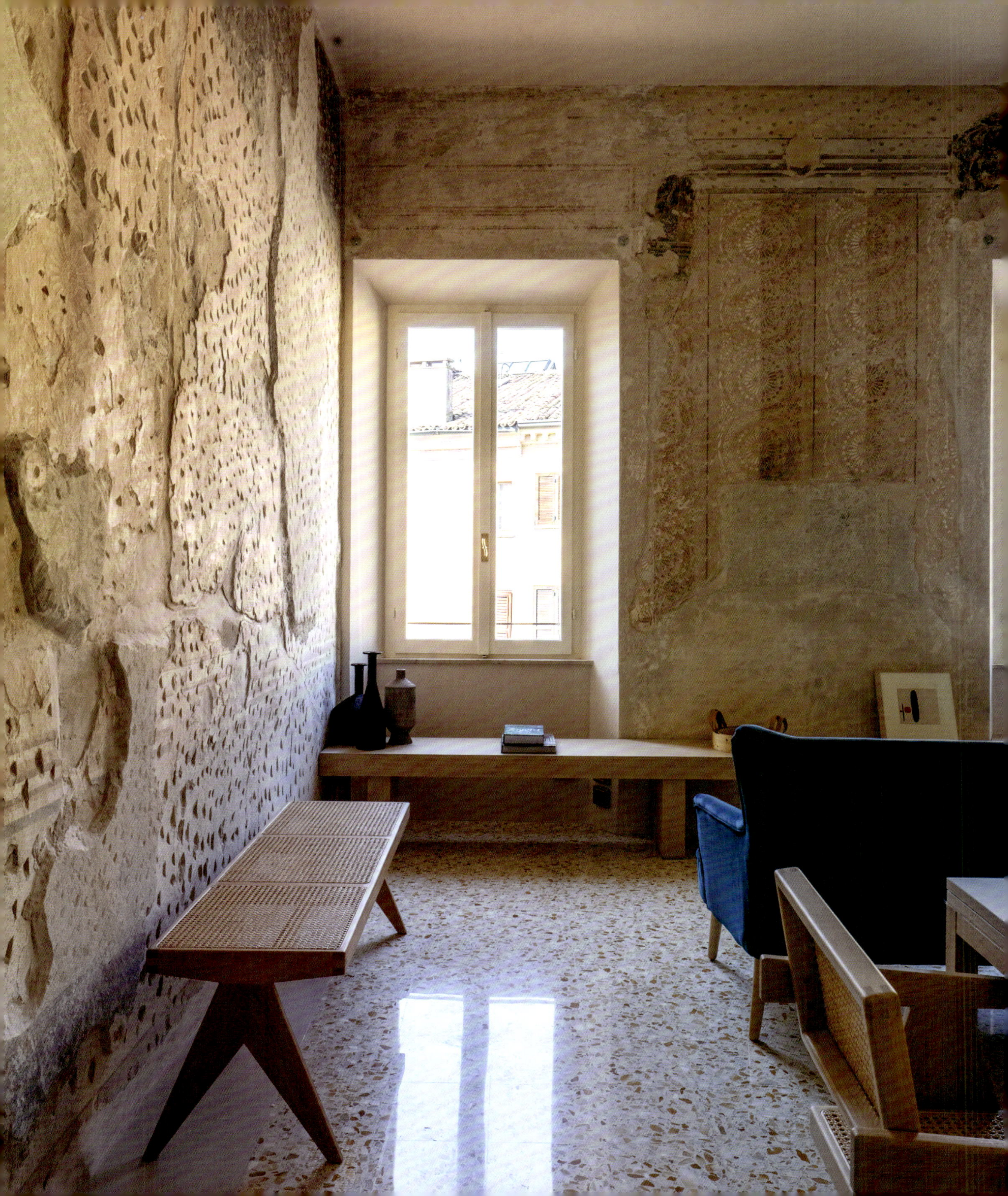

Monolocale EFFE

36m² / 387ft²
Archiplanstudio
Mantova, Lombardy

Like the city of Mantova in Italy's Lombardy region – known for its grand palaces and renaissance architecture – Monolocale EFFE is full of architectural surprises. Archiplanstudio's client's brief was to create two homes out of his grandmother's apartment, but the architects didn't yet know the hidden treasure that was literally waiting to be uncovered.

Located in a 15th-century building, the 36-sq-m (387-sq-ft) apartment was created from the two original bedrooms. A wall was knocked down between them and a new entrance, kitchen and bathroom were added, as well as a floor-to-almost-ceiling bedroom cube in the centre of the space.

In the early stages of the renovation, beautiful frescos were discovered underneath years of paint and render. These exhumed layers of history sharpened the focus of the design language for the home.

The first glimpse of the past meeting the present is in the home's entryway: there are exposed walls, simple wooden hooks for hanging coats and a glass-fronted cabinet for storing shoes.

The living room, kitchen and dining room exist in one area and are seamlessly united by custom oak furniture designed by Archiplanstudio. A long bench, which can be decorated or used for additional seating, sits along the length of one wall. A dining bench sits flush against the wall of the sleeping cube. The small square dining table, ordinarily used for working from home, can be extended to seat up to eight guests.

On the wall adjacent to the dining table, there is a simple-yet-polished kitchen. The lower cabinet doors are finished in brass and bring warmth to the space. The wall-mounted induction plate is only placed on the benchtop when needed, leaving the area free for mise en place.

The bathroom starts just outside the bedroom entrance. A square, resin sink sits on an oak bench, mirroring the bench in the living area. The toilet and shower room are concealed behind a sliding door. The fresco wall brings soft, raw texture to an otherwise minimal space.

The cementing di graniglia concrete tile floors were installed in the 1960s. To begin this new chapter, they were lightly sanded and treated with a protective topcoat.

Saving the best for last, the bedroom cube sits in the centre of the home. Its walls purposely do not reach the ceiling, to aid visual cohesiveness and airflow through the apartment. A double bed sits on a wooden platform with built-in storage underneath. Floating shelves line the wall above the bed and, much like a submarine's portholes, circular cut-outs are situated throughout the bedroom so the fresco walls can be glimpsed from within the cube.

Monolocale EFFE is a prototype for contemporary living in an ancient city. Seamlessly combining centuries of history and a fresh take on modern minimalism, it is a home that honours the past and looks to the future.

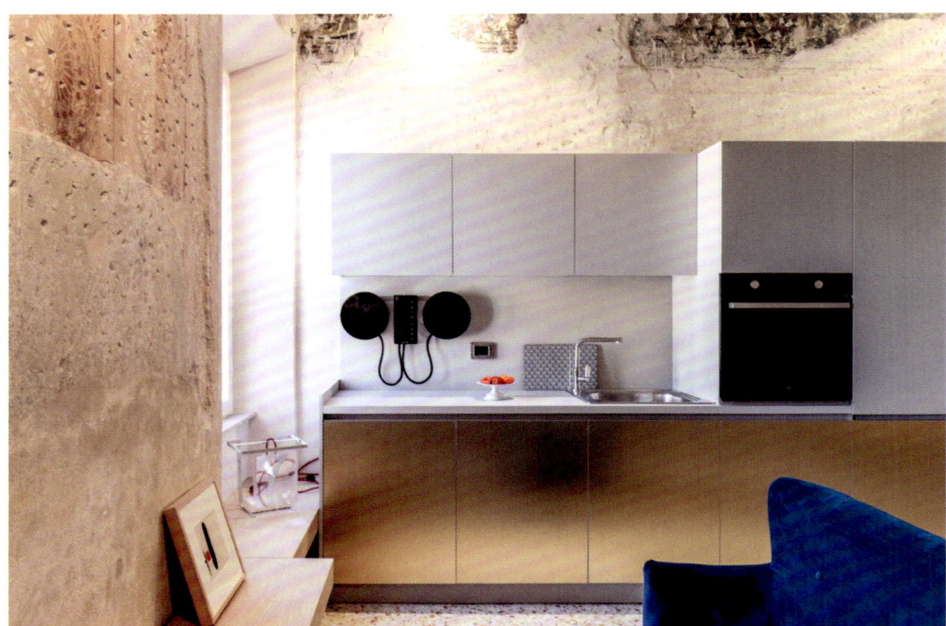

PAGE 162 During the renovation, beautiful frescoes were discovered under layers of paint and render. These walls immediately became a central focus of the design.

RIGHT The induction hob is wall mounted to free up bench space. The dishwasher and refrigerator are built in to continue the clean cohesive look.

AFTER

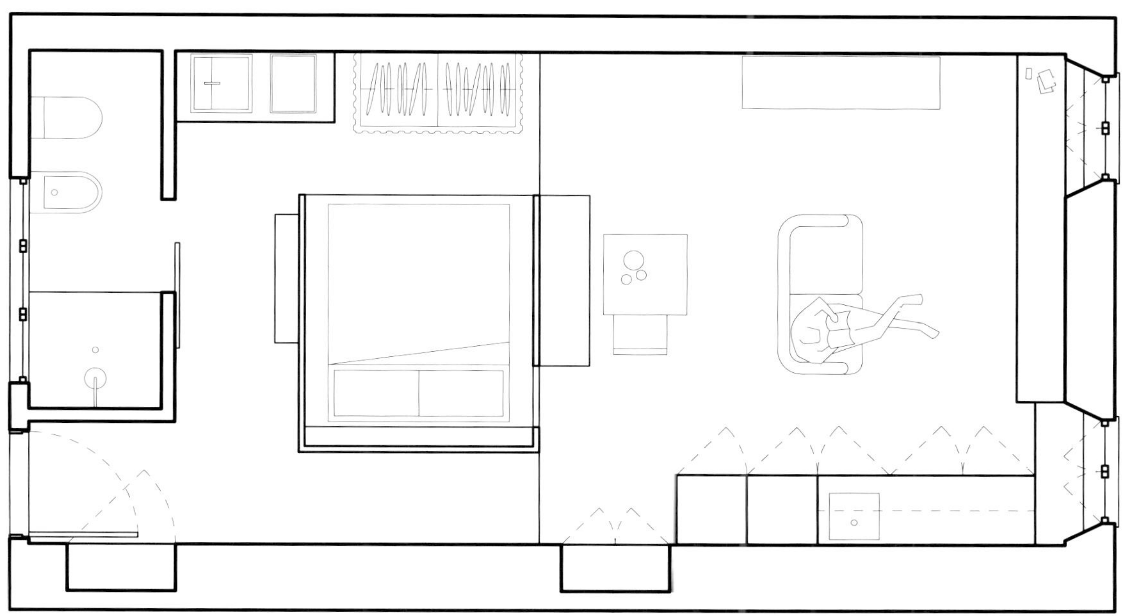

BEFORE

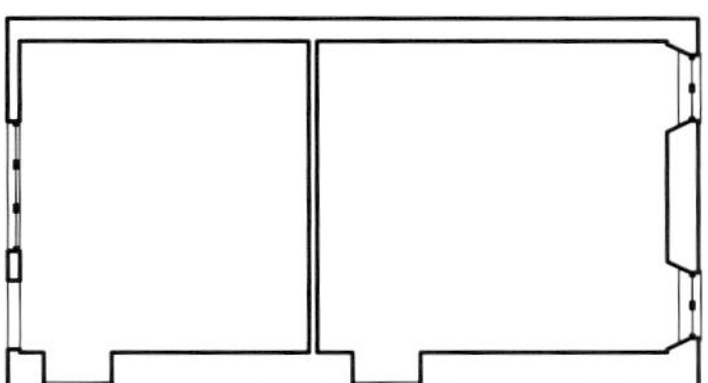

Scale 1:100

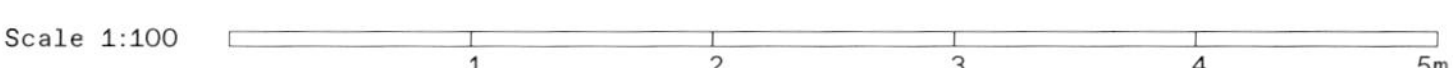

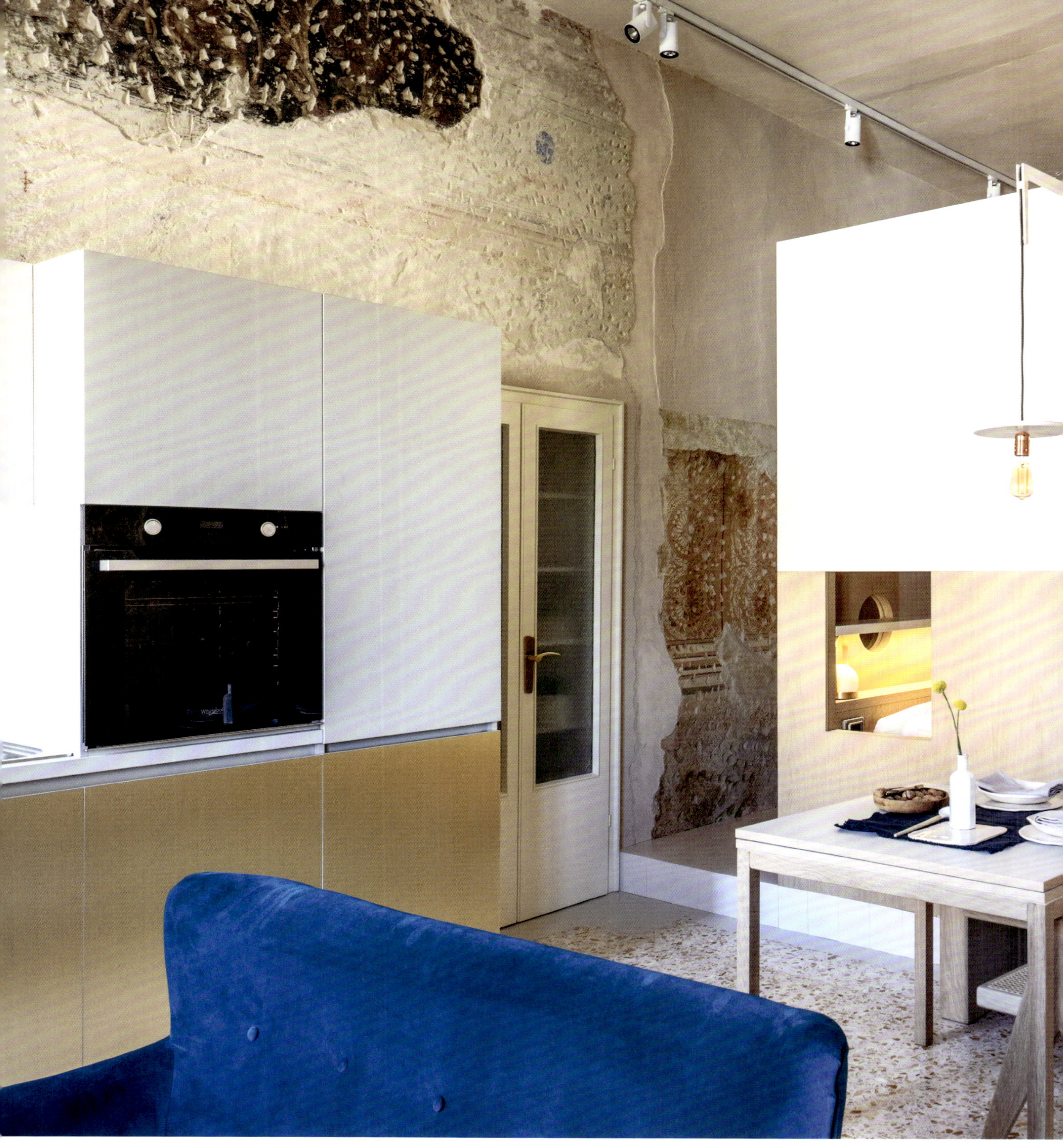

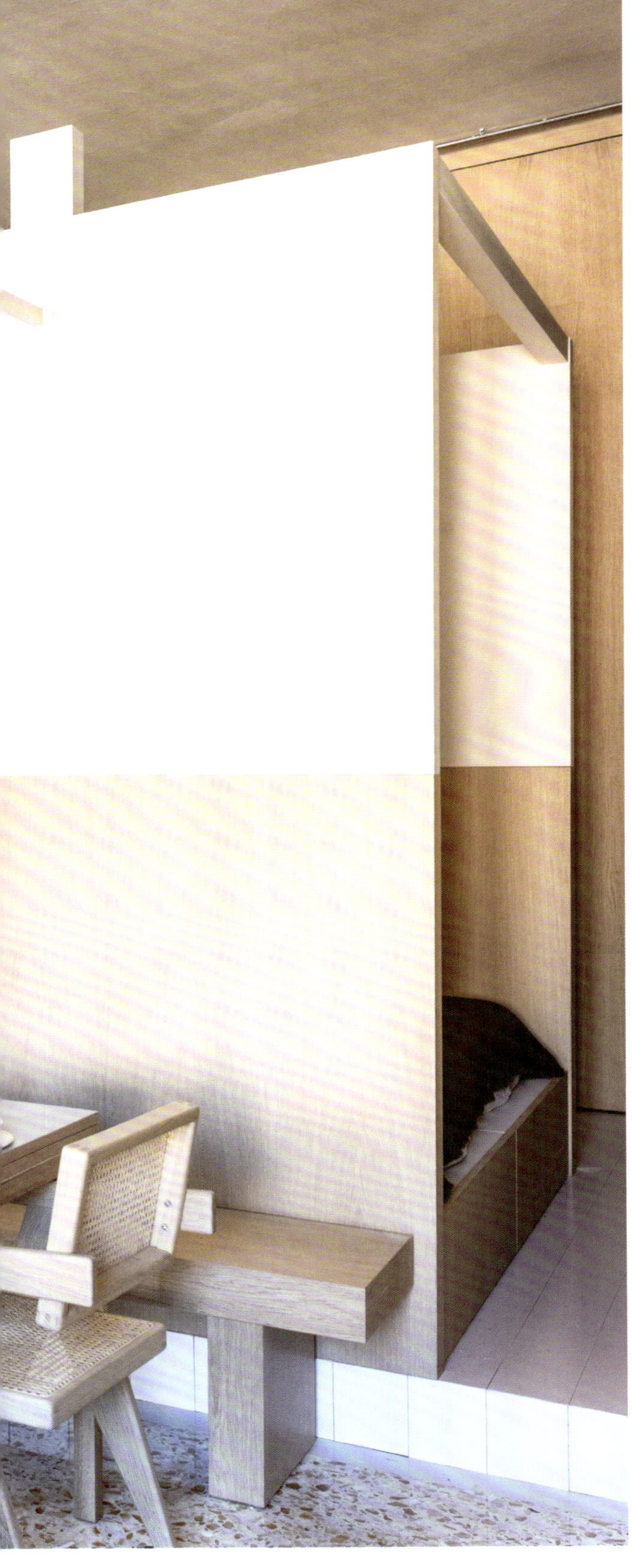

Monolocale EFFE is a prototype for contemporary living in an ancient city.

OPPOSITE Once the fresco walls were discovered, a 'central element' was needed to ground the space, so a bedroom cube was created. An extendable dining/work table sits alongside the bedroom cube.

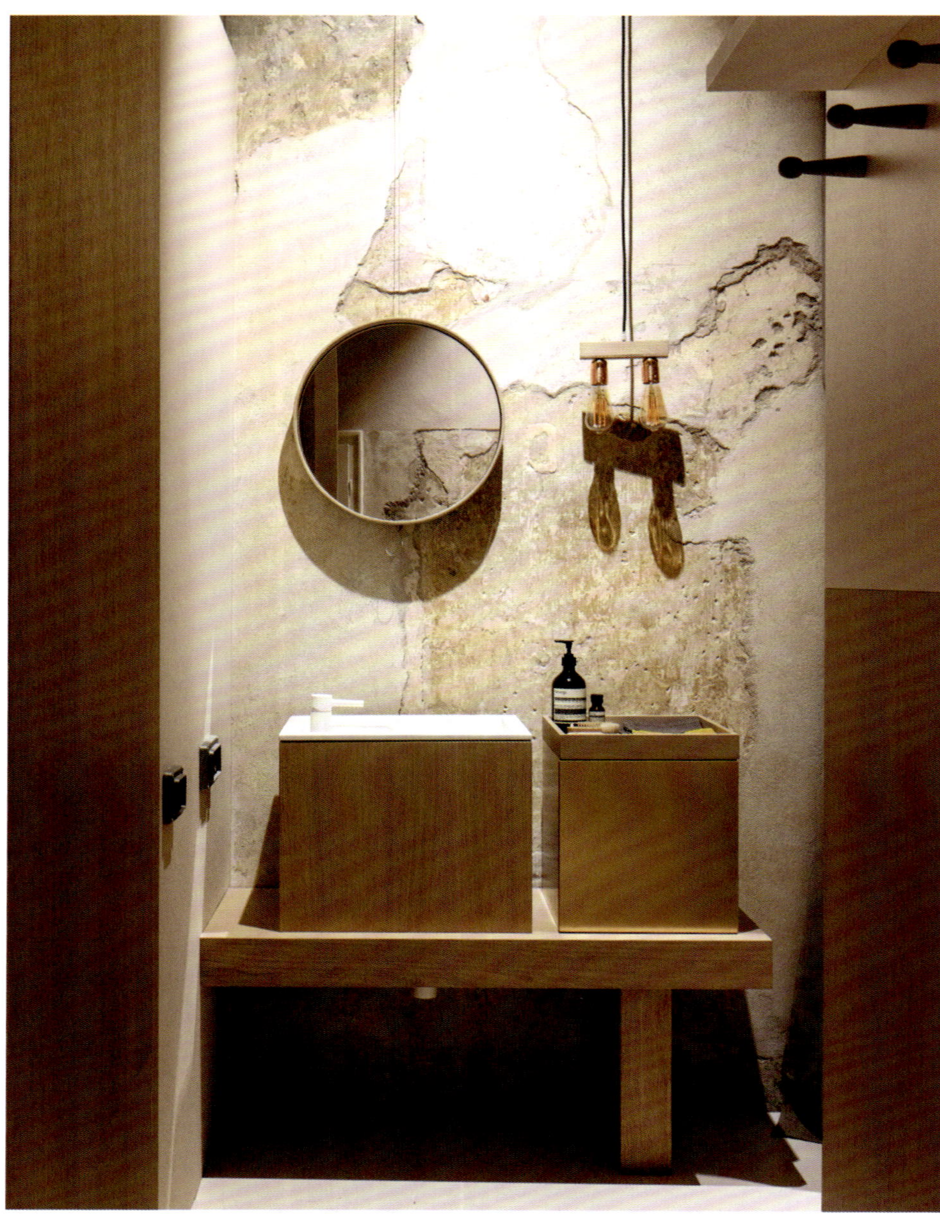

LEFT To keep the bathroom as minimal as possible, the plumbing was placed in the base of the sink. Next to the sink is a custom brass storage box.

OPPOSITE Inside the cosy bedroom cube, the integrated headboard has built-in shelves for a lamp and displaying personal belongings.

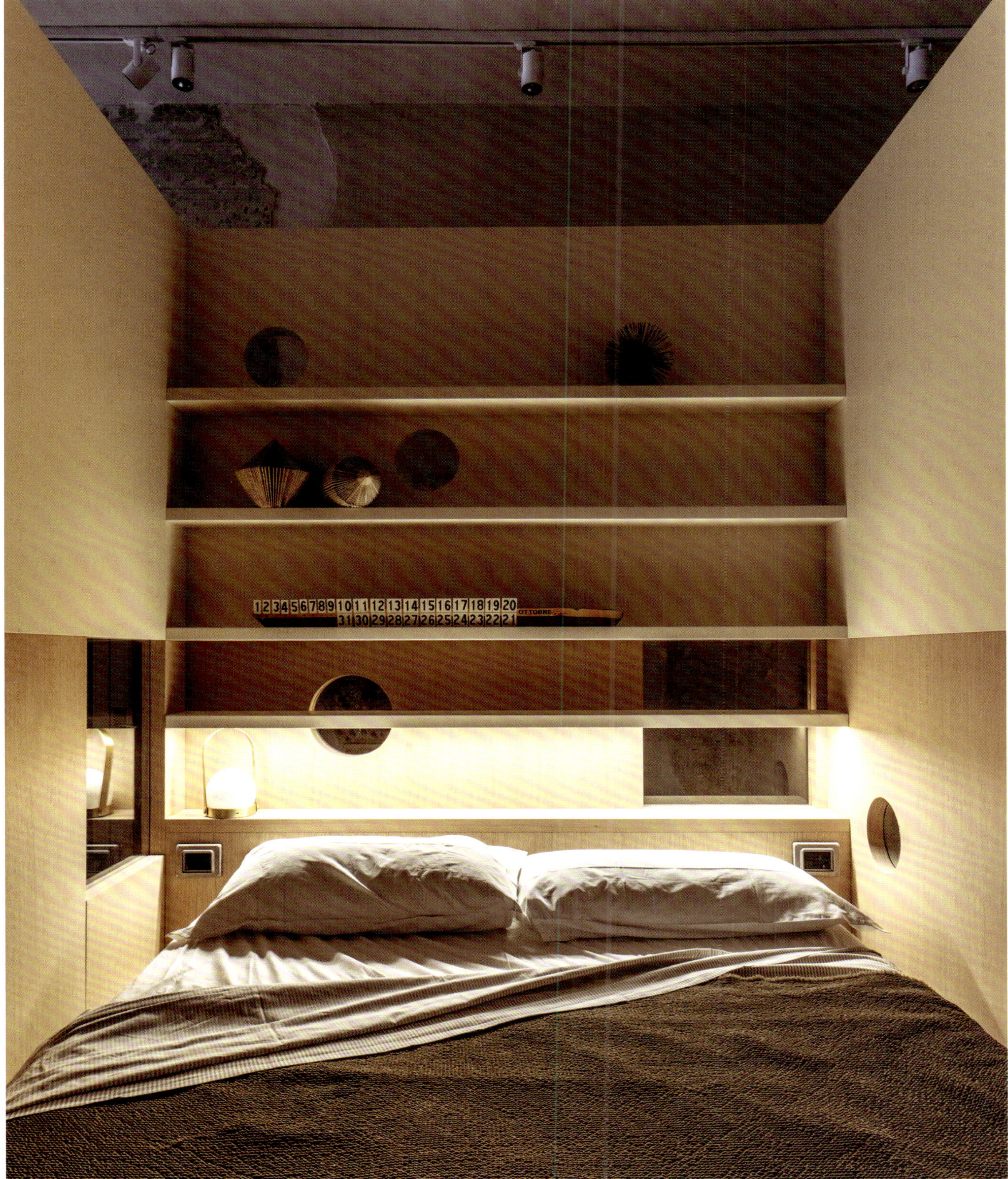
1 2 3 4 5 6 7 8 9 10 11 12 13 14 15 16 17 18 19 20
31 30 29 28 27 26 25 24 23 22 21
OTTOBRE

4

Experimental approaches in small-space design allow us to challenge preconceived notions, break free from the confines of traditional design constraints and unleash our creative potential. They invite us to question the status quo, daring us to ask: What if? What if we incorporate unconventional materials or reimagine the function of a particular space? What if we blur the lines between different areas, creating a seamless flow of energy and purpose? It is through experimentation that we can find answers to these questions and unlock new perspectives on how we live within compact environments.

At first, the concept of experimentation may seem daunting or unnecessary when dealing with such limited spaces. After all, wouldn't it be easier to stick to tried-and-true methods, following established norms and design conventions? However, by shying away from experimentation, we risk confining ourselves to a world of missed opportunities and unexplored possibilities.

Consider the Maximalist Mini Loft, which is a testament to the power of bold experimentation. Its daring colour palette – including vibrant pink doorknobs and a 3D-printed coffee table by architect and owner Anthony Authié – challenges conventional norms and injects personality into the space. By playing with different sizes of grains on the floor tiles and the tabletops, the loft embraces patterns and textures, transforming a small area into a visually captivating experience.

In Barcelona, EG112 simple dwelling is a prime example of how experimental approaches can enhance functionality and create a unique atmosphere. The open bathroom, featuring mustard-coloured

Experimental Approaches

tiles, becomes a striking focal point that integrates seamlessly with the overall aesthetic. Adopting a nautical theme, Jacobo Valentí created the ambience of being inside a boat, showcasing how experimental design choices can create a sense of wanderlust and charm. The clever utilisation of IKEA hacks demonstrates how even the most accessible solutions can be transformed into something extraordinary.

Candy Cube Residence by NC Design & Architecture Limited embraces the power of colour. This whimsical abode playfully combines vibrant hues, demonstrating how experimentation can bring joy and creativity to life. From the lighting in the bathroom, artfully imitating natural skylight, to the wave-like ceiling design subtly demarcating the space, every aspect of Candy Cube Residence showcases the transformative effects of experimental approaches.

By embracing experimental approaches, we open ourselves up to a world of limitless creativity and innovation. It is through experimentation that we discover unexpected solutions, ingenious hacks and game-changing designs that redefine what is possible in small-space living. Each step we take towards experimentation enables us to reimagine the boundaries and challenge the conventional limitations of space, materials and functionality.

Experimental approaches not only enhance the aesthetic appeal of small living, but contribute to their practicality and sustainability. They prompt us to explore alternative construction, eco-friendly materials and energy-efficient solutions. Experimentation is not only about creating visually striking spaces; it is about finding sustainable ways to utilise resources and minimise our ecological footprint.

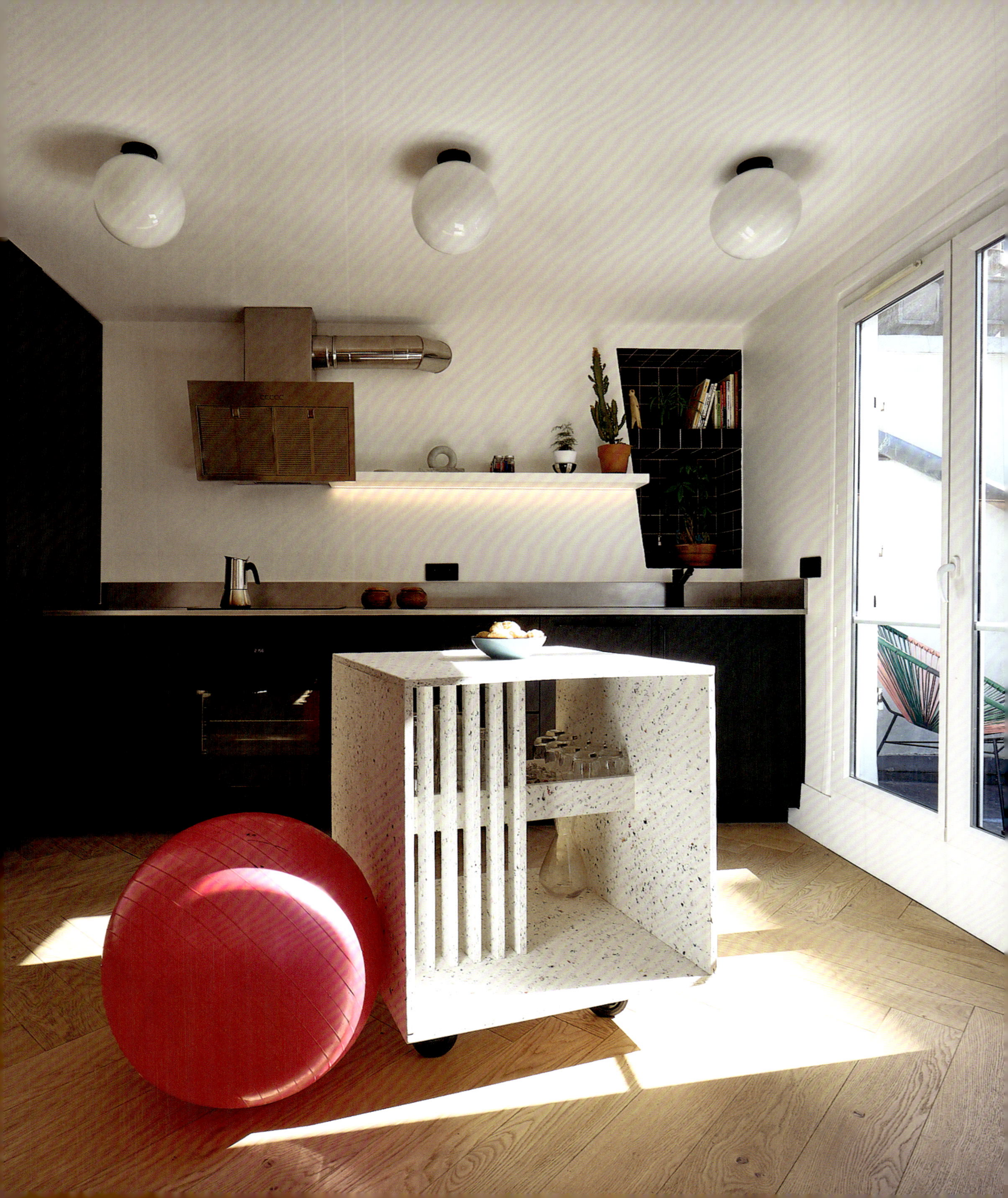

Stroboscope

42m² / 452ft²
studiobravo
Opera District, Paris

Rumoured to have once been the next-door neighbour of Napoleon, Stroboscope sits on the fifth floor of a Haussmann-style building constructed after the French Revolution. Like so much of Paris, it seems history happened here.

When architects Marion Richards and Thomas Pellerin first saw it, the 'overall heritage style of the apartment was already lost'. The rooms were dark and completely disproportionate to the space, and a thorough overhaul was needed. They reimagined the layout so that the original kitchen, which was the darkest area, became the bedroom, and a new kitchen and bathroom were built.

From the entryway there is a sightline through the 42-sq-m (452-sq-ft) apartment and out to a large balcony overlooking the facades of the 9th district of Paris. On one side of the entry, there is a wall lined in cork sheeting – a simple way of personalising the space and changing the decor as the client desires. On the other side, through a set of double-glazed doors, there is the arresting blue bedroom. The vibrancy of this blue, thanks to International Klein Blue, makes the colour sing even in the apartment's darkest room. There are two narrow walk-in wardrobes: one niche is for the client's clothes and the other is a compact laundry.

Light washes into the room via a skylight and the bathroom is a white-tiled, dark-grouted minimal space complete with translucent glass walls with black oblique lines. Tucked away at the back of the bathroom is the toilet. Unlike the bathroom, it is tiled in black.

PAGE 172 The eye-catching kitchen island was custom made from recycled plastic and can be moved around the room as needed.

BELOW A multifunctional bench in the living area lines the wall. It acts in part as a dining area, lounging area and can fold out to a single bed.

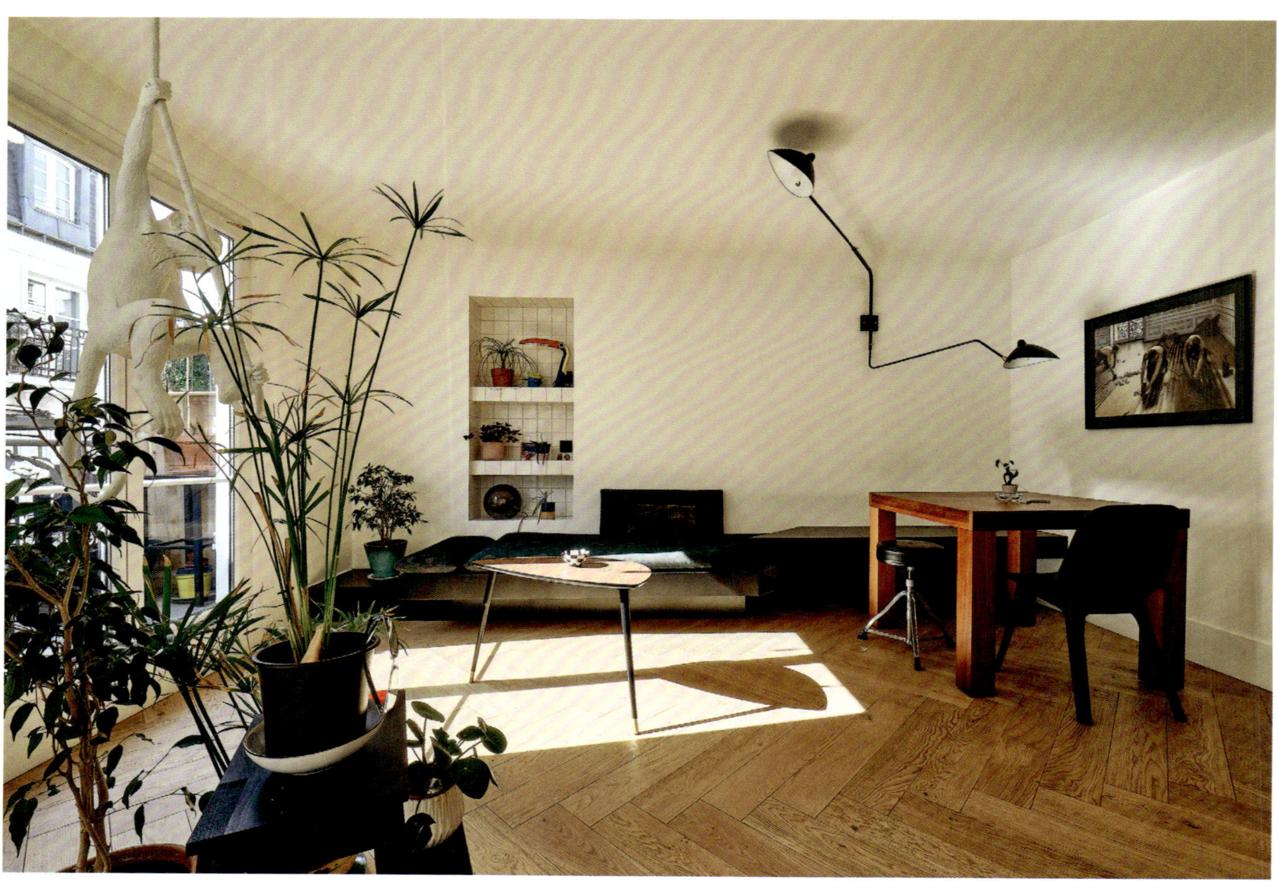

AFTER

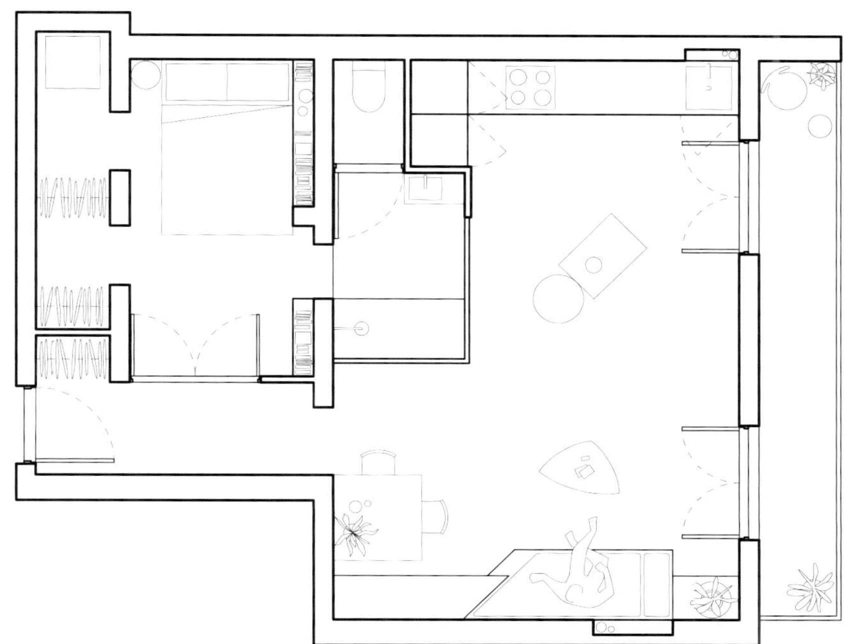

BEFORE

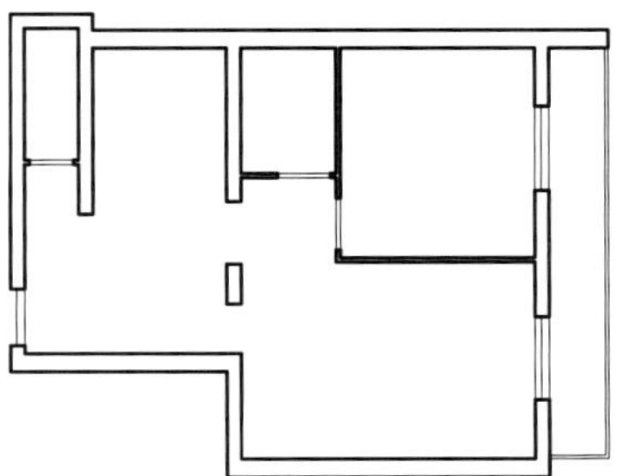

Scale 1:100

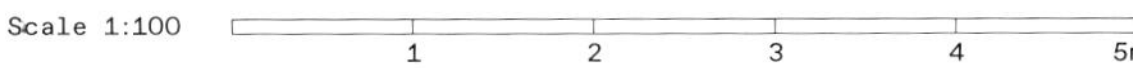

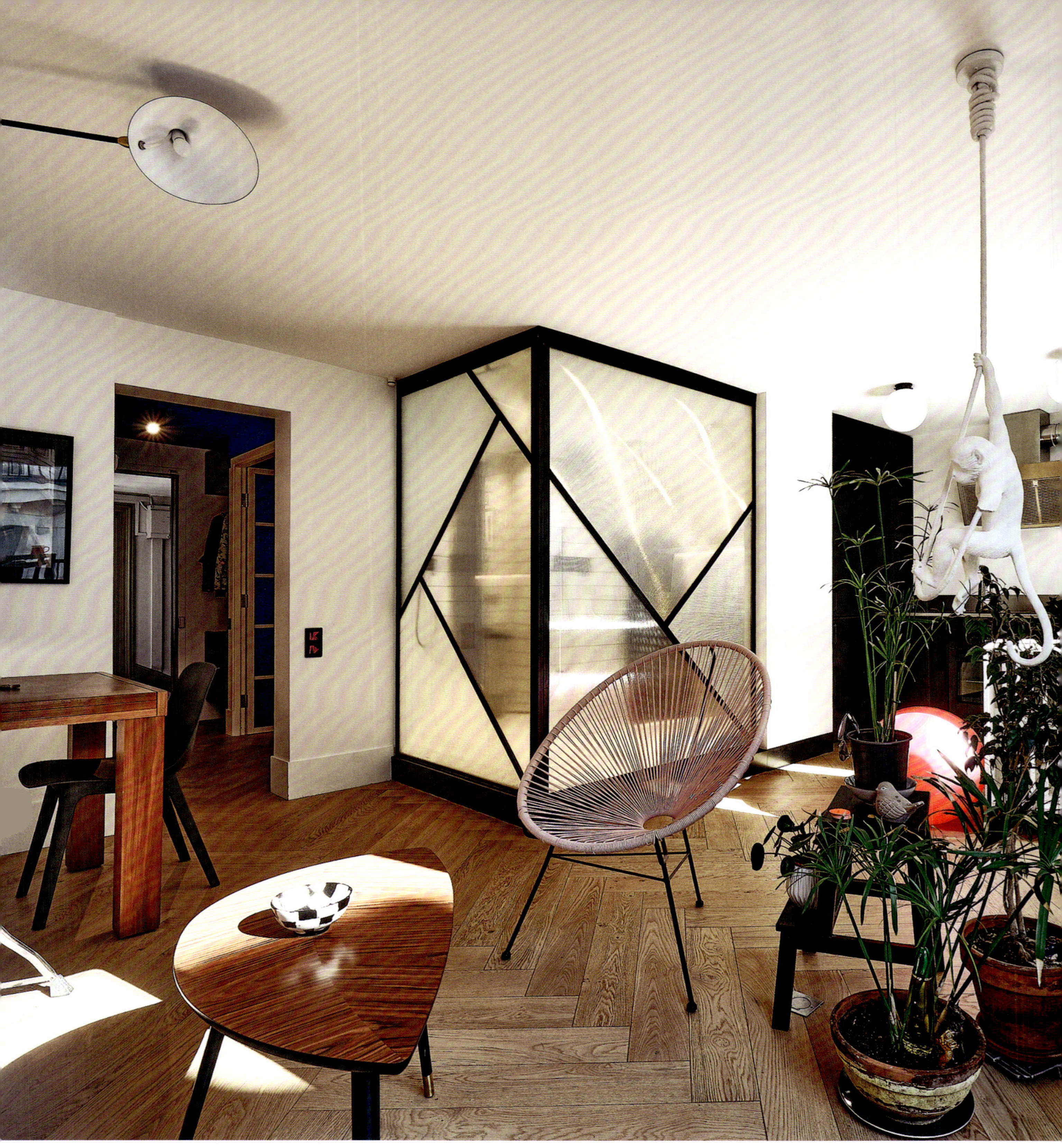

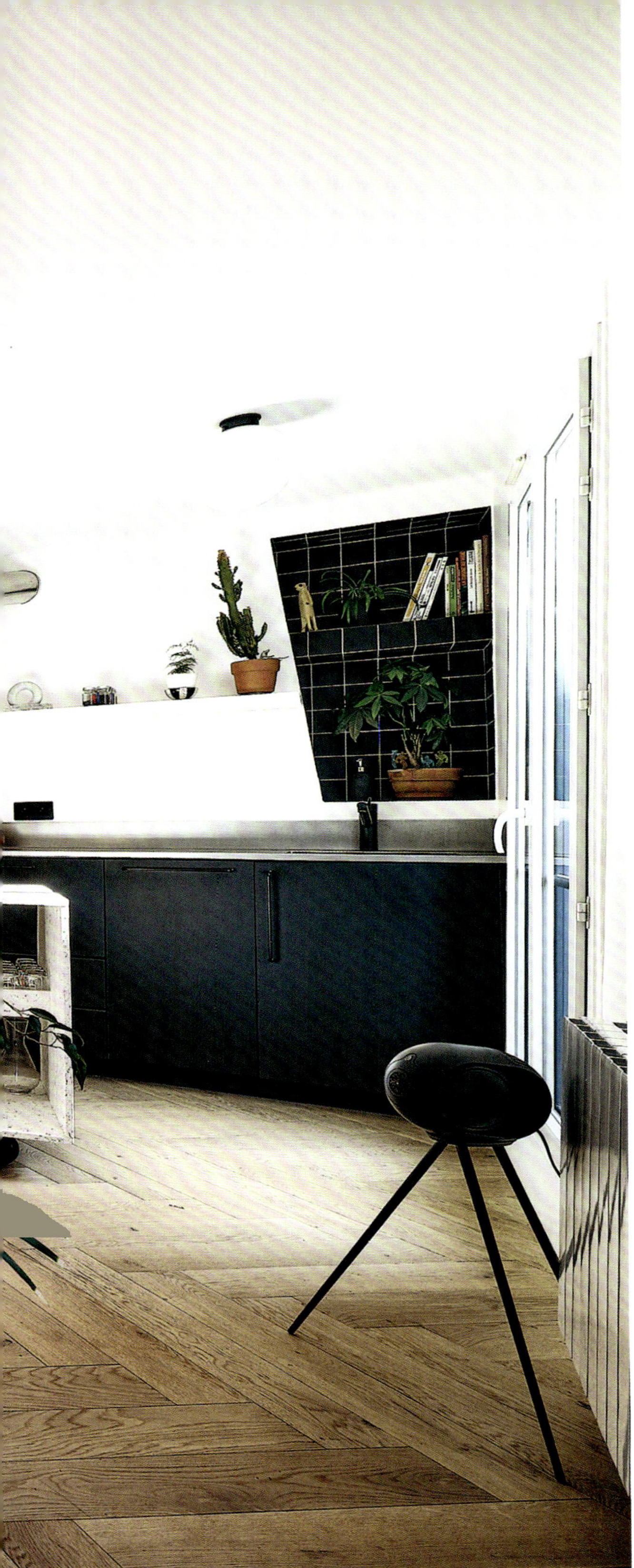

As there were windows on only one side of the apartment, the glass walls in the bathroom serve multiple purposes. During the day they lend natural light to the bedroom and at night, they turn the bathroom into a huge lightbox that illuminates the whole apartment.

The studiobravo team explains that 'maximising light in all areas with transparent walls while keeping a sense of intimacy was inspired by the work of Charlotte Perriand in her Japanese projects'.

On the other side of the glass wall is the living room. Here the wall also serves as a feature of the space. The living room is a generous area that was kept purposely minimal to accommodate visitors. A multifunctional bench in black wood lines the wall. Designed on two levels, it appears to be levitating off the floor. The upper side is seating for the dining area and the lower side is a couch. Leftover white tiles from the bathroom were used to line the open shelves.

The fully equipped kitchen has stainless-steel benchtops and ample storage. The recessed shelving, covered in black tiles, mirrors the white shelves in the living room. The kitchen island, a custom piece made from recycled plastic, provides more workspace and storage, and can be moved around as needed.

In Stroboscope everything ties together with a black bow. The kitchen facades and living room bench are black, matching the structure of the feature glass wall. The black taps and faucets in the bathroom tie into the black tiles used in the powder room and shelving in the kitchen.

This home is not trying to be a warm embrace. Instead, it celebrates rare-yet-decadent minimalism while confidently ticking all the boxes required to be a completely unique dwelling in the heart of Paris.

LEFT One of the client's goals was to have a home with as much light as possible. Pellerin captured the light in a previously dark area of the home by creating a 'lightbox' effect with the glass bathroom walls.

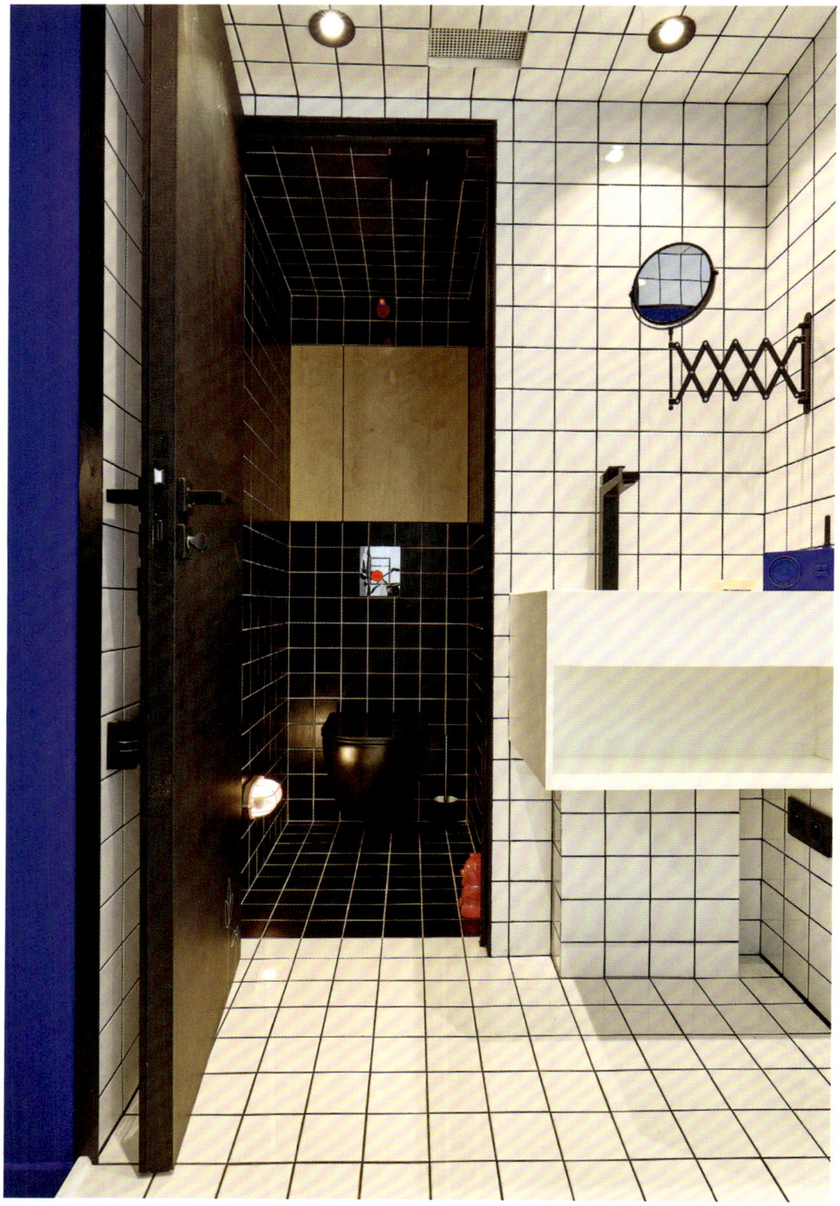

LEFT Black accents reign throughout the home. The black tapware in the bathroom ties in with the black tiles in the toilet room.

OPPOSITE The striking International Klein Blue bedroom features a large wooden beam that was left exposed to 'pay homage to the history of the building'. It was also painted the same distinct shade of blue and acts as a sculptural element in the room.

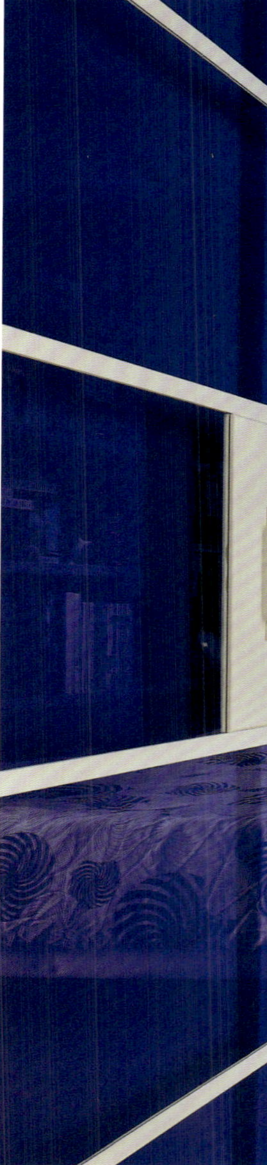

In Stroboscope everything ties together with a black bow.

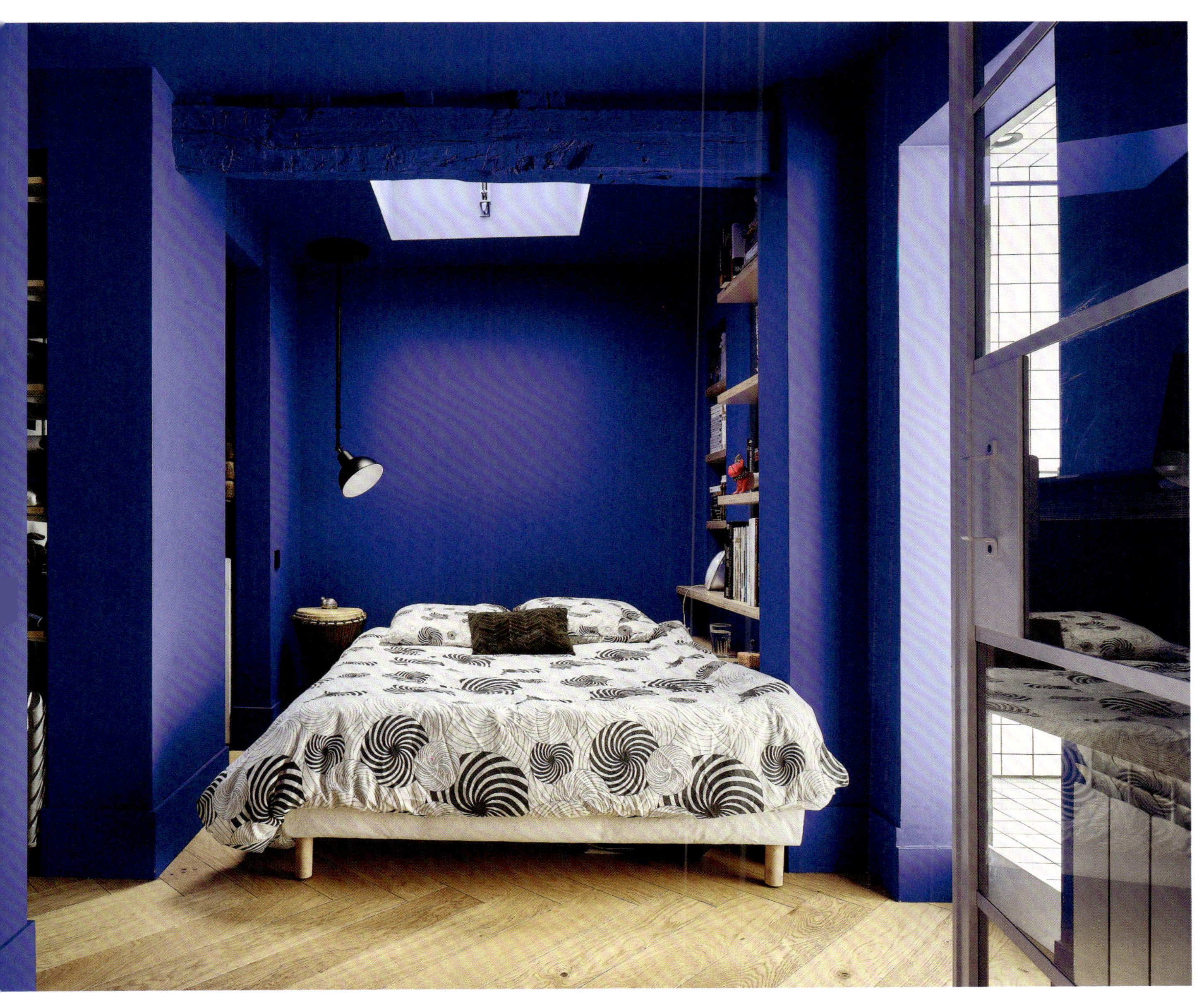

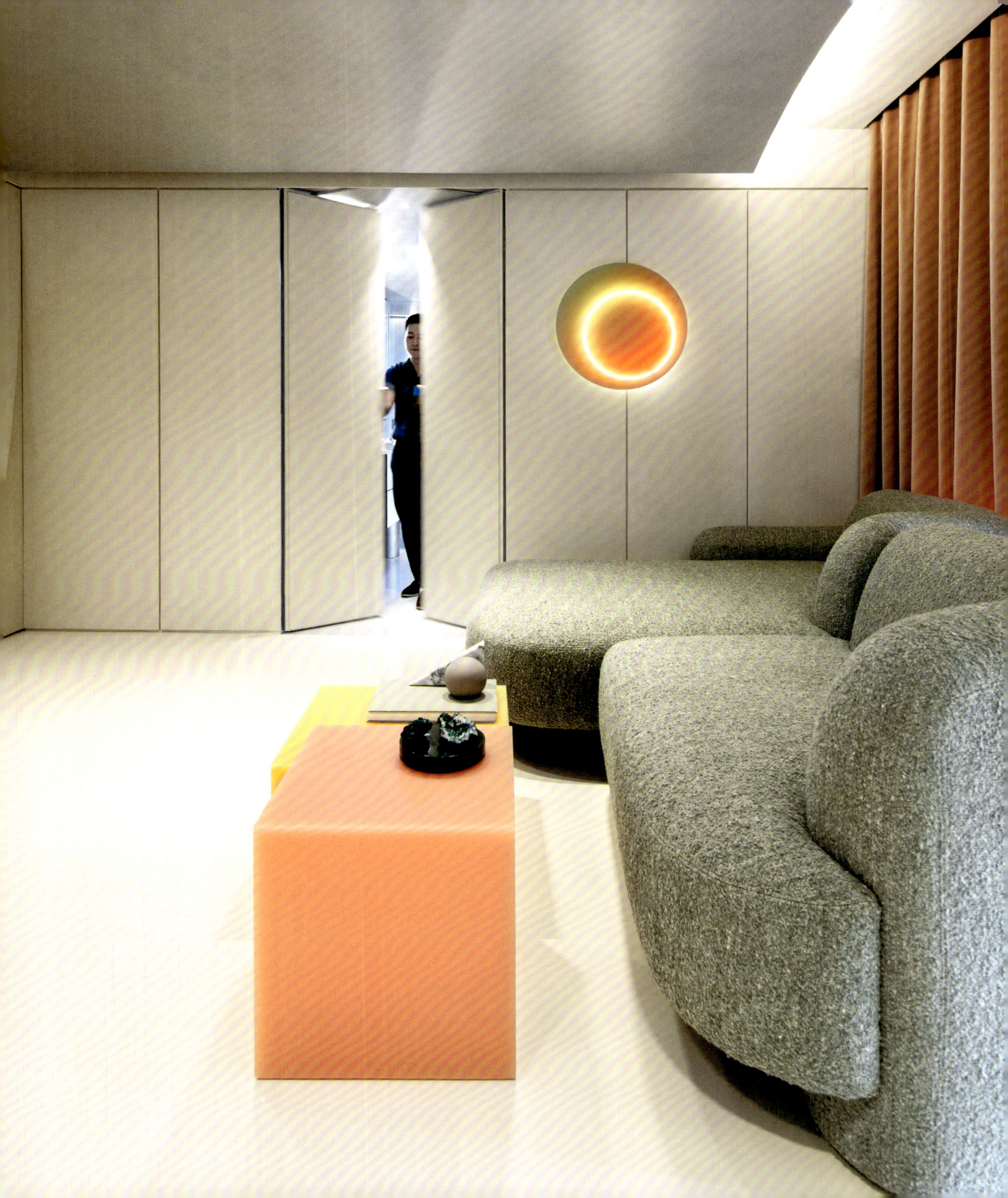

Candy Cube Residence

59m² / 635ft²
NC Design & Architecture Limited
Tai Hung, Hong Kong

A little bit of sweetness in a heaving, thriving city is how Nelson Chow's Candy Cube Residence feels. Designed for a close friend who wanted a fun, colourful and futuristic home with generous storage, the bustle of Hong Kong is left behind when you step into this apartment.

Chow and his team of designers at NC Design & Architecture Limited felt that the original floor plan was not utilised to its full potential, so they removed the internal walls and opened the space up into a single large room with a separate area for the bathroom and kitchen. In doing so, they maximised the generous 59-sq-m (635-sq-ft) floor plan.

The living room is like a sugary treat, while the kitchen, stark and metallic, is like the spoon it is served on. It is long and narrow with a door at either end, one of which serves as the entrance to the apartment. The balcony lets in a good amount of natural light, making the kitchen brighter than the space should allow. Upon stepping through the kitchen into the main room, you're transported to a different era.

Curved walls, moveable dividers and vivid furniture complement each other and create a critical role in dividing the home's various functions. The finishes and lighting are futuristic, but the colours are 70s-inspired, creating an 'Asimovian' atmosphere.

PAGE 180 A vision as bold as Candy Cube Residence had to be executed precisely. Custom furniture and a considered approach to colour are key to its success.

BELOW White walls and cabinets are offset with bursts of colour and light.

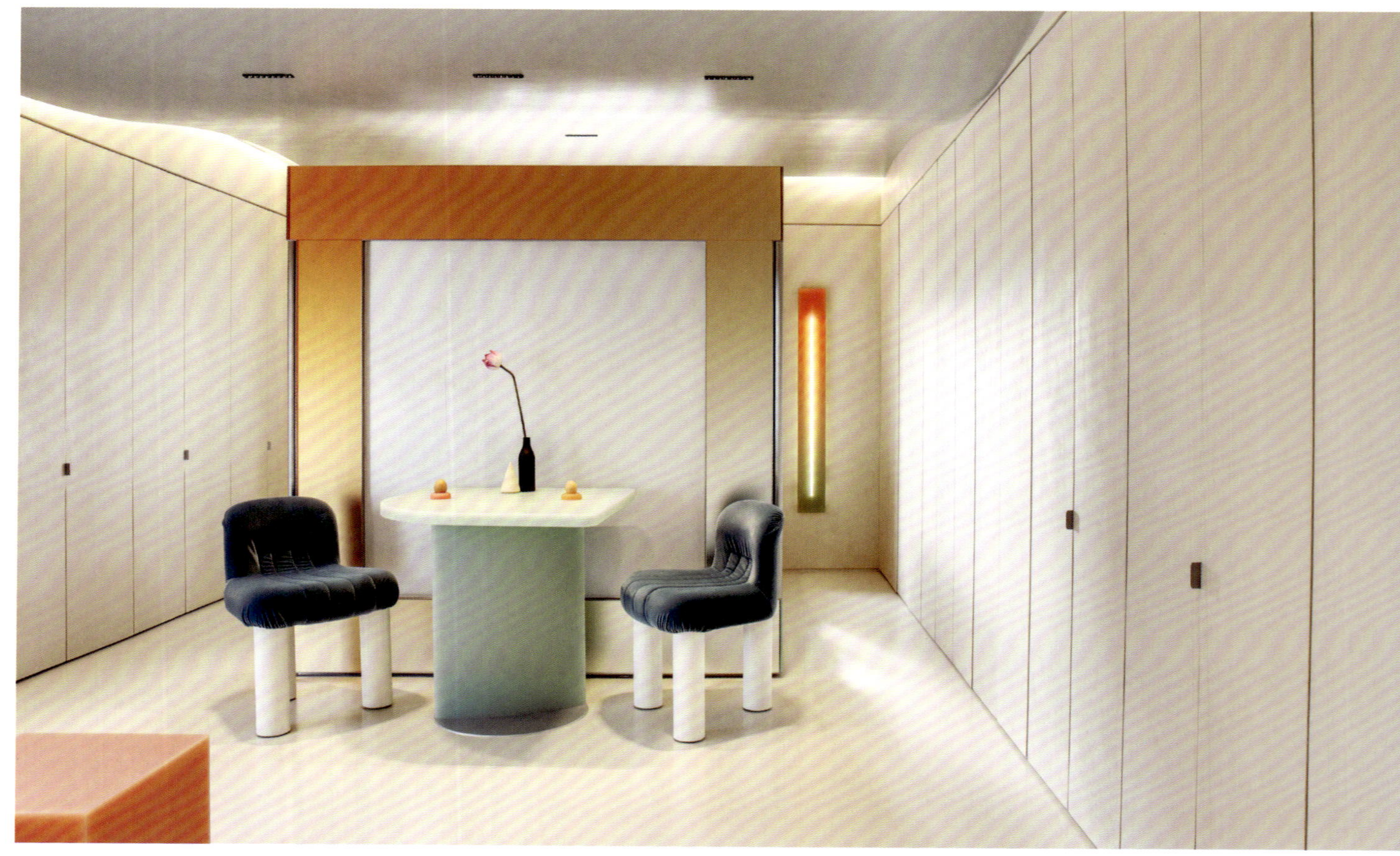

AFTER

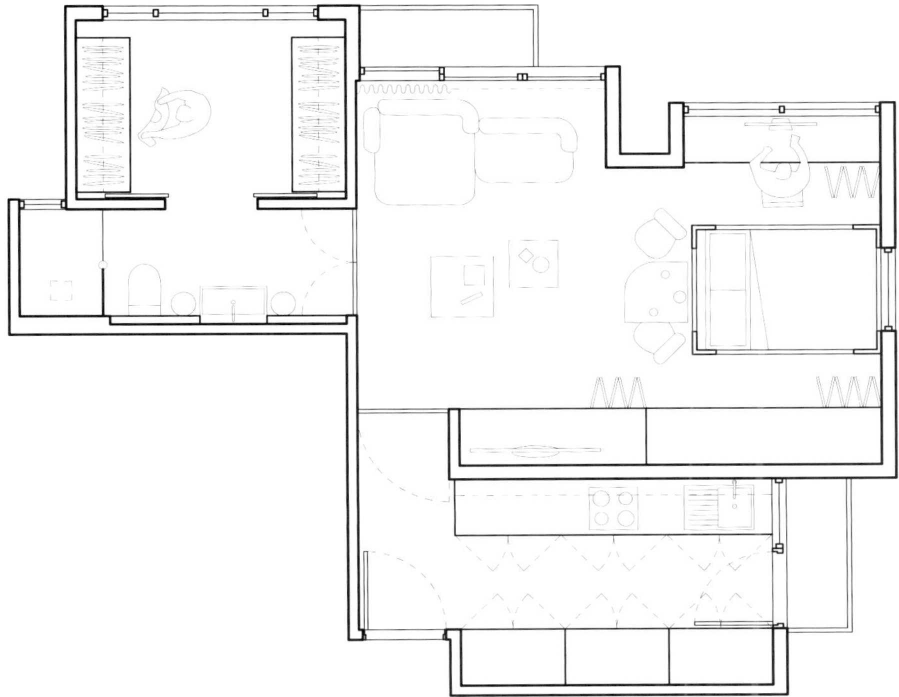

BEFORE

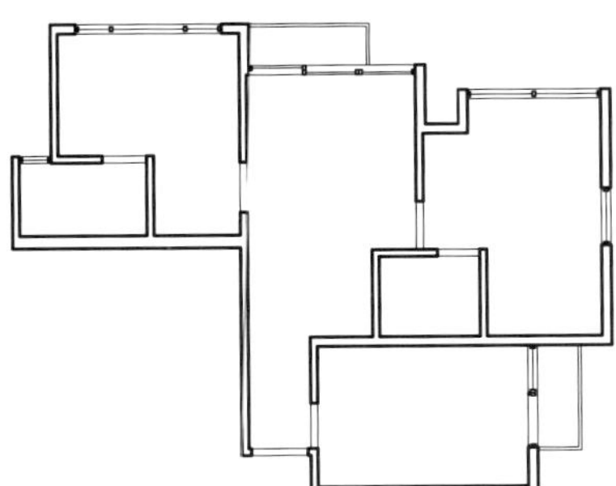

Scale 1:100

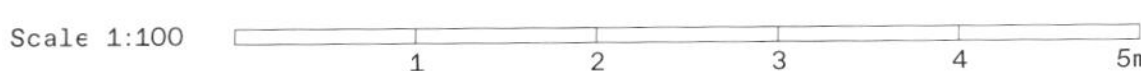

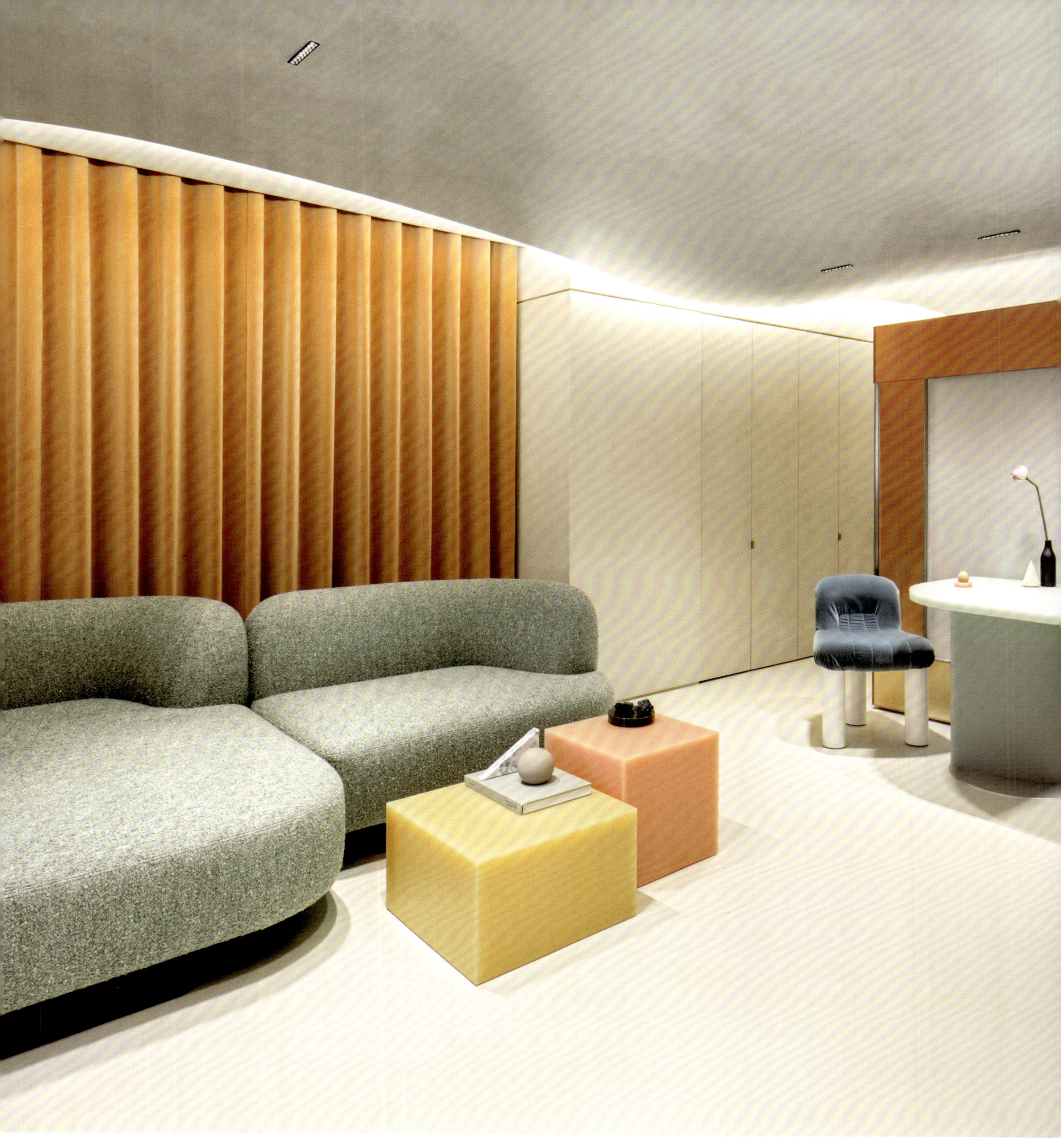

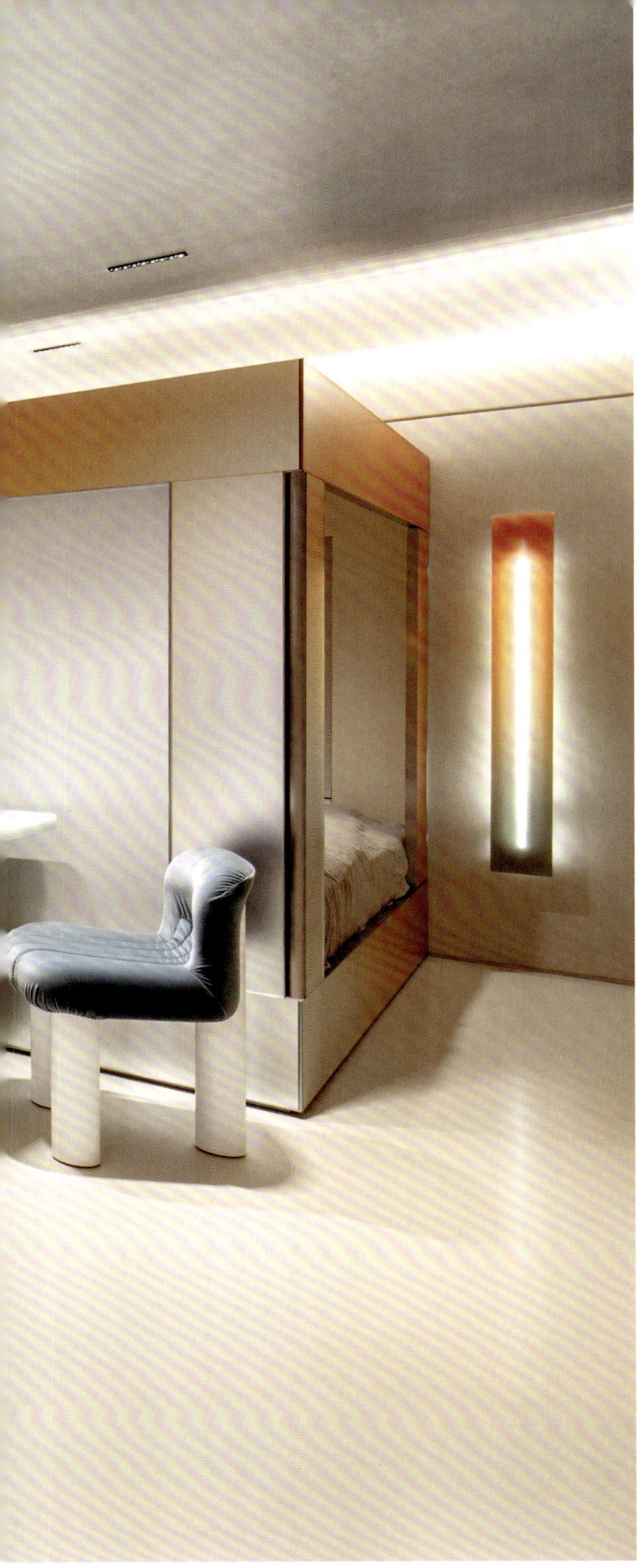

The living, dining and sleeping areas are all in this space and are defined by custom furniture that tastefully decorates each zone. The bed itself is housed in a cube, divided from the living room by a bright wall that acts as a backdrop to the larger area. Accessible from both sides and with plenty of natural light, the team has managed to make the space feel very cosy and while integrated, quite separate. All the furnishings were carefully selected and designed for this home, from the custom curved kitchen door with a sculptural handle to the Cini Boeri Botolo armchairs with wheels that serve as both dining and office chairs.

Chow worked with Sabine Marcelis to design one-off, sculptural resin pieces, including the candy-coloured coffee tables and the semi-transparent soap dining table that emits a soft glow. The lighting in the apartment is called Dawn Lighting and gradates from orange to green, adding to the playful atmosphere of the space.

With its custom furniture, hidden details and bold use of colour, Candy Cube Residence is a work of art, or, as Chow describes it, 'a futuristic space that feels like a gallery'.

LEFT The primary bedroom is a peaceful space enclosed within the 'cube'. A feng shui master was consulted on the best orientation for sleeping.

The living room is like a sugary treat, while the kitchen, stark and metallic, is like the spoon it is served on.

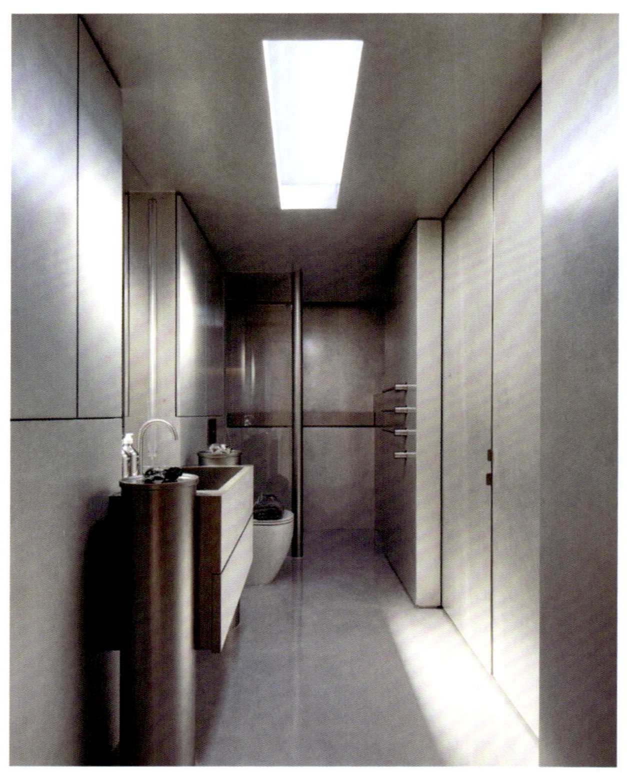

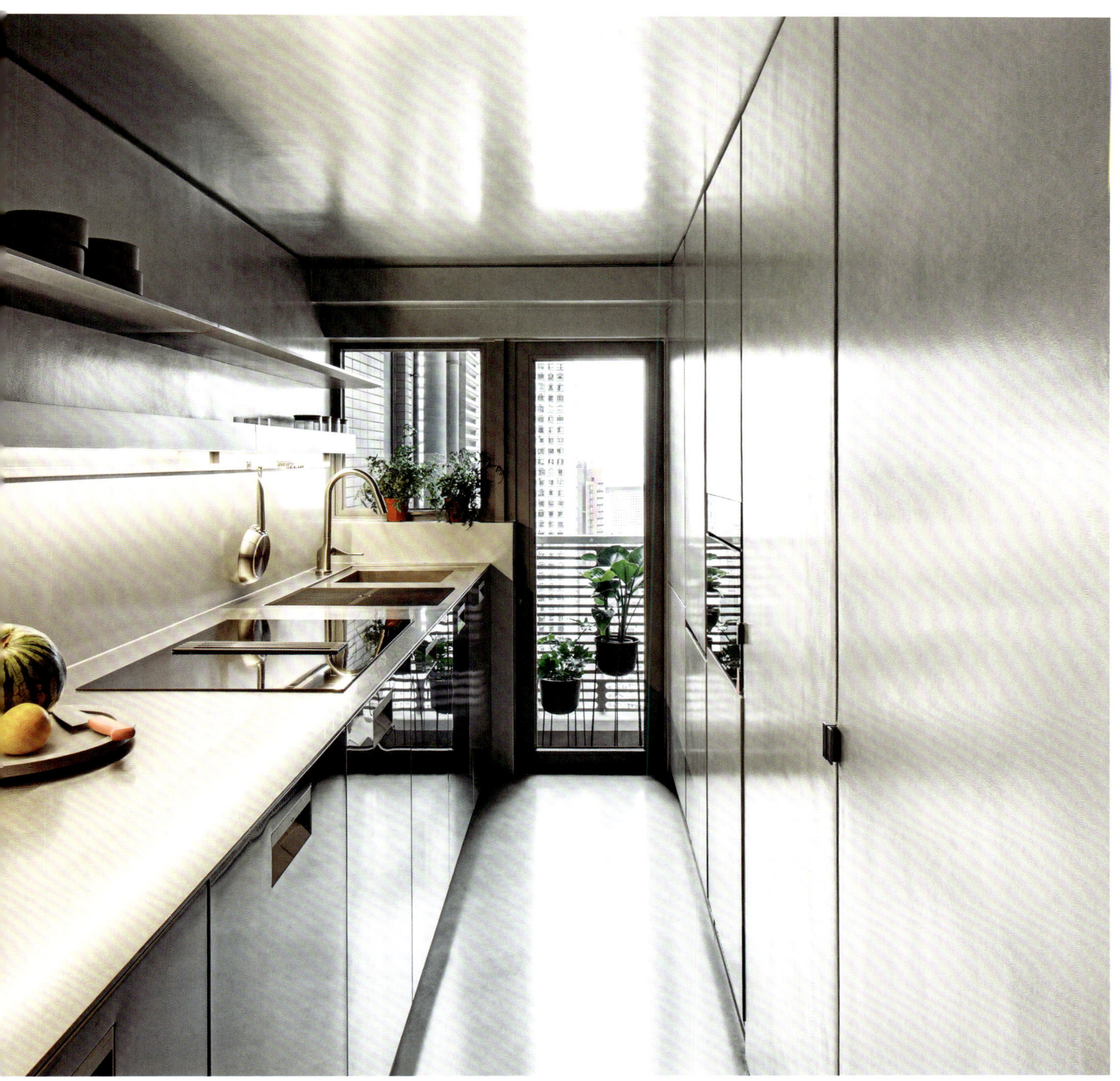

OPPOSITE Chow describes the team's inspiration for the bathroom was 'a space that feels like you're entering a spaceship'.

ABOVE The narrow kitchen is offset by its length and ample bench space. Using metallic finishes also makes it feel larger, as light bounces off surfaces.

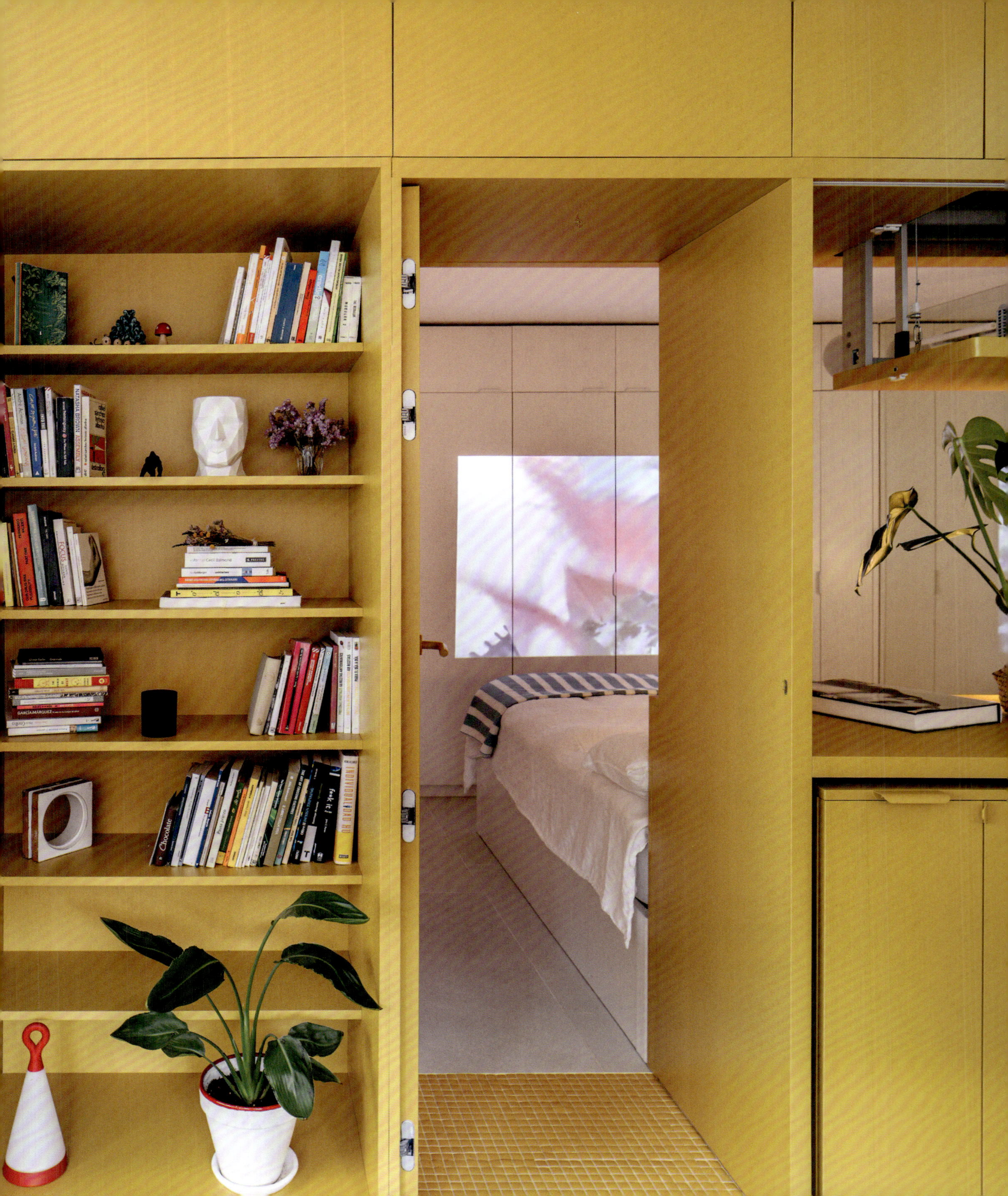
NATASHA BROWN
Chocolate

Casa Gialla

47m² / 506ft²
gon architects
Sol, Madrid

When Gonzalo Pardo and the team at gon architects were renovating a one-bedroom apartment on a budget, form and function were top of mind. Located in La Puerta del Sol, one of Madrid's busiest squares, their client wanted a space big enough for her and her partner that was stylish and functional with clever storage. Inspired by the bold use of colour and geometry of 1960s Italian apartments, Casa Gialla was transformed according to three principles – demolish, drill and equip.

‘The load-bearing wall between the bedroom and the living/kitchen/dining room was removed to generate unity,’ explains Pardo. ‘Then new perforations were made in the roof to introduce as much natural light as possible.’ A bright yellow floor-to-ceiling storage system was also erected along the perimeter to maximise storage in the living, kitchen and office/utility areas.

This unique wall design, which extends along the entire length of the 47-sq-m (506-sq-ft) apartment, allows for the option of enclosing or opening the bedroom up to the rest of the living space. A curtain can be drawn to completely close off the bedroom when the owners have guests over or when they want to make it feel extra cosy. A projector was integrated into the storage area, which can be directed towards either the living area or the bedroom.

The main area of the apartment features a spacious rectangular layout that offers versatility through the various functions of the feature wall for different events and occasions – whether it’s hosting a party, entertaining friends, watching a movie or enjoying a quiet night in. An abundance of custom cabinetry hides a table, laundry appliances and even a Murphy bed for when guests stay.

To ensure a seamless transition from indoor to outdoor space, the design utilises large tiles that extend towards a bi-fold door leading out to the terrace and an outdoor shower and bathtub.

Despite the limited budget, the apartment is functional and a visually pleasing space. The team chose to save on IKEA storage solutions for areas like the bedroom wardrobe and spend their furniture budget on the striking floor-to-ceiling yellow storage unit. This focus on design has produced a home that is both bright and inviting with a stylish flair that’s evident in every corner.

PAGE 188 Flush joinery and integrated shelves were elevated by the explosion of sunny yellow.

AFTER

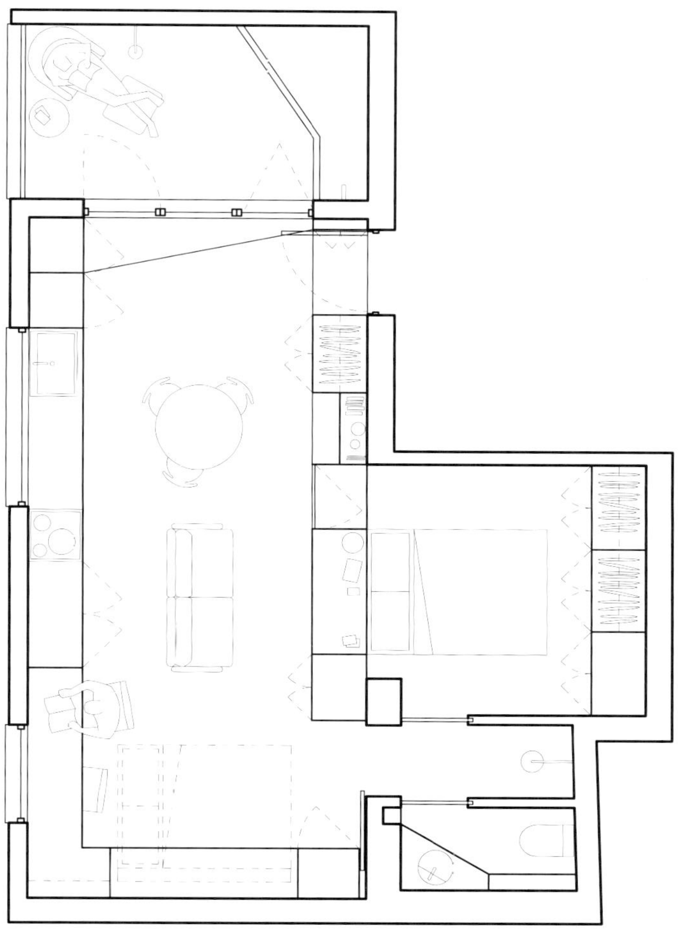

BEFORE

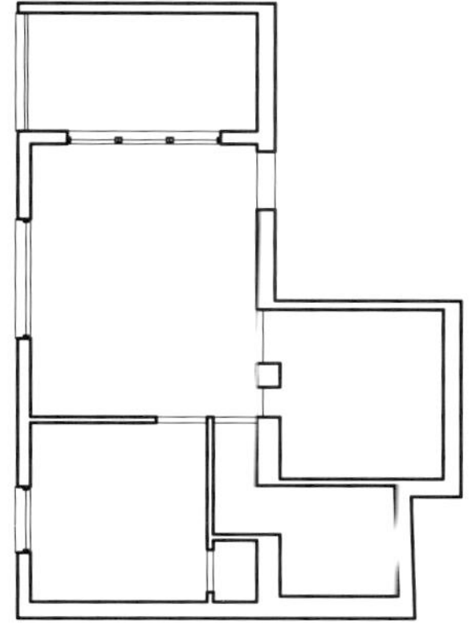

Scale 1:100 1 2 3 4 5m

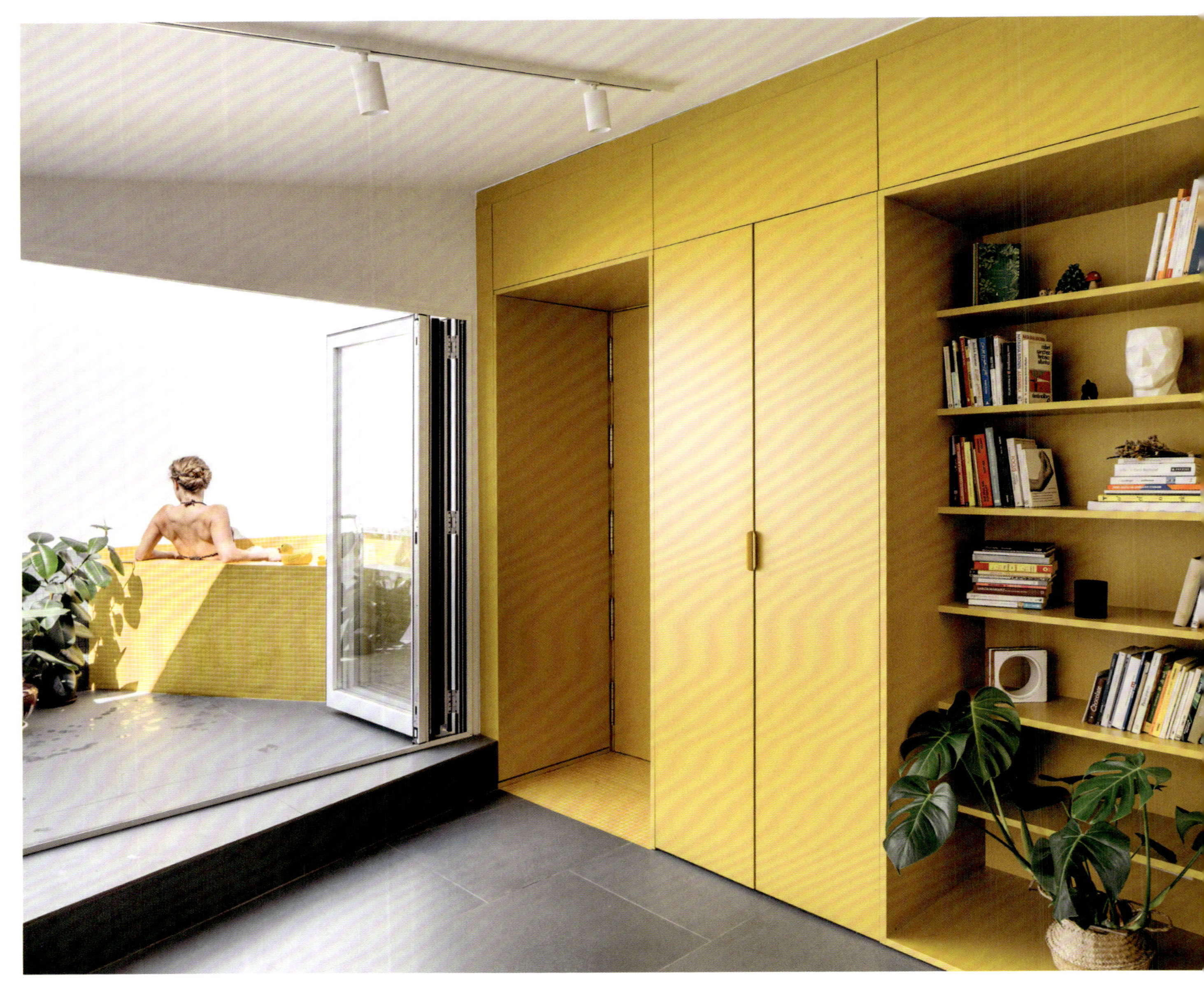

Casa Gialla was transformed according to three principles – demolish, drill and equip.

OPPOSITE The grey tiling continues up and over the step to merge the indoor and outdoor areas.

BELOW In the bedroom, the yellow transitions suddenly into white and the room becomes a calmer, more peaceful space.

BOTTOM Curtains can be drawn to create privacy in the bedroom.

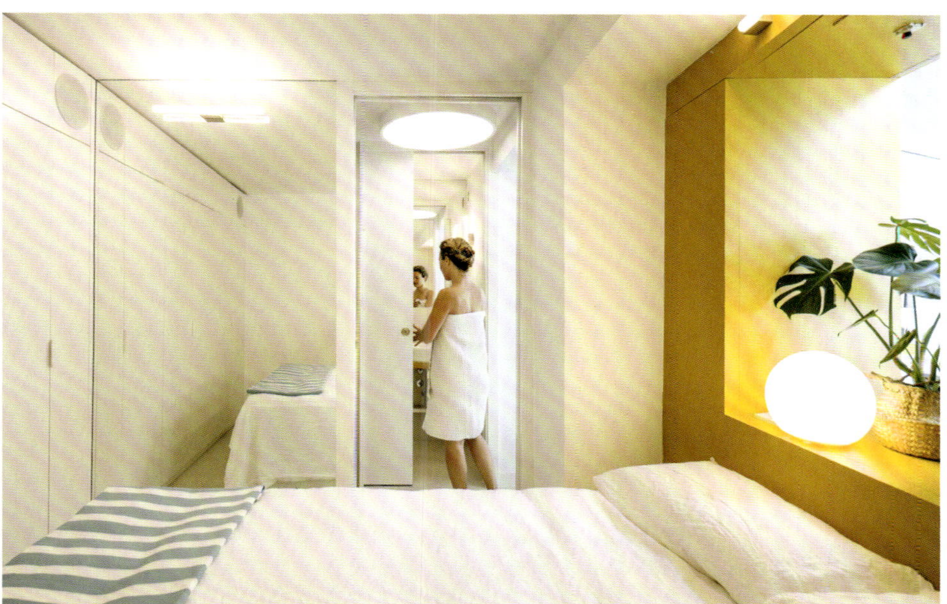

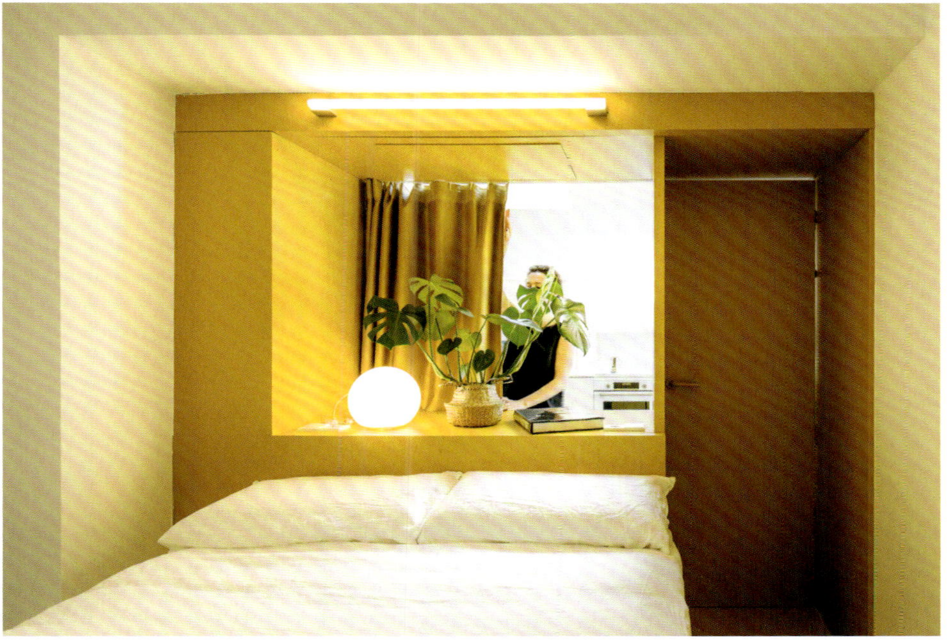

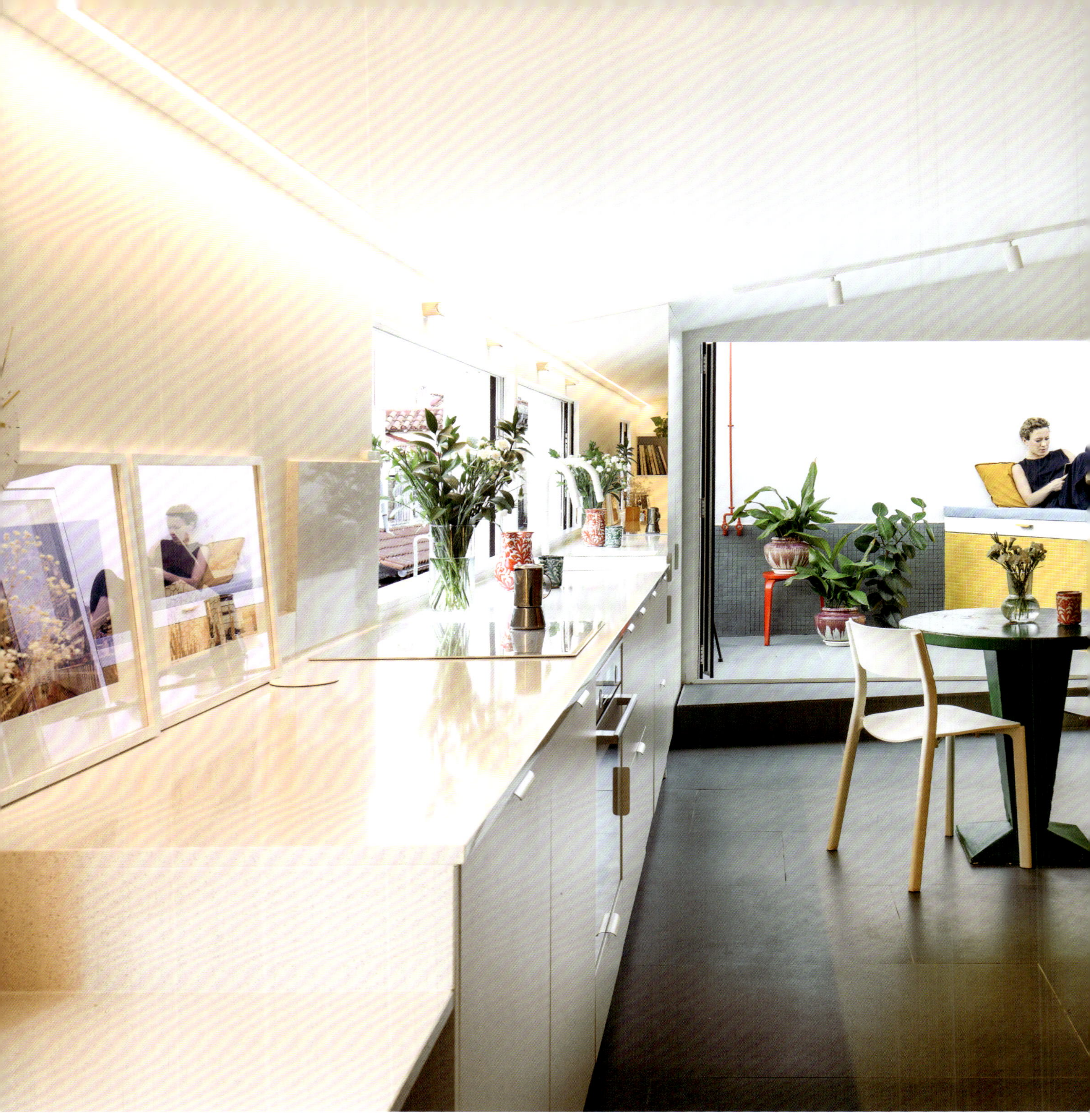

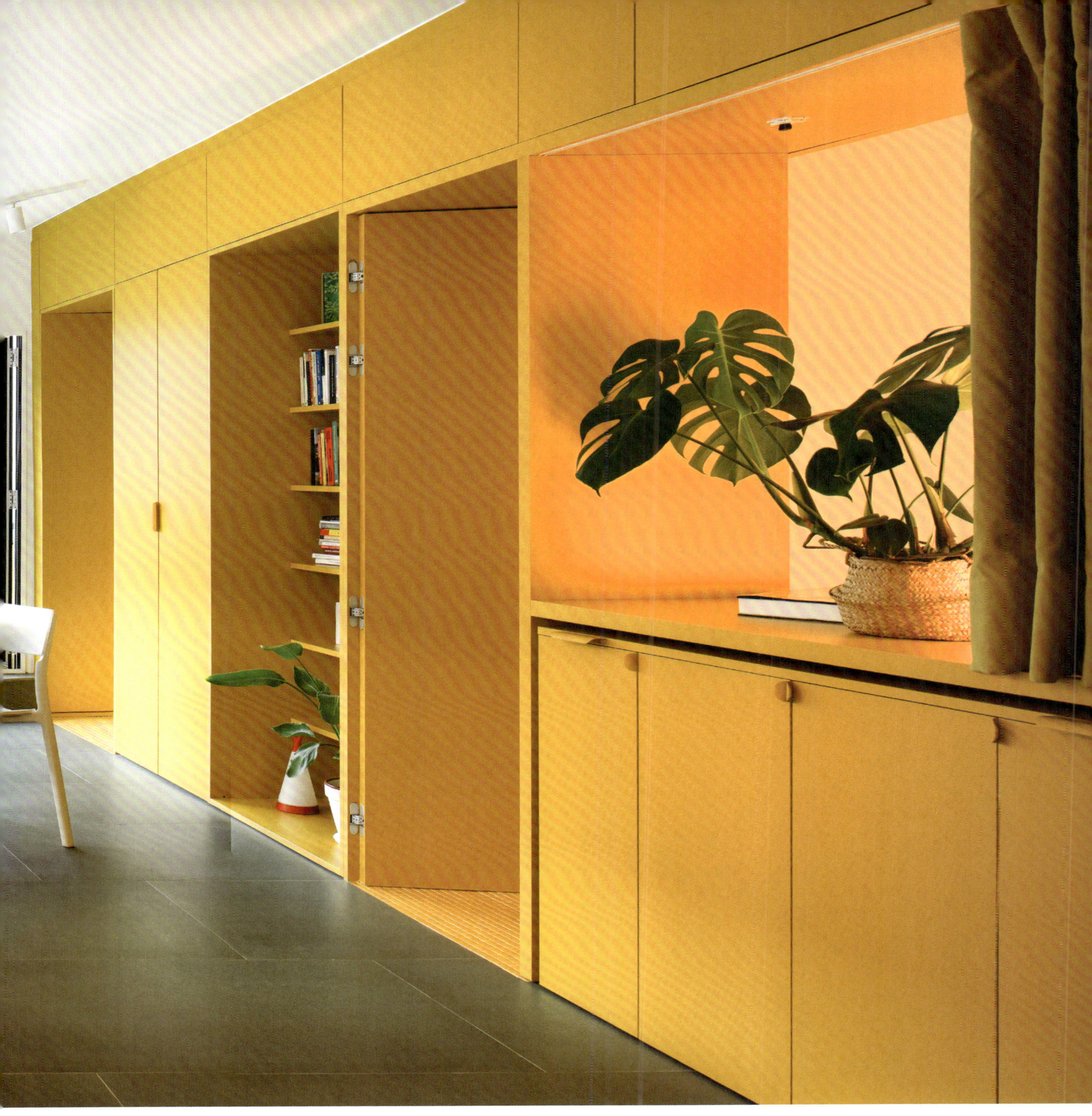

ABOVE The pitched ceiling was taken into account when designating the utility of the indoor zones.

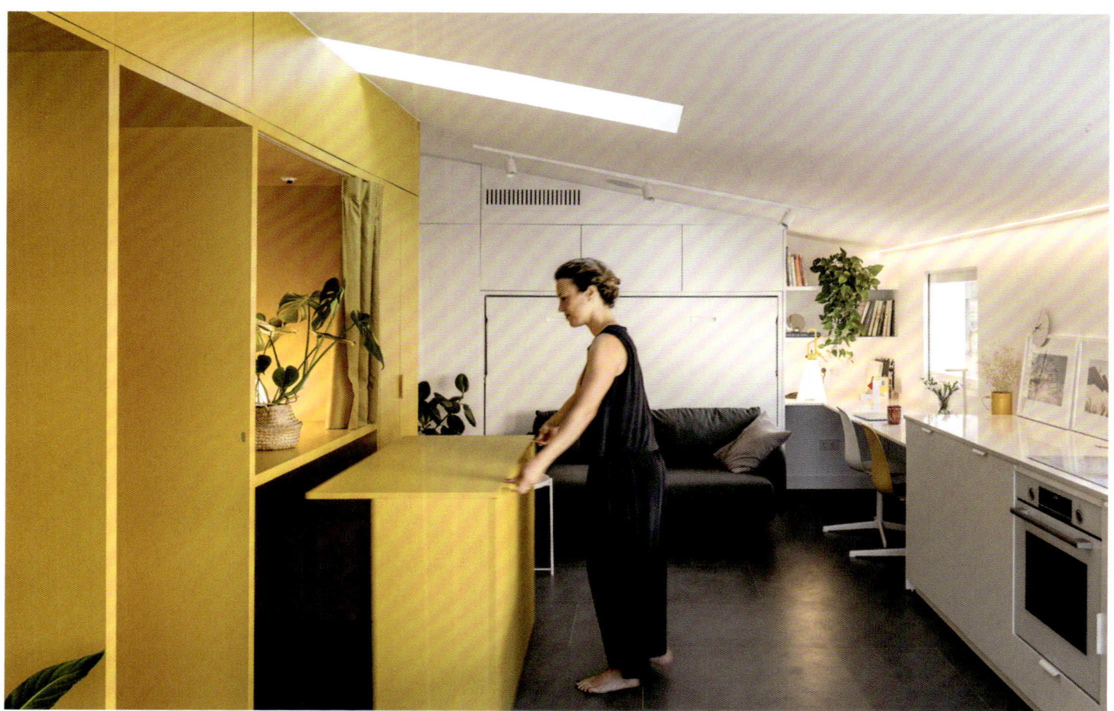

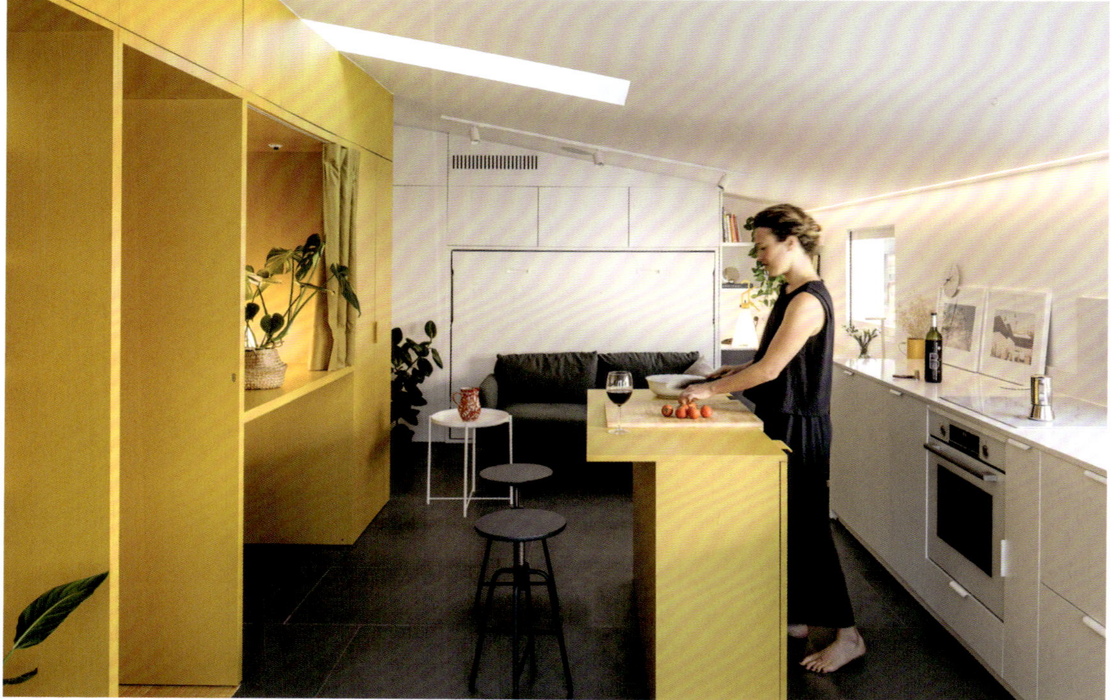

TOP The kitchen island can be pushed under the custom joinery when not in use to free up floor space.

BOTTOM Despite the kitchen's compact size, the portable island means there's always room for meal prep.

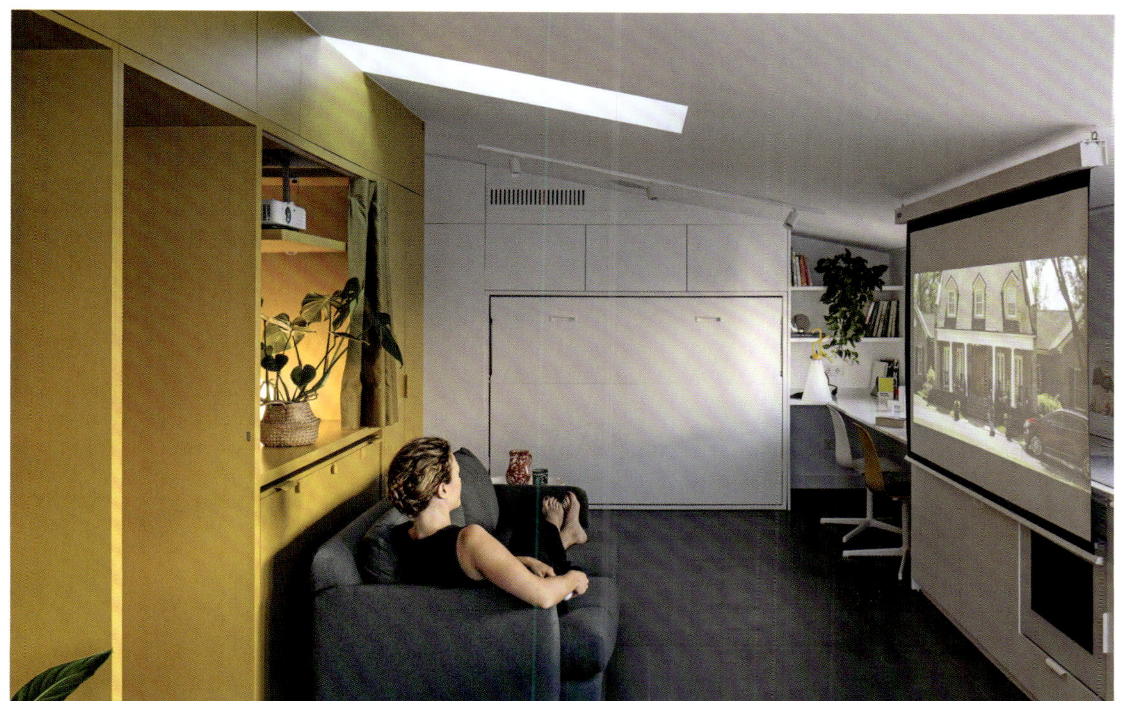

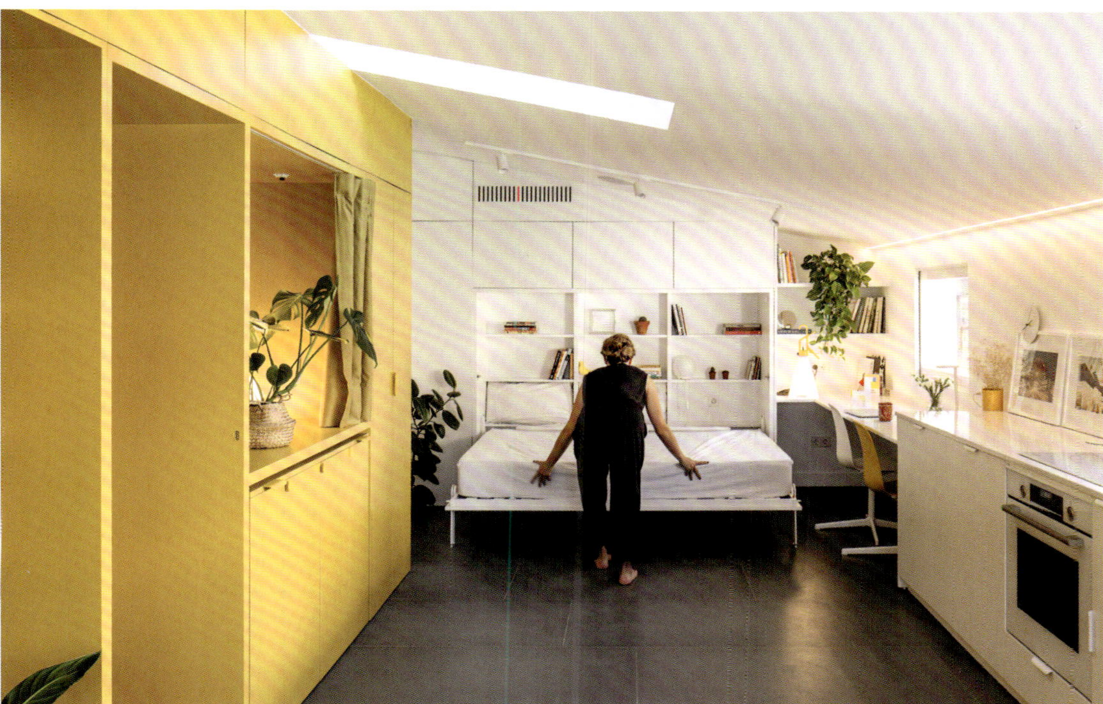

TOP The couch can be drawn into the centre of the room to watch the drop-down projector screen.

BOTTOM A Murphy bed can be folded down for guests, revealing additional recessed shelving.

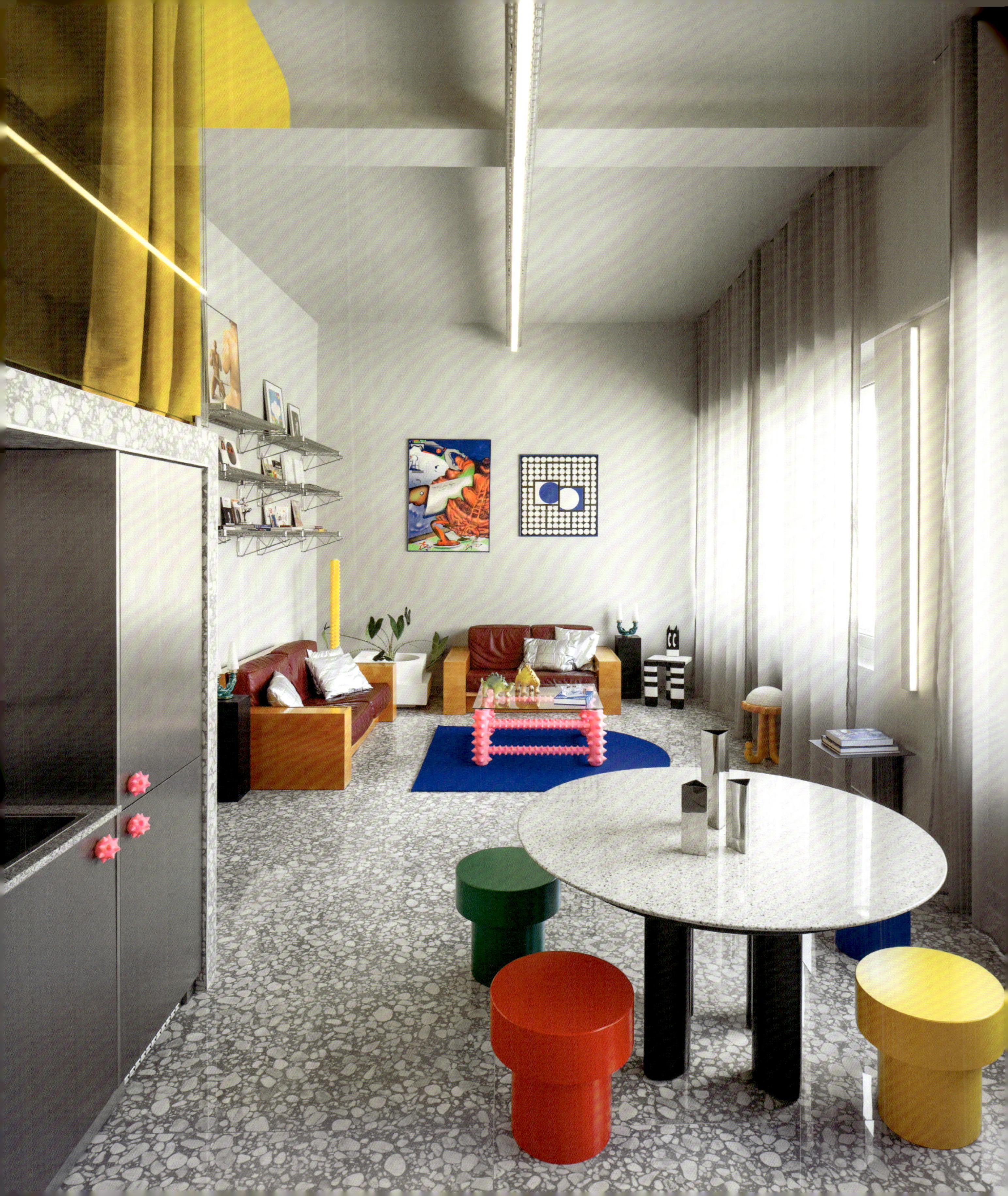

Maximalist Mini Loft

57m² / 614ft²
Zyva Studio
Bagnolet, Paris

'I like to think of spaces and pieces of furniture like fictional characters just like the toys in *Toy Story* that come to life as soon as Andy leaves the room,' says architect and designer Anthony Authié. 'I see them as actors in my architectural narrative.'

Authié took inspiration from the Nintendo games, animated movies and LEGO of his childhood to invent 'a new hybrid architectural form' where fun and colour reign.

'We wanted to create a fully fledged and unique aesthetic that reflected who we are,' he says of the 57-sq-m (614-sq-ft) loft apartment that he shares with his wife and their dog. And unique it is.

Situated in an old building in Bagnolet, an eastern suburb of Paris, the property was initially used by a company that made wood flooring in the 1980s and was converted into a residential space in the early 2000s. The original apartment, which was all white with wood floors, underwent surprisingly few structural changes to become what it is today. The kitchen was extended, the staircase was modified to open the space and a small wall was removed from the bathroom to add a closet.

The fun starts in the home's entry: an L-shaped hallway with bright-yellow walls and grey terrazzo flooring. Just off the hallway through a yellow door is the bathroom. Its floor and walls are also grey terrazzo. The generous proportions of the room, an open shower design and large green closets give the space a 'walk-in wardrobe' feel. It's a one-stop space to shower, dress and do laundry. A separate toilet shares the bathroom's aesthetic.

The themes of colour and texture continue in the apartment's main room, which contains the living and dining areas, as well as the kitchen. The space is essentially a large grey box with 4.2-m-high (13.7-ft-high) ceilings. It's filled with playful nods to 1980s video games and pop culture. The spiked base of the coffee table in the living room and the door handles and light fittings seen throughout were specifically inspired by Koopa Troopas in Super Mario Bros. games. They were all 3D-printed in Authié's studio.

Above the red leather couch, there are metallic kitchen shelves that double as a display area for art and books. 'I thought it would be fun to make a fully metallic kitchen inspired by Mr Freeze in Batman,' Authié says of the metallic doors and grey granite benchtops in the kitchen. 'I often think of kitchens as a cold science lab where experiments are conducted and things are preserved.'

The dining table is made of the same granite as the kitchen benchtop and Authié chose the bold, primary coloured OHM Studio stools because they reminded him of the pipe tunnel in Super Mario Bros.

Up the staircase, in what appears to be a big yellow box when the outer layer of curtains is closed, is the bedroom. Once inside, red and orange flame curtains that Authié designed and had printed provide a slightly unnerving yet humorous contrast to the bright yellow walls. The lighting on either side of the bed is inspired by the industrial lights in Paris metros.

Authié's philosophy when designing a small space is 'to create a truly unique experience, as if you are entering into a time machine and travelling through unexplored worlds'. And this is exactly what he has done with his own home.

PAGE 198 On the grey terrazzo used throughout his home, Authié says: 'I always try to create rhythm like in a song. The terrazzo allows me to play with these variations. Its repetitive pattern allows me to create noise and contrast with the yellow and green in the bedroom and the bathroom.'

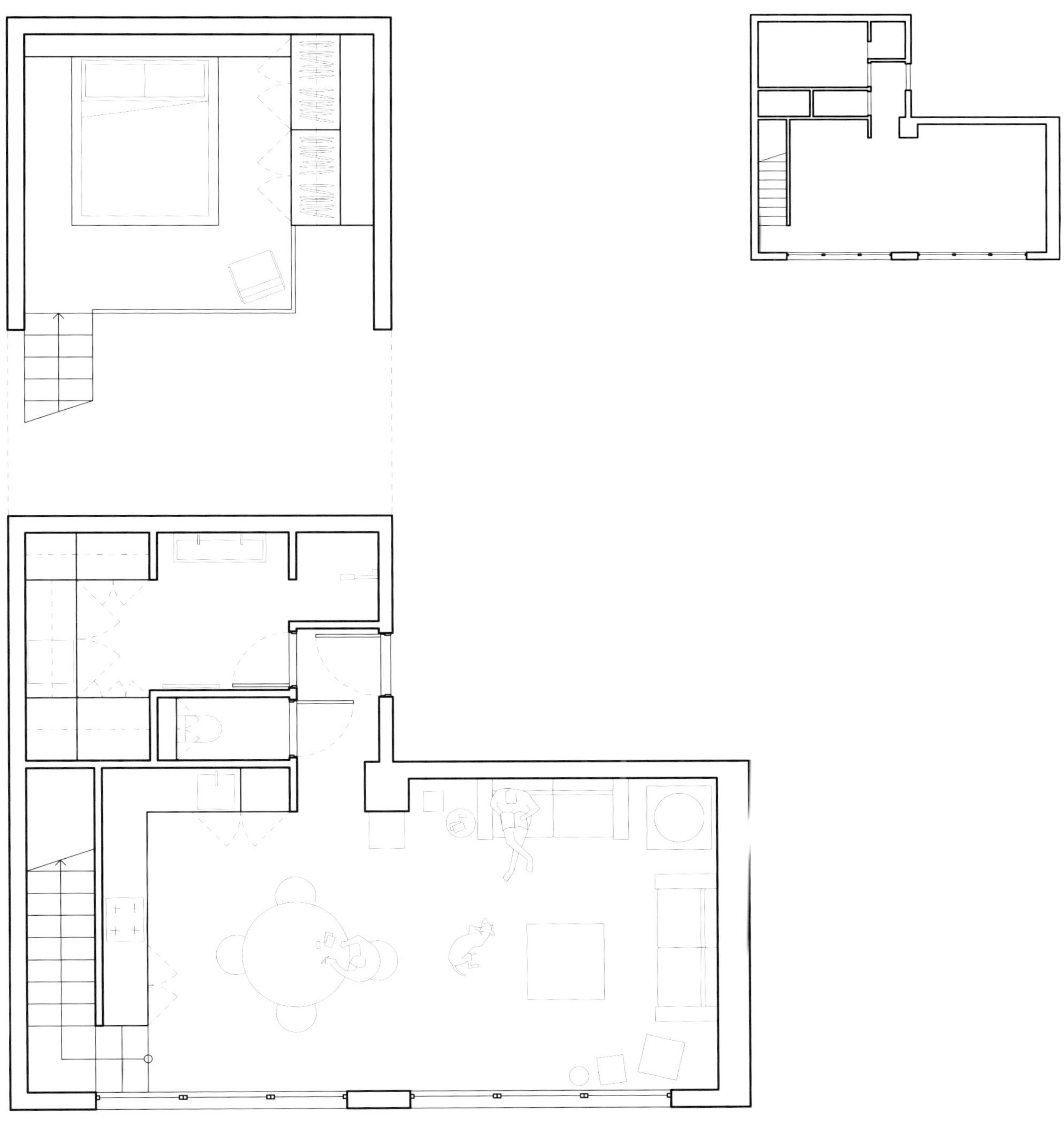
AFTER
BEFORE
Scale 1:100
1
2
3
4
5m

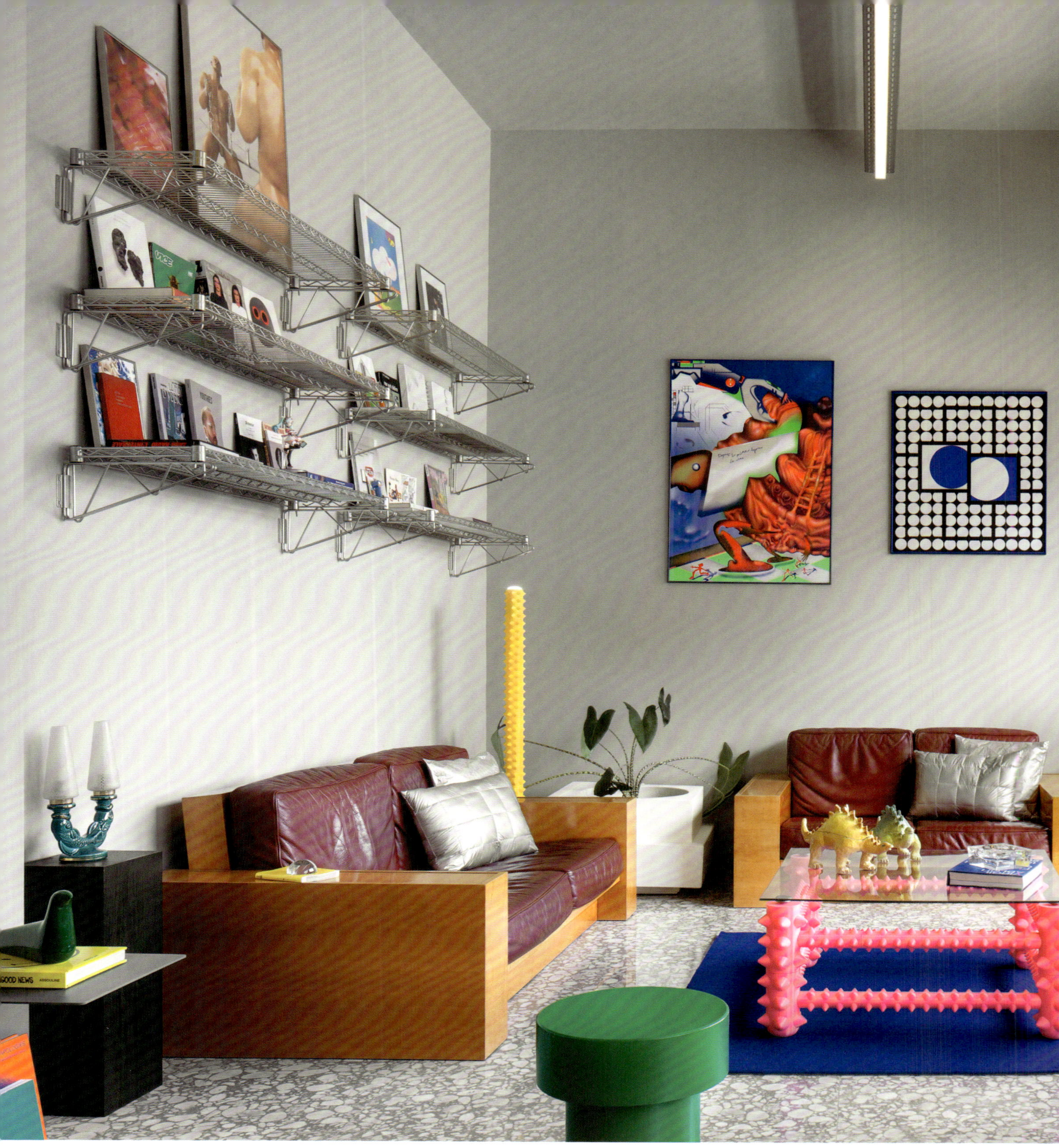
VICE
GOOD NEWS

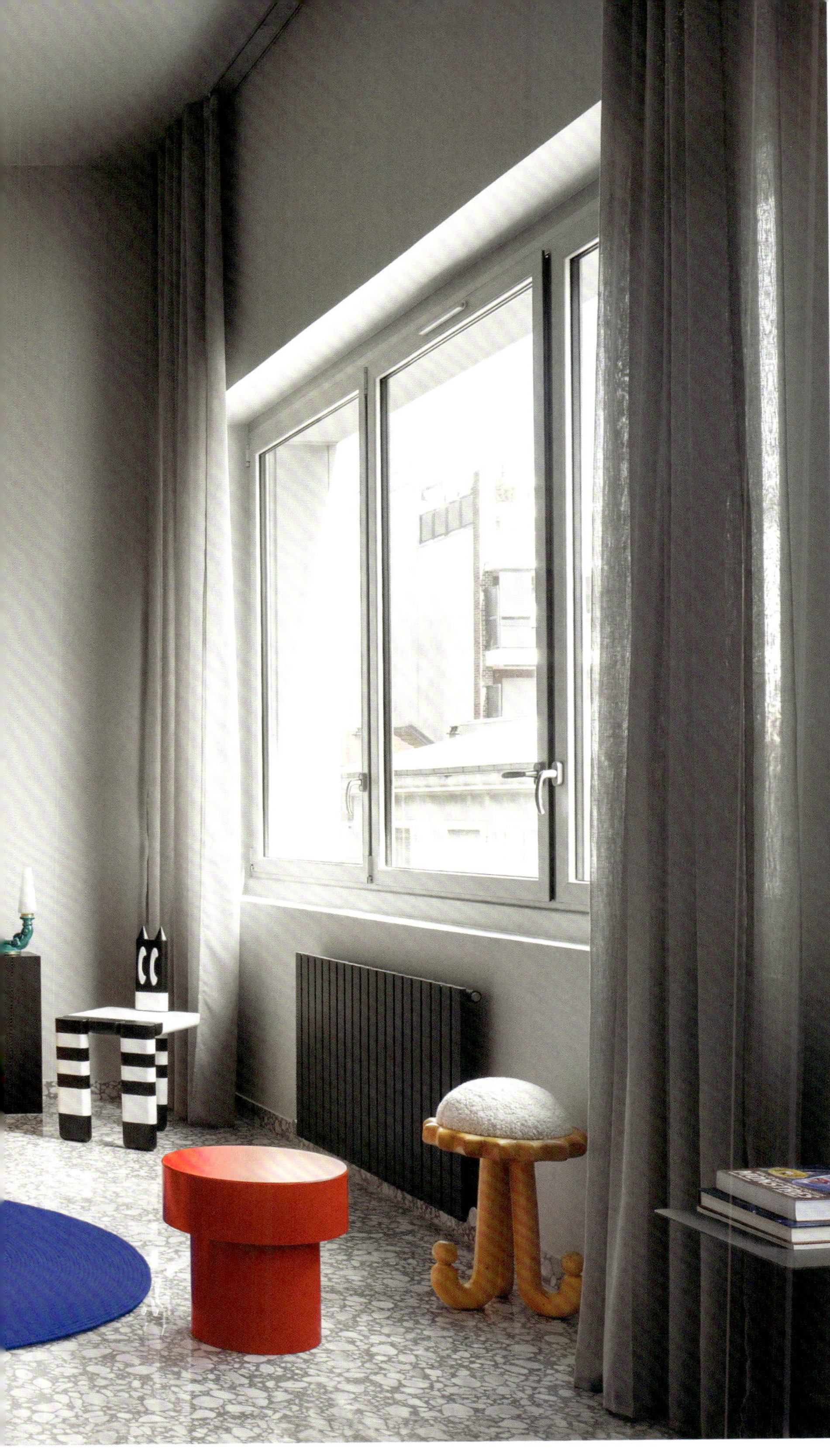

LEFT In the living room, artist Alix Coco's JOJO stool was chosen by Authié because it reminded him of an octopus. A small herd of Coco's dinosaurs also take up residence here.

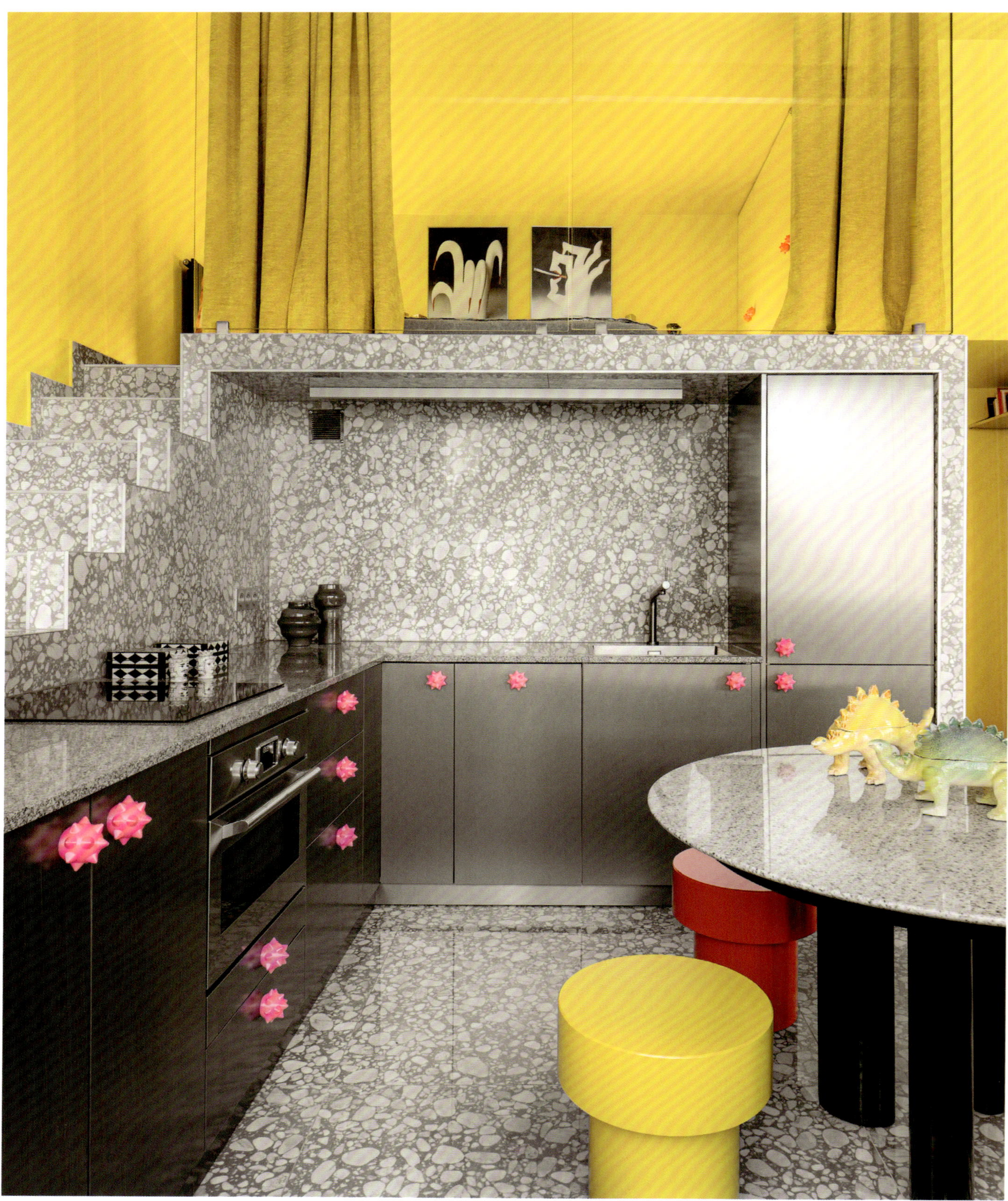

OPPOSITE The dishwasher and refrigerator are integrated into the kitchen for a more seamless look.

BOTTOM LEFT The staircase to the bedroom acts as a wall for one side of the kitchen.

BOTTOM RIGHT The bathroom sits under the stairs. It's another example of bold, playful colour against the texture of the grey terrazzo.

Authié took inspiration from the Nintendo games, animated movies and LEGO of his childhood.

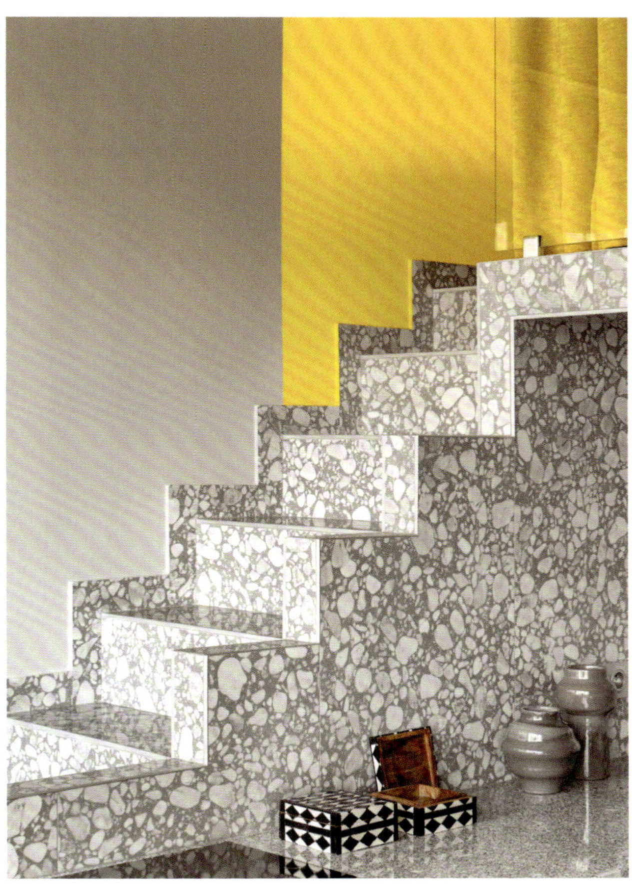

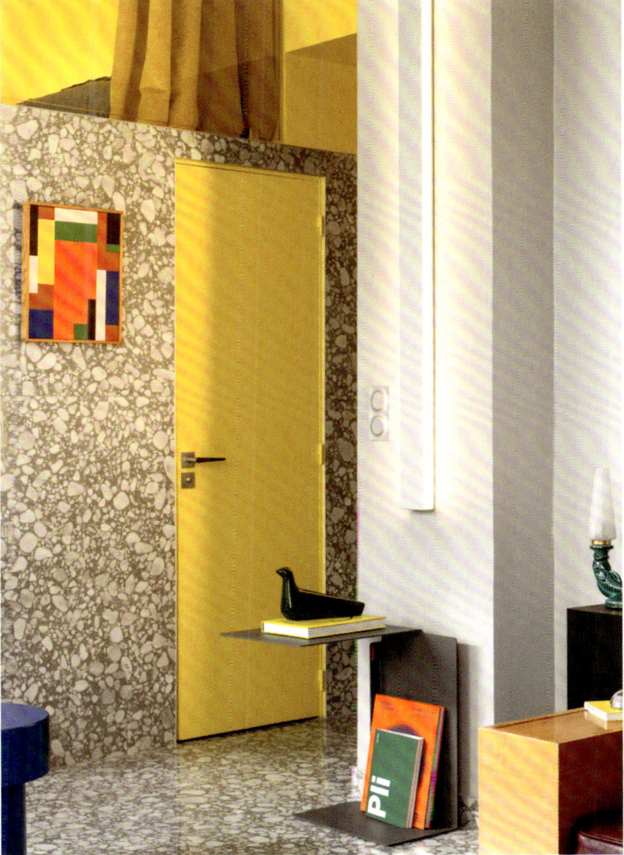

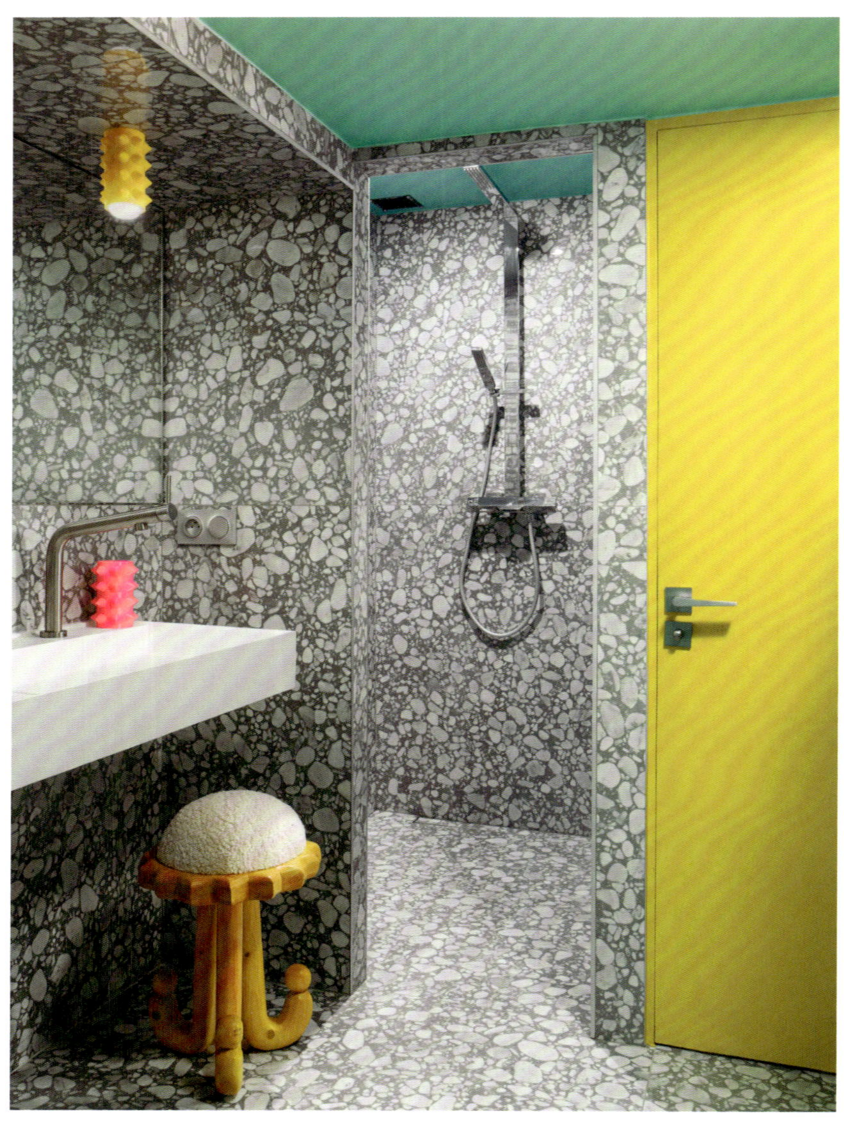

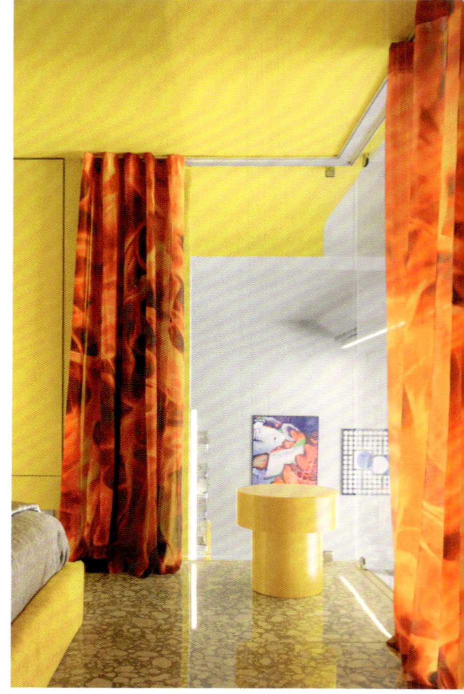

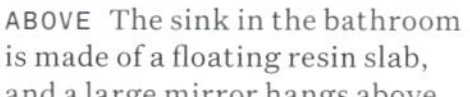

ABOVE The sink in the bathroom is made of a floating resin slab, and a large mirror hangs above.

RIGHT Authié designed and printed the bedroom's flame curtains.

OPPOSITE The base of the bed was made using the same fabric as the yellow block-out curtains. On the right wall there is storage for clothes.

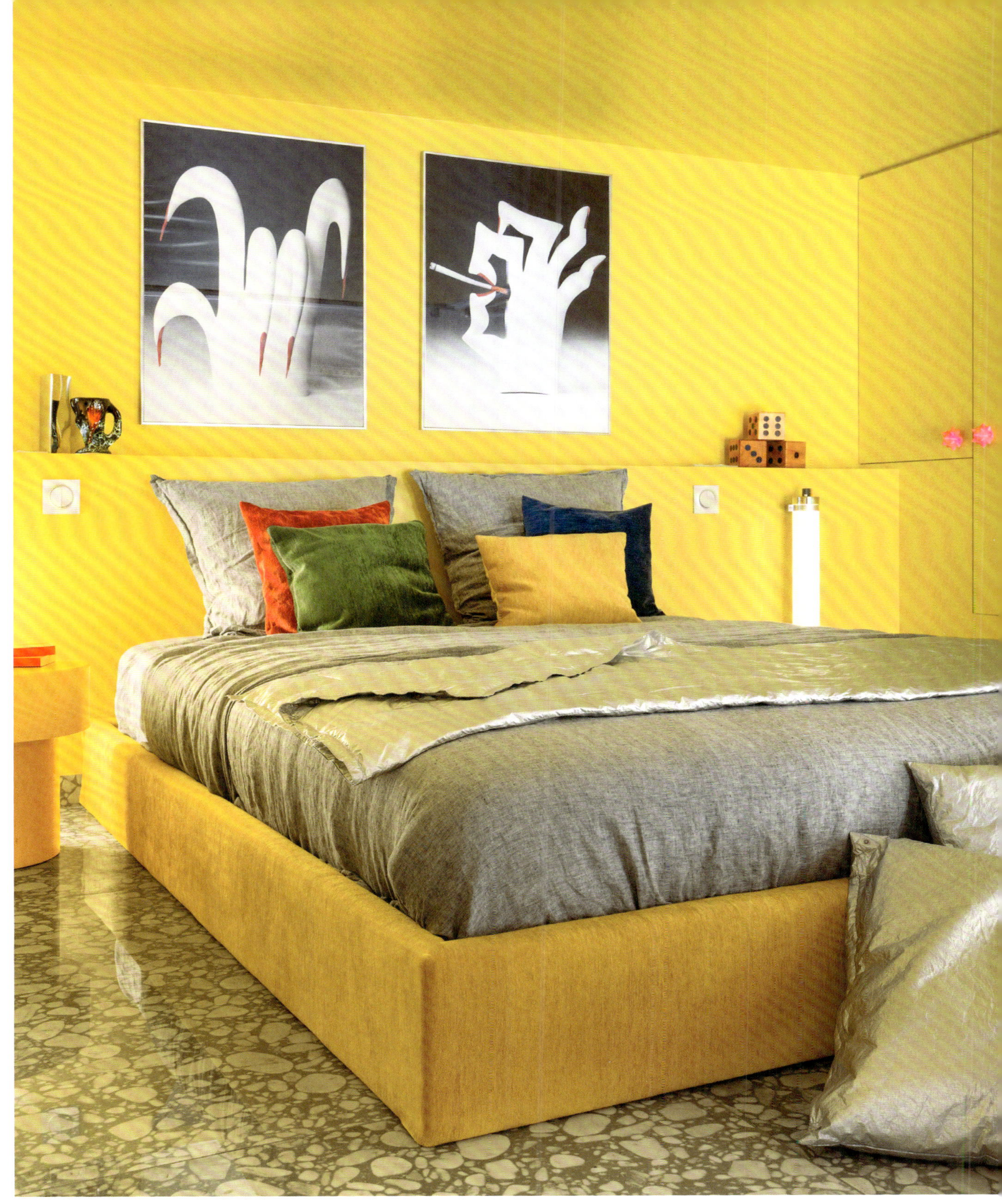

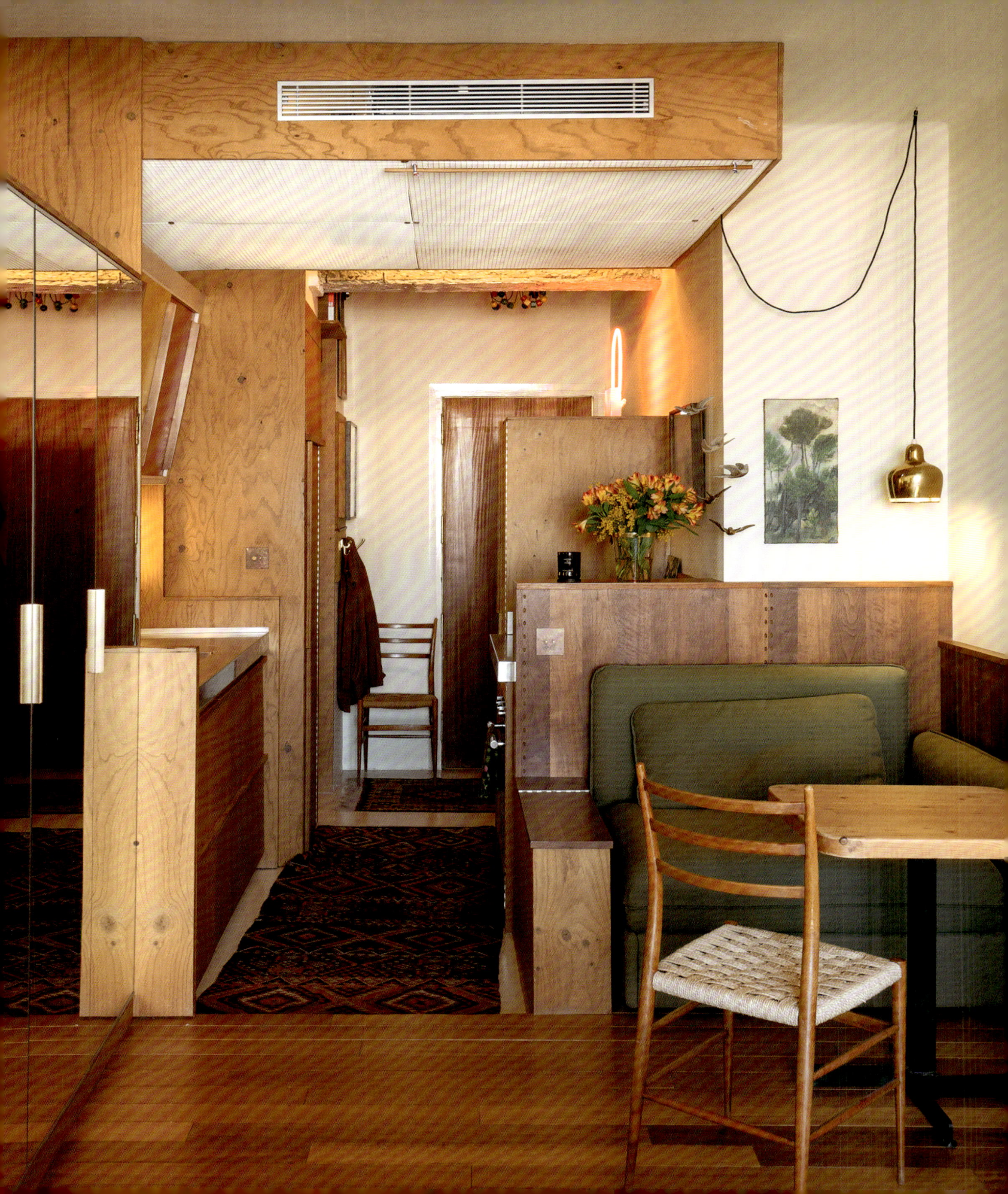

EG112 simple dwelling

34m² / 366ft²
Jacobo Valentí
Eixample, Barcelona

In the heart of Barcelona is the bustling neighbourhood of Eixample. In Catalan, Eixample means 'to make something wider', which was exactly what was happening to Barcelona in the 19th century. The implementation of the Eixample plan established a link between the historic city centre and the suburban areas, thereby expanding the city's size tenfold. The plan involved the creation of a grid of squares with green spaces in every block, fostering a tranquil and healthful environment.

At that time, Barcelona was a rich and modern city with a blossoming culture. The wealthiest families were competing for the best pieces of land in Eixample to build their homes in the modernist style, with Gaudi being the most notable architect. Sagrada Familia, Pedrera and Casa Batlló are just three examples of modernist architecture that can be found in this special neighbourhood.

Given all this, the location was the main attraction for owner and architect Jacobo Valentí who was looking for something for himself that was small and easy to renovate. He was particularly keen on a top-floor apartment with natural light and great views. Upon seeing this 34-sq-m (366-sq-ft) space, he immediately fell in love with it and recognised its potential, despite the obvious need to remove walls and change the layout to make the most of the floor plan.

Valentí found inspiration from various sources but was heavily influenced by Charlotte Perriand's interiors, particularly the materials and colours used in 'La unite d'habitation' Marseille, as well as 'Le cabanon' by Le Corbusier. He was also a big fan of mid-century furniture and challenged himself to create the perfect space around a unique piece, a kitchen cabinet by Charlotte Perriand from a Le Corbusier building, which he has made a central piece in the kitchen.

Valentí commenced his renovation in 2019, but the pandemic disrupted his plans. During lockdown, he and J.Dom, a friend and carpenter, worked on the apartment every day, dedicating significant attention to every detail. The renovation resulted in significant changes to the original plan, including the modification of the floor plan, the elimination of the false ceiling and the removal of faux doors. In addition, they opened a previously unused 1-sq-m (10-sq-ft) space, which allowed more natural light to enter the apartment. The removal of an oversized bathroom and a redundant corridor also helped to brighten up a formerly dark area of the apartment. The bathroom was divided into two sections, with the toilet at one end and the shower niche next to the terrace.

Valentí's vision stretched further than just the interior: he wanted more outdoor space so he transformed a portion of the indoor area into an extension of the terrace, spanning over 3 sq m (32 sq ft). This terrace is the part of the apartment that he cherishes the most. 'Terraces are a must in Mediterranean cities,' he says. 'This was a really good decision because it has become the area that I use the most and in summer I eat most of my meals out there.'

Despite the exceptional quality throughout the home, Valentí says that the renovation cost less than the price of the furniture within. 'These tiny projects offer the opportunity to invest in the best materials and solutions, no matter what they cost, because of the limited quantities needed.'

PAGE 208 Different tones of wood and a pop of green create an eclectic forest feel in Jacobo Valentí's home.

BELOW As colourful as Barcelona itself, the bathroom is a scarlet dream.

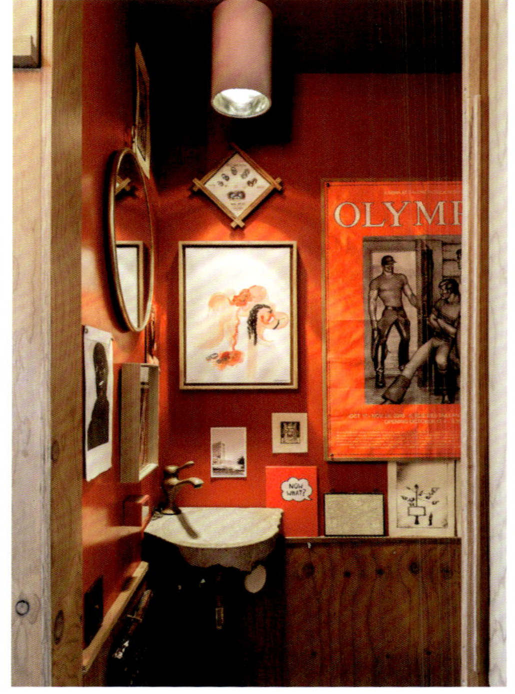

AFTER

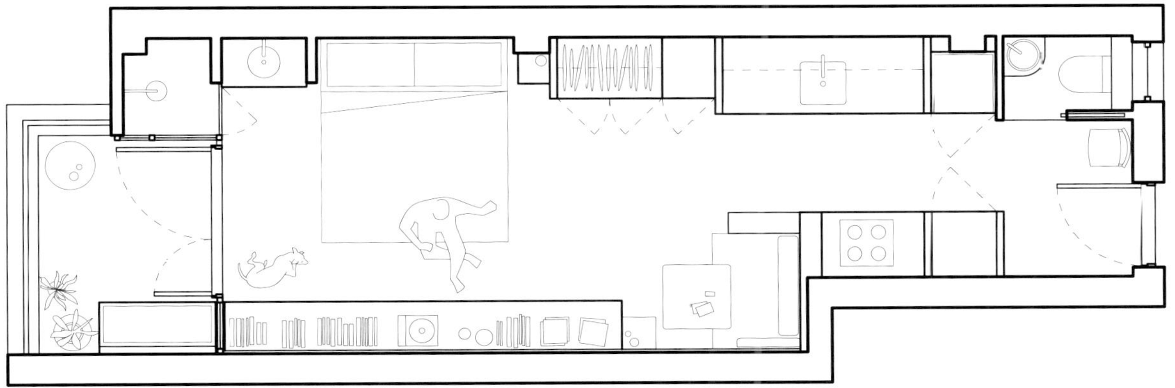

BEFORE

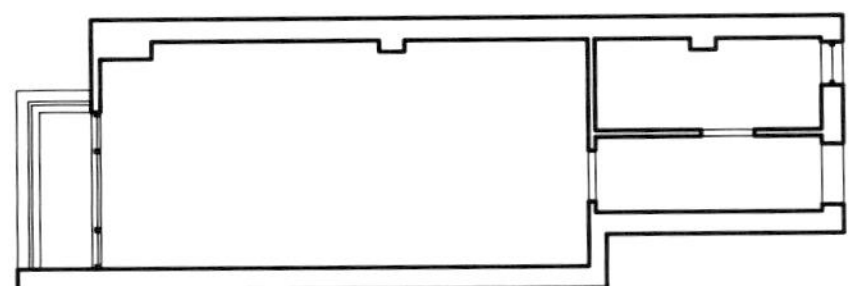

Scale 1:100

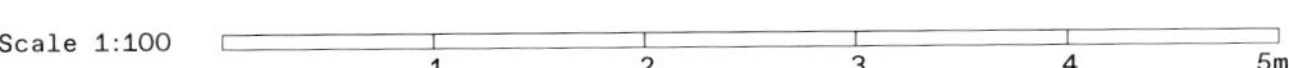

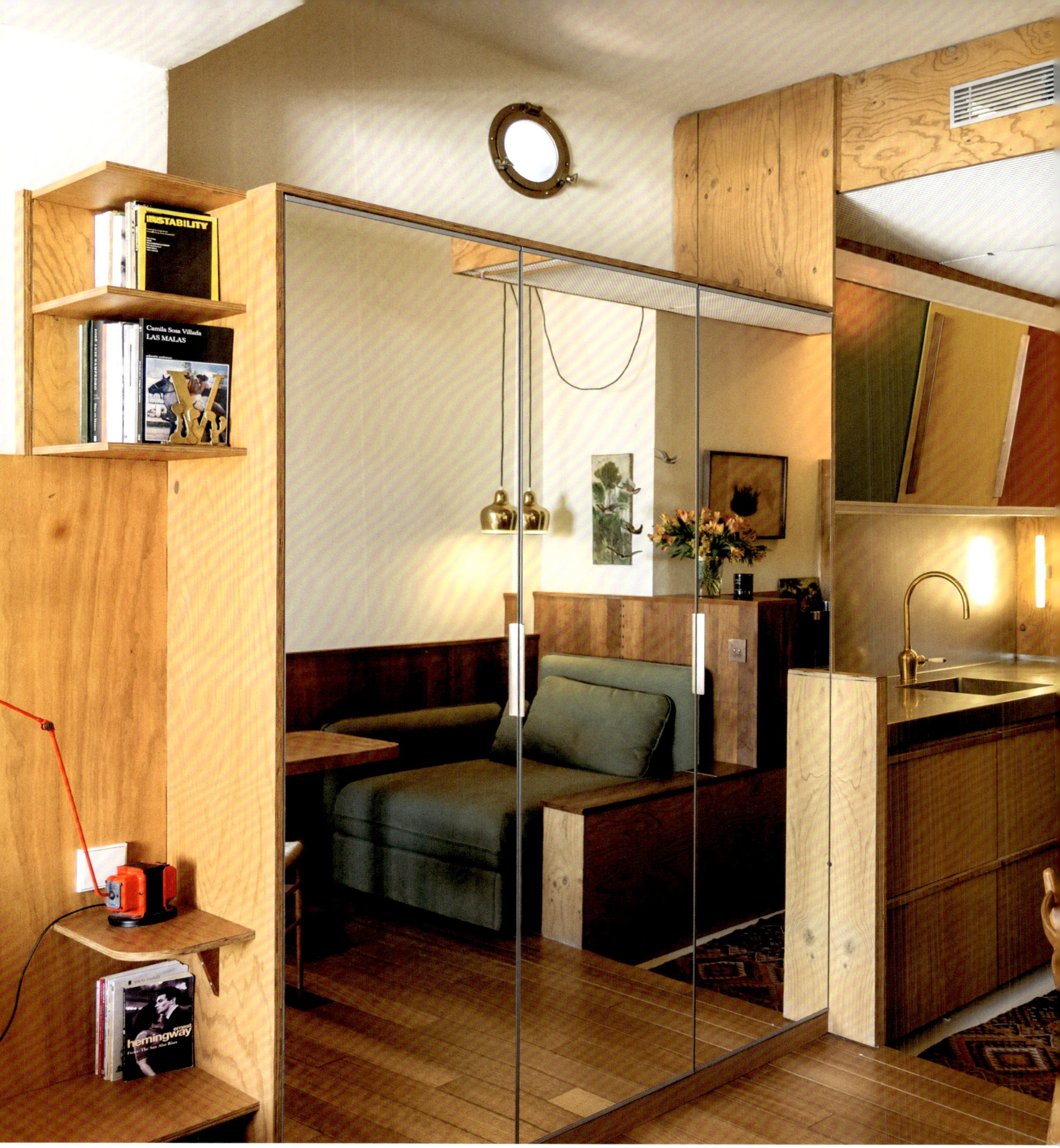
INSTABILITY
Camila Sosa Villada
LAS MALAS
ernest
hemingway

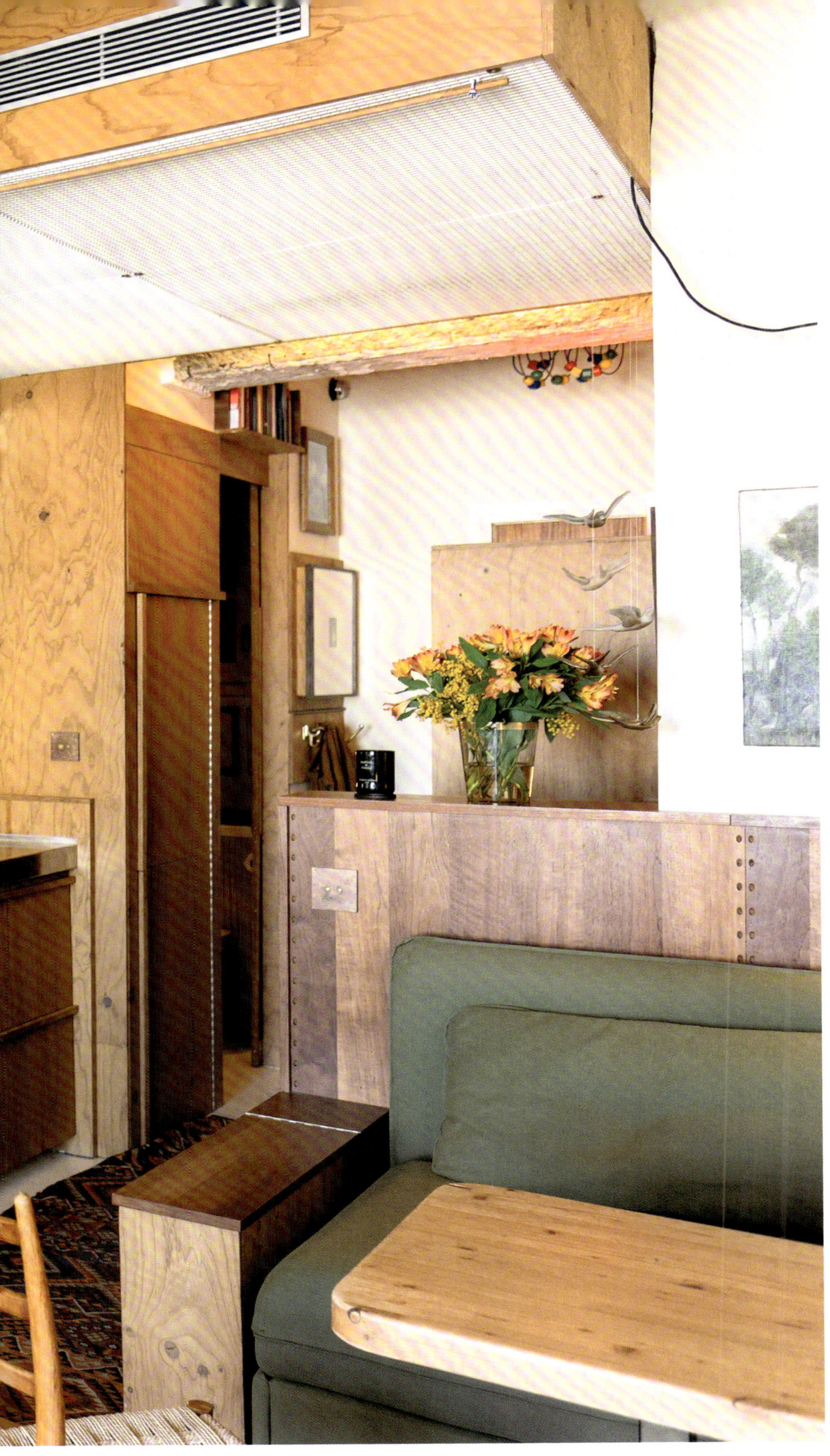

LEFT One of Valenti's most prized possessions is the kitchen cabinet by Charlotte Perriand.

'Tiny projects offer the opportunity to invest in the best materials and solutions.'

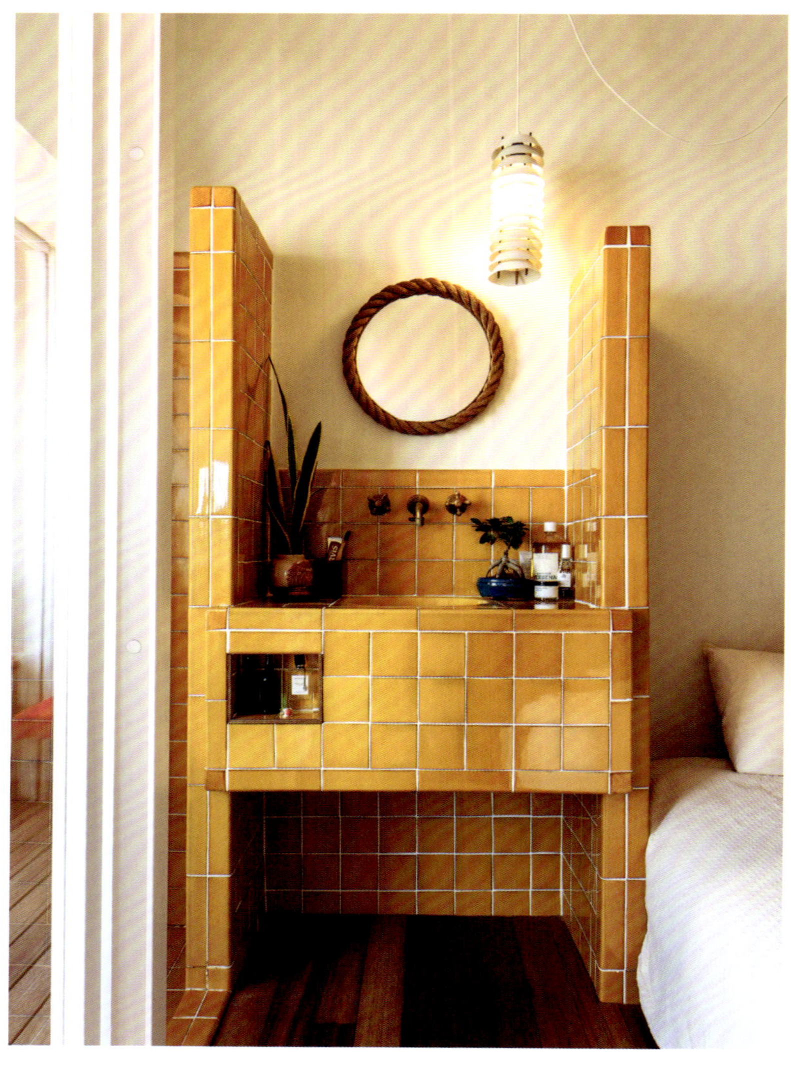

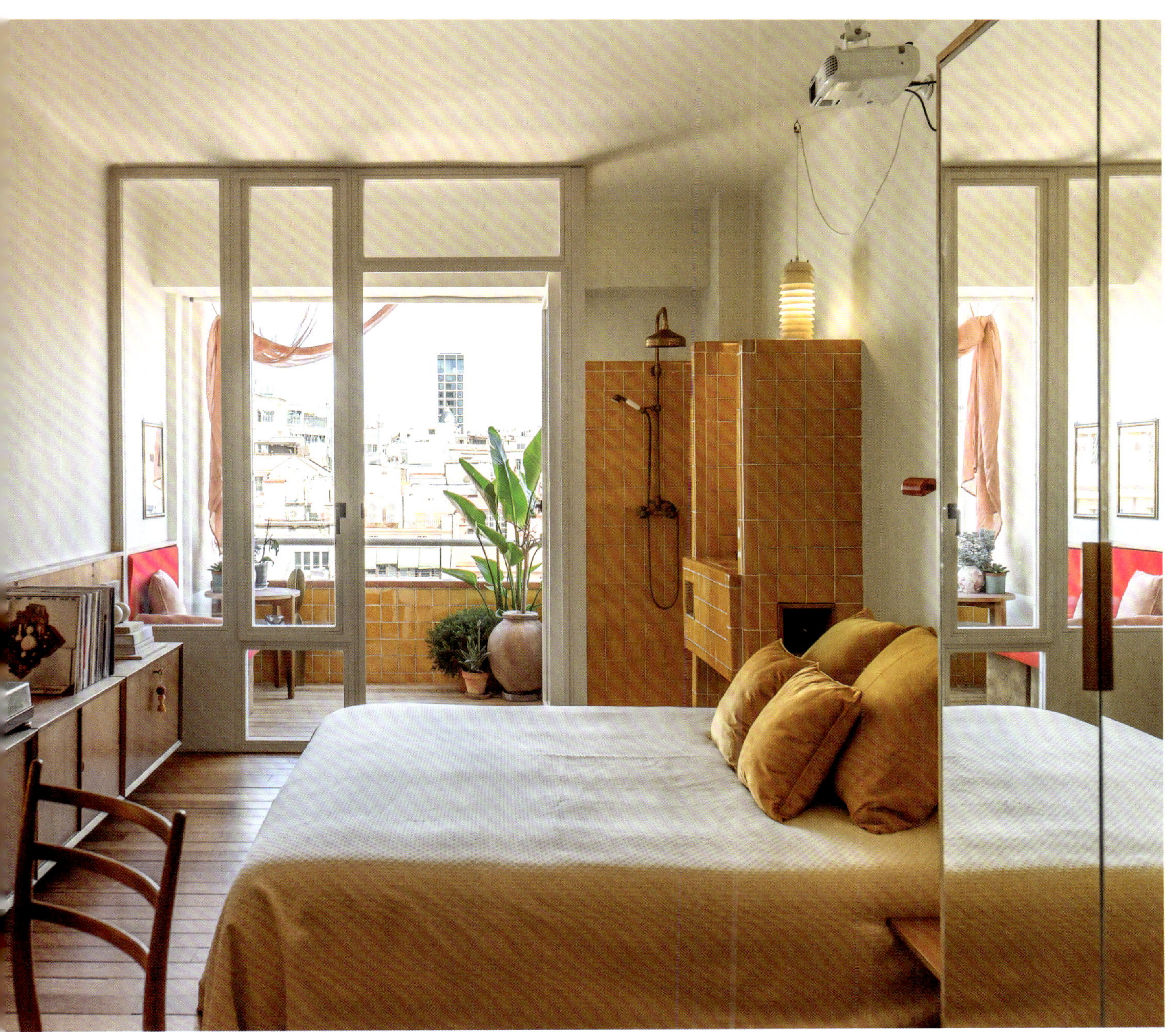

OPPOSITE Another zone means another colour. Yellow tiles define the bathroom, which is tucked in the corner of the bedroom area.

ABOVE The yellow tiling flows out to the balcony and the Barcelona sunshine.

5

When it comes to small-footprint living, sustainability is not an afterthought – it's an integral part of the design process. The projects in this section demonstrate a harmonious blend of creativity, efficiency and conscious decision-making. They encompass a holistic approach that considers the environmental impact of materials, energy usage and overall utilisation of resources. From the initial construction phase to the ongoing operations of the home, sustainability is at the forefront. Innovative design strategies, such as passive heating and cooling, maximise energy efficiency and reduce reliance on traditional heating and cooling systems while thoughtful selection of materials such as reclaimed wood and other eco-friendly materials not only minimises waste, but also adds character and uniqueness to the home.

Jourdain by BILOBA.archi in the heart of Paris exemplifies the fusion of affordability and sustainability by utilising materials like French pine plywood. The built-in furniture and sleeping loft, crafted from this eco-friendly material, not only provide functional and elegant solutions but also contribute to a reduced carbon footprint. Owner and architect Matthieu Torres's home fully embraces sustainability by incorporating salvaged and second-hand furniture, as well as giving new life to cherished items passed down through generations of his and his partner's families.

Another remarkable sustainable solution can be seen in owner and builder Adam Souter's Pepper Tree Passive House where nature and sustainability seamlessly converge. Rather than removing a majestic pepper tree, this

Sustainable Solutions

tiny home was carefully constructed around it, preserving the beauty of the natural surroundings of Unanderra in southern NSW. It was of the upmost importance to Souter and architect Alexander Symes that Pepper Tree Passive House embodied passive design principles, harnessing passive heating, cooling and natural lighting to minimise energy consumption. By strategically placing windows and utilising efficient insulation, this home remains comfortable year round while reducing its reliance on energy-intensive systems.

In Amsterdam, Scheeps, a waterfront apartment, offers a compelling example of sustainability through upcycling and DIY principles. This small-footprint design showcases how resourcefulness and creativity can transform discarded materials into a charming and sustainable living space. By incorporating second-hand furniture and fittings, designers, makers and owners Fadime Gökkaya and Koen Fraijman breathed new life into items that might have otherwise been destined for landfill. This approach not only reduces waste, but also adds character and uniqueness to the home. Scheeps is a testament to the possibilities that lie within our everyday surroundings, inspiring us to think outside the box and reimagine our own living spaces.

As you peruse this section, we ask that you consider how designing with sustainable solutions in mind is not only a responsible choice for the planet, but also shows how a simpler, more intentional way of living prioritises our connection to the environment.

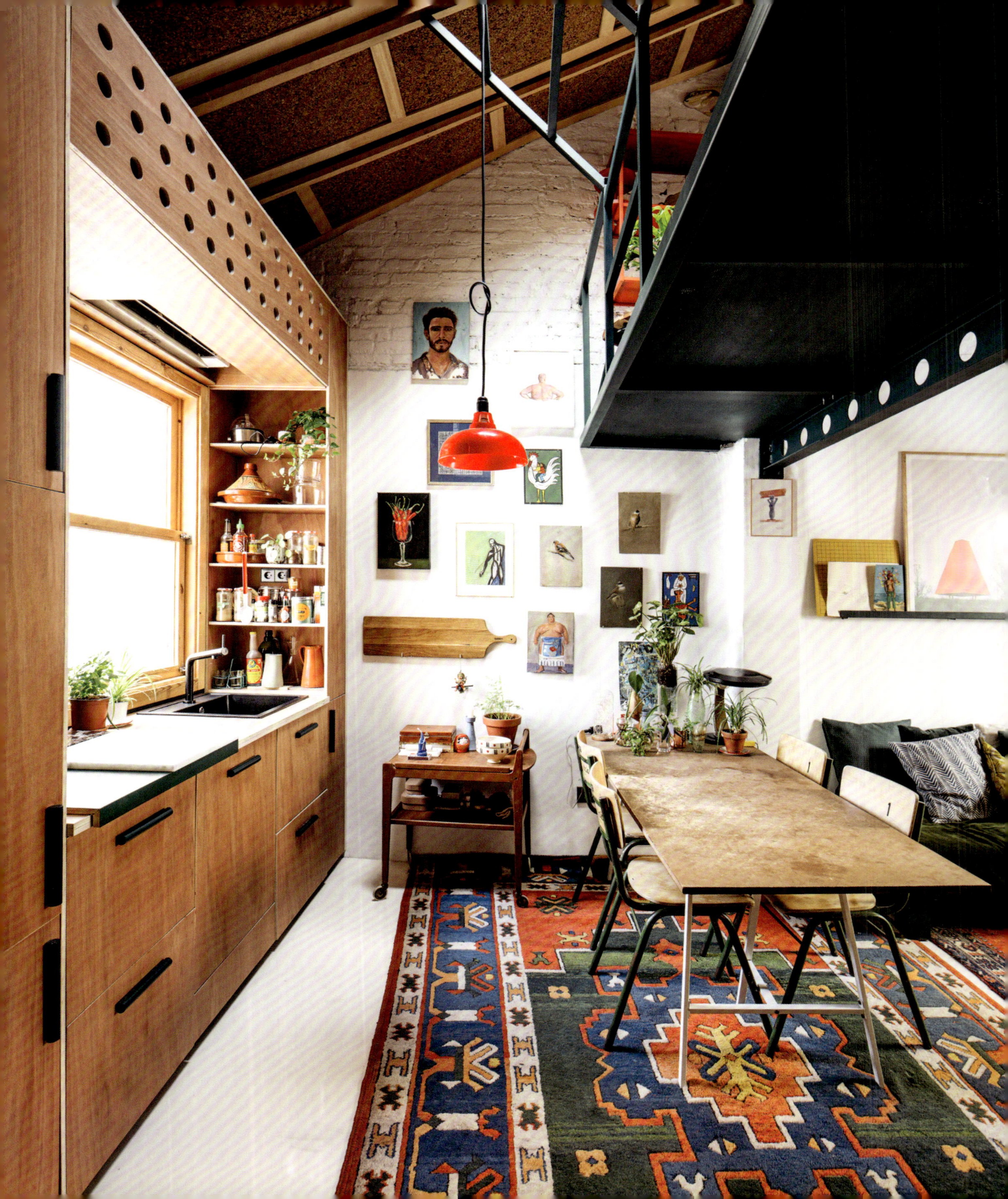

House for Cosimo Piovasco

45m² / 484ft²
Mariana de Delás
Rastro, Madrid

In the enchanting neighbourhood of Madrid's Rastro, Mariana de Delás's apartment symbolises creativity and innovation. The neighbourhood feels timeless – groups of relaxed neighbours gather on the streets and this strong community spirit has a special place in de Delás's heart.

Constructed in 1940, the apartment building was initially designed as a residential space for out-of-city workers. De Delás's vision for her apartment has breathed new life into the space by transforming it into an awe-inspiring home where functionality meets a sense of adventure in every corner. In fact, this apartment is one of the tiniest yet most captivating in Madrid.

Inspired by Italo Calvino's novel *The Baron in the Trees*, de Delás envisioned her apartment as a treehouse-like dwelling, capturing the essence of growing in altitude and embracing a sense of playfulness. In doing so, she needed to look within herself and work out what she needed to make her home a 'happy place'.

'It's easier getting to know oneself when deciding to live in a small space,' she says. 'Everyone can live in a big space but in a small space you have to prioritise. Some people may prioritise hidden storage, a minimal lifestyle or a big kitchen. For me, it was a great opportunity to know what I really wanted to have and what I could live without.'

The apartment originally featured low gypsum false ceilings and a cramped layout. Originally 29 sq m (312 sq ft), the apartment gained an additional 15 sq m (161 sq ft) through the creation of metal gangways suspended from a 3 × 3 tubular stairway. The gangways house a relief panic storage space with an extra study table overlooking the main area, and a tucked in bedroom that sits on top of the bathroom and entry hallway. These elements created a harmonious balance between openness and functionality. The elevated gangways have an added benefit, providing peeks of the neighbouring rooftops.

Right at the entrance, a hidden bathroom concealed behind a wooden panel adds an element of surprise. The hallway is adorned with red plywood, creating a textured 'grounded' atmosphere. This complements the green metal elements of the gangway, which are an homage to the branches of trees, softening the steel and providing a feeling of being under a forest canopy.

The living area is an open space, featuring a steel fold-out couch and a custom-made hanging staircase-cum-cabinet. A TMC floor lamp by Catalan designer Miguel Milá illuminates the space, while carefully selected rugs, plants and artwork add to the cosiness.

In the kitchen and dining area, a portable electric hob in place of a traditional stove keeps the benchtop clutter free. The walls are adorned with art pieces by local artists, another nod to community.

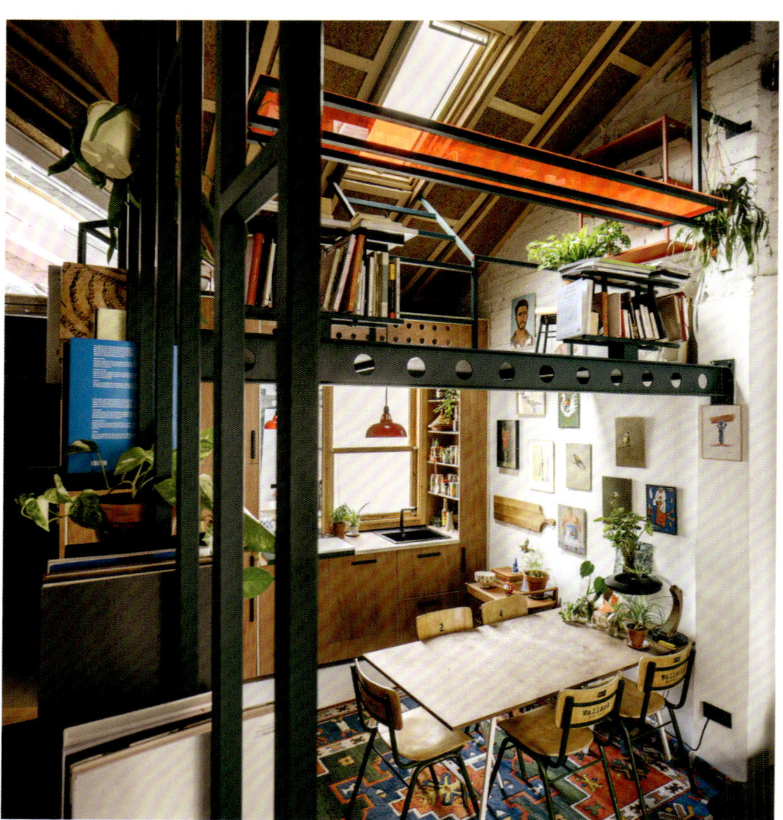

PAGE 218 High ceilings provide so much opportunity for extending up.

RIGHT A mezzanine doubles the floor space, allowing for work and sleep to be separated from living and dining.

AFTER

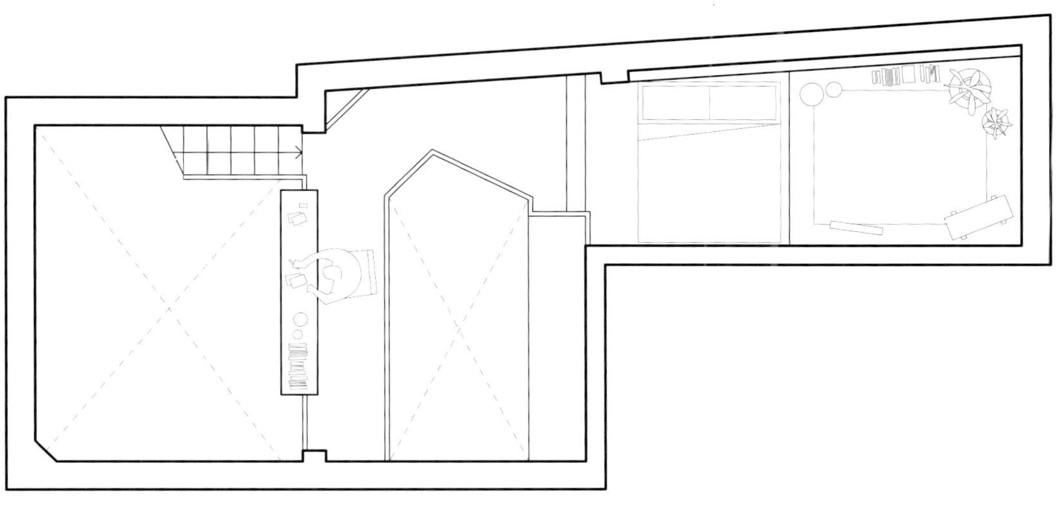

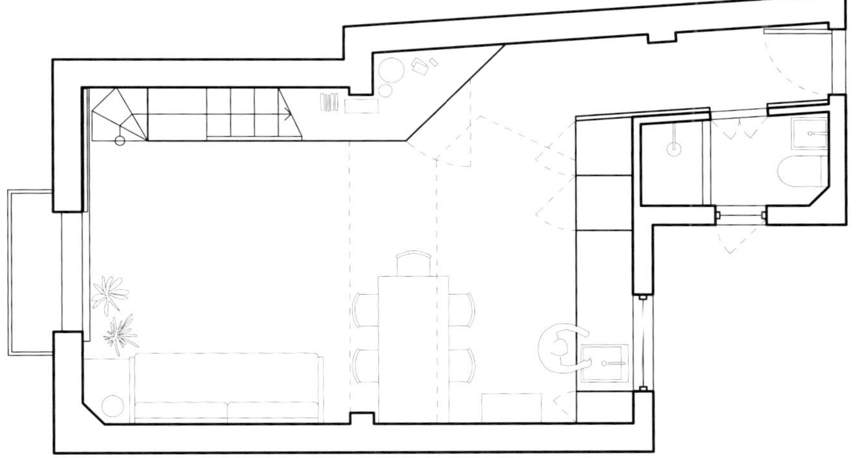

BEFORE

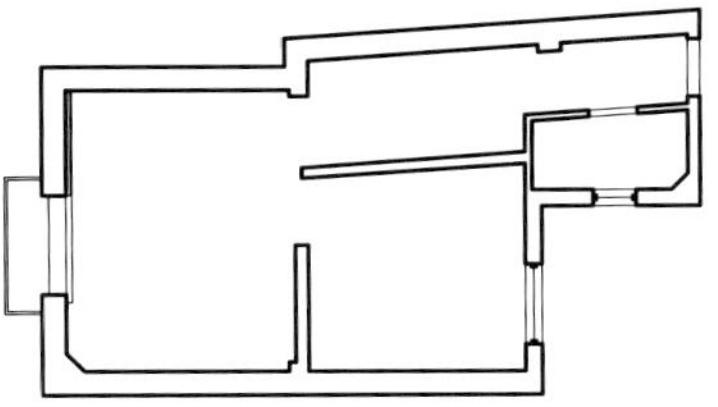

Scale 1:100

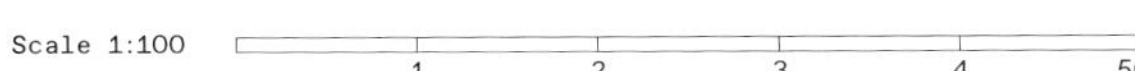

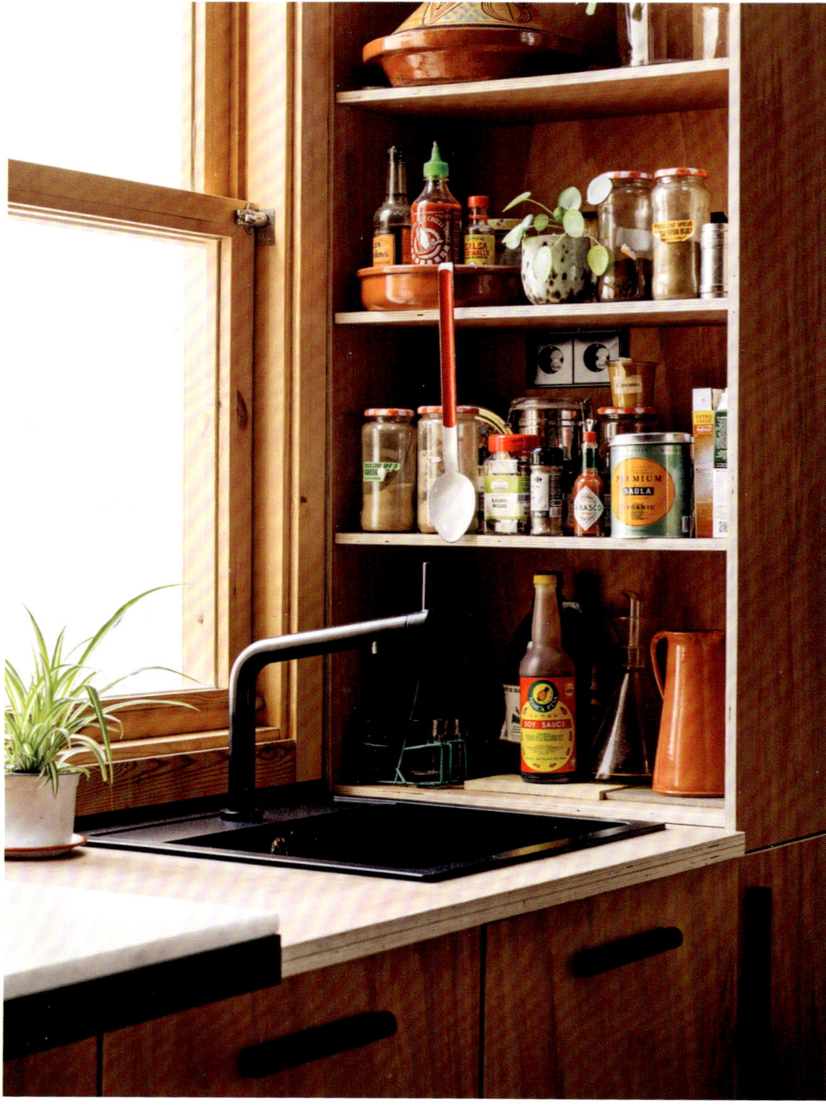

LEFT There is ample pantry space for a resident who takes cooking seriously.

OPPOSITE The ply stairs extend into custom cabinets that run the length of the stairs. The staircase continues as a tubular hanging staircase.

The sleeping area, on the mezzanine created by the gangway, is designed to evoke a sense of tranquility akin to resting among the trees, with a skylight for glimpsing the moon and stars. Additional space beside the bed has been transferred into a cubby filled with art and pillows and storage compartments hidden beneath. The bathroom is a world of its own with green and white tiles, the leaves of the canopy meeting the clouds. The use of unique wood window systems adds character and experimentation to the space.

The apartment's top gangway is a bonus space with various uses. 'We dry the clothes in the railing, have a more intimate study area on the table above, which at the same time acts as a very warming lamp, and the orange plexiglass creates a super warm environment at night,' says de Delás.

While the interior is a sanctuary, the way de Delás speaks of her neighbourhood is a good reminder of why so often tiny apartments are in trendy locations. With a lot of larger homes in desirable neighbourhoods out of the financial reach of young singles and couples, small apartments provide access to areas that would otherwise be unattainable. And designers like de Delás do a great job of making these small homes just as attractive.

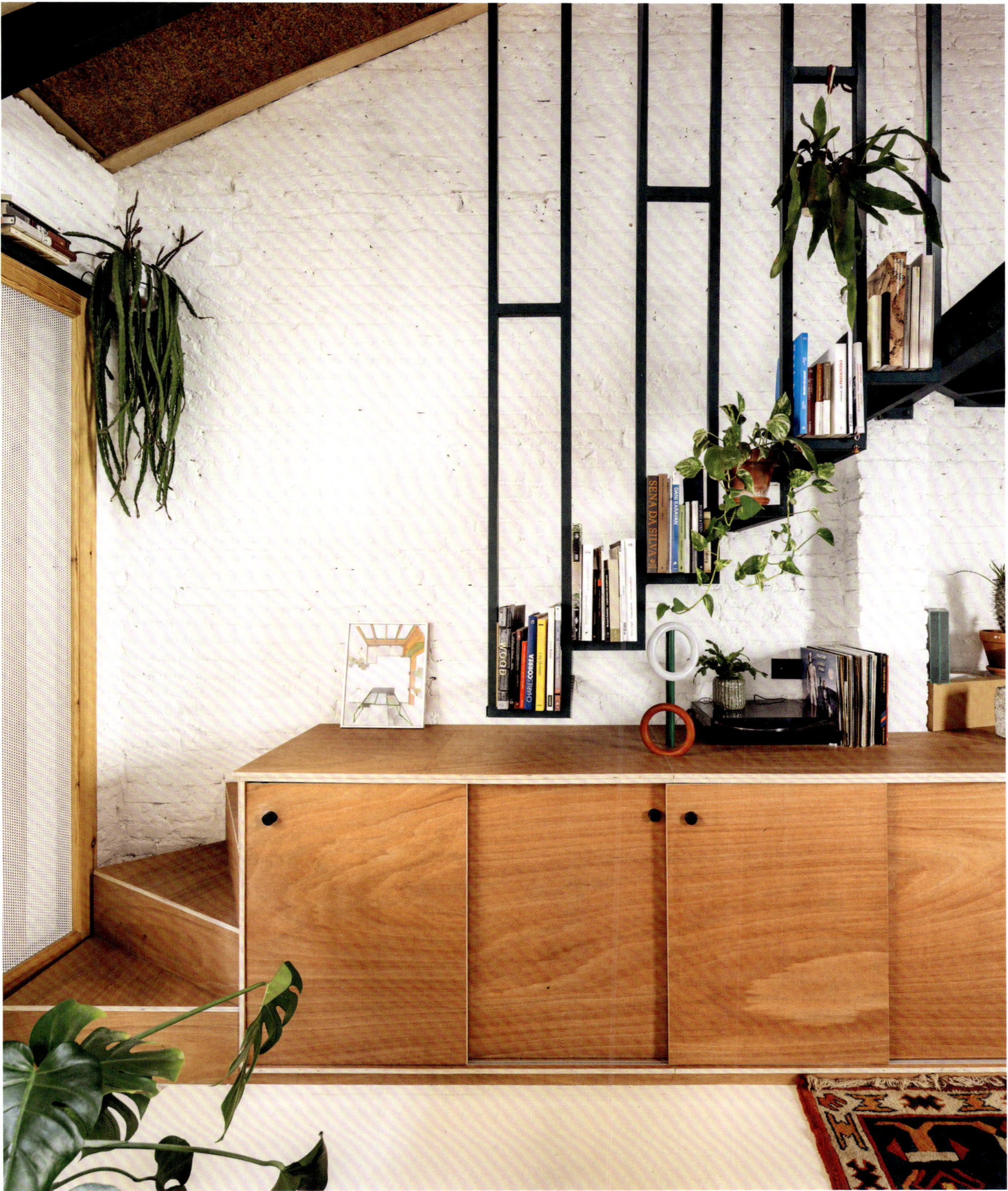

WOOD
CHARLES CORREA
City Quarters
SENA DA SILVA
DANI KARAVAN

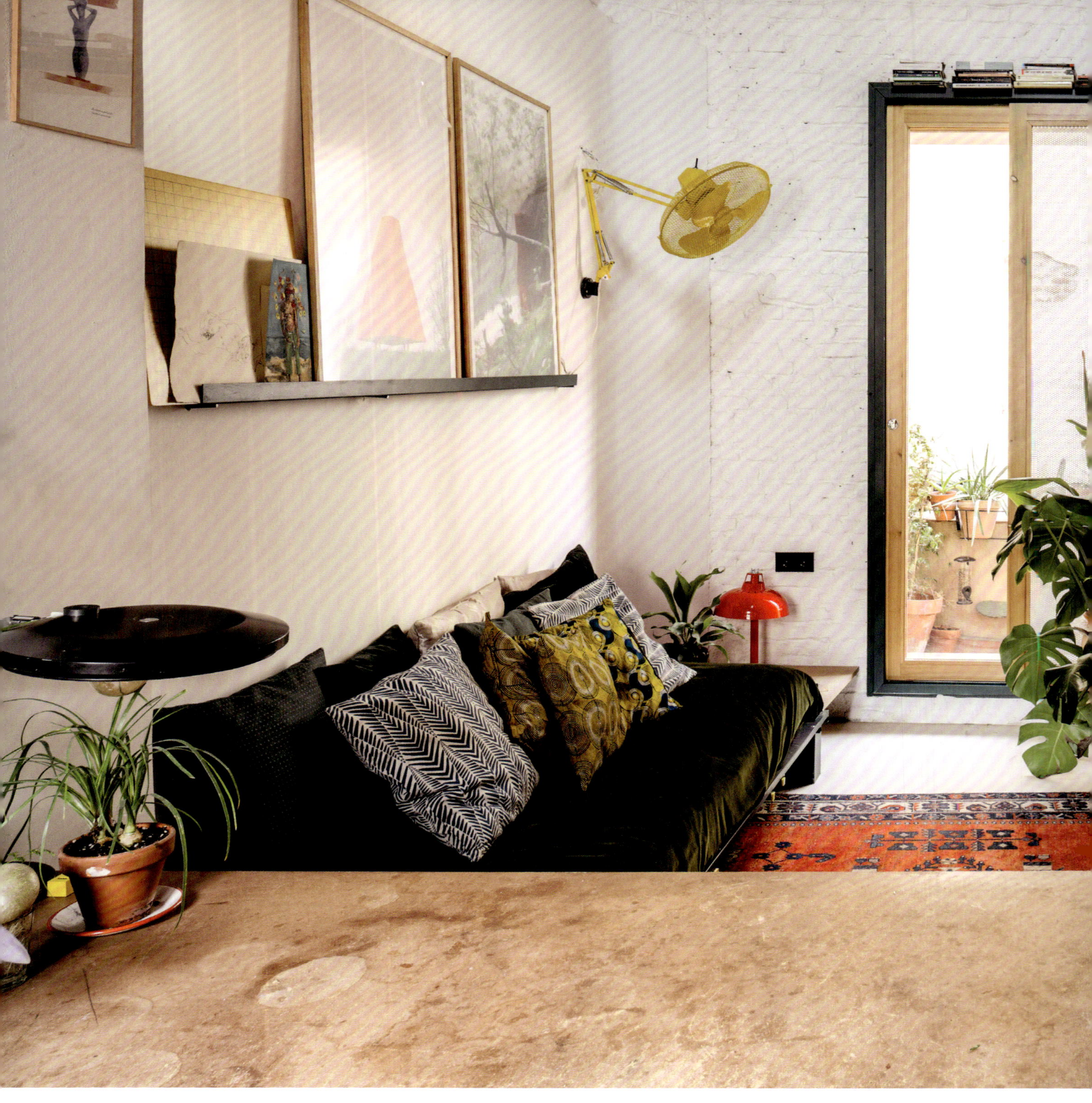

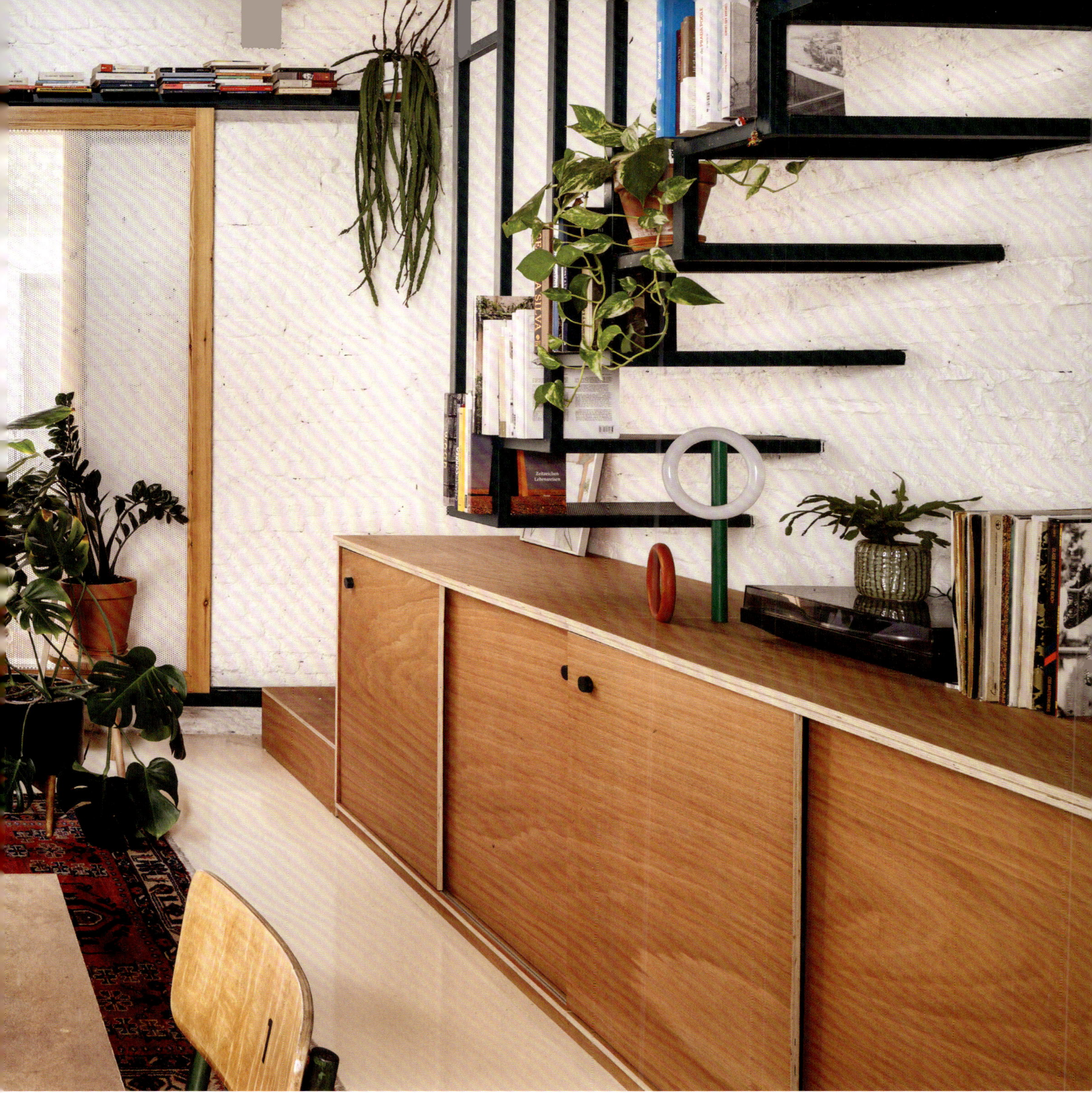

ABOVE Forest green touches and plants warm up the timber and painted brick.

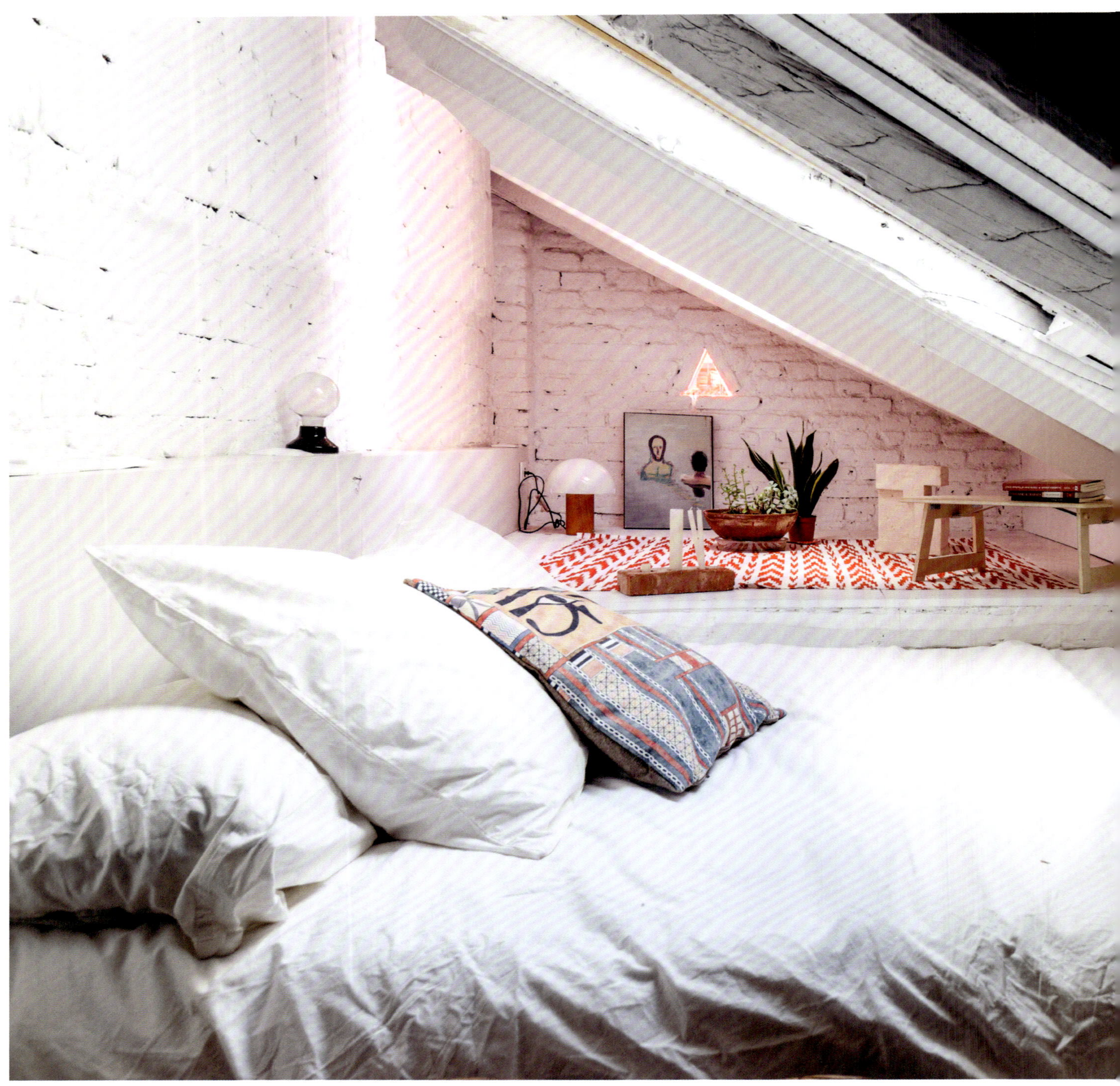

ABOVE There is just enough space to sit up in bed under the pitched roof.

OPPOSITE The green and timber theme is continued in the bathroom.

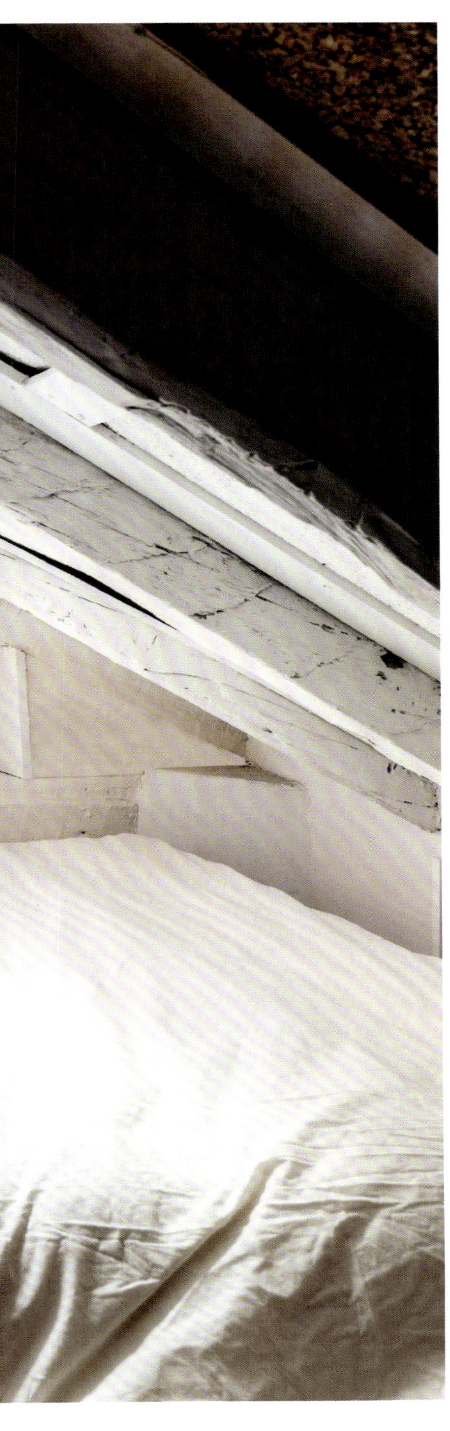

This apartment is one of the tiniest yet most captivating in Madrid.

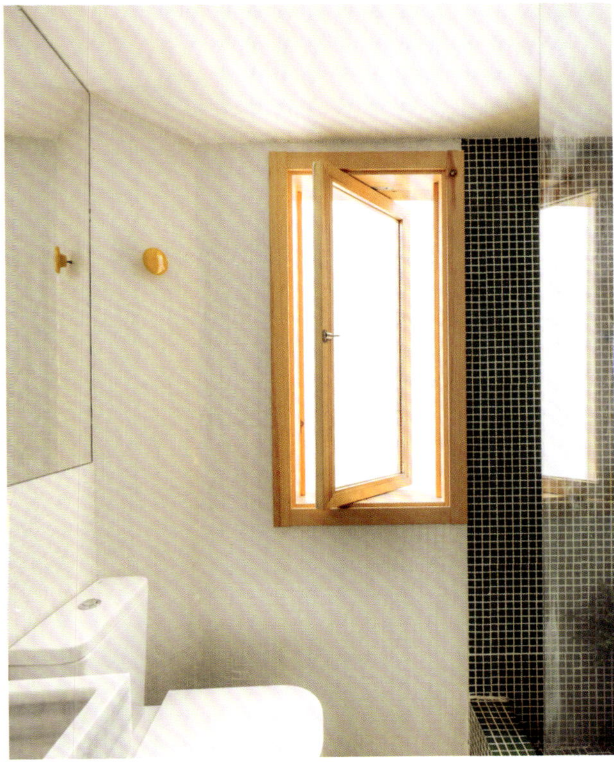

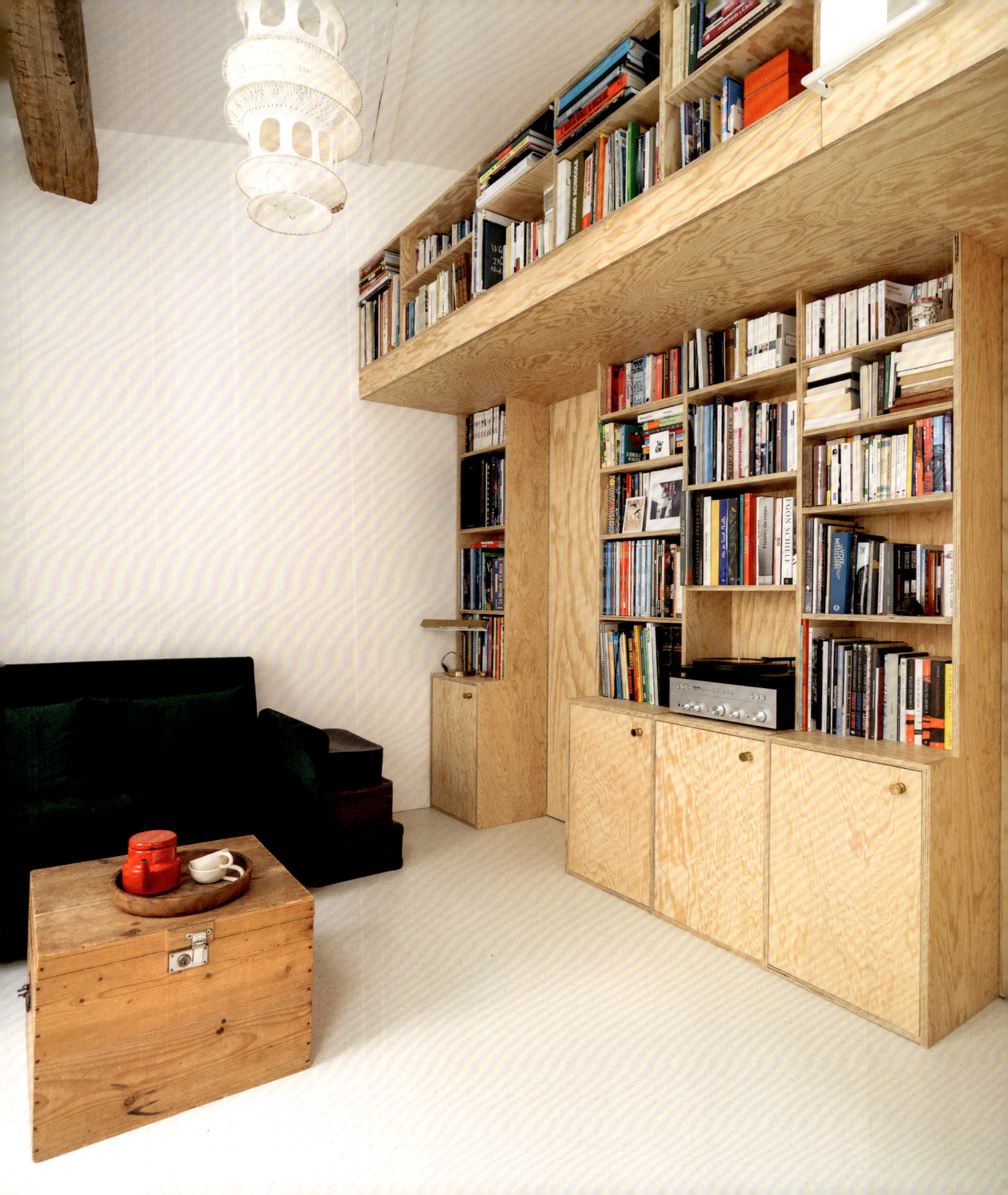
DELACROIX
EGON SCHIELE

Jourdain

24m² / 258ft²
BILOBA.archi
Jourdain, Paris

The story of this home's creation reads something like an architectural fairytale. A young couple rescues a dark dilapidated apartment and transforms it into a natural-light-filled home decorated with carefully considered finds and thoroughly sentimental pieces passed down through both sides of the family.

Located in a tiny and modest building in the 20th district of Paris, Jourdain is the unassuming feat of owner and architect Matthieu Torres and his partner. 'Our main goal was to make this apartment as sustainable and economical as possible,' explains Torres. Most of the renovation was done by the couple themselves to 'save money, take good care of the details and to improve [our] building skills'.

Torres started by gutting the whole interior, which included three tiny rooms and low, constricting ceilings. Hidden above the damaged ceiling boards was enough volume to add a small mezzanine level, and so the 24-sq-m (258-sq-ft) space became a 31-sq-m (333-sq-ft) apartment. The original space also had no bathroom or toilet, so the addition of a bathroom had to be considered in the budget as well.

The entryway is a bright and airy double-height space. Three skylights were added to keep the home perpetually full of light. The exposed original wooden beams, what Torres terms 'the skeleton of the apartment', add an earthy quality.

French pine plywood, chosen for its durability, the couple's desired aesthetic and to fit their limited budget, was used for much of the joinery. The mezzanine level was added by creating a 'compact furniture unit', which includes the bathroom, built-in bookshelves, a walk-in wardrobe and the bedroom in the space above the unit.

The mezzanine bedroom, accessed by a foldable ladder, is a simple-yet-warm space. A skylight 'provides a little window to the skyscape' and a plywood box forms the headboard, which doubles as a shelf.

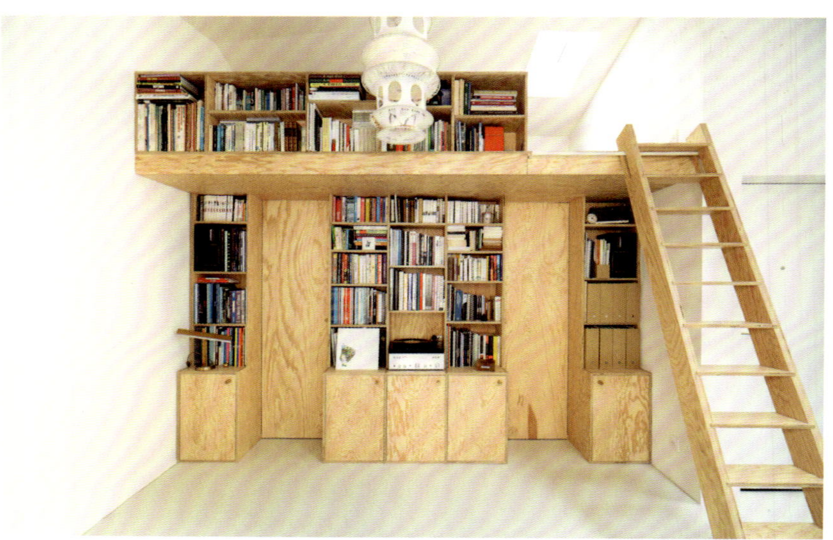

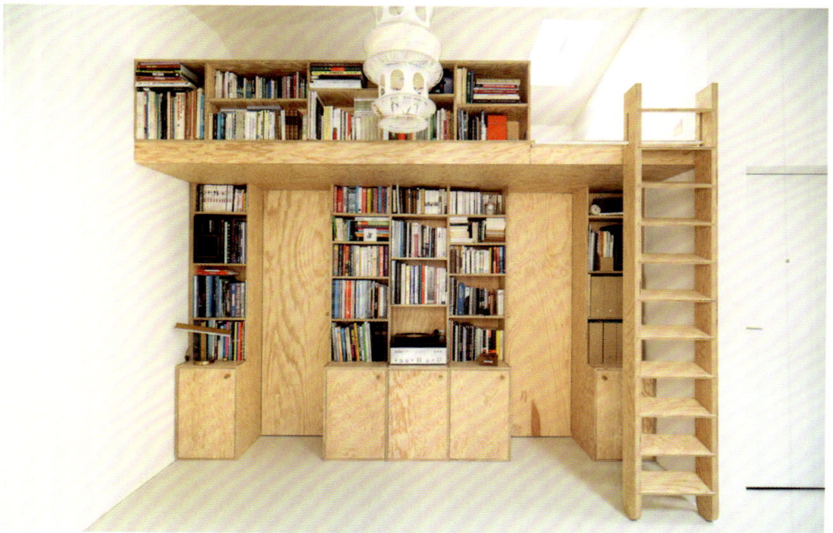

PAGE 228 The couple loves books and music so lots of bookshelves were included in their design and span the height of the first and mezzanine levels.

TOP RIGHT A ladder provides easy access to the mezzanine-level bedroom.

RIGHT The joinery unit was a major design element, or as the couple calls it: 'the core of the house'.

AFTER

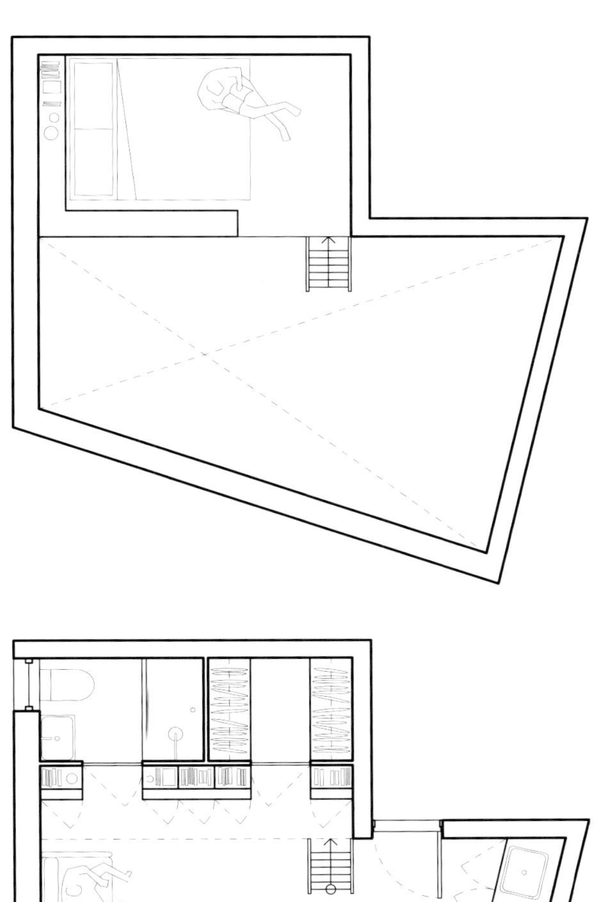

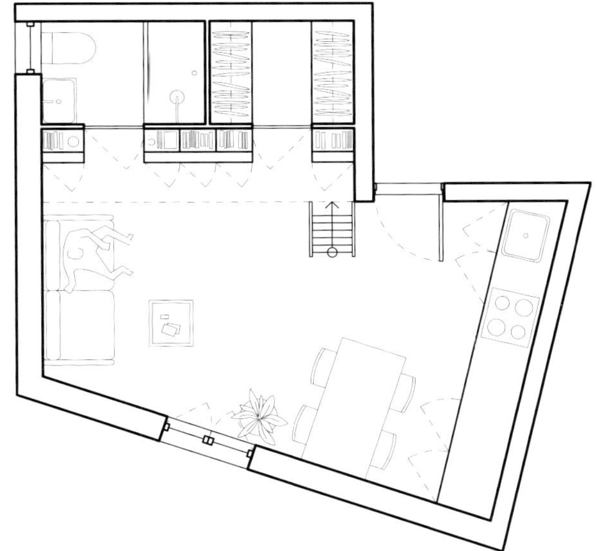

BEFORE

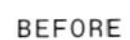

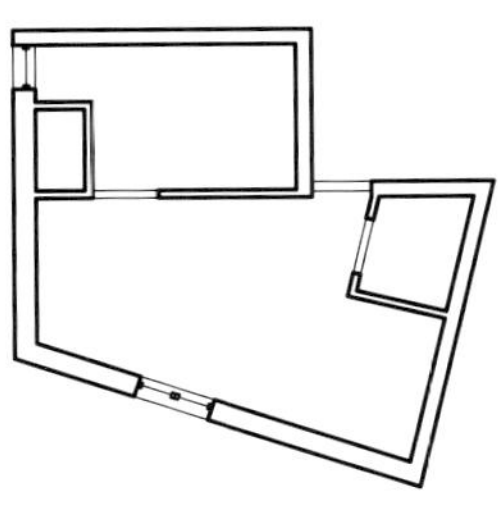

Scale 1:100

1 2 3 4 5m

Back down the ladder, the bathroom has been designed around a small window. White tiles, white taps and a white showerhead were chosen to create the impression of more volume. The white elements also act as a light-bouncing backdrop for the room's showpiece – a playful shower curtain made from a shiny gold emergency blanket.

Next to the bathroom is a compact walk-in wardrobe, fitted with a bench and storage. Both the bathroom and the wardrobe act as buffers to filter noise from the neighbours and common areas of the building.

As the couple love to cook together, the kitchen became the main feature of the apartment. A 'funny boot-shaped' cover was designed for the rangehood and ample storage was created below the counters to keep the wall free of clutter and cupboards.

'We like the idea of simplicity, irregularity and imperfection,' Torres says. 'Almost all of our furniture pieces are simple and meaningful items that we inherited or found on the street.' These sentimental pieces include the doorknobs on the built-in joinery unit that were salvaged from Torres's grandparents' apartment and an old workshop table that belonged to the grandfather of Torres's partner and now serves as their dining table.

So many things about Jourdain just feel right. Mostly, it demonstrates the possibility of a home being deeply personal and seemingly easy to replicate, and in doing so inspiring innovation at its most attainable.

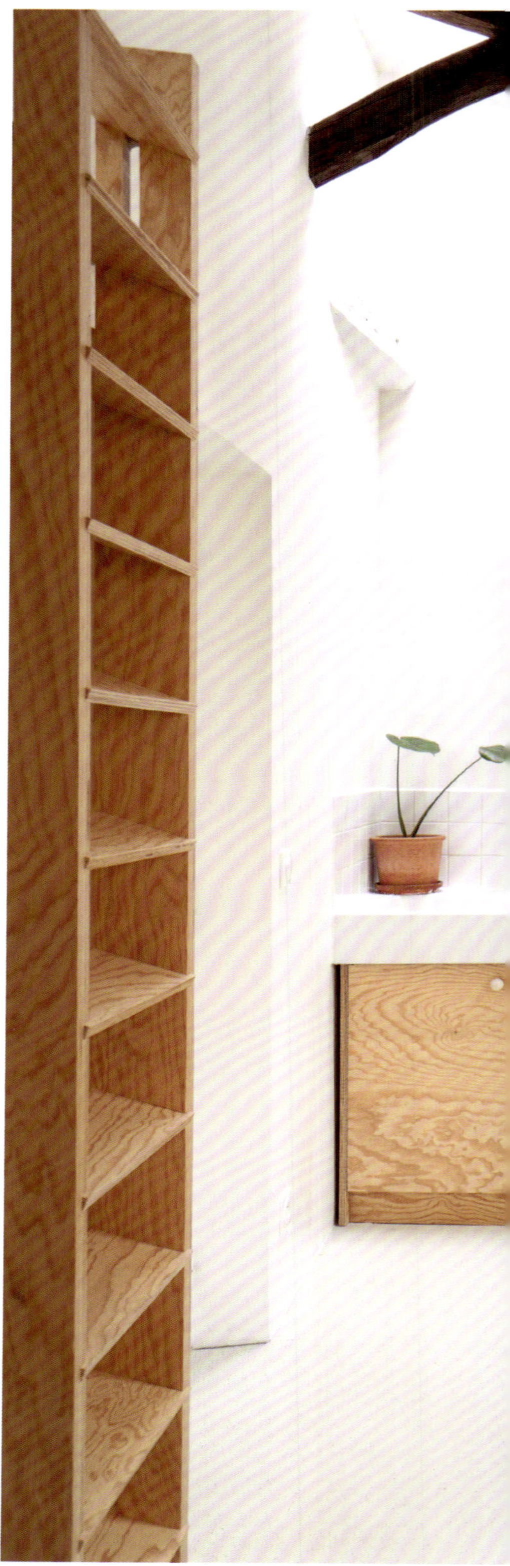

RIGHT The couple asked a friend who is a ceramicist to create the knobs for their kitchen cabinets. 'It is a pleasure to see and touch the designer's work everyday,' says Torres.

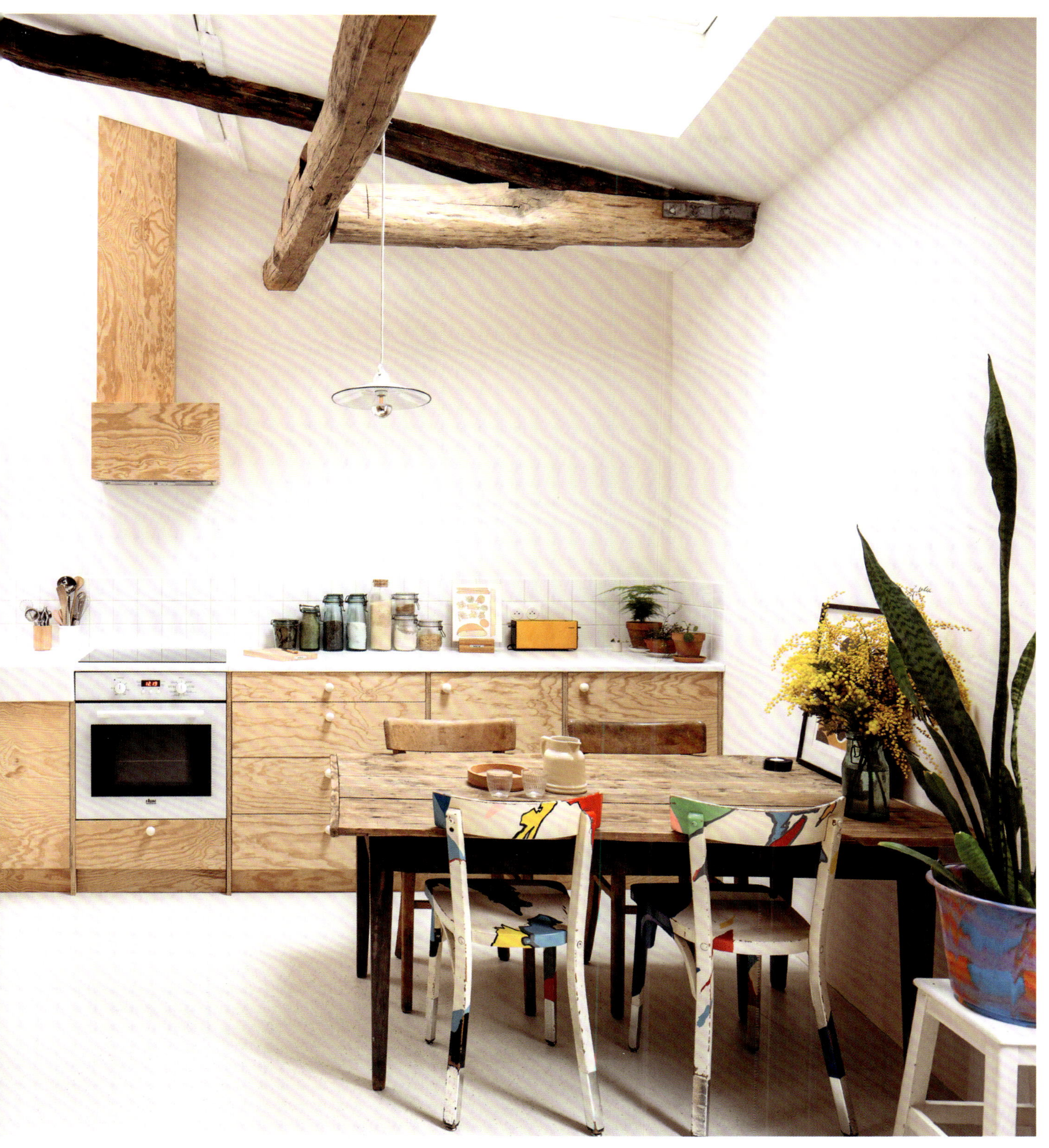

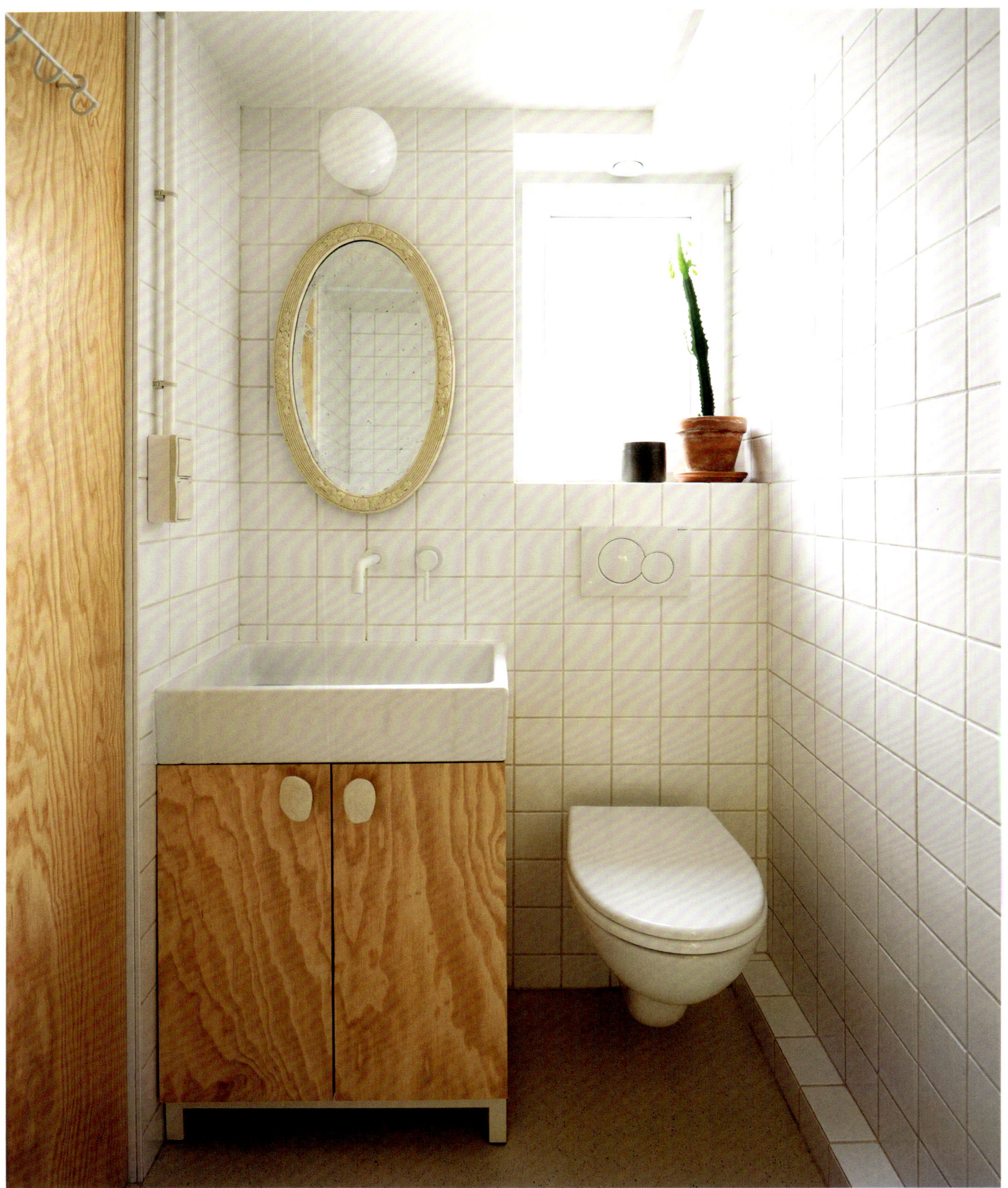

OPPOSITE In the bathroom, the mirror above the sink came from a relative – yet another sentimental touch. The sink was found on the street months before the apartment renovation.

RIGHT The mezzanine-level bedroom was kept simple with plywood framing and a small shelf above the bed for more books and other small items.

BELOW 'We love the warm, shiny reflections that it brings all over the space,' Torres says of using an emergency blanket as a shower curtain.

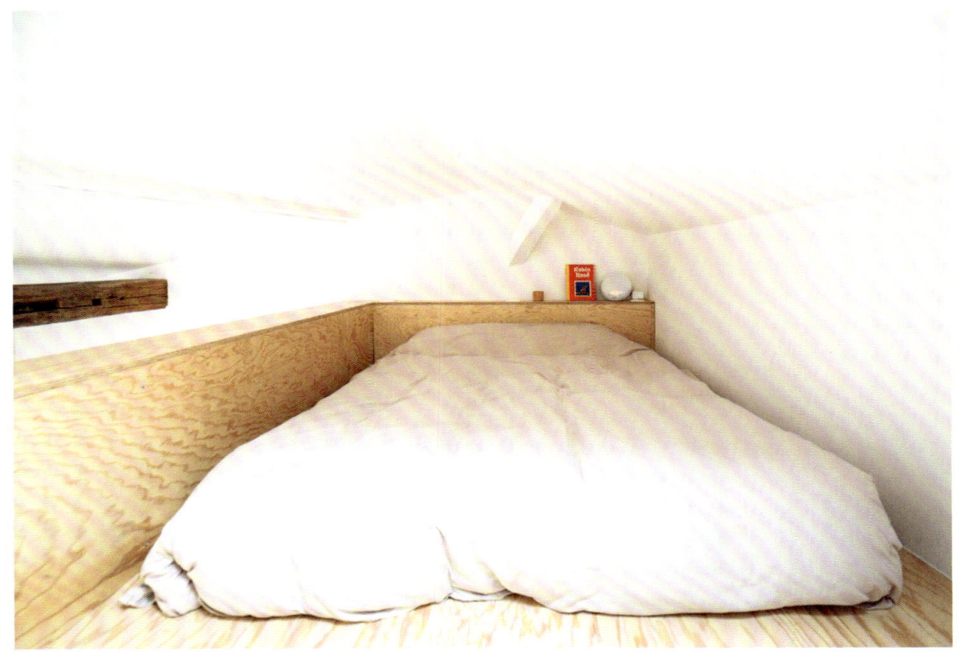

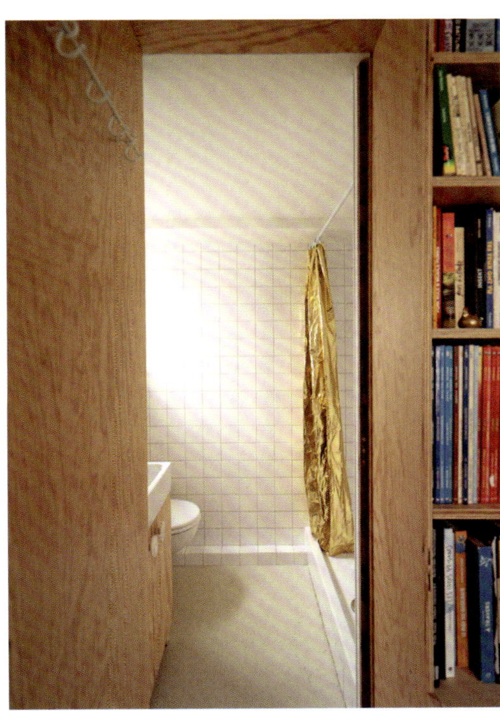

'We like the idea of simplicity, irregularity and imperfection.'

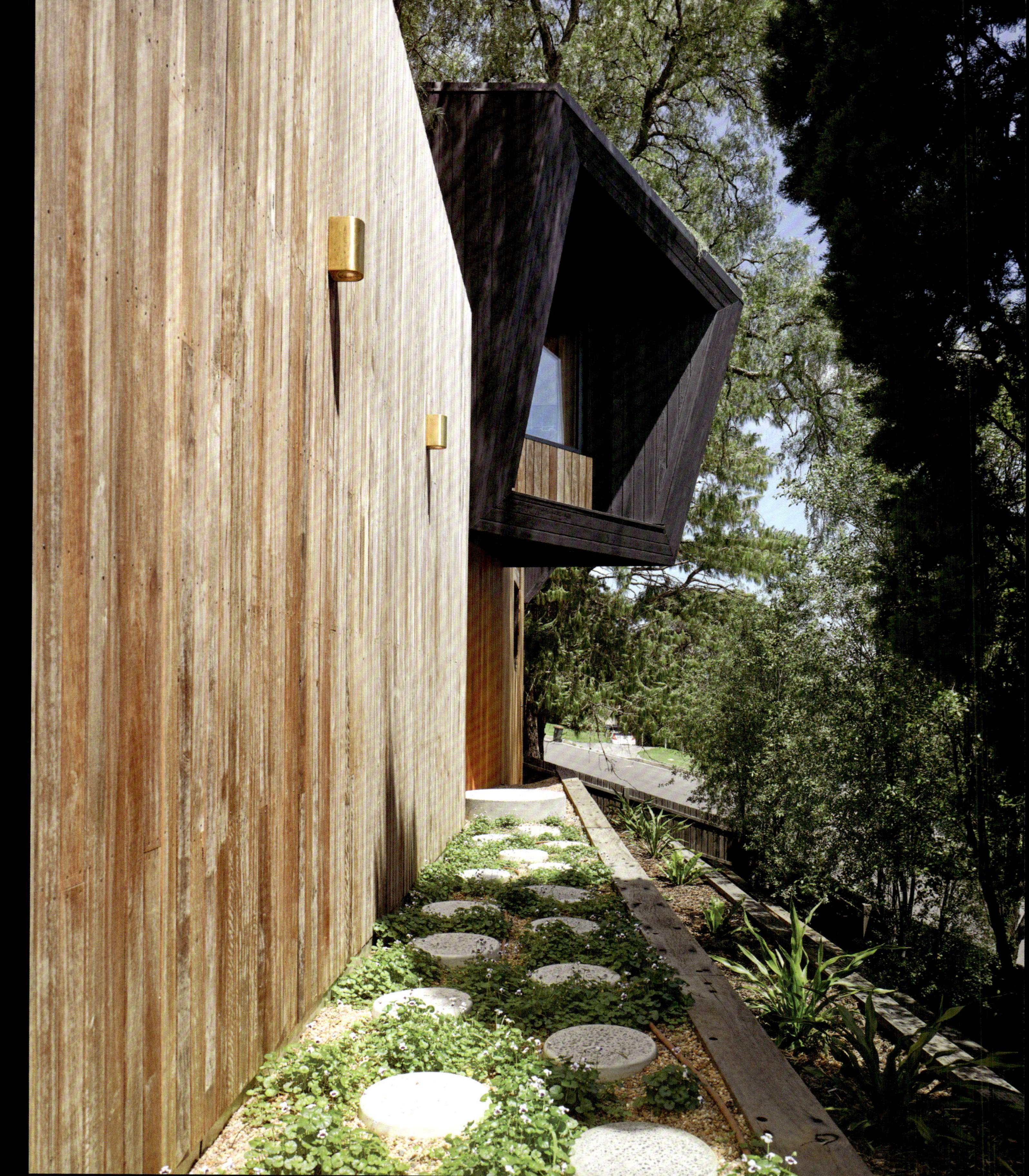

Pepper Tree Passive House

54m² / 581ft²
Alexander Symes Architect & Souter Built
Unanderra, Wollongong

The pepper tree is a hardy and resilient plant that is loved by landscapers due to its bright red berries and delicate foliage. In the case of Pepper Tree Passive House, a 60-year-old pepper tree is so revered the home has been built around it, allowing it to continue to thrive, and become an ever-changing feature of the home.

A remarkable example of sustainable architecture and harmonious design, Pepper Tree Passive House was designed by Alexander Symes in collaboration with owner-builder Adam Souter. Located in Unanderra, just an hour-and-a-half south of Sydney, the 54-sq-m (581-sq-ft) house meets the five critical factors of International Passive House standards: advanced insulation performance, high-performance glazing systems, minimal air infiltration, a heat recovery ventilation system and thermal bridge reconstruction. To achieve this, sustainable materials and technologies were utilised. For example, bifacial solar panels serve a dual purpose of generating electricity and providing shade.

Despite the challenging steep slope of the site, the house blends in harmoniously with the surrounding landscape. The pathway to the house consists of concrete stepping stones made from surplus material from the slab pour that lead to a set of stairs constructed from reclaimed timber and wedged between the original building and the new secondary structure. This use of salvaged and waste materials is a key feature throughout.

The entrance of the home is through a triple-glazed door that not only lets in northerly light but helps the house's performance. This leads to a wing with a living room at one end and the kitchen at the other. The living area features a custom-made daybed, constructed in-house using leftover flooring material. The daybed has an integrated side piece cut on an angle to allow for easy movement throughout the living area. At night, the trundle can be pulled out to create a second bedroom.

PAGE 236 Pepper Tree Passive House's timber exterior is a nod to the natural structure the home is built around.

BOTTOM LEFT Varying shades of timber contrast against the sky and trees above.

BELOW In the middle of it all, the pepper tree provides shade and is a magnificent beauty to behold.

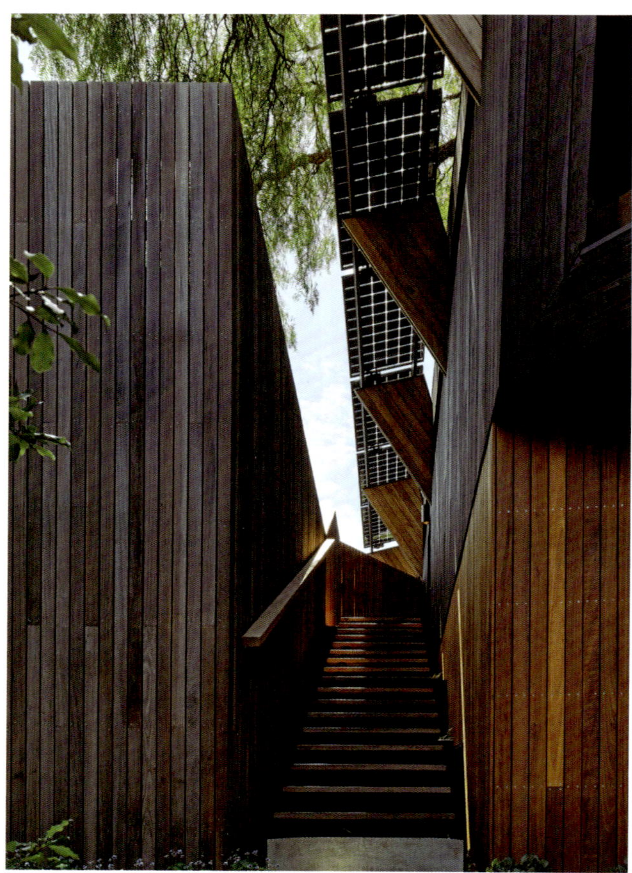

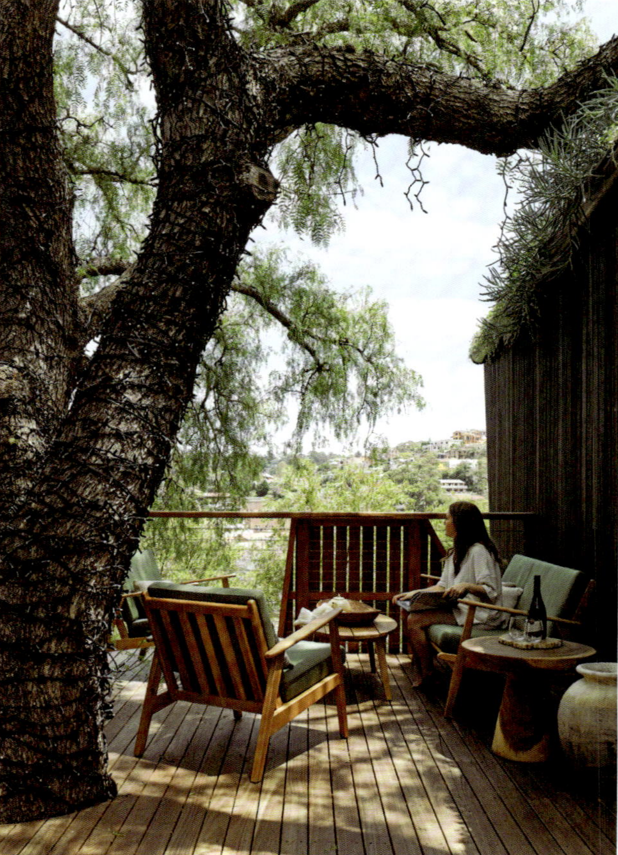

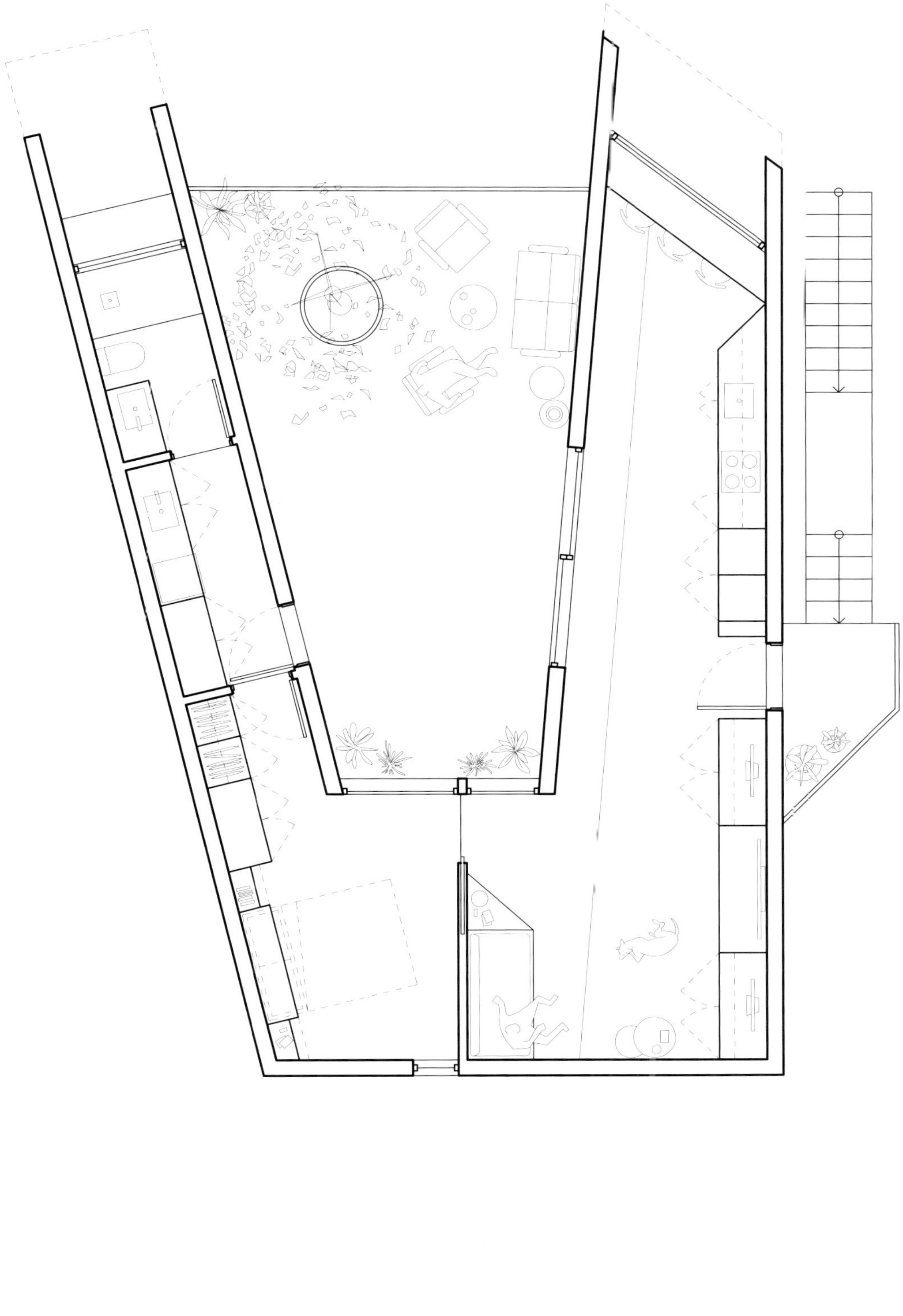

Scale 1:100

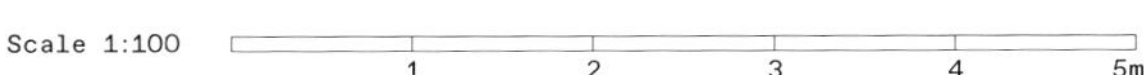

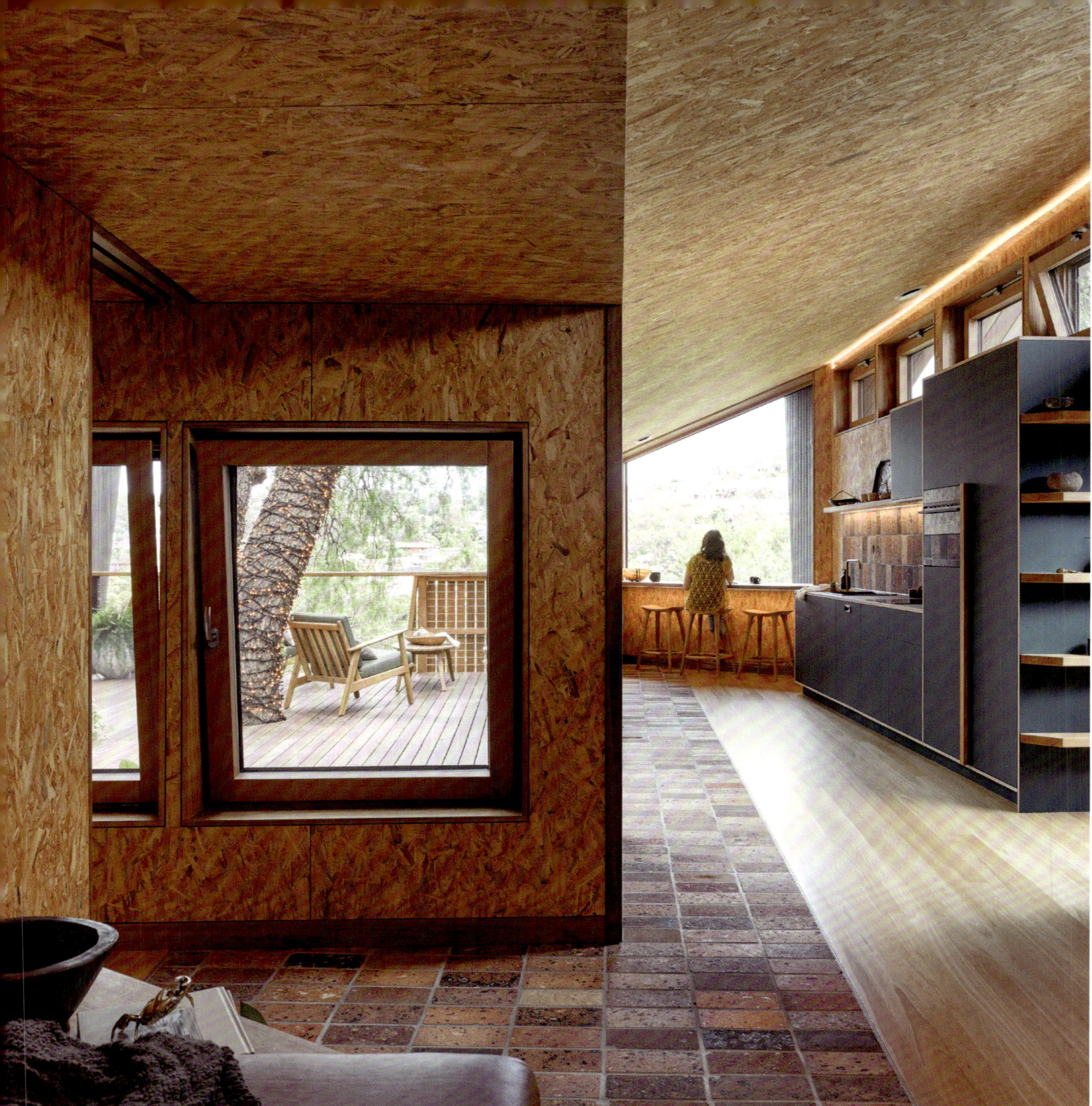

ABOVE Exterior and interior meet through the continuation of wood finishes and ample windows.

OPPOSITE LEFT Ambient lighting makes even a functional space like the laundry feel warm and welcoming.

OPPOSITE RIGHT The convict brick splashback is illuminated by an LED light under the kitchen shelf.

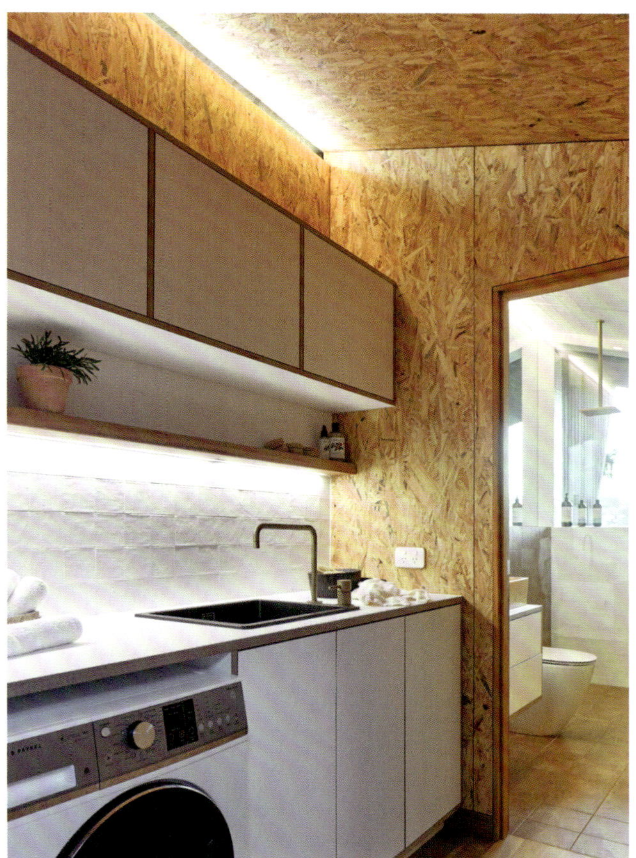

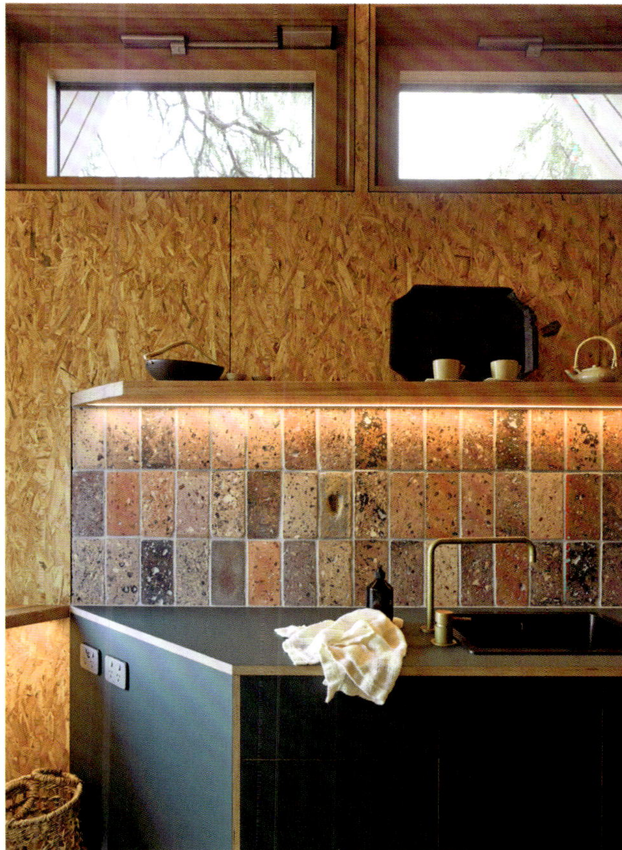

The kitchen includes a large sink, an induction cooktop, a rangehood, an integrated dishwasher, a combo microwave oven and a hidden fridge. A floating timber shelf with an LED light underneath provides lighting for the benchtop and washes light over the recycled convict-brick splashback. Instead of a traditional dining table, there is an angled breakfast bar, which is a more spatially efficient use of the dining area.

The bedroom is accessed through a custom-made OSB sliding door that seamlessly slides into a pocket in the wall. The bedside tables are floating shelves that were integrated into the joinery to save space. The wardrobe has an area for storing clothes, but also an office nook which is revealed behind a bi-fold pocket door. It was important to Souter that the home was dual purpose, functioning as both a home and office, so during the day the Murphy bed can be pushed up to reveal a drop-down desk tucked away underneath it.

This aesthetically pleasing and functional house conforms to modern living standards while reducing its environmental impact. Like the pepper tree, the home is resilient and sustainable. The exterior walls of the building are clad in burnt Shou Sugi Ban timber, a Japanese treatment of charring the wood that makes it termite-resistant and fire-retardant. Pepper Tree Passive House demonstrates how to live more intelligently and efficiently, with fewer resources and in a way that is sympathetic to our natural surrounds.

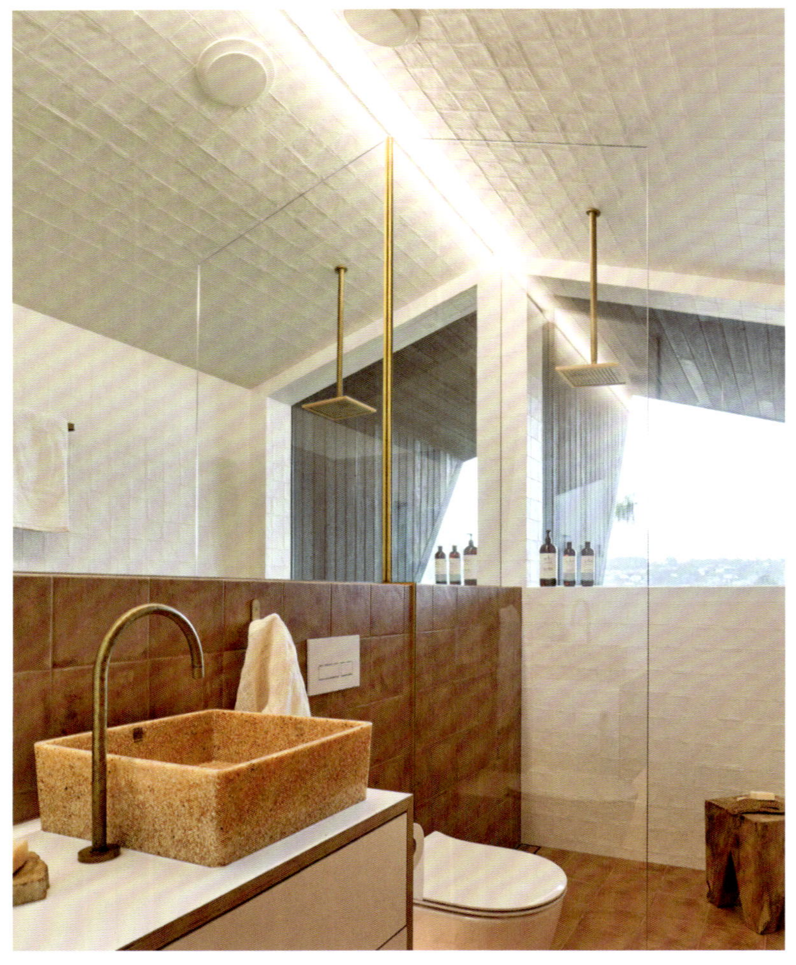

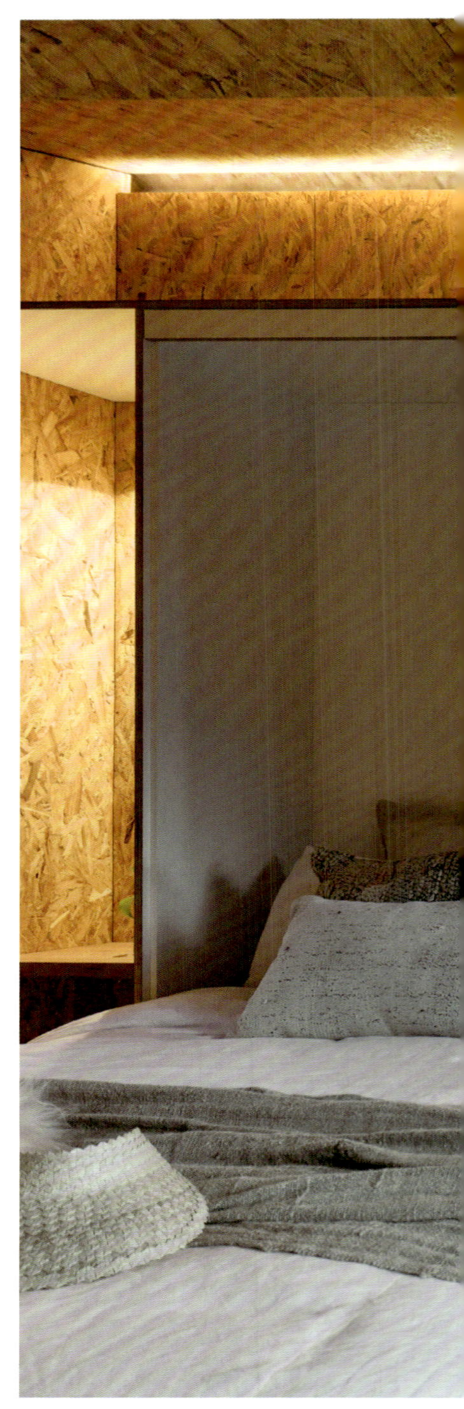

Pepper Tree Passive House demonstrates how to live more intelligently and efficiently, with fewer resources and in a way that is sympathetic to our natural surrounds.

OPPOSITE Mirrors and windows mean less electricity is needed to light up the home.

BELOW A nook provides a cosy spot for the head of the bed.

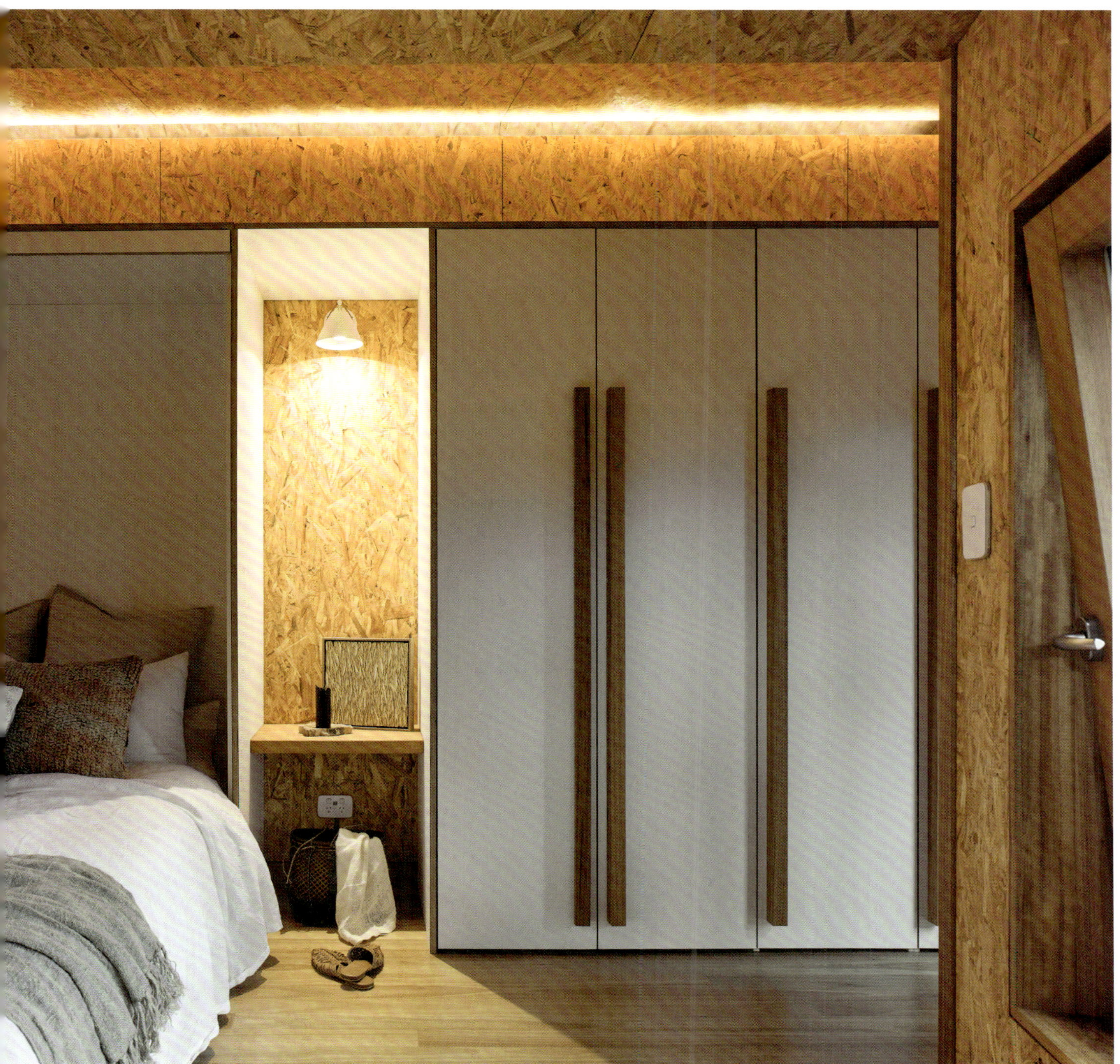

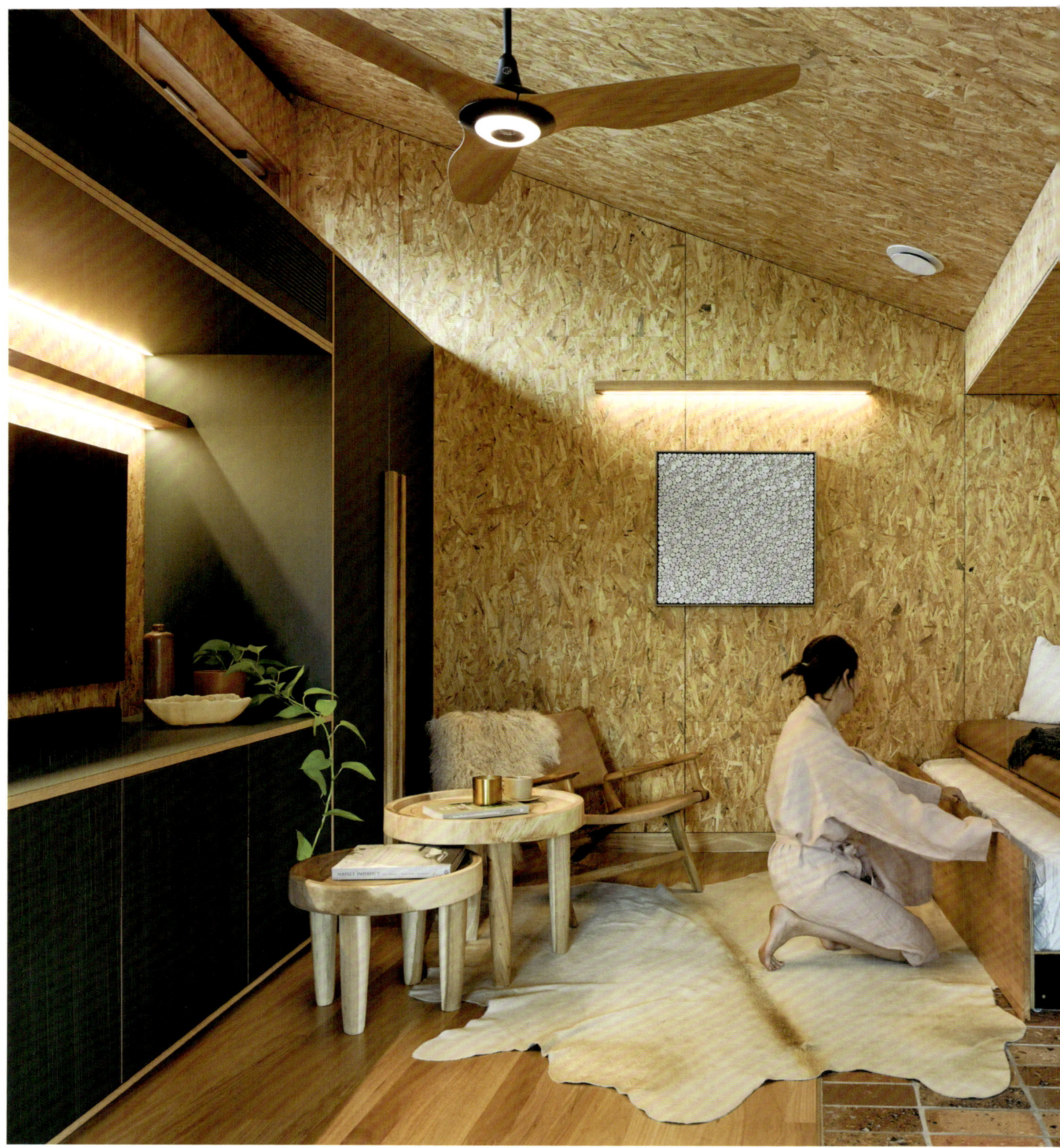

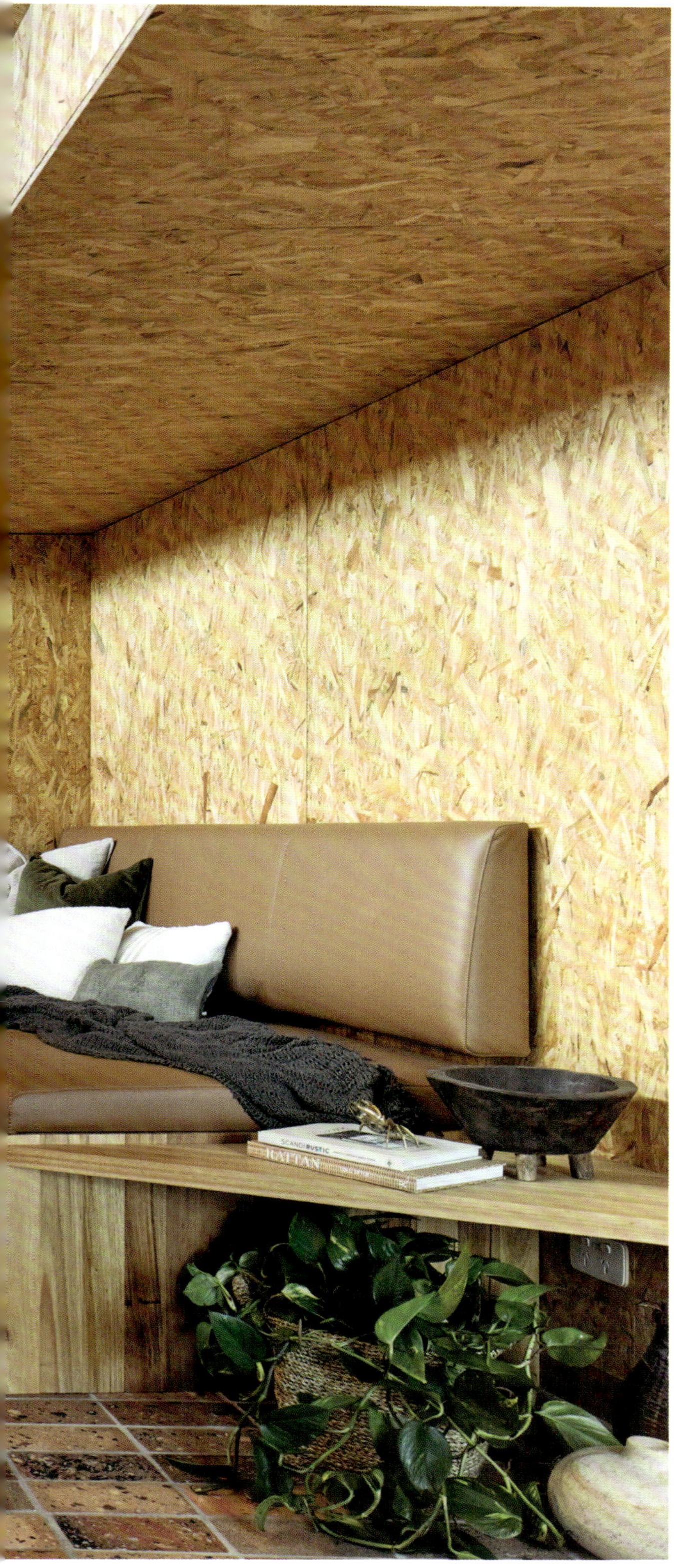

LEFT A well-designed small home will often have integrated and multipurpose hidden furniture like this slide-out trundle bed under the couch.

BELOW A custom joinery wall features a home office and a kitchenette.

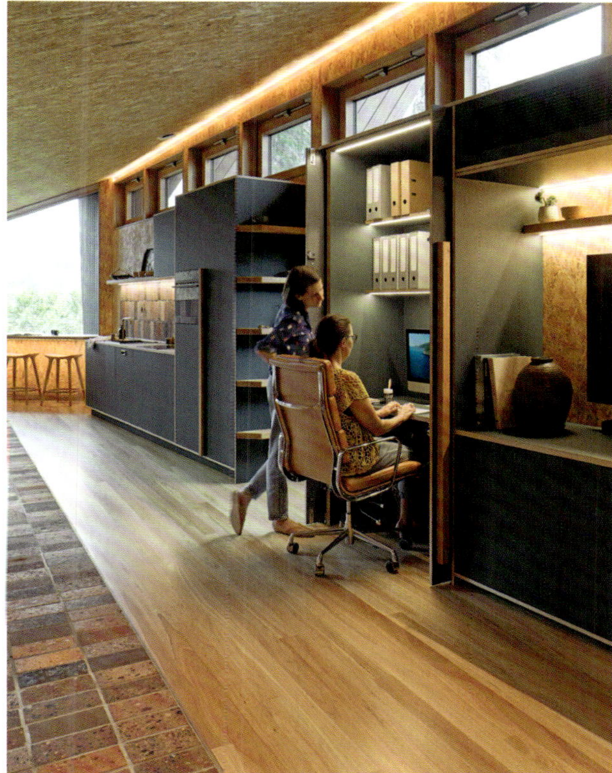

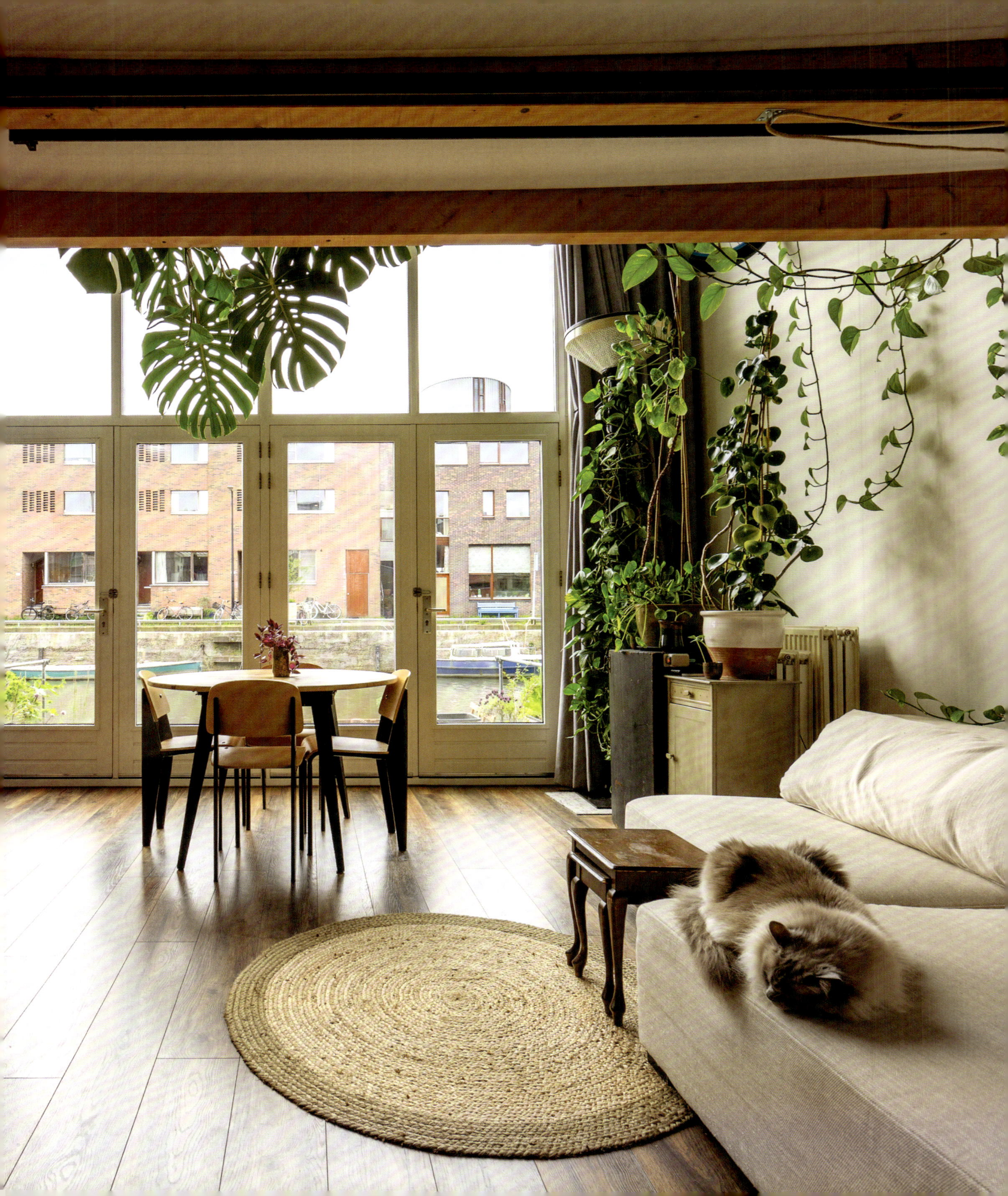

Scheeps

45m² / 484ft²
Fadime Gökkaya & Koen Fraijman
Eastern Harbour District, Amsterdam

Scheeps is the home of modern-day inventor, designer and maker, Koen Fraijman and his partner Fadime Gökkaya. Much of the home's magic is due to the couple's ability to repurpose found objects in unexpected ways to create furniture specifically for the space. The duo are not afraid to bring home cumbersome treasures sourced from surprising locations in their hand luggage either.

The 45-sq-m (484-sq-ft) space sits on the waterfront of Amsterdam's East Harbour District. 'Our vision was formulated in "interactions" with the house and not in square metres or materials,' Fraijman says of living in the loft for years before buying it from his mother.

The couple undertook the renovation themselves. They loved the high ceilings and big windows that opened to the waterfront and were drawn to the playfulness of the layout so they made very few structural changes to the loft. They added a kitchen island, built a frame around the bed and extended the terrace by adding a floating deck. The deck, however, was no small feat as it had to be built indoors, partially disassembled to manoeuvre around a central column and then reassembled outside.

Unusually, the front door opens onto a split-level entrance so the design rationale here was to keep the area clear so as not to disrupt the sightline through the house and out to the water. There are still some unique elements though, like the ceiling light hanging in the hallway. Fraijman and Gökkaya found the light in an abandoned factory in Istanbul – it's one of the treasures that travelled home in their hand luggage.

The bathroom sits just off the entryway. Once Fraijman and Gökkaya had figured out the placement of the plumbing pipes they custom built a cabinet for the washing machine and basin. This cabinet also houses a built-in litter box for Sok the cat.

PAGE 246 Sok the cat lounges in front of the big windows that open up to the waterfront floating deck.

BELOW The view of the apartment from the water. Assembling the deck was no small feat as it had to be partially disassembled to get past the central column of the home and then once outside, reassembled on the water.

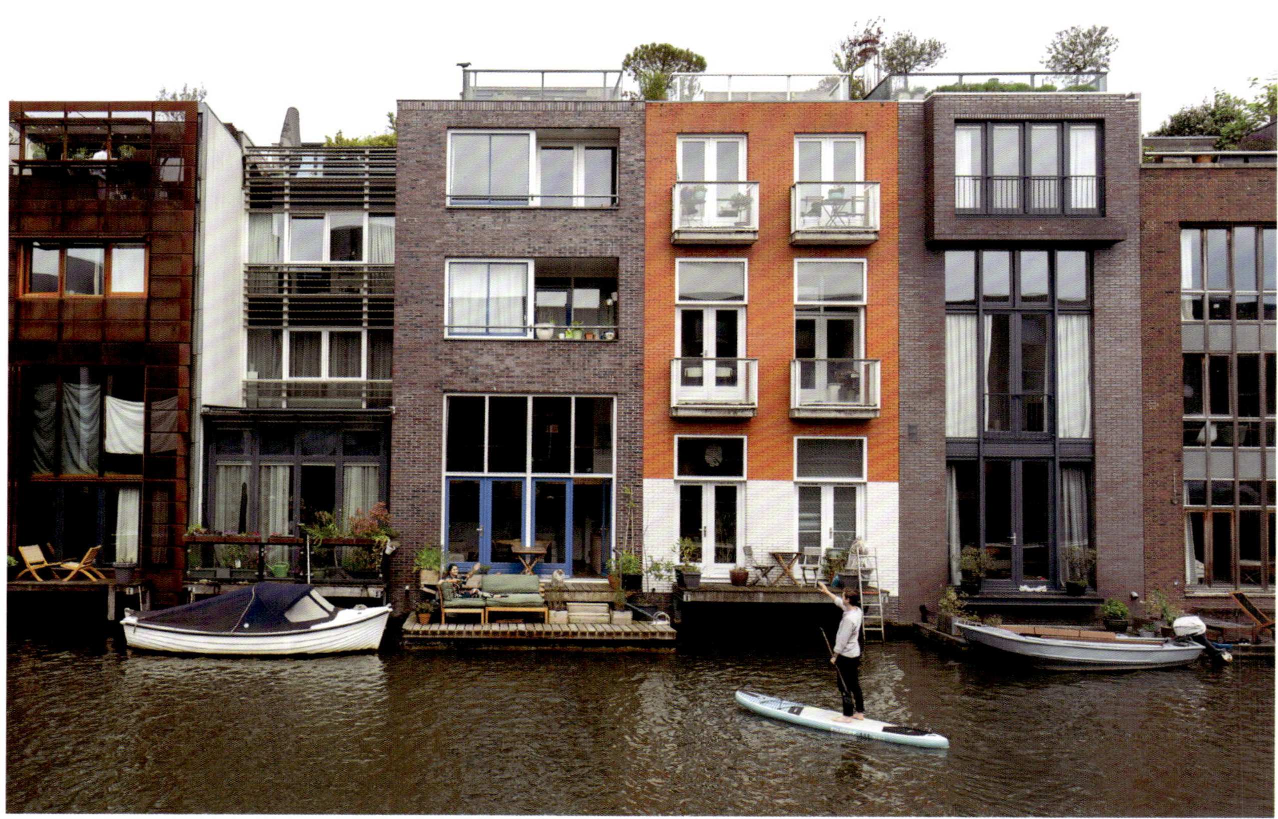

AFTER

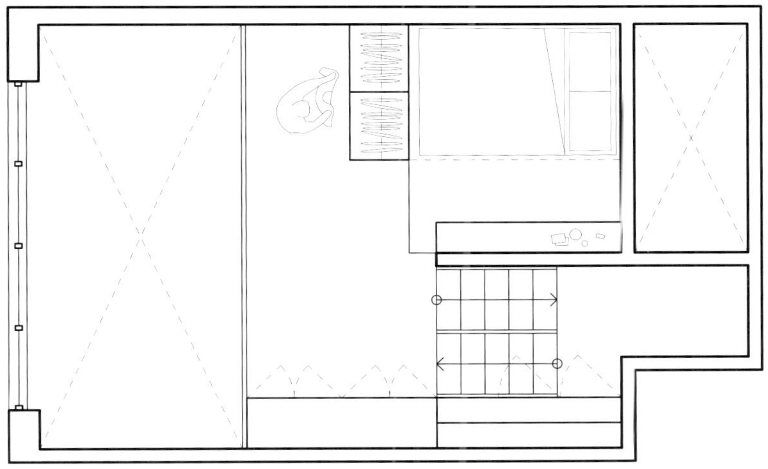

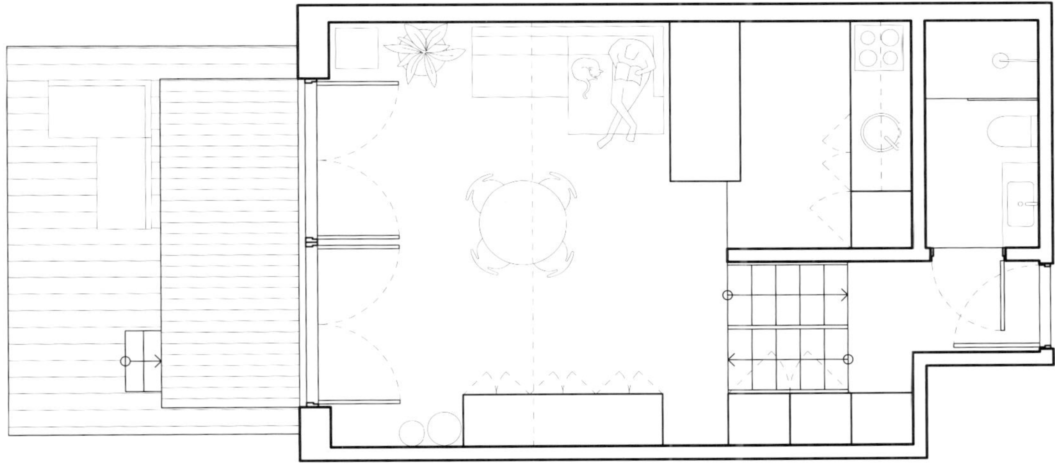

BEFORE

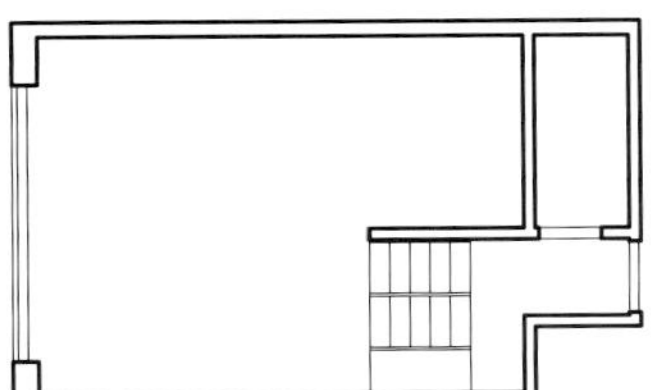

Scale 1:100

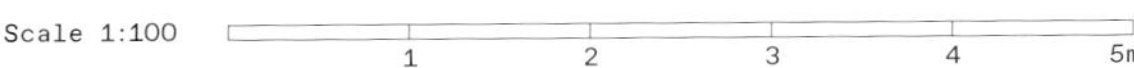

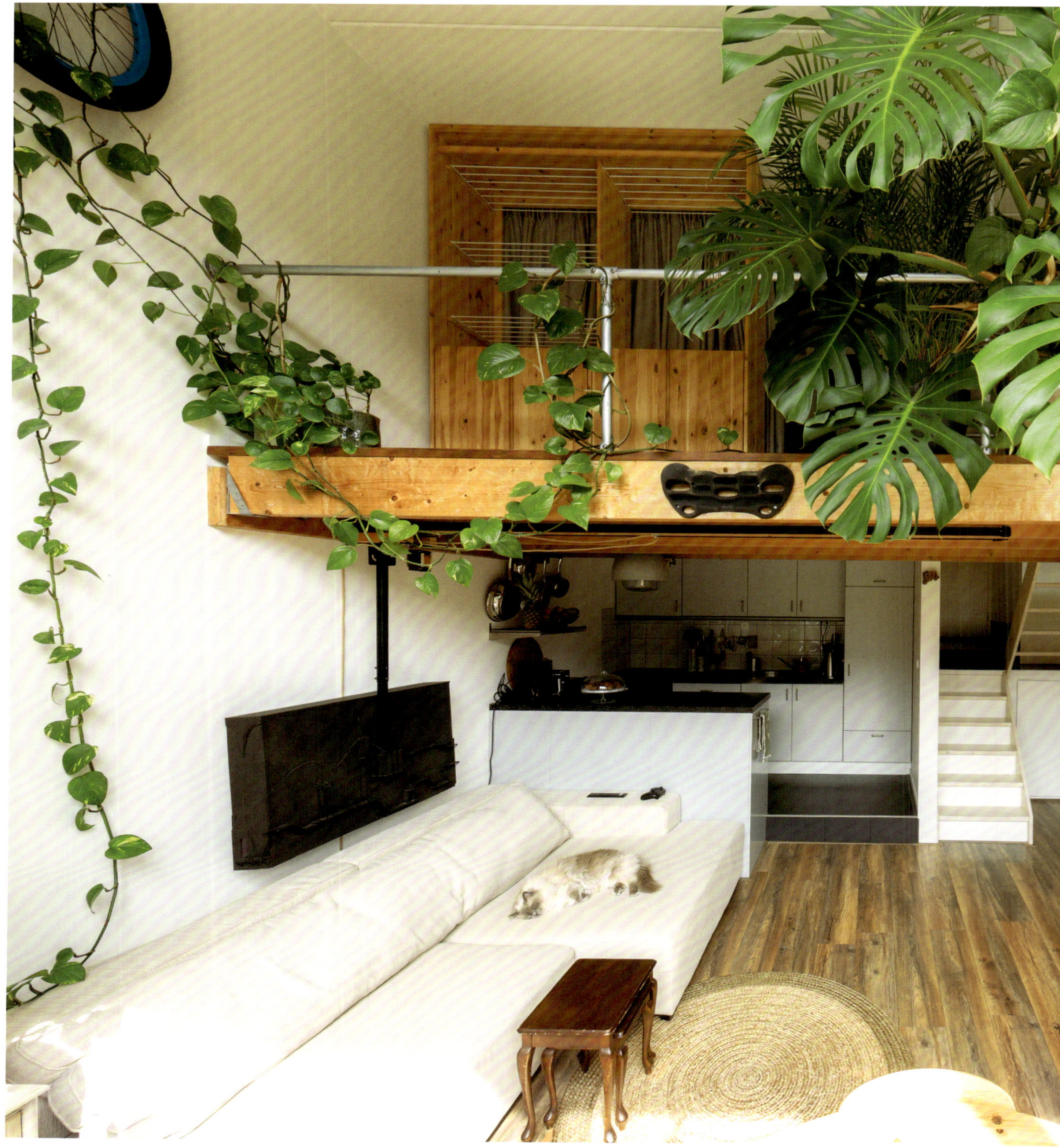

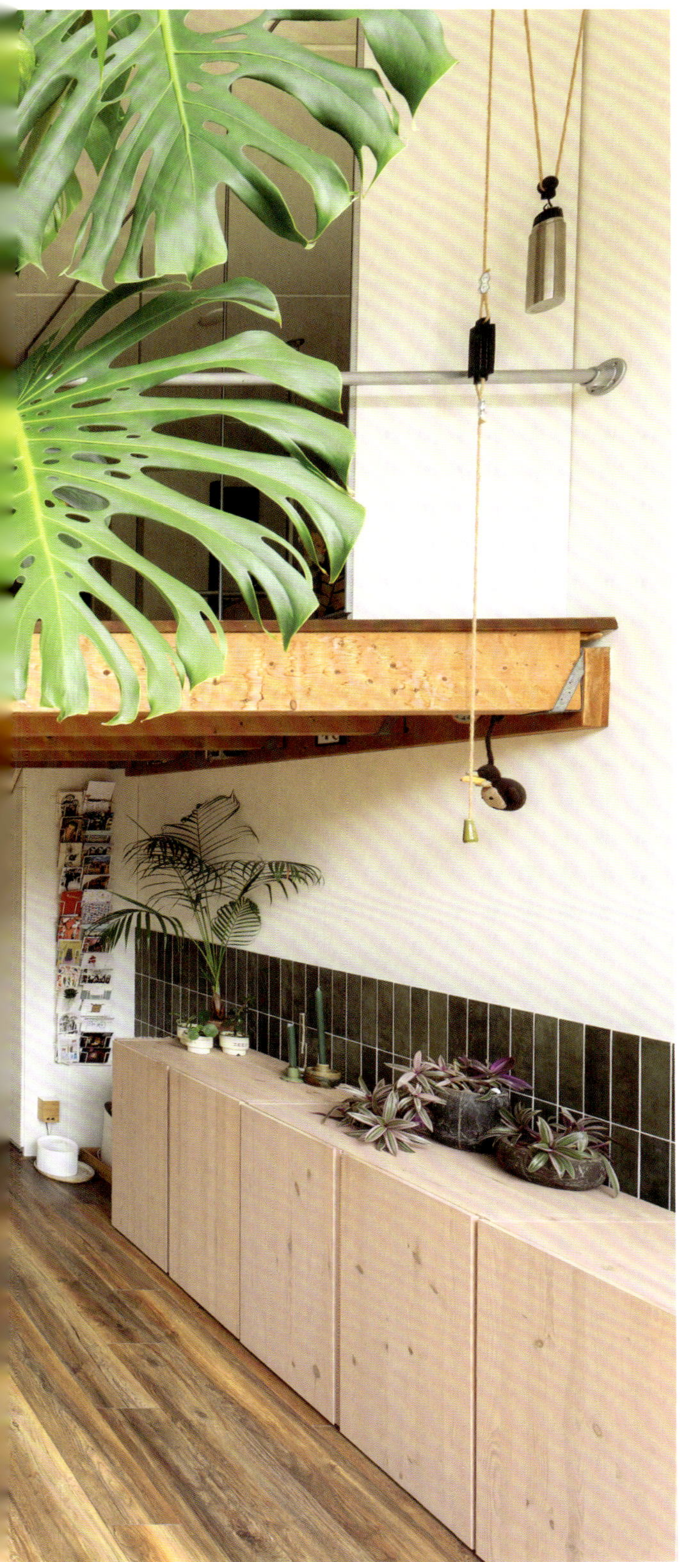

In the living area, a plethora of plants happily reach toward the light streaming in through the south-facing windows. On the opposite wall, a tiled green wall and a distinctive blush-pink cabinet make for an eye-catching duo. The cabinet is used for storage but also features a fold-out desk and a hiding place for Sok.

Of all the clever custom-made pieces, Fraijman is most proud of the television rig. Suspended by a rail on the ceiling, the television can be moved from against the wall to the middle of the room. When not in use, it's pulled back against the wall to show off a sculpture on the back of the rig. This adaptation is one of the many ways the designers have used their ingenuity to customise their home

The couple liked the 'simplicity and calmness' of the original grey kitchen so their only change was adding a kitchen island and building a large spice rack into the area above it. Another interesting find is the kitchen light that was originally a streetlamp from the municipality.

Up a few stairs to the bedroom, the bed sits within a wooden frame and is surrounded by curtains that help to keep the mosquitoes out and block out light at nighttime. The wooden structure at the end of the bed doubles as a drying rack and room divider.

During the day, small electric blinds on the south-facing windows help deflect the sun. There was only one remote for these blinds so Fraijman created a playful solution by attaching the remote to a pulley system that sits between storeys. The light switches were also located at the front entrance, which was very inconvenient when lying in bed, so Fraijman connected them to a comically large industrial switch that he found in an abandoned factory in Belgium.

'I like to make things myself and that really creates a certain style,' Fraijman says of his and Gökkaya's entirely unique and inventive waterfront home.

LEFT Plants and the couple's inventive pulley system feature in the living room, along with the television rig with a sculpture on the back of it.

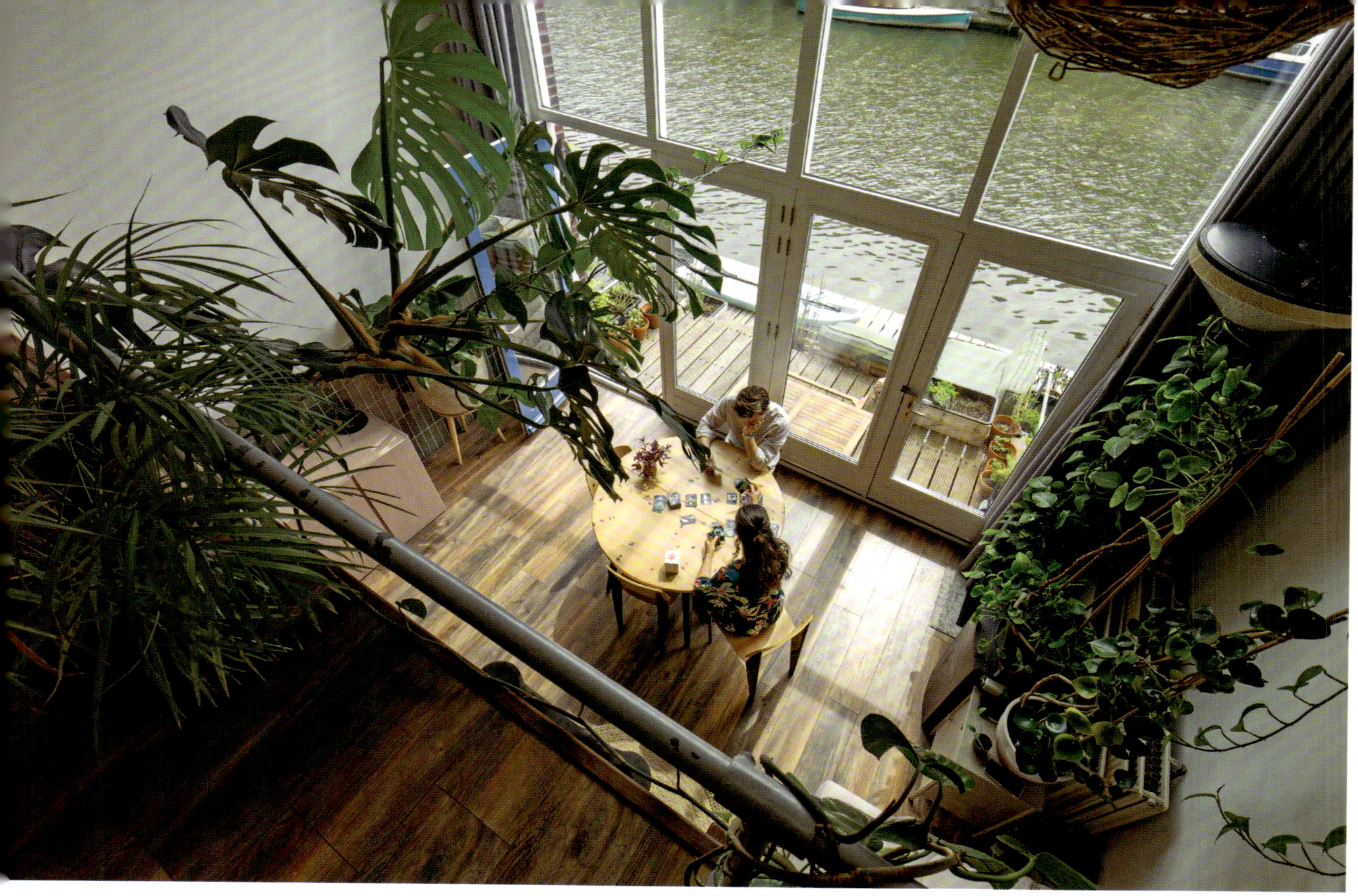

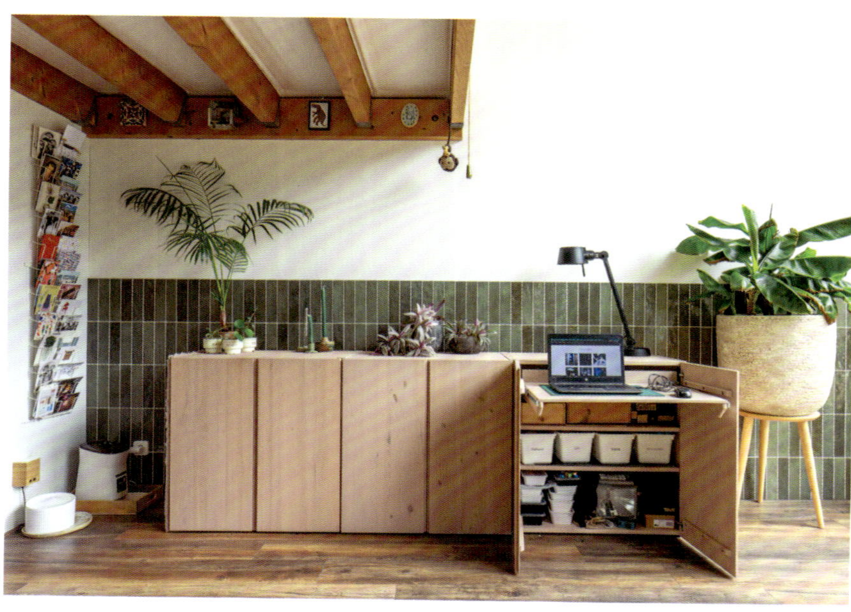

‘Our vision was formulated in “interactions” with the house and not in square metres or materials.’

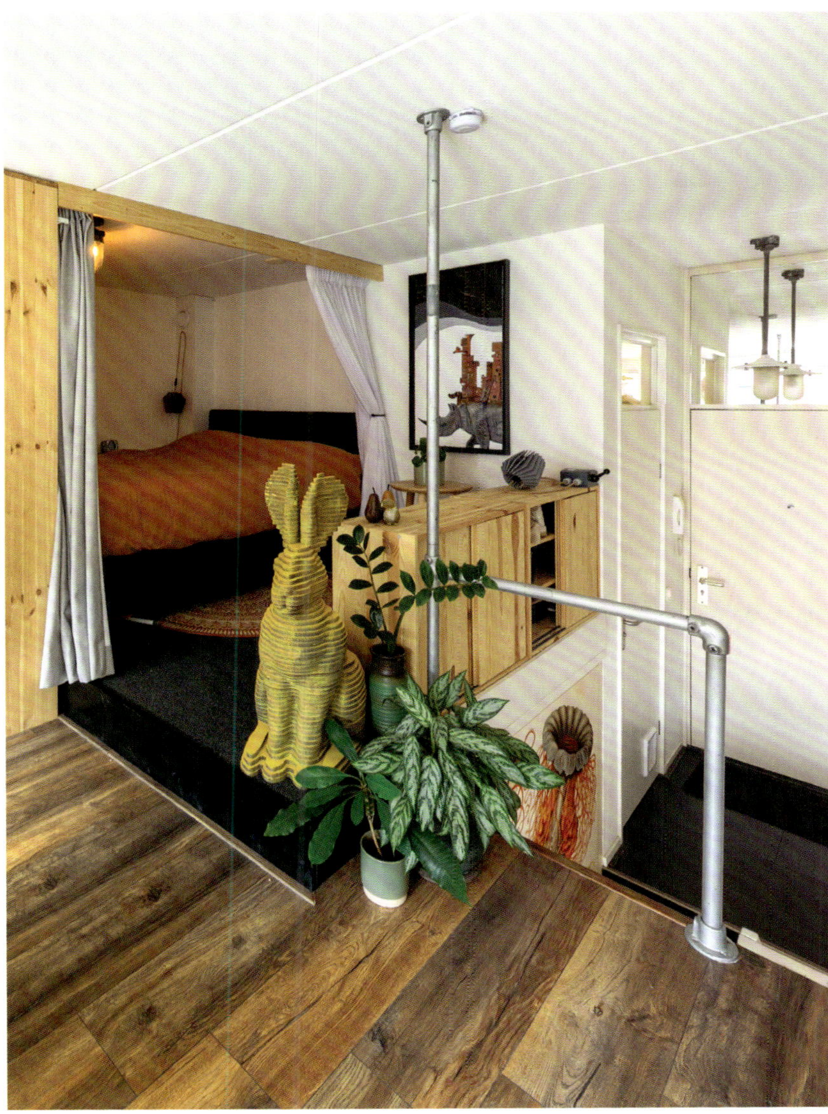

OPPOSITE TOP Although it appears to be small, the dining table can seat up to eight people. The couple chose the round table to contrast with all the other angular furniture pieces.

OPPOSITE BOTTOM The pink cabinets were made by combining and painting three IKEA cabinets. The cabinets feature a hidden desk and a hiding place and scratching surface for Sok.

RIGHT The pendant light in the entry was found in an abandoned factory in Turkey and came home via Fraijman’s hand luggage.

BELOW Fraijman buit a custom cabinet around the washing machine. This cabinet also hides Sok's litter box.

RIGHT The bedroom cube is surrounded by personal details like the comically large industrial switch and a sentimental art installation – Fraijman's bike that he used to go to school on.

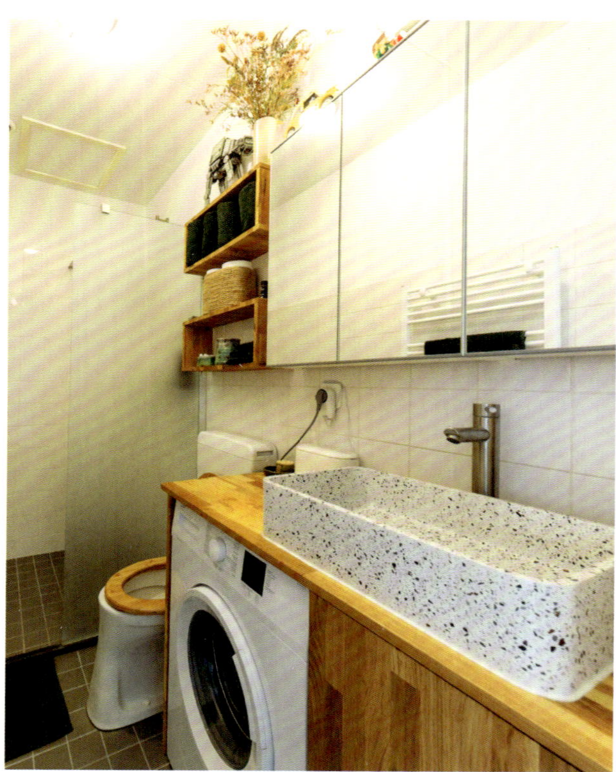

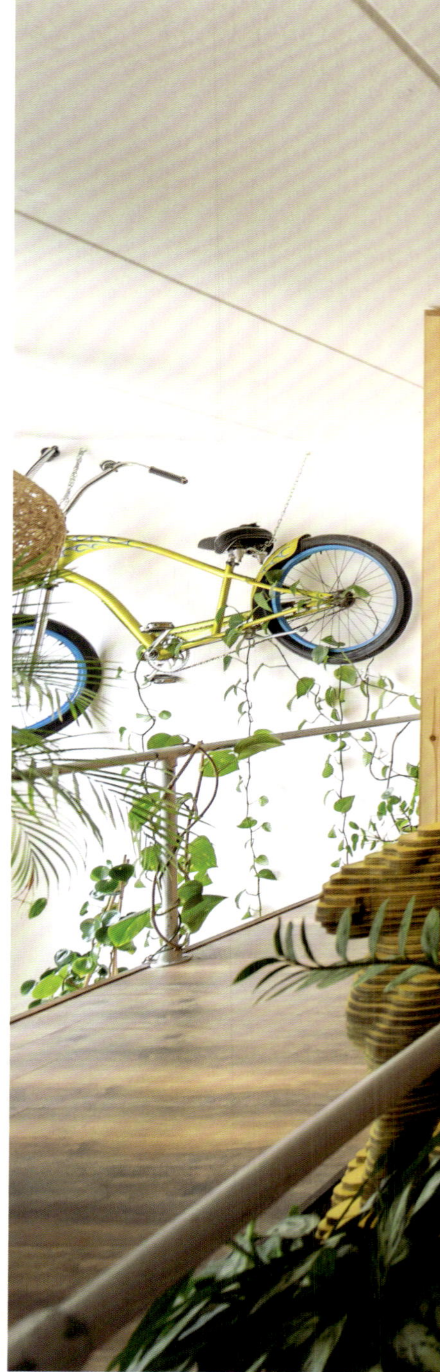

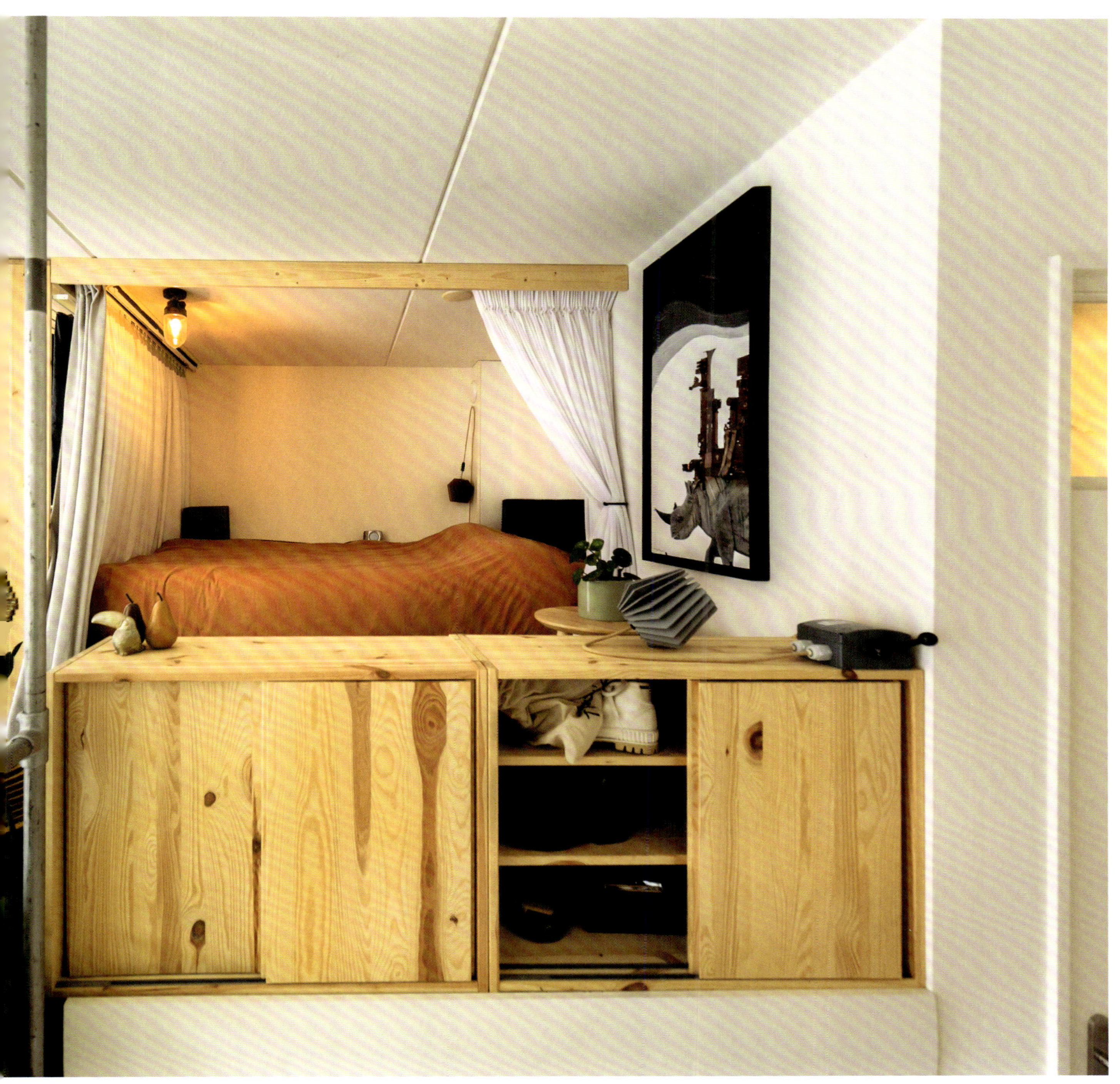

6

Small-footprint design can often be misrepresented as homes for singles or couples. Yet increasingly, we are seeing a trend toward families choosing to live in smaller homes in urban centres rather than in the suburbs.

So how have architects and designers responded to their new clientele and the challenges that the adapting needs of families present? From curtain partitions that serve as flexible walls to cleverly integrated furniture, this section showcases the ingenious ways in which families have chosen to live in small-footprint homes.

One such remarkable example is F-house, a thoughtfully designed abode in Osaka, Japan, that maximises every inch of available space to suit the needs of a family of four. Due to the limitations of height and width in its construction, coil kazuteru matumura architects decided to focus on expanding the dimensions vertically. While the ground floor features a standard ceiling, the second floor extends the height to its maximum potential, creating a loft that serves both as a storage area and a play haven for the children.

Another striking example of compact family living is the Crussol residence in central Paris. Here, what could have been a standard nursery was designed to evolve as the architects/owners Edouard Roullé-Mafféïs and Ophélie Doria's child grows. With the use of modular furniture and no built-in fixtures, the room can be easily rearranged and adapted for the child's changing needs and interests. Furthermore, throughout the home, furniture is cleverly used as dividers, delineating distinct areas while maintaining an open and airy feel.

Family-Friendly Homes

Also in the French capital, Paris Duplex Extension is a small apartment that exemplifies the concept of closely integrated family living. The kitchen, designed with meticulous attention to detail, allows for seamless interaction between family members. By incorporating varying heights of joinery, including a low built-in bench seat, the young child of architect Olivier Menard can climb up and share in preparing family meals. This home also extends vertically, creating a second level that further maximises space to meet the needs of an expanding family.

With an eye towards the future, the designers of the F-house, Crussol and Paris Duplex Extension have prioritised versatility and adaptability. This emphasis on flexibility ensures that these homes can accommodate changing lifestyles in the long term and allow families to truly make the space their own.

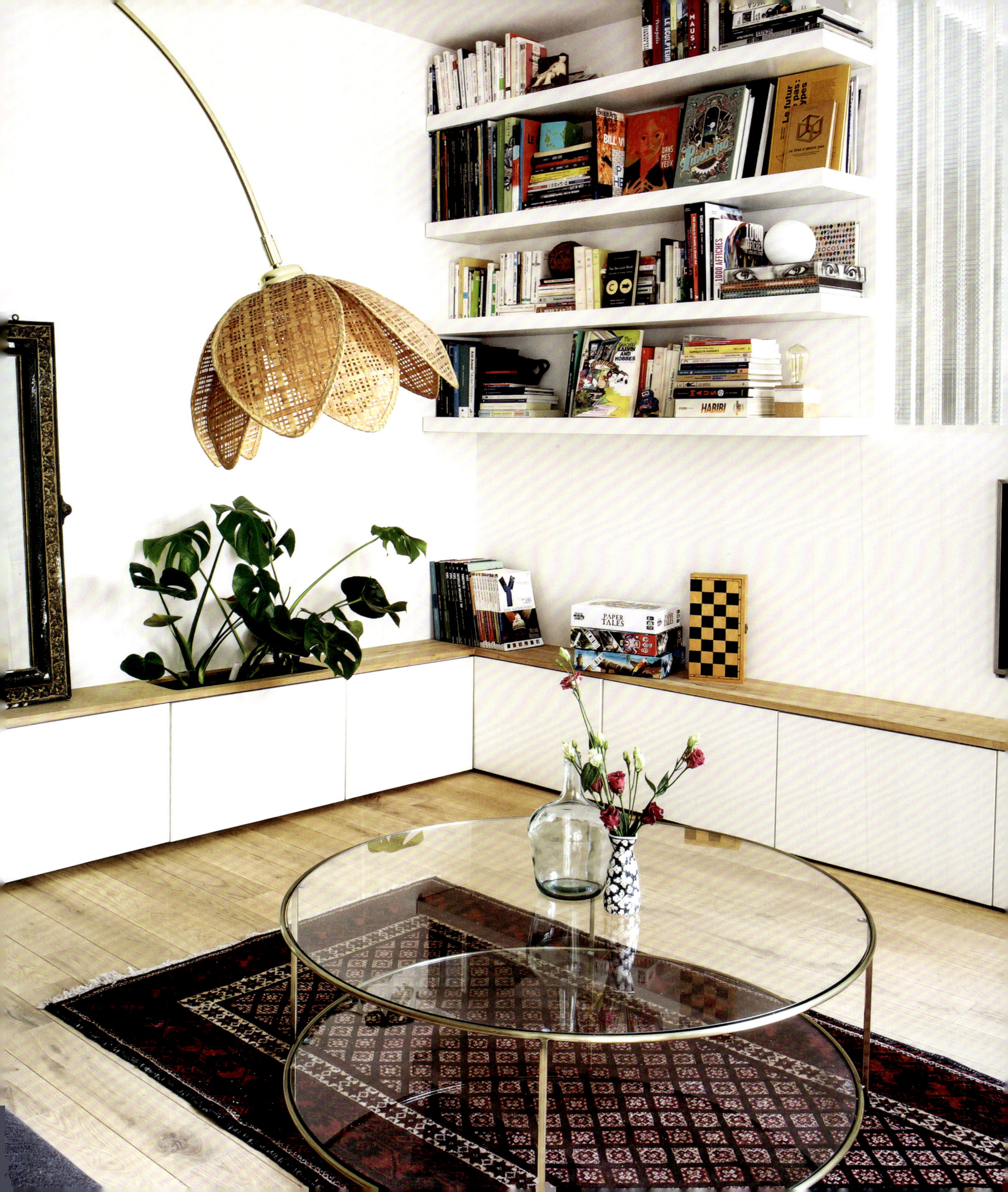

LE SCULPTEUR
MAUS
DANS MES YEUX
1000 AFFICHES
CALVIN AND HOBBES
HABIBI
PAPER TALES

Crussol

54m² / 581ft²
Space Factory
Oberkampf, Paris

When Edouard Roullé-Mafféïs and Ophélie Doria found Crussol – a mid-20th-century painter's workshop and gallery space located in Oberkampf, in the historic 11th district of Paris – it was kismet. Acting as both architect and client, their brief had been to 'find a place with a soul and make it an apartment' and Crussol couldn't have been a better discovery.

But with two separate entrances, a single half wall and no existing rooms, the narrow 54-sq-m (581-sq-ft) L-shaped property was not without its challenges.

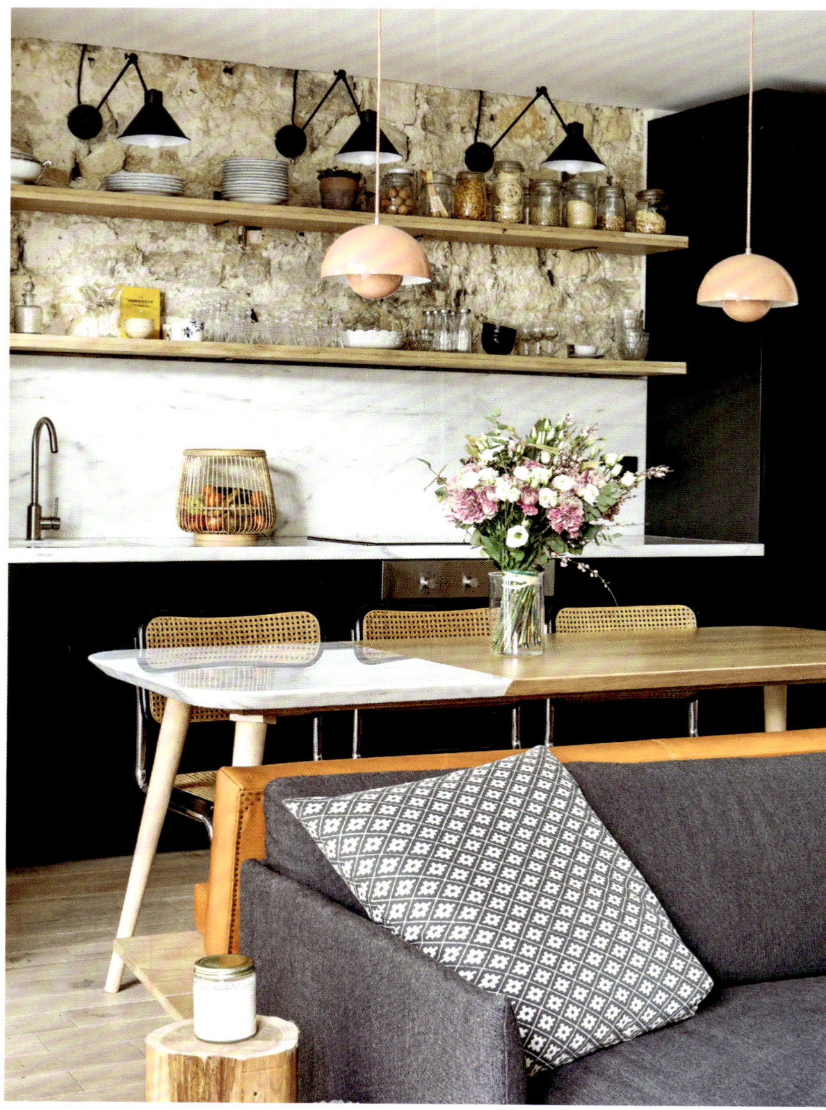

PAGE 258 The low storage unit wraps around the wall and features a planter and ample surface area to personalise with decor as the owners desire.

LEFT Instead of building a wall, the living and kitchen area are divided using a couch and a custom bench seat.

Undeterred, and charmed, by the original windows and the potential of a character-filled family home, Roullé-Maffëïs and Doria sectioned off the entrance and created a kitchen, a primary bedroom and an ensuite bathroom. They also removed the second entrance door and replaced it with a window, and added a mini loft above a room, which became a nursery.

In terms of design, it was important to find a world that worked for their opposing aesthetics – Roullé-Maffëïs favours object-filled spaces while Doria gravitates towards simplicity and clean lines. And so, '*L'atelier rangé – dérangé* (a tidy and busy workshop)' was born.

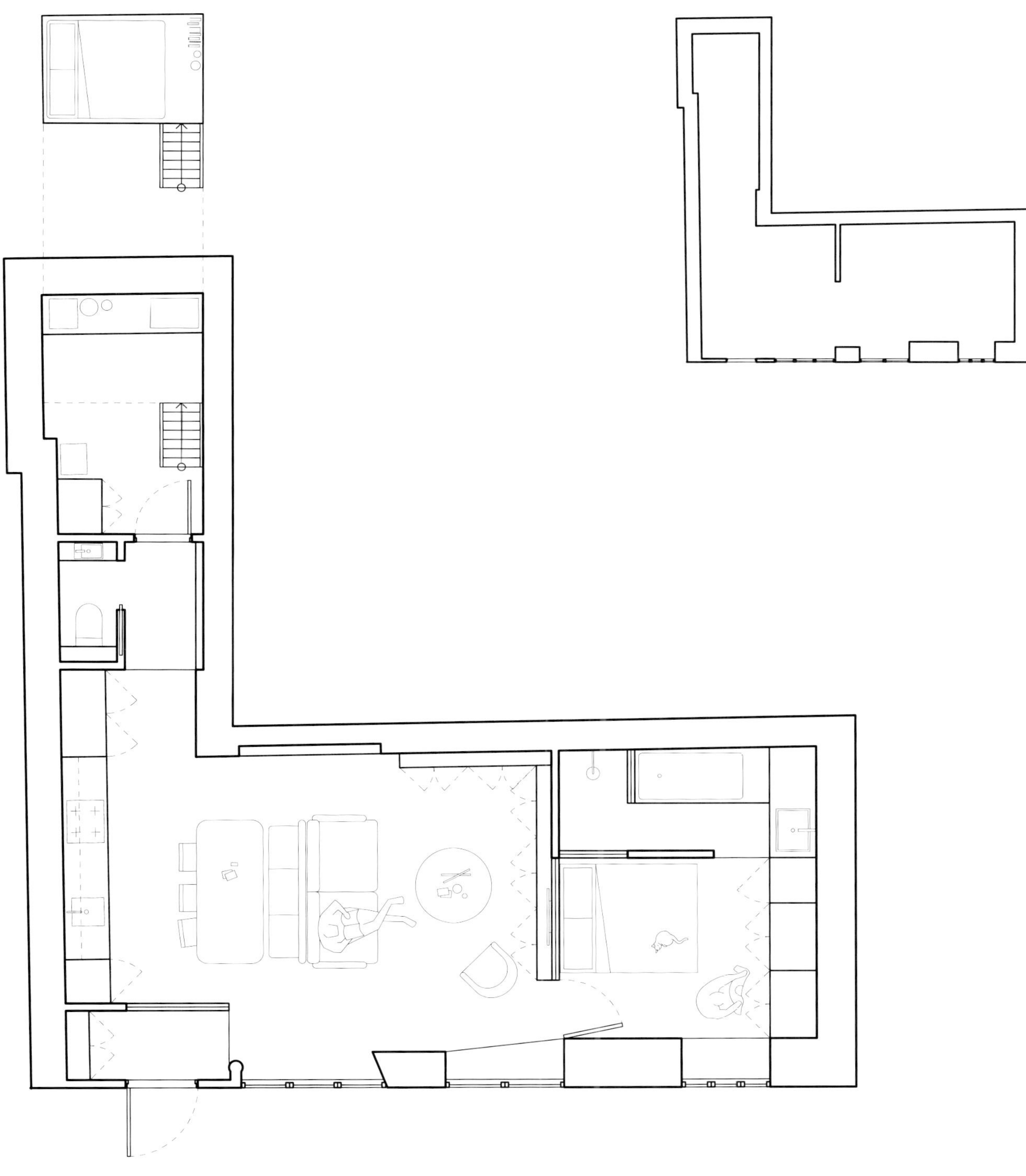

Scale 1:100

1 2 3 4 5m

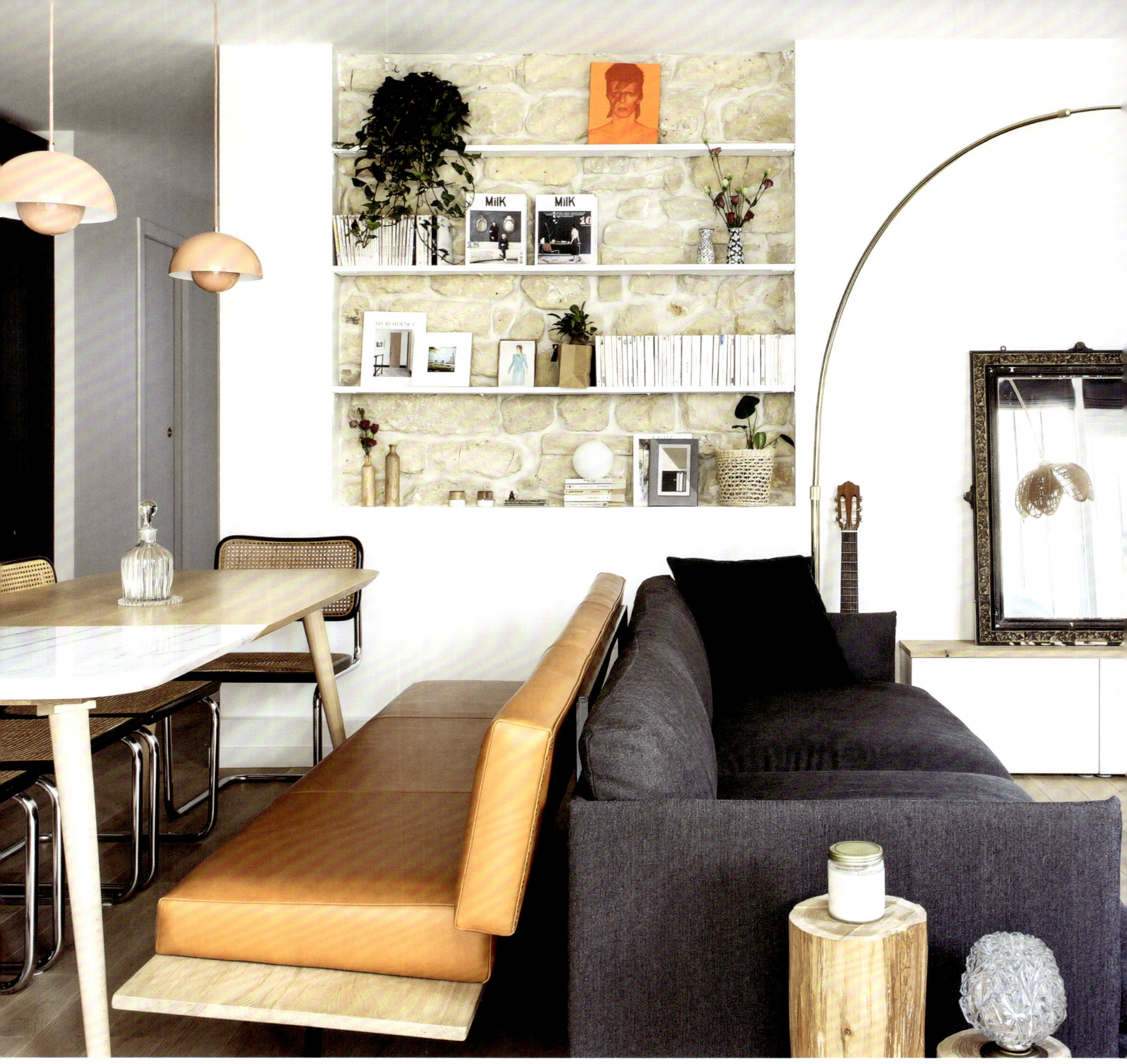

‘We wanted to respect the soul of the original workshop.’

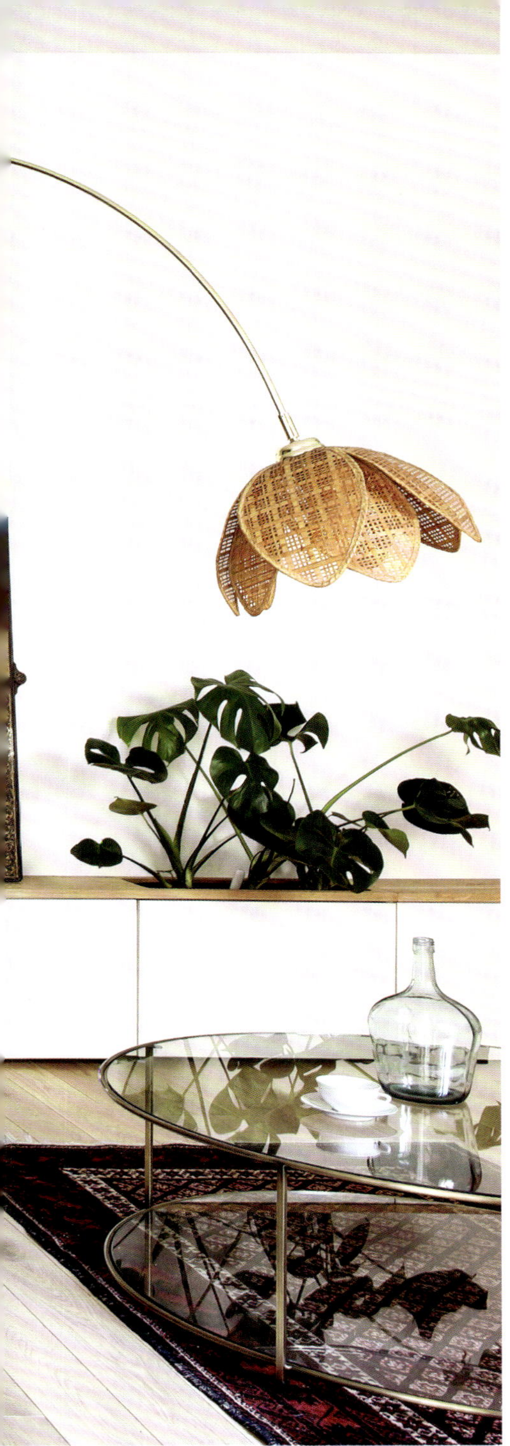

This motto became the roof under which both designers' aesthetics could reside. Simple, light-filled, open-plan spaces include busy zones, such as bookshelves, kitchen shelves and niche shelving in the living room.

'We wanted to respect the soul of the original workshop,' explains Doria. For instance, the same glass used in the original windows was brought in to create a divider in the entryway. A large metal standing beam was also left exactly where it was found at the entrance of the home.

Almost 30 sq m (322 sq ft) of the 54-sq-m (581-sq-ft) space is dedicated to the living area. With their design motto in mind, low storage units wrap around two of the walls of the space. Floating shelves were added to a section of beautiful white stone and brick wall, unearthed during the renovation – and left as is to pay homage to the existing building.

In the kitchen, matte black was chosen for the cabinetry to highlight another stone wall in the home that was discovered during construction.

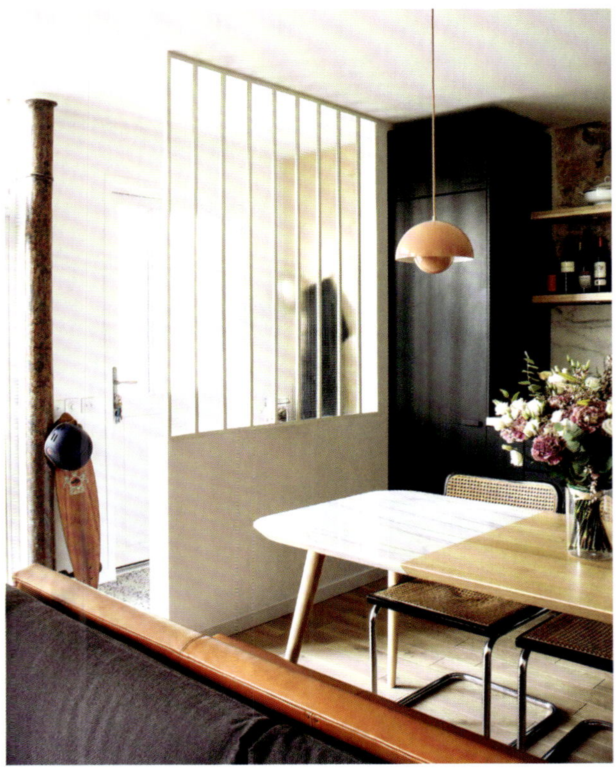

ABOVE To maximise space, the dining table bench and the couch were positioned back to back.

RIGHT The entryway glass divider allows natural light to flow into the kitchen while maintaining privacy.

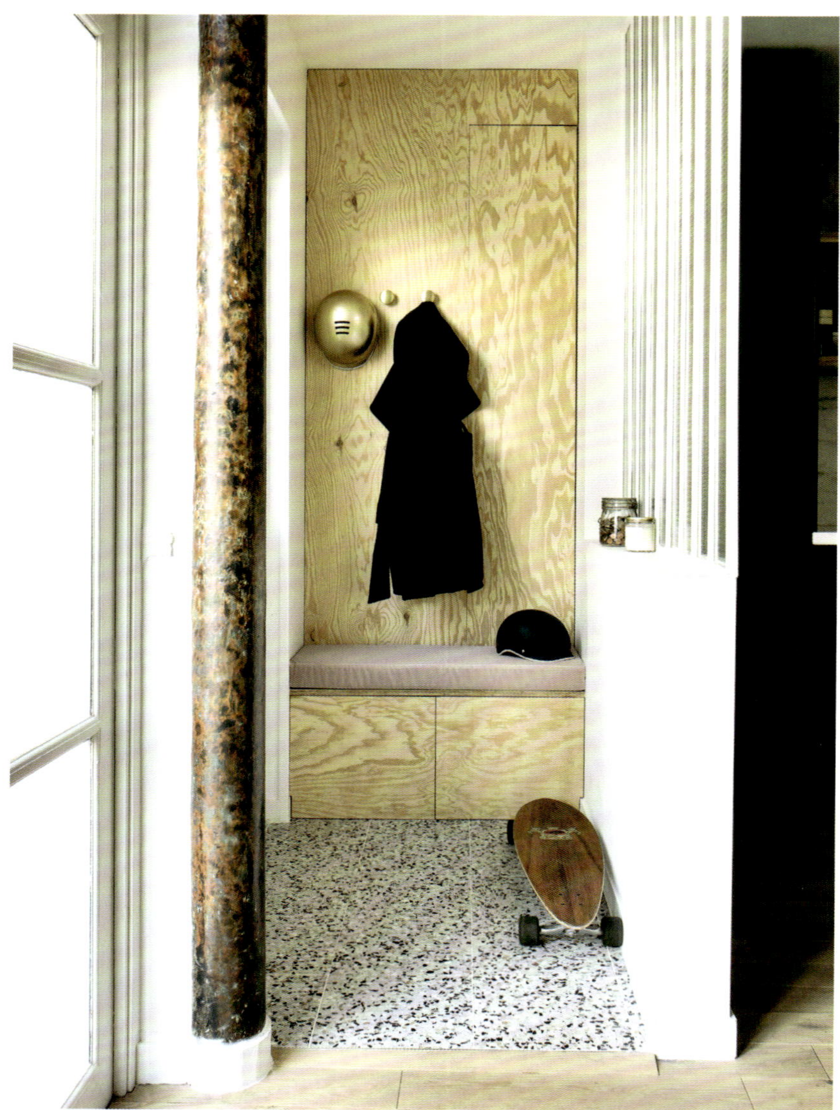

LEFT In the entryway the pinewood wall has hidden storage and bench with shoe storage underneath.

BELOW Recycled glass windows were used in the bedroom to allow the light from the bedroom to be shared with the living room.

OPPOSITE LEFT Even though the bathroom is small, the couple didn't want to compromise on comfort.

OPPOSITE RIGHT The bathroom was thoughtfully designed so it could include a shower, bath and vanity unit.

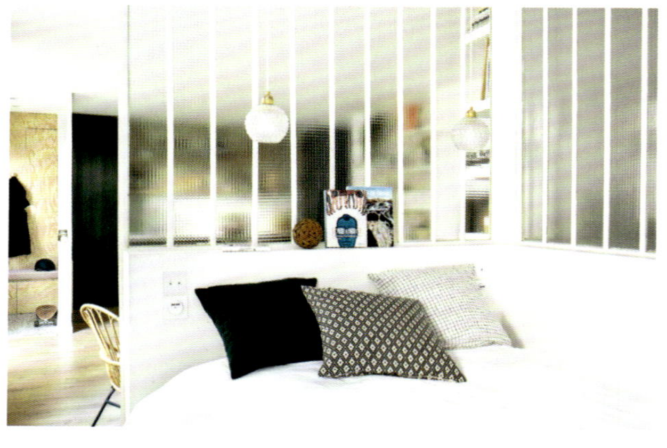

The bedroom, separated from the living area with recycled glass windows, is a compact space with a custom-made queen bed and a closet. A small bench wraps around the heater, creating a cosy reading nook like the one in the living room. On having a full-size bath in a tiny ensuite bathroom Roullé-Mafféïs says: 'We didn't want the apartment to lack the comforts of a bigger space.' The side of the bath is also mirrored to create the illusion of a bigger bathroom.

The family's 'fluffy roommate', Noon the cat (Noon because that is when she wakes up), was thought of too. She comes and goes through a cat hole in the door and shelves were built for her to access her hammock that lives next to the window. 'So that she can always be on the lookout and be the tiny concierge she truly thinks she is,' the couple explains.

Through a hallway past the kitchen is a small nursery with big design ideas. The custom-made closet, change table, armchair and cot can be transformed: first into a toddler bed and then a full-size bed as their baby daughter grows. The duo's ideology – 'It's not the square metres that matter, it's what we do with them' – could not ring truer here.

Like many soulful places, Crussol is filled with gentle contradictions. It is refined yet relaxed, full of personality but not packed with stuff. It is a home that feels fresh and exciting, but also like one that has always been here.

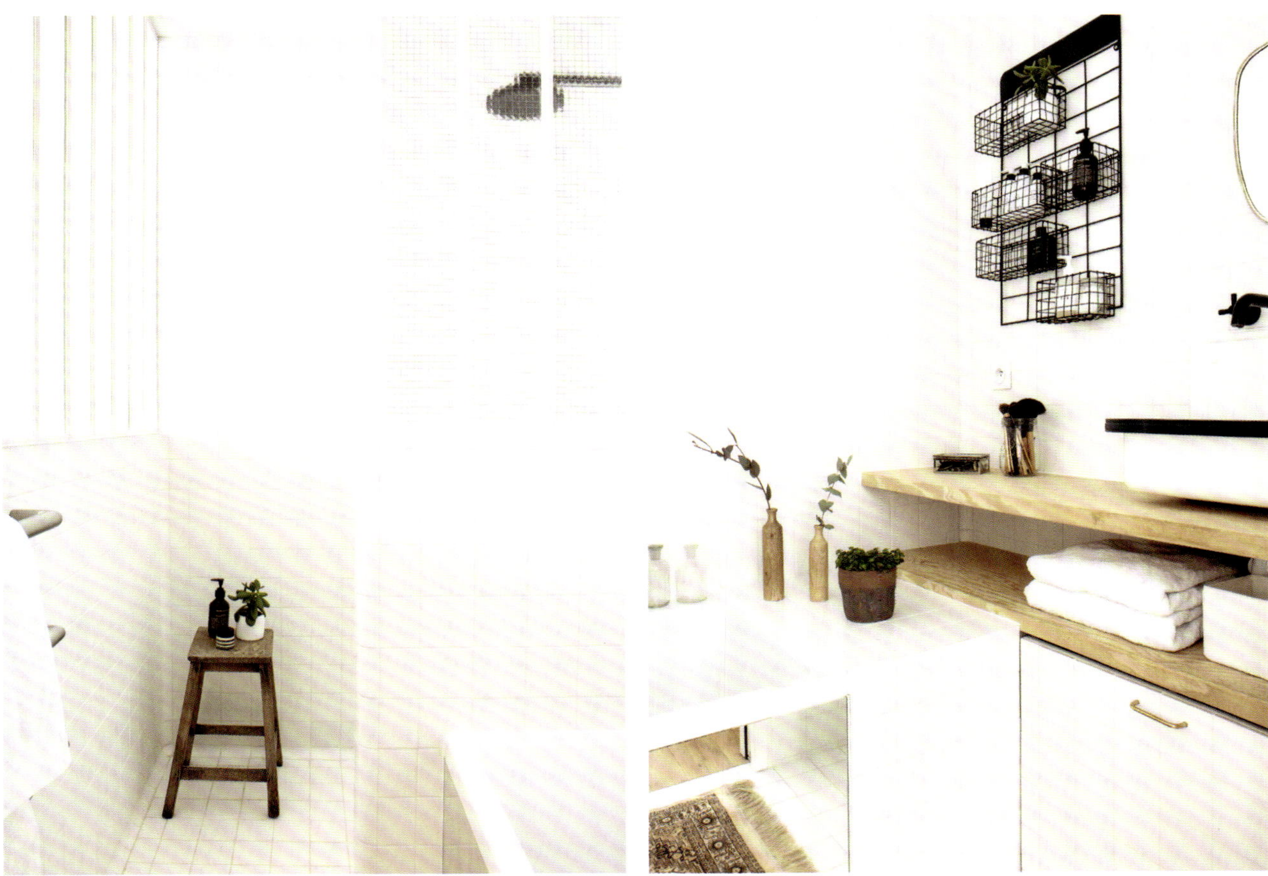

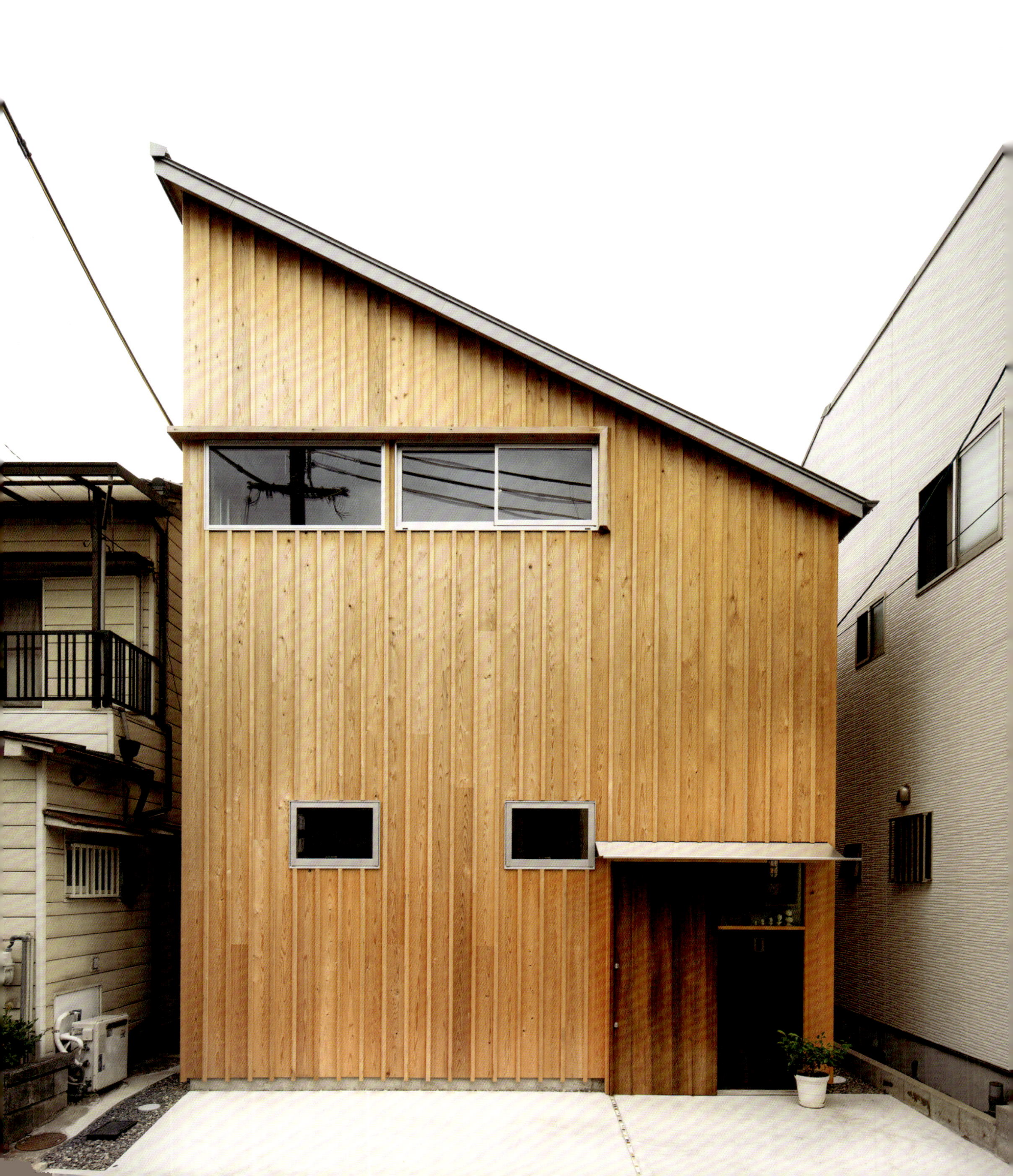

F-house

57m² / 613sqft²
coil kazuteru matumura architects
Hirakata-shi, Osaka

On a quiet street of a quiet neighbourhood in Osaka, Japan, sits a compact wooden house with a sliding front door, a stainless-steel portico and a shed roof. It could be almost anywhere in the world: on any street, in any city. It's home to a family of four and holds books and toys, family photos, old furniture, an office and everyday kitchen bits and bobs – happy household stuff.

However, what makes this three-storey home unique was the architects' ability to use what already was. Designed around the family's existing furniture, the 57-sq-m (613-sq-ft) house doesn't have a vacant white wall or edgy custom piece of multiway folding furniture in sight.

The house was built with Yoshino Japanese cedar and mukunoki tree. Masaaki Okimoto, the lead carpenter, gave the home character through this material use. But the story of the woodwork's creation is also charming. Mr Okimoto invited the client's children to experience and take part in the construction process – and subsequently, ebullient easter eggs of wood inlay details are dotted around the home.

Mosaic tile art of various shapes and sizes, a playful hint of what's to come, is one of the first details you'll notice. The other eye-catching detail is the use of large cream curtains – a budget-friendly solution – that divide many areas throughout the house. On the first floor, they are used to separate the bathroom from the sleeping areas, and in between the parents' and children's bedrooms. Head architect Kazuteru Matumura explains the rationale for using the curtains was 'creating an open and flexible atmosphere'.

The children's bedroom is a sunny and simple collection of store-bought bunk beds, a desk on wheels and the obligatory stuffed animals and toys. In comparison, the primary sleeping area quietly exudes a serene simplicity. At the end of the two beds in the primary bedroom, a closet is hidden behind more cream curtains.

With a brief from the family to be able to 'gather together in one open space', the architects created a large area for the kitchen, dining room and living room on the second floor. It's an open-plan space with a ceiling high enough to accommodate a tiny third-floor loft, accessible by a ladder, or a climbing wall, which is used for additional storage as well as a kids' play area.

The living room is separated from the staircase by the family's preloved bookshelf that was custom fit to double as the handrail. The cream curtains feature here again, too. All the living room furniture is preowned and gives the area a memories-are-made-here feel.

And then, there's the climbing wall. Complete with rainbow-coloured climbing holds, it is an unexpected-yet-needed contrast among all the warm wood and soft folds of cream.

The architects designed the galley kitchen stove and sink section to be the same width as a dining room table that the family already owned. Retroactively fitting the home to what already existed is a clever way of streamlining the space. The rest of the kitchen paraphernalia, of which there is no shortage, is tucked away behind even more curtains.

This family home brings small-space living out of the shiny, white-walled museum of minimalism. It is unique in its extreme specificity, but also its extreme relatability.

PAGE 266 F-house is in a quiet residential area with a large park nearby – a perfect location for a family.

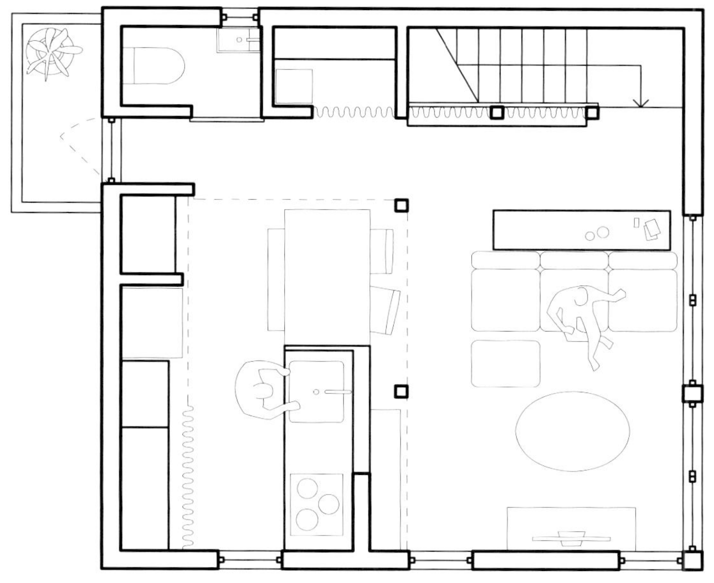

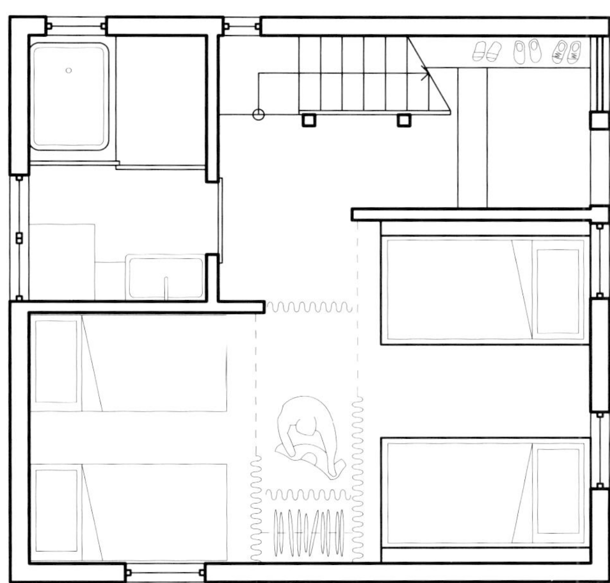

Scale 1:100

1 2 3 4 5m

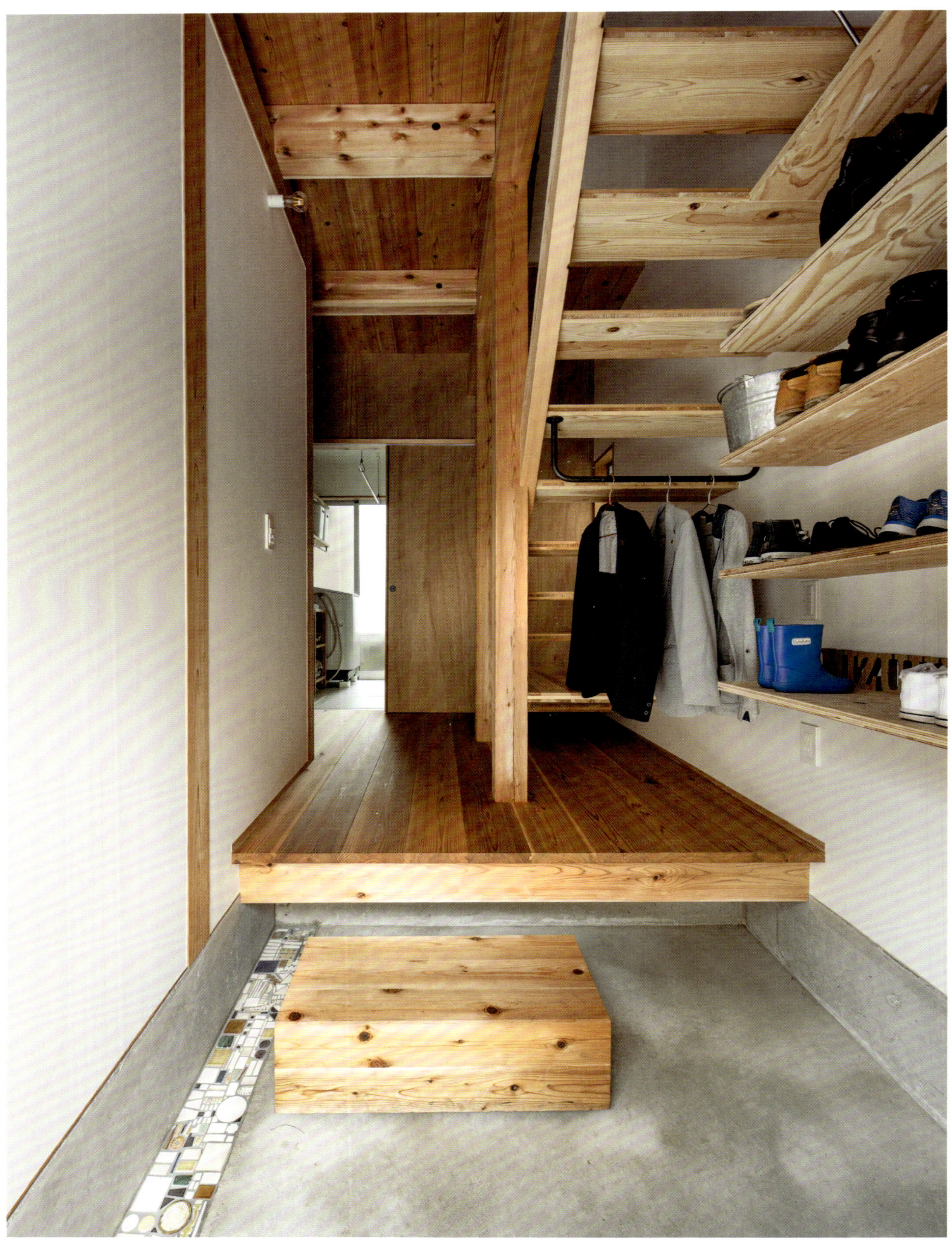

OPPOSITE The home's entryway is simple and functional.

BELOW Mosaic tiles are embedded into the earthen floor in the entryway. They are one of many artisan details throughout the home.

RIGHT The bathroom's large rectangular sink is a fugitive from a science lab and is one of the many pragmatic design choices made to keep costs down.

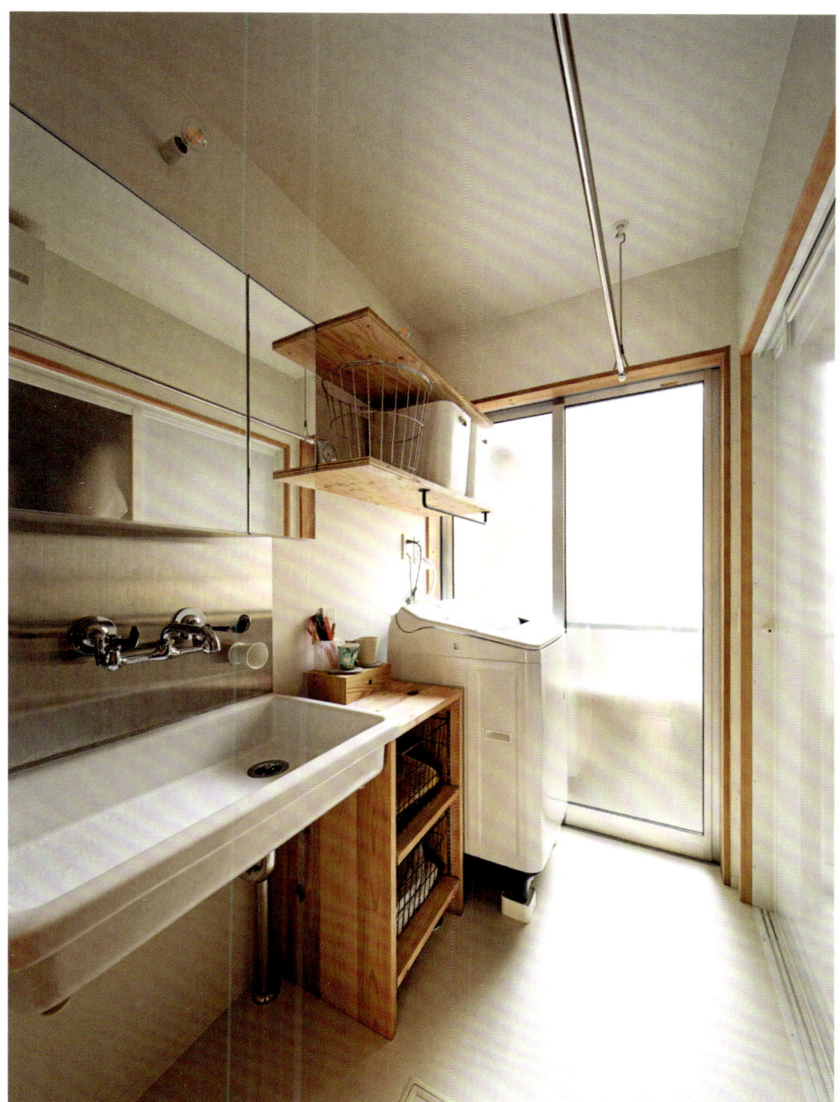

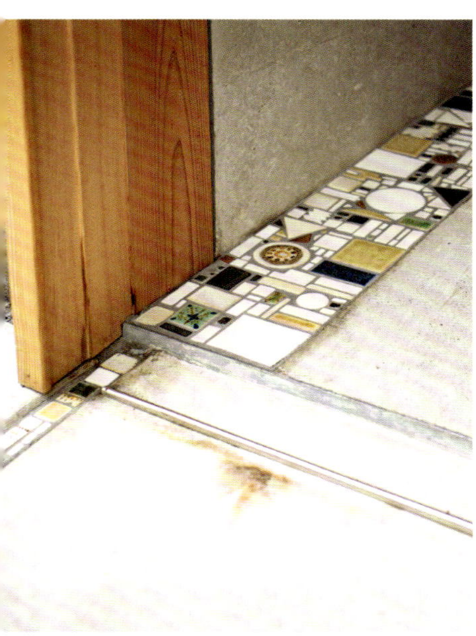

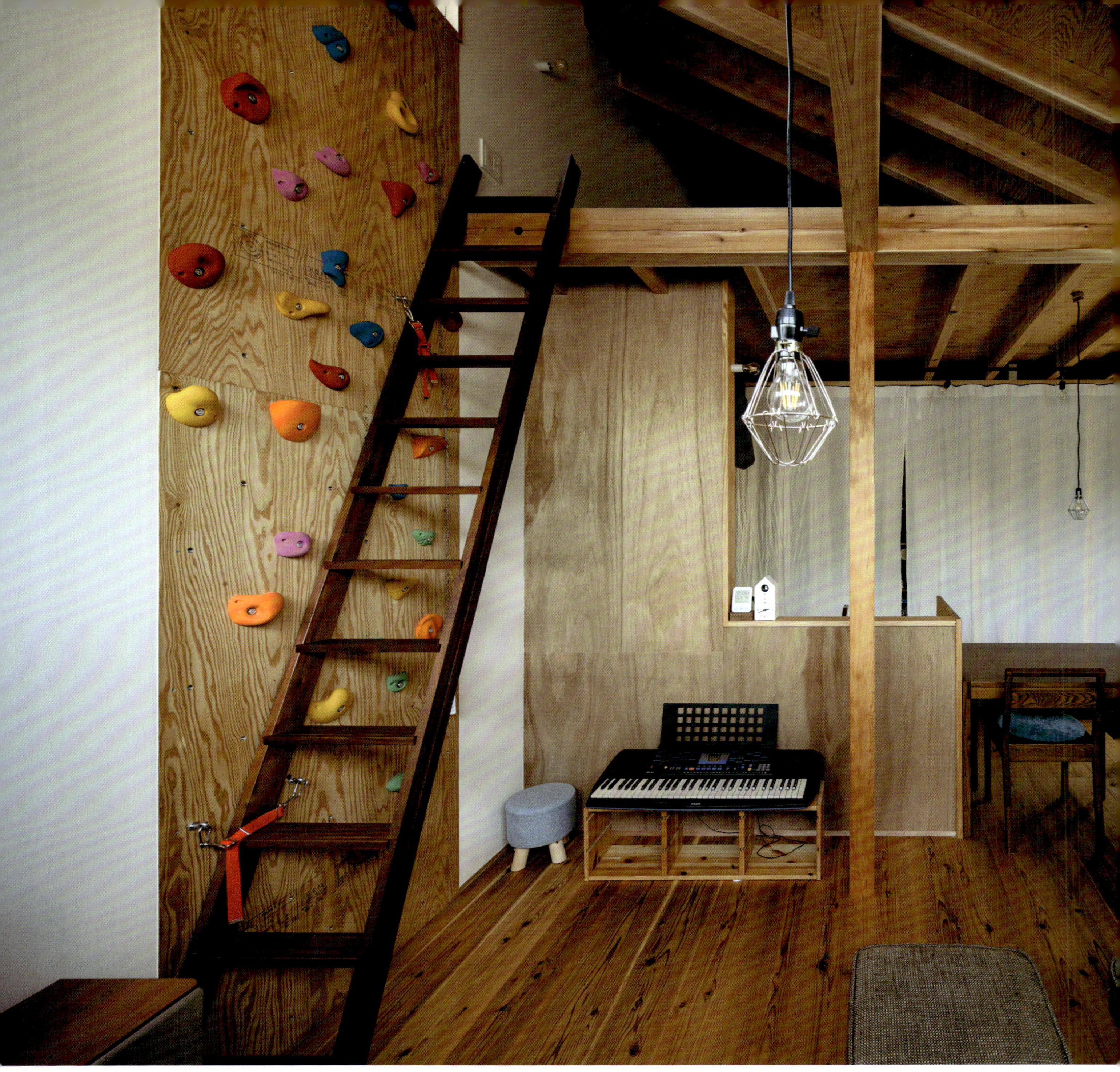

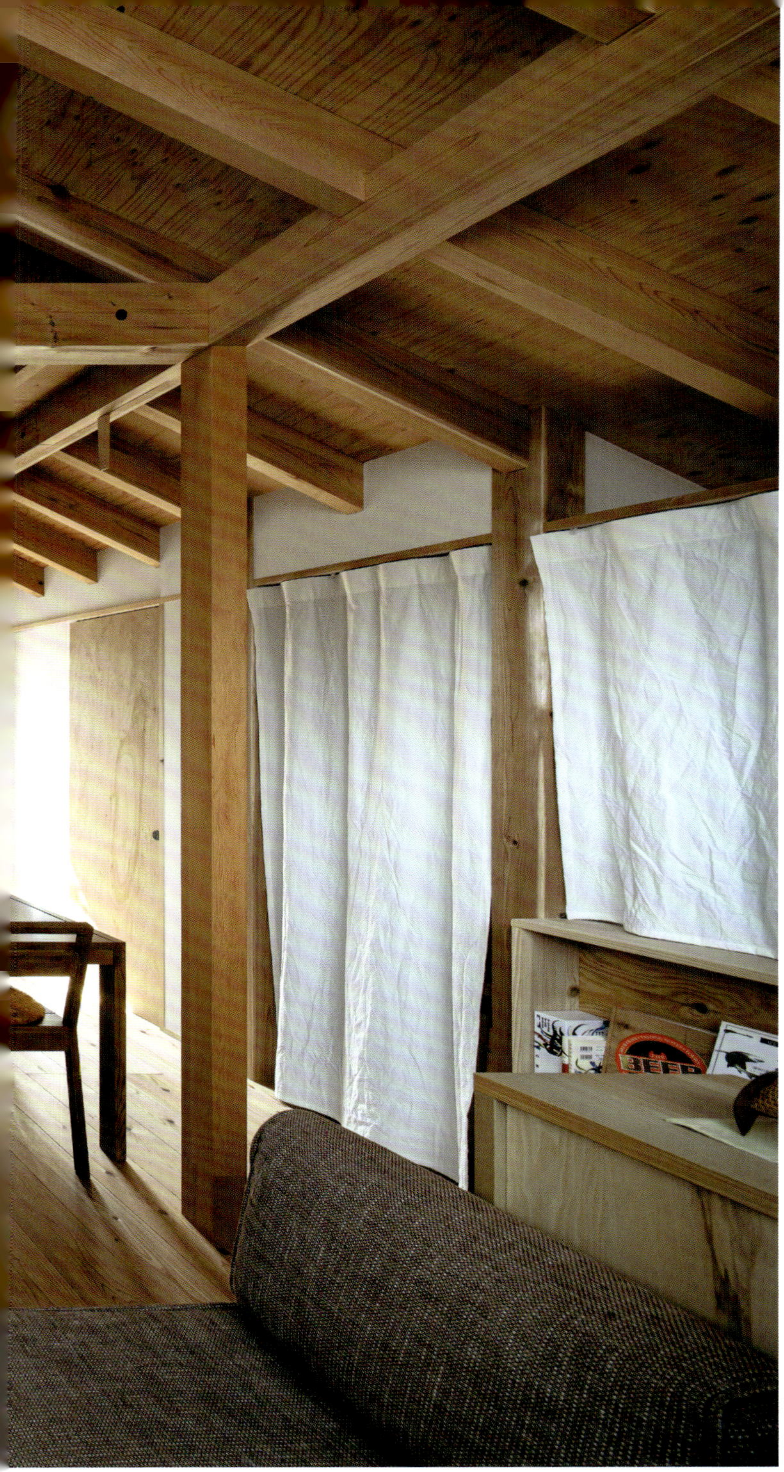

OPPOSITE Curtains were used throughout the home to divide areas without sacrificing light or flow, as well as to 'reduce labour when changing the floor plan in the future'.

BELOW The climbing wall and a ladder are the two playful options to access the small loft area.

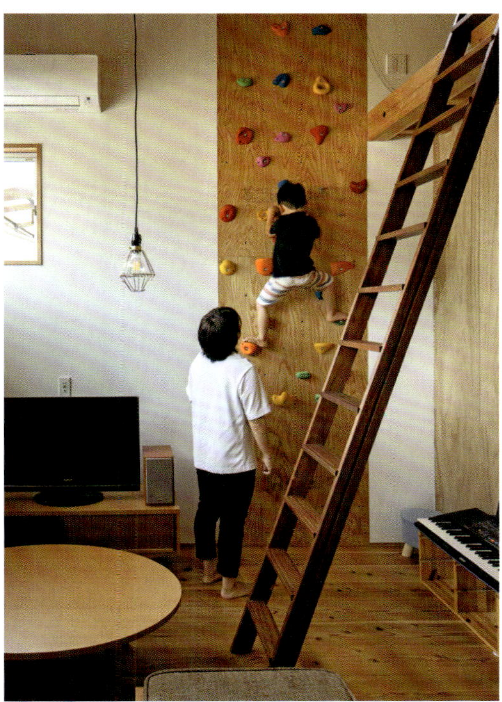

This family home brings small-space living out of the shiny, white-walled museum of minimalism.

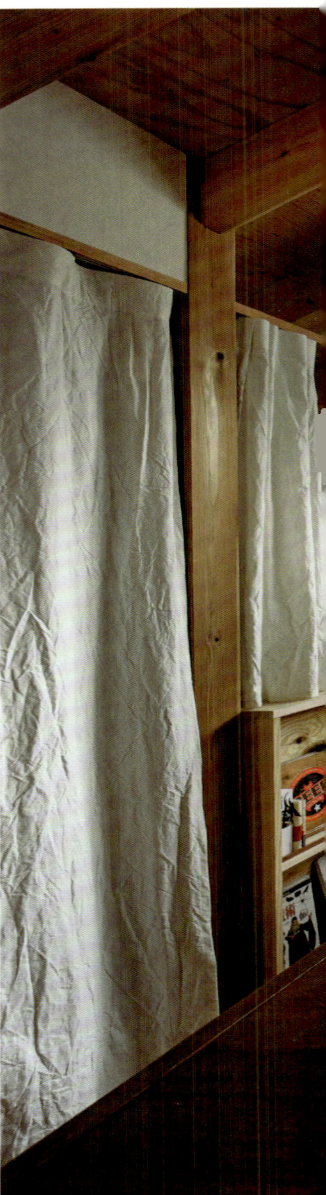

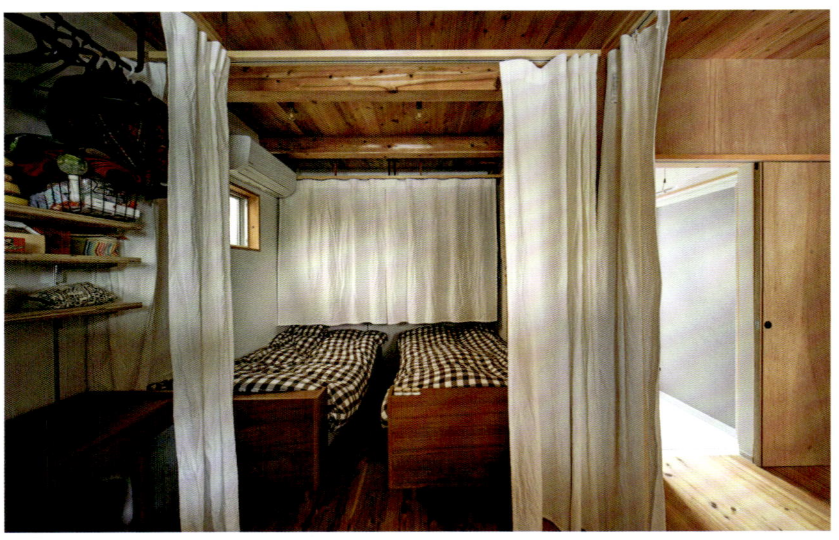

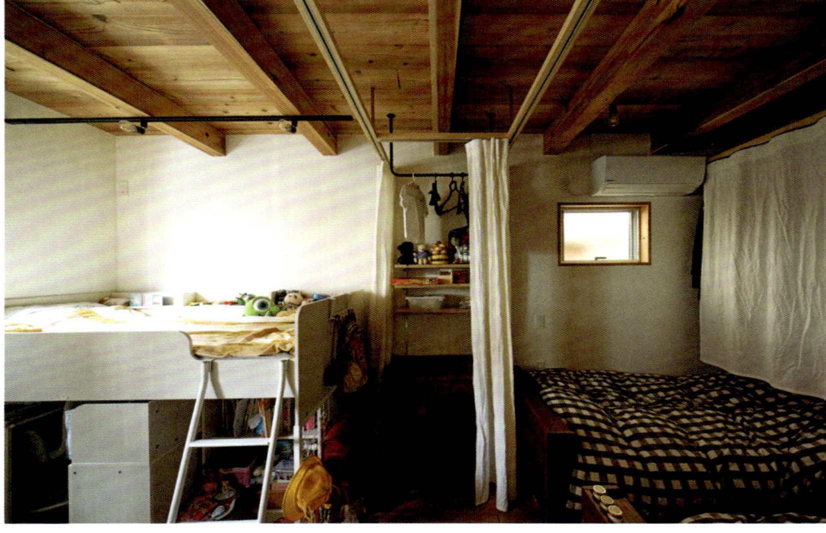

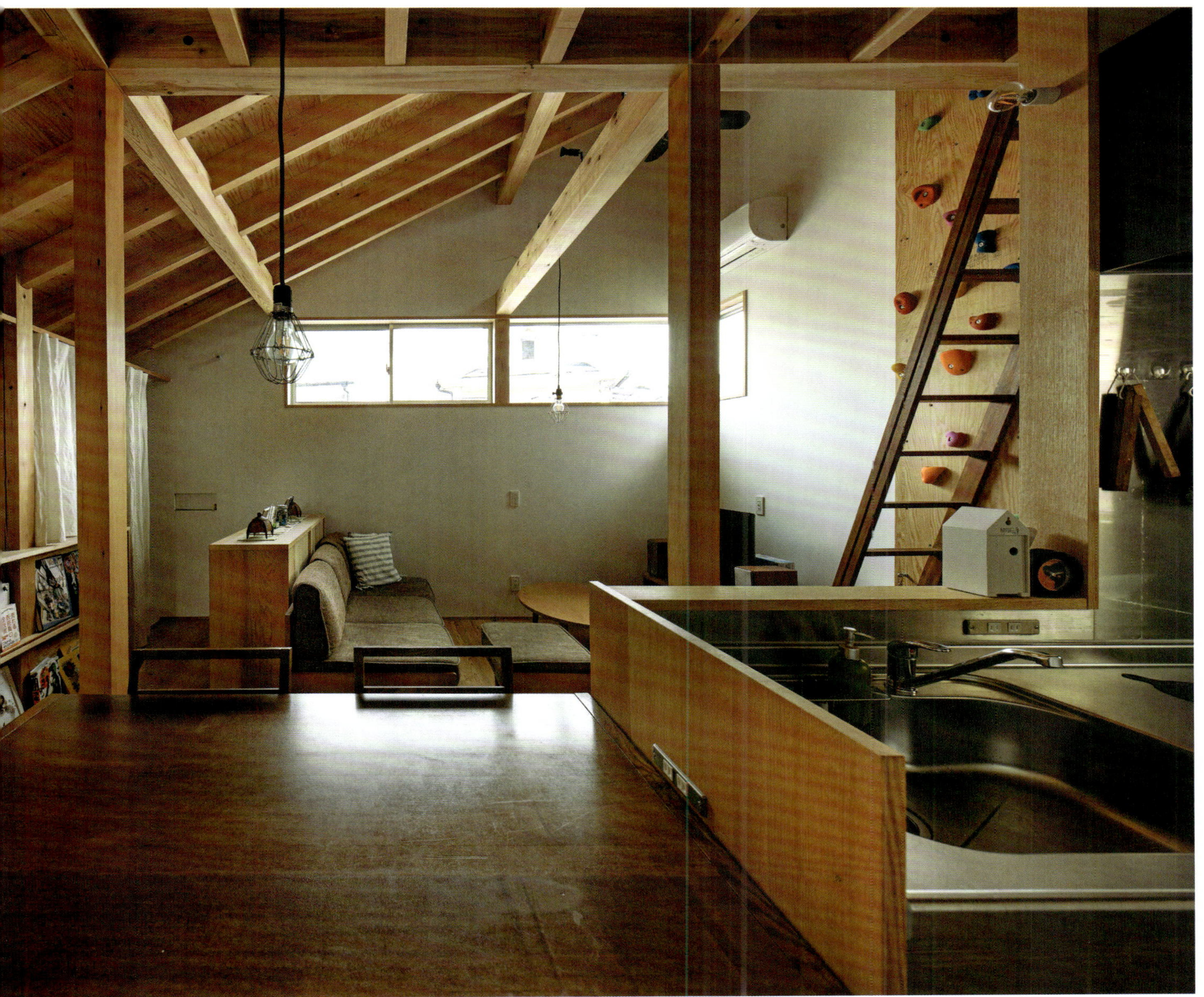

OPPOSITE TOP Curtains enclose the primary bedroom and conceal clothes storage above the head of the beds.

OPPOSITE BOTTOM The children's bedroom – separated from the primary by curtains – is filled with beloved toys and budget-friendly furniture.

ABOVE On designing a space around furniture the family already owned Matumura says: 'They wanted to live a life where they could make good use of their favourite furniture.'

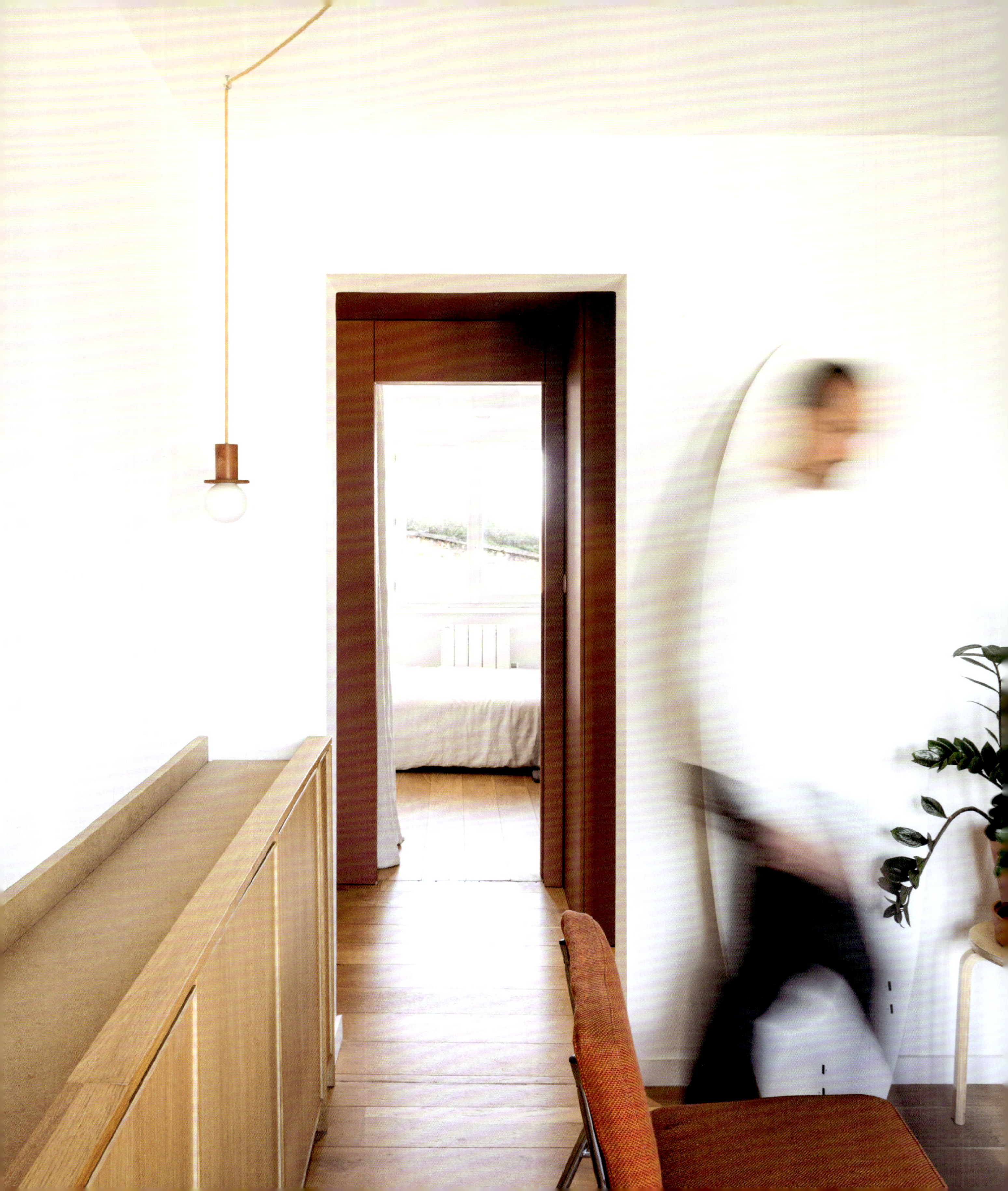

Fourvière Apartment

57m² / 613ft²
MURA architectes
Fourvière, Lyon

Fourvière Apartment's balcony floor is painted Majorelle Blue 'just for fun'. It's a delightful lesson that a thoughtfully designed space doesn't have to take itself too seriously.

When architects and owners Maxime Hurdequint and Mary Bravard first saw the apartment, they fell in love with its incredible views. To the west, there are sunsets over the Mont d'Or hills; to the east, sunrises overlooking the river, the city centre of Lyon and the Alps.

Completed in 1959 as part of the post-World War II reconstruction program, the 57-sq-m (613-sq-ft) apartment's layout was original when Hurdequint and Bravard came across it. They reconfigured the space to accommodate their need for a bright, two-bedroom home that could host up to 10 friends and had a large shower space 'like a hotel room'.

In search of as much light as possible, they also made sure all the doors aligned with the windows so that light, especially at sunrise and sunset, could wash through the apartment.

The colour palette of terracotta and olive green starts right from the entrance with a corridor painted floor to ceiling in a bold terracotta. This corridor connects every room in the apartment. On the left, the pre-existing area was narrowed to gain closet and storage space. And on the right hang several of Hurdequint's own art pieces. A full-length mirror fills the wall at the end of the corridor to visually extend the space.

Upon entering the living room, the line of sight leads to the balcony with its Majorelle Blue floor. The living room furniture is a mix of colourful vintage finds, gifts from family members and serendipitous finds on the streets of Paris. Along the back wall there's a long IKEA cabinet with oak doors. Wooden slots were added to the sides of the piece so that it appears custom made. The empty wall above it is used for projecting films onto.

The designers wanted the living room to feel spacious and airy, so in contrast the kitchen was designed to be understated. Cabinets were installed only below the quartz benchtop. The gable wall above the benchtop was scrapped to highlight the rough, concrete texture. A small adjoining room was custom made into a pantry or 'cabistou', as the couple call it. This hides the oven, fridge, space for a vacuum cleaner and room to store groceries.

Hurdequint and Bravard 'love the way the light reveals the texture of the concrete' in the primary bedroom. In fact, the floor-to-ceiling wardrobe doors were custom made and painted white to blend in with the walls.

Because the bathroom has a concrete sunshade, the shower was placed in front of the window so they can enjoy the landscape while showering. Built-in storage accommodates the washing machine and hot water tank. Most of the surfaces here are covered with a waxed concrete, giving the room a refined, serene feel.

This home has two 'temperaments': the warm, rich tones of the terracotta-painted corridor, and branching off, like ribs from a spine, the bright, largely white, light-filled rooms. They work together to create an effortlessly styled and simple family home.

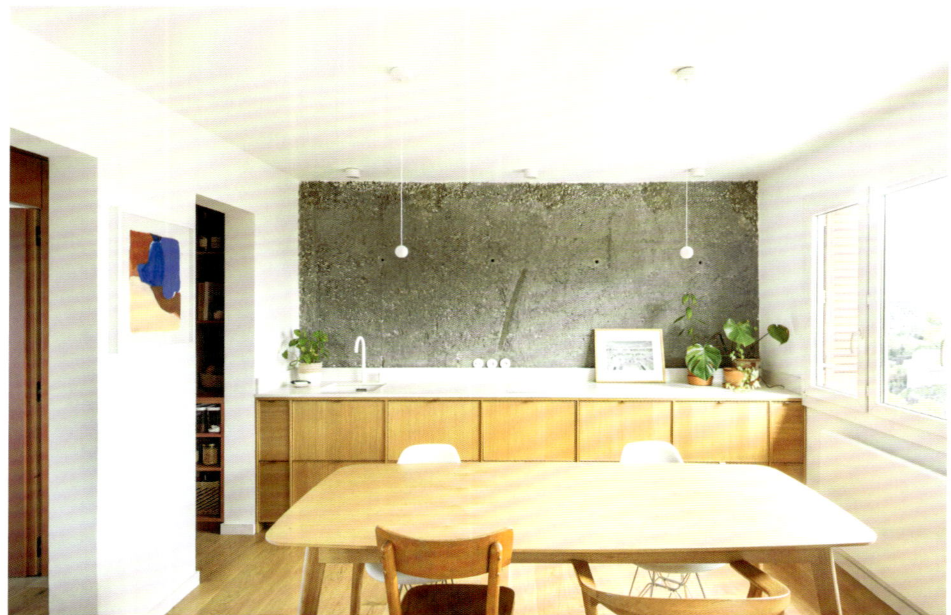

PAGE 276 The view from the living room into the primary bedroom highlights the contrast between the terracotta corridor and the bright bedroom beyond.

LEFT The dining table, placed between the kitchen and the living area, is finished in oak and can, as per the brief, seat up to ten people.

AFTER

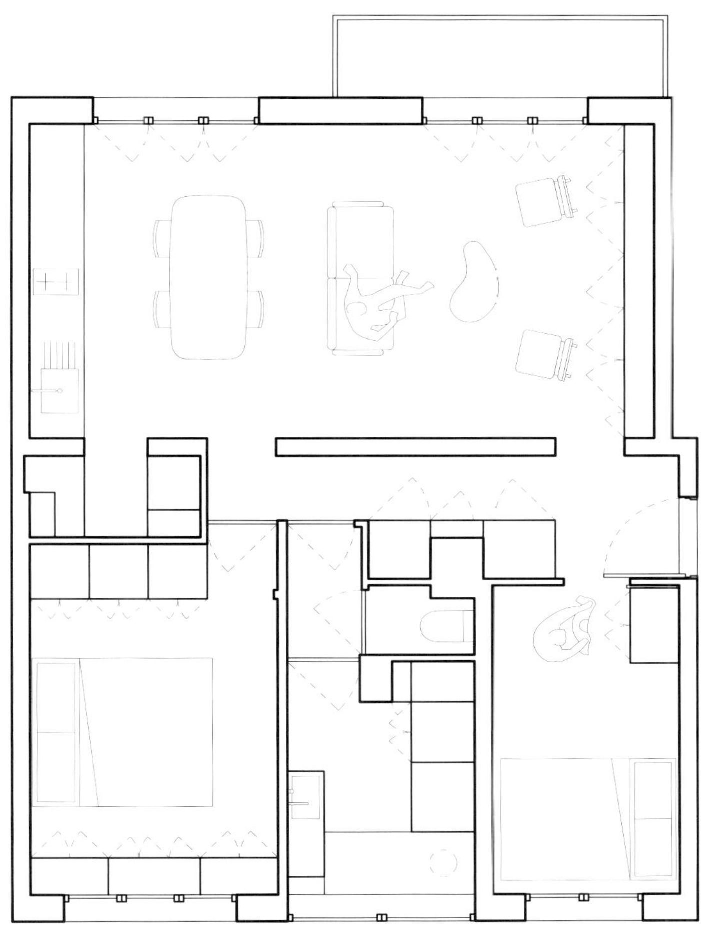

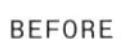

BEFORE

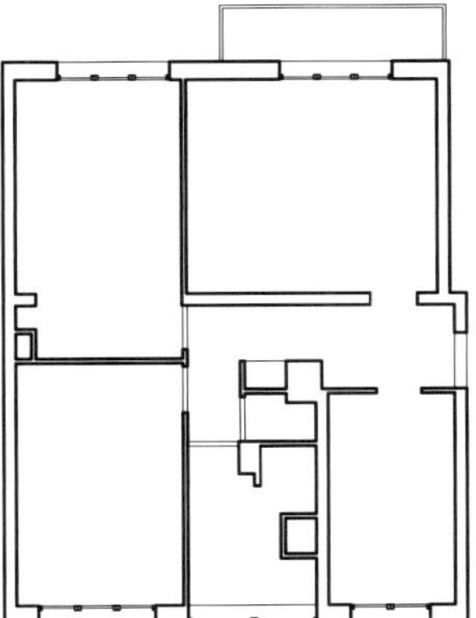

Scale 1:100

1 2 3 4 5m

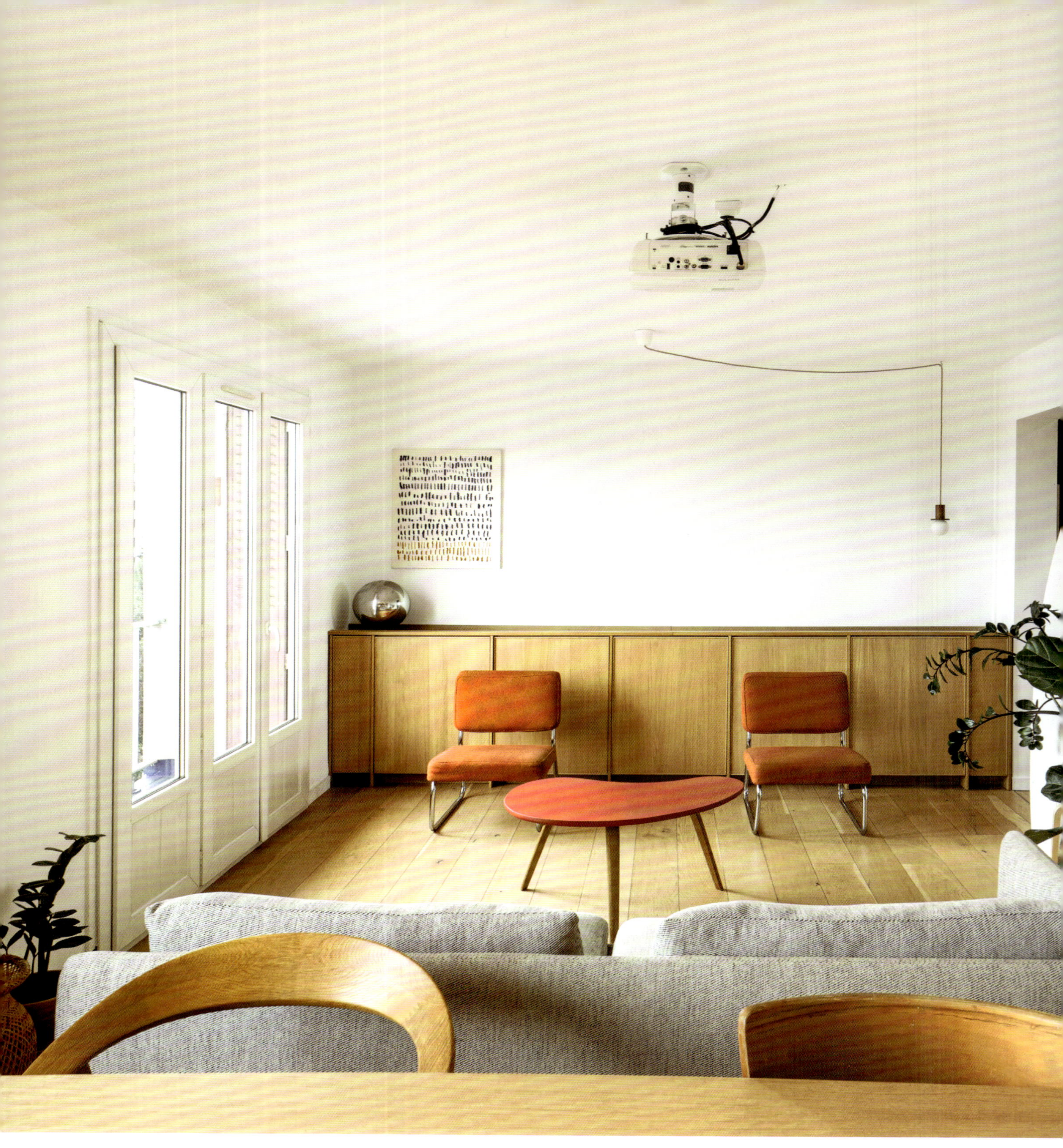

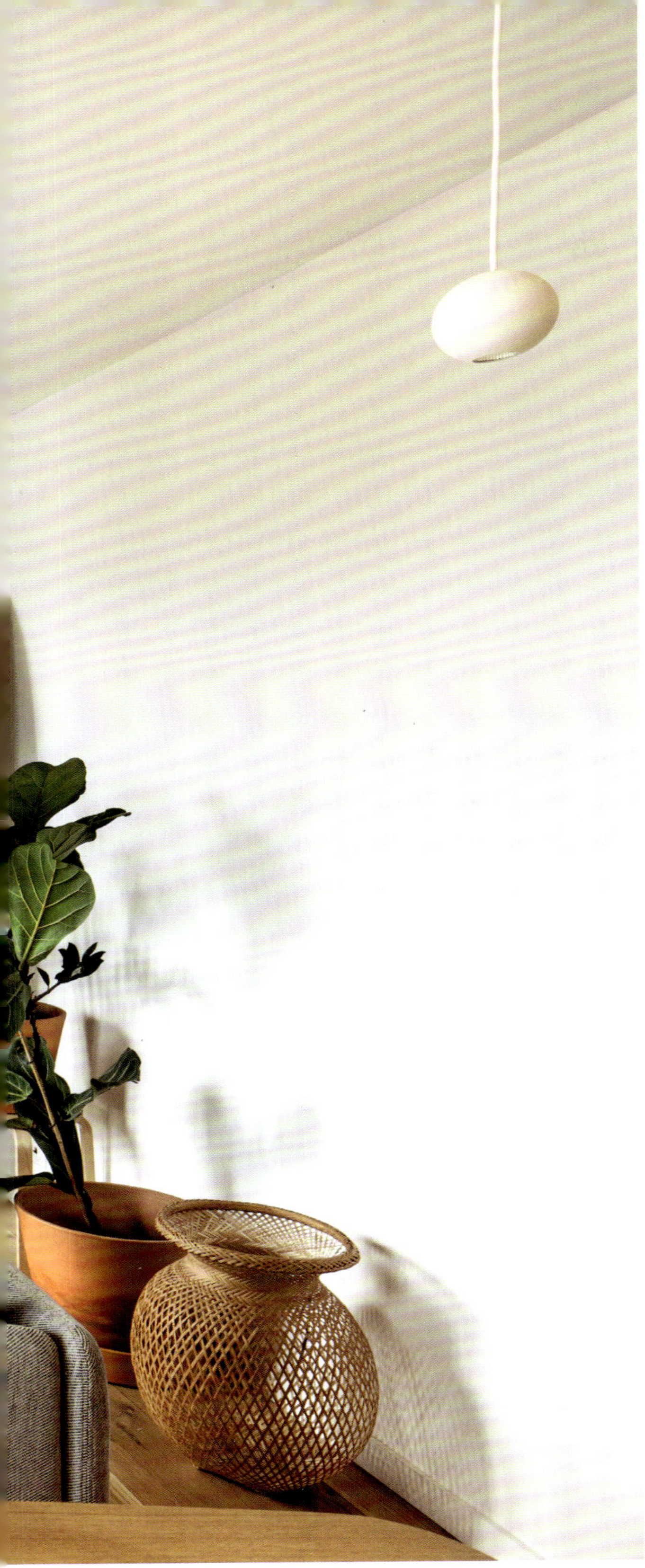

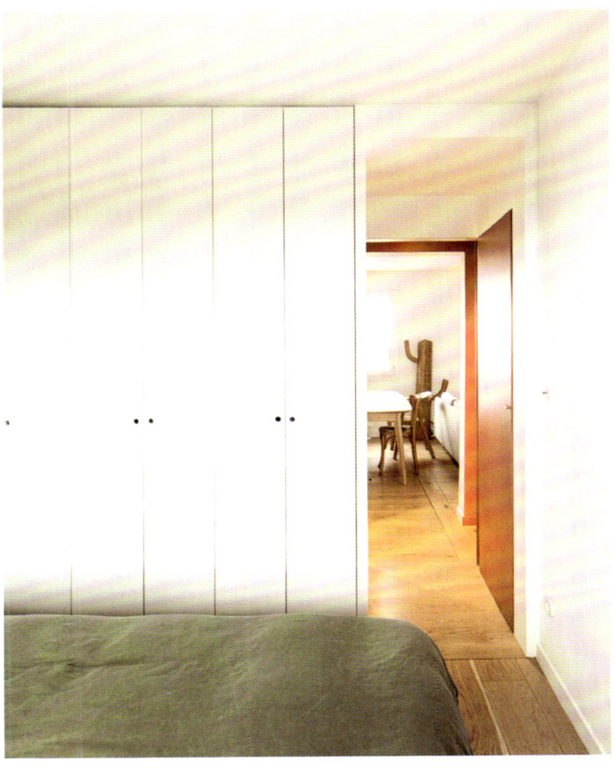

OPPOSITE The wall above the cabinet is nearly completely blank so there's room for projecting movies on it. The armchairs and coffee table are vintage finds from the 1960s.

ABOVE Custom-made built-ins abound in the primary bedroom.

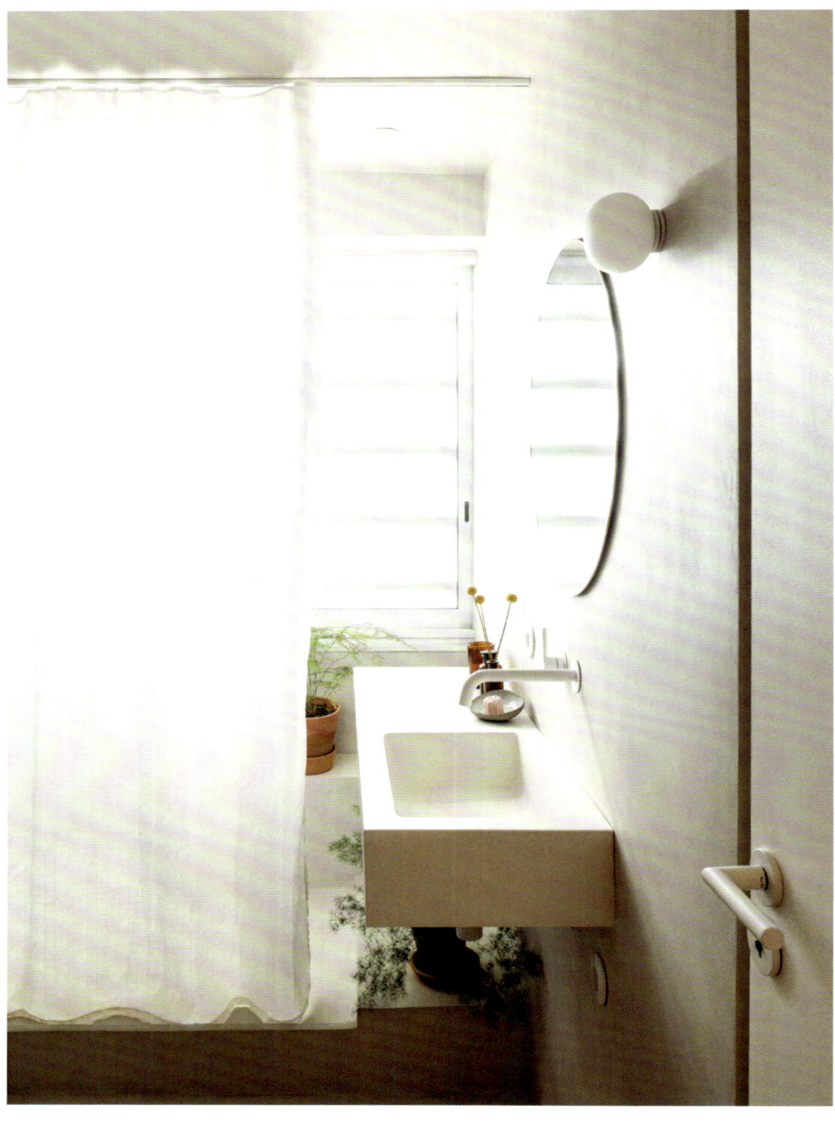

LEFT The wall-mounted basin extends into the shower area.

BELOW The bathroom's serene energy is enhanced by waxed concrete surfaces.

OPPOSITE Artworks by Hurdequint hang in the terracotta entry corridor.

In search of as much light as possible, they also made sure all the doors aligned with the windows.

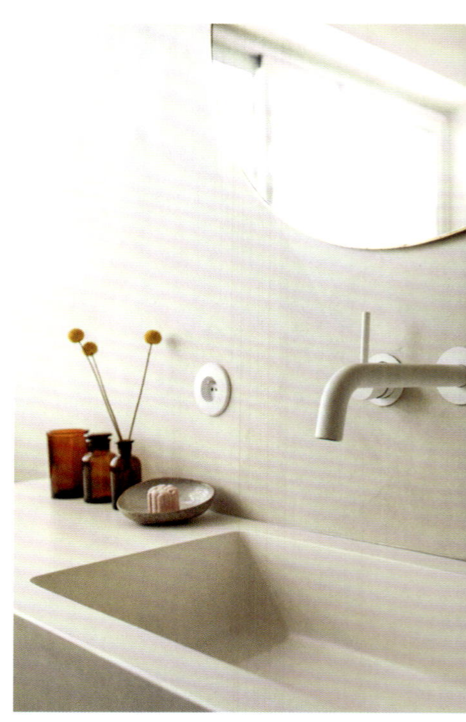

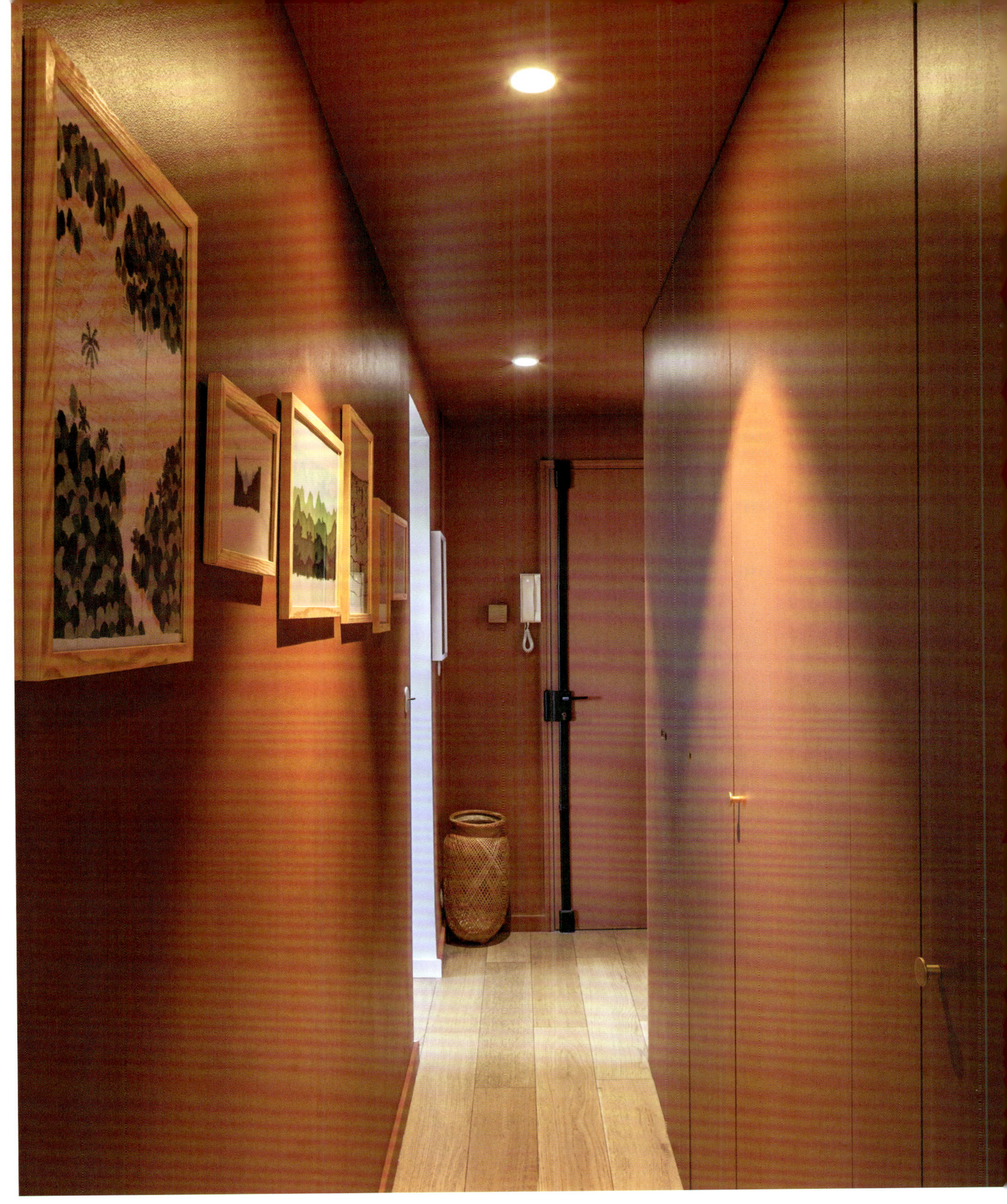

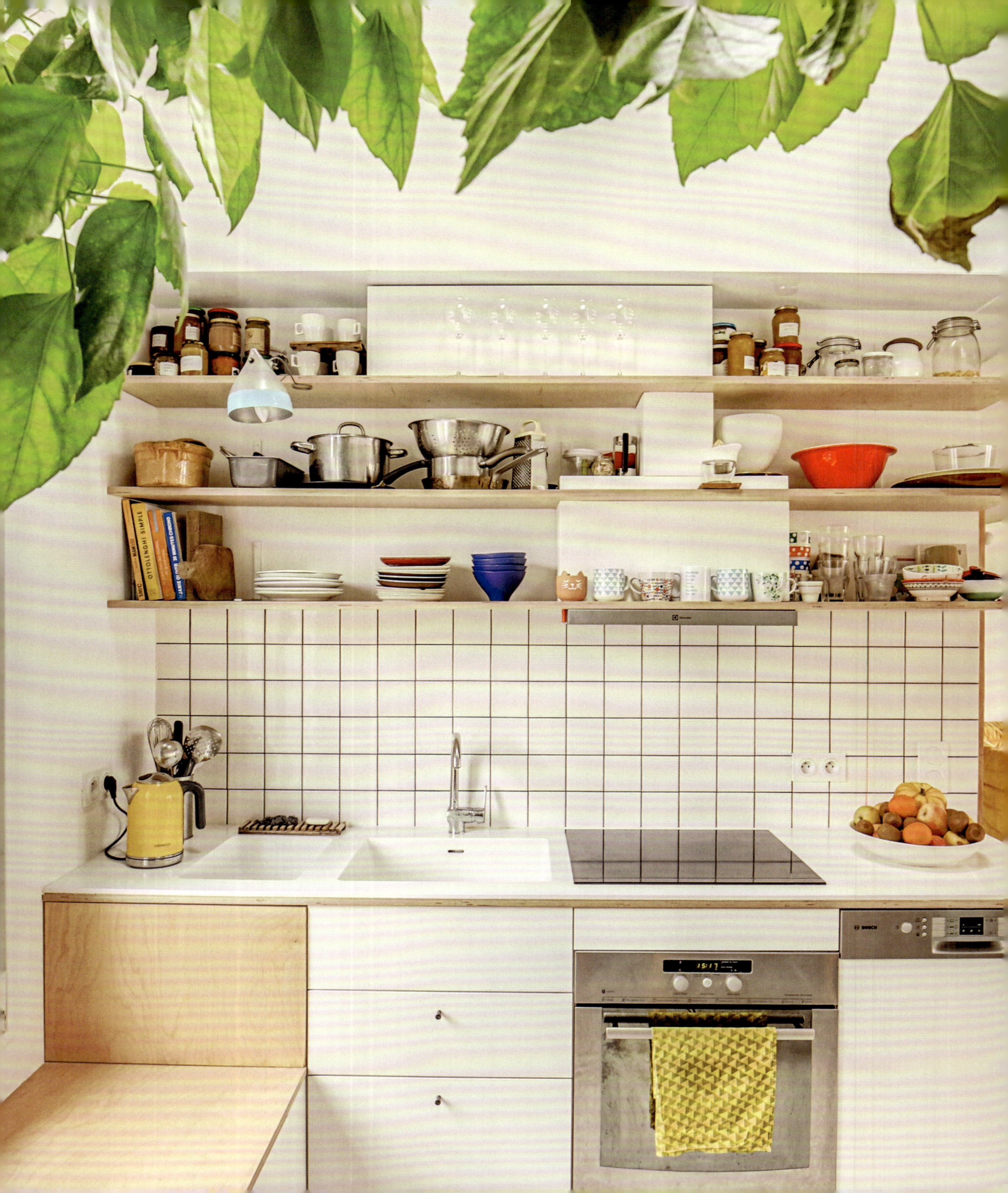
OTTOLENGHI SIMPLE
30 MINUTES CHRONO
BOSCH

Paris Duplex Extension

45m² / 484ft²
Archibien
Porte d'Ivry, Paris

Architect Olivier Menard of Archibien faced a common dilemma when he and his wife found out their family was growing – they would need more space. The couple loved their existing apartment in the culturally rich Parisian suburb of Porte d'Ivry and when the apartment above them serendipitously became available, they decided to extend up.

Believed to have been constructed in the 1870s to accommodate working-class families, the building was once owned by a single family before being subdivided into smaller flats.

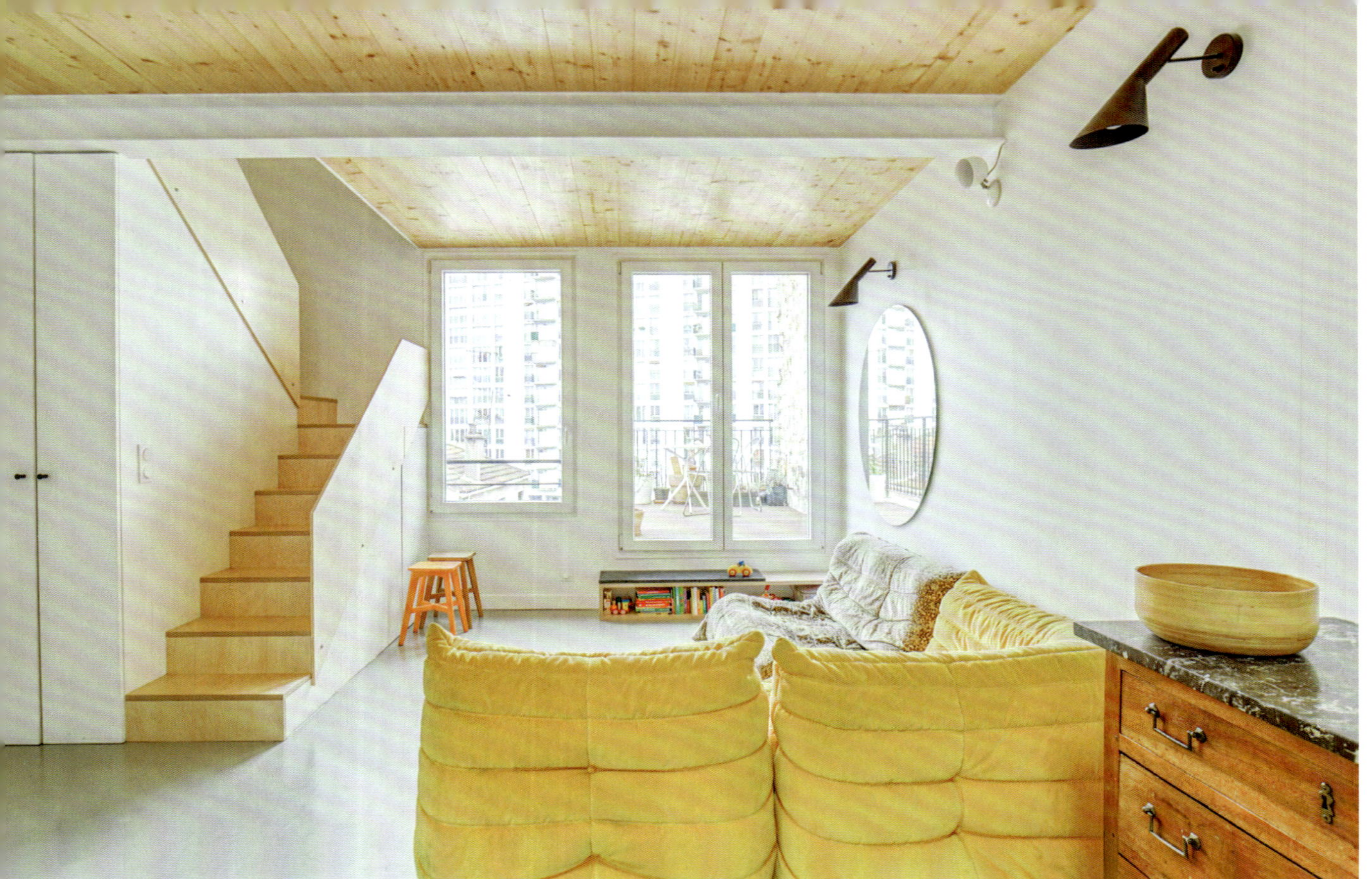

Archibien's vision was to optimise every inch of the 45-sq-m (484-sq-ft) space and create a greater sense of volume by constructing two zones with elevated ceilings: the living area with an open staircase, and a double-height space above the kitchen/dining area that features a skylight to allow natural light in.

The materials used also maximise the feeling of spaciousness. A composite steel and concrete slab coated with a light grey epoxy resin was chosen to create a smooth and cohesive floor. The L-shaped kitchen was designed with low cabinets and a bench seat under the window to give the impression of a more open space. The countertop was fashioned from Hi-Macs, a material better known by its commercial label, Corian, and paired with birch plywood. It featured a joint-free surface with integrated sinks. The splashback was composed of plain white ceramic tiles with black grout, adding both brightness to the kitchen and providing an easy-to-wipe surface.

Situated above the living area is the primary bedroom, complete with a skylight and a ceiling fan. The most prominent feature is a sizeable, double-glazed window that affords a view of the kitchen below. A desk positioned near the window enables the room to double as a workspace – a clever use of an area that would otherwise remain unused during the day. The team at Archibien incorporated customised storage for the couple's clothing and personal items, and designed a simple nursery that could adapt and evolve as the couple's child grows up.

AFTER

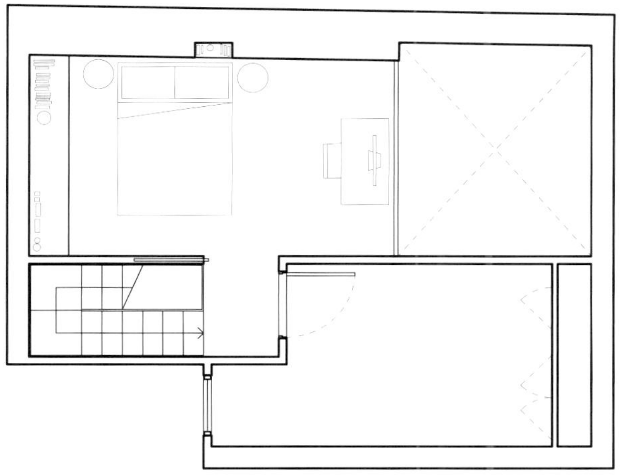

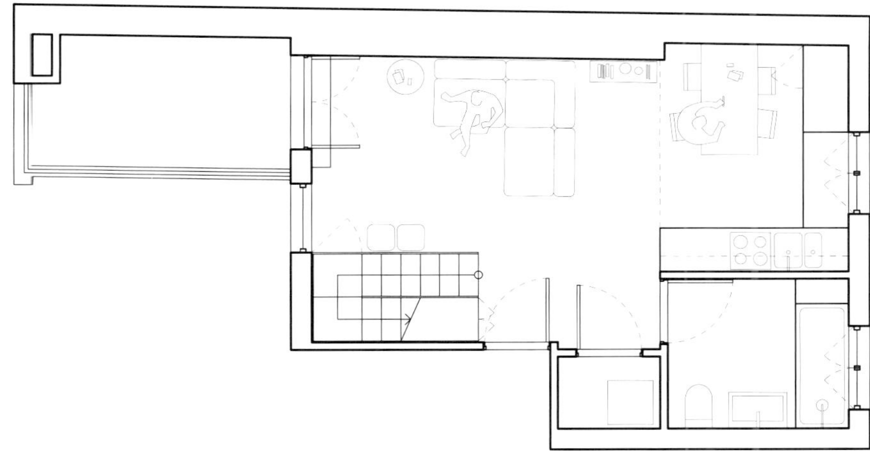

BEFORE

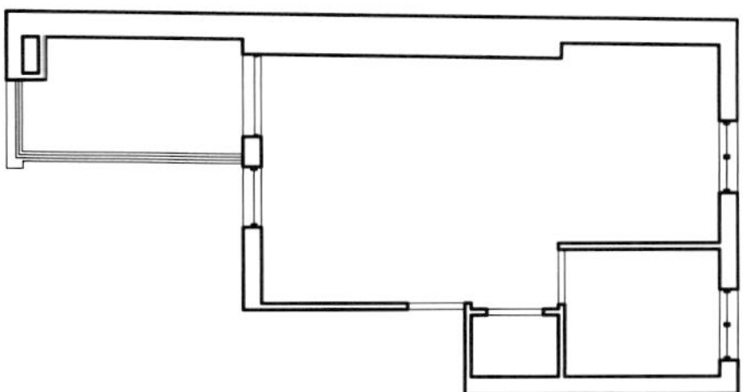

Scale 1:100

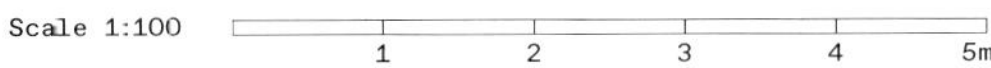

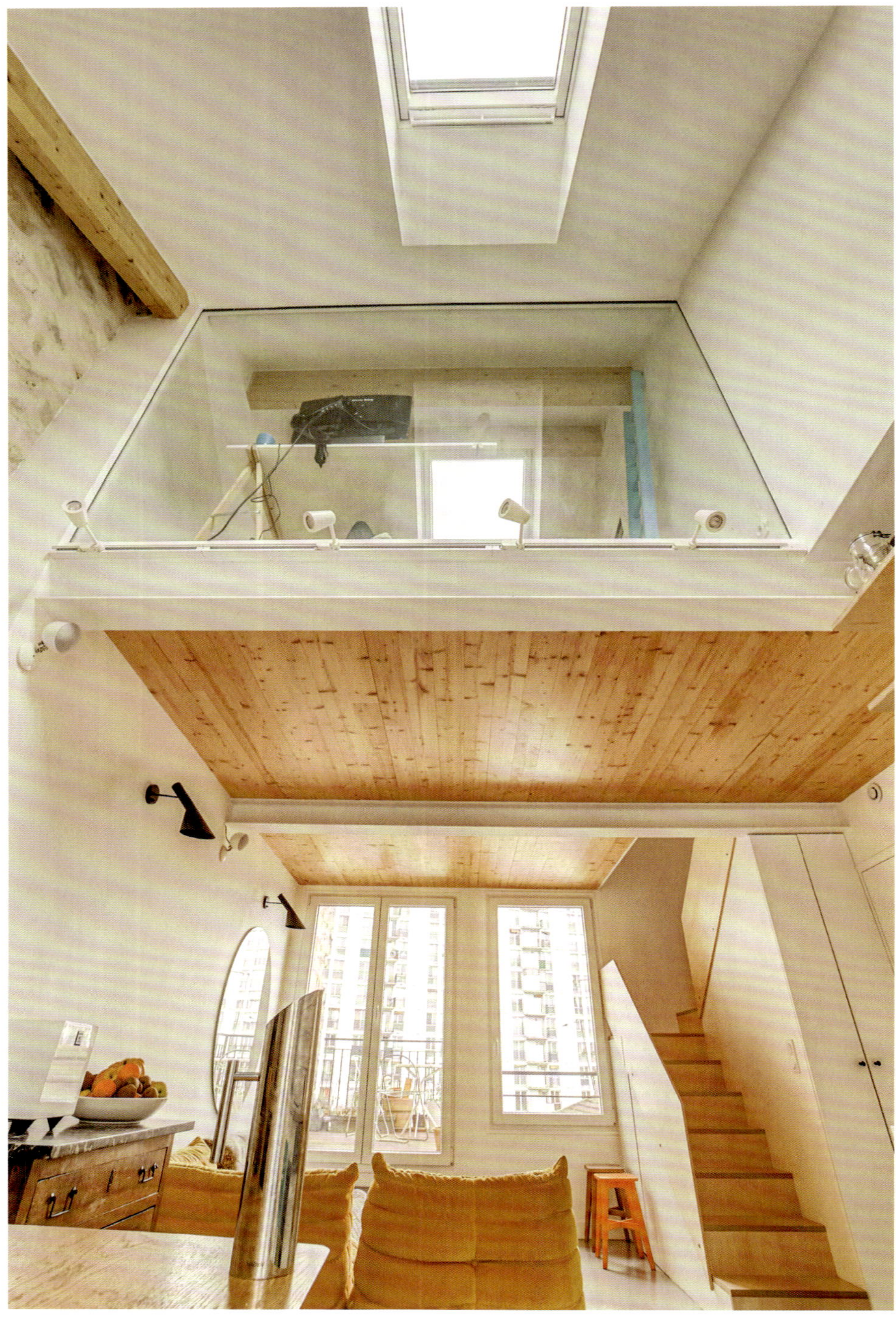

PAGE 284 A small but serious kitchen serves this family well.

PAGE 286 When the apartment above became available, Menard and his wife decided to extend up.

LEFT A floor-to-ceiling glass wall in the primary bedroom was introduced to maximise natural light.

OPPOSITE TOP Timber was used for the beams, a ceiling fan and recessed shelves in the primary bedroom, mirroring the timber flooring.

OPPOSITE BOTTOM Colourful furniture was cleverly used to break up an otherwise neutral materials palette.

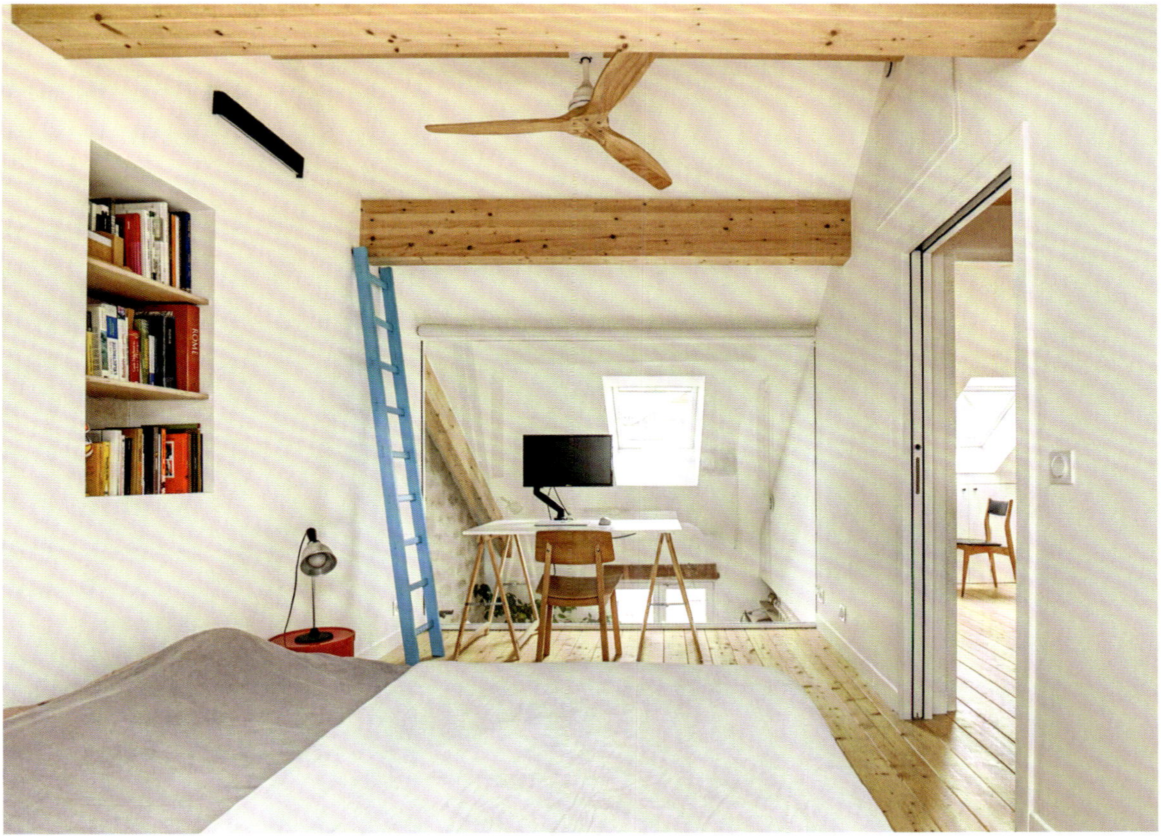

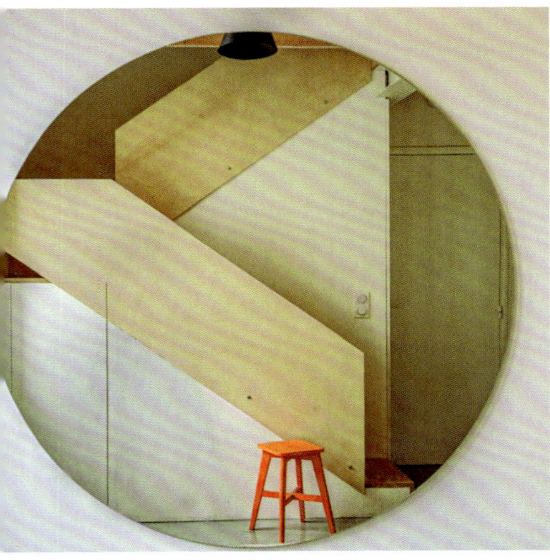

Archibien maximised the potential of the apartment by undertaking a vertical expansion. Adding vertical extensions to current buildings, where possible, is a logical way of accommodating more individuals in urban areas. This approach leverages the pre-existing electrical, water and sewage infrastructure, as well as established transportation systems, schools, hospitals, parks and other amenities. In heavily populated urban centres like Paris, as space grows increasingly limited and resources become scarcer, it makes sense to reside in smaller homes.

Archibien's creation is a testament that small family homes can be every bit as cosy and visually pleasing as their more extensive counterparts. And Menard takes pleasure in designing spaces that many architects might consider challenging because 'beauty and comfort come out of practical, technical, physical and economical constraints'.

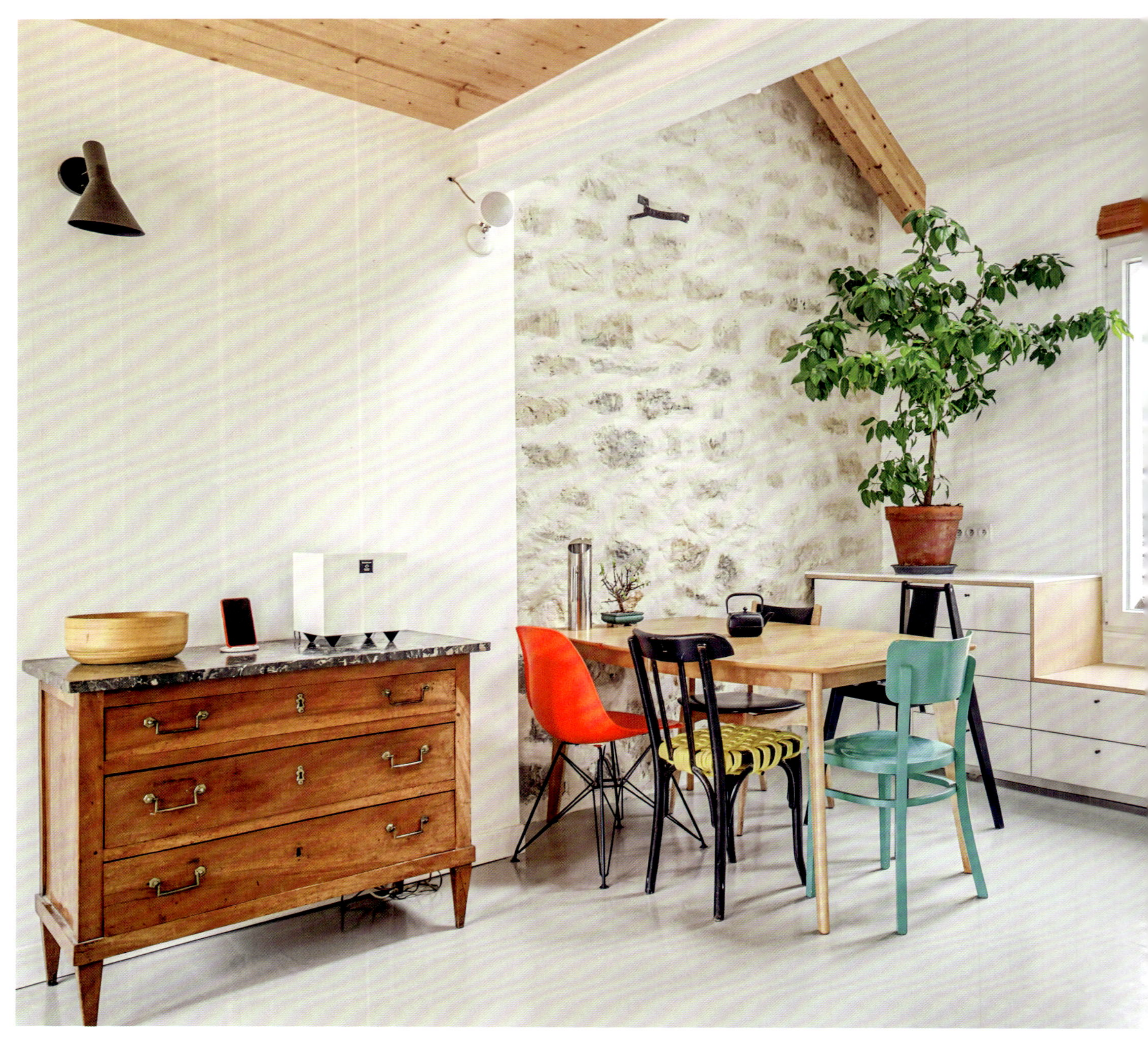

ABOVE The stone wall, untouched by render, adds a homely feeling to the kitchen and dining area.

OPPOSITE The bathroom has a bath, a rarity in a home of this size, but useful for a family with young children.

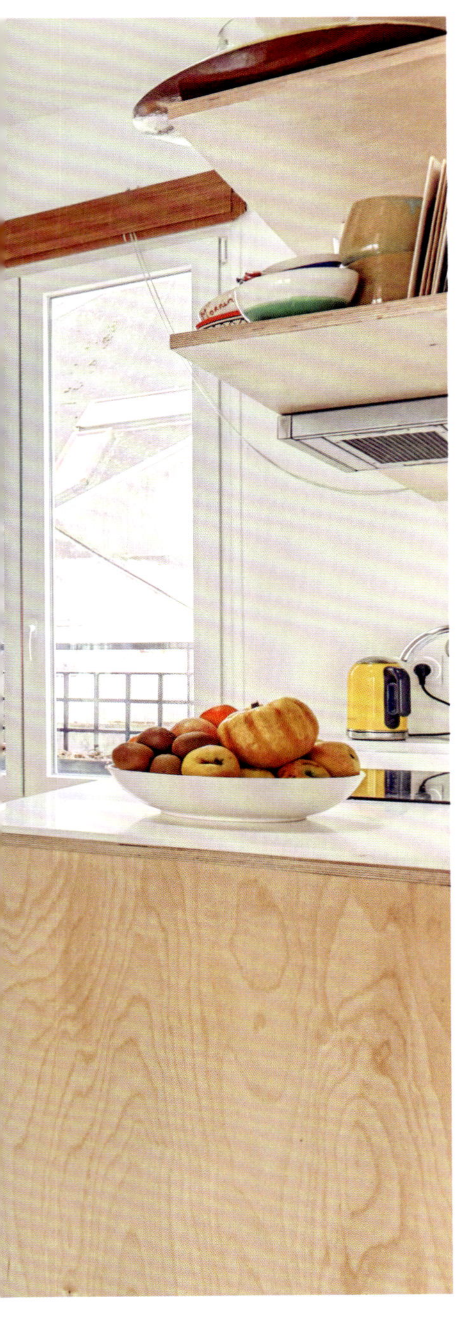

Small family homes can be every bit as cosy and visually pleasing as their more extensive counterparts.

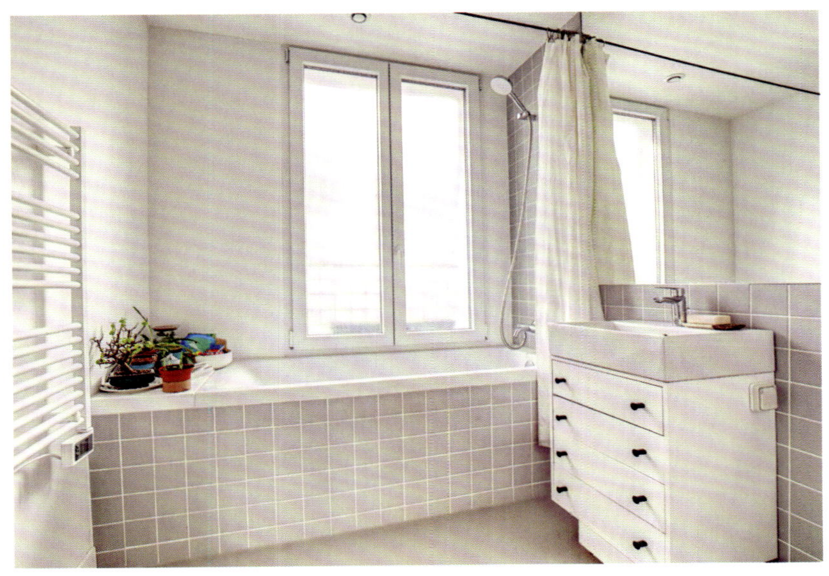

Credits

beâCHâlet p. 12

51m² / 549ft²
Bronte, Sydney

ARCHITECT
mattr.studio
Matt Reynolds

PHOTOGRAPHER
Guy Wilkinson Photography
guywphoto.com/index

DESIGN MENTOR
Jenny Reynolds

CARPENTRY COACH
Geoffrey Reynolds

ELECTRICIAN
Heath Vincent at Safelectric

Candy Cube Residence P. 180

59m² / 635ft²
Tai Hung, Hong Kong

ARCHITECT
NC Design & Architecture Limited
Nelson Chow
ncda.biz

PHOTOGRAPHER
HDP Photography
hdp-photographyservices.com

CONTRACTOR
DDL Contracting limited,
HKAGCM limited.

Casa Cubo P. 22

59m² / 635ft²
Parque Chacabuco,
Buenos Aires

ARCHITECT
Arqs. Michatek Skarstad
Torunn Vaksvik Skarstad
and Matias Michatek
michatekskarstad.wixsite.com/website

PHOTOGRAPHER
Javier Agustín Rojas
javieragustinrojas.com

Casa Gialla P. 188

47m² / 506ft²
Sol, Madrid

ARCHITECT
gon architects
Gonzalo Pardo
gon-architects.com

PHOTOGRAPHER
Imagen Subliminal
(Miguel de Guzmán
+ Rocío Romero)
magensubliminal.com

CONSTRUCTION
Redo Construcción
@redo.construccion

Crussol P. 258

54m² / 581ft²
Oberkampf, Paris

ARCHITECT
Space Factory
Ophélie Doria and Edouard
Roullé-Mafféïs
spacefactory.fr

PHOTOGRAPHER
Hervé Goluza
@herve_goluza

EG112 simple dwelling P. 208

34m² / 366ft²
Eixample, Barcelona

ARCHITECT
Jacobo Valentí
jacobovalenti.com

PHOTOGRAPHER
Juan Serlo
@juanserlo

WOODMAKER
Javier Dominguez

F-house P. 266

57m² / 613ft²
Hirakata-shi, Osaka

ARCHITECT
coil kazuteru matumura architects
Kazuteru Matumura
coilkma.com

PHOTOGRAPHER
YFT, YAMADA FOTO TECHNIX,
Keishiro Yamada
yamada-foto-technix.com

CARPENTER
Kisaburo, Okimoto Masaaki
kisaburo.info

Flat Eleven P. 136

50m² / 538ft²
Oltrarno, Florence

ARCHITECT
Pierattelli Architetture
Claudio Pierattelli
pierattelliarchitetture.com

PHOTOGRAPHER
Iuri Niccolai
iuriniccolai.it

Fourvière Apartment P. 276

57m² / 613ft²
Fourvière, Lyon

ARCHITECT
MURA architects
Maxime Hurdequint
and Mary Bravard
mura.archi

PHOTOGRAPHER
Mathieu NOËL
mathieu-noel.com

House for Cosimo Piovasco P. 218

45m² / 484ft²
Rastro, Madrid

ARCHITECT
Mariana de Delás
marianadelas.com

PHOTOGRAPHER
Imagen Subliminal
(Miguel de Guzman + Rocio Romero)
imagensubliminal.com

Home in Akatsutsumi P. 86

46m² / 495ft²
Setagaya, Tokyo

ARCHITECT
Small Design Studio
Kumiko Ouchi
small-design-studio.com

PHOTOGRAPHER
Yumi Saito
yumisaitophoto.com

Ilioupoli Apartment P. 144

55m² / 592ft²
Ilioupoli, Athens

ARCHITECT
Point Supreme Architects
Konstantinos Pantazis
and Marianna Rentzou
pointsupreme.com

PHOTOGRAPHER
Yiannis Hadjiaslanis
hadjiaslanis.com

IT's House P. 30

70m² / 753ft²
Wenshan District,
Taipei City

ARCHITECT
2 Books Design
Jeff Weng
2booksdesign.com.tw

PHOTOGRAPHER
Lucas K. Doolan
studiomillspace.com

Jourdain P. 228

24m² / 258ft²
Jourdain, Paris

ARCHITECT
BILOBA.archi
Matthieu Torres
@biloba.archi

PHOTOGRAPHER
Matthieu Torres
@matthieu__torres

Kolonaki Apartment P. 154

48m² / 516ft²
Kolonaki, Athens

ARCHITECT
Cluster Architects
Lora Zampara and
Michalis Saplaouras
cluster-architects.com

PHOTOGRAPHERS
Studiovd
Nikos Vavdinoudis and
Christos Dimitriou
studiovd.gr

Limit House P. 76

28m² / 301ft²
DaTong District,
Taipei City

DESIGNER
Republic Design
Joanne Wang, Jia-Bao Dong,
Chris Choo
rd-interior.com

PHOTOGRAPHER
Yu Chen Chao Studio
@yuchenchao_studio

Lwowska P. 40

32m² / 344ft²
Podgórze, Kraków

DESIGNER
pigalopus
Karolina Chodur and
Malwina Borowiec
pigalopus.pl

PHOTOGRAPHER
Michał Lichtański
@lichtanskimichal

Mark II P. 96

27m² / 291ft²
Rushcutters Bay, Sydney

DESIGNER
Nicholas Gurney
nicholasgurney.com.au

PHOTOGRAPHER
Kat Lu
katherinelu.com

Marvila Attic P. 48

60m² / 645ft2
Marvila, Lisbon

ARCHITECT
KEMA studio
Eliza Borkowska and Magdalena
Czapluk
kema.pt

PHOTOGRAPHER
@Alexander Bogorodskiy © KEMA
studio Eliza Borkowska

Maximalist Mini Loft P. 198

57m² / 614ft²
Bagnolet, Paris

ARCHITECT
Zyva Studio
Anthony Authié
zyvastudio.com

PHOTOGRAPHER
Yohann Fontaine
yohannfontaine.com

Monolocale EFFE P. 162

36m² / 387ft²
Mantova, Lombardy

ARCHITECT
Archiplanstudio
Jacopo Rettondini, Diego Cisi and
Stefano Gorni Silvestrini
archiplanstudio.com

PHOTOGRAPHER
Barton Taylor
bartontaylorphotography.com

Paris Duplex Extension P. 284

45m² / 484ft²
Porte d'Ivry, Paris

ARCHITECT
Archibien
Olivier Menard
archibien.com

PHOTOGRAPHER
©Archibien.com
archibien.com

PARTNER
M. Cardines

CONSTRUCTION
Humeau Eco Construction
AFB
SIMA

Park Street Apartment P. 58

42m² / 452ft²
Brunswick, Melbourne

DESIGNER
Alex Antoniadis
@xand.who.are.you

PHOTOGRAPHER
Nam Tran
nevertoosmall.com

Pepper Tree Passive House P. 236

54m² / 581ft²
Unanderra, Wollongong

ARCHITECT
Alexander Symes Architect
alexandersymes.com.au

BUILDER
Souter Built
souterbuilt.com.au

PHOTOGRAPHER
Barton Taylor
bartontaylorphotography.com

INTERIOR DESIGNER
Eliesha Keenan
paianodesign.com

Pinkyellow P. 68

32m² / 344ft²
Fayna Town, Kyiv

DESIGNER
Olha Bondar Design
olgabondar.net

PHOTOGRAPHER
Alexander Kondriyanenko
brizmaker.com

Project #13 P. 104

64m² / 688ft²
Serangoon, Singapore

ARCHITECT
Studio Wills + Architects
William Ng and Keguang Kho
studio-wills.com

PHOTOGRAPHERS
Khoo Guo Jie
khoogj.com
Finbarr Fallon
finbarrfallon.com

ENGINEER
CAGA Consultants Pte Ltd

CONTRACTOR
Wah Sheng Construction Pte Ltd,

CARPENTER
Sin Hiap Chuan Wood Works

Scheeps P. 246

45m² / 484ft²
Eastern Harbour District,
Amsterdam

DESIGNERS AND MAKERS
Fadime Gökkaya and Koen Fraijman
fraijman.nl

PHOTOGRAPHER
Rem Burger
remberger.nl

Stroboscope P. 172

42m² / 450ft²
Opera District, Paris

ARCHITECT
studiobravo
Marion Richard and Thomas Pellerin
@studiobravo.archi

PHOTOGRAPHER
Bertrand Noël
bertrandnoel.com

CARPENTER
Sergiu Stici / EURL S.T.I.C

CARPENTER KITCHEN ISLAND
Le pavé ®

VM36 P. 114

53m² / 570ft²
Pigalle, Paris

ARCHITECT
JMLC STUDIO
Jean-Malo Le Clerc
jmlcstudio.com

PHOTOGRAPHER
Juan Jerez Studio
juanjerezstudio.com

CONTRACTOR
Ge Renov
ge-renov.com

Waterloo Street P. 124

59m² / 635ft²
Bugis, Singapore

ARCHITECT
Three-d conceptwerke
Dess Chew
three-d-conceptwerke.com

PHOTOGRAPHERS
Justin Loh
@justinloh911
Wong Weiliang
crispcontrasts.com.sg/wong-weiliang-interior-architectural-photography

Floor Plans

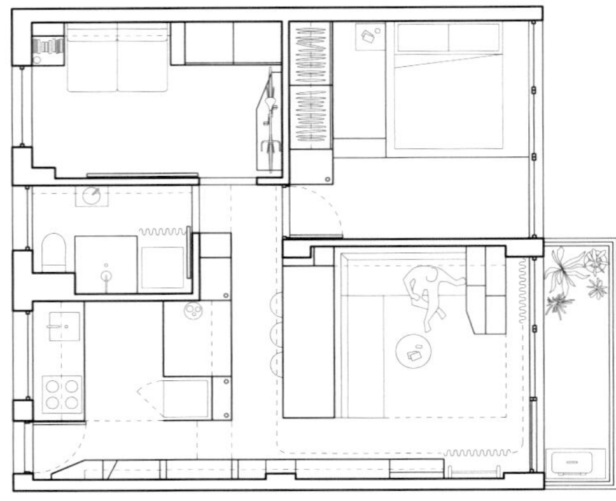

beâCHâlet p. 12

$51m^2$ / $549ft^2$
Bronte, Sydney

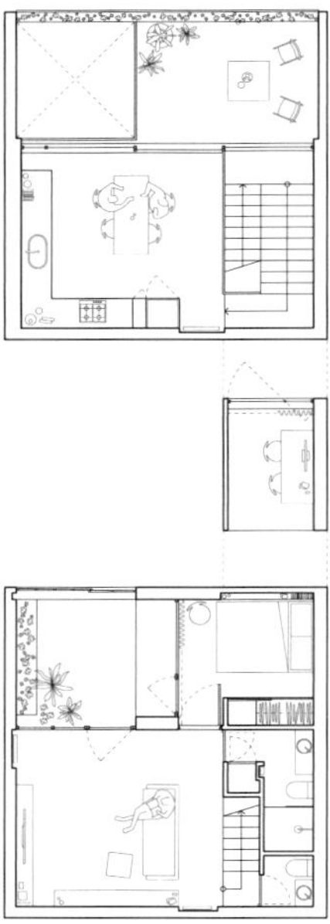

Casa Cubo P. 22

$59m^2$ / $635ft^2$
Parque Chacabuco,
Buenos Aires

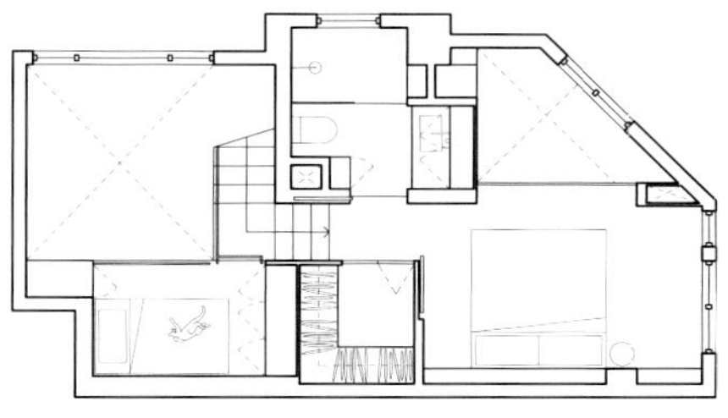

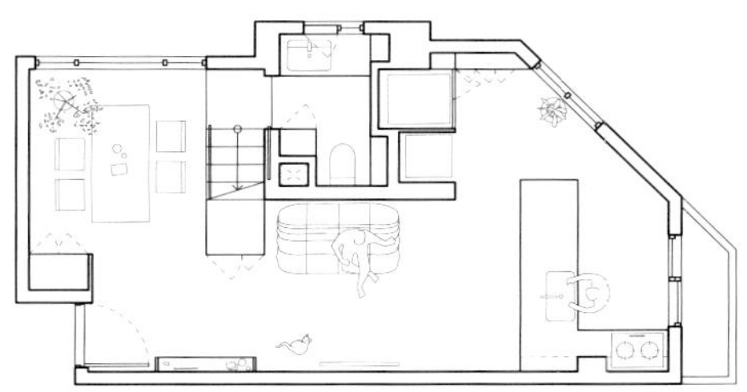

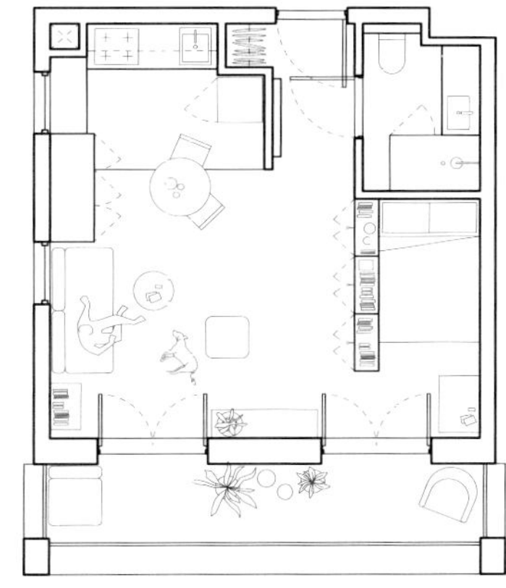

IT's House P. 30

70m² / 753ft²
Wenshan District,
Taipei City

Lwowska P. 40

32m² / 344ft²
Podgórze, Kraków

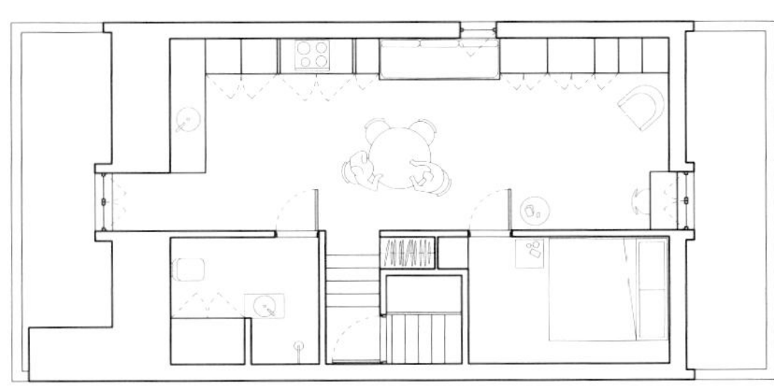

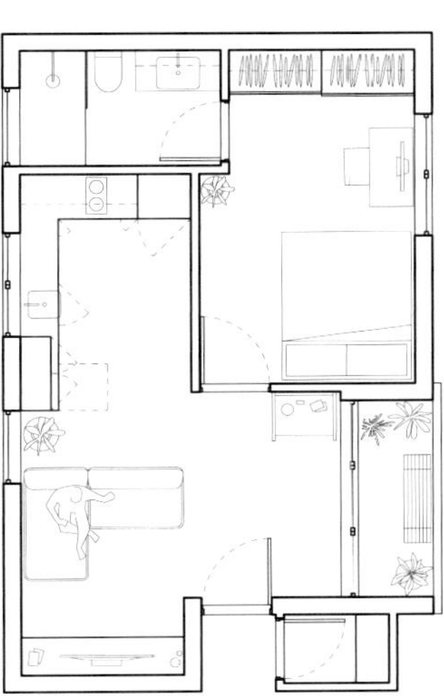

Marvila Attic
P. 48

60m² / 645ft²
Marvila, Lisbon

Park Street Apartment P. 58

42m² / 452ft²
Brunswick, Melbourne

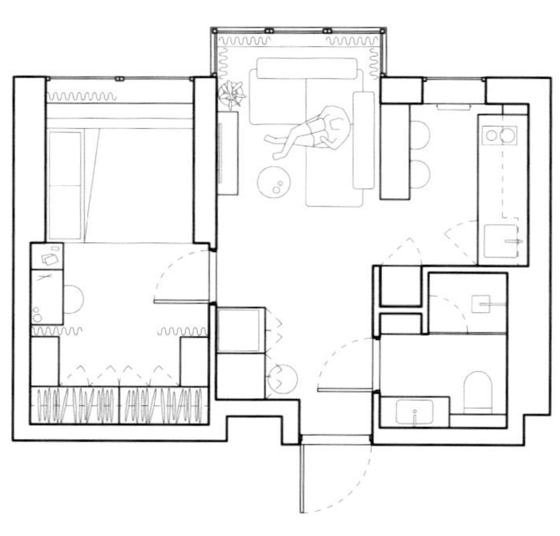

Pinkyellow P. 68

32m² / 344ft²
Fayna Town, Kyiv

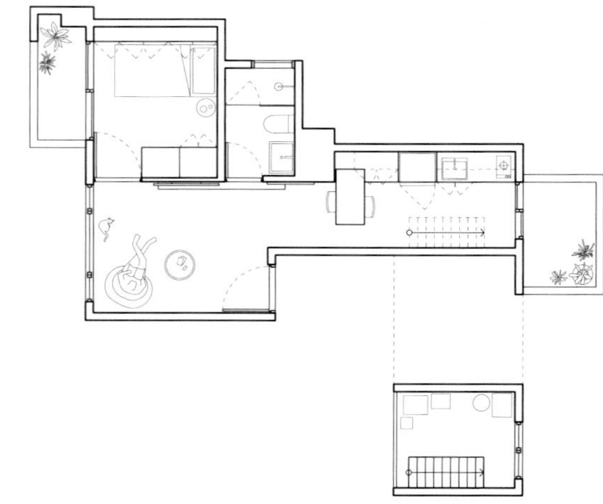

Limit House
P. 76

28m² / 301ft²
DaTong District,
Taipei City

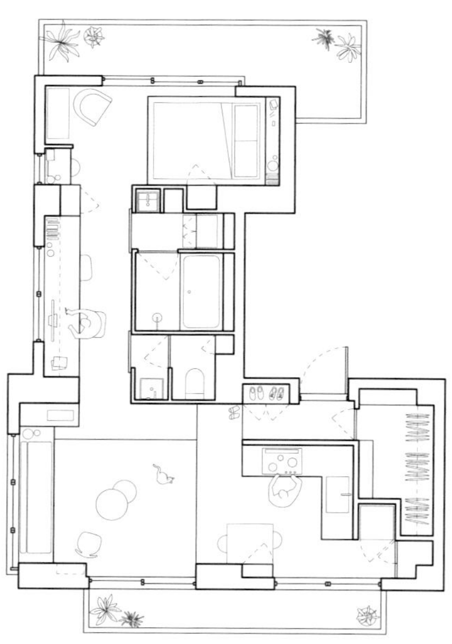

Home in Akatsutsumi P. 86

46m² / 495ft²
Setagaya, Tokyo

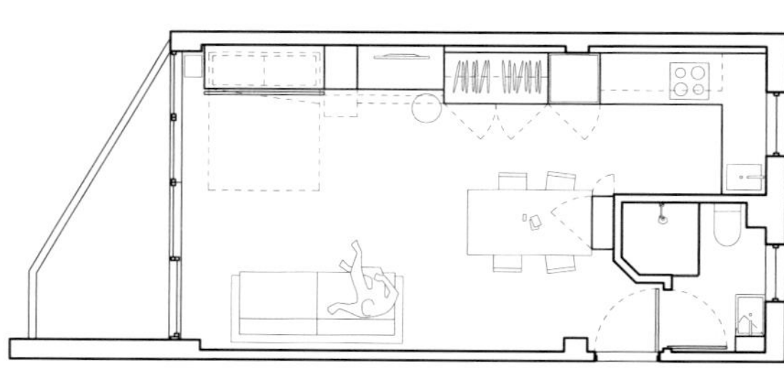

Mark II p. 96

27m² / 291ft²
Rushcutters Bay, Sydney

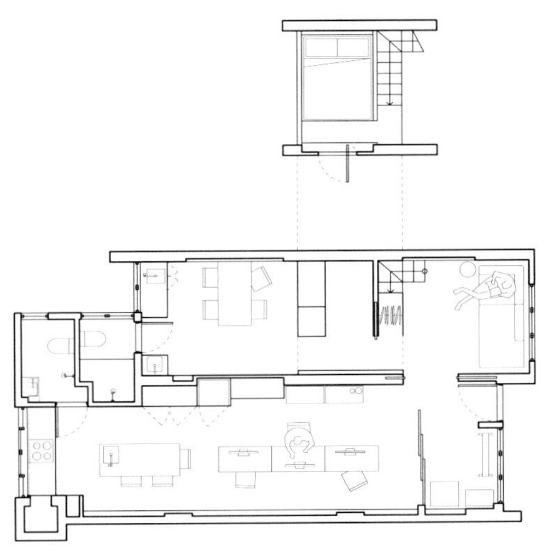

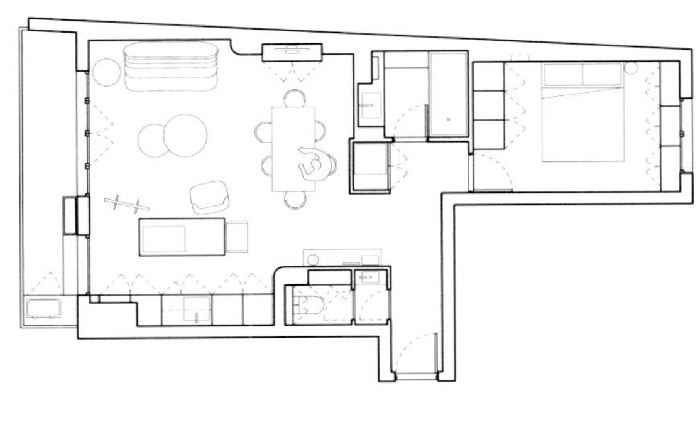

Project #13
P. 104

64m² / 688ft²
Serangoon, Singapore

VM36 P. 114

53m² / 570ft²
Pigalle, Paris

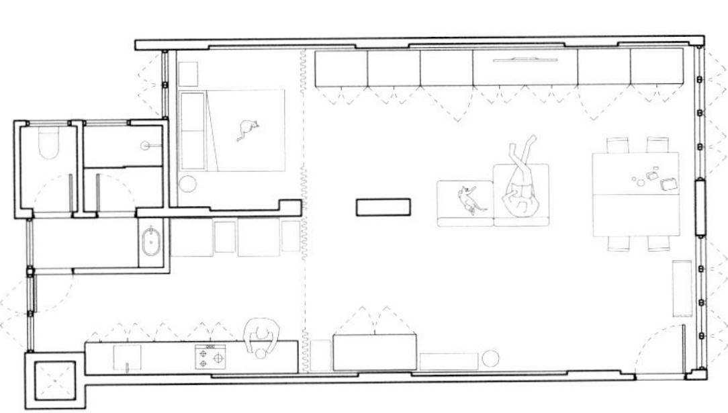

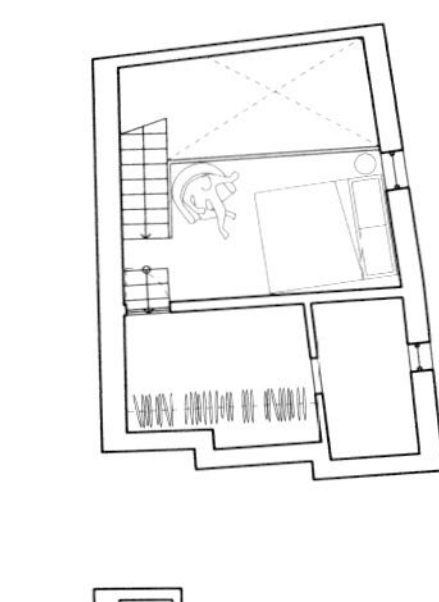

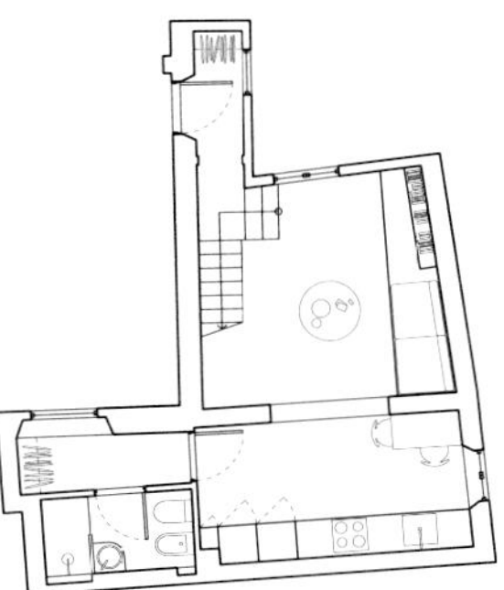

Waterloo Street P. 124

59m² / 635ft²
Bugis, Singapore
Three-d conceptwerke

Flat Eleven P. 136

50m² / 538ft²
Oltrarno, Florence

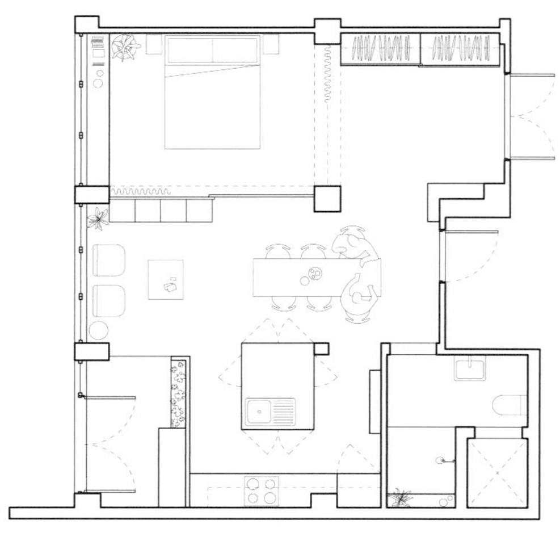

Ilioupoli Apartment P. 144

55m² / 592ft²
Ilioupoli, Athens

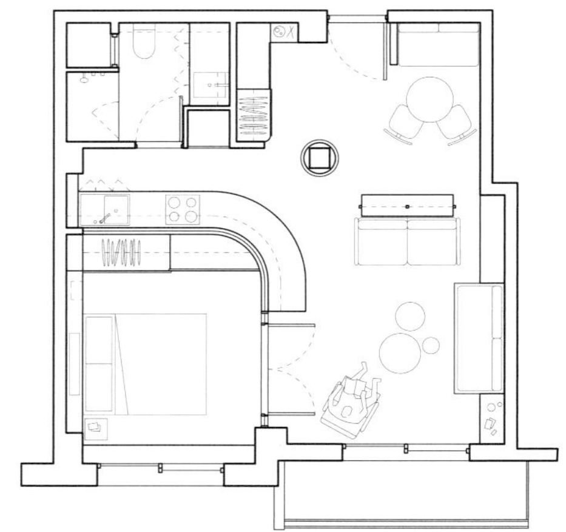

Kolonaki Apartment P. 154

48m² / 516ft²
Kolonaki, Athens

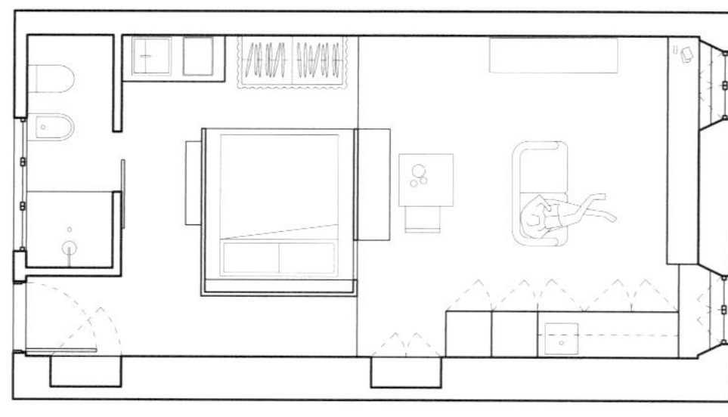

Monolocale EFFE P. 162

36m² / 387ft²
Mantova, Lombardy

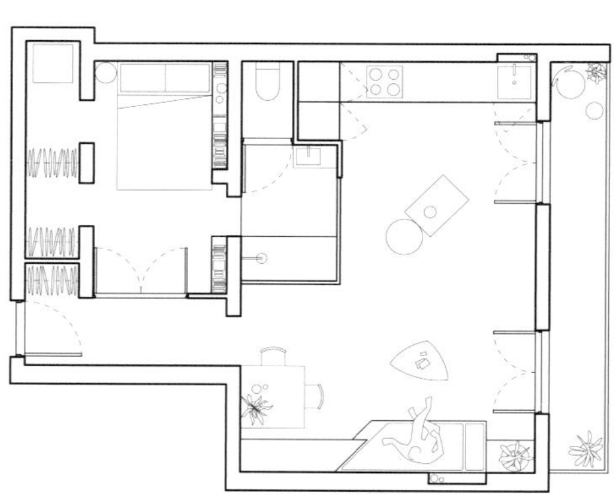

Stroboscope P. 172

42m² / 450ft²
Opera District, Paris

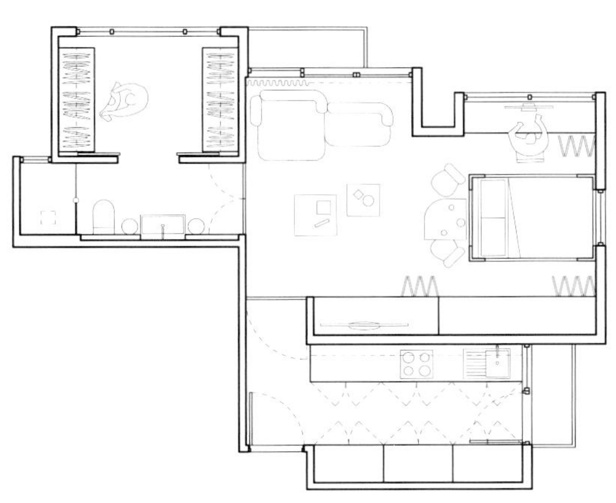

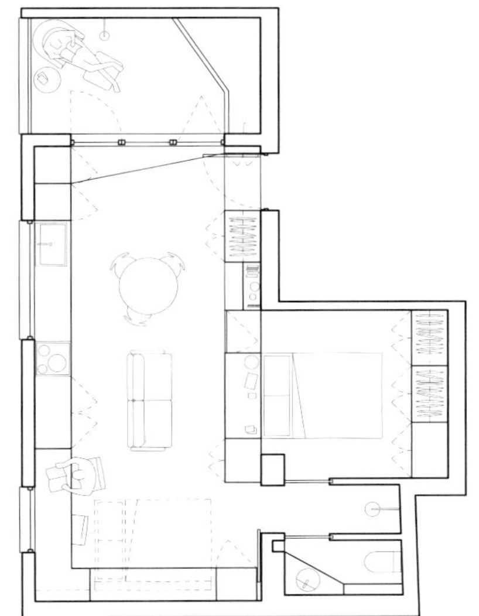

Candy Cube Residence P. 180

59m² / 635ft²
Tai Hung, Hong Kong

Casa Gialla
P. 188

47m² / 506ft²
Sol, Madrid

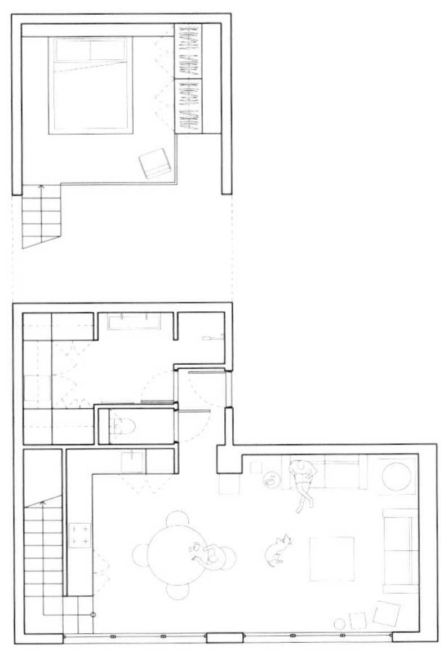

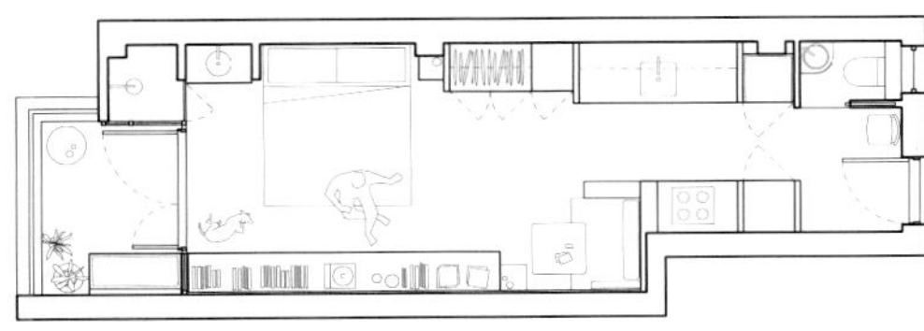

Maximalist Mini Loft P. 198

57m² / 614ft²
Bagnolet, Paris

EG112 simple dwelling P. 208

34m² / 366ft²
Eixample, Barcelona

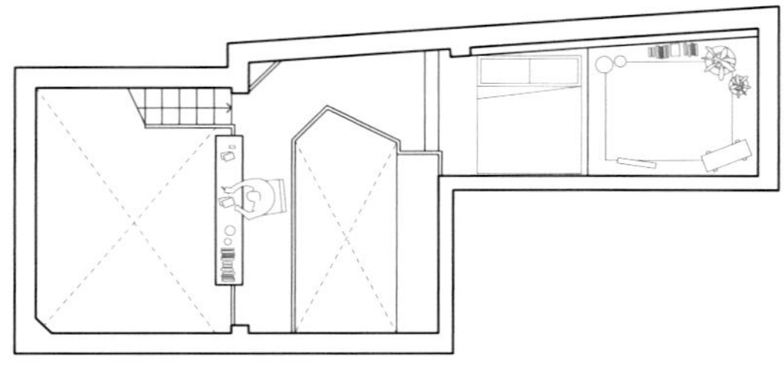

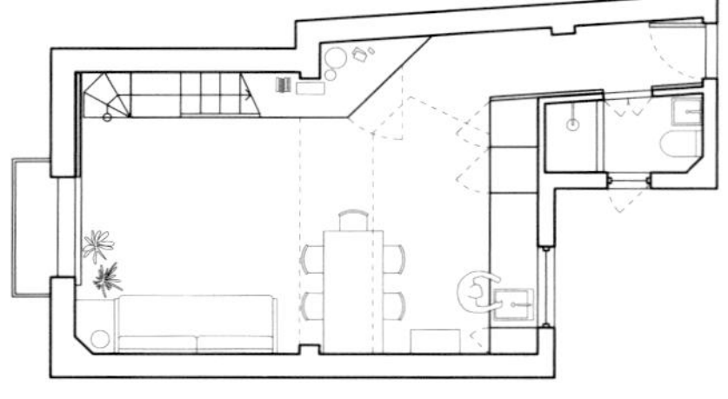

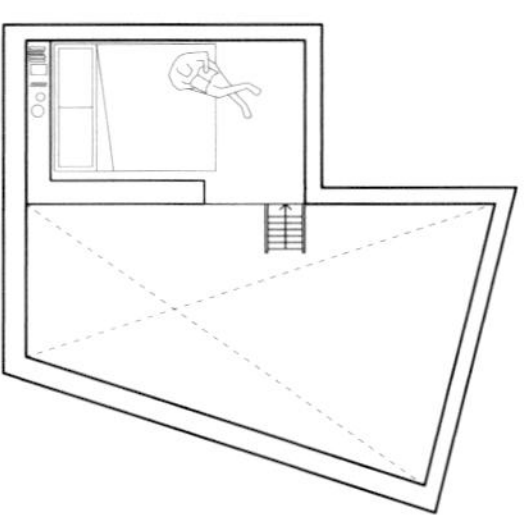

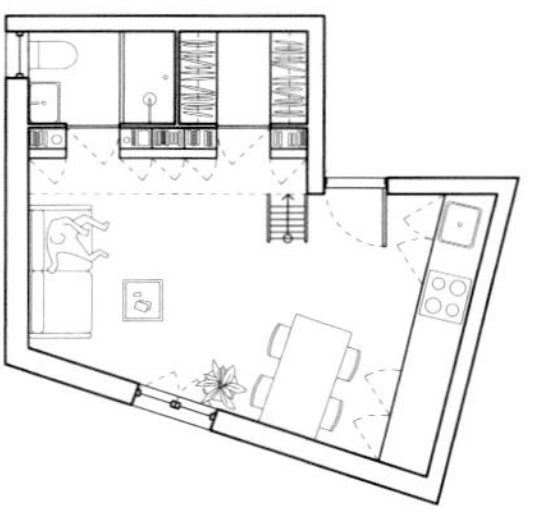

House for Cosimo Piovasco P. 218

45m² / 484ft²
Rastro, Madrid

Jourdain P. 228

24m² / 258ft²
Jourdain, Paris

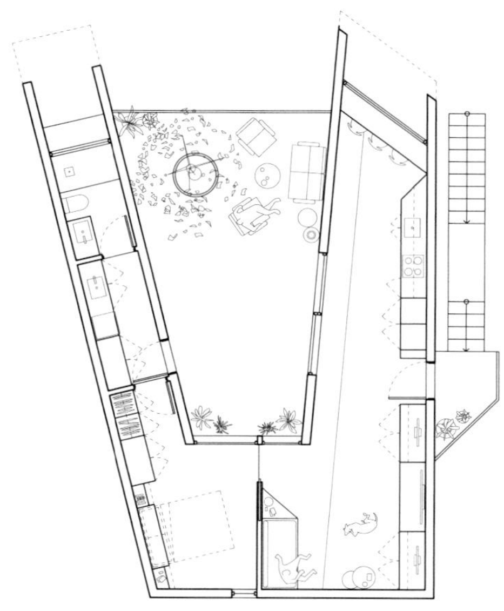

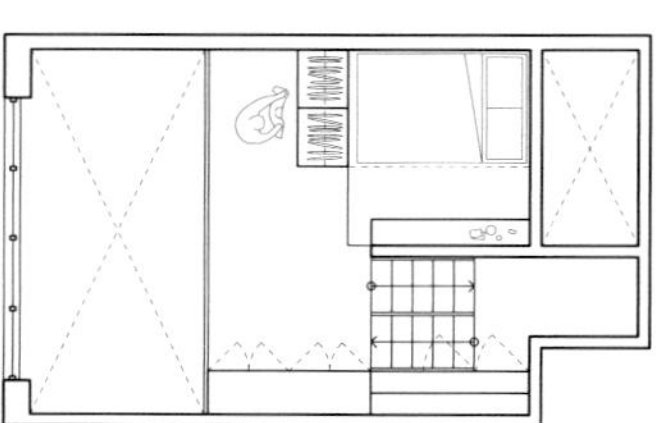

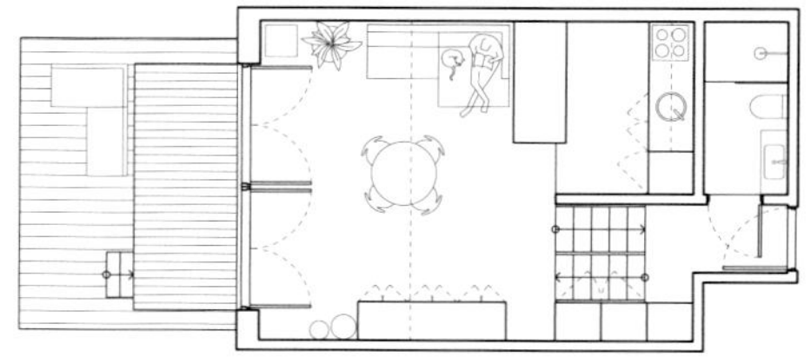

Pepper Tree Passive House P. 236

54m² / 581ft²
Unanderra, Wollongong

Scheeps P. 246

45m² / 484ft²
Eastern Harbour District, Amsterdam

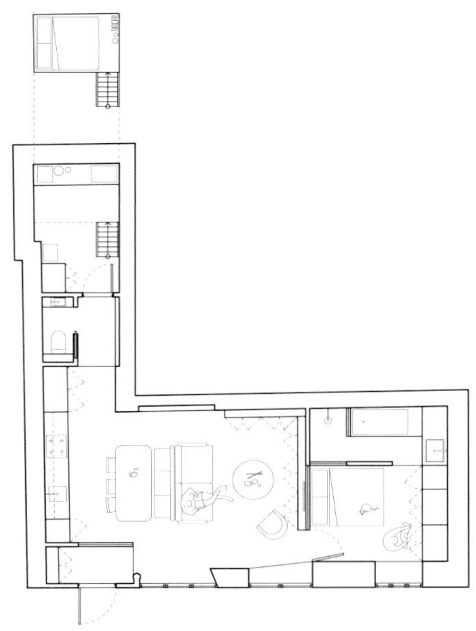

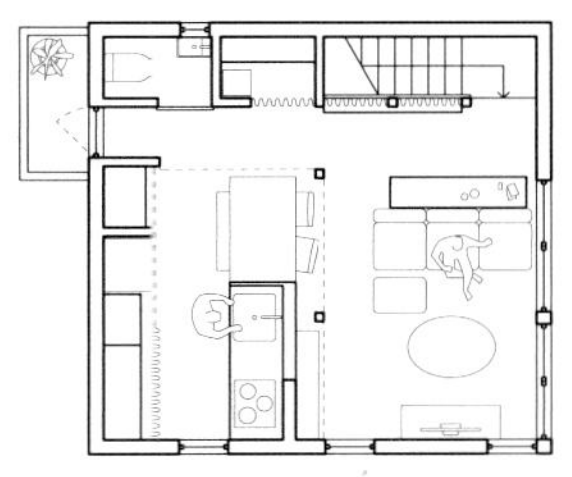

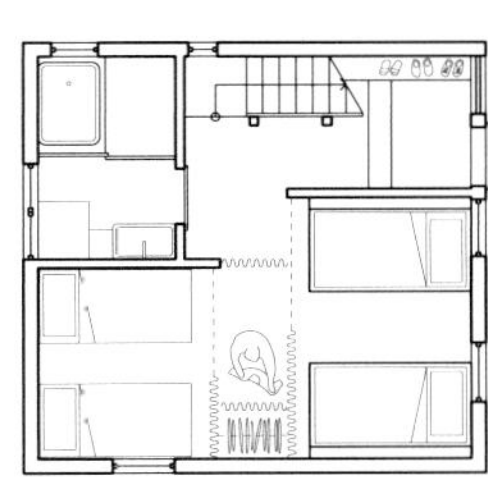

Crussol P. 258

54m² / 581ft²
Oberkampf, Paris

F-house P. 266

57m² / 613ft²
Hirakata-shi, Osaka

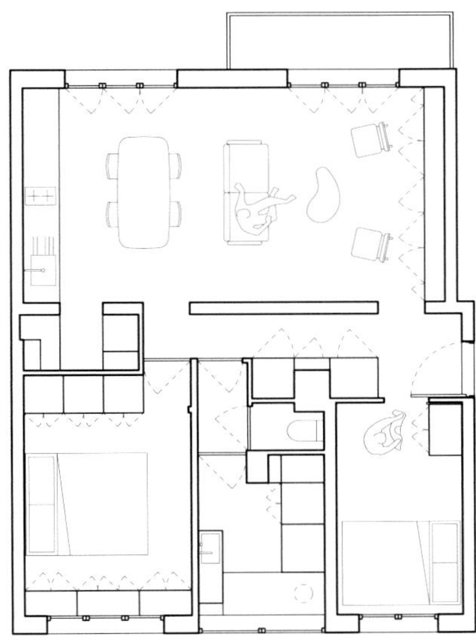

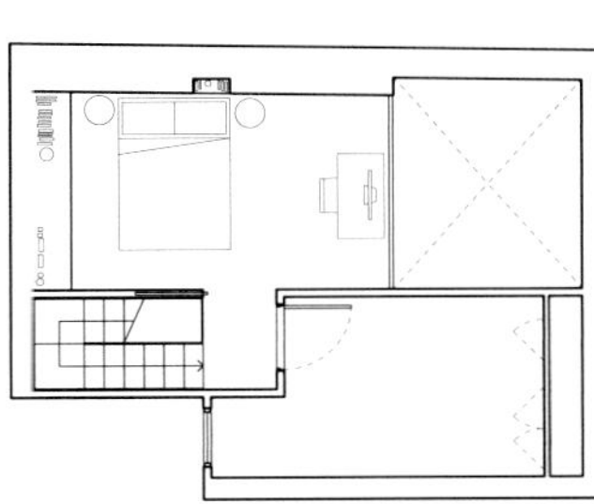

Fourvière Apartment P. 276

57m² / 613ft²
Fourvière, Lyon

Paris Duplex Extension P. 285

45m² / 484ft²
Porte d'Ivry, Paris

Thanks

We owe the quality of this book to the amazing designs it showcases. First and foremost, we want to thank the architects and designers who allowed us to feature their magnificent projects. Without your work, Never Too Small wouldn't exist. Thank you for inspiring us and for generously supporting Never Too Small. Thank you to the owners and residents of the homes we've featured for generously allowing us into your space and trusting us to share your beautiful residences with our audience.

Thank you to our photographers and videographers who capture such high-quality images of these wonderful homes. We love that we can display them so lovingly and surround them with our words and descriptions. We hope you love seeing them on our channels and in print as much as we do!

To the Smith Street team: Paul, Evi-O.Studio and Tahlia, thank you for backing us to create book two! We're really proud of our collaboration and we just love working with you all to capture these beautiful profiles.

To our audience, this book only exists because you were incredibly supportive of our first book. Your emphatic response gives us the encouragement we need to keep creating high-quality products for you to engage with. We are always and forever so grateful.

To the Never Too Small crew – James, Lindsay, Nam, Jess, Luke, Elizabeth, Petrina, Reco, Seb and Claryss – thanks for keeping the engine running while we run off to create these products. We love our little team and we're inspired by you all every day. This is your book too.

Finally, to everyone who has adopted, or hopes to adopt, some of the principles we try to live by. Thank you for doing your part in making your homes, community and the world a better place.

– Colin, Joel and Camilla

I would probably need ten pages to thank all the people who have contributed to this book and who have supported Never Too Small for all these years. But you know who you are!

I want to express a big heartfelt thank you to our wonderful team at Never Too Small and our publisher, Smith Street Books. A particular mention is due to Joel Beath and Camilla Janse Van Vuuren for their beautiful writing in this book. Thank you, my beloved powerhouse producer Lindsay Barnard. And, of course, thank you to our publisher Paul McNally for believing in us and making my dream of having a Never Too Small book on Tate Modern's bookshelves come true. Fingers crossed.

Thank you to all the architects and designers who have been willing to share their designs and knowledge with us to create this second book. I also want to extend my gratitude to the talented team at Evi-O.Studio for designing this gorgeous book. Nic Agius and George Mollett, thank you for drawing the floor plans that everyone loves.

I would also like to thank my parents and siblings for their unconditional love and belief in my dream. And a special thank you to Mark Alexander for your continuous support and love.

Finally, I want to express my deepest gratitude to you – yes, you, who is reading this right now – for supporting us on this wonderful journey. I am forever grateful.

– Colin

Thanks to my father, Ross Beath, who would have loved to have slowly gone through this book and read each of my words. Despite it not being within his sphere of interest, he would have found something to be curious about and would have loved to have had a conversation with me about it. He was proud of me for writing my first book and would have been just as proud about this second one. He's a man that deserves to be remembered. A good man to know.

Thanks to Camilla who jumped onboard to co-write this with me. Thanks for taking the job so seriously and crafting your words so carefully.

Lindsay, just like last time, you're the reason this book exists. Without your fastidiousness, mixed with your understanding of the creative process, this would be an unorganised, unfinished jumble of ideas. Thank you, you deserve more credit than a note at the end of the book.

Thanks Colin, I love how you see the world and I love how passionate you are about making sure our audience promise is delivered and that the people who engage with our products receive value. Thanks for holding us to your high standards.

NTS team, what an incredible little team we have. I'm so proud of our ambition and work ethic and what such a small team can create.

To our audience – this book is only possible because you supported us so generously with our first book. Thank you and please rest assured we have tried to lift the bar with this, our second book. We hope you love it even more.

Paul, Tahlia and Evi O, thanks crew. Paul, love working with you. Love your pragmatism and vision. Tahlia, these are your words too. Thank you for your patience and thoroughness. Evi O, thanks for bringing our words to life through your beautiful design.

To my mum, Gaye, and my siblings, Ben and Kate, it's been a tough couple of years without Dad. Love you all so much. Foxy, Haddles and Lawsy, you guys are everything. Love forever and always.

— Joel

I'd like to firstly acknowledge the Never Too Small team for welcoming me on this journey with open arms. Thank you for trusting me with this precious enterprise. I have truly loved the process.

Joel, thank you for your confidence in me as your writing partner. And for giving me free rein to let the words fall as they wanted.

Tahlia, for the e-mail tennis match you so willingly played and for making the editing process less daunting – thank you.

Ant Lucille, thank you for your consistent writing encouragement and guidance over the years. Your enthusiasm to dive right in, send me articles and examples, ideas and suggestions, is always appreciated.

Kezia, for giving me the nudge I needed all those years ago to start sharing my writing beyond incredibly long and elaborate text messages to friends, thank you! It was a good idea.

Gilli, I will always be grateful for your rare and unique skill to pack volumes of wisdom, encouragement and humour into brief conversations. Thank you for saying the things I needed to hear. Thank you for London.

Lauren Pie, for your support and enthusiasm of this project. And all the projects! Thank you for your years of friendship. They keep a big piece of my soul.

To my mom, Maureen, and my dad, Timothy, thank you for creating a family culture where creativity was the norm. It took me until adulthood to realise how unique and precious that is. And for a literal lifetime of unending love and support, thank you. I love you.

Tyron and Joel, one of us, one of us! You're the best brothers an author could ask for. I love you both.

Christian, thank you for holding my hand through adventures big and small. For all your incredible hard work and support. For all your love. I love you.

Harriet, you're the best three year old I know. Thank you for drawing me pictures while I was busy tap-tapping away on my laptop and for saying 'you're do it, Mama!' just when I needed to hear it. I'm so lucky to be your mom. I love you, Harriet Wilder.

And Lindsay-Jane, for this opportunity, for your life-changing, life-affirming friendship, for your belief in me, your advice, feedback, love, humour, ideas and more love. For all of it, thank you. Always.

— Camilla

About Never Too Small

Never Too Small was born out of a desire to make living in small spaces better. From humble beginnings as a YouTube channel, Never Too Small has grown into a modern media company that shares knowledge and inspiration for better small-footprint living with a growing global audience across its YouTube series, its limited documentary series, its multiple broadcast television series, its multiple books (the second of which you are now reading) and its series of digital guides. A desire to share and inspire continues to be at the core of all things Never Too Small as it increasingly assumes the role of advocate – actively championing more creative, considered and sustainable ways to design and live.

Never Too Small's content has been featured in the *Wall Street Journal*, *The New York Times Magazine*, the *Guardian* and *Elle Decor*, and Colin Chee, Never Too Small's creator and creative director, has been invited to speak at events around the world. Colin and his core team are based in Melbourne, Australia, but are supported by a talented and highly valued team of international collaborators. Together they share a vision for a more sustainable, inclusive and resilient future for our cities in which small-footprint design and thinking play a central role. For more about Never Too Small, visit nevertoosmall.com

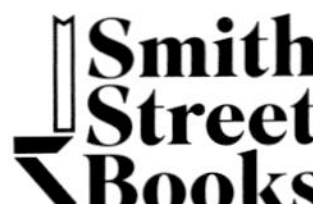

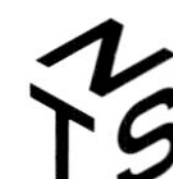

Published in 2024 by Smith Street Books
Naarm (Melbourne) | Australia
smithstreetbooks.com

Distributed outside of ANZ, North & Latin America by
Thames & Hudson Ltd., 6–24 Britannia Street, London, WC1X 9JD
thamesandhudson.com

EU Authorised Representative: Interart S.A.R.L.
19 rue Charles Auray, 93500 Pantin, Paris, France
productsafety@thameshudson.co.uk; www.interart.fr

ISBN: 978-1-9230-4907-9

Smith Street Books respectfully acknowledges the Wurundjeri People of the Kulin Nation, who are the Traditional Owners of the land on which we work, and we pay our respects to their Elders past and present.

Publisher: Paul McNally
Editor: Tahlia Anderson
Designers: Susan Le & Katherine Zhang | Evi-O.Studio
Typesetting: Matthew Crawford | Evi-O.Studio
Floor plans: Nic Agius and George Mollett
from Aguis Scorpo Architects
Printed & bound in China by C&C Offset Printing Co., Ltd.

Book 312
10 9 8 7 6 5 4 3

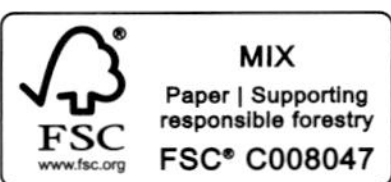